S0-AFM-999

HITLER'S PRE-EMPTIVE WAR

HITLER'S
PRE-EMPTIVE WAR
The Battle for Norway, 1940

By
HENRIK O. LUNDE

CASEMATE
Philadelphia & Newbury

Published in the United States of America in 2010 by
CASEMATE
908 Darby Road, Havertown, PA 19083

and in the United Kingdom by
CASEMATE
17 Cheap Street, Newbury, Berkshire, RG14 5DD

© 2009 by Henrik O. Lunde

ISBN 978-1-935149-33-0

Cataloging-in-publication data is available from the Library of
Congress and from the British Library.

All rights reserved. No part of this publication may be reproduced,
stored in a retrieval system or transmitted, in any form or by any
means, electronic, mechanical, photocopying, recording or
otherwise, without the prior permission of the publishers.

Printed and bound in the United States of America.

For a complete list of Casemate titles, please contact

United States of America
Casemate Publishers
Telephone (610) 853-9131, Fax (610) 853-9146
E-mail casemate@casematepublishing.com
Website www.casematepublishing.com

United Kingdom
Casemate-UK
Telephone (01635) 231091, Fax (01635) 41619
E-mail casemate-uk@casematepublishing.co.uk
Website www.casematepublishing.co.uk

Mixed Sources
Product group from well-managed
forests and other controlled sources
www.fsc.org Cert no. SW-COC-002283
© 1996 Forest Stewardship Council
FSC

CONTENTS

PREFACE AND ACKNOWLEDGMENTS

There are many cogent reasons why the 1940 campaign in Norway has an enduring importance and why its study should be basic reading for students of military history, for military planners and operators, and for policymakers. The fact that it was the first campaign in history in which land, sea, and air forces were fully involved is sufficient to meet the above criteria. However, there are other compelling reasons.

For both the Germans and the Allies, the war in Scandinavia demonstrated the extreme risks and dangers inherent when undertaking a preemptive war or a war of choice. The Norway campaign remains a perfect example of how things can quickly unravel when the underlying assumptions governing plans are fallacious. Furthermore, the Allied and Norwegian responses to the manner and pace of the German attack provide classic examples of the results of the problems that have always faced military planners in democracies relying on poorly trained and equipped conscript forces.

Many writers have concluded that the German plans and preparations were kept so secret that the attack came as a complete surprise to the Norwegians and the Allies. In fact, there were numerous intelligence reports pointing to imminent German actions in Scandinavia. Policymakers and planners gave little credit to these reports because of their preconceived ideas about German capabilities and intentions; hence they failed to draw the conclusions that, perhaps, ought logically to have followed.

The rough geography and severe climate of Norway encouraged the Norwegians to believe that their country was easy to defend. This belief, combined with the scarcity of resources in the interwar period, left the country with inadequate military forces to meet a determined aggressor. The operations in north Norway show clearly that to commit forces in the Arctic without adequate equipment and training is a recipe for disaster.

The war was the first direct clash between German and Allied land and air forces. It was a testing ground for the innovations in equipment and doctrine developed since World War I. The effect of air power on both land and naval operations, little understood in Norway and Great Britain, was demonstrated clearly during the war in Norway, and caused a fundamental shift in how this new weapon was viewed. The campaign also saw the first use of airborne troops to seize airfields and key objectives far behind enemy lines.

The Norwegian campaign revealed serious deficiencies in Allied command structures and inter-allied coordination and cooperation. Failure to achieve unity of command plagued both sides, but with the Germans the command difficulties were largely overcome by a high degree of professionalism at the operational level.

Finally, the campaign in Norway provides a textbook example of two military operational philosophies: centralized versus flexible control.

The German invasion of Denmark and Norway is usually dealt with in a few pages in the better-known political or military histories of World War II. This is understandable. The campaigns of the war were spread across nearly six years around the world, and the one in Norway was a comparatively small affair, both in the size of forces involved and in the number of casualties.

Several accounts of the campaign were written shortly after the war by authors from all participating countries. *The Campaign in Norway* by T.K. Derry in 1952, which became the official British history of the campaign, is undoubtedly the most authoritative and most widely read account in English. However, this excellently written book suffers from some of the same problems that David Reynolds finds in Churchill's multi-volume history of World War II. Both authors present British motives and actions in the most favorable light. For the most part, facts are presented correctly, but the reader is often misled or influenced by omissions, lack of balance, distortions, and the shifting of blame for failure. Although a number of books have been written by British authors since the 1950s, they are largely unknown on this side of the Atlantic. These works were primarily written for the British public, and deal mainly with Allied operations, in particular the naval aspects. Some accounts, by omission or through a narrow perspective, paint an inaccurate picture of events. While there are some well-written German and Norwegian accounts, they have not been translated and are therefore practically unknown outside their own countries.

There are a number of biographies of individuals involved in the Norwegian operations, both political and military, as well as a number of personal accounts and unit histories. These sources are valuable but must be treated with care. For example, it is often the case that writers of a biography fall in love with their subjects and therefore lose their objectivity, sometimes downplaying, overlooking, or excusing their subjects' flaws and weaknesses.

A review of the studies available in English led this author to the conclusion that the treatment of the campaign, with few exceptions, is unbalanced. The operations of French, Polish, and Norwegian troops are invariably given far less coverage and credit than they deserve. Inconsistencies between national accounts are numerous and the impact of such factors as terrain, climate, training, and personalities are seldom addressed adequately.

The intent of this book is to treat planning and operations in a balanced manner, without a national focus, using sources from all participating countries. The planning and operations are analyzed in the light of what the participants knew or could have been expected to know. Hindsight analysis is avoided as far as possible. It is always easy to be wise after the event. While few things are more dangerous in the writing of a military history than hindsight, the mere recounting of events without analysis and objective critique makes it a useless exercise. The focus of this book was originally on military operations in and around Narvik and on the political decisions and planning leading up to those operations. However, while Narvik had a seemingly magnetic effect upon military planners before and during the war—out of all proportion to its actual military importance—these operations cannot be understood in isolation. I soon realized that limiting my book to Narvik was unrealistic because that campaign was entwined with the whole of the war in Norway as well as in Europe generally.

I owe a special debt to those who have written about the various aspects of the war in Norway, and they are frequently referenced in text and notes. Among those who deserve special mention is retired Norwegian Major General Torkel Hovland, a former commander in north Norway. He provided a number of references at the outset that would otherwise have been difficult to locate.

The same is true for Hans Haugse, a retired Norwegian headmaster, who also put me in contact with Petter Sandvik, an individual with personal experiences from Narvik in 1940. Mr. Sandvik, in addition to his personal observations, provided materials from various institutions that proved useful.

Lieutenant Colonel Palle Ydstebø of the Norwegian Defense Staff was kind enough to make available helpful information on the historical aspects of the defenses in north Norway. Magnor Kr. Fjellheim kindly provided photographs of the area around Narvik that illustrate the formidable terrain and climatic challenges to military operations. Colonel (US Army, Ret) Henry Gole reviewed the draft manuscript and provided valuable perspectives on the issues during our frequent discussions.

I am grateful to a number of institutions and wish to give the staff of three a specific mention: the US Army Military History Institute in Carlisle, Pennsylvania; the Library of Congress in Washington, DC; and the Coyle Free Library in Chambersburg, Pennsylvania. The friendly and helpful staff at the Coyle Library helped locate and obtain access to sources from all over the United States.

My friend, Dr. Enoch Haga, has expertly guided me through this project, from beginning to end. He read every draft and made very helpful suggestions as to subject matter, organization, style, composition, and illustrations. Whenever pessimism began to rear its ugly head, Dr. Haga was always there to provide encouragement and support.

Finally, it is obvious that without the great patience and understanding on the part of my family, as I became increasingly absorbed in this work over the past three years, it would never have seen the light of day. My debt to them is immense.

Despite the diligence of those who provided assistance, comments, and advice, I must stress that I take full responsibility for all conclusions and such errors as this book may inadvertently contain.

PROLOGUE

"A power that wants to land in Norway, whether in
the south or in other places, must rule the sea, and the
power that rules the sea has no need to land in Norway."
STATEMENT TO THE PRESS ON JANUARY 14, 1939 BY ADMIRAL HENRY E. DIESEN,
COMMANDER-IN-CHIEF OF THE NORWEGIAN NAVY.

Norway's Strategic Importance

Located east of the British Isles, Norway is situated on one side of the route used by German ships heading to or returning from the Atlantic. In the south, Norway forms the northern shore of the waters leading to and from the Baltic approaches. With the advent of air power, the possibilities that control of the Norwegian coastline offered to the belligerents, particularly Germany, were obvious. The Baltic, its approaches, and German harbors in the Baltic were within reach of both long range and shorter range British bombers operating from Norwegian airfields. An Allied presence in Norway would virtually bottle up the German Navy and cut off much of the merchandise that flowed through Scandinavia. This was a serious concern since the very effective Allied blockade during World War 1 was a fundamental reason for Germany's defeat in that war. On the other hand, a German presence in Norway would secure the Baltic approaches. German bombers operating from Norwegian airfields could cover the whole of the North and Norwegian Seas, as well as portions of the Faeroe-Iceland gap, critical for naval access to the North Atlantic. The sea routes to Soviet harbors on the Arctic coast could also be interdicted by naval and air forces operating from bases in North Norway. This consideration, however, only became important later in the war.

In World War 1, to prevent German access to the North Atlantic, the Allies decided to create a mine barrier across the North Sea, from the Orkneys to a point three miles off the Norwegian coast, near the town of Haugesund. The United States was the major participant in this enormous project. The U.S. Navy laid almost 57,000 of the 70,000 mines. The barrier stretched over a distance of 230 miles and varied in width from 15 to 35 miles. The mines were laid in several layers at various depths. The British Navy complained that the barrier, on which enormous labor and money was spent, would be ineffective unless the corridor between the mine barrier and the Norwegian coast was closed, and all Allied governments put the strongest pressure on the Norwegians to close it themselves.

This immense barrier took a long time to complete, and by then there was little doubt about how the war would end. It had become clear to the Norwegians that Germany no longer possessed the means to invade Scandinavia. Still, it was not until October 1918 that Norway laid two minefields in territorial waters to close the gap.

During World War II, both Germany and the Allies imported raw materials from Scandinavia, but in Germany's case, these imports were critical. The German war industry lacked two important raw materials, oil and iron. Most of the iron ore coming from mines in Sweden was shipped from the port of Luleå when the Baltic was ice-free. During the months when Luleå was blocked by ice, the ore was shipped to Narvik in Norway and from there in ships along the Norwegian coast to Germany. The importance of the iron ore and the role it played in the plans of the belligerents is discussed in the first two chapters.

Opposing Policies at the Outset of World War II

When war broke out in Europe at the beginning of September 1939, none of the belligerents planned for or expected Scandinavia to become a theater of operations. Germany viewed a neutral Norway as in their best interests. When Norway issued a declaration of neutrality on September 1, 1939 the German response came on September 2. The Germans stated that they would respect Norwegian neutrality as long as that neutrality was maintained in an uncompromising manner. If not maintained in such a manner or if a third power violated Norwegian neutrality, Germany would be forced to protect its interests in ways and by means dictated by the situation at the time. While the statement signaled Germany's views that it considered Norwegian neutrality to be in its best interests, it also gave a clear warning that Germany would not tolerate a tilt in Norwegian neutrality towards the Allies or an actual Allied presence in Norway. The British and French did not issue an immediate response to Norway's declaration of neutrality but in answer to a query from the Norwegian Foreign Minister, Halvdan Koht, the British Government stated it would respect Norwegian neutrality in the present war. However, a German attack on Norway would be considered an attack on Great Britain and would be met with force. There may have been several objectives behind this British declaration. First, a way to close some of the loopholes in the British blockade was to prevail on the Norwegian government to interpret their responsibilities as a neutral party in a manner favorable to the British; and secondly, to lessen Norwegian fears of the German threat. In addition, it was critically important for the British to obtain the services of the large Norwegian merchant fleet.

The British achieved this last objective when the Norwegian Shippers Association chartered the largest and most modern ships in their fleet to the British on November 11, 1939. British achievement of this important goal was not the end of the matter. Policy makers had to keep in mind that hostilities with Norway would nullify the agreement. To balance the scales, Norway signed a trade agreement with Germany on February 23, 1940 stipulating that Norway would continue to provide exports to Germany at the 1938 level.

The British policy of appeasement in the 1930s was aimed at maintaining peace and the status quo in Europe. To this end, British leaders were willing to accommodate some of the German government's grievances resulting from provisions forced on it at Versailles at the end of World War I. This British policy did not end entirely with the declaration of war on Germany on September 3, 1939. Prime Minister Neville Chamberlain and his Foreign Secretary, Lord Halifax, continued to cling to the desperate hope that the German people would overthrow Adolf Hitler. In the light of Hitler's continued aggressive tactics, it is clear that Chamberlain and Halifax misjudged and underestimated Hitler and his ambitions and overestimated the ability and willingness of the German people and their armed forces to take action against their own government. Nevertheless, this policy partially explains Allied reluctance and timidity towards offensive operations in 1939 and early 1940.

Another factor influencing reluctance to initiate operations in the west was the four-year bloodletting in the brutal trench warfare of World War I, still fresh in French and British memories. Many people, including Winston Churchill, believed that the nation's resources were badly spent in this war of attrition and that a repeat of that calamity must be avoided in any future conflict. This feeling strengthened Churchill's existing fascination with flank strategies.

In accordance with their policy, Chamberlain and Halifax were eager to prevent the war from escalating to the point where it took on a life of its own. This view soon collided with that of Churchill, who pressed for action in Scandinavia, as well as with that of the French leadership, keen on distracting German attention from its own doorsteps.

Norwegian Policies

It is impossible to understand Norwegian policies and actions in 1939–40 without considering how the country viewed its own interests as well as those of the belligerents. Great Britain enjoyed considerable good will among the Norwegians, who still attached some importance to their common historical heritage which dated back to the Scandinavian settlements in England and Scotland. They saw in the growth of British democracy over the preceding century a close parallel to developments in Norway during the same period. British support during the dissolution of the Swedish-Norwegian union in 1905 was not forgotten. The Norwegian royal family was closely related to the British royal family. King Håkon VII, who married his cousin Princess Maud, the youngest daughter of Edward VII and Queen Alexandra in 1896, was King George VI's uncle.

The economic bonds to Britain were strong and the very survival of Norway's large merchant fleet and its future as a trading nation were closely tied to British fortunes. Norway had the fourth largest merchant marine in the world. This fleet, in particular the modern tanker part of 1.5 million tons, was of vital importance to the Allies. The British needed iron ore that came through Narvik, as well as annual imports of 10,000 tons of aluminum and 70,000 tons of carbide from Norway. The Norwegian policy makers felt, therefore, that a war with England had to be avoided at all costs.

This feeling was well known to the British and that, plus the sorry state of Norwegian defenses, emboldened the Allies to violate Norwegian sovereignty. Rowland Kenney, the press attaché at the British Embassy,[1] had a discussion with Finn Moe, a member of the Norwegian Labor Party. This was shortly after Foreign Minister Koht delivered a speech attacking the British. Finn Moe assured Kenney that the foreign minister was resolute in his view that if Norway entered the war, it had to be on the side of the Allies, something he could not say openly.[2] While the statement appears to give a correct picture of Koht's views, to provide this information to Kenney could only encourage the British leaders in their continued violations of Norwegian neutrality.

The friendship between Germany and Sweden at the beginning of the 20th century when Norway asserted its independence also had a tendency to cause anti-Swedish sentiments to take the form of friendship and sympathy for the British. The activities in Germany in the 1930s had created both disgust and alarm, and the Norwegian leaders took some actions that were sure to irritate the Germans. In 1935, the Nobel committee awarded the Nobel Peace Prize to Carl von Ossietzky, who was in a German concentration camp when nominated. Four years later, Norway rejected a German offer of a non-aggression pact. The historical relationship with Great Britain and Germany and the policies of the latter's government go a long way to explain the consensus in Norwegian political circles in 1940 that a war with Great Britain had to be avoided.

Most members of the Norwegian government were ill equipped to deal with the events that unfolded in 1939 and 1940. Most had little interest in military affairs and foreign policy. Prime Minister Johan Nygaardsvold was a former lumberjack and labor union offical, Minister of Justice Trygve Lie was also a former labor union official, and Minister of Defense Carl F. Monsen was a conscientious objector and had been arrested for pacifist agitation. Foreign Minister Koht was a professor of history and well qualified for his job, but in this, he was a lone figure among his colleagues.

The Norwegian Terrain

To understand the magnitude and difficulties faced by anyone undertaking military operations in Norway, it is important to keep the country's geography in mind. Norway is slightly larger in area than Great Britain but over 95 percent of the country consists of mountains, deep valleys, extensive forests, and thousands of islands along the coast. These features resulted in enormous internal communications problems. The population, which was slightly over three million in 1940, was concentrated in a few cities, the main valleys in the eastern part of the country, and along a narrow strip of coastline.

Cold and heavy snow is the normal winter climate in the eastern and internal portions of central Norway. The coastal areas of western and northern Norway, in contrast, have relatively mild winters because of the Gulf Stream. However, the darkness, frequent and violent storms, and the spring thaw complicate both military and civilian movement.

The primary means of communications was by sea, or by the railroad system that had not yet reached Narvik. The road network was susceptible to interdiction in the narrow, precipitous valleys, in the mountains, and along the coast where the use of ferries was required to cross the numerous fjords. There were no roads linking Narvik and the two northern provinces, Troms and Finnmark, to the rest of the country.

The rough geography and severe climate, while presenting an invader with serious problems, encouraged the belief that the country was easy to defend. This belief, in turn, contributed to the scarcity of resources allocated for defense.

The Norwegian Military

Norwegian policies and the level of preparedness of her armed forces in 1940 can be explained partly by the country's experience in World War I, or rather by the failure of its leaders to interpret correctly the reasons for that experience. While the country managed to avoid direct involvement in that conflict, the Norwegian merchant marine, mostly in the service of the Allies, suffered losses that were proportionally greater than those suffered by the British. More than half of the Norwgian merchant fleet and 2,000 sailors were lost, primarily to German submarine warfare. Although the country had to endure severe blockade measures and the war involved great costs to the Norwegian population, Norwegian companies, industrialists, and shipping magnates reaped huge economic benefits.

Johan Nygaardsvold and his government hoped to remain neutral in World War II, and perhaps to reap similar economic benefits. However, Norway's strategic and economic importance for the belligerents had increased during the inter-war period because of the German need for iron ore. In addition, air power had come of age. There were also other important differences between the situation in 1914 and that in 1939.

The Norwegian armed forces were modern and well trained in World War I, following a deliberate program of force build-up and modernization in preparation for the separation from Sweden only nine years earlier. One reason for scrupulously defending Norwegian neutrality in World War I had to do with the likelihood that Norway and Sweden, if involved in the war, would be on opposite sides.

By 1940, the situation in the armed forces was completely different. Norwegians were caught up in the general pacifist feelings prevailing in much of Europe and the expression that World War I was "the war to end all wars" was more than a slogan. Norwegians were ardent supporters of the newly formed League of Nations and some even viewed that institution as a substitute for national defense. High unemployment levels in the 1920s and 1930s, up to 42% among organized labor in 1932, also contributed to a general unwillingness to increase spending on defense.

These pacifist feelings and severe economic conditions were contemporaneous with the rise of the Labor Party, which viewed the professionals in the military services as opponents of its social service programs. Annual defense expenditure had fallen to less than $9 million in 1935. Thereafter, it increased but even the 1938 budget allocated only $12 million, supplemented by a $13 million loan, to the armed forces. However, the scarcity in the defense budget was only part of the problem. This is demonstrated by the fact that almost $10 million were on hand and unused when war broke out. Much of the materials needed to rearm and modernize came from sources outside Norway and these became more and more difficult to acquire.

Both the navy and coastal artillery were fully mobilized from the first to the last day of World War I. Minefields protecting the coastal fortresses were laid and all forts had infantry protection against coastal attack. The minefields were under army control until 1936 when the control passed to the navy. In 1939, in contrast, the navy and coastal artillery were only partially mobilized, the minefields were not laid, and no infantry protection was provided for the forts.

While the neglect of defenses was serious, it was not total. There was a system of compulsory military service dating back over 300 years. The conscripts were, for the most part, hardy individuals used to outdoor life in a severe climate and most individuals had access to and were proficient in the use of firearms. However, the military training period was short and the equipment was old, if not obsolete. Antiaircraft guns were scarce and there were no tanks and antitank weapons.

Despite these shortcomings, more could have been done after the outbreak of war in Europe with the resources on hand. In addition, quick and resolute actions at the time of the invasion could have made the assault very costly for the attacker. It appears that both politicians and a number of military officials lacked the will to take effective measures.

The Norwegian Army was organized into six divisional areas in 1940. The 1st and 2nd Divisions were located in eastern Norway, the 3rd Division in the southern part of the country, the 4th Division in the Bergen area, the 5th Division in the Trondheim region, and the 6th Division in North Norway. These divisions were not expected to operate in the same manner as those of major powers. The geography of the country dictated a different and more flexible approach. The divisions were territorial in nature and the operational concepts were built around infantry regiments that were expected to operate under the decentralized control of the divisions. The 1st, 2nd, 5th, and 6th Divisions each had three regiments. The 3rd and 4th Divisions each had two regiments. In addition, there were combat units of cavalry, artillery, engineers, and so on. These units were normally parceled out to the regiments, making those units theoretically capable of operating as independent entities. There were three cavalry regiments, three artillery regiments, three mountain artillery battalions, and two named infantry battalions (Alta and Varanger) in North Norway. At full mobilization, the army was expected to field approximately 119,000 men. However, this number gives a false impression. Most of these troops were not trained and the equipment needed to sustain a full mobilization was not available.

Plans for partial mobilization relied on telegrams or letters while full mobilization called for notification by any means, including radio. The depots for the units to be mobilized were located near population centers and this proved to be a serious problem. Five of the divisional areas each had one battalion in training at the time of the invasion, but these units were located some distance from the German landing sites. The 6th Division was partially mobilized because of the Finnish-Soviet conflict, and the area from Narvik to the border with Finland and the Soviet Union can be viewed as reasonably well prepared. The total on duty strength of the Norwegian Army at the beginning of April 1940 amounted to about 13,000 troops and almost half of this force was stationed in the northern part of the country.

Training and exercises of larger formations were two of the most serious weaknesses affecting the Norwegian Army. The lack of maneuvers by larger units resulted in a reduced competence level among the higher-ranking officers in the army, an item noted by the Germans in their after-action reports. A recruit drafted into the infantry served only for 72 days, the shortest training and service period of any country in Europe. In addition, the number of eligible draftees called up each year was continually reduced, first by overly restrictive medical standards, thereafter by a raffle, and finally by the exclusion of several categories of conscripts. By 1940, there were only 20,000 draftees trained to use modern equipment and weapons. It would have taken several years to train the force adequately at that rate. In most respects, except for familiarity with the terrain and experience in the severe climate, the Norwegian Army was poorly prepared to cope with the German Army and its blitzkrieg doctrine.

The Royal Norwegian Navy, including the coastal forts, was partially mobilized at the outset of hostilities in Europe and its primary task was to enforce the neutrality laws and regulations along the extensive Norwegian coast. The navy was divided geographically into three naval districts. The 1st Naval District included the coastline from the Swedish border to a point just south of Stavanger. The 2nd Naval District included the coastline from south of Stavanger to the provincial boundary between Nord-Trøndelag and Nordland. The 3rd Naval District included the coastline from where the 2nd Naval District left off to the Soviet border. The navy was small compared to that in 1914. The total tonnage in 1914 was about 34,600 while the total tonnage in 1940 came to only 10,300. In addition, the construction program in 1914 called for eight coastal defense ships, two monitors, six destroyers, 40 torpedo boats, and 12 submarines. The building program in 1939 consisted of only two destroyers, three torpedo boats, one submarine, and one motor torpedo boat.[3]

The relatively small navy in 1940 consisted of two coastal defense ships (an additional two in mothballs), 10 minelayers, three older destroyers of the *Draug* class, four newer destroyers of the *Sleipner* class, three larger torpedo boats of the *Trygg* class, and 14 other torpedo boats. There were also six *B* class and three *A* class submarines, eight minesweepers, and six patrol ships. Another 49 leased or requisitioned vessels served as patrol boats. A significant portion of the fleet of 111 ships available in April 1940 was obsolete by the standards of the time. Only one minelayer and four destroyers could be considered modern warships. There were 5,200 officers and men on duty in the navy in April 1940.

The coastal fortifications, one of the most neglected elements of the Norwegian defense establishment, were only partially mobilized. Many of the officers earmarked for mobilization had not been on active duty since 1918 and some batteries had not fired a live round since the 1890s. Several of the main batteries were not manned and only a few of the forts had operational antiaircraft guns. The gun-pits were open and exposed to air attacks. The planned minefields were not laid. Under the full mobilization scenario, the coastal forts should have a total strength of 8,424 officers and men. The actual strength in April 1940 was only 2,403. The coastal forts also suffered from a lack of infantry to defend any inland approaches.

There was no Norwegian air force as such. All aircraft were assigned to either the army or the navy. The Army Air Corps was in the middle of reorganization and receiving new aircraft. The period of reorganization and retraining was to have been completed by July 1, 1940. The reorganization called for the establishment of two squadrons of fighters consisting of Curtis Hawk P36s purchased from the United States and two bomber squadrons consisting of Italian Ca 312s. These aircraft were delivered but they were still in their crates when the Germans attacked. Another 129 aircraft were ordered but not delivered.

The Army Air Corps consisted of 62 aircraft at the beginning of 1940 but only 19 of these were modern operational aircraft: nine British Gladiator fighters, four Italian Ca 310 bombers, and six Heinkel (He-115) torpedo aircraft.[4] About 42 naval airplanes were assigned to seven coastal stations and were a mixture of reconnaissance, torpedo, and training aircraft. Again, the aircraft were old and ill suited for modern warfare. Neither the army nor the naval aircraft were capable of meeting the onslaught of the Luftwaffe and, despite valorous individual deeds, had no significant effect on operations.

Norway's neglect of its armed forces in the inter-war period was well known to the belligerents and the poor state of its defenses, when compared to a generation earlier, served as an invitation to violate the country's neutrality. Both the German and the British leaders viewed the Norwegian military as a minor obstacle to their plans.

NOTES

1 While foreign representatives in the Scandinavian countries and Scandinavian representatives in other countries were known as "ministers" and their offices "legations," I have chosen to use the more recognized terms "ambassadors" and "embassies."

2 Bjørn Bjørnsen, *Narvik 1940* (Oslo: Gyldendal Norsk Forlag, 1980), pp. 146-147.

3 Rolf Hobson and Tom Kristiansen, Norsk Forsvarshitorie. Bind 3 1905-1940. Total krig, nøytralitet og politisk splittelse (Bergen: Eide Forlag, 2001), p. 248.

4 Michael Tamelander and Niklas Zetterling, *Niende april. Nazi-Tysklands invasjon av Norge* (Oslo: Spartacus, 2001),

1

ALLIED PLANS: FLAWED, INADEQUATE, AND HESITANT

"I think the whole thing is hare brained."

CHIEF AIR MARSHAL SIR CYRIL NEWALL'S COMMENT ON ALLIED
PLANS FOR OPERATIONS IN SCANDINAVIA.

Plan *Catherine*

Winston Churchill, who turned 65 in November 1939, was appointed First Lord of the Admiralty at the outbreak of World War II. He had a fascination for the indirect approach in warfare and for striking at what he perceived to be enemy vulnerabilities or weaknesses. This fascination led to the debacle at Gallipoli and goes far to explain Britain's preoccupation with flanking strategies in the Balkans, southern Europe, and Norway. In 1939, Churchill advocated taking strong action in response to what he perceived as German weaknesses.

Churchill had his first conceptual plan of action against the German northern flank ready the very instant he returned to his old job in the Admiralty. He discussed the plan with Admiral Dudley Pound, the First Sea Lord, on September 3, 1939. The operation he had in mind is reminiscent of the Dardanelles operation that cost him the job as First Lord of the Admiralty in 1915. Churchill's plan called for forcing an entry into the Baltic for the purpose of attacking the German fleet and cutting the German supply route from Sweden. Churchill recalled to active duty an old friend, 65-year-old Admiral of the Fleet William Boyle, who had inherited the title of Lord Cork and Orrery, for work on this project. Admiral Cork had a personality akin to that of Churchill's. He had vast energy, an offensive spirit, and a feared temperament—and he was apparently the only one who expressed any enthusiasm for Churchill's scheme.

By September 12, 1939, an outline plan, codenamed *Catherine*, was ready. In broad terms, it called for a force of two or three battleships, one aircraft carrier, five cruisers, a detachment of submarines, and two destroyer flotillas supported by a fleet of tankers and supply ships. The fleet was to remain in the Baltic for several months and it was assumed that Danish and Swedish bases would be available after the fleet had been there long enough to remove Scandinavian fears of the Germans. It was further hoped that the presence of the British fleet would cause Sweden, Denmark, and Norway to join the war on the side of the Allies.

It is hard to understand the logic behind these assumptions. The opposite is more likely to have occurred. Sweden and Denmark could interpret the passage of a large fleet of warships through the narrow strait between them for attacking a state bordering the Baltic (Germany) as contrary to their international obligations. It is equally logical that forcing these approaches and seizing bases could bring Sweden and Denmark into the war on the side of Germany. Sweden would not have reacted kindly to having its trade with Germany and to other parts of Europe through Germany interrupted in this manner.

Moulton writes that the plan should "not be dismissed too lightly," although it seemed "in retrospect clumsy and improbable" because "it seemed to offer the prospect of a relatively easy and bloodless way of winning the war by stopping Swedish ore."[1]

That prospect was rather dim. The Germans could hurl at least 1,300 combat aircraft at the British ships from nearby bases. Moulton writes that the fleet was expected to operate in the Gulf of Bothnia, thereby placing it beyond the range of German bombers. However, to reach its destination, the fleet would have to make a long passage well within the range of German aircraft, and we can assume that the Germans would make every effort to ensure that the British fleet would not escape from what may well have become a deadly trap. The project shows that Churchill had not yet realized the effects of air power on naval operations, effects that proved enormously detrimental to operations in Norway within seven months. Furthermore, the Kiel Canal offered the Germans the opportunity to move ships between the North Sea and the Baltic without the use of the Baltic approaches.

The plan seems not to have been supported by the Navy. Admiral Pound pointed out that several conditions would have to be met before the operation could be carried out: active Swedish support, no opposition from the Soviet Union, upgrading the ships to withstand air attacks, and an ice-free Baltic. The last two conditions postponed any possibility of carrying out *Catherine* until the following spring, while the first two had the practical effect of eliminating any prospect of launching it. Admiral Pound may have hoped that by spring Churchill would have turned his boundless energy to other projects.

Iron Ore and Other Motives

Churchill began looking around for other immediate opportunities to strike at the enemy. He advanced the idea that the British government should take immediate action to prevent German ships from using Norwegian territorial waters for transit to Germany. Most of Churchill's colleagues agreed with his reasoning, but their respect for the neutrality of small states and their hope for a peaceful settlement with Germany prevented them from making an early decision. Churchill presented his views to the Cabinet on September 19, 1939.

Churchill suggested that certain steps were necessary before a closing of the corridor within Norwegian territorial waters could be undertaken. First, the negotiations with the Norwegians for chartering their merchant fleet had to be completed. Second, in order to prevent a quarrel with the Swedish government, the British Board of Trade should arrange to buy that country's iron ore, which would otherwise go to Germany.

The suggestions advocated by Churchill proved to be more difficult to achieve than envisioned. Negotiations with the Norwegians for the use of their fleet had been underway since the war began. The Norwegians were aware of their fleet's value, used it to obtain advantage, and dragged out the negotiations. A major agreement was signed in mid-November 1939, but many issues were not settled until March 1940. The Allies realized that any massive violation of Norwegian neutrality would end the negotiations. This consideration, the neutrality arguments, and the hope for a peaceful resolution of the war meant that Churchill's ideas languished, although he provided the War Cabinet with a more detailed memorandum on September 29.

In addition, there had been a marked decline in the iron ore traffic to Germany via Narvik. One contributing factor was that the crews of merchant ships were unwilling to sail through dangerous waters in wartime, but in addition the German decision-makers diverted some of the Narvik ore to Luleå to be stored. The shipments had declined from 457,482 tons in February 1939 to only 99,391 in February 1940. During the same period, the shipments to Great Britain had more than doubled. These figures, made public by the Norwegians, apparently gave Churchill some temporary concerns.

Before submitting his more detailed memorandum to the War Cabinet on September 29, Churchill asked the Naval Staff to reconvene the committee on iron ore and look over his draft memorandum in order to insure that he was not completely off the mark. He wrote, "It is no use my asking the Cabinet to take the drastic action suggested against a neutral country unless the results are in the first order of importance." He had heard that the shipment of iron ore from Narvik was much reduced and that the Germans were stockpiling ore in southern Sweden for shipment to Germany during the winter months. He wanted to know if these statements were true and stated, "It would be very unpleasant if I went into action on mining the Norwegian territorial waters and was answered that it would not do the trick."[2]

Since Churchill did submit his memorandum to the War Cabinet on September 29, it seems that the Naval Staff dispelled some of his concerns. The memorandum takes note of the decline in shipments from Narvik, but urges more dramatic action if they start moving again. Churchill concluded that the prevention of the Narvik supplies would greatly reduce Germany's power of resistance. By December 1939, he tried to convince his reluctant colleagues that the interruption of the ore coming through Norway could be decisive for the outcome of the war.

Churchill was a man of vast knowledge and experience; however, it is difficult to square his stated views with realities. It was obvious to Churchill and his colleagues that mining Norwegian waters would stop only that portion of iron ore shipped via Narvik. Other efforts were required to achieve a great reduction in Germany's warmaking power. However, stopping iron ore shipments along the Norwegian coast was for Churchill only a means to an end. It became obvious in the months after his initial flurry of memoranda dealing with the iron ore issue that he and a few other members of the British Government wanted to expand the war into Scandinavia, particularly Norway. To accomplish this, Germany had to be provoked. The mining of Norwegian territorial waters would serve as that provocation. The expected German counteraction presented possibilities for easy military victories because of the vast superiority of the British fleet, and would give the Allies reasons to occupy various parts of Norway. This would accomplish four important goals: 1) Stop the flow of ore along the coast; 2) Make the blockade of Germany more effective; 3) Increase the air threat to German Baltic and North Sea harbors; and 4) Bring Sweden under Allied influence. While these points remained unstated at the outset, they were undoubtedly the strategic reasons for the preoccupation with the flow of iron ore along the coast, the stoppage of which would only have a minor effect on German war industry.

The belief that stopping German ore shipments from Sweden would be an immediate and decisive factor in the war was overstated. Germany's import of high-grade iron ore from Sweden came mostly from deposits in the Kiruna and Gällivare regions of northern Sweden, while a small amount came from mines in central Sweden. From May to November, the ore from the Kiruna/Gällivare region reached Germany by sea via the port of Luleå at the northern end of the Baltic Sea (Gulf of Bothnia). This port was normally ice-bound from December to April and the ore was then shipped by rail to the ice-free Norwegian port of Narvik. It was estimated that the Germans imported 22 million tons of iron ore in 1938. About nine and one-half million tons came from sources that were no longer available to Germany after the outbreak of war. The Allies estimated that another nine million tons came from Sweden.[3] The scheduled deliveries to Germany for 1940, as specified in the German-Swedish agreement, were actually 10 million tons. The Swedes considered it necessary to ship two to three million tons of this commitment through Narvik.

The Germans were prepared to ship about three million of the 10 million tons via rail to the ice-free port of Oxelösund or other ports in southern Sweden, provided arrangements were made for storage during the winter months.[4] This would almost remove their reliance on Narvik as a shipping port. Churchill's plans to sever the ore shipments from Narvik by mining Norwegian territorial waters would therefore have little impact on Germany's receipt of Swedish iron ore, while risking driving Norway into the German camp. Churchill's plans also risked alienating public opinion in neutral countries, particularly in the United States.

One reason the Allies believed that the imports of iron ore from Sweden were all-important to Germany's war industry can be traced back to statements made by the prominent German industrialist Fritz Tyssen, who lived in exile in Switzerland. He concluded that Germany would not be able to wage active war for more than one year if the supplies from Sweden were cut off. The Ministry of Economic Warfare appears to have endorsed Tyssen's view without a detailed examination of its validity.

The later years of the war demonstrated that the use of scrap iron, German domestic supplies of low-grade ore, and stockpiling had been severely underestimated. The German capture of the Lorraine fields in May 1940 reduced the importance of Swedish ore. However, while there is little doubt that a successful Allied invasion and seizure of the iron ore districts in northern Sweden would have led to acute shortages of high-grade ore in Germany, the likelihood of driving Norway, Sweden, and possibly the Soviet Union into the German camp was a high price to pay for this advantage.

The Winter War and Contending Plans

The outbreak of the Winter War between Finland and the Soviet Union on November 30, 1939 put the Scandinavian question in a new light. There was a strong desire in both France and Britain to help the Finns with volunteers and materiél. The only possible route for such help was through Norway and Sweden. The Allied Supreme War Council decided on December 19, 1939 to send help to Finland if requested.

The Allied governments recognized that this new situation would give them a chance to interrupt Germany's ore supplies. It would certainly be easy to prevent shipment of iron ore to Germany through Norwegian waters if Narvik became an Allied supply base for the Finns. However, Churchill was still arguing for the more limited action of mining Norwegian territorial waters. He hoped that the consequent interruption of iron shipments would lead to German counter-action and the opening of a new front where Allied naval superiority would lead to military victories. Furthermore, the British War Cabinet believed that German counter-action was likely to add Norway and Sweden to the Allied camp.

Chief of the Imperial General Staff, General Edmund Ironside, was even more ambitious. He argued for the occupation of the Swedish mining districts. At the same time, he argued against mining Norwegian territorial waters since that would make a move against Narvik and the Swedish iron districts more difficult and could push the Norwegian government into alliance with Hitler. While this was a logical assumption, it appears that General Ironside did not recognize that direct aid to the Finns through Scandinavia—against the wishes of the Scandinavian states—and the occupation of the iron ore districts in Sweden could have a far graver repercussion, by pushing Josef Stalin, the Russian leader, into backing Hitler. To assume that the Swedish and Norwegian governments would acquiesce in the use of their territories for direct aid to the Finns, particularly since they were well aware of the real objective of the operation, was unrealistic, as events were to prove.

Ironside's plan, if successful, might stop Germany's importation of Swedish ore, but it was ill-founded. In December 1939, a report from the intelligence division of the British War Office estimated that Germany would need 25–30 divisions for a successful invasion of Sweden and Norway.[5] In spite of this, Allied war planners never considered using anything near that force level in their own plans in Norway and Sweden. At the most, they considered that only a few brigades were required and, if the Germans intervened, a force of no more than

150,000. Part of this force was also intended to aid the Finns in their campaign against the Soviet Union.

Chamberlain and Halifax were still hoping for a change of leadership in Germany that could lead to peace, a chance that could be destroyed through aggressive actions in Scandinavia. However, members of their own party were demanding action, and the two leaders turned the differences in the plans of Churchill and Ironside to good advantage. Churchill's more limited plan could be executed within a few days, but would not assist the Finns, while Ironside's proposal would take months to prepare.

In a memorandum dated December 16 and considered by the war cabinet on December 22, Churchill attempted to secure approval for his scheme of mining Norwegian waters. In this memorandum he states:

> The effectual stoppage of the Norwegian ore supplies to Germany ranks as a major offensive operation of the war. No other measure is open to us for many months to come which gives so good a chance of abridging the waste and destruction of the conflict, or of perhaps preventing the vast slaughters which will attend the grapple of the main armies... If Germany can be cut from all Swedish ore supplies from now onwards till the end of 1940, a blow will have been struck at her war-making capacity equal to a first-class victory in the field or from the air, and without any serious sacrifice of life. It might indeed be immediately decisive.[6]

However, Churchill knew that the mining would not cut Germany off from all Swedish ore supplies and he was already thinking about submarine mining of the approaches to Luleå and sabotage action ("methods which be neither diplomatic nor military") at Oxelösund.[7]

The distinct possibility that the contemplated actions in Scandinavia would bring additional countries into the German camp and severely damage Allied reputations in the Dominions and among neutrals did not seem to worry Churchill. In a memorandum to the War Cabinet dated February 19, 1940, dealing with the stoppage of German traffic in Norwegian territorial waters, he wrote:

> Finally I do not hesitate to say that if the worst case came to worst and Norway and Sweden joined Germany and invited their troops into their country to protect them, a step which would be fatal to their

independence and also extremely unpleasant for them at the time, even so, a state of war with Norway and Sweden would be more for our advantage than the present neutrality which gives all the advantages to Germany for nothing and imposes all disadvantages upon us. Germany would then have to defend and victual the Scandinavian peninsula, thus diverting her strength and consuming her strained supplies. Our blockade would become far more effective, and using sea-power we could easily supply ourselves with varying temporary bases on the Norwegian coast.[8]

Some of these conclusions are certainly open to question. It is difficult to see how it would be more advantageous for the British to have the Scandinavian countries in the German camp rather than neutral. The loss of the large Norwegian merchant fleet and the raw materials coming from Norway and Sweden would certainly lead to a strained situation for the British, and seems a strange contention in view of Churchill's emphatic statement two months earlier that "it cannot be too strongly emphasized that British control of the Norwegian coast-line is a strategic objective of first-class importance."[9] That the British forces would be able to establish and supply themselves at temporary bases on the Norwegian coast using sea power was a dangerous assumption.

Furthermore, it was unlikely that the Germans would need to move any forces into Sweden for that country's defense. What they needed to move into Norway were primarily air and naval forces. This move, which was being urged by high officials in the German Navy, would immediately improve the German strategic position without a shot being fired.

While Allied policy was shortsighted, the military planning for carrying it out was ineffective. The expeditionary force would risk facing not only Norwegian resistance but also that of Sweden, a country with a large citizen army that was better trained and equipped than that of its neighbor to the west. In addition, the expeditionary force could expect to meet the full fury of the German armed forces, as well as those of the Soviet Union if the Allies made good on their promise to help the Finns.

It appears that the Allied policy makers had become so preoccupied with the importance of interrupting Germany's importation of iron ore, and of embroiling that nation in military operations in Scandinavia, that they ignored realities and the obvious risks to themselves.

Chamberlain and Halifax came down on the side of Ironside. In this way, they demonstrated willingness to aggressively pursue the war and to bring help to the Finns, while winning precious time for their desired peaceful solution to the war. Such action was also in line with Chamberlain's well-known anti-Soviet views and the views of the military leaders that supporting the Finns was necessary not only to prevent a Soviet attack on Norway and Sweden but also to protect Allied interests against possible Soviet aggression in other areas of the world. Churchill, on the other hand, had expressed considerable understanding for the Soviet demands vis-à-vis Finland, and he viewed a war between the Scandinavian countries and the Soviet Union as an advantage to the Allies, since it would give them excellent reasons for establishing themselves in Scandinavia.[10] A number of key Allied policy-makers believed that the landings could be carried out with the approval of Norway and Sweden and would therefore not be regarded by the United States and the Dominions as a breach of neutrality in the way that mining Norwegian waters almost certainly would be.

The proposed help to Finland camouflaged the real objective: to occupy Narvik and secure control over the Swedish mining district. The French government under Edouard Daladier had another hidden objective in mind in helping the Finns. The French faced the German Army on their eastern border. Memories of the enormous suffering and destruction during World War I were still fresh in French memories, and Daladier also hoped for a change of leadership in Germany that could lead to peace. In the meantime, however, the French government viewed operations in Scandinavia as an excellent opportunity to divert the war to someone else's territory while pacifying the demand from the French populace that action be taken to aid the Finns.

A French plan formulated in the middle of January 1940 sought to avoid the necessity of asking the Swedish and Danish governments permission to breach their neutrality. It called for British and French forces to land at Petsamo, in former Finnish territory and for a naval blockade of the Soviet coast between Murmansk and Petsamo. The British objected to this plan since it would certainly lead to war with the Soviet Union. Why the British did not think that active Allied intervention on the side of the Finns would lead to a similar result is difficult to understand, unless one assumes that the policy-makers never intended for Allied forces to advance further than to the Swedish iron ore districts.

The only measures undertaken at the War Cabinet meeting on December 22, 1939 were to make diplomatic protests to Norway about the misuse of its territorial waters by Germany and to provide instructions to the military chiefs to consider the implications of any future commitments in Scandinavia. The cabinet authorized the military to plan for a landing at Narvik in the north and to consider the consequences of a German occupation of southern Norway.

The military chiefs had been somewhat skeptical about the risks involved in an operation against the iron ore districts in northern Sweden. Some of this skepticism now began to fade. General Ironside, while stating that it would not be an easy matter to reach the iron ore districts in snow and difficult terrain, concluded that the Allies could reach the mines before any possible Russian counter-moves. He further concluded that, if the British army were to be confronted by superior forces, a line of retreat was available after the mines were destroyed. He estimated that a force of three or four thousand men on skis or snowshoes would be sufficient.[11] Admiral Pound tried to ease worries that the Germans might occupy southern Sweden and Norway by stating that the disadvantages if they did so would be more than offset by cutting the iron ore supplies to Germany. The danger of war with the Soviet Union was now viewed as an acceptable side-effect of an operation that could cut the iron ore supplies to Germany. Fears of the Soviet military machine were somewhat abated when it was stopped in its tracks by the small Finnish conscript army. Military planners no longer considered the Soviets capable of creating problems for the Allies in other parts of the world or of providing a great deal of help for Germany in Scandinavia.

The military chiefs also focused on the advantages of shifting the war to Scandinavia, where they reasoned that the Germans would need at least 20 divisions while the Allies, with the help of the Swedes and Norwegians, could make do with a much smaller force. It was believed that the German army had only limited reserves of iron ore on hand, and the chiefs concluded that this fact would force the Germans to attack in the west in the near future or to invade Sweden to secure the Swedish ore. Such an action would also require the Germans to invade Norway, and these combined operations would demand resources on a scale that would force them to postpone indefinitely an attack in the west.

The chiefs gave their blessings to the proposed operations in northern Norway and Sweden, and recommended that the first part of the force be dispatched no later than March 1940 in order to secure the mining districts and the port of Luleå before the northern Baltic became navigable. No direct military action was contemplated against the iron ore mines in central Sweden. They were to be made inoperable by sabotage.

The military chiefs' acquiescence in the operation against northern Scandinavia carried with it several assumptions. It was imperative to obtain the cooperation of the Norwegian and Swedish governments, although such cooperation would place both those nations at odds with Germany and very possibly the Soviet Union as well.

The chiefs expected that an operation against Narvik would cause German counter-action in southern Norway and Sweden. The Scandinavian nations would be promised help and this help would come primarily through Trondheim in central Norway. The forces landed there would proceed to Sweden, and in cooperation with that nation's military, establish a defensive line south of Stockholm. Since a German occupation of southern Norway would place Trondheim within the reach of their air force, it was deemed necessary to also occupy Bergen and Stavanger. It was considered essential to carry out these operations almost simultaneously, and this required much shipping and very large naval forces.

Churchill kept pressing for his more limited option of mining the territorial waters. He presented a five-point plan to the War Cabinet on December 29 calling for quick action, pending execution of Ironside's more ambitious plan:

1. Send a note to Norway and Sweden promising Allied help in certain circumstances.
2. Notify Norway on January 1 that the British intended to retaliate for the sinking of ships in Norwegian territorial waters.
3. Send a British flotilla to Norway.
4. Begin seizing German ships in Norwegian territorial waters.
5. Take measures against the iron ore facilities in Oxelösund by end of January 1940.

As already stated, Churchill was well aware that the elimination of the iron ore shipments through Norwegian waters would not alone have a severe effect on German war industry. His plans in the fall of 1939 and spring of 1940 were simple. He hoped for a German reaction to interference with their ore shipments. This would provide the Allies with the requisite excuse needed to move into Scandinavia and eliminate the source of iron ore and other valuable supplies for Germany. The northern blockade would be much more effective with British bases on the Norwegian coast. While Churchill hoped that the Scandinavian countries would resist a direct German attack and become part of the Allied camp, he was not overly concerned if, instead, there was a hostile reaction by these countries to British actions and a request from them for

German assistance. While the cabinet members were impressed with Churchill's arguments, they made no decision.

The military Chiefs of Staff, with Air Chief Marshal Sir Cyril Newall as spokesman, advised against Churchill's proposal on January 2 when they presented the plan they had developed. They reasoned that Churchill's plan could lead to German countermeasures that would jeopardize the larger project—the seizure of Narvik and the Swedish iron ore districts. This was in accordance with views expressed by Ironside at the War Cabinet meeting on December 22. Furthermore, the army was not prepared to counter a German move against southern Norway. While expressing favor for Churchill's project, Chamberlain used the Chiefs of Staff's objections to delay any actions except for the dispatch of a note to Norway.

The minutes of the meeting on January 2 clearly indicate that there was no realistic understanding of possible Swedish, Norwegian, and German reaction to an Allied entry into northern Scandinavia. They also demonstrate lack of understanding for the complexities of operations in a rugged, roadless arctic wilderness. Churchill maintained that Allied forces were sufficient to seize the iron ore districts regardless of Norwegian and Swedish reactions. The Dominions Secretary, Anthony Eden, suggested that 5,000–7,000 Canadians could be available for the operation in March. When it was pointed out that the Canadians were not trained on skis, General Ironside noted that they had snowshoes, and felt that was sufficient. The lack of reality of these and other assumptions by Allied leaders was quickly demonstrated when they sent forces to Norway in April.

British Note to Norway on January 6, 1940

Lord Halifax delivered the British diplomatic note to the Norwegian Ambassador in London, Erik Colban, on the evening of January 6. The note used the sinking of one Greek and two British merchant ships in 1939—*Thomas Walton* on December 8, *Garoufalia* on December 11, and *Deptford* on December 13—as examples of Norwegian failures to prevent the misuse of its territorial waters.[12] The note, a copy of which was provided to Sweden, stated it would be necessary in the future to permit British warships to operate in Norwegian waters because the Germans had turned them into an operational area.

The Norwegian reaction was stronger than the British had anticipated. The Norwegians viewed the note as the most serious threat yet against their neutrality. They were probably aware that some British officials, Churchill among them, were hoping for a German reaction. In Churchill's view, the

Scandinavian countries were afraid of Germany and they would react favorably to Allied demands only if they were more afraid of them than the Germans. Foreign Minister Koht probably selected his words deliberately when he voiced the suspicion "that the British Government's goal was to bring Norway into the war."[13] To the Norwegians, the note sounded suspiciously like the unreasonable accusations that sometimes preceded action by major powers. In addition, they felt particularly offended that this note was directed at a nation that had lost many lives and much property bringing supplies and foodstuffs to Great Britain through the German blockade.

The Norwegian government viewed the British threat so seriously that they prevailed on King Håkon VII to send a telegram on January 7 to his nephew, King George VI, asking for his personal intervention. George VI answered that it was necessary in this period for his country to defend its interests. The official Norwegian protest pointed out that British actions of the type threatened would lead to German counter-measures, and that the Norwegian Navy had orders to repel any violations of Norwegian neutrality by all means, regardless of the perpetrator's nationality.

At least one writer claims that the exchange of letters between the two monarchs had a significant impact. Kersaudy writes, "Actually, the intervention of such an eminent personality as King Haakon of Norway was more than enough for Neville Chamberlain to give up even the semblance of any warlike initiative."[14] It is more likely that Chamberlain and Halifax used the strong Norwegian response to the British note, along with a very negative response from Sweden, as reasons to put the brakes on Churchill's plans.[15] In the middle of January, the British government shelved Churchill's plan for immediate action against the iron ore traffic.

There followed over the next month a series of note exchanges between the British and Norwegians. Lord Halifax suggested to the Norwegian Ambassador that Norway take steps to close its waters, and an aide memoir of January 22 made the same suggestion. The Norwegian answer in early February stated that the Norwegian government would examine measures to protect its territorial waters, including mining. It was not until March 20 that the Norwegian Defense Ministry was asked to examine the possibility of mining specific points along the coast. Rear Admiral Henry E. Diesen, Commander-in-Chief of the Norwegian Navy, recommended on April 2 that if the government deemed it necessary, mine barriers should be laid south of Stadt. The Allies did not wait for the Norwegians to make a final decision.

Allied Military Plans

The British and French military staffs presented their plans to the Allied Supreme War Council in Paris on February 5, 1940. The War Council, based on these plans, approved a British motion to prepare and dispatch a military expeditionary force of several brigades of British, French, and Polish troops to the Finnish front. The expedition would be under British command. The primary objective of this force, which was to proceed to the Finnish front through Norway and Sweden, is actually found in another plan, code-named *Avonmouth*. The iron ore mines were included in the objectives of the expeditionary force.

The plan required Allied forces to land in Narvik and advance along the railroad to Kiruna and Gällivare, and on to Luleå on the Baltic. It was planned that the brigades would be positioned along this line before the middle of April, when Luleå would again be free from ice and open to German ore traffic. The unreasonableness of the assumption that Allied forces would be able to accomplish this in the roadless arctic wilderness was confirmed when elite British troops proved unable to undertake any off-road operations, and French Alpine troops were deemed unsuited for operations in the mountains around Narvik by their commander as late as May. Only part of the expeditionary force would proceed to Finland, and there is no doubt that the main objective was to halt the export of iron ore to Germany under the guise of helping the Finns.

The Allied plan anticipated a strong German reaction to the occupation of parts of northern Norway and Sweden. However, the planners did not expect Germany to be in a position to act effectively until late spring when the Baltic was ice-free. Nevertheless, to meet possible German countermoves, the Allied plans called for the occupation of the cities of Trondheim, Namsos, Bergen, and Stavanger by five British territorial brigades. This part of the operation was code-named *Stratford*. The occupation of these cities would provide bases from which to defend Norway, and open an alternate route to Finland via Trondheim. That city, along with Namsos, would serve as the main Allied base. Bergen would be an important secondary base and serve as the eastern terminal of a planned North Sea mine barrier. The planned operation against Stavanger can best be characterized as a raid. The city was to be held only long enough to destroy the Sola Airfield in order to deny its use by the Luftwaffe.

The plan for actions in Norway and Sweden called for reinforcements to be sent via Trondheim to take part in possible operations against Germans in southern Sweden, code-named *Plymouth*. These forces would consist of about

100,000 British and 50,000 French troops. Two British divisions due to embark for France were held back in Britain to be available for the Scandinavian operations. The port facilities in Trondheim were limited and it was estimated that it would take one month to get about 24,000 combat troops to link up with Swedish forces in positions to oppose a German advance. The rest of the force was needed to hold bases and keep lines of communications open. Over 40 destroyers were required as close-in escorts for the troop transports. The mission of the Home Fleet, strengthened by units of the French fleet, was to protect the transports against attacks by enemy surface units and the Luftwaffe. The air force contingent consisted of only six and one-half squadrons, three of which were fighters. In addition, four squadrons of heavy land-based bombers were placed at the disposal of the operation. While these were large commitments at this stage of the war, their inadequacy is confirmed by Britain's own intelligence estimate, mentioned earlier, of what the Germans needed to carry out a similar operation. Derry maintains that these commitments were not large if the military chiefs were right in their opinion that it was their first and best chance to grab the initiative and shorten the war.

Even if the military chiefs were right in their assessment of the effects on the German war effort, the resources were inadequate against the logical reactions of the two Scandinavian countries, and particularly against the probable reactions by Germany and the Soviet Union. The issue of what to do if Norway and Sweden resisted, a probability Churchill claims to have recognized, was never faced by the Supreme War Council.

Preliminary requests to Norway and Sweden on March 2, 1940 about free passage of Allied troops to Finland were rejected quickly and firmly. In spite of this refusal and strong indications that Sweden and Norway would resist, the planners made no increase in the planned force levels. The likelihood of Norwegian resistance was eventually accepted, but the operation proceeded despite this probability. The military planners questioned what to do if the Norwegians and Swedes resisted, but the issue was studiously avoided by decision-makers. A note in Ironside's diary is illustrative.

As the attitude of the Norwegians was in doubt, the commanders were instructed to land provided there was no serious fighting. The British had no intention of fighting their way through Norway and into Sweden. On the other hand, the commanders were not to be deterred by a show of resistance.[16]

Another astonishing excerpt from the instructions to the commanders was:

> It is not the intention of this government that the force should fight its
> way through either Sweden or Norway. Nonetheless, should you find
> your way barred by Swedish forces, you should demand passage from the
> Swedish commander with the utmost energy.[17]

These were early examples of the many muddled statements and directives
that were to emanate from the British command authorities during the
Norwegian campaign. Chief Air Marshal Newall was on the mark when he said
at the time, "I think the whole thing is hare brained."[18]

The *Altmark* Incident

On February 16, 1940 an episode occurred that proved tailor-made for
Churchill's plans. At the same time, the outcome was such that future violations
of Norwegian neutrality by the Allies would be viewed with greater
understanding both domestically and in neutral countries. The episode involved
violations of Norwegian neutrality by both the German and British navies, and
the Norwegians can certainly be blamed for not enforcing their own rules and
for handling the incident in a clumsy manner.

The German pocket battleship *Admiral Graf Spee* had raided shipping in the
South Atlantic before it was scuttled off Uruguay's Platte River on December 17,
1939. Survivors from merchant ships she had sunk had been transferred to one
of her supply ships—*Altmark*—before the pocket battleship encountered the
Royal Navy. The *Altmark*, commanded by Captain Heinrich Dau, headed back
to Germany with its cargo of prisoners after the demise of the *Admiral Graf Spee*
and entered Norwegian territorial waters on February 14.

The Norwegians had their suspicions about the ship's cargo but allowed it to
proceed along the coast under naval escort. The ship flew the German naval flag,
but despite this fact, Dau allowed three visits by Norwegian naval personnel on
February 15. The German captain reported that the ship had participated in
exercises in the Atlantic and was on its way from Port Arthur, Texas to Germany
with a cargo of 8,500-tons of oil, that the ship was armed with 20mm antiaircraft guns, but that these were stowed away before entering Norwegian waters.

Rear Admiral Carsten Tank-Nielsen, the commander of Norway's 2nd Naval
District, was in a dilemma. If *Altmark* was a merchant ship, it had the right,
under the neutrality regulations, to sail through the restricted area around

Bergen after being inspected. A warship, on the other hand, could not sail through the area. Classified as a naval auxiliary, the ship did not fit neatly into either of the two categories.

The Norwegian destroyer *Garm*, with Admiral Tank-Nielsen aboard, and the minelayer *Olav Tryggvason* intercepted *Altmark* well within the restricted area, escorted by the torpedo boat *Snøgg*. The acting chief of staff of the naval district and *Snøgg's* captain boarded *Altmark* and conferred with Captain Dau. The Norwegians informed Dau that either he had to submit to a search or he would not be allowed to proceed through the restricted area. Captain Dau stated that the ship was a naval auxiliary and he would not permit a search. He was then ordered to take his ship out to sea, around the restricted area.

While this conference was underway, the Germans broke radio silence and sent a report to the German Embassy in Oslo. Norwegian naval communicators intercepted the radio message and the military control office in Oslo stopped the telegram from reaching the German Embassy. Captain Dau was admonished not to use his radio while in Norwegian waters. The German captain apologized but asked the Norwegians to notify the German Embassy that he had refused inspection and was taking his ship out to sea. Admiral Tank-Nielsen agreed to this request. *Altmark* withdrew from the restricted area to await an answer from the German Embassy. Norwegian warships remained in the vicinity to ensure that the German ship did not reenter the restricted area.

The destroyer *Garm* had been close enough to *Altmark* for sailors to report that SOS whistle signals were heard from the German ship and that white handkerchiefs had been displayed at the portholes. *Garm* also reported that the Germans had started up the on-board cranes and other machinery, obviously in an attempt to drown out the signals.

Admiral Tank-Nielsen sent the following message to the Norwegian Naval Staff: "The ship has refused supplemental visitation and its passage through the restricted area has been denied. Probably prisoners aboard. Inform the Commander-in-Chief."[19] The telegram reached Admiral Diesen at 1554 hours. Diesen conferred with the Norwegian Foreign Office. Both the Foreign Office and Admiral Diesen appear to have felt there had been enough visitations to the German ship, and that Admiral Tank-Nielsen was not handling this problem in accordance with supplemental instructions after a somewhat similar situation in November 1939.[20] Diesen and the Foreign Office decided to send the German ship on its way at once. The Norwegians were eager to get this embarrassing and potentially dangerous ship out of its territorial waters as quickly as possible.

The report from *Garm* about suspicious activities aboard *Altmark* did not reach the Norwegian naval headquarters until after Admiral Diesen's decision, but he stated later that receipt of the report would not have altered his decision. Admiral Tank-Nielsen was ordered to let *Altmark* pass in its capacity as a naval auxiliary and to provide an escort. The passage through the restricted area was accomplished in darkness, an action contrary to the navy's own neutrality regulations.

Meantime, a report of *Altmark's* presence in Norwegian waters had reached Rear Admiral H. Boyles, the British Naval Attaché in Oslo. Boyles passed this report on to the British Admiralty. Churchill recognized the potential opportunities in the situation and acted quickly. He instructed Admiral Pound that he should not hesitate "... to arrest *Altmark* in territorial waters should she be found. The ship is violating neutrality in carrying British prisoners of war to Germany. ... The *Altmark* must be regarded as an invaluable trophy."[21]

Three reconnaissance aircraft from Coastal Command were dispatched to locate *Altmark*. She was sighted in Norwegian waters south of Stavanger. The escorting Norwegian patrol boat *Firern* had no antiaircraft guns and could only signal the British aircraft that they were violating Norwegian airspace, and warn them to stand off.

A British destroyer flotilla of six ships commanded by Captain Philip Vian (later Admiral of the Fleet) in the destroyer *Cossack*, intercepted *Altmark*, now escorted by the Norwegian torpedo boat *Skarv*, outside the entrance to Jøssingfjord, halfway between Egersund and Flekkefjord. Three destroyers made the initial intercept: *Cossack*, *Intrepid*, and *Ivanhoe*. At first, they stopped short of Norwegian territory and signaled *Altmark* to proceed on a westerly course, out of Norwegian waters. *Altmark* ignored the signal and proceeded on its previous course. At that point, *Intrepid* and *Ivanhoe* entered Norwegian waters despite protests from the Norwegian torpedo boat. *Ivanhoe* tried to position itself to block *Altmark* but the Norwegian torpedo boat took up a position between the two ships and moved to within hailing distance of the British destroyer, which fired a warning shot toward *Altmark*.

The *Altmark* slowed down and a boat was launched from *Ivanhoe* with the intention of boarding the German ship. Lieutenant Hansen, the commander of *Skarv*, protested the British breach of Norwegian neutrality. Captain Gordon answered the protest by telling the Norwegian officer that he had orders to capture the German ship. Captain Dau used the delay to move *Altmark* at full speed towards the Jøssingfjord entrance. Three additional British destroyers arrived on the scene, and a second Norwegian torpedo boat, *Kjell*, took up a position between the British force and the entrance to Jøssingfjord.

A very dangerous situation had developed. The six modern British destroyers were vastly superior to the two Norwegian torpedo boats.[22] However, the sinking of Norwegian naval vessels, with loss of life, in their territorial waters would probably lead to war between Britain and Norway.

Lieutenant Halvorsen, *Kjell's* commander, was the senior Norwegian officer on the scene and took command of the Norwegian force in the area. He protested verbally to Captain Hadow, the *Ivanhoe's* skipper. For unknown reasons, Captain Hadow initially addressed Halvorsen in German. Hadow switched to English after the Norwegian lieutenant told him, to the great amusement of the destroyer crew, "Please, speak English, Sir."[23] With these pleasantries out of the way, Lieutenant Halvorsen demanded that the British force leave Norwegian territorial waters immediately. Captain Hadow informed the Norwegian that *Altmark* carried 400 British prisoners, and that he had orders to free them and bring them to England. Nevertheless, the British withdrew. On the advice of Norwegian pilots, *Altmark* used the time to enter Jøssingfjord. Captain Dau again used his radio to send a message to the German Embassy in Oslo via a coastal radio station. Norwegian authorities stopped the message.

Skarv remained with the British destroyers while *Kjell* followed and hailed *Altmark*. Captain Dau informed Halvorsen that Norwegian warships from the 2nd Naval District had visited the ship repeatedly and he had received permission to use Norwegian territorial waters. No mention was made of prisoners. *Kjell* returned to the British destroyer force, tied up alongside *Cossack*, and Halvorsen boarded the British ship for a conference with Captain Vian. To Vian's statement that *Altmark* carried British prisoners, Halvorsen replied that he had no knowledge of any prisoners. However, even if this was the case, he maintained the British had no rights to violate Norwegian neutrality, and demanded that the British force depart as quickly as possible in order to avoid serious consequences.

The Norwegian torpedo boats had received orders from Rear Admiral J. Smith-Johannsen, commander of the 1st Naval District (which included the Jøssingfjord area), that force should be used to oppose any British attempt to seize *Altmark*. Vian suggested that Norwegian and British officers should inspect the ship, but the Norwegian turned down this suggestion, since allowing foreign officials to inspect ships in Norwegian waters was a serious infringement of the nation's sovereignty. Halvorsen pointed out that the German ship was in Norwegian waters, had been inspected by Norwegian warships, and had been permitted to proceed. Vian agreed to leave territorial waters, but stated that his force would remain outside to wait for *Altmark*.

Reports of what was transpiring on the Norwegian coast reached Churchill, and with the concurrence of the Foreign Office he sent Captain Vian the following order:

> Unless Norwegian torpedo-boat undertakes to convoy *Altmark* to Bergen with a joint Anglo-Norwegian guard on board, and a joint escort, you should board *Altmark*, liberate the prisoners, and take possession of the ship pending further instructions. If Norwegian torpedo-boat interferes, you should warn her to stand off. If she fires upon you, you should not reply unless the attack is serious, in which case you should defend yourself, using no more force than is necessary and ceasing fire when she desists.[24]

By this stage, the German Ambassador and his naval attaché had become involved, lodging protests. Admiral Boyes visited the Norwegian Naval Staff that evening. In addition to protesting the British action, Norwegian officers pointed out that it was not necessary for the British to attack *Altmark* in its present position. The Norwegians showed Admiral Boyes maps illustrating that *Altmark* would be forced to leave Norwegian territorial waters to avoid the ice in the Skagerrak, and that British forces could easily intercept the ship at that time. It would be logical for Admiral Boyes to forward this information to the British Admiralty. The official Norwegian naval history states that there is no evidence he forwarded the information, but if he did, it had no influence on the events that were unfolding.

The urgency of the British action raises questions about their motives, aside from the obvious one of freeing their fellow citizens. *Altmark* was trapped in Jøssingfjord and going nowhere, with a force of six British destroyers outside the entrance. If Churchill's suggestion of a joint escort of *Altmark* to Bergen or another suitable harbor had been made to the Norwegian government, rather than through Captain Vian to a low-ranking Norwegian naval officer, it is quite possible that a solution agreeable to both parties would have been found. Similarly, the information given to Admiral Boyes by the Norwegian Naval Staff was certainly available to the British Admiralty, even if Boyes did not make a report. There are good reasons to believe that the British (probably Churchill and the Admiralty), knowing there were acceptable alternatives to confrontation, chose the latter. A confrontation would certainly focus public attention on German misuses of Norwegian waters, plus Norway's failures to enforce its neutrality, and could lead to the kind of German countermeasures Churchill desired.

Admiral Smith-Johannsen rescinded his order to use force to prevent the seizure of *Altmark* after he discussed the matter with his superior, Admiral Diesen. Captain Vian had meanwhile received Churchill's order and decided to carry it out using his own destroyer. Halvorsen hailed him at the mouth of the fjord and Vian stated what his orders were. Halvorsen, who was personally convinced the German ship carried no prisoners, asked for ten minutes to examine the German ship. Reports from the 2nd Naval District indicating that prisoners might well be aboard the ship were apparently not relayed to the 1st Naval District. Captain Vian rejected the Norwegian suggestion and proposed instead that Halvorsen accompany the British boarding party as a representative of the Norwegian authorities. He also suggested that the boarding take place from the Norwegian torpedo boat. Halvorsen rejected the suggestion. However, since he was convinced there were no prisoners aboard *Altmark*, he consented to be present on HMS *Cossack* as an observer.

After he realized what was happening, Dau managed to ram *Cossack* with the aft end of *Altmark*, without causing any significant damage. The British boarding party entered the German ship and, according to German and Norwegian sources, opened fire on its crew resulting in five (seven according to some sources) dead and a number of wounded. The British reported that they had fired in self-defense after coming under fire from the Germans. Captain Dau denied that the Germans had fired a single shot. Lieutenant Halvorsen left the British destroyer in protest when the firing started, and reported later that he observed the British firing at German crewmembers fleeing on the ice. Two hundred and ninety-nine prisoners were freed and transported to England. Norwegian destroyers escorted *Altmark* to repair facilities and the ship eventually returned to Germany.

Norway protested the British action. On the legal side, Norway based its position on the claim that *Altmark* was a warship. "Warships have the rights to passage through neutral waters and the fact that it is carrying prisoners does not change this fact."[25] The British rejected the Norwegian protest. Chamberlain deplored the views of the Norwegians since "it would in their [British] view legalize the abuse by German warships of neutral waters and create a position which His Majesty's Government could in no circumstances accept."[26]

The *Altmark* affair had no direct effect on Allied planning except for the conclusion that the Norwegians were either in no position or were not inclined to prevent German misuse of their territorial waters. The passive reaction by the Norwegian Navy may also have emboldened the British dramatically to increase their violations, both in number and scope, over the next few weeks. A passage from the Norwegian naval history is illustrative.[27]

> The belligerents' activities on the Norwegian coast showed a strong increase during March and the first days of April 1940. The number of intentional or unintentional neutrality violations by both warships and aircraft increased continually. From the middle of March until Norway became a participant in the war, there was thus seldom a day when the country's neutrality was not violated one or several times. . . . Most violations were, as earlier, carried out by British warships and aircraft . . .

In the opinion of the Allies, the *Altmark* incident strengthened their moral justification for their planned action in Scandinavia. Such an underpinning was badly needed since it appeared that the Finnish-Soviet conflict was reaching a climax and could cease to be a motivation for action in Scandinavia.

End of the Winter War and its Effect on Allied plans

The great Soviet offensive against the Finnish Army on the Karelian Isthmus opened on February 1, 1940. It lasted for 42 days. Ten days of heavy bombardment by over 500 aircraft and Soviet guns, massed wheel to wheel, preceded the attack by two armies consisting of 54 divisions. After 12 days of ferocious fighting, resulting in enormous Russian casualties, the Mannerheim Line was breached on February 13, and by March 1 the Finnish right flank was pushed slowly back to the city of Viipuri. The situation for the Finns had become desperate. They were short of ammunition and their troops were exhausted. The hoped-for assistance from the West had not materialized. The total number of foreign volunteers in Finland numbered only 11,500, and 8,275 of these were from Sweden and Norway, mostly from Sweden. The volunteers also included 300 men in the Finnish-American Legion who received their baptism of fire in the last days of the war.

A Finnish delegation proceeded to Moscow to discuss armistice terms on March 7. The Soviet terms were surprisingly lenient, almost the same as those contained in their demands in November 1939 that led to the war. The Russian losses in the war have never been published but most observers believe they suffered more than 200,000 killed and another 400,000 wounded. The Soviets were also alarmed by the cool attitude displayed by Germany in early 1940, and by the prospect of a war with England and France unless they came to quick terms with the Finns. The Finns accepted the Soviet terms on March 12.

The conclusion of peace between the Soviet Union and Finland rendered the underpinnings of Allied plans obsolete. With unenthusiastic agreement by the French leader, Daladier, the British government decided on March 14 to set aside plans for operations in Scandinavia. Since there was no longer the slightest chance that Sweden and Norway would acquiesce to an Allied presence in their countries, active resistance had to be anticipated. This would throw the Scandinavian countries into the arms of Germany.

It is easy to recognize that Allied policy and plans were shortsighted and inadequate. While execution of the policy may have achieved some success against Germany's peripheral interests, it carried with it huge long-term risks that seriously damaged the Allies' claim to the high moral ground. The slow-moving Allied planning and preparation machinery was undoubtedly very fortunate for their war effort. Operations in Scandinavia and assistance to Finland would probably have resulted in war with the Soviet Union, while Sweden and Norway might have become Germany's reluctant allies. This could have had enormous consequences for the outcome of WWII.

The conclusion of peace between the Soviet Union and Finland also saved Chamberlain and Halifax from the precarious position of having to carry out an operation that they believed would remove all possibilities of peace. They no doubt welcomed the news that the Soviet-Finnish conflict had ended, and to remove any possibility that an operation on the scale anticipated could be carried out, they quickly dispatched the two regular divisions (held back for operations in Scandinavia) to France. By reducing the force available for use in Scandinavia to 11 battalions, they hoped to discourage their use. This became a major factor in the debacle following the decision to dispatch troops to Norway.

Churchill's Mining Plan Approved

Plans for Allied action in Scandinavia, particularly in Norway, continued due to Churchill's persistence. Information about Allied plans to help the Finns leaked to the press, and their failure to carry them out resulted in a storm of criticism directed at the governments in Britain and France. Daladier's government fell, and the more aggressive Paul Reynaud replaced him as prime minister. The new French Prime Minister was more congenial to Churchill's designs. He advocated an aggressive war effort and revisited the question of operations in Scandinavia, including taking control of the Norwegian coast.

Churchill and Reynaud had similar views as to the purpose of operations in Scandinavia, differing only when it came to details. Churchill's primary goal was to entice the Germans into an area where British naval superiority could bring victories. In the process, the Allies would increase the effectiveness of the blockade, eliminate iron ore shipments to Germany via Norway, and possibly bring Sweden under their sway. This was only different from the views of Reynaud in scope and emphasis. He wanted to send an expedition into Norway in order "to create a new theater of war in which the Germans would use up their men, their materiel, and in particular their air force, and above all, their reserves, especially of petrol."[28] Chamberlain and Halifax were facing severe criticism in the press and from their colleagues, and it seems they were ready to do anything as long as it looked as if they were doing something.

Reynaud and his colleagues came to London on March 28, 1940 for a meeting of the Supreme War Council. Prime Minister Neville Chamberlain finally threw his support behind Churchill's long-standing proposal to cut Germany's import of iron ore from Narvik. Reynaud readily agreed, and it was decided to mine Norwegian waters beginning April 5. The participants in the meeting agreed that a good pretext would have to be found to alleviate the adverse reactions such an operation would have in neutral countries, particularly in the United States. It was agreed that diplomatic notes should be sent to Norway and Sweden before the mining. These notes would state that the neutrality policies of the Scandinavian countries gave great comfort and help to Germany, and the Allies could not ignore these facts. In effect, this was tantamount to saying, "Either you are with us or against us." They would remind the recipients that Hitler was diametrically opposed to the autonomy and rights of small nations, a cause for which the armies of both France and Britain were fighting.

The plan called for delivery of these notes to the Norwegian and Swedish governments on April 1 and 2. The mining operations, code-named *Wilfred*, were thereupon to proceed without further warning to the Norwegians. These operations were expected to result in German retaliation, and British and French troops were held in readiness for a rapid occupation of Narvik, Trondheim, Bergen, and Stavanger (Plan *R4*).

It was hoped that the Norwegians, who were expected to be aware of possible German counter-measures, would not resist the mining, and in fact might welcome the Allied action. The planners were less certain about the Swedish reaction. It was hoped that Allied troops in Narvik would be able to move against the iron ore mines in Sweden and be in position to help that country against a German attack. The plan also called for mining the Luleå harbor with aerial deployed mines.

There can be no doubt that the sympathies of Sweden and Norway were with the Allies; nevertheless, it was over-optimistic to hope that they would not resist an attack. A more pragmatic approach would have been to assume that Sweden, in the face of Allied landings in Narvik, their advance on the iron ore district, and the mining of Luleå, would have acquiesced to German assistance if they thought it necessary. The subsequent Allied operations in North Norway demonstrated clearly that they would have been incapable of reaching the Swedish iron ore districts if faced with Norwegian and Swedish resistance, so Sweden may not even have needed to call on Hitler's help.

The propaganda value to the German leaders of an Allied attack on two small neutrals was obvious. The Allies may well have lost the moral high ground they had secured after the German aggressions against Czechoslovakia and Poland. Even Churchill's eloquence may not have been able to overcome the negative effects among neutrals.

It is difficult to understand why such intelligent and experienced policy-makers and military planners could have been so confident of Norwegian and Swedish support for their proposed gross infringement of neutrality. One possible explanation is that the Allies were so captivated by the perceived advantages of widening the war that they glossed over any serious objections.

In order to disrupt river traffic, the Supreme War Council also agreed to drop mines in the Rhine River and its canals at the same time, in an operation code named *Royal Marine.*

By including an attack directly against Germany as part of the plan, the Allies likely hoped to deflect some of the anticipated criticism that their first offensive operation of the war was carried out against a neutral country rather than the aggressor.

The French War Committee objected to Operation *Royal Marine* on April 3. Daladier, who was now Minister of Defense, argued that *Royal Marine* would lead to German reprisals against French industries. He pointed out that the fighter aircraft of the French Air Force would need three months before they were ready to protect French industries against German air attacks.

An irritated Chamberlain dispatched Churchill to Paris to try to convince the French to carry out both operations. In the meantime, however, those operations were put on hold. Churchill met Daladier on April 5. He was not particularly interested in *Royal Marine* and did not press Daladier to change his mind as Chamberlain had hoped. Churchill told Chamberlain and Halifax that the French arguments against *Royal Marine* were well grounded, but that the mining of Norwegian waters should proceed. Both the prime minister and his foreign secretary appear to have reached that decision even before Churchill's return. The British War Cabinet decided to carry out Operation *Wilfred* in the early morning hours of April 8. Halifax favored proceeding with *Wilfred* since he feared that not doing so could cause the Reynaud government to fall. He realized that Reynaud's resolute offensive spirit was largely motivated by a desire to avoid the fate of Daladier. The delay in launching the Allied operation from April 5 to April 8 had a huge effect on events in Norway.

The decision to proceed with the operations in Norway caused a feeling of relief and optimism among the people of London and Paris. The optimistic mood is reflected in Chamberlain's speech to a gathering of conservative politicians and supporters on April 5. He pointed out to the audience that Hitler, in not going on the offensive over the past seven months, had failed to exploit his initial military superiority. He continued:

> Whatever may be the reason—whether it was that Hitler thought he might get away with what he had got without fighting for it, or whether it was that after all the preparations were not sufficiently complete—however, one thing is certain: he missed the bus.[29]

Chamberlain's statement that Hitler had missed the bus was as ill advised as his claim of "peace in our time" after his earlier meeting with Hitler in Munich. As he addressed the House of Commons on May 7 in an emotionally charged atmosphere, when things were unraveling for the Allies in Norway, his speech was continually interrupted by shouts of "Hitler missed the bus!" and "Who missed the bus?"

To meet the contingency of a German reaction, Operation *Wilfred* had a complementary plan named *R4*. This was scheduled to go into operation when "the Germans set foot on Norwegian soil, or there was clear evidence that they intended to do so."[30] This plan included provisions for a British brigade (the 24th Guards) and a French contingent to be dispatched to Narvik to clear that port and advance to the Swedish border. Another five battalions were destined for

Stavanger, Bergen, and Trondheim to deny those cities to the enemy. Plan *R4* was allocated no air support. It was apparently expected that the infantry units, once ashore, would be able to hold these cities against all threats. It was hoped that the Norwegians would welcome the British and French troops as allies. There were no contingencies covering the real possibility that the Norwegians would resist.

The primary objective of the expedition in Norway was Narvik and the railroad leading to the Swedish border. Later, as opportunity presented itself, the Allied troops were to advance into Sweden and occupy the iron ore districts of Kiruna and Gällivare. The brigade destined for Narvik was to be brought there in a transport escorted by two cruisers. These ships were to leave their debarkation port a few hours after the minefields were laid. It is evident from this timeline that a landing in Narvik was to take place even if there was no immediate German counter-move. A gradual buildup of forces in Narvik was anticipated until the strength of the units there reached approximately 18,000. This force would be composed for the most part of French alpine troops. If an advance into Sweden became an actuality, one squadron of fighters would support these troops. The plan—especially the assumptions and force allocation parts—strikes one as tentative, nonchalant, and unrealistic when compared to what the Germans were planning.

Allied Diplomatic Notes on April 5, 1940

The British and French notes were delivered to Norway and Sweden on the evening of April 5. The gist was contained in paragraph five of the documents:

> The Allies, seeing that they are waging war for aims which are as much in the interests of smaller States as in their own, cannot allow the course of the war to be influenced against them by the advantage derived by Germany from Norway or from Sweden. They therefore give notice that they reserve the right to take such measures as they may think necessary to hinder or prevent Germany from obtaining from these countries resources or facilities which for the prosecution of the war would be to her advantage or to the disadvantage of the Allies.[31]

Koht received the note as he was preparing to attend a dinner at the residence of the U.S. Ambassador, Mrs. Harrimann. He addressed the Norwegian Parliament with carefully chosen words to conceal his mixed feelings of fear and anger and to avoid creating a sense of alarm in the country. His speech was directed more at the diplomatic corps and the foreign press representatives than at the Norwegian people. He stressed that the Allies had nothing to gain by closing Norwegian waters since the country traded more with Great Britain than with Germany, and more iron ore from Narvik went to the Allies than to Germany. He reminded the listeners that the Allies had approved the trade agreements and signed treaties to that effect. To force Norway to abandon these agreements would be a breach of neutrality and Norway would find itself at war.

The British government had little information about Koht's reaction to the note when some of the War Cabinet members met on Saturday, April 6. However, there was no doubt about the Swedish reaction. The Swedish ambassador to Great Britain had stated immediately that it could become necessary to reexamine the trade agreements between Sweden and England. The British ambassador in Stockholm reported that the Swedish Foreign Minister, Christian Günther, had stated that the notes brought his country to the edge of war. The British ambassador expected Sweden to mobilize the following day and had great difficulties persuading the foreign minister not to release the notes to the press. However, in a conversation with Koht, Günther opined that the notes were not as ominous as they sounded, and that they were probably designed to silence domestic critics in Great Britain and France.[32]

Chamberlain and Halifax decided to send a message to calm Swedish fears and anger. Despite the fact that British naval forces were already at sea, and troops were in the process of embarking for landings in Norway, the British message assured the Swedes that they had no intention of landing in Scandinavia unless they were forced to do so by a similar German action. This was also the day on which the British government approved military orders to execute the mining operations and the landing of troops in Narvik.

Allied Operations Begin

Four destroyers of the 20th Destroyer Flotilla, commanded by Captain Bickford, left Scapa Flow on April 5 with a course for Vestfjord, to lay a minefield. They were accompanied by four more destroyers of the 2nd Destroyer Flotilla, under the command of Captain Warburton-Lee. His mission was to cover Bickford's destroyers during the mine-laying operation and later to guard the minefield. Another force left Scapa Flow on the same day. It consisted of the minelayer *Teviot Bank*, escorted by four destroyers under the command of Captain Tod. The mission of this force was to lay mines off Stadt (north of Bergen). British destroyers would also simulate laying a minefield near the town of Molde.

Chamberlain and Halifax were nervous about the possibility of armed conflict with the Norwegian Navy during the mining operations. An agitated Koht had recently protested to the British Embassy about continued British violations of Norwegian waters, and stated that such violations would no longer be tolerated. Henceforth, the Norwegians would use force. Admiral Pound explained that the British warships would not let themselves be chased away by Norwegian warships. The mines would be laid, but only minimum force would be used. He agreed there could be some exchange of fire since, according to recent intelligence, the Norwegian Navy had orders to use force against neutrality violations. However, the Norwegians had concentrated their naval forces near the larger cities, and since the minefields were located far from these cities, he did not anticipate a quick reaction.[33]

The British Navy would not interfere with Norwegian operations to sweep the minefields; it would just lay a new field in a slightly different location. If the Norwegians challenged the British destroyers guarding the minefields, they were to be told that they were there on humanitarian grounds, to keep innocent ships from being sunk. Thereafter, they were to withdraw from Norwegian waters and leave the guard mission to the Norwegians.

It was planned initially that the cruiser *Birmingham* and two destroyers hunting for a German fishing fleet near the Lofoten Islands would cover the mining operation in Vestfjord. The final decision was to send the battle cruiser *Renown*, flagship of Vice Admiral W.J. Whitworth, as a show of force to discourage the Norwegians from trying to hinder the operation with their coastal defense ships *Norge* and *Eidsvold*. *Renown*, escorted by the destroyers *Greyhound*, *Glowworm*, *Heron*, and *Hyperion*, left Scapa Flow late in the afternoon of April 5. On their way to Vestfjord, they were joined by the eight destroyers that had departed Scapa Flow earlier the same day.

Nineteen submarines, including two French and one Polish, were directed to the Kattegat and Skagerrak on April 4. Their mission was to frustrate any German attempt to interfere with the British mining operations or the bringing of troops to Norway.

In readiness to protect the operation against German counter-measures were the 2nd Cruiser Squadron in Rosyth, consisting of two cruisers and 15 destroyers, and the 18th Cruiser Squadron in Scapa Flow, consisting of two heavy cruisers and five destroyers. Vice Admiral G. F. B. Edward-Collins commanded the 2nd, and Vice Admiral G. Layton commanded the 18th. The Home Fleet, commanded by Admiral Sir Charles Forbes, was also in Scapa Flow, ready for operations. It consisted of the battleships *Rodney* and *Valiant*, the battle cruiser *Repulse*, the cruiser *Sheffield*, and 10 destroyers.[34]

Admiral Sir Edward Evans was designated naval commander of the expedition against Narvik. He hoisted his flag on the cruiser *Aurora* in the Clyde on April 4. This ship, together with the cruiser *Penelope*, was ordered to escort a large troop transport that embarked troops on April 7. The ship took aboard one battalion of the 24th Guards Brigade, the First Scots Guards. The other two battalions of the brigade were on their way to the embarkation point on April 7. This force was scheduled to depart the Clyde early in the morning of April 8.

The orders for the operation were similar to those issued for *Plymouth* earlier. The main difference was that the force would advance to the Swedish border and await further instructions. However, if the opportunity presented itself, the force would continue on to the iron ore field at Gällivare.

Some confusing statements in the military order perplexed even Halifax. He noted that one paragraph stated that the Allied forces were to land only after agreement with the Norwegian government, while the next paragraph stated that they should tolerate some losses if the Norwegians opened fire. Ironside explained that this provision was included since it was possible that even if the Norwegians decided to cooperate, local military commanders might be confused or out of communications with their superiors. The parenthetical reference to the precondition of Norwegian cooperation was removed from the document.

Major General Pierce C. Mackesy, the designated ground-force commander for Narvik, explained to Halifax what was meant by the phrase that called for landings provided it could be done without serious fighting. The troops were to accomplish their missions by methods like those used against civilians: persuasion, pressure, rifle butts, and fists. The troops were expected to tolerate seeing some of their own shot before resorting to deadly force. Thereafter, it was permitted to use as much force as necessary to protect themselves.[35]

One battalion of the 146th Infantry Brigade, destined for Trondheim, was embarked on another transport on April 7. Two battalions of the 148th Infantry Brigade, to be landed in Bergen and Stavanger, were at the same time embarked on the cruisers *Devonshire*, *Berwick*, *York*, and *Glasgow* in Rosyth. Admiral J.H.D. Cunningham commanded this squadron. The force was scheduled to leave Rosyth early on April 8.

The commanders of the forces for Trondheim and Bergen had some special instructions. The landings were to take place only after German "hostile actions," unless the Norwegians extended an invitation. If the force destined for

Bergen was unable to land, it should try to do so in Trondheim. If that also proved impossible, the forces were to return to Great Britain. Cooperation with Norwegian military forces was important, but this should not divert the Allies from their primary goals.

A British brigade of three battalions was held back as a reserve, to be transported to Narvik as soon as the 24th Brigade had occupied that city. A French force of about 14,000 men was also destined for Narvik. However, its first part, a combined alpine brigade of six battalions, was not scheduled to sail from France until eight days after the first British troops had sailed.

The Allied operations in Norway were underway. Their origins can be traced to the political leadership in both Great Britain and France. While the ideas were Churchill's, he had the wholehearted support at the highest levels in the French government (Reynaud and Daladier). Chamberlain and Halifax gave their reluctant support only after the storm of criticism that broke out following their failure to take timely action to help the Finns. It is important to keep the strategic credentials of these policy makers in mind. Kersaudy has commented, "With the exception of Winston Churchill, the War Cabinet ministers had not the slightest notion of strategy, and they knew it; as for Churchill's notions, they were highly imperfect—and he did not know it."[36] The British naval leadership supported the operation because it held out promise for action that could cripple the German Navy, prevent the latter from improving its strategic position, and strengthen the naval blockade. The other services in Britain were much less enthusiastic, particularly the air force. They were concerned about the diversion of scarce resources away from the main theater of operations in France.

There is no doubt that what the Allies contemplated constituted aggression; but any clear-cut interpretation becomes muddled because of almost simultaneous German action. Similarity of intent should not be inferred because of the coincidental timing of the operations. Moulton draws the distinction by writing that the German intent was to occupy the capital and country, while the Allies were involved in a small naval operation to mine the territorial waters with a small military force in British ports in case of a German reaction. While this sounds reasonable, we have seen that the naval forces were not small; the military force designed to occupy the main population centers on the coast was small because it was all that was immediately available, and that this force was to sail before or simultaneously with the mining operation. The fact that they did not sail as scheduled was due to a British Admiralty decision that all ships were needed for naval action when it became aware that the Germans were at sea.

NOTES

1 J. L. Moulton, *A Study of Warfare in Three Dimensions: The Norwegian Campaign of 1940* (Athens, Ohio: The Ohio University Press, 1967), p. 44.

2 Winston Churchill, *The Gathering Storm* (Boston: Houghton Mifflin Company, 1948), p. 536.

3 William Norton Medlicott, *The Economic Blockade* (London: HMSO 1952-59), vol. 1, chapter 4 Section 6.

4 Memorandum by the War Economy and Armament Division of the OKW, dated February 22, 1940, contained in *Fuehrer Conferences on Matters Dealing With the German Navy 1940* (Translated and printed by the Office of Naval Intelligence, Navy Department, Washington, D.C., 1947), vol. 1, pp. 18-19.

5 Maurice Harvey. *Scandinavian Misadventure* (Tunbridge Wells: Spellmount, 1990), p.33.

6 Churchill, *Gathering Storm, pp.* 544-547.

7 Ibid, 544-545.

8 United Kingdom Public Record Office (PRO), *War Cabinet (CAB)*, 66/5 WP (40) 60, 19 February 1940.

9 Churchill, *Gathering Storm, p.* 546.

10 See Patrick Cosgrave, *Churchill at War, alone 1939–1940* (London, 1974), vol. 1, pp. 120-128.

11 Bjørnsen, *Narvik 1940* (Oslo: Gyldendal Norsk Forlag, 1980), p. 55.

12 An investigation by the Norwegian Navy was inconclusive. It could not ascertain with certainty that the sinking of two of the three ships took place within Norwegian territorial waters. They felt relatively certain that *Deptford* was sunk in territorial waters. This sinking claimed 30 lives, including two Norwegian pilots. It was determined during the Nuremberg Trial that the German submarine *U38* had sunk all three ships.

13 Letter from Ambassador Wollbæk on January 12, 1940, quoted in E. A. Steen, *Norges Sjøkrig 1940-1945. 1. Sjøforsvarets nøytralitetsvern 1939-1940. Tysklands og Vestmaktenes planer og forberedelser for en Norgesaksjon* (Oslo: Den Krigshistoriske Avdeling, Forsvarstaben. Gyldendal Norsk Forlag, 1954–1958), p. 57.

14 François Kersaudy, *Norway 1940* (New York: St Martin's Press, 1987), p. 24.

15 The Swedish Cabinet Secretary, Erik Boehman, had a stormy meeting with Pollock, the First Secretary of the British Embassy in Stockholm about the British note. Boehman asked Pollock if the British Government had not already sufficient number of small nations, whose destinies they had ruined, on their conscience (PRO, *CAB* 66/3, January 7, 1940). Bjørn Prytz, the Swedish Ambassador in London, espoused a completely different line after having delivered the Swedish protest to Halifax. In commenting on Boehman's outburst in a conversation with Charles Hambro in the Ministry of Economic Warfare, Prytz mentioned that he personally felt that the British should carry out their threatened action. He stated that the Norwegians would only complain loudly and try to blame Sweden (PRO, *FO* 371, 24820 WM (40) 7 CA, January 9, 1940).

16 Roderick Macleod and Denis Kelly (eds), *Time Unguarded. The Ironside Diaries 1937-1940* (New York: David MacKay Company, Inc., 1963), p., 228.

17 Sir John Kennedy, *The Business of war: The War Narrative of Sir John Kennedy* (Edited by Bernard Fergusson. London: Hutchinson, 1957), p. 49.

18 Ibid, 48.

19 Steen, *Norges Sjøkrig 1940-1945,* vol. 1, p. 69.

20 The armed merchant ship *Westerwald*, flying the German naval flag, had been allowed to

proceed through Norwegian territorial waters without inspection after a decision by the Norwegian Foreign Office. It was also allowed to proceed through the restricted area around Bergen under escort during daylight hours.

21 Churchill, *Gathering* Storm, p. 561.

22 Each torpedo boat had a crew of 21. *Kjell* had one 76mm (3-inch) gun and three torpedo tubes. *Skarv* had two 47mm cannons and three torpedo tubes. The patrol boat *Firern* arrived on the scene during the confrontation. This 247-ton vessel with a crew of 12 and a single 76mm gun did not change the enormous odds facing the Norwegians.

23 Steen, *Norges Sjøkrig 1940–1945,* vol. 1, p.71.

24 Churchill, *Gathering* Storm, p. 562. The British later claimed that Captain Vian suggested the joint escort to Bergen to Lieutenant Halvorsen during their conference. Halvorsen denied that any such exchange had taken place. Churchill sent his orders to Vian at 1725 hours and it is therefore unlikely that Vian had these instructions at the time he talked to Halvorsen.

25 Steen, *Norges Sjøkrig 1940-1945,* vol.1, p. 90.

26 Churchill, 564.

27 Steen, 1:99. It should be noted that Germany also violated Norwegian neutrality during this period. A German submarine – *U21* – ran aground in Norwegian territorial waters on March 27, and it was captured and interned. A German aircraft made a forced landing in Norway on April 3. The crew destroyed the aircraft before they were captured by Norwegian forces.

28 Christopher Buckley, *Norway. The Commandos. Dieppe*, 13.

29 Churchill, *Gathering Storm,* p. 584.

30 Steen, *Norges Sjøkrig 1940-1945,* vol 1, p. 166.

31 Ibid, vol 1, p. 106.

32 Bjørnsen, *Narvik*, pp. 222-223.

33 Ibid, p. 220.

34 The actual composition of the various cruiser squadrons and destroyer flotillas changed frequently, as ships were attached or detached.

35 PRO, *CAB* 65/6 WM (40) 83, April 6, 1940. Also, Bjørnsen, *Narvik*, pp. 182 and 223.

36 Kersaudy, 26.

2

GERMAN PLANS: BOLD, IMAGINATIVE, AND RECKLESS

"The operation in itself is contrary to all principles in the theory of naval warfare."

STATEMENT TO HITLER BY GENERAL ADMIRAL ERIC RAEDER ON MARCH 9, 1940.

Norway in German Strategic Planning

When World War II began, Germany had no plans to invade Norway. In a conversation with Count Ciano, the Italian Foreign Minister, on August 12, 1939, Hitler stated that he was convinced none of the belligerents would attack the Scandinavian countries, and that these countries would not join in an attack on Germany. There are no reasons to doubt the sincerity of this statement, and it is confirmed in a directive on October 9, 1939.

At the outset of war in 1939, Hitler considered it advantageous to have a neutral Scandinavia. The same views also prevailed initially among the staff of the German Armed Forces Headquarters (Oberkommando der Wehrmacht, or OKW). The members of the OKW considered it foolish to initiate an attack on Norway unless the British and French tried to spread the war to that area. They viewed a campaign in Norway as a risky drain on troops and resources from the main front in the west.

When the idea of invading Norway began to take shape, it did not originate with Hitler, but from members of the German Navy. In fact, he needed considerable persuasion before accepting what some considered a necessity. Eventually, he became convinced of the need for a preemptive strike to forestall a British move against Norway. Liddell-Hart wrote that "Hitler, despite all his unscrupulousness, would have preferred to keep Norway neutral, and did not plan to invade her until he was provoked to do so by palpable signs that the Allies were planning a hostile move in that quarter."[1]

German war planners considered Norway of great importance to Germany in a prolonged war. However, since initially they did not anticipate a long war, Norway's role was reduced to keeping sea traffic flowing without interference from the enemy for a relatively short period. The OKW strategic plan for the war was simple. The main attack would be directed against France and, after an expected victory, Britain would be presented with a generous peace offer that the political leadership felt confident would be accepted.

The navy's reason for pushing to secure Norway may be traced back to that service's experience in World War I, when the large German fleet failed to reach the open sea. The isolated ships that did reach open waters had to cross the dangerous North Sea before they could pierce the British blockade. Many German naval officers saw their only hope for useful service during World War II to be contingent on the German Navy acquiring bases in locations that would avoid or complicate British blockades.

Vice Admiral Wolfgang Wegener wrote a book about this subject in 1929 titled *Die Seestrategie des Weltkriges*. This book was well known in the German Navy and it influenced the strategic thinking of many of its key officers in the late 1930s. Wegener argued that the primary mission of the German Navy in any future conflict was to keep the sea lanes open for German merchant shipping, and that this could not be accomplished from German or Danish harbors. Wegener saw two possible solutions. One was to capture bases on the French coast. The other involved the seizure of bases in Norway. Although he does not directly say so, Wegener appears to view the acquisition of bases in Norway as the easier of the two solutions. This was natural since he was writing based on the experience of World War I, when the German army failed to reach the French coast. With respect to bases in Norway, he wrote, "England would then be unable to sustain a blockade line from the Shetlands to Norway but would be forced to withdraw to approximately a Shetlands-Faeroes-Iceland line. However, this line was a net with very wide meshes."[2]

Wegener concluded that, while it would be difficult for the British to defend the new line because of its proximity to German bases in Norway, the only way to eliminate the possibility of a blockade was to seize the Faeroes or the Shetland Islands. This would eliminate the dangers of a blockade and would place the German Navy in a position to interdict British supply routes, an objective that could not be achieved from bases in Norway. Wegener judged the seizure of the Faeroes or the Shetland Islands as beyond German capabilities, and this in turn reduced the value of bases in Norway.

Grand Admiral Erich Raeder, the commander-in-chief of the German Navy, did not have a large fleet at his disposal in 1939, but his surface raiders and submarines faced the same obstacles as those Wegener had pointed out ten years earlier. Furthermore, the German Navy had not given up on its plans to play a significant role among the armed services. Hitler approved the navy's plans for a gigantic fleet rearmament, the so-called *Z-plan*, in January 1939.[3] Hitler not only approved the rearmament program but ordered that it should begin immediately and should take priority over other needs, including the rearmament requirements of the other services. It is therefore not surprising that the German Navy, at an early date, turned its attention to the possibility of extending its operational range. The naval officers did not share the optimism of their army and air force counterparts that the war would be short and that bases would soon be available on the French coast. They were also deeply skeptical about the English government accepting a peace offer after a French defeat.

There was no unanimity of views in the German Navy on either the desirability of establishing bases in a Norway, or the service's ability to do so. However, new support for Wegener's ideas surfaced in the late 1930s when some of the officers who favored his approach to naval strategy began to occupy key positions and the question of bases assumed increasing importance in operational planning. There is little doubt that Raeder, too, although not a follower of Wegener, was favorably disposed to his ideas. Gemzell points to convincing similarities between the reasoning contained in a briefing Raeder gave Hitler and others on February 3, 1937 and what Wegener wrote almost a decade earlier.

The similarities in views between Wegener and Raeder have been challenged in a recent article in the Naval War College Review. Commander Hansen describes how Wegener and Raeder, who came into the navy together and were close friends, drifted apart and became bitter enemies.[4] Hansen maintains that the two saw the importance of Norway in different ways. For Wegener, bases in Norway represented a "gate to the Atlantic," while Raeder was more concerned with "the absolute necessity to the German war effort of Swedish iron ore." However, Raeder's preoccupation with the iron ore issue was closely tied to his desire for a large fleet, which could challenge the British Navy in ways very similar to those put forward by Wegener. When Raeder warned that the loss of Swedish iron ore would quickly destroy the German armament industry, he was also perhaps worried about what such a loss would do to the naval construction program.

The German fleet was divided geographically into the Eastern Group Command in the Baltic under Admiral Rolf Carls and the Western Group Command in the North Sea under Admiral Alfred Saalwächter. Saalwächter sent a report to the Naval High Command (Oberkommando der Kriegsmarine, or OKM) on March 2, 1939 in which he openly discussed the acquisition of bases in Norway. He cautioned that the British Navy would close the northern approach with a mine barrier, including mining Norwegian territorial waters. The Norwegian government's ability to prevent such an action was judged as being limited. Saalwächter's report stressed both the dangers to Germany of British dominance in Norwegian waters and the favorable change in the geo-strategic position that a German occupation of Norway would bring about.[5]

The OKM was also concerned about the effects of a mine barrier. As a result of the increased range of air power, they considered it likely that the new barrier would be located further north than the one in World War I, and that the only option available to change this strategic fundamental would be through the acquisition of bases in central or northern Norway. The OKM, however, continued to believe that the best solution to the strategic problems of the German Navy was through the acquisition of bases on the French coast.

Admiral Carls had been a longtime follower of Wegener's ideas.[6] He was the third highest-ranking officer in the navy and a dominant personality, known among his colleagues as the "Blue Czar." According to Carls, the only way the navy could achieve decisive results in a war was to adopt a two-pronged strategy that concentrated on holding open German sea-routes while attacking British overseas trade. While favoring Wegener's views, he also considered the acquisition of bases in France the best solution, since the German Navy could not eliminate the effects of a British blockade and pose a threat to that country's supply routes from Norway. These ends could only be accomplished by capturing the Faeroes or the Shetland Islands, objectives beyond Germany's capabilities.

In an appraisal of the political-military situation on September 4, 1939, Admiral Carls pointed out the strategic importance of Scandinavia and the danger to Germany if the British Navy was to obtain bases in that area. At every opportunity in September 1939, he emphasized the dangers posed to Germany by British naval and air bases in southern and western Norway. He continually stressed the importance of making plans to counter the possibility of the British establishing themselves on the Norwegian coast.

Raeder claims in his autobiography that "our armament industries would have died overnight" had it not been for the 10 million tons of Swedish iron ore used in German steel production. He goes on to say that the trade through Norwegian waters was going so well that it was taken for granted. He claims:

> Never having studied seriously a war with England until that war practically broke out, we had not seriously questioned how far Norway could guarantee her neutrality and the security of the Narvik route in case of war between England and Germany.

In addition, he continued, "Nobody in the Navy, and probably almost nobody else in Germany gave the Norwegian problem a second thought during the first month of the war."[7]

These statements are not supported by facts and they misrepresent the navy's role in planting the seeds and establishing the intellectual framework for the necessity of the Norwegian operation.[8] Raeder's assessment that the war economy would have died overnight if Swedish ore were unavailable is no doubt influenced by his realization that the navy would be the first to suffer if further prioritizing became necessary. By stressing this point in his testimony before the International Military Tribunal, he was undoubtedly trying to depict his activities in the months leading up to the invasion of Norway as responsible pre-emptive planning.

In his testimony at the Nuremberg Trial, Admiral Raeder states that he had not concerned himself with the Norwegian question until he received several intelligence reports during the last week of September 1939.[9] He is less than candid. The question of bases in Norway surfaced numerous times in the period after 1935. In a post wargame statement on April 12, 1938, Raeder dealt with the subject of base acquisition for improving the navy's operational possibilities. The planning committee in 1938 considered a partial occupation of Norway, but its final report concluded that while such a move would improve Germany's strategic position, it would require substantial forces that could be used better elsewhere. However, the idea was kept alive as an acceptable alternative to the acquisition of bases on the continent's open Atlantic coasts.

Admiral Carls kept a journal that was read regularly by Raeder, and entries in that journal in September 1939 pointed out the risk of British footholds in southern and western Norway and the necessity for planning German counter-measures.[10]

The intelligence reports that Raeder refers to in his testimony at the

Nuremberg Trial included reports from the German Naval Attaché in Oslo, Lieutenant Commander Richard Schreiber, and a rare personal visit by Admiral Wilhelm Canaris, head of the Abwehr (Department for Foreign Intelligence and Security within OKW) who informed him that there were signs "that the British intended to occupy bases in Norway."[11] The next impetus came from Admiral Carls, who was privy to the same intelligence reports as Raeder. He made a telephone call to Raeder during one of the last days of September to explain that he had prepared a private letter for him. The letter dealt with the dangers to Germany of a British occupation of bases in Norway, and raised the issue of whether Germany should forestall such an attempt by the British. Raeder states that he received the letter at the end of September or beginning of October. He testified at his trial that the letter impelled him to pose a series of questions to the Chief of Staff of the Naval Staff (Seekriegsleitung, or SKL) examining the danger of English occupation of Norwegian bases as well as the pros and cons of a German expansion to the north.[12] The questions Raeder posed to the SKL were also given to Rear Admiral Karl Dönitz, the commander of German submarine forces, for comments. Dönitz proposed the establishment of a major submarine base in Trondheim and a fuel/supply depot at Narvik.

The SKL reached mixed conclusions on Admiral Carls' letter and on the questions posed to them by Raeder. In a document prepared by the Operations Divisions of the Naval Staff on October 9, their opinion was one of caution.[13] The naval staff saw no pressing reasons why Germany should establish itself forcefully on the Norwegian coast. First, the occupation of bases on the Norwegian coast would not bring any decisive advantages to Germany's strategic position, particularly if it were necessary to secure such bases with force. Second, SKL viewed continued Norwegian neutrality as a definite advantage to Germany. They concluded that the German ore traffic would be safer with a neutral Norway than it would be after an eventual German occupation, provided the British forces respected Norwegian territorial waters. The naval staff saw the obvious advantages of Norwegian bases in a naval war against Britain, but they also saw clearly the hazards involved in an effort to expand the operational theater in face of superior British naval power.

On the other hand, the SKL considered it absolutely necessary to prevent a British occupation of Norway or the seizure of bases in that country. They argued that a British presence in Norway would bring Sweden into the British sphere of influence and possibly end Swedish iron ore exports to Germany. Their temporary conclusions were that bases in Norway would not significantly enhance Germany's strategic position.[14] The fact that Germany was negotiating with the Soviet Union for the lease of a base near Polarnoje (in Kola Bay) may have influenced the SKL conclusion. The lease of the base took effect in November, and German submarines used it frequently.

Raeder Briefs Hitler

Raeder had a routine meeting with Hitler on October 10, 1939 and used the opportunity to bring up the subject of Norway.[15] He took a more aggressive approach than that contained in the SKL answers to his questions on October 3. Raeder pointed out that the establishment of British naval and air bases in Norway would be a very dangerous development for Germany. The importance of Norway for aerial warfare was a factor that was not present in World War I, but which had since considerably increased the importance of that country to the belligerents. Raeder stated that Britain would not only be able to control the entrance to the Baltic, but would be in a position to outflank German naval operations in the North Sea and German air attacks on Great Britain. The flow of iron ore from Narvik would end, and the Allies would be able to exert strong pressures on Sweden.

Having alerted Hitler to the obvious dangers, Raeder proceeded to mention possible solutions. He pointed out the advantages that would follow from German occupation of certain strategic points along the Norwegian coast, the major one being virtually unhampered naval access to the Atlantic. By dwelling on the dangers to Germany of a British presence in Norway and the advantages of a German presence there, rather than on the advantages of the status quo, Raeder showed that he was more in tune with the ideas of Wegener and Carls than those of his own staff. He was also exploiting Hitler's paranoia. Hitler, who was preoccupied with the planned attack in the west, was noncommittal. He asked Raeder to leave his notes, promising further consideration.

There were, of course, officers within the SKL who favored the idea of acquiring bases in Norway. Two of these, mentioned by both Salewski and Gemzell, had close personal relationships with Raeder. One was Lieutenant Commander Heinz Assmann, the second Admiralty Staff Officer, an influential position within the Operations Department. He was involved in operational planning, kept the war diary, and prepared Raeder's reports to Hitler. These confidential duties indicate that he was held in high regard and caused him to have frequent contacts with Raeder. The second officer was Captain (later Admiral) Erich Schulte Mönting. He had been Raeder's aide-de-camp and then became chief of his personal staff. As such, he had important coordinating duties, including the supervision of German naval attachés in foreign countries and contacts with foreign naval attachés in Germany.

Admiral Raeder continued his interest in the establishment of German bases in Norway after his conversation with Hitler on October 10. He received valuable support from Lieutenant Commander Schreiber and from Alfred Rosenberg, the semi-official philosopher of Nazism and chief of a special office concerned with propaganda in foreign countries.

Schreiber was assigned as naval attaché to Norway on the recommendation of Admiral Carls. He had served on Carls' staff and he was well acquainted with that admiral's views on the Norwegian question. Soon after his arrival in Oslo, Schreiber established contact with Vidkun Quisling, the leader of the Norwegian fascist party.

The strategic importance of Scandinavia took on greater importance in both Berlin and London when the Soviet Union attacked Finland on November 30, 1939. Schreiber kindled Raeder's interest by his reports of rumors of Allied plans to occupy strategic points along the Norwegian coast. These reports reinforced similar information in the Western press and from German diplomats in neutral countries.

The possibility that the war would be longer than previously thought began to arise in November 1939. This possibility brought the economic warfare issue to the forefront, and Hitler issued a directive on this subject on November 29. Raeder quickly exploited this new emphasis by pointing out that Great Britain received substantial supplies from the three Scandinavian countries. He indicated that much of the export from these countries passed through Norway and then via convoys to Great Britain. The resources going to the Allies would go to Germany if that country came under German control. Denial of British access to these valuable raw materials and foodstuffs would serve to shorten the war.[16]

Hitler Meets Vidkun Quisling

Alfred Rosenberg sponsored a visit to Berlin by Quisling in December 1939. Rosenberg and Quisling had met for the first time in 1933. Quisling had been a reserve officer in the Norwegian Army and the Norwegian Minister of War from 1931 to 1933. It was after his stint as cabinet minister that he founded *Nasjonal Samling* (National Unity), a party with an ideology similar to Nazism. Its platform was pan-German, anti-Soviet, anti-British, and anti-Semitic. Rosenberg and Quisling's organizations maintained regular contact. Quisling and Rosenberg met again in June 1939 when the former spoke to a convention of the Nordic Society, a Nazi organization for cultural and trade relations with Scandinavia.

Quisling arrived in Berlin on December 10, 1939, and the next day Raeder was informed that Quisling had requested an interview, based on a recommendation by Rosenberg. The interview was arranged quickly. The traditional view, as reported by historian Telford Taylor, is that Rosenberg was behind this meeting as well as the later ones with Hitler. Ralph Hewins, Quisling's biographer, has called this into question. He claims that Raeder knew all about Quisling and his party, and that he may have used the Rosenberg organization to establish formal contact.[17]

There is evidence to support Hewins' claim. Admiral Schniewind, Chief of Staff of SKL (a position comparable to that of Fritz Halder on the General Staff), has written that many important issues were classified "political," kept from the SKL, and handled by Schulte Mönting. Schniewind claims Schulte Mönting arranged the contact with Quisling.[18] Raeder's adjutant, Freiwald, worked for Schulte Mönting and he reports that Schulte Mönting and Viljam Hagelin, a Norwegian business executive who was Quisling's representative in Germany, were old friends.[19] Hans-Dietrich Loock claims that there were close contacts between Schulte Mönting, Rosenberg's people, Quisling, and Hagelin.[20]

Raeder related at his trial that Schulte Mönting informed him that Quisling had asked for a meeting. This request came through Hagelin who apparently had been sent by Rosenberg. In the same testimony, Raeder claims, "Up until 11 December I had neither connections with Herr Rosenberg, except for the fact that I had seen him on occasion—nor, above all, did I have any connections with Quisling about whom I had heard nothing up to that point."[21]

It was natural for Raeder, on trial for his role in the attack on Norway, to downplay his connection with Rosenberg and Quisling. However, it is not believable that Raeder had not heard about Quisling in the many reports from Schreiber, his naval attaché in Norway, who had excellent contacts with Quisling and his organization. In addition, Raeder had probably heard about Quisling from his Chief of Staff, Schulte Mönting.

Raeder was an astute politician, and his motive in arranging the meeting with Quisling through Rosenberg may have been calculated to ensure that any unpleasantness following the meeting of Hitler and Quisling fell firmly at Rosenberg's door. However, by participating in these meetings, Raeder assured himself of some of the credit in case the enterprise proved successful.

Hagelin accompanied Quisling to the meeting with Raeder. Quisling told Raeder that the Norwegian foreign policy was "controlled by the well-known Jew, Hambro (President of the Norwegian Parliament), a great friend of Hore-Belisha (British Secretary of State for War)," and that British landings near Stavanger and Kristiansand were under consideration. Quisling claimed that Hambro and his followers were counting on Britain to keep the Soviets out of Scandinavia, but he saw it as a pretext for Britain gaining a foothold in Norway. Quisling and his followers wished "to anticipate any possible British step in this direction by placing the necessary bases at the disposal of the German Wehrmacht."[22] Admiral Raeder did not comment on Quisling's statements but agreed to bring the matter to Hitler's attention.

Rosenberg prepared a memorandum on Quisling's visit. While the memorandum recognizes the growing anti-German feeling in Norway, due partly to the war between Finland and the Soviet Union, it is full of praise for Quisling and overestimated highly that individual's influence and support among the Norwegian people and within the Norwegian Army.

Admiral Raeder made good on his promise to bring the matter to Hitler's attention by briefing Hitler on December 12 in the presence of Generaloberst Wilhelm Keitel, Chief of the OKW, Major General Alfred Jodl, Chief of Operations at OKW, and Hitler's naval adjutant, Lt. Commander Karl von Püttkammer. Raeder's briefing is in agreement with Rosenberg's memorandum with respect to what Quisling is alleged to have said, but it is less laudatory. With respect to Quisling's offer of cooperation, Raeder stated, "It is impossible to know with such offers how much the people concerned wish to further their own party schemes and how important German interests are to them."[23]

Raeder recommended a cautious approach to the issue. He advised that Norway must not be allowed to fall into British hands, as such an event "could be decisive for the outcome of the war." It is alleged that he went as far as telling Hitler that Quisling believed there was an agreement between Norway and Great Britain about an occupation of Norway.[24] Raeder pointed out that British occupation of Norway would most likely turn Sweden against Germany and this could jeopardize Germany's naval position in the Baltic and prevent German ships from reaching the high sea. The admiral tempered this by stating that German occupation of bases on the Norwegian coast would result in strong British countermoves, that the navy could not cope with the intense surface warfare that would surely develop over a sustained period, and that the free flow of iron ore from Narvik could be interrupted.

Hitler concurred that a British occupation of Norway was unacceptable, but stated that he wanted to hear Rosenberg's opinion on the advisability of a personal meeting with Quisling. Raeder concluded his briefing by asking that, if Hitler was favorably impressed with Quisling, the OKW should "be permitted to make plans with Q. for preparing and executing the occupation" by peaceful means or by force.[25]

Hitler's decision to receive Quisling, pending a recommendation from Rosenberg, resulted in consultations between Rosenberg and Raeder on December 13, and a letter from Rosenberg to Raeder stating that he would take Quisling to meet Hitler on December 14.[26] Those present at the first meeting between Hitler and Quisling included Raeder, Keitel, Hagelin, and Hans Wilhelm Scheidt, head of Rosenberg's Northern Department. Rosenberg was unable to attend because he had sustained an injury, but he had prepared a memorandum for Hitler on Quisling and his party, and Scheidt served as Rosenberg's representative at the meeting. Raeder also visited Rosenberg at his home in the morning of December 14, before taking the two Norwegians to see Hitler.[27]

Although no record of this relatively long meeting has surfaced, Hitler must have been favorably impressed with Quisling, since he ordered OKW to "investigate how one can take possession of Norway."[28] The investigation was to focus on two alternative schemes. One involved minor German military support for a coup by Quisling and his followers, while the second was a military occupation of the country.

Churchill writes that Quisling arrived in Berlin with a "detailed plan" for political action in Norway and that "Hitler's decision to invade Norway . . . was taken on December 14."[29] This is misleading. Hitler only directed OKW to *investigate* how to take control of the country. Churchill's statement makes it appear that the Germans decided to invade Norway before they actually did.

If Hitler's order to the OKW to study the matter is viewed as a decision to invade Norway, then the December 22 British War Cabinet directions to the Military Chiefs to plan for operations in Norway must be viewed in the same way. Furthermore, the British Chiefs presented their plans on January 2 and the Allied Supreme War Council was briefed on the final plans on February 5. The German plan was briefed to Hitler on February 29 and his directive was issued the following day. The two events—Hitler's order after meeting Quisling and the War Cabinet's directive to the Military Chiefs on December 22—should be viewed as part of contingency planning and were not invasion decisions.

Telford Taylor writes that there were two more meetings between Hitler,

Quisling, and Hagelin, on 16 and 18 December. Most sources, including Quisling's writings, mention only two meetings in total, those on 14 and 18 December. Taylor may have based his statement on Raeder's testimony at the Nuremberg Trial where he states, "The Fuehrer had two more conferences with Quisling on 16 and 18 December at which I was not present."[30] I believe there were only two meetings, on 14 and 18 December. The second meeting lasted about one hour. Hitler let it be known at the meeting that his preference was for a neutral Norway, but that if the enemy tried to extend the war into this area, he would be forced to react accordingly. He promised monetary support for Quisling and his followers, but Hitler did not inform Quisling that he had directed OKW to explore the feasibility of occupying Norway.

The primary sources of information we have about the two meetings Hitler had with Quisling are from the testimony of Raeder at Nuremberg and Quisling's writings from prison. We should treat these with care. The charges against Raeder dealt largely with his role in planning the attack on Norway. It is reasonable to assume that he tried to downplay his role in the events leading up to Hitler's decision. Likewise, Quisling wrote his account while in a Norwegian prison awaiting trial and execution for treason. An excerpt from Quisling's writing on this subject might be worth repeating:

> During all this [discussions with Hitler, Raeder, etc.] there was no question of any German occupation of Norway, certainly not of my giving any guidance and advice with a view to such an occupation. Hitler was, however, emphatically clear that if Norway did not vindicate her neutrality vis-à-vis Great Britain, Germany would attack with all her power. One may take if for granted that the German authorities themselves knew best how to carry out such a counter-action and that they were not willing to discuss it with a foreigner whom they were meeting for the first time. . . .

Rosenberg's writings about the political preparations for Germany's operations in Norway, and other more circumstantial evidence, suggest that Quisling not only warned the Germans against real or imagined British plans in Scandinavia but also offered his and his party's assistance to the Germans. The Germans were eager to use Quisling as a source of information, but they were not willing to compromise their thoughts or plans by sharing them with the leader of a small political party with little credibility in its own country. They merely supplied money to Quisling's party and received periodic reports about conditions in Norway.

There is no evidence to suggest that the information received from Quisling had any major effect on German preparations, or that Quisling had any knowledge about Germans plans. Claims by some British authors, such as Churchill and Adams, that Quisling provided the Germans with detailed information on the Norwegian military and its facilities, are not supported by subsequent developments or by information in German sources. The fact that German intelligence was wrong on several issues well known to Quisling and his followers suggests that they provided little or no information of military value.

It made good sense for the Germans to keep Quisling in the dark. It would have been extremely foolish and reckless for the Germans to share their plans with Quisling and his followers, or to request the kind of information that would lead them to the obvious conclusion that an invasion was being prepared. Writers during and after World War II have blown the effect of Quisling and his followers on German plans and operations all out of proportion. It served as a convenient explanation by both the British and Norwegians for an embarrassing military defeat, but there is almost no evidence to support the various claims that are made to support this theory.[31]

Studie Nord

The wheels were now in motion. In response to Hitler's directive, Jodl's staff made a preliminary examination titled *Studie Nord* that outlined a plan for the occupation of Norway. A very small group headed by Colonel (later General) Walter Warlimont, deputy chief of the OKW operations staff, completed this study. Warlimont recommended that a staff headed by a Luftwaffe general with a chief of staff from the navy and an operations officer from the army should further develop the study. Hitler had instructed Keitel and Jodl to keep knowledge of the Norwegian study severely restricted, and this instruction was evidently followed to the letter.

Raeder recognized that the Norwegian venture carried great risk and that a truly neutral Norway would best serve Germany's interests. Nevertheless, he kept up the psychological pressure on Hitler. The SKL received numerous alarming reports in December 1939 from Schreiber. These reports pointed to disturbing signs of British plans to land in Norway, using help to Finland as a pretext.

Raeder warned Hitler on December 30, 1939, in the presence of Keitel and Püttkammer, that under no circumstances should Norway be allowed to fall into

Great Britain's hands. He suggested that the British could carry out an "unobtrusive occupation" of Norway and that no serious opposition would be offered by either Norwegians or Swedes to such an event. Raeder went on to admonish, "Therefore it is necessary to be prepared and ready."[32]

Studie Nord was completed on December 28, but on Hitler's instruction it was not distributed for evaluation and comment to the three service headquarters until January 10, 1940. It appears that only OKM considered *Studie Nord* in a serious manner, but even this headquarters recommended that no action be taken unless it became clear that the British intended to move into Scandinavia. On this, there was complete agreement between Raeder and his staff, but there were differences when it came to what emphasis should be placed on the danger of a British occupation of Norway.

Raeder was convinced that Britain would occupy points on the Norwegian coast in the near future, to stop the iron ore traffic from Sweden and hinder German naval operations in the Atlantic and North Sea. He also believed that the Norwegian government would cooperate with the British, or at least fail to offer effective resistance. The accuracy of Raeder's assessment of British intentions is remarkable.

The operational branch of the SKL, under Admiral C. Fricke, did not believe that a British occupation of Norway was imminent. The SKL took a conservative military view of the forces the British would require for the operation and concluded that Britain did not have the forces necessary to carry out an occupation of Norway and thereafter secure that position against German threats. Fricke and his planners believed that a British occupation of Norway would cause a strong reaction from the Soviet Union.

The SKL viewed a preemptive German strike against Norway as disadvantageous. German imports of iron ore currently proceeded safely through Norwegian territorial waters and this situation would continue as long as Great Britain respected Norwegian neutrality. A German occupation would result in the necessity of providing naval escorts for the ore traffic, and this would put a great strain on the navy. A German strike against Norway would demand almost every ship in the navy for it to have even the slightest chance of success against British superiority at sea. The occupation was a grave decision to make in view of the fact that a successful occupation of Norway would not be a decisive factor in the war against France and Britain. An action against Norway in the absence of a British move in that direction would also be difficult to justify. Hubatsch writes that it was only at the last moment that the SKL agreed that nothing short of force could solve the Norwegian problem.[33]

Caution was also the view of Captain Theodor Krancke, who represented the SKL at OKW on matters dealing with Norway, and was the chief of staff of the group tasked to further develop *Studie Nord*. However, despite doubts, the operational branch of the SKL agreed that it would be prudent to undertake preparations for an operation against Norway in case British actions made it necessary.

The caution that prevailed in the operational branch of the SKL was also prevalent in the German Foreign Office. This organization underlined the fact that Germany had lost much goodwill in the Scandinavian countries because of its association with the Soviet Union and the Soviet-Finnish war. However, the diplomats expressed fear that the Allies could find a justification in the occupation of points on the Norwegian coast under the guise of helping the Finns. The German Foreign Office concluded that the Norwegian government would oppose an Allied invasion with all means at its disposal, but it was less certain about the reaction of the Norwegian people. The Foreign Office based its conclusions primarily on reports received from Dr. Curt Bräuer, the German Ambassador in Oslo.

Commander Schreiber and Hans Wilhelm Scheidt, Rosenberg's personal representative in Norway, did not share Bräuer's views. They concluded that Norway was not enforcing its neutrality and would not oppose a British invasion. They made their views known in numerous messages and in person when they visited Berlin in January 1940. Subsequent events illustrated that the two representatives had good reasons for these claims. The *Altmark* affair, and frequent British violations of Norwegian neutrality in the aftermath of that incident, did not lead to any meaningful measures on the part of the Norwegians to enforce their neutrality.

The operational branch of the SKL had worked out an expansion of *Studie Nord*. This is contained in an SKL operational branch document titled *Überlegungen Studie Nord*, dated January 19, 1940 and summarized by Ziemke in the cited work. The SKL envisioned requirements for naval support for landings from Oslo to Tromsø, and considered surprise the key element in the operation. The whole fleet had to participate to carry out the navy's part of the operation. They foresaw no difficulties on the outward journey if surprise could be achieved. The Norwegian warships were not considered a threat to even a single light naval unit, and the coastal fortifications were not viewed as serious obstacles. However, it was important to capture these fortifications intact as quickly as possible in order to use them against expected British counterattacks.

The SKL calculated that the assault force should consist of an airborne or mountain division. Transportation would be provided through the combined resources of the Luftwaffe and the navy. The problem of weather was recognized. Air force participation would be limited by the typical winter weather both in the target areas and along the routes to those areas. On the other hand, the expected weather conditions would favor the navy. The darkness, fog, and stormy weather would shield the fleet from British observation and help achieve surprise.

The SKL considered sending the troops that were not air transported by merchant ships, disguised as ore transports. This idea was rejected because a large number of ships would be required, the navy could not afford them protection, and there was a risk of discovery by Norwegian authorities. A second possibility considered was to transport the assault troops aboard fast-moving warships. The disadvantage here was that the number of troops would be severely restricted, and that there would be little room for supplies and equipment. A combination of the two proposals was deemed the most suitable. Assault elements would be carried in warships while reinforcements, supplies, and equipment were to be transported in merchant ships.

The operational staff of the SKL considered the attitudes of Denmark, Sweden, and the Soviet Union, and offered recommendations for each. The staff suggested that Germany should seize bases at the northern end of the Jutland Peninsula in Denmark as a means to dominate the Skagerrak and the southern portion of the North Sea. The Soviet Union should be assured that the occupation of bases in North Norway was only for the duration of the war. Sweden would be informed pointedly that the only way to preserve its independence was to adopt a pro-German neutrality policy.

Hitler Moves Planning to OKW

Hitler was still preoccupied with plans for the campaign in the West, but when bad weather forced a postponement of the that offensive, he turned his attention to the Scandinavian situation. On January 23, he ordered *Studie Nord* recalled and directed that all future work on this project take place at OKW under his personal guidance. Up to then, the review and planning for *Studie Nord* was carried out by the services and the OKW. Security may have been one of the major considerations in Hitler taking this unusual step. Some of the plans for the Western offensive had fallen into enemy hands when a German officer's airplane had made a forced landing in Belgium earlier in January.

Keitel informed the service chiefs on January 27 that he would take over supervision of a working staff consisting of one officer from each of the three services experienced in operational planning and with some background in organization and supply. The group's chief of staff, and senior member of this inter-service team, was Captain Theodor Krancke, commander of the heavy cruiser *Admiral Scheer*. The code-name *Studie Nord* was now replaced by the more secretive code-name *Weserübung*. (The Weser was a German river; "übung" means exercise or drill.) The group held its first meeting on February 5.

The close working relationship between OKW and SKL has led some writers to suggest that there existed an axis between the two organizations, or between Raeder and Jodl, on the subject of Norway.[34] There is no doubt that OKW was tuned to Raeder's ideas and supportive of his views. As opposed to General Halder, Jodl took a positive view of the feasibility of securing bases in Norway as early as October 1939, and "thought it could be easily accomplished." The OKW had made its own study on the possibility of acquiring bases in Norway and concluded that, although it would require considerable forces, it was feasible and should be considered if other possibilities (e.g. the base on the Russian coast) proved inadequate. A copy of this report was given to Raeder.[35] The views of the OKW appear to be more in tune with the views expressed by Raeder in the fall of 1939 and the early winter of 1940 than with the more cautious attitude in the SKL.

The OKW and Hitler had definitely taken a lead in the invasion plans by March 1940, and during February and March of that year, Raeder had become a cautious follower.

Centralizing the planning for the Norwegian operation in OKW made sense since it involved elements of all three services, and because there was no precedent in German military history for the type of combined arms operation envisioned. However, the action was the first of several that eroded the influence and prestige of service commanders. Oberkommando des Heeres (Army High Command, or OKH) still constituted the famed German General Staff and it was not to be expected that it would relish seeing its planning and operational functions taken over by what amounted to Hitler's personal military staff. The army and air force harbored similar feelings, and it was therefore not surprising that these two organizations reacted vehemently a few weeks after Hitler had taken this action. Walter Goerlitz writes the following about Hitler charging OKW with planning the Norwegian operation and the creation of a theater command directly answerable to him and his staff:

> This practice, which was soon to be extended to other military undertakings, really amounted to the creation of a second General Staff. It was Hitler's answer to the General Staff's opposition. Its result was that Jodl, as head of the *Wehrmachtführungsstab*, was now recognized at the Führer Headquarters as the leading military personality of the day.[36]

Hitler's unprecedented disregard for the General Staff has been explained in various ways, but there is no doubt that Goerlitz is on the mark. Halder's diary entry on February 21 notes, "Headquarters XXI Corps is to be placed under OKW in order to avoid difficulties with the Luftwaffe." Later events indicated that this was just an attempt by Keitel and Jodl to soothe bruised feelings at OKH. Another reason advanced for Hitler and his staff taking direct control of the planning and execution of *Weserübung* was that it would relieve OKH of some work, since that headquarters was deeply involved in preparations for the attack in the West. However, the workload of OKH was not reduced by the new procedures. The various branches of OKH were still involved in force readiness, movement, transport, and supply, and it could be argued that the new command arrangements created more work and greater stress since the various staff sections of OKH and its subordinate organizations now had to answer to two masters. The fact that these command arrangements became a prototype for similar arrangements later in the war tells us that OKH's workload was not a prime consideration.

The Krancke Staff

The OKW work group that became known as the Krancke Staff produced the first real plan for the Norwegian operation. It used the work of the SKL as a point of departure, but its mission was nevertheless formidable. Information on Norway, its armed forces, and its facilities was limited, since it had not enjoyed a high priority within the German intelligence services. The personnel limitations dictated by secrecy were handicaps and the lack of such basic items as maps became serious problems. However, within three weeks the staff produced the first practical plan.

The plan called for the capture of seven ports simultaneously: Oslo, Kristiansand, Arendal, Stavanger, Bergen, Trondheim, and Narvik. These cities constituted the population centers in Norway and contained many of the country's industries. Furthermore, the capture of these cities would gain control of almost all Norwegian naval facilities, forts, most operational airfields, and more than half of the supply depots the Norwegian Army needed for mobilization.

The Krancke Staff increased the force level from the one division envisioned by SKL to an army corps consisting of one airborne division, one mountain division, one motorized brigade, and six reinforced infantry regiments. The Krancke Staff planned to transport the troops in three ways: by aircraft, by warships, and by merchant ships.

Eight transport groups of the 7th Air Division would bring five parachute battalions in the first wave. The rest of the assault wave would arrive on warships. The second air transport wave would bring about half of the airborne division over a period of three days, while the third and fourth echelons of the troops would arrive by sea on the fifth day. The Krancke plan envisioned that about half of the assault echelon would arrive on warships while aircraft transported the rest. The Trondheim and Narvik assault units would all arrive on warships since these cities were outside the range of transport aircraft.

The Krancke Staff concluded that the Norwegian armed forces had neither the desire nor the ability to offer any effective resistance, and that the Germans could consolidate their positions after the landings through diplomatic means. The plan urged that the Norwegians be assured of maximum independence in internal affairs, that Germans take over all forts and supply depots, that the Norwegian armed forces be reduced to a caretaker status except for the units along the Finnish border, and that no Norwegian mobilization take place without prior German approval.

With respect to Denmark, the Krancke Staff believed that airfields in northern Denmark could be acquired peacefully by threatening to take them by military force. The SKL proposed that the threat against Sweden should be dropped, and instead both the Soviet Union and Sweden were to receive assurances that the occupation would only be for the duration of the war and that Germany guaranteed Norway's borders.

The Krancke plan was a great improvement over the more rudimentary work of the SKL. However, it contained serious flaws. The combined services operation was the first of its kind to be undertaken by Germany and the plan underestimated the potential problems posed by Norwegian and British forces. The will and fighting abilities of the opponents were minimized. The underlying assumption in the plan was that the operation would remain shrouded in complete secrecy until the actual landing of German troops on Norwegian soil. This was an unrealistic military assumption in view of the buildup requirements. Over 100,000 troops along with thousands of tons of supplies and equipment, required movement to debarkation ports, and the shipping to carry these had to be assembled in a very limited number of north German ports. There were no good reasons to believe that this would not be observed or commented on.

Hitler Expedites Planning and Appoints a Commander

Whatever the legal pros and cons of the *Altmark* incident described earlier, they mattered little to Hitler. As Churchill and his supporters may have hoped, it was the event that energized him into action. Hitler was convinced that the British government would no longer respect Norwegian neutrality—a conclusion supported by the dramatic increase in British violations over the weeks that followed—and that Norwegian territorial waters would no longer offer a safe route for the transport of iron ore. On February 19, Hitler ordered the planning for *Weserübung* expedited and forces designated for the operation.

In addition to the *Altmark* affair, Hitler had other reasons to be worried. In the middle of February, German naval intelligence succeeded in breaking British naval codes, and this gave them important and accurate information about Allied activities and intentions. The information gathered was provided to OKW. The intercepts indicated that intense Allied preparations were underway for operations against Norway under the pretext of helping Finland. This confirmed Raeder and Hitler's conclusions about British intentions.

When Hitler decided to expedite *Weserübung*, Jodl suggested that a commander for the operation be selected, and he and Keitel, apparently without consulting the army,[37] recommended the 54-year old General der Infanterie Nikolaus von Falkenhorst, born in Breslau and a descendant of a military/ aristocratic family named von Jastrzembski.[38] In 1918, at the end of World War I, von Falkenhorst had served as operations officer of General von der Goltz's division in Finland. Von Falkenhorst had commanded the XXI Army Corps in the Polish campaign. He was still commander of the XXI Corps, stationed at Bacharach, and its troops were undergoing training in Grafenwöhr. Jodl and Keitel recommended von Falkenhorst for the Norwegian operation because of his experience in Finland. Hitler accepted the recommendation and Falkenhorst was summoned to Berlin.

Hitler interviewed von Falkenhorst on February 21, and the following day, after he had reviewed plans prepared by the Krancke Staff, Hitler confirmed his appointment. Hitler told von Falkenhorst he would have five divisions for the operation.

In a statement to the Norwegian High Command (Forsvarets overkommando) on September 30, 1945, General von Falkenhorst related how General Brauchitsch viewed the Norwegian operation. He let von Falkenhorst understand that he did not agree with Hitler's decision and opined that the operation did not serve any useful purpose. Brauchitsch pointed out that his opinion had not been solicited, that Hitler alone had made the decision, and that he was now making all arrangements with the help of Admiral Raeder.[39]

Von Falkenhorst brought a select group of staff officers from the XXI Corps to Berlin and they began their work on February 26, among them Colonel Erich Buschenhagen, the corps chief of staff. These were combined with the earlier Krancke Staff and the new organization was designated Group XXI or Army High Command, Norway (Armee-oberkommando Norwegen, i.e., AOK Norwegen).

The intelligence estimate contained in the plan produced by Falkenhorst's staff placed the peacetime strength of the Norwegian Army at about 40,000, with a 3,000-strong permanent cadre. Despite recognizing the excellent physical condition of the majority of the population, the army was given only a moderate rating because of the short training period, an over-aged officer corps, the perceived lack of competence among non-commissioned officers (NCOs), and lack of modern equipment. The conclusion was that the Norwegian Army could not offer any resistance worth mentioning against a major power, and units would quickly break when faced with surprise and bold action. German intelligence considered the ships in the navy too old to pose any problems for an attacker. The same was true for the aircraft assigned to the navy and army. They concluded that the coastal forts were unmanned in peacetime and therefore no obstacles as long as the element of surprise was maintained. Generally, the Germans overestimated the strength of the Norwegian military forces (except for the navy) while underestimating their fighting capability. With the exception of their conclusion regarding the coastal forts, however, the shortcomings in the intelligence estimate caused only minor difficulties.

Von Falkenhorst presented his plan for the invasion of Norway to Hitler on February 29. In addition to the increase in force levels, there were several changes to the earlier Krancke plans. These changes made the undertaking more realistic militarily. The increased force levels reflected a more reasonable view of the difficulties confronting the German armed forces in some of the most inhospitable areas on the globe, opposed to an army very familiar with the terrain and climate. It also recognized that the various landings had to be self-sustained until link-ups, a task not easy in difficult terrain with poor internal lines of communications. Finally, it represented a more sober assessment of the threat posed by the British Navy.

Krancke's group had recognized the importance of bases in northern Denmark, but had suggested that these should be acquired through diplomatic pressure. This was also how OKW viewed the issue, although the threat of military force might have to be used and the forces should therefore be ready. The occupation of Luleå in Sweden and the railroad leading from that city to Narvik was also considered, but the OKW, in the person of Colonel Warlimont, changed these ideas in reviewing a February 26 working paper from von Falkenhorst's staff on February 27. There was to be no action against Sweden, and the acquisition of bases in Denmark was no longer left to diplomatic pressures. The seizure of bases in Denmark by force was also in accordance with von Falkenhorst's views since he did not want to leave the outcome of this important part of his operation to the uncertainties of diplomatic negotiations. He requested an additional corps headquarters and two divisions to seize the Jutland Peninsula and possibly the rest of Denmark if the Danes resisted.

Up to now, it was assumed that the attack on Norway would be carried out either just before or after the attack in the West. Jodl now proposed that *Weserübung* be carried out independent of that offensive. Hitler's agreement to this proposal was contingent on an examination of the practicability of such a solution.[40] The carrying out of the two operations independent of each other involved scaling back on some of the parachute troops the Krancke Staff had considered necessary for the operation.

Hitler approved von Falkenhorst's plans on February 29 but insisted that the capture of Copenhagen also be included as a mission. Hitler again directed Rosenberg that there should be no attempt to enlist Quisling's support for the operation "in any form."[41]

In the meantime, Raeder continued to feed Hitler a mixture of caution and alarm. On February 20 and again on February 23, Hitler asked Raeder about maintaining the ore traffic from Narvik following the occupation of Norway.[42] Raeder answered that the "best thing for maintaining this traffic as well as for the situation in general" was the maintenance of Norwegian neutrality. However, he went on:

. . . what must not be permitted, as stated earlier, is the occupation of

Norway by Britain. That could not be undone; it would entail increased pressure on Sweden, perhaps extension of the war to the Baltic, and cessation of all ore supplies from Sweden.

Raeder stated that the ore traffic from Narvik, which amounted to 2,500,000 to 3,500,000 tons, would have to be suspended for a time since the protection of this traffic through the 800-mile passage along the coast would require large naval and air resources. He advised Hitler that there were alternatives available in case the transport of ore through Norwegian territorial waters proved too risky. Six million tons of the anticipated supply of 10 million tons could be shipped through Luleå during the months that city was not ice-locked. Another three million tons could be stored and/or shipped south by rail to the port of Oxelösund, south of Stockholm. That would leave about one million tons to be shipped through Narvik instead of the much higher tonnage normally associated with that city. He cautioned that not all of this would be achieved in 1940 since it appeared the weather conditions would keep Luleå ice-bound longer than normal. Finally, Raeder pointed out that all supplies would be cut off if the British occupied Norway while a German occupation of Norway would oblige Sweden to meet Germany's demands.

So far, the army and air force had been kept in relative darkness about the Scandinavian operation. However, this now changed since the actual forces to participate had to be designated. This led to serious inter-service wrangling and to disputes between OKW and the service chiefs.

Von Falkenhorst and his chief of staff had their first meeting with General Halder, the Army Chief of Staff, on February 26. Halder took a hard attitude with respect to von Falkenhorst's troop requirements. He requested full and timely information about all future requests. He insisted that OKH should be fully informed about future requirements before they became formal OKW demands, and received von Falkenhorst's verbal assurance to this effect.

The OKW issued the directive for *Weserübung* on March 1, over Hitler's signature. The directive was issued in nine copies. Five copies were for OKW and one each for von Falkenhorst and the service chiefs. On the same day as Hitler signed the *Weserübung* directive, OKW presented the services with the force requirements. This came without prior consultations despite von Falkenhorst's assurances to the contrary three days earlier. The requirements presented to OKH included a corps headquarters, two divisions, and a motorized brigade for Denmark, as well as five divisions and a number of special units for Norway. The requirements caused anger in the services and a flurry of wrangling and power struggles between the service chiefs and OKW over the next week.

The army managed to obtain some reduction in forces they were required to provide. However, Luftwaffe chief Hermann Göring caused most of the difficulties. He had a large ego, felt slighted, and refused to tolerate subordinating air force units (except for tactical control) to any other service or joint commands. While the attack on Denmark and Norway was the first combined operation of the war, any semblance of a unified command structure for Group XXI disappeared because of Göring's protests. The air force component of *Weserübung*, X Air Corps, was removed from von Falkenhorst's control. It would now report to Oberkommando der Luftwaffe (Air Force High Command, OKL) and von Falkenhorst would have to submit his requirements and requests to OKL. To compensate for the lack of a unified command structure, OKW had to make detailed decisions about command relationships and even had to exercise direct control in certain cases to ensure smooth cooperation between the services.

However, Göring also caused difficulties for the other service chiefs. He was very critical of previous planning, and the result was that the concessions OKH had wrung from the OKW were not only rescinded, but the original requirements were increased. In a directive on March 7, the number of requested divisions rose from seven plus to nine plus. The navy had planned on a rapid return of its warships, in order to escape the expected furious counterattacks by the British Navy. They were now required to keep ships in Norwegian harbors, particularly in Narvik.

The Army commander-in-chief, General Brauchitsch, did not raise further issues about the size of the army requirements. He appears to have been satisfied to take a back seat in all future planning for the Scandinavian venture. He did not even attend Hitler's final conference with the service chiefs and General von Falkenhorst about *Weserübung* on April 2. OKH had been opposed to the Scandinavian adventure from the very start, regarding it as a lunatic idea. Brauchitsch's absence from the conference on April 2 is only one of many indications that the army wanted nothing to do with *Weserübung*, an operation with so many inherent flaws and dangers that they fully expected it to fail.

There had been an undercurrent of opposition to Hitler among high-ranking members of the army, if not outright plotting. Their goal was the removal of Hitler and a conclusion of peace with the Allies. To have any hope of success they needed the support of Brauchitsch and Halder. There were no prospects of these two officers turning against Hitler, to whom they were bound by both traditional loyalty and fear, as long as he remained popular and respected by the German people. His popularity had increased over the years after a series of successes, often achieved despite doubts or opposition from the armed forces. It may well be that the army leaders believed strongly that the Scandinavian adventure was doomed. The failure could then be laid squarely at Hitler's feet and would be a serious blow to his prestige and standing with the German people. The prestige of the General Staff, on the other hand, would be enhanced by its non-participation in the preparation for and execution of *Weserübung*. Under such conditions, the time could be ripe for planning a regime change.[43]

The Germans were increasingly concerned that the Allies would soon make their move in Scandinavia and present the Germans with the worst of all possible scenarios. Speed had become a necessity. On March 3, Hitler called for a substantial speed-up of preparations and indicated that he would not tolerate any delays by the services. He directed that the forces for *Weserübung* assemble by March 10 and be ready to launch within four days. During a stormy session with the service chiefs on March 5, Hitler again reiterated that he wanted preparations for the Scandinavian operation hastened.

The German Navy was well pleased with the developments in the plans for *Weserübung*, with one major exception. Almost the entire surface fleet would participate in the attack on Norway, and a few older ships would be used against Denmark. The outward journey to Norway would be hazardous, and the return journey, after the British had a chance to recover from what the Germans hoped would be surprise, would involve extreme risks for the units deployed to central and northern Norway. The navy considered the critical point of the outward journey to be at the latitude of the Bergen-Shetland Islands. There was a good chance that the German ships would be discovered by the British in this area, and it was planned that they would pass during the hours of darkness. If the German naval units were discovered before reaching this point, operations north of Bergen could well become impossible because of the proximity of the British naval bases in Scotland.

The one exception to the navy's satisfaction was the requirement that it should leave naval units in Norwegian harbors. To do so without air support amounted to suicide in the views of the naval staff. Admiral Raeder, who was more adept at handling Hitler than his army counterpart, wasted no time in appealing the decision to leave naval units in Norwegian harbors after the invasion. He wrapped this appeal very nicely into an overall appreciation of the Norwegian situation that he presented to Hitler on March 9.[44] Hitler was impressed by Raeder's arguments, but because of Göring's objections, the matter remained unsettled for nearly two weeks.

Peace negotiations between the Finns and Soviets were underway, but the Finnish Foreign Minister had made it known that if the Soviet demands were too harsh, Finland would ask for Allied assistance. The British Prime Minister stated on March 10 that help would be provided if asked for. Also that day, public reports and German knowledge of the concentration of British naval forces in Scotland caused the German Naval Staff to conclude that preparations for an Allied invasion of Norway might already be completed and carried out as early as the following week. SKL made this accurate assessment in its journal:

> The enemy can not see any possibility of obtaining victory in the European theater of war. The enemy views the spreading of the theater of war into the north to cut off Germany's import of iron ore as a strategic necessity. Because of Finland's predicament, such an operation would have to take place soon, and the Finnish situation gives the enemy the justification to carry it out before the anticipated German offensive in the west. The ice conditions in the Baltic Sea prevent Germany from carrying out operations there.[45]

It appears that Raeder had lost some of his earlier enthusiasm for the Scandinavian venture by February and March 1940. We can only guess at the reasons. The navy had three objectives in mind in its initial planning for an operation against Scandinavia. One was the securing of iron ore from Sweden, so important for the shipbuilding program. Second, bases in Norway would improve the German navy's strategic position. Third, preventing British occupation of bases in southern Norway would secure the Baltic approaches and increase the security of naval facilities in the Baltic against air attacks. It was not at all certain in the autumn of 1939 that the war would be short, and securing the great French mines in Lorraine was by no means assured. Under these circumstances, Raeder saw a chance for his service to play an important role and he attempted to draw Hitler's attention to the north, away from the great offensive in the west. However, by the spring of 1940, it had become obvious to Raeder that Hitler could not be distracted from his western plans.

The prospects for success in the west were improved greatly by the plan General Erich von Manstein developed and sold to Hitler. It was now more reasonable to assume that a breakthrough to the English Channel would succeed. This would provide the navy with bases on the French Atlantic coast and force the French to retreat from the Lorraine region. Norwegian bases no longer had the same importance. Equally significant to Raeder was a decision taken by Hitler on January 17, 1940 with respect to the long struggle over rearmament priorities. Hitler decided that the army should have priority, and he even suggested that it could become necessary to disband large naval units. Raeder's protests over this decision were not successful.[46]

The blow to Raeder's hopes of having a navy in the mid-1940s that could secure Germany's trade routes while threatening those of Great Britain, together with a more promising chance of securing naval bases in France at virtually no cost to the navy, must have caused him to have second thoughts about the wisdom of attacking Norway. The preservation of the navy now assumed greater importance. The greatest concentration of British sea power in North Sea harbors since World War I threatened the very existence of the German Navy, unless complete operational secrecy was maintained. Raeder's concerns are shown by the fact that he expressed doubts to Jodl about the importance of "playing a preventive role in Norway." There also appears to have been some reluctance within von Falkenhorst's command, based on entries in Jodl's diary: "Certain naval officers seem to be lukewarm about *Weserübung* and need a shot in the arm. Even von Falkenhorst's three immediate subordinates bring up points that are none of their business."[47]

There remained the objective of securing the flow of Swedish iron ore, and this was the argument used by Raeder in his meetings with Hitler in the spring of 1940.[48] The availability of this source and the prospect of the Lorraine fields preserved the chance that Hitler could still be prevailed upon to shift the armament priority to the navy after a successful campaign in the west. The loss of the Swedish ore, while a severe blow to the German war industry, would be particularly devastating to the navy.

The conclusion of peace between Finland and the Soviet Union on March 12 caused problems not only for the British but also for the Germans. An entry in Jodl's diary on March 10 warned, "For us the situation is troublesome because the justification for Falkenhorst's action becomes difficult if peace (between Finland and Russia) is soon concluded." Notations in the same diary from March 12 to 14 indicate that Hitler was also searching for a way to justify

Weserübung. For example, an entry for 13 March reads, *"*Fuehrer does not give the order for 'W' [*Weserübung*]. He is still trying to find a justification.*"*

As noted, Raeder appears to have become somewhat more cautious, and there was disagreement among senior members of his staff, as well as within von Falkenhorst's staff, about the necessity for and wisdom of the Norwegian operation. For his part, Hitler would probably not have minded a delay in *Weserübung* as evidenced by his order on March 13 for the planning to continue "without excessive haste."[49] However, he agreed with Raeder that the British had not abandoned their strategic objective of eliminating German ore imports through Norwegian territorial waters and that, for this reason, Scandinavia would remain an area of unrest that had to be dealt with eventually. Hitler reaffirmed his intention to carry out *Weserübung* before the attack in the west.

Hitler left Berlin on March 17 for a meeting with Benito Mussolini, the Italian fascist leader, at the Brenner Pass. There are no indications that he mentioned anything to Mussolini about his plans for Norway and Denmark. Hitler spent the following days at Obersalzberg, and called for an immediate meeting with Raeder, Keitel, and Jodl when he returned on March 26.

Raeder reported to Hitler that he no longer considered a British landing in Norway imminent, but that their goal of cutting off Germany's iron ore import remained. He expected this to take the form of disruption of the ore traffic in Norwegian waters in the hope that this would create a pretext for action against Norway. Raeder concluded that the Germans would be forced to carry out *Weserübung* eventually and argued for early action. He pointed out that the new moon on April 7 would provide favorable conditions, and that the northern nights would be too short after April 15; that German U-boats covering the planned operation could remain in position for only two or three additional weeks; and that the anticipated foggy and overcast weather conditions in early April favored the Germans. Hitler agreed that the landings should take place on April 7, but the following day, March 27, he told Halder that he wanted the operation to take place on April 9 or 10. We do not know what caused this postponement, which was strongly opposed by the navy, but it probably had something to do with a new round of inter-service squabbling.

Raeder wanted the air force to drop mines in all major British estuaries in order to hamper the movement of their fleet during the most critical part of the operation. Göring resisted this request and offered instead to bomb Scapa Flow. The navy believed bombing would be ineffective in preventing the movement of the fleet. Raeder also wanted the German ships to return to Germany as quickly as possible after landing the troops. Göring argued that the ships should remain to support the operations, and it appears that Hitler was also leaning in this direction. Raeder considered this a life and death issue for the German Navy, and after the regular meeting with Hitler, General Keitel, General Jodl, and Commander von Püttkammer in the afternoon of March 29, 1940, he requested to see the Führer privately. Hitler still wanted to leave naval forces behind in Narvik and Trondheim, but after Raeder had again enumerated the many arguments against such an idea, Hitler relented and allowed for the ships in Narvik to return to Germany immediately after landing the troops and refueling. With respect to Trondheim, he asked Raeder to "investigate the matter once more."[50]

Hitler held a final review of the *Weserübung* plan and preparations on April 1. Von Falkenhorst, the senior officers from each service, and the commanders of each landing force gave the briefing. Hitler gave the plan and preparations his blessings and concluded with a short pep talk to those present, including his justification for carrying out the operation. He stated that, while he had full confidence in the carefully prepared operation and its commanders, the time between this review and the completion of the operation would impose on him the greatest nervous anxiety of his life.[51] Rosenberg's diary entry for April 9 depicts a more euphoric Hitler, who is alleged to have said, "Just as Bismarck's Reich was born in 1866, the Great German Reich will be born from what is going on today."[52]

The following day Hitler set the date and time for the operation as April 9 at 0415 hours. He also relented in his desire to keep warships in Trondheim.

The Operational Plan

Von Falkenhorst, his staff, and other headquarters within the Wehrmacht tasked to support *Weserübung* had been busy during the month of March. The German military officers at times displayed some weaknesses when it came to strategic assessments, and political, economic, and psychological considerations were often not given the proper weight. However, the officers were superb when it came to operational planning. The final operational plans for *Weserübung*, which were issued on March 5, 1940 and for Narvik on March 12 are excellent examples of meticulous planning. But they are remarkable plans not only for their attention to details and close cooperation between the services, despite the failure to achieve a unified command structure, but also for their display of imagination, innovation, and the assumption of calculated risks. This superb planning was combined with boldness and skill in execution. These were important factors in making an operation that the General Staff regarded as "lunatic" a stunning operational success. In both planning and execution, *Weserübung* stands in sharp contrast to the dilatory and rather unprofessional efforts on the part of the Allies.

Nevertheless, it must be recognized that the operation was a gamble, and the German General Staff could well have been proven correct in its expectation of failure. While superb planning and bold execution were important factors in its eventual success, the element of luck, hoped for but not planned for in military operations, was equally important. If the Norwegians and the British had heeded the many warnings they received, the stunning operational success could easily have turned into military disaster.

It is rather amazing that the operation succeeded as well as it did, not only because of those risks already alluded to, but also because of the rather makeshift command and operational control mechanism. Much of this can be traced back to inter-service rivalries, but German lack of experience in combined operations also played a large role. Von Falkenhorst commanded only the ground forces, and had no command authority over the naval and air force components, who instead took orders from their respective services. Requirements for the other services were passed from Group XXI to the services, usually through OKW.

This three-way command relationship existed not only for the passage and landing but also for the entire operation. A territorial command for the air force was established, and this with General Erhard Milch's Fifth Air Fleet absorbed the X Air Corps on April 12. All naval units in Norway after the landings would come under the leadership of Admiral Boehm, with headquarters in Oslo. He established subordinate naval commands in Bergen and Kristiansand.

At the various landing sites, an army officer was designated as commander of the landing forces and for operations to secure the landing site. The senior officer present from either the navy or the army would assume command after the landings were carried out. However, he could only issue orders to the other services within his area in emergencies.

Von Falkenhorst had his headquarters in Hamburg during the actual attack and was directly subordinate to Hitler through OKW. A group was established at OKW, including officers from each service, to serve as a link with Group XXI and as a coordination point, particularly for the flow of reinforcements and supplies after the initial landings. X Air Corps, under Lieutenant General Hans Geissler, also had its initial headquarters in Hamburg. The command and control of naval operations for the attack was divided. OKM decided that the operations in the Baltic, Kattegat, and part of Skagerrak should be under Admiral Carls with his headquarters in Kiel. Operations in the North Sea were under Admiral Saalwächter with his headquarters in Wilhelmshaven.

The fact that the planning for and conduct of the operation proceeded relatively smoothly must be attributed to the personalities and professionalism of the officers at the working level. This is also the conclusion reached by Group XXI in its after-action report:

> That the commands and troop contingents of the three armed forces branches worked together almost without friction cannot be credited to purposeful organization of the commanding staff. It was, instead, entirely an achievement of the personalities involved who knew how to cooperate closely in order to overcome the inadequacies of the organization.[53]

The invasion plan called for one major naval expedition along the Norwegian coast to land the lead elements of the three assault divisions. The assault force designated for the attack was divided into six task forces in addition to a naval covering force. The assault troops were carried on warships. These task forces were scheduled to arrive at the entrance to all target ports shortly after 0400 hours, and the assaults were to be carried out within 30 minutes of arrival.

The targets were geographically separated by about 1,000 miles of water, so the ambitious timetable required not only precision planning and execution but also considerable luck. The dangers for the Germans were much greater in Narvik and Trondheim than at the other ports, which meant that those units would have to be self-sufficient until they linked-up with forces landed in other parts of the country. The Germans might get away with one naval sortie to Narvik, but a second expedition along the coast was completely out of the question. The situation in Oslo and the other parts of southern Norway was considered more favorable since those operations would, at least in part, be under the protective umbrella of German aircraft after the initial landing. A rapid build-up of forces in Oslo was considered feasible, and these forces would push inland as quickly as possible to prevent or disrupt Norwegian mobilization and to establish overland connections with other beachheads.

Task Forces 1 and 2, destined for Narvik and Trondheim respectively, sailed together, escorted by the battleships *Gneisenau* and *Scharnhorst*. Each battleship had a crew of 1,800. Admiral Wilhelm Marshall, Fleet Commander, should have commanded this combined force but he was ill and Vice Admiral Guenther

Lütjens assumed command. The two battleships and the ships destined for Trondheim and Narvik were to sail together to designated locations. The battleships would then proceed on a northerly or northwesterly course in an attempt to draw any major British surface forces away from the Norwegian coast. The two battleships, Task Force 1, and Task Force 2 departed various north German ports shortly before midnight on April 6, joined forces at 0200 hours on April 7, and proceeded toward their destination. The fleet was given a strong fighter escort during daylight hours on April 7.

Task Force 1, commanded by Captain Friedrich Bonte, who flew his flag from the destroyer *Wilhelm Heidkamp*, consisted of ten destroyers. There were 3,140 officers and crew aboard the ten destroyers. The assault elements of Task Force 1 were commanded by Major General Eduard W.C. Dietl and consisted of the reinforced 139th Mountain Regiment, advanced headquarters and staff elements of the 3rd Mountain Division, and various support elements. The approximately 2,000 troops were distributed equally on the ten destroyers.

The naval elements of Task Force 2, under the command of Captain Hellmuth Heye, consisted of the heavy cruiser *Admiral Hipper* and four destroyers. These ships had a crew of 2,860 officers and men. The landing force, commanded by Colonel Weiss, consisted of two battalions of the 138th Mountain Regiment, an engineer company, artillery battery, and support units. Total strength of the landing force was 1,700.

Task Force 3, which had the mission of capturing Bergen, departed Wilhelmshaven and Cuxhaven shortly before midnight on April 7. It consisted of the light cruisers *Köln* and *Königsberg*, the naval artillery training ship *Bremse*, two torpedo boats, five motor torpedo boats, and the support ship *Karl Peters*. The ships were manned by 2,420 officers and men and were commanded by Rear Admiral Huber Schmundt. The Bergen landing force, commanded by Major General Tittel, consisted of elements of the 69th Division staff, two battalions of the 159th Infantry Regiment, two engineer companies, two naval artillery batteries, and various support units. The total strength was 1,900.

The mission of Task Force 4 was to capture Kristiansand and Arendal and Captain Rieve was the navy commander. The naval force consisted of the light cruiser *Karlsruhe*, three torpedo boats, seven motor torpedo boats, and the artillery training ship *Tsingtau*. This task force departed Wesermünde at 0400 hours on April 8. The officers and men on the ships totaled 1,767. Colonel Gihr commanded the landing force, which consisted of one battalion plus one company of the 310th Infantry Regiment, one motorcycle squadron, and some naval artillery personnel. The strength of the landing force was 1,100.

Task Force 5 had as its mission the capture of the Norwegian capital, including the government and king if that was possible. The naval contingent of Task Force 5 consisted of the heavy cruisers *Blücher* and *Lützow*, the light cruiser *Emden*, three torpedo boats, eight R-boats (small minesweepers), and two auxiliaries (armed whalers). *Blücher* was the newest of the major German surface units, launched on June 8, 1939 and commissioned on September 10, 1939. Its actual displacement was 18,200 tons although it was officially listed at 14,050 tons. Sea trials had just been completed prior to the Norwegian invasion. The *Lützow* was originally classified as a pocket battleship and named *Deutschland*. It was reclassified as a heavy cruiser on January 25, 1940 and given a new name. Hitler thought there would be undesirable psychological and propaganda consequences if a ship named *Deutschland* should be sunk. The ships of Task Force 5 carried a combined crew of 3,800. Rear Admiral Kummetz commanded the naval component. The landing force consisted of two battalions of the 307th Infantry Regiment, one battalion of the 138th Mountain Regiment, plus various artillery, engineer and support units. The strength of the landing force was 2,000. Major General Engelbrecht commanded the landing force.

Task Force 6 was the smallest. Its mission was to capture Egersund on the southwest coast. The Germans considered this small coastal town important enough to be included as a target for the first day because it was the eastern terminal of the underwater cable to England. Task Force 6 assembled in Cuxhaven and sailed from the Elbe estuary at 0445 hours on April 8. Captain Kurt Thomas was the task force's naval commander, and he had at his disposal four minesweepers with a combined crew of 328 personnel. Captain Eichorn of the cavalry commanded the landing force and had one motorcycle squadron of 150 soldiers for his mission.

Nearly every ship in the German Navy participated in *Weserübung*. In addition to the protective group consisting of the two battleships mentioned earlier, 36 German U-boats took up positions along the Norwegian coast and in the areas around the Shetland Islands and the Orkneys. The submarines were divided into eight designated groups and four boats operating independently in the waters between Orkneys-Shetlands-Bergen.

The only major units of the German Navy not participating in the Norwegian attack were the pocket battleship *Admiral Scheer*, the light cruisers *Leipzig* and *Nürnberg*, six destroyers, and four torpedo boats. These were all undergoing repairs. The Luftwaffe had sunk two German destroyers by mistake in February 1940.

The army divisions assigned for operations in Norway consisted of the 3rd and 2nd Mountain Divisions, the 69th, 163rd, 181st, 196th, and 214th Infantry Divisions. The two mountain divisions were elite units, consisting of a mixture of German and Austrian troops. The 2nd was not on the original list of units for the invasion but was added and moved to Norway when it became apparent that mountain troops were necessary to establish contact between the Trondheim landing force and that in Narvik.

While the main army units constituting the invasion force did not possess nearly a uniform level of personnel, training, equipment, and experience, they were considered fully combat ready. While some of the troops could be considered old for combat duty, this was compensated for by experience. The 214th Infantry Division, for example, consisted primarily of militia or territorial solders as well as veterans from World War I. A number of the units were armed and equipped with captured materiel (Austrian, Czechoslovakian, and Polish).

Training time varied. Some German units had not trained for winter and mountain operations, and all units lacked training in amphibious operations. These were serious shortcomings that had to be overcome. All units were extensively trained in offensive operations, and all ranks were expected to show themselves capable of flexibility, initiative, and improvisation.

Air Corps X, under Lieutenant General Hans Geissler's command, was tasked with providing air support for the Norwegian operation and was considerably augmented for this mission. Air Corps X employed more than 1,000 aircraft in the Norwegian operation, including approximately 500 transport aircraft.

Air Corps X consisted of three squadrons and one group of fighter-bombers. Each squadron normally consisted of three groups and each group had 27 aircraft. There was also one group of dive-bombers, two groups of fighters, 18 reconnaissance aircraft, one group of seaplanes, and seven groups of transport aircraft. The Luftwaffe also provided three anti-aircraft battalions, one parachute battalion, and several air landing units. The navy also had under its own command three groups of reconnaissance aircraft. The mission of Air Corps X was to transport parachute and other troops to Oslo, Kristiansand, and Stavanger, to protect the troop transports and the landing of troops in Norway against enemy aircraft, to provide close air support for the troops, and to capture and expand Norwegian airfields.

Only light equipment and limited supplies could accompany the small number of personnel in the attack groups; that is, those transported on warships. It was therefore of great importance that heavier weapons, equipment, and reinforcements for the initial landings arrive in Norwegian harbors on the day of the attack. The timely availability of fuel was particularly critical for the returning warships. Several transport groups were organized to bring the heavy weapons, supplies, equipment, reinforcements, and fuel to Norway. One was referred to as the Export Echelon (Ausführ-Staffel) and consisted of seven merchant ships that were to sail individually from Hamburg to Narvik, Trondheim, and Stavanger with weapons and supplies for those troops that were landed by sea or air. The ships were to pretend to be merchant ships on their way to Murmansk and were to arrive at their real destinations *before* the warships or airplanes.

The 1st Sea Transport Echelon consisted of 15 merchant ships that assembled in Stettin on March 12 and began loading units from the 69th and 163rd Infantry Divisions on April 4 (3,761 troops, 672 horses, 1,377 vehicles and 5,935 tons of supplies). These forces were earmarked for Oslo, Kristiansand, Stavanger, and Bergen. Two large tankers loaded with fuel sailed from Wilhelmshaven: one to Narvik and one to Trondheim. Another large tanker sailed from Murmansk to Narvik. Five smaller tankers would later bring fuel from Hamburg to Oslo, Stavanger, Bergen, and Trondheim. The ships of the 1st Sea Transport Echelon and the tankers sailed individually, and no visible protective measures were taken. For security reasons, none of the ships from the Export Echelon, the 1st Sea Transport Echelon or the tankers was allowed to leave German harbors earlier than six days before the day of the attack. The time allowed for these ships to reach their destination proved inadequate in many cases and led to serious supply difficulties. However, it was the limited number of tankers for Narvik that caused the most serious problems for the navy.

The 2nd Sea Transport Echelon consisted of 11 merchant ships and carried troops from the 196th Infantry Division (8,450 troops, 969 horses, 1,283 vehicles and 2,170 tons of supplies). It sailed from Goetnhafen (Gdynia) and Köningsberg to Oslo. These ships were scheduled to arrive in Oslo two days after the invasion.

The 3rd Sea Transport Echelon consisted of 12 merchant ships that were to proceed from Hamburg to Oslo with 6,065 troops, 893 horses, 1,347 vehicles and 6,050 tons of supplies. These ships were scheduled to arrive in Oslo six days after the invasion. Further reinforcements and supplies, consisting of 40,000 troops, 4,000 horses, 10,000 vehicles, and 40,000 tons of supplies were to be brought to Oslo as quickly as possible. The returning ships of the 2nd and 3rd Sea Transport Echelons would be used in this effort.

The German attack on Norway was fully underway when the last task force, Task Force 6, departed the Elbe estuary at 0445 hours on April 8, 1940. The first attack wave carried more than 30,000 German sailors and soldiers.

This operation was an extremely hazardous undertaking, and its success rested on three pillars: complete tactical surprise, the determination and professionalism of those involved, and mistakes by the enemy. There was an extremely slim margin between success and failure. The key element of achieving tactical surprise carried enormous risks. Any action or intelligence that aroused suspicions in Britain or Norway could lead to catastrophe. The overwhelming British naval forces present in or around the North Sea presented a grave threat to the German attack groups. A mobilization of the Norwegian Army as late as April 8, providing additional personnel for the coastal fortresses, and laying the planned minefields, could have made the German landings very costly. Mobilization before the German capture of the depots would have opened the possibilities of Norwegian counterattacks against the isolated German landing forces. Admiral Carls' assessment on the evening of April 7 was somber, realistic, and prophetic.

> The risks are great, and there will be losses. But in view of the great significance of the operation, the price to be paid will not be too great if most of the surface fleet is lost. One must be prepared for the loss of at least half of the committed naval forces if Norwegian or British resistance is encountered.[54]

The eagerness to carry out Operation *Weserübung* exhibited by many officers in the German Navy is traceable to their desire to avoid the conditions that prevailed in World War I by acquiring operational bases on Europe's open coastline that would make a British blockade difficult or impossible. This would greatly simplify and extend the navy's operational range. It is therefore strange that they were prepared to sacrifice most the navy in this endeavor, particularly in view of Hitler's shift of priority to the army and the improved prospects of acquiring bases on the French coast. An outcome along the lines anticipated by Admiral Carls seems to go directly against the objectives the German Navy was trying to achieve.

The Views of the Opposing Admiralties

Did the two admiralties think with precision along the same lines in correct strategy as claimed by Churchill in his now famous quote? Strategy is driven by objectives and capabilities. There was a distinct, although subtle, difference in the objectives of the two sides. Churchill's desire was to provoke the Germans into operations in Scandinavia, operations that he believed could be challenged effectively and successfully by the Allies and thereby bring quick military victories in a war that had stagnated. Threatening the German source of badly needed iron was a means of provoking this confrontation. The French, likewise, wanted to open a new front in order to divert German attention and resources from their border. They also viewed the threat against the flow of iron ore as a means by which to open the new front. Both Churchill and his friends across the Channel felt that if they succeeded in this process, the maritime blockade of Germany would become more effective, especially if they succeeded in severing the flow of iron ore. To this end, they were willing to accept great political and military risks.

The Allies certainly possessed the capability to bring on the confrontation desired by Churchill and Reynaud. It is a much different question to ask if they could have succeeded in cutting the flow of iron ore to Germany. A realization of the difficulties involved in doing so may help explain Churchill's lukewarm support for Ironside's project of invading northern Sweden. The Allies lacked expertise in arctic warfare and were ignorant as to the problems of geography, climate, and the lack of lines of communications in northern Norway and Sweden. In retrospect, it is difficult to see how the Allies could have captured the iron ore districts in northern Sweden in the face of almost certain Norwegian and Swedish resistance, even without German intervention in that area. The goal of doing so was unrealistic in view of their capabilities.

The senior officers in the German Navy had served during the four years of relative inactivity of the High Seas Fleet in World War I, imposed largely by geographical limitations. They had seen the effects of the previous war's blockade on the German people and witnessed the drop in morale in the navy that eventually led to a mutiny of the High Seas Fleet. They were determined to avoid a similar situation arising in World War II. Their desire for bases in Norway was driven by a wish to complicate British blockade measures and open the door to the Atlantic.

Raeder shared this view, but he was in less of a hurry to acquire those bases. However, the urgency of acquiring them increased as evidence suggested that the

British intended to seize the bases for themselves. Raeder was encouraged by Hitler's approval of the *Z Plan*, but realized that if the iron ore supplies were limited the navy might suffer as a result of priority being given to the demands of other branches of the services. In the short term, therefore, his primary concern was to keep Swedish iron ore flowing to the benefit of the naval building program. Hitler's main concerns were the uninterrupted flow of iron ore, not primarily for the benefit of the navy, but to the benefit of the German armament industry as a whole. He was also concerned with the air threat to Germany by Allied air forces operating from bases in Scandinavia. The other military services in Germany were far less in favor of the Scandinavian operations because they viewed them as distractions from the main effort in the west.

Hitler certainly had the ground and air assets to undertake the Scandinavian operations, as well as troops trained and capable of operating in the arctic mountain wilderness. The navy did not have the resources required by a thoughtful military plan, particularly as it involved Narvik and, to a lesser, extent Trondheim. The Germans could have carried out the operation in Norway without landing in Narvik, but it would have been more difficult. For the German Navy, it was an extremely high-risk affair. While the Allies risked losing ships, the Germans ventured their whole navy. Whether or not this happened hinged on secrecy and slow, irresolute, and faulty reactions by the Norwegians and the Allies, hardly the assumptions required in a prudent military plan.

The debate over motives and capabilities will never be settled. However, Churchill's statement that the two admiralties thought in precision along the same lines and in correct strategy—while an excellent one-liner—fails to tell the story.

NOTES

1 Basil H. Liddell-Hart, *History of the Second World War* (New York: G.P. Putnam's Sons, 1971), p. 52.

2 Wolfgang Wegener, *Die Seestrategie des Weltkrieges* (Berlin: E. Mittler & Sohn, 1929), p. 49.

3 The Anglo-German Naval Agreement in 1935 fixed German naval tonnage at one-third of the British fleet. However, the German Navy's desire to play a major role is demonstrated by the *Z Plan*, which called for the construction, by 1945, of 10 battleships, 13 pocket battleships (*Panzerschiffe*), four aircraft carriers, five heavy cruisers, 44 light cruisers, 68 destroyers, 249 large, medium, and small submarines, and 90 torpedo boats. Hans-Martin Ottmer, *Weserübung. Der deutsche Angriff auf Dänemark und Norwegen im April 1940* (Oldenburg: Militärgeschichtliches Forschungsamt, 1994), p.13.

4 Kenneth P. Hansen, "Raeder Versus Wegener: Conflict in German Naval Strategy," in *Naval War College Review*, September 22, 2005. Raeder was godfather to one of Wegener's children and describes him as an intimate friend in his memoirs, but they developed such an animosity that Raeder refused to deliver the eulogy at Wegener's funeral in 1956.

5 Quoted in Carl-Axel Gemzell, *Organization, Conflict, and Innovation. A Study of German Naval Strategic Planning 1888-1940*. (Lunde: Esselte Studium), pp. 286-287.

6 Gemzell writes, "Moreover, the results of our investigation make it possible to establish with certainty that, from the start of the war, Carls was greatly involved in the Scandinavian question and advanced opinion about the importance of bases in Denmark and Norway." (*Organization*, p. 381)

7 Erich Raeder, *My Life* (Henry W. Drexel, transl. Annapolis: United States Naval Institute, 1960), p. 300.

8 Michael Salewski writes, "The 'Norwegian case' remained, as already demonstrated, permanently in the considerations of the Naval Staff since 1937" (*Die deutsche Seekriegsleitung 1935-1945*. Volume I. *1935-1941* [Frankfurt am Main: Bernard & Graefe Verlag für Wehrwesen, 1970], p.177).

9 International Military Tribunal (IMT), *Trial of the Major War Criminals before the International Military Tribunal, 14 November 1945-1 October 1946* (Nuremberg: 1947-49), vol. 14, pp. 85-86.

10 See Carl-Axel Gemzell, *Raeder, Hitler und Skandinavien. Der Kamp für einen Maritimen Operations-plan* (Lund: C.W.K. Gleerup, 1975), pp. 301-308 and 380 for detailed discussions of these events. Also Ottmer, *Weserübung*, pp. 17-20.

11 IMT, *Trial of the Major War Criminals*, vol. 14, pp. 85-86.

12 IMT, *Trial of the Major War Criminals*, vol. 14, p. 86. An entry in the *Kriegstagebuch der Seekriegsleitung 1939–1945* (hereinafter *KTBS*), for October 3, 1939 confirms Raeder's testimony and treats the questions that needed to be answered by the study in more detail. See also IMT, document C-122, GB-8.

13 The document titled "Überlegungen zur Frage der Stützpunktgewinnung für die Nordsee-Kriegführung" appears in Salewski, *Die deutsche Seekriegsleitung* , vol 1, pp. 563-565.

14 *KTBS*, October 9, 1939 and Steen, *Norges Sjøkrig 1940-1945*, vol 1, pp. 126-127.

15 *Fuehrer Conferences On Matters Dealing With the German Navy 1939* (Translated and printed by the Office of Naval Intelligence, Navy Department, Washington, D.C., 1947), pp. 12-14.

16 *Fuhrer Conferences*, December 8, 1939, p. 46.

17 Ralph Hewins, *Quisling. Prophet without Honour* (New York: John Day Company, 1966), pp. 178-179.

18 Letters between Admirals Böhm and Schniewind as quoted in Gemzell, *Organization*, p. 389 n. 43.

19 Gemzell, *Skandinavien*, p. 270.

20 Hans-Dietrich Loock, *Quisling, Rosenberg und Terboven. Zur Vorgeschicte und Geschichte der national-sozialistischen Revolution in Norwegen* (Stuttgart: Deutsch Verlags-Anstalt, 1970), pp. 207-209.

21 IMT, Trial of the Major War Criminals, vol. 14, pp. 92-93.

22 *Fuehrer Conferences 1939*. Annex 1 – Minutes of a Conference on December 11, 1939 at 1200, p. 56.

23 *Fuehrer Conferences*, p. 54.

24 Loock, *Quisling*, p. 371.

25 *Fuehrer Conferences 1939*, p. 54.

26 Hewins (*Prophet without Honor*, p. 179) reports that the first meeting between Hitler and Quisling took place on December 15 but this is apparently an error. The *Jodl Diary* gives the date of the first meeting as December 13, but this is also most likely a mistake since Raeder's handwritten note at the bottom of the letter he received from Rosenberg on December 13, refers to the meeting scheduled for December 14.

27 This according to Telford Taylor, *The March of Conquest. The German Victories in Western Europe, 1940*. New York: Simon and Schuster, 1958, p. 88.

28 Entry in the *Jodl Diary* for December 13 – a probable error in date as already noted – and in the *Halder Diary*, dated December 14, 1939.

29 Churchill, 537 and 564. [add title]

30 IMT, 14:95.

31 There has been considerable speculation about what was discussed at a meeting between Colonel Hans Piekenbrock, Chief of the Abwehr's espionage section (Abwehr 1 – Nachritenbeschaffung) and Quisling at the Hotel d'Angleterre in Copenhagen on April 4, 1940. There is no evidence that Quisling was informed about the impending invasion. The Germans made a mention of this meeting (see IMT, *Trials of the Major War Criminals*, vol. 14, p. 41) but they also state, "Quisling and Hagelin, according to orders, could not be informed of the imminence and the time of operation." See also Walter Hubatsch, *Die deutsch Bezetsung von Dänemark und Norwegen 1940*. Gottingen: Wissenschaftlicher Verlag, 1952, p. 55 and n. 33 on that page. It is more likely that the meeting was an attempt by the Germans to see if Quisling knew anything that would indicate an intelligence leak. To tell Quisling about the operation five days before the landings would be very reckless and not in keeping with the security measures adopted to protect the whole venture. It would have been contrary to specific orders issued by Hitler on February 29, 1940.

32 *Fuehrer Conferences 1939*, p. 62.

33 Hubatsch, *Die deutsch Bezetsung*, pp. 40-41.

34 Ib Damegaard Petersen, "Aksen OKW-OKM," in *Historisk Tidsskrift*. Copenhagen: 1966, 12. Række, 2:1:92-122. It appears Gemzell (*Organization*, pp. 397-399) supports the views expressed by Petersen.

35 Gemzell, *Skandinavien*, p.227 and *Organization*, p. 399.

36 Walter Goerlitz, *History of the German General Staff 1657-1945*. New York: Praeger, 1957, p. 371.

37 However, an entry in the *Halder Diary* for February 21 states that von Falkenhorst had been placed in charge of preparations for the Norwegian operation and that Hq. XXI Corps would be placed under OKW "in order to avoid trouble with the air force." There is also a note by Halder, "Not a single word has passed between the Fuehrer and ObdH [Commander-in-Chief of the Army, Generaloberst Walther von Brauchitsch] on this matter, this must be put on record for the history of the war. I shall make a point of noting down the first time the subject is broached, not until 2 March."

38 General von Falkenhorst was tried and found guilty of war crimes by an American–British–Norwegian military tribunal in 1946 and sentenced to death. The sentence was subsequently reduced to 20 years' imprisonment. He was released from prison in 1953 because of

health problems. Von Falkenhorst died in 1968.

xxxix Steen, *Norges Sjøkrig 1940-1945*,vol. 1, pp. 134-135.

40 Kurt Assmann, *The German Campaign in Norway*. Admiralty: Naval Staff, 1948, p. 4 n. 7. See also, *Jodl Diary*, 5 and 7 March 1940.

41 Hans-Guenther Seraphim, *Das politische Tagebuch Alfred Rosenbergs aus den Jahren 1934/35 und 1939/40*. Göttingen: Musterschmidt-Verlag, 1956, p.102.

42 *Fuehrer Conferences 1940*, February 23, 1940, vol. 1, p. 14.

43 John W. Wheeler-Bennet, *The Nemesis of Power. The German Army in Politics 1918-1945*. New York: St Martin's Press, Inc., 1954, p. 494.

44 *Fuehrer Conferences 1940*, March 9, 1940, vol. 1, p. 20.

45 *KTBS*, March 10, 1940.

46 Salewski, *Die deutsche Seekriegsleitung*, p. 147. As the Norwegian operation was underway (April 29), Hitler ordered severe curtailment in the navy's shipbuilding program. Construction on two aircraft carriers, one battleship, and three light cruisers was terminated.

47 Entry in *Jodl's Diary* for March 14, 1940: "Ob.d.M. ist zweifelhaft, ob es jestz noch wichtig ist, in N. das preventive zu spielen. Fraglich ob man nicht Gelb vor Weserübung machen soll." By hinting at delaying the attack on Norway until after the attack in the West, Raeder was obviously thinking that the very hazardous operation in Norway might not be necessary if the attack in the West was successful. See also *Jodl's Diary* entries for March 21 and 28, 1940.

48 See *Fuehrer Conferences 1940*, "Report of the Commander in Chief, Navy to the Fuehrer on 9 March 1940 at 1200", vol. 1, pp. 20-21 and "Report of the Commander in Chief, Navy to the Fuehrer in the Afternoon of 26 March 1940", vol I, pp. 22-24.

49 Earl F. Ziemke, *The German Northern Theater of Operations 1940-1945*. Washington, D.C.: Department of Army Pamphlet 20-271, 1959, p.20.

50 *Fuehrer Conferences 1940*, March 29, 1940, vol. 1, p. 29.

51 *Gruppe XXI Kriegstagebuch* (hereinafter *XXIKTB*), 1 April 1940 as quoted in Ziemke, *German Northern Theater*, pp. 21-22.

52 Extract from the *Private Diary* of Reichsleiter Alfred Rosenberg, April 9, 1940, p. 17, quoted in Hubatsch, Appendix J, 454.

53 Quoted in Ziemke, 32.

54 Admiral Carls' assessment of the situation in the evening of April 7, 1940. Quoted in Steen, 1:149.

3

IGNORED WARNINGS: SHIPS PASSING IN THE NIGHT

"I wish I could believe this story. German intervention in Scandinavia is just what we want."
NOTATION BY LAURENCE COLLIER, A HIGH BRITISH FOREIGN OFFICE
OFFICIAL, ON RECEIPT OF NEWS THAT THE GERMANS WERE ABOUT
TO INVADE NORWAY.

German Intelligence and Security

Already on January 4, the Abwehr reported that one division of alpine troops had been pulled out of the Maginot Line and the agent who made the report concluded that these troops were destined for northern Europe. On March 7, the Germans learned that 16,000 troops were being redeployed from France to England. The increased British naval activities off the Norwegian coast and repeated violations of that country's territorial waters in March and early April were unmistakable signs that something more ambitious than troop redeployment might be afoot.

One source for German intelligence was Taylor G. Kent, who worked in the code room of the American Embassy in London. Since October 1939, he had forwarded important messages that came through the deciphering machine to the German Embassy in Rome. From there they were sent to Berlin. These messages included private communications between Churchill and Roosevelt.[1]

Reports received by the German intelligence services, particularly the SKL, indicated that the Allies would invade Norway and possibly Sweden even after the conclusion of peace between Finland and the Soviet Union. There were indications, supported by notations in the SKL journal on 15 March, that the peace had postponed but not altered Allied plans. These notations were based on intercepted and partially deciphered radio messages. A message from the British Admiralty to the commander of the Home Fleet on March 14 indicated that a large-scale embarkation of troops had been completed. The transports were prepared to sail and the troops were ready to board. The transports were to leave British Channel ports and proceed north on 48 to 80 hours notice depending on the political situation. Raeder and the SKL believed that *Weserübung* had developed into a race with similar British plans and they urged that landing operations be undertaken as quickly as possible. This influenced the selection of April 7 as the day of attack, later changed to April 9.

While Hitler's decision on March 26 to launch the invasion in early April was primarily due to anticipated weather conditions, the correctness of that decision in Hitler's mind was reinforced by continuous reports of Allied intentions to land in Norway. The Germans learned about the decision taken by the Allied Supreme War Council on March 28 and German intelligence intercepted a diplomat's report on March 30 of a conversation with Paul Reynaud. This report indicated that the Allies would launch operations in northern Europe within the next few days.[2]

Hitler had placed stringent restrictions on the number of individuals who knew about the impending operations. However, this circle had to be widened as the date for the operation drew closer. The Germans tried to disguise their troop movements as maneuvers and some troops were left in the barracks to suggest ongoing normal activity. The risk of discovery increased when the troops and shipping for the operation began assembly in the north German ports of Stettin, Hamburg, Wesermünde, Cuxhaven, Swinemünde, and Wilhelmshaven. Any intelligence forces monitoring German troop dispositions would have had ample reason to suspect that an important operation was underway.

Betrayal

Admiral Canaris, Chief of the Abwehr, was an opponent of Hitler and his policies, and that included the Scandinavian operation. Colonel Hans Oster, Chief of Staff at the Abwehr, was the center of Abwehr opposition and more aggressive than his superior in his anti-Hitler activities. Both eventually paid for their actions with their lives. Oster and others hoped to remove Hitler and come to an understanding with the British. They believed that a confrontation with the Allies in Scandinavia would harden British determination and make it difficult or impossible to arrive at an agreement. With respect to this issue, the views of the opponents of Hitler in Germany paralleled those of Prime Minister Chamberlain and Lord Halifax in Great Britain.

As a last resort Colonel Oster and his associates decided to leak information about the impending operation as soon as they had certain knowledge about its details. They may have felt this treasonous act as being justified by their belief that they were acting for the greater good of their country. They hoped that their warnings would lead the British and Norwegians to take countermeasures that would spoil the German operation, or plans for that operation. They anticipated that the Germans would detect active Norwegian and British preparations to meet the threat and therefore cancel the operation. To this end, Colonel Oster passed information about the operation to his contact in the Vatican and to his friend Major Gijsbertus J. Sas, the Dutch Military Attaché in Berlin, on April 3. Oster informed Sas that the German invasion of Norway and Denmark would take place early the following week (April 8-10) and asked that this information be passed to the Norwegians, Danes, and British.[3]

The information was passed to the Dutch War Ministry in two messages on April 3 and 4. Sas had a casual friend at the Norwegian Embassy, Councilor Ulrich Stang. Sas met Stang at the bar in the Adlon Hotel in the afternoon of April 4 and they had lunch together. Sas told Stang the Germans would invade Norway and Denmark on Tuesday (April 9) and that the attack in the west was sure to follow in short order. Stang dismissed the warning, stating that he did not believe it. Both Deutsch, in his book, and Roger Manvell and Heinrich Fraenkel, in their book, write that Sas did not know that Stang was a Quisling follower and claim that Stang never forwarded the warning to Oslo.[4]

Sas also informed Commander Kjølsen, the Danish Naval Attaché in Berlin, who forwarded the warning to the government in Copenhagen by courier, concluding that it was an OKW plant. His superiors in Denmark apparently shared this conclusion. Kjølsen met Arne Scheel, the Norwegian Ambassador in Berlin, the same day (April 3) and told him about the conversation he had with Major Sas. While Kjølsen's report to Scheel was less precise than Sas' statement to Stang, it is obvious that both the Norwegian Ambassador and his Councilor received clear warnings of an impending German attack.

In 1945, the Norwegian Investigative Commission looked into what the Norwegian Embassy did with these warnings. Scheel's explanation was never obtained since he died during the war. Scheel sent the following message to the Foreign Office in Oslo on April 4:[5]

The military attaché at one of the neutral nations legations here has today—in strict confidence—stated to one of the Legation's officials that according to information he had received from a responsible source, one should expect an attack on Holland in the near future, possibly already next week. . . . The Legation repeats the above—with all possible reservations—because the military attaché in question is known as a sober minded and well-informed man, and this Legation does not wish to fail to report the matter. The military attaché also hinted at a German invasion of Denmark with the intention of acquiring air and submarine bases on the west coast of Jutland.

The report failed to mention the warning about a German invasion of Norway on April 9. Another message the next day (April 5) from the Norwegian Embassy in Berlin read:

> The same report that is treated in my message 683 (above) was also received by the Danish Legation, which also heard rumors about occupation of points on the southern coast of Norway. The objective of the attacks that the rumors deal with was to step up the tempo of the war and to forestall the Allies.

Again, there is no mention of the direct warning from Major Sas about a full-scale invasion. The message on April 5 is obviously based on Scheel's conversation with the Danish Naval Attaché. The 1945 Investigative Commission concludes that Sas' report to Stang was forwarded in a misleading manner and that Scheel's report of his conversation with Kjølsen was only "a weak echo" of what was actually said. It is possible that Stang only reported to Scheel that part of the conversation with Major Sas that dealt with the anticipated attack in the west and possible moves against Denmark, conveniently leaving out the part that dealt with a direct attack on Norway.

Dutch intelligence ignored Sas' request to inform the British. Sas was not aware that his information was not forwarded to its intended recipient. If he had known, he may have employed other means to get the intelligence to the British. The failure to pass the information to the British intelligence and the failure of the Norwegian Embassy in Berlin to forward all the information it received to Oslo may not have changed the lethargic behavior of the two governments since other signs of impending events were ignored, discounted, or misinterpreted. However, it is possible that if the information had reached the right people, precautions could have been taken in London and Oslo that would have resulted in a calamity for the Germans.

Ottmer writes that the German Abwehr, and therefore presumably the

Chancery, knew the facts of the betrayal. They did not know, however, how the enemy would react to this information. Ottmer also writes that it seems this "factor of uncertainty" was not made known to Group XXI.[6] If the German authorities knew about this breach of security, they obviously did not know who had made the disclosure.

Warnings Received by the Norwegians

Intelligence about suspicious activities in northern Germany reached the Scandinavian countries at least a week before the date set for the attack. Reports from Sweden, Denmark, and Germany about unusual activities began to flow into offices in Oslo during the last week of March 1940. These included rumors that the Germans were preparing to cross the Danish border and that military leaves had been cancelled. The Swedish Naval Staff believed these reports indicated that the Germans were preparing to seize Norwegian harbors and airfields.

Ambassador Scheel had already sent a warning message to the Norwegian Foreign Office on April 1 where he reported the embarkation of German troops in Stettin. Scheel's conclusion was that these troops were probably part of operations against Sweden or other areas of the Baltic and that he saw no connection between these activities and possible German operations against Norway. The Norwegian Foreign Office did not forward this report to the Norwegian military authorities.

The Swedes were concerned about what was going on in Germany's Baltic and North Sea ports. Swedish intelligence officers, who believed that the assembly of German troops and ships in Stettin pointed to an overseas expedition, informed the intelligence division of the Norwegian Naval Staff. The Swedish Ambassador in Berlin asked the German Foreign Office for an explanation on April 2. The Swedish Naval Attaché in Berlin also forwarded a report that day stating that he had been informed that the Germans were preparing an operation against Norway in order to preempt British landings in that country. While the source for this report is unknown, the wording is similar to Ambassador Scheel's message on April 5. However, if the date of the report is correct, neither Scheel nor the Danish Naval Attaché could be the source since they did not receive their information until the following day.

A Norwegian newspaper reporter for *Aftenposten* in Berlin, Theo Findahl, notified his editorial office in Oslo on April 5 that there were rumors of large troop concentrations in northern Germany. He called the same editorial office on April 7 with the news that there were plans to land 1,500,000 troops on Norway's southern coast. The newspaper called the Norwegian Naval Staff and informed the duty officer, Captain Håkon Willoch. Admiral Diesen instructed Captain Willoch to call the Foreign Office and ask them not to print Findahl's report. Admiral Diesen assumed full responsibility for this action before the Investigative Commission in 1946.[7]

The Norwegian Naval Staff received an even more ominous report during the evening of April 7 from the Norwegian Embassy in Berlin via the Norwegian Foreign Office that appeared to substantiate the earlier reports from the Swedes:

> Information from a reliable source that the troop transports mentioned in my 611 message [April 1 message], 15 to 20 ships with a combined tonnage of 150,000, departed Stettin on a westerly course on the night of April 4–5. We are informed that the destination is to be reached on April 11, destination unknown.

Despite these alarming and accurate reports, neither Admiral Diesen nor his staff believed there was any danger of a German attack. The reports were discussed but the conclusion was that they dealt with German landings in the Netherlands in conjunction with an overland attack. Sir Llewellyn Woodward writes that Diesen concluded that the concentration of German troops and shipping in northern Germany was connected to the Allied plans to help the Finns.[8] The Finnish-Soviet conflict had ended almost a month earlier and there is no support for Woodward's claim in Norwegian sources. Of all reports forwarded to the navy by the Norwegian Foreign Office, only the last (Scheel's report on April 7) was forwarded to the naval district commanders and its dispatch was delayed until the afternoon of April 8, almost a full day after receipt by the naval staff.

Some in the Norwegian Army took a more serious view of the situation and Colonel Rasmus Hatledal, the Chief of the General Staff, called for partial mobilization on April 5. The government turned down this suggestion. Hatledal was an energetic officer who was not afraid to take initiative and responsibility. This was in sharp contrast to his superior, General Kristian Laake, the Commander-in-Chief of the Army.

The warships comprising TF 5 (destination Oslo) sailed through the Great Belt, the main strait between the Danish islands, in clear weather and full daylight on April 8. The progress of the group was followed closely by Danish observation posts and reported to the Danish Naval Ministry. These reports were passed on to the intelligence section of the Norwegian Naval Staff throughout the day.

However, the first report about major German naval movements on April 8 came from the Swedish Defense Staff at 1000 hours. The report read "German naval forces consisting of the battleship *Gneisenau*, the heavy cruiser *Blücher* and the light cruiser *Emden* have, accompanied by numerous smaller vessels, passed through the Great Belt during the morning on a northerly course. Destination unknown."

The Norwegians called their contact at the Danish Naval Ministry for confirmation and further information. They received a quick reply at 1043 hours:

Forty-six German *räumboote* [small minesweepers] and 38 armed trawlers have, according to a report from Østre Flakk Lightship, spread out in northern Kattegat but have not yet passed Skagen [the northernmost point on the Jutland Peninsula]. *Gneisenau, Leipzig* and *Emden* passed Langeland between 0600 and 0700 hours on a northerly course, followed by three torpedo boats and six armed trawlers.

Both the German and British Naval Attachés visited the Norwegian Naval Staff in the course of the morning of April 8. Lieutenant Commander Schreiber, the German Naval Attaché, was the first visitor to Captain Steen, chief of the naval intelligence division. Steen asked Schreiber if the German Ambassador had protested the British breach of Norwegian neutrality (that had occurred when the British laid mines that morning) to the Norwegian Foreign Office. Commander Schreiber answered that this had not been done and he did not think a protest would be made. When Schreiber left, he told Steen, "Goodbye Captain, thank you for the enjoyable time we have spent together." Captain Steen was a little surprised at this statement and asked if Schreiber was leaving. The German answered no, but that he still wanted to say goodbye.

A short time thereafter, Admiral Boyes, the British Naval Attaché, arrived. His visit was to have a serious effect on Norwegian expectations and preparations. Boyes asked Steen to report to Admiral Diesen that he had reason to believe that a British fleet was on its way to meet the German naval forces that were reported at sea. Captain Steen assumed that the admiral was speaking about the German naval units in the Kattegat and Skagerrak, but the British in fact had no intention of meeting those units. Instead, Boyes may have meant the German naval forces that the British had sighted on a northerly course in the North Sea the previous day (see later in this chapter). The Norwegian Naval Staff did not know about this sighting.

The information provided by Admiral Boyes led Admiral Diesen and his staff to conclude that they could expect a major collision between German and British naval forces within a short time and they expected the Germans to be driven back with heavy losses. Admiral Diesen passed this information on to the 1st Naval District.

New information from the Swedish Defense Staff, received around noon, confirmed the earlier reports about strong German naval units heading north. The Swedes also reported that infantry and artillery units were observed near Rendsburg, heading north towards the Danish border. The Swedes intended to conduct aerial reconnaissance over the Kattegat and report the results to the Norwegians but no further reports were received.

There were several incidents during April 8 which, taken together with the flow of intelligence reports of German naval and troop movements, should have energized the Norwegians to take immediate precautions. The first incident was the sinking of the German transport *Rio de Janeiro* in international waters off the southern coast of Norway by the Polish submarine *Orzel*. This happened at 1115 hours. *Rio de Janeiro* was one of the 15 merchant ships in the 1st Sea Transport Echelon that had departed German ports on April 4. This ship was carrying troops and equipment destined for Bergen. It was exactly the type of incident the SKL had feared would negate the element of surprise and the reason they had so strenuously opposed the early sailing of the ships in the 1st Sea Transport Echelon.

The destroyer *Odin*, the patrol ship *Lyngdal*, and Norwegian fishing vessels brought about 100 survivors from the sinking ship into Kristiansand and other harbors during the day. These turned out to be uniformed soldiers and naval personnel who reported they were on their way to Bergen to help the Norwegians in accordance with a request from the Norwegians.

The second incident was the sinking of *Posidonia* at 1330 hours in international waters at the mouth of Oslofjord by the British submarine *Trident*. *Posidonia* was not part of the German operation. However, a small tanker, *Stedingen*, scheduled to bring fuel to Stavanger also fell victim to *Trident* on the same day. Finally, a British submarine intercepted *Kreta* of the 1st Sea Transport Echelon and it sought refuge in Norwegian territorial waters. *Kreta*, on its way to Kristiansand, was hailed by a Norwegian patrol boat but allowed to proceed. *Kreta* arrived in Kristiansand on April 13, four days late.

The Norwegian Naval Staff received two messages during the afternoon from their contact person in the Danish Navy. They received the first message at 1535 hours: "Two ships of the *Gneisenau* class, one of the *Deutschland* class, one of the *Emden* class and three torpedo boats of the *Möwe* class passed Anholt at 1205 on a northerly course and two auxiliary or mining ships painted a gray color passed Korsør at 1500 on a northerly course." The second message at 1820 hours read:

> A division consisting of *Gneisenau, Deutschland* [*Deutschland* had been renamed *Lützow* but was still referred to in intelligence reports by its former name], *Emden* and three torpedo boats of the *Möwe* class passed Hirtsholm at 1715 hours on a northerly course. Two armed 6,000-ton merchant ships passed through Storebelt on a northerly course. Many people observed on board, possibly troops. Seventeen trawlers also passed that location.

Twenty minutes earlier, a telegram from the British Admiralty via the Norwegian Embassy in London arrived at the Norwegian naval headquarters:

> German naval forces were observed in the North Sea traveling in the company of what is believed to be a merchant ship, possibly troop transport. Their leading elements were observed this morning outside the Norwegian coast on a northerly course. It is assumed for certain that the goal is to undertake operations against Narvik and they could arrive there before midnight. Admiral Phillips [vice chief of the British Naval Staff] added that the Germans could be in Narvik at 10 P.M. today.

This was the only warning message the British sent the Norwegians on April 8. Faced with all these alarming reports and incidents, why did the Norwegians not take immediate precautions to meet an obvious threat? While there were divided views about the purpose of the German naval movements, the consensus was that these activities had nothing to do with an attack on Norway. Such an eventuality was ruled unrealistic in view of the Allies' estimation of German capabilities and overwhelming British superiority at sea.

A final intelligence report from Denmark seemed to support this conclusion.

At 2311 hours the Danes reported that three large warships were observed at 1900 hours, 12 nautical miles north of Skagen Lightship (the northern point of the Jutland Peninsula) on a westerly course at high speed. They stated that these were the same three ships reported on earlier in the day. The westerly course of the German ships appeared to confirm the view held by Admiral Diesen and his chief of staff that the destination was not Norway and they appear to have persisted in their view despite the warning from the British five hours earlier. There were many who viewed the British warning as an attempt to distract the Norwegians from dealing with the British minefields.

Admiral Diesen refused to believe the statements by the German survivors from *Rio de Janeiro* that they were headed for Bergen. He believed their statements camouflaged a German operation against a more westerly target, possibly the Shetland Islands or the Faeroes. It is difficult to see how he arrived at this conclusion since he also believed that a German attack against Norway was improbable due to British naval superiority. If he ruled out German operations against Norway because of British naval strength, it seems surprising that he then ruled in operations by the Germans in Britain's backyard. Furthermore, the naval staff apparently did not find it strange that the reports included a large number of smaller ships (small minesweepers, trawlers, and torpedo boats) unsuitable for distant operations. If these were destined for the Netherlands, they would surely have used the Kiel Canal rather than the long, circuitous, and exposed route around the Jutland Peninsula.

However, most government officials and members of the Norwegian parliament shared Diesen's view that the German naval activity did not have Norway as a target and that the Germans would wait to see what the Norwegians did about the British mining before taking any actions. This was a big mistake on the part of the Norwegian military leaders. They failed to appreciate that air power had significantly changed the old concept of naval superiority. Furthermore, they violated an important principle by basing their plans and actions on what they perceived the German intentions to be. It would have been more prudent to base their plans and preparations on German capabilities and the German course of action most dangerous to Norwegian interests. Finally, British actions over the last 24 hours had already given the Norwegians ample reasons to make plans and preparations necessary to defend the country.

Instead, only minor precautionary measures were taken. At 1820 hours, Admiral Diesen ordered the 1st Naval District to call up additional personnel for the forts. A request for two infantry companies to protect the Bergen and

Trondheim forts was passed to the army at 2215 hours but it could not be acted on in time. On recommendations from the commanders of the 1st and 2nd Naval Districts, Diesen ordered the lighthouses from the Swedish border to the entrance of Bergen extinguished. A statement over the national broadcasting system announced this action at 2218 hours. The lighthouses in the 3rd Naval District (and the rest of the 2nd Naval District) were not included in this order, even though the British had reported that German naval forces could be expected in Narvik before midnight.

The acting commander of the 3rd Naval District pointed out to Admiral Diesen at 2345 hours that there were 14 German merchant ships in Narvik harbor and asked for instructions in case of a British attack on these ships. Admiral Diesen answered 10 minutes later that a British attack on German shipping in Narvik was to be met with force. Similar messages were not sent to the 1st and 2nd Naval Districts but the fact that such messages were even considered necessary tells much about the irresolute nature of the Norwegian Government and its military officials.

Diesen did not order his forces to the highest state of alert. The 1st Naval District gave a second-stage alert warning to its forces after it was told by Diesen not to activate the highest state of alert "because it would just scare people." Some lower echelons misinterpreted the 1st Naval District order and proceeded to the highest state of alert. The 2nd Naval District had already ordered its ships to their assigned war stations after the British mining.[9]

Crisis Provoked by the British Mining of Norwegian Waters

Some of the lethargy of the Norwegian authorities can be explained by the fact that they were already trying to manage another crisis, Allied mining of Norwegian waters. The rapidly unfolding events of April 8 were propelling the country precipitously into a war it wanted to avoid at all costs. These events were so confusing that even those who had concluded that the country would find itself at war within a very short time did not know before midnight on April 8 whether they would be fighting the British or the Germans.

Information about British mining operations in Norwegian territorial waters reached Norwegian authorities at 0420 hours on April 8. Norwegian naval vessels intercepted the British destroyers in territorial waters off the coast near Molde. No armed clashes took place, despite the Norwegian Foreign Minister's earlier warning to the British that future violations would be met with force. The British action was different from earlier violations of the country's neutrality: it was an act of war. Norwegian officers protested the mining and the British destroyers left Norwegian waters before noon after Norwegian assurances that they would assume responsibility for warning merchant traffic. The Norwegians received sketches of the simulated minefield.

At 0600 hours, the British and French Naval Attachés delivered notes to the duty officer at the Norwegian Naval Staff that Norwegian territorial waters had been mined in three places. Only one minefield was actually laid but the Norwegians did not know this until later.

The British and French diplomatic representatives in Oslo also delivered simultaneous notes to the Norwegian Foreign Office about the mining operations. Koht called the Prime Minister at 0630 hours and requested an emergency meeting of the cabinet. Prime Minister Nygaardsvold decided to consider the problem first at a Foreign Relations Committee session despite Koht's protest that this would lead to delay.

Admiral Diesen and Defense Minister Birger Ljungberg met between 0900 and 1000 hours. Diesen recommended that the minefield in Oslofjord be laid as quickly as possible. This act required defense department approval. Commodore Corneliussen, the Admiralty Chief of Staff, was also present. He noted that the Hague Convention required that the mining by neutrals of their territorial waters had to be announced well beforehand and that it would present risks to merchant traffic since there was an insufficient number of patrol vessels available. Why this had not been recognized as a problem earlier is not explained. While two of the nine patrol boats assigned to the 1st Naval District were undergoing repairs, the district had eight torpedo boats and some of these could have filled the void temporarily. Ljungberg did not make a decision but said he would bring the matter to the attention of the cabinet. Diesen raised the issue again later in the day but he was never given authority to mine the approaches to Oslo.

A joint meeting of the cabinet and the foreign relations committee of the parliament began at 1000 hours, breaking up at 1130. This was about the time that the Norwegians began receiving reports of German naval units on a northerly course through the Great Belt and Kattegat. However, it appears that these events were not discussed. The focus was on what to do about the British mining operations. A decision was made to lodge strong protests against the Allied action and to clear the minefields. Diesen was ordered to prepare to sweep the mines. It was obvious to those present at this meeting that such action could draw Norway into the war, since clearing the minefields would probably lead to clashes with British forces; but if the steps announced were not taken the Germans would have good grounds to take strong measures. The underlying tone at this and subsequent meetings of the Norwegian Government on April 8 was that whatever happened, war with Great Britain was to be avoided. The instructions for clearing the minefields cautioned that force should not be used against overwhelming odds and that the navy should not engage in armed conflict with British destroyers near the minefields except in self-defense.

The Norwegian protest to the British and French governments was approved at a cabinet meeting that began immediately after the joint meeting of the cabinet and foreign relations committee broke up. The protests were sent to all Norwegian overseas embassies and released to the press at 1255 hours. The Parliament met in open session from 1715 to 1735 hours to hear a report by Foreign Minister Koht. He stated that the Allies were apparently trying to expand the war to Norway and reported on the protests that had been made. The parliament expressed unanimous support for the actions.

A closed meeting of the parliament started at 1800 hours and lasted until 1915. The Commander-in-Chief of the Navy, the Commanding General of the Army, and their respective chiefs of staff were present. There was a discussion about what do if the neutrality policy failed and Norway was forced to enter the war. This meeting also reached consensus that the Norwegian Government should seek to avoid being drawn into a war against the British. The results of the various meetings appear to give some authority to the conclusions reached by the various political and military leaders in Germany that the Norwegian Government was not willing to enforce its neutrality and that it would probably not offer any meaningful resistance to Allied attempts to occupy strategic points on the Norwegian coast. However, it should be borne in mind that occupation was a very different matter to the mining of waters, and it is possible that the Norwegian Government's reaction to such an invasion would have been more forceful.

Warnings Received by the British

Operations *Wilfred* (the Allied mining of territorial waters) and *R4* (the occupation of designated cities) were originally scheduled to begin April 5 but were postponed to April 8.

Part of the mining operation was carried out, so what of Allied plans to occupy portions of Norway? To answer this question we must go back and look at the intelligence received by the Allies about German movements, and the consequent decisions that were taken.

The British received many reports about concentrations of German forces in Baltic and North Sea ports. They also knew that a German intelligence collection ship, *Vidar*, was positioned off the Norwegian coast. The British decided to leave the ship alone in the hope of breaking the German radio code. As in the case of the Norwegians, the British did not properly piece together the various items of information arriving at the Foreign Office and the three services. This failure properly to coordinate, correlate and interpret the various warnings was a major blunder.

On March 26, the British Ambassador in Stockholm reported that the Germans had concentrated air forces and naval shipping in Baltic harbors and that their plans might involve the occupation of Norwegian air bases and ports. This was followed by a report by Admiral Darlan that the Germans had assembled shipping for an expedition against ports in southern Norway and Sweden. The Swedish military attaché in Finland, Curt Kempff, had a discussion with his German colleague on April 2 about the German activities in the Baltic. The German assured him that he had no knowledge about German plans in the Baltic and that all the activity had to do with Norway.[10] A report of this conversation was forwarded to Stockholm and the Swedes provided the information to the British.

On April 3, the British War Office received a report that there was a large buildup of German troops near Rostock and that 200,000 tons of shipping had assembled in Stettin and Swinemünde with troops on board. Their alleged purpose was the invasion of Scandinavia. The British concluded that the Germans had taken these steps in order "to deliver a counter-stroke against a possible attack by us upon Narvik or other Norwegian ports,"[11] which was precisely the response Churchill was hoping for. Part of the British failure to take these reports as an indication that Germany was preparing to invade Scandinavia can be traced back to the estimate made by the intelligence branch of the British War Office in December 1939, which concluded that 25-30 German divisions would be required for an attack on Norway and Sweden. Intelligence reports about the assembly of a few divisions in northern Germany were discounted since such force levels appeared inadequate for an invasion.

The most important and accurate report received by the British was one on April 6 from a neutral observer in Copenhagen. The report stated that a German division had embarked on ten ships and that the troops were to land at Narvik on the night of April 8-9. Even this report failed to energize the British. The Admiralty did not believe its accuracy and did not seriously consider the possibility that the Germans might reach Narvik before them. Consequently, the report was not forwarded immediately to the Commander-in-Chief of the Home Fleet, Admiral of the Fleet Sir Charles Forbes.

The British continued to believe that any German operation would be in reaction to their own operations and did not consider it possible that the Germans might be planning the first strike. This mistaken evaluation based on faulty interpretation of intelligence, underestimation of German capabilities, and an uncompromising belief that the vastly superior Royal Navy ruled out any possibility of a German attack in North Norway had serious consequence for the development of the situation in Norway. This attitude is well illustrated by a notation by Laurence Collier, a high Foreign Office official on a report about German intentions and preparations, "I wish I could believe this story. German intervention in Scandinavia is just what we want."[12]

The British Cancel *R4* and Sail to Intercept the German Navy

British aircraft made the first sighting of German forces in the North Sea at 0848 hours on April 7. They reported seeing one cruiser and six destroyers escorted by eight fighters. A partial report reached Admiral Forbes at 1120 hours and the full report 30 minutes later. At about this same time, Forbes was given the intelligence report that the British Admiralty had received the day before from the neutral observer in Copenhagen. However, the message from the Admiralty ended on an unhelpful note, "All these reports are of doubtful value and may well be only a further move in the war of nerves."[13]

Admiral Forbes also received a report about three German destroyers near the same position observed by the aircraft in the morning, and on a southerly course. He began to doubt the objective of the German thrust and remained in Scapa Flow while ordering the fleet to be ready to sail on an hour's notice. He was also awaiting results of a bombing attack against the German naval units.

The attack by 12 Blenheim bombers took place at 1330 hours. The German ships were now 78 nautical miles north of where they were sighted earlier. The attack was unsuccessful but the aircraft reported that the German naval force consisted of one ship of the *Scharnhorst* class, two cruisers, and ten destroyers. Repeated radio reports by the aircraft giving the German strength, course, and speed did not reach Forbes and he did not receive their report until 1730 hours, after the planes had landed.

One is entitled to ask why Admiral Forbes remained in harbor after the first sighting. The explanation that he awaited the results of the bombing is not convincing. He could easily have received that report while at sea. With what appeared to be a sizable German foray into the North Sea (complemented by previous intelligence reports), it would seem prudent for the admiral to have taken his fleet to sea and await developments in a more central North Sea location. Whatever the German intentions, this would have placed him in a much better position to take action and could have changed the outcome of the German operations against ports in northern and central Norway.

The British concluded, from the new position of the German ships, that they were directed against a northerly goal but they could not be certain what that goal was. It could be part of a German attack against Norway, but it could also be an expedition against shipping in the Norwegian Sea or the Atlantic. They did not rule out the possibility that the Germans intended to carry out a bombardment against the southern coast of England. This would seem extremely unlikely since the Germans would not only face vastly superior British naval forces but they would also be exposed to British air power. While they were uncertain about the objective of the German force, the British military leaders, like their Norwegian counterparts, failed to settle on the one potential German course of action most detrimental to their interests.

The Home Fleet finally sailed to intercept the Germans at 2015 hours. Moulton reports that the last ships of the fleet cleared Scapa Flow at 2115 hours. The fleet consisting of the battleships *Rodney* (the largest in the Royal Navy in 1940) and *Valiant*, the battle cruiser *Repulse*, the cruisers *Sheffield* and *Penelope*, and ten destroyers, headed on a northeasterly course at 20 knots. A French cruiser and two destroyers were also attached to the Home Fleet. At the same time, the Germans were proceeding northward at 29 knots.

The 2nd Cruiser Squadron, consisting of the cruisers *Galatea* and *Arethusa* and 15 destroyers, had left Rosyth with orders to proceed to a position about 80 miles west of Stavanger. The 18th Cruiser Squadron, consisting of two cruisers and seven destroyers, was already at sea escorting a convoy of merchant ships to Norway. This squadron was ordered to send the merchant ships back to Scotland and to join the hunt for the German ships.

The main German force under Admiral Lütjens passed the latitude of the Shetland Islands in the early morning hours of April 8 without encountering British forces. The weather had deteriorated during daylight hours on April 7. Low cloud cover and fog prevented British aircraft from locating the German ships after their unsuccessful bombing attempt at midday. The wind increased to gale force during the night.

The British were meanwhile canceling their planned operations against the Norwegian coast. Admiral Pound was away from the Admiralty on April 7 and returned late in the evening. With Churchill's apparent knowledge and concurrence he made decisions that were to have far ranging implications for events in Norway. The third mine-laying expedition at Stadt, on the Norwegian coast, was abandoned and the minelayer and four destroyers that had been tasked with this mission were recalled. The battleship *Warspite* and the aircraft carrier *Furious*, both located in the Clyde, were ordered to join the fleet at sea. The departure of *Furious* was so hurried that its fighter squadron of Skuas was left behind, on orders from the Admiralty.[14] The cruiser *Aurora* and six destroyers, also located in the Clyde, were preparing to escort the troop transport to Narvik. This mission was now canceled and the cruiser and destroyers were ordered to proceed to Scapa Flow and thereafter join the fleet. The Admiralty also ordered that the 1st Cruiser Squadron in Rosyth, consisting of four heavy cruisers and escorts, should disembark the troops destined for Norway and quickly join the fleet. The order reached the cruiser squadron early in the morning of April 8 and the troops were disembarked hurriedly. In the process, they became separated from much of their equipment.

The Admiralty had decided that every ship was needed for naval purposes. In the process, it abandoned *R4* at the exact moment when the conditions for which it was planned were at hand, namely when German forces set foot on Norwegian soil or there was clear evidence this was about to happen. Chamberlain and Admiral Forbes, who already had greatly superior forces at his disposal, were not consulted but it is doubtful that their views would have altered the instructions given.

The abandonment of *R4* did not help secure an encounter with the German ships and the best chance the Allies had for influencing events ashore in Norway was lost. The decision to cancel R4 is an excellent example of how the insistence on overwhelming force to defeat an enemy can led to serious consequences.[15] It is likely that if the 1st Cruiser Squadron had departed with the embarked troops in the morning of April 8 as planned, it would have been able to land the troops in Bergen and Stavanger that same evening, several hours before the German arrival. The squadron would then have been in position to intercept and destroy the German task force bound for Bergen. The abandonment of *R4* served no valid purpose and, along with the late departure of the Home Fleet, was the most monumental British mistake in the early part of the Norwegian Campaign.

It is true that the British might have encountered Norwegian resistance in

Bergen and Stavanger if they landed in the evening of April 8, particularly coming on top of their massive violations of Norwegian sovereignty that morning. The Norwegian directive that British and French warships should not be fired on was not issued until the early morning hours on April 9 when the identity of the attackers was established. However, in view of their instructions not to land if faced with Norwegian resistance, the troops would probably have remained on the warships pending a resolution of that issue. The British would have been in a perfect position to engage TF 3 on its way to Bergen. This would have involved a naval engagement with troops aboard but this was also true for the Germans. There can be no doubt that the four heavy cruisers of the 1st Cruiser Squadron, *Devonshire*, *Berwick*, *York*, and *Glasgow* and their escorts, clearly outmatched the Germans.

The British Navy appeared to have their eyes fixed on the possibility that the Germans were attempting a breakout into the Atlantic. The appearance of the German warships in the North Sea, if correlated with earlier intelligence of troopship concentrations in north German ports and reports that a division had embarked for a landing at Narvik, should have led the Admiralty to the conclusion that they were not dealing with a breakout. Furthermore, it was not logical for the Germans to take along almost half their destroyer force, which had a limited cruising range without refueling, on a dash into the Atlantic. Finally, the Home Fleet had an enormous superiority over their opponents without using the ships designated to support *R4*.

Both Admiral Forbes and leaders at the Admiralty must have realized that Home Fleet would not be able to intercept the German forces that were sighted if these were heading for Narvik. The difference in the location of the German fleet from the time it was sighted until it was bombed indicated that it was traveling north in excess of 20 knots. There would have been an excellent chance of intercepting the Germans if the Home Fleet had departed as quickly as possible after the sighting but the delay of over 12 hours removed that possibility. Admiral Lütjens' force had already passed the latitude of Scapa Flow by the time Forbes' ships finally lifted anchor. The Home Fleet headed on a northeasterly course for 24 hours until it passed the latitude of Trondheim, without any contact with the German ships.

Glowworm's Valorous Fight

One British warship made an accidental contact with German naval units in the early hours of April 8. The destroyer *Glowworm* was part of Admiral Whitworth's force heading north to cover the mining operations in the approaches to Narvik. The ship had lost a man overboard and dropped behind to try to pick up the missing sailor. *Glowworm* was not able to rejoin Whitworth's force due to heavy seas and poor visibility.

Glowworm was northeast of Trondheim when she sighted two destroyers from TF 1, *Hans Lüdemann* and *Bernd von Arnim*. The German ships had become separated from the rest of the Task Force in the gale and heavy seas. The destroyers were battered heavily and army supplies were washed overboard, as were a number of men, most of them soldiers. Speed was reduced to 22 knots but the formation became scattered.

Glowworm opened fire on *Hans Lüdemann* and the German ship immediately increased its speed and headed away from the British destroyer. *Bernd von Arnim* was further south. It engaged the British ship in a running battle on a northerly course. The German ship was larger and outgunned the British destroyer. However, *Glowworm* proved more seaworthy and her captain, Lieutenant Commander Gerard Broadmeade Roope, handled her in an excellent manner. *Bernd von Arnim*, on the other hand, had a hard time in the heavy seas, took considerable damage from the waves, and its target acquisition and gunnery suffered as a result.

The only German destroyer that attempted to come to *Bernd von Arnim's* aid was *Paul Jacobi*, a ship of the same class as *Bernd von Arnim*. However, *Paul Jacobi* took a 55-degree roll in heavy seas, five men were swept overboard, and she lost the use of some of her boilers. *Bernd von Arnim* also lost two men overboard when she increased her speed to 33 knots in an attempt to outrun her adversary. Neither side scored any hits since gunnery became virtually impossible as the ships were tossed around in the heavy seas.

Admiral Lütjens ordered the heavy cruiser *Admiral Hipper* to turn around and deal with the British destroyer. *Hipper* came upon the two destroyers, which were still engaged violently in heavy seas, around 0900 hours. Both destroyers momentarily mistook her for a British cruiser and *Bernd von Arnim* even sent a couple of salvos in her direction. *Hipper* opened fire on *Glowworm* at a distance of 9,000 meters and hit the destroyer's bridge with the first salvo. *Glowworm* answered with a salvo of torpedoes, and tried to escape. *Hipper* laid a smoke screen, avoided *Glowworm's* torpedo salvo by some quick maneuvering, and entered the smoke screen. According to German sources, Captain Heye, *Hipper's* skipper, feared additional torpedo salvos and decided to ram the British destroyer. According to British sources, *Glowworm's* captain, realizing that his chances of escape were next to nil, also decided to ram his adversary. The heavy cruiser was slower to respond to the helm and the result was that the British destroyer hit *Hipper* and tore away about 150 feet of the ship's outer armor plating and the starboard torpedo tubes. Heye stated later that the ramming by *Glowworm* resulted in less damage to his ship then his own attempt at a head-on ramming is likely to have caused. *Glowworm* was almost crushed by the impact with her adversary, fell away in the heavy sea, and blew up within a couple of minutes.

Glowworm's class of destroyers normally carried a crew of 145 men. *Hipper* managed to rescue 38 despite the rough sea. *Glowworm's* captain was among those the Germans tried to haul onto the cruiser deck. However, before reaching safety, he fell back into the ocean and perished. Lieutenant Commander Roope was awarded the Victoria Cross for his gallantry.

British Miscalculations

Glowworm provided a valuable service for the British fleet. She sent a series of radio messages starting at about 0800 hours, reporting the location and strength of the enemy force. She continued her reporting until she blew up. The British were able to determine from these reports that the German force, on a northerly course, was located about 300 nautical miles north of the Home Fleet and about 140 nautical miles south of the battle cruiser *Renown*, now near the entrance to Vestfjord. There were also eight British destroyers in Vestfjord engaged in mining activities.

Admiral Whitworth, with the battle cruiser *Renown* and the destroyer *Greyhound*, turned south at about 0830 hours upon hearing the *Glowworm's* report. He had detached the destroyers *Hyperion* and *Heron* the previous afternoon to lay the dummy minefield near Molde.

Admiral Forbes realized he had little chance of reaching the Germans from the south with the main fleet. He therefore detached the faster battle cruiser *Repulse* (*Renown's* sister ship), the cruisers *Penelope* and *Birmingham*, and four destroyers to head north at top speed. Later, it became necessary to detach *Birmingham* in order that she could return to Scapa Flow to refuel. The British were well positioned to bring on a major naval battle with the German surface fleet, but then the situation began to unravel.

The Home Fleet continued north during the day without making enemy contact. The weather was unfavorable for aerial reconnaissance but a seaplane scouting ahead of the Home Fleet sighted enemy ships around 1400 hours well out to sea north-northwest of Trondheim. The German ships were on a westerly course and were reported by the aircraft as consisting of one battle cruiser, two cruisers, and two destroyers. This was actually TF 2, *Hipper* and four destroyers. Admiral Lütjens had detached them around 1100 hours and they were steering various courses while waiting for the designated time to enter Trondheim. The British aircraft was fired on, damaged, and landed in Norway where the crew and aircraft were interned. Later attempts to locate the German ships failed.

The Home Fleet was about 150 nautical miles south of the German ships but the course reported by the reconnaissance aircraft had a major effect on Admiral Forbes' subsequent tactical decisions. He had been steering a northeast course, which could have resulted in the Home Fleet meeting the German ships as they eventually steered a southeasterly course to enter Trondheimfjord. However, the report that the German fleet was heading away from the Norwegian coast caused Admiral Forbes to alter his course first to north and then, at about 1600 hours, to north-northwest. In this way, he moved away from the Norwegian coast and allowed a clear path for the Germans to enter Trondheim.

Admiral Lütjens continued north with the *Scharnhorst*, *Gneisenau*, and the ten destroyers of TF 1. He was in a precarious position. A force of eight British destroyers was based at the entrance to Vestfjord, between him and his target, and Admiral Whitworth was steaming towards him from the same area with one battle cruiser and one destroyer. Another battle cruiser, a cruiser, and four destroyers were coming up quickly from the south-southwest. The main force of the Home Fleet was further south.

The British Admiralty now intervened in tactical operations. It was beginning to have second thoughts about the accuracy of the report from the neutral diplomat in Copenhagen on April 6 that a German division, embarked on ten ships, was to land in Narvik during the night between 8 and 9 April. They had initially discounted the information as just another move in the war of nerves. In view of all reports coming in about German naval movements, the Admiralty staff were no longer as skeptical as they had been about the veracity of the April 6 report.

The first precautionary step by the British Admiralty was to release the eight destroyers from their guard duty in Vestfjord, where they were to have remained for 48 hours and to order them at 0945 hours to join Admiral Whitworth. It is claimed that Whitworth was not made aware of the orders to the destroyers until 1045 hours and he was given no reason for the Admiralty's interference in fleet operations. While this may be true, it is strange that the order to the destroyers was not overheard by the radio operators on *Renown* and reported to the admiral. I believe the destroyers and Whitworth were notified at the same time and that the one-hour discrepancy in time is due to some authors working on Norwegian local time while others used Greenwich Mean Time. At 1115 hours, the Admiralty also passed on to Admiral Whitworth their newfound concerns that the Germans might actually be heading to Narvik.

Most British sources report that Whitworth received the Admiralty message ordering the destroyers to join him while he was still on a southbound track and that this is what caused him to head north.[16] The official Norwegian naval history reports that Whitworth turned north because he realized he would arrive too late to assist *Glowworm*, and that he received the message from the Admiralty after he had already turned back north. However, Whitworth's mission was not to assist *Glowworm* since she was presumed lost, but to intercept and destroy the force that *Glowworm* had engaged. It makes more sense, therefore, that Whitworth turned north after the Admiralty's orders, in other words after 1115 GMT but probably closer to 1300 hours. Whitworth may have continued south after the Admiralty message at 1115 hours in the hope of intercepting any northbound German forces. At some point in the next two hours, he must have decided to turn around and link up with the destroyers from Vestfjord. The reduced visibility may have convinced him that he ran the risk of the Germans slipping past him and engaging the destroyers at the entrance to Vestfjord, which would have been a very unequal match.

Admiral Whitworth's decision to turn north may have been fortunate. Had *Renown* and *Greyhound* continued on their southward track they may well have encountered Admiral Lütjens who was heading north towards the entrance to Vestfjord at 24 knots. On opposite tracks, the two forces may have been less than one hour apart (about 50 miles) when Whitworth turned north. An encounter between *Renown* with its lone destroyer and two German battleships and ten destroyers could have been catastrophic for the British fleet.

The Admiralty's meddling in operational affairs had other unfortunate results. If the eight British destroyers had remained in the vicinity of the minefield as originally planned, they would probably have encountered the ten German destroyers loaded with troops, now separated from the battleships and almost out of fuel, on their way to Narvik. Whatever the outcome of such an encounter, it would have adversely affected TF 1's mission.

It made good sense for the British to concentrate their forces in view of reports of heavy German surface units at sea. The location of that concentration and Admiral Whitworth's decision after linking up with the destroyers had unfortunate results. The Admiralty now viewed Whitworth's primary mission as preventing the Germans from reaching Narvik. It also appears that this view was transmitted to the admiral.

According to the Norwegian naval history, Admiral Whitworth linked up with the destroyers 20 nautical miles west of Skomvær Lighthouse at 1715 hours, two hours and 45 minutes before Admiral Lütjens detached the destroyers of TF 1 for their run up the Vestfjord to Narvik. The British literature is imprecise as to the location of the rendezvous point. Harvey and MacIntyre place it at or near the Skomvær Lighthouse, Moulton fails to mention the location, and Dickens writes that it was 23 miles south of the lighthouse. Whatever the exact location, the important point is that it was not the best place to intercept the Germans if they were heading for Narvik. The logical place to concentrate to prevent the Germans from reaching that city would have been at the entrance to Vestfjord, northwest of the British minefield. This would also have brought the British ships into a position somewhat in lee of the Lofoten Islands and the later problems with the weather would have been diminished.

The gate to Narvik was left wide open when Whitworth took his ships, as soon as they were assembled, on a westerly course away from the Norwegian coast. What led the admiral to make this perplexing move in view of the information passed to him earlier that the Admiralty had concluded that the Germans might well be heading for Narvik?

It is true, as some defenders of Admiral Whitworth have pointed out, that his instructions were either lacking or vague. However, the most damaging enemy course of action would be an attack on Narvik and the Admiralty had strongly alluded to this possibility. The approach to Narvik from the south was through Vestfjord, which is why the mines were laid there. The defenders also point out that the admiral was bombarded by a mass of irrelevant incoming messages as he headed north, that the required intense and critical evaluation of the situation was inhibited by increasingly rough weather, and finally that he was placed in a position where he was forced to second-guess the desires of his superiors.

These explanations are less than convincing, except that Whitworth may have given his superiors' well-known fears of a German breakout into the Atlantic more consideration than it warranted. The earlier aerial reconnaissance reports about German ships on a west-northwest course off Trondheim may have caused him to think, as it did Admiral Forbes, that the German intention was to break into the Atlantic. However, by comparing the reconnaissance report from 1400 hours with the report of the bombers from 1330 hours on the previous day, it should have been apparent that something was wrong. The report from 1400 hours reported five ships while the report from the previous day had reported thirteen ships. In any case, Whitworth ordered his ships to look for the British west of the Lofoten Islands.

Admiral Whitworth listed the possible enemy courses of action after the encounter with *Glowworm* as follows: 1) return to Germany, 2) head for Iceland, 3) make for Murmansk, or 4) attack Narvik. It is difficult to understand why he placed the possibility that the Germans were heading for Iceland ahead of an attack on Narvik. The likelihood that the Germans were heading for Murmansk also did not make sense. Why would the Germans risk their ships in a dash for Murmansk, and for what purpose? The British should also have realized that, without refueling, both these destinations were beyond the range of the destroyers in the German force. Whitworth placed the possibility of an attack on Narvik last, notwithstanding intelligence to the contrary and despite the obvious fact that this was the enemy course of action most damaging to British interests. At the entrance to Vestfjord, Whitworth's battle cruiser and nine destroyers would have been in an ideal position to bring on a major naval engagement and probably thwart the German attack on Narvik. In retrospect, positioning himself near the British minefield would have led to a German disaster since the battleships had separated from TF 1 and headed into the open sea. Instead, Whitworth apparently planned to be in a position to meet the Germans if they should attempt to pass northward, outside the Lofoten Islands. This fateful decision opened the gate to Narvik just as Admiral Forbes' decision to alter course to the north and then north-northwest opened the gate to Trondheim.

At 1752 hours, shortly after Admiral Whitworth began to head away from the Norwegian coast and into the Norwegian Sea, he received a cautionary message from the Admiralty. It stated that since the aircraft that had sighted the Germans ships west of Trondheim had only spotted part of the enemy force, it was possible that the rest were still headed towards Narvik. Other than noting that the missing ships were two cruisers and 12 destroyers, Whitworth took no action.

The officials in London now had a clearer appreciation of German intentions than did Admiral Whitworth. At this time, the German destroyers were still about three hours from the entrance to Vestfjord, and so about two hours from separating from the battleships. Every minute counted. This was the proper time for the Admiralty to intercede and at 1850 hours a message was sent to Whitworth that should have left no doubt in his mind as to the appropriate action to take: "To Vice-Admiral Commanding Battlecruisers, repeat to Commander-in-Chief. Most immediate. The force under your orders is to concentrate on preventing any German force proceeding to Narvik. May enter territorial waters as necessary."[17] Admiral Whitworth received the message by 1915 hours. There was no doubt that the message was an order. The words "is to concentrate" should have left no doubt.

Admiral Whitworth did not immediately take the action necessary to carry out the Admiralty order but continued on his westward course. At 2014 hours, he signaled his force: "Our object is to prevent German forces reaching Narvik. My present intention is to alter course at 2100 to 280 degrees (to north-northwest), and to turn 180 degrees to starboard (east-southeast) in succession at midnight." These course changes left the British fleet steering away from the Norwegian coast for almost five hours after receipt of the Admiralty order.

The weather was now dictating Admiral Whitworth's course of action. The conditions had deteriorated to a point never experienced by some of the seasoned sailors aboard the British ships. During the night the wind reached Force 11 on the Beaufort scale, a speed of 64 to 72 miles per hour, with towering 50-foot waves. The destroyers became almost unmanageable in the heavy seas and Whitworth felt it necessary to keep his fleet together and steer a course that would avoid sea damage to his ships. His explanation is as follows:[18]

> On receipt of this signal (Admiralty 1850 hours message) I calculated that the enemy had had ample time to reach my vicinity if they were proceeding direct to Narvik. Assuming that they had not yet passed me I decided to proceed up Vestfjord with the object of placing myself between the enemy and his objective. There were two objections to this course of action. One was the possibility of being brought to action by a superior force (four of my destroyers had no torpedoes and only two guns).[19] The other was the navigational danger of approaching a dangerous coast in low visibility without having been able to fix the ship's position for three days.
>
> The weather at this time showed signs of improving and I decided to disregard both these objections. But the improvement proved to be only a lull and it came on to blow with great force from the northwest,

accompanied by rain and snow squalls with prolonged periods of bad visibility. This sudden deterioration in the weather decided me to change my plans, because I felt that the enemy would make little progress and not try to make Vestfjord during the dark, and would probably stand to seaward during the dark hours, so I decided to do the same.

A few observations regarding this appraisal are in order. The British ships had been on a westerly course for about two hours when Admiral Whitworth received the Admiralty order. The Norwegian lighthouses were not extinguished until after 2200 hours, and the order only pertained to those located south of Bergen. Skomvær Lighthouse sends out a powerful beam that should have been visible from the *Renown* in periods between squalls, and from the destroyers, which passed near the lighthouse to arrive at their rendezvous point. This should have given the British ships a sufficiently accurate fix on their position that positioning themselves at the over 30-mile-wide entrance to the fjord should not have presented an unacceptable navigational hazard. Furthermore, the destroyers obviously had a good fix on their position since they gave the Norwegians an accurate geographic diagram of the minefield they had laid.

Whitworth completely misjudged his opponents and overestimated the difficulties he faced. His reasoning that the Germans would not enter Vestfjord in poor visibility and in a violent storm was dead wrong. The German Naval Staff's operational order emphasized that the operation was to be carried out despite navigational problems or bad weather. Captain Bonte displayed both skill and determination as he led his destroyers into the dark and dangerous fjord. Admiral Raeder's proclamation, provided to every naval officer after departure from German harbors, reads:[20] "Surprise, speed and quick action are the necessary prerequisites for operational success. I expect all task force commanders and all ship captains to be imbued with an unbreakable will to reach their assigned harbors despite all difficulties that may develop …"

It is doubtful that the British could have intercepted the German fleet before TF 1 was detached for its run up Vestfjord at around 2000 hours, even if Admiral Whitworth had implemented his order immediately upon receipt. After separating from TF 1, the German battleships were on a parallel track with Whitworth's force, off the British port quarter, possibly 30 miles apart. If Whitworth had turned around, he may have encountered the battleships. The German ships had radar and this gave them a significant advantage in the near zero visibility that prevailed that night.

Admiral Lütjens' orders, after detaching TF 1, were to draw any major British surface units away from the Norwegian coast but at the same time, he was instructed to avoid a decisive engagement. A British defeat would have been a serious blow to the Allies and would have left the German Navy in control of the northern waters for more than 24 hours, sufficient time for the destroyers in Narvik to refuel, if the tankers showed up, and start their return voyage to Germany.

Admiral Whitworth was notified about 2130 hours that the battle cruiser *Repulse* and its accompanying ships were on their way to join him. He reported his position to this force at 2200 hours as being 67° 09 North, 10° 10 East on a course of 310°. This shows that he was 40 nautical miles further out to sea than he had been at 1715 hours.

The weather in the Norwegian Sea improved somewhat during the night, and Admiral Whitworth finally turned east towards the Norwegian coast at 0240 hours on April 9, almost seven hours after receipt of the Admiralty order. Before long, Whitworth's force found itself in battle with the *Scharnhorst* and *Gneisenau*.

Battleship Action

Admiral Lütjens detached TF 1 at 2000 hours and started his planned diversion to the north and west. Western Group Command informed him at 2133 hours that two British warships of the *Renown* class were at sea and that an enemy cruiser and destroyer had been sighted in Vestfjord. He later received several reports about enemy naval forces, one that placed a British force very close to his own position.

Mountainous seas confronted Lütjens' ships as they started their diversionary run on a course of 290°, and speed was reduced to 7 knots although it was later increased to 12 knots. The German battleships were about 80 nautical miles west-south-west of the Lofoten Islands at 0400 hours on April 9 when they made radar contact with an enemy force 18,500 meters to their west, 280° from their position. Soon, they observed a large enemy warship and the German ships altered their course to north.

On their way to the Vestfjord, the British were actually the first to sight the enemy when their lookout spotted two ships between themselves and the coast at 0337 hours. The early British sighting was probably because the German ships were silhouetted against the dawning eastern horizon. Whitworth reported to the Admiralty that a ship of the *Scharnhorst* class and a cruiser of the *Hipper* class confronted him. This left the Admiralty and Forbes guessing as to the location of the other German battleship they knew was at sea.

Whitworth continued on his southeastern course until 0359 hours, and then changed his course to 305° before opening fire with his main armament against *Gneisenau* and the secondary armament against *Scharnhorst*. The range was 17,000 meters and the time was 0408 hours. The Germans returned fire three minutes later. The British destroyers also opened fire with their 5-inch guns but they began to fall behind in the heavy sea. *Renown* also reduced speed in order to use her forward guns. Lütjens had orders to avoid decisive combat if possible and this was apparently the reason he changed course away from the British. In doing so, he placed his ships in a position where they could only use their aft guns.[21]

Whitworth changed course to northeast at 0418 hours. The German ships were now off his starboard bow and the distance had decreased to 15,000 meters. A 15-inch shell hit the *Gneisenau*, destroyed her forward fire control system, and made her main armament temporarily inoperable. *Gneisenau* sustained two more hits. One damaged the door to her forward turret and this caused the seas that were sweeping over the forward portions of the battleship to flood the turret, resulting in severe electrical damage. Three 11-inch projectiles also hit *Renown* but the damage was not serious. *Scharnhorst* was not hit and was able to assist *Gneisenau* by crossing behind her and laying smoke. The German battleships increased speed to 28 knots and *Renown* started falling behind. Frequent snow squalls also reduced the visibility. *Renown* increased her speed to 29 knots for a few minutes but after some ineffective salvos by both sides, the Germans disappeared from sight at 0615 hours. Whitworth thereupon detached the destroyers to guard the entrance to Vestfjord. *Repulse* and her accompanying ships, still more than seven hours away, were given the same mission.

Renown continued on a northwesterly course in the hope of reestablishing contact with the German ships in case they turned south. At 0900 hours, Admiral Whitworth received orders from the Admiralty to undertake operations to prevent German landings in Narvik and he thereupon concentrated all his forces on this mission. The southern approach to Narvik was finally closed, but long after the Germans had sailed through and attacked that city.

Admiral Lütjens has been criticized for lack of aggressiveness in not turning his battleships around and destroying his adversary. This criticism is unfair. His mission, after detaching TF 1, was to draw main surface units of the British fleet away from the Norwegian coast and the landing areas. Lütjens looked upon the engagement with *Renown* (the Germans identified their opponents as two or three large ships) as proof that he had successfully carried out his mission. His further orders were to avoid enemy contact and bring his ships back to Germany. It was possible for Lütjens to score a spectacular victory if he had turned on his opponent and approached him from different directions thereby dividing the enemy fire, but this was by no means certain. The British destroyers would have joined such an engagement and they presented a serious torpedo threat. Admiral Raeder, in his report to Hitler on April 13, fully endorsed Lütjens' conduct:[22]

> The Commander in Chief, Navy fully endorses the conduct of the Fleet Commander. It would have been wrong to have all-out battleship operations off the Lofoten Islands; the tactical situation was very unfavorable, with the enemy disposed along the dark western horizon, our ships along the clear eastern horizon, and the wind strength 10.

Group Command West and reports from aircraft and submarines kept Lütjens informed during the day about British fleet movements and he started his return voyage to Germany in the evening of April 9. The battleships linked up with *Hipper* and reached Wilhelmshaven in the afternoon of April 12 without encountering British naval forces. It was planned that the destroyers from Narvik would join the battleships for the return voyage but this was not possible.

British Hesitation

The Home Fleet was on a north-north-westerly course away from the Norwegian coast at 1600 hours, slightly north of Trondheim's latitude. This allowed TF 2 to slip safely into Trondheim during the night. The Admiralty informed Admiral Forbes at about 1500 hours that a large German naval force had been observed in the Kattegat and Skagerrak on a northerly course.[23] These were the ships in TF 5. This complicated the situation for Forbes. He knew there were sizable German forces to his north. He did not expect to catch up with these but he hoped Admiral Whitworth would intercept them.

The battle cruiser *Repulse*, the cruiser *Penelope*, and four destroyers had been sent ahead since their higher speeds gave them a better chance to catch up with the German ships. These ships were formally detached from the Home Fleet at 2000 hours and placed under Admiral Whitworth's operational control. In addition to serving as reinforcements for Whitworth, they also served as an assurance that the Germans would be intercepted if they turned south. At the same time, Forbes turned the rest of the Home Fleet around and headed south.

Most British writers imply that the decision to turn south was Admiral Forbes', influenced by his view, as opposed to his colleagues in the Admiralty, that a full-scale German invasion of Norway was in progress.[24] There are reasons to question this conclusion.

First, the Admiralty sent Forbes a message at 1842 GMT laying out their objectives, which were to prevent the return of the German ships to his north and to intercept the force reported heading north in the Kattegat and Skagerrak. It appears that both the Admiralty and Admiral Forbes considered these forces a more promising target for the Home Fleet. This is a strange assessment since the logical targets for the ships steaming north through the Skagerrak were ports in southern or southwestern Norway. However, it seems that both Forbes and his colleagues in the Admiralty continued to be haunted by fears of a German breakout into the Atlantic. A look at the composition of the reported forces (included torpedo boats, small minesweepers, and trawlers), taken together with the Admiralty's own conclusion as to the target of the German forces to the north, should have put these fears to rest.

A second reason to doubt that Forbes had concluded that a full-scale invasion of Norway was in progress at the time *Glowworm* was sunk is the disposition he made of the forces at his disposal. If he had reached the stated conclusion, his logical action would have been to position his forces to cover the obvious targets on Norway's west coast: Trondheim, Bergen, and Stavanger. Instead, he turned away from the Norwegian coast, kept his fleet 80 to 100 miles from the Norwegian coast, even after turning south, and kept the 1st, 2nd and 18th Cruiser Squadrons that had been attached to him in the middle of the North Sea. Such a disposition only made sense if his primary concern was a German breakout into the Atlantic. Some writers maintain that the Admiralty, not Admiral Forbes, stipulated the dispositions of the naval forces in the North Sea in the evening of April 8.[25] However, the official history of the Norwegian campaign makes no mention of any Admiralty orders with regard to the tactical disposition of forces in the North Sea until they issued the order for the cruiser squadrons to link up with the Home Fleet.

It may well be that, after turning south, Admiral Forbes began to give more credence to the possibility that the German forces observed in the Skagerrak were heading for ports in Norway, a possibility also alluded to in the Admiralty's message at 1842 hours. This explains his orders to the 1st and 2nd Cruiser Squadrons. However, he must still have viewed this as a less likely possibility than a breakout since he continued the Home Fleet on a southerly course far out to sea, and had the 18th Cruiser Squadron sweep towards the Home Fleet, also far out at sea. Forbes ordered Admiral Cunningham's 1st Cruiser Squadron, now reinforced by the French cruiser *Emile Bertin* and two French destroyers, and Admiral Edward-Collins' 2nd Cruiser Squadron to proceed to a point off the Norwegian coast between Stavanger and Bergen. They were to start a northward sweep at 0500 hours on April 9. If carried out, the sweep would undoubtedly have led to an engagement with TF 3, destined for Bergen.

Task Force 3 Eludes the British Navy

The ships constituting TF 3 were located in three harbors in northern Germany on April 7. The light cruisers *Köln*, *Königsberg*, and the auxiliary *Bremse* were located in Wilhelmshaven and cleared that harbor before 2340 hours on April 7. The torpedo boats *Wolf* and *Leopard*, and the depot ship *Karl Peters* left Cuxhaven about the same time. The motor torpedo boats left from Helgoland. Plans called for the three elements of TF 3 to rendezvous near the southern coast of Norway, 56° 20 North, 06° 20 East, at 1015 hours on April 8. The three elements picked up an escort of He-111s at dawn on April 8.

Admiral Huber Schmundt's assessment of the situation was not very optimistic. He realized that the German groups destined for Narvik, Trondheim, and Bergen were dangerously exposed to British interception and counterattacks. Narvik and Trondheim were located far from British naval bases, but Bergen was within eight or nine hours' sailing distance from Scapa Flow and Schmundt believed that the British would launch their main naval effort against Bergen with secondary attacks against Narvik and Trondheim. Much of TF 3's passage took place in daylight since its speed was limited to 18 knots because of the slow moving *Bremse* and *Karl Peters*. Schmundt assumed that the German ships destined for Narvik and Trondheim, which had departed a day earlier, would encounter British naval forces. This would make it very difficult for TF 3 to proceed along the Norwegian coast in clear weather.

The Germans were lucky because the weather deteriorated as they headed north and because the British made mistakes and were indecisive. The fog that hid the Germans ships from the British also prevented the German ships from making their scheduled rendezvous off the coast of southern Norway. Admiral Schmundt's orders stipulated that he should let nothing interfere with his mission and therefore he proceeded towards Bergen at 18 knots, despite the fact that visibility was less than 500 meters.

It was not until around 1600 hours on April 8 that *Karl Peters* and the torpedo boats joined the main force. The Germans were in great peril during their voyage along the Norwegian west coast. Admiral Schmundt received a message from Naval Command West that numerous British warships were located between TF 3 and Bergen. This was an accurate report. As the fog lifted and the ships of TF 3 assembled, except for the motor torpedo boats, a British naval force of two modern light cruisers and 15 destroyers was located only 60 nautical miles to the northwest, between TF 3 and the southern approach to Bergen. This was the 2nd Cruiser Squadron, which had reached its start point for next morning's sweep. The weather was clear and visibility good as TF 3 continued towards Bergen at a distance of 12 to 15 miles off the Norwegian coast.

The Admiralty now made another unfortunate intervention in tactical operations and the outcome was again harmful to the British and beneficial for the Germans. Worried that the cruiser squadrons off the Norwegian coast, which were about 135 nautical miles from the Home Fleet, could be caught between the German naval forces in the north and the ones reported in the Skagerrak, the Admiralty annulled Admiral Forbes' plan for a cruiser sweep along the Norwegian coast. Instead it ordered the 1st and 2nd Cruiser Squadrons to join forces about 100 miles off the Norwegian coast and steer towards the Home Fleet. The 18th Cruiser Squadron had received a similar order earlier.

The British also failed to have reconnaissance aircraft aloft along the Norwegian coast after the fog lifted late in the afternoon on April 8. Reconnaissance aircraft might have spotted the German ships before the 2nd Cruiser Squadron started towards the Home Fleet and the attack on Bergen could have had a different outcome. As with Narvik and Trondheim, the British left the door to Bergen wide open at the last moment.

The Home Fleet continued on its southerly course during the night and when the Germans attacked Bergen, it was located only 90 miles off the Norwegian coast between Bergen and Stavanger. This enormous concentration of naval power was completed when the cruiser squadrons joined the Home Fleet early in the morning of April 9. Admiral Forbes had already learned from the Admiralty that German warships were engaged by fortresses covering the approach to Oslo and that German forces were attacking Trondheim, Bergen, Stavanger, and Kristiansand. This information must have convinced him that he was chasing a phantom enemy in the open waters of the North Sea while a full-scale German invasion of Norway was in progress. The question was what to do about it. Here again, we see the dramatic differences between the decentralized and swift German operations as opposed to the centralized and hesitant British response.

Forbes knew that German warships were in Bergen but he kept worrying about their strength. Although the picture of what was happening was still very murky, it was probably possible for Forbes and his staff to draw accurate conclusions about the strength of German force in Bergen, if they had pieced together accurately the reports about German naval movements that had been received since April 6. They estimated that the German force to their north (near Narvik) consisted of one battleship, two cruisers, and ten destroyers. It was actually two battleships and ten destroyers. The German force observed steering away from the Trondheim area was estimated to consist of one battleship, two cruisers, and two destroyers. It was actually one heavy cruiser and four destroyers. Information was now flowing in that one German light cruiser was in action at Kristiansand and that two heavy cruisers and one light cruiser were attacking Oslo.

The British knew that the German surface navy included two battleships, one armored cruiser (*Admiral Sheer*, not yet re-classified as a heavy cruiser), three heavy cruisers, six light cruisers, and 22 destroyers. They may have been aware that *Admiral Sheer*, two light cruisers, and six destroyers were undergoing repairs. However, even without possession of this fact, a review of recent intelligence reports could have let them deduce that both battleships, eight of the 10 cruisers, and 12 of the 22 destroyers were accounted for. From this, it would be logical to assume that the German naval forces in Bergen consisted at the most of two cruisers and a few destroyers. A further consideration was that it would take some time before the Germans would have the forts around Bergen operational, if they were captured, and that the Luftwaffe was not a serious threat until established at Norwegian airfields. The situation called for a quick and decisive strike against the Germans in Bergen before they were able to consolidate and the situation changed to their advantage.

Instead, Admiral Forbes entered into a discussion with the Admiralty about the situation, starting at 0620 hours. He mentioned that he contemplated making a strike against Bergen with cruisers and destroyers and asked for information about German strength in that city. About four hours passed before the Admiralty signaled approval for the attack by instructing Forbes to:

> Prepare plans for attacking German warships and transports in Bergen
> and for controlling the approaches to the port on supposition that the

defences are still in the hands of the Norwegians. Similar plans as regards Trondheim should be prepared.[26]

Forbes finally sent Vice Admiral Layton's 18th Cruiser Squadron with four cruisers and seven destroyers at 1130 hours on April 9 to attack the German naval units in Bergen.

The Home Fleet was only 90 nautical miles from Bergen at 0620 hours when Admiral Forbes mentioned to the Admiralty that he contemplated an attack on Bergen. However, the Home Fleet continued on its present southward course, leading it away from Bergen. This meant that when Admiral Layton's cruisers and destroyers were dispatched to Bergen they had to sail northward in the face of a strong northerly gale. The destroyers were only able to make 16 knots in the heavy seas. At that rate, the ships would not reach the entrance to the Bergen approaches before nightfall.

The plan called for the destroyers to attack Bergen harbor from the north and south supported at a distance by the cruisers. An aerial reconnaissance of Bergen at 1400 hours revealed that there were two German cruisers in the harbor and the British became suspicious that the Germans might already have captured the coastal fortresses. Layton began to doubt the wisdom of the plan but neither he nor Forbes had called it off when a message from the British Admiralty canceled the attack.

If Admiral Layton's force had entered the harbor after dark as planned, it would have found only one badly damaged cruiser, one damaged naval artillery support ship, and four serviceable motor torpedo boats. There was practically no danger to the British ships from the captured Norwegian shore batteries since they did not reach partial operational readiness until April 10 and full readiness on April 13. There were some dangers from mines laid by the Norwegians but there were still Norwegian naval units in each of the approaches that, no doubt, would have been happy to lead the British safely past the minefields. Again, lack of information, and an unwillingness to take risks meant that the Home Fleet missed an opportunity to inflict significant damage on the German Navy.

If the British had continued on towards Bergen, there is also some possibility that they might have encountered the cruiser *Köln* and the two torpedo boats at the start of their return voyage to Germany. However, it is equally possible that German aerial reconnaissance would have spotted the approaching British squadron, in which case *Köln* and her escorts may have elected to remain in Bergen. These ships left Bergen after darkness and sought refuge in a fjord when they were informed that strong British naval forces were near the route they planned to take back to Germany.

The Home Fleet's final chance to deal a blow to the German Navy in western Norway was lost the following morning when Forbes ordered naval forces away from the Norwegian coast and left the door open for the three ships to escape.

Air Power Shakes British Confidence

The Luftwaffe was not established ashore in the early hours of April 9, so this would have been the best time for the British to strike. An attack on the city late on April 9, or thereafter, may have proved costly in view of growing German air power projected from Sola Airfield and the fact that the Germans laid their own minefields in the Bergen approaches on April 10.

German aircraft began attacking British naval forces early in the evening of April 9. The Luftwaffe first attacked Admiral Layton's force on its way back to the Home Fleet after the cancellation of its planned operation against Bergen. Two cruisers received minor damage from near misses and one of the new *Tribal* class destroyers, the *Gurkha*, was sunk. The Germans also carried out several attacks against the Home Fleet. A 1000-lb bomb struck the battleship *Rodney*, Admiral Forbes' flagship, but the damage and loss of life was not serious. Three cruisers sustained minor damage from near misses and only one German aircraft was shot down. The damage to Forbes' confidence, however, was considerable.

The Home Fleet steered north for several hours to get out of the range of German bombers, then Admiral Forbes turned westward during the night. He did not head back towards the Norwegian coast until after *Warspite* and *Furious* joined him. He also recommended to the Admiralty that British surface vessels only attack German naval units in northern waters and that naval operations near the south and west coast of Norway be limited to submarines. He also recommended that *Furious*, who had left her fighter squadrons behind in Scotland, should not be used without fighter escorts in areas where she would be exposed to German aircraft. The Admiralty accepted these sensible recommendations. Without adequate air cover, naval operations near the Norwegian shore would have exposed the ships to furious attacks by a Luftwaffe that was growing rapidly in strength at Norwegian airfields.

NOTES

1 Ladislas Fargo, *The Game of the Foxes* (New York: D. McKay Co., 1971), pp. 431-436.

2 David Irving, *Hitler's War* (New York: The Viking Press, 1977), p. 94.

3 Harold C. Deutsch, *The Conspiracy against Hitler in the Twilight War* (Minneapolis: The University of Minnesota Press, 1968), p. 320.

4 Deutsch, *The Conspiracy against Hitler*, p. 321, and Roger Manvell and Heinrich Fraenkel, *The Canaris Conspiracy. The Secret Resistance to Hitler in the German Army* (New York: Pinnacle Books, 1972), pp. 122-123. Stang was not a member of *Nasjonal Samling* at this time but joined that party after his return to Norway. In the trials following World War 2 Stang was prosecuted for failing to forward Sas' warning. He claimed that he had not knowingly kept this information from the Norwegian Government and the court found him innocent of this charge. However, he was sentenced to four years of hard labor because of his party membership.

5 This and the other intelligence reports received by the Norwegian Naval Staff and used in this book are copied in Steen, *Norges Sjøkrig 1940-1945*, vol. 1, pp. 199-204.

6 Ottmer, *Weserübung*, p. 61.

7 "Norge visste, ingen gjorde noe," *Aftenposten*, June 14, 2005.

8 Sir Llewellyn Woodward, *British Foreign Policy in the Second World War* (London: HMSO, 1970), p. 114.

9 Admiral Diesen had ordered his forces to the highest state of alert on a couple of occasions during the winter when the situation appeared threatening. He had received a reprimand from the Foreign Minister on the last occasion and this may have contributed to his lack of enthusiasm for taking this step, but his own views of the nature of the threat were probably of equal importance.

10 Bjørnson, *Narvik*, p. 210.

11 Churchill, *The Gathering Storm*, p. 459.

12 PRO, *FO* 371/24815 N 3602/2/63. Laurence Collier, considered a Norwegian expert, was Dormer's designated replacement as British representative in Norway.

13 T. K. Derry, *The Campaign in Norway* (London: HMSO, 1952), p. 26.

14 Harvey, *Scandinavian Misadventure*, p. 56.

15 The Home Fleet in Scapa Flow consisted of two battleships, one battle cruiser, three cruisers (including one French), and 12 destroyers (including two French). Another battleship and an aircraft carrier (without fighters) were on their way from Clyde to join the fleet. In addition, there was the 2nd Cruiser Squadron at Rosyth with two light cruisers and eight destroyers. One battle cruiser, one heavy cruiser and 16 destroyers were at sea or off Norway's northern coast. Then there was the 18th Cruiser Squadron consisting of two heavy cruisers and five destroyers in the North Sea along with one large minelayer and four destroyers. The addition of four cruisers and two destroyers (1st Cruiser Squadron) was not a significant augmentation in view of the damage the disembarkation of troops caused to Allied plans for landing troops in Norway.

16 See, for example, Peter Dickens, *Narvik: Battles in the Fjords* (Naval Institute Press, 1974), pp. 25-26 and Donald MacIntyre, *Narvik* (London: Evans Brothers Ltd, 1959), pp. 35-36.

17 Quoted in Dickens, *Narvik*, p. 30.

18 Ibid.

19 The four destroyers that laid the minefield had undergone a conversion. Both torpedo tubes and two guns were removed in order to compensate for the weight of the mines.

20 Quoted in Steen, *Norges Sjøkrig 1940-1945*, vol. 1, pp. 154-155.

21 *Renown* had a displacement of 32,000 tons, could reach a speed of 29 knots, and carried a crew of 1,200. Her main armament consisted of six 15-inch guns and her secondary armament consisted of 20 4.5-inch guns. The German battleships had a displacement of 31,850 tons, and were capable of a speed of 31.5 knots. Each had a crew of about 1,800, a main armament of 11-inch guns, and 12 6-inch and 14 4-inch guns as secondary armament.

22 *Fuehrer Conferences 1940*, April 13, 1940, vol. 1, p. 36.

23 Admiral Forbes received several intelligence reports from the Admiralty on April 8, but they were not all timely. The Polish submarine *Orzel* sank the *Rio de Janeiro* about 1015 hours GMT on April 8. The Admiralty learned about this in the early afternoon and it was reported by Reuters from Oslo at 1930 GMT. However, Admiral Forbes was not given this information until 2255 GMT.

24 See, for example, Moulton, *Study of Warfare*, p. 102; MacIntyre, *Narvik*, pp. 29-33 Dickens, *Battles in the Fjords*, p. 28. Stephen Wentworth Roskill writes, "Admiral Forbes has stated that by this time (after the *Glowworm* engagement) he was convinced in his own mind that a German attack on Norway had started." (*The War at Sea 1939*-1945 [London: HMSO, 1954], vol. 1, p. 160).

25 See, for example, MacIntyre, *Narvik, p.* 33.

26 MacIntyre, *Narvik*, p. 52.

4

NARVIK AREA DEFENSES

'The defense of Narvik stands or falls on the
defense of the Ofotfjord entrance."

STATEMENT BY COLONEL GEORG STANG,
A FORMER NORWEGIAN MINISTER OF DEFENSE.

The Norwegian military forces stationed in North Norway in 1940, particularly
the land forces, were better prepared for hostilities than those in other areas of
the country. In the first place, the war between Finland and the Soviet Union
resulted in the movement of relatively large forces to Finnmark. It was necessary
to insure that neutrality was not violated and that the war did not spill over into
Norway. Another reason for a higher level of preparedness was the obvious Allied
interest in the iron ore shipments through Narvik.

Naval Forces

A sizable proportion of the naval force stationed in North Norway during the
Winter War was redeployed to other parts of the country after the conclusion of
peace between Finland and the Soviet Union. This included three modern
destroyers, two submarines, and one torpedo boat. Some of the warships that
were earlier stationed in Tromsø were organized into a separate division, called
the Ofot Division, and moved to Narvik. This concentration of forces was aimed
at hindering or discouraging British warships from entering Ofotfjord to destroy
the many German merchant ships involved in the iron ore shipments during the
winter of 1939-40. The prevailing view in the Norwegian Government was that
the British posed the greatest danger to Narvik and consequently very little
thought was given to any possibility of confronting German naval forces.

The 3rd Naval District, with its headquarters in Tromsø, was responsible for
the naval defense of the long coastline from the provincial boundary between
Nord-Trøndelag and Nordland to the Finnish border. This was a relatively new
organization, created in January 1937, and at the outset, it had no assigned naval
units. Commodore L. Hagerup commanded the 3rd Naval District, but he

departed for a leave in southern Norway on April 5. Captain Per Askim, the Ofot Division commander, acted as district commander in Hagerup's absence. In addition to these duties, Askim was the skipper of the coastal defense ship *Norge*.

The ships available to the 3rd Naval District were organized into two divisions as of March 31: the Ofot Division and the Finnmark Division. In addition, eight patrol vessels reported directly to the naval district. Most of the ships in the Finnmark Division were reassigned after the Winter War and it had only five patrol vessels on April 8. The Ofot Division consisted of the two coastal defense ships *Norge* and *Eidsvold*. The division was also assigned the 3rd Submarine Division, which comprised the submarines *B3* and *B1* as well as the submarine tender *Lyngen*. Finally, there were three patrol boats, *Michael Sars*, *Senja*, and *Kelt*. All Ofot Division's ships were in Narvik on April 8.

The aircraft assigned to the naval district consisted of three Heinkel-115 torpedo aircraft and two MF-11 reconnaissance aircraft. The three torpedo aircraft were stationed at the Tromsø Naval Air Station. There were no torpedoes available and the aircraft were therefore rigged to carry 500-lb and 150-lb bombs. The two reconnaissance aircraft were stationed in Vadsø, near the Soviet border.

The naval forces assigned to the 3rd Naval District were inadequate in both numbers and quality to meet an attack by a modern navy. The two coastal defense ships were 40 years old. They had a displacement of 3,645 tons, a crew of 229, and could muster a maximum speed of only 17 knots. Each was armed with two 8.3-inch guns, six 6-inch guns, and six 76mm guns. This was a large number of heavy weapons for ships of their size but the ranges of the heavier caliber guns were short. The antiaircraft defenses were inadequate. They consisted of two 76mm and two 20mm guns as well as two 12.7mm and four 7.92mm machineguns. The fire direction system was outmoded and the same was true for the watertight compartment and bottom hull construction. The ships were severely limited in their capacity to fight modern warships and aircraft. They were best suited as floating batteries.

The two submarines were built between 1922 and 1925 from old plans that did not incorporate the lessons learned from World War 1. They were especially hampered by the long time it took to dive. Each had a 76mm gun and four torpedo tubes. The larger patrol vessels were not warships in the traditional meaning of that term. The use of these vessels was limited to escort, patrol, and guard duties. Their armaments ranged from 4-inch down to 37mm guns. Of the three patrol boats in the Ofot Division, *Michael Sars* carried two 47mm guns, *Senja* had only one, and *Kelt* had one 76mm gun.

Army Forces

Major General Carl Gustav Fleischer, the commander of the 6th Division, commanded all army forces in North Norway. His geographic area of responsibility coincided with that of the 3rd Naval District. The country's three northern provinces were sparsely populated and mobilization called for the introduction of forces from other areas of the country. Fleischer was designated as wartime commander of all forces in North Norway, army as well as navy. When war broke out in Europe in September 1939, a so-called neutrality watch, which was a very limited mobilization, was organized throughout the country. Since the Soviet Union was not a belligerent, the neutrality watch in North Norway was limited to two infantry battalions and a garrison company. One line battalion and the garrison company were located in East Finnmark and the other battalion in the Narvik area.

The looming crisis between the Soviet Union and Finland in October 1939 resulted in a further buildup of forces in North Norway. The Alta Battalion was mobilized and the forces in East Finnmark were strengthened by the addition of engineers and artillery. When war broke out in Finland, the Alta Bn and the 1st Bn, 15th Inf Regt at Elvegårdsmoen were sent to East Finnmark. In addition, the 1st Bn, 14th Inf Regt was mobilized in December and sent to East Finnmark. The 1st Bn, 16th Inf Regt was also mobilized but remained at Setermoen in Troms Province. Since the buildup in East Finnmark exceeded three line battalions, Colonel W. Faye, who commanded the 6th Field Brigade, was designated as the overall commander in that area and given a special staff. Colonel Kristian R. Løken took over as commander of the 6th Field Brigade and the Troms area.

The Norwegian Government viewed the situation in Finland with alarm and the 6th Division was ordered partially mobilized in January 1940. In addition to various staff elements, support and service support units, two infantry battalions and one artillery battalion were mobilized. The Varanger Battalion was stationed at Nyborgsmoen in East Finnmark. The 2nd Bn, 15th Inf Regt and the 3rd Mountain Artillery Bn remained at Setermoen. At the same time, a redeployment of forces took place. The Alta Bn was demobilized. The 1st Bn, 15th Inf Regt returned to Elvegårdsmoen where it was demobilized and replaced by a battalion from Trøndelag, the 1st Bn, 13th Inf Regt. Another battalion from

Trøndelag, the 1st Bn, 12th Inf Regt was moved to East Finnmark. The final major change in the disposition of forces in North Norway took place on March 15, 1940 when the 1st Bn, 14th Inf Regt in East Finnmark was replaced by the 2nd Bn from the same regiment and the 1st Bn, 16th Inf Regt at Setermoen was demobilized.

Thus, while each of the other divisional areas in the country had only one infantry battalion on active duty at the time of the German attack, the 6th Division in North Norway had five battalions assigned. The units in North Norway were better equipped than the units in other areas of the country. All field units were outfitted with skis and winter gear. What was lacking was procured or produced by civilian industry within the divisional area. Various women's organizations provided a valuable service by making winter clothing, including white winter camouflage materials for covering regular uniforms.

The three northern provinces were well stocked with food and fuel. For most foodstuffs there were sufficient quantities on hand to last up to nine months in case the area became isolated from the rest of the country. A concerted effort was made in early 1940 to distribute these vast stores to smaller warehouses throughout the countryside. This distribution served a dual purpose. First, it increased the security of the stores by making their capture or destruction more difficult. Second, the wide distribution made access easier for both the military and the population at large, particularly in areas that could become isolated either through enemy action or because of the severe winter weather.

The units mobilized for the neutrality watch were expected to conduct such training and exercises as would improve their ability to operate in war. There was an acute shortage of both junior officers and NCOs despite efforts to bring some in from other parts of the country. Many of the enlisted and lower ranking NCOs in the units that were mobilized came from older age groups and the recruit training period for some had been as short as 48 days. Since a number of years had passed since these enlisted men were trained or on active duty, it became necessary to restart their training. Officers and senior NCOs were much older than their counterparts in the German Army, well past their prime for the physical demands likely to be faced by company grade officers in combat. Furthermore, they did not have experience to fall back on since they had seen little service and few had the opportunity in the 1920s and 1930s to attend refresher courses, or to become familiar with new weapons and equipment.

A look at the ages of the officers in the 1/13th Inf Regt, which had the mission of defending the Narvik area, illustrates this problem. This unit was activated in Nord-Trøndelag Province on January 5, 1940 and arrived in Narvik on January 13. The battalion commander was 58 years old. The ages of the five captains ranged from over 40 to 62 years of age. The situation was similar among the 26 lieutenants assigned to the battalion. Their average age was 37.5 years, with the two youngest being 25 and the two oldest 56. The lack of combat experience, inadequate training, limited periods of active duty and age are the major factors that determined the performance of this battalion in the campaign.

Lack of quarters resulted in units being spread out over relatively large areas. Combined with the severe winter weather and the lack of daylight during the winter months, the dispersion of the units made training very difficult.

The units in East Finnmark were required to patrol and outpost long stretches of the border with the Soviet Union and Finland. This mission made unit training and exercise at company and battalion level impossible for them.

The situation was better in Troms and Ofoten. Here it was possible to conduct maneuvers at battalion and brigade level. Two such maneuvers were conducted in February and March. The first was a defensive exercise, while the second involved movement to contact and attacks against prepared defensive positions. A maneuver by the 1/13th Inf, scheduled to begin on March 8, was cancelled due to continual snowstorms. A report by the 6th Division on December 18, 1939 summarizes the combat readiness of its battalions and the statements are equally applicable to the units in its command in April 1940:[1]

> The resulting experiences are that our battalions after the end of their mobilization—despite obvious deficiencies in organization, training, and equipment—can be assigned simple tactical missions which, at the outset, should be limited to defense.
>
> They can quickly become capable of movement through various terrains but are hardly able to undertake missions involving maneuvering in war until they have undergone extended training under favorable conditions. This is dictated by the weaknesses in the level of individual training and commanders' exercise experience.

Despite all shortcomings, there is no doubt that the battalions involved in the neutrality watch in North Norway benefited from that experience in both operational readiness and morale. It is to General Fleischer's credit that he managed, despite serious obstacles, to bring the 6th Division to a state of readiness that permitted the start of offensive operations within a relatively short time after absorbing the first shocks of war. Fleischer wrote, "The units suffered much hardship but developed toughness, became skilled at operating together, and learned to manage on their own. They became units that could be used in war."[2]

For these reasons, the campaign in North Norway started out with advantages that were not present in other areas of the country. General Fleischer was able to begin operations almost immediately with mobilized units and fully functional and provisioned supply and support organizations. Except for the units that lost their supplies and equipment when the Germans captured Elvegårdsmoen, the 6th Division was able to mobilize according to plans without any serious enemy interference.[3] The units in southern and central Norway had their mobilization disrupted by the immediate loss of depots and population centers. In addition, they had to cope with enemy air supremacy and a rapid build-up of his forces.

General Fleischer had his headquarters in Harstad, but he and his chief of staff had departed for an inspection of the forces in East Finnmark on April 3, 1940. They were at Nybergsmoen near Kirkenes on April 8 to observe an exercise by the Varanger Battalion. Colonel Lars Mjelde, the 6th District Commander, supervised the division staff during Fleischer's absence.

North Norway was divided into five sectors, but battalion-size or larger formations were located in only three area commands on April 8, 1940:

1) East Finnmark Command under Colonel Wilhelm Faye. This command's mission was to guard the eastern border during the Winter War. It was kept mobilized afterward, at the request of the Finns. The Finns wanted the Norwegian forces in East Finnmark maintained until the Soviets withdrew from areas scheduled for return to Finland. Faye's command consisted of the Varanger Inf Bn at Nybergsmoen; 1/12th Inf; 2/14th Inf; a reinforced garrison company in Sør Varanger; two motorized artillery batteries (one split up and used in static positions); a platoon each from the 6th Signal Company, 6th Engineer Company, and 6th Transportation Company; and the 6th Field Hospital.

2) Troms Command under Colonel Kristian R. Løken, who also commanded the 6th Field Brigade. The following units were assigned to him: The 6th Field Brigade Staff; 2/15th Inf at Setermoen; 3rd Mountain Artillery Bn at Målselv consisting of two horse-drawn field artillery batteries and one motorized battery; 6th Signal Company minus one

platoon; 6th Transportation Company less one platoon; 6th Medical Company; 6th Veterinary Unit; and the 6th Division NCO School.

3) Nord-Hålogaland Command under Colonel Konrad Sundlo. Sundlo was assigned as commander of the 15th Inf Regt when he was promoted to colonel in 1933. The following units were under his command on April 8, 1940: 1) Regimental staff. This was a skeletal, peacetime organization as opposed to the staffs of the other two major operational units under General Fleischer's command. It lacked adequate personnel in intelligence, communications, and civil affairs and no staff or telephone journals were kept due to lack of personnel. In addition, several officers on the staff were absent on April 9. The inadequate staffing was testified to at Colonel Sundlo's trial in 1947. 2) 1/13th Inf. This unit was located at Elvegårdsmoen with one company and one machinegun platoon in Narvik. The units in Narvik were ordered there by General Fleischer on February 17, 1940 in the wake of the *Altmark* affair. 3) 6th Engineer Co of the Hålogaland Engineer Bn, minus one platoon. This reserve company was mobilized in October 1939. Its mission was to construct bunkers and other defensive positions in Narvik and along the Ofot Railway.

4) 6th Anti-Aircraft Battery with four 40mm cannons and two machinegun platoons, each with three antiaircraft machineguns. This battery was mobilized on January 8, 1940.

5) An armored train unit from the 3rd Mountain Artillery Bn. 6) A guard detail on the Nordal Railway Bridge between Narvik and the Swedish border.

A functional radio net was established shortly after the outbreak of war in 1939 and it was in operation until October 10, 1939. It provided radio communication between the District Command in Harstad, Colonel Sundlo's headquarters in Narvik, and Colonel Løken's headquarters in Troms. Telephone was the only means of communication between the three major subordinate commands, the District Command, and General Fleischer's headquarters after October 10, 1939. There were no direct communication links between navy and army commands in the Narvik area, although there was frequent personal and telephone contact between Colonel Sundlo and Captain Askim. The failure to provide the army headquarters in Narvik with a radio link to the Ofot Division caused serious problems. While the Ofot Division had radio communications with the 3rd Naval District, that organization relied on telephone to communicate with army headquarters in Harstad.

The Hålogaland Air Group, established in January 1938, came under General Fleischer's direct command. This unit had its headquarters at Bardufoss Airfield and it had six Fokker CVE aircraft (Dutch built light bomber-reconnaissance aircraft), one transport, and three Tiger Moth aircraft assigned. Three Fokker aircraft, the transport, and one Tiger Moth were stationed in Seida in East Finnmark. The rest were at Banak in West Finnmark. There were two antiaircraft platoons at Seida and one at Banak. Each platoon had three Colt machineguns. The aircraft were outfitted with skis and were therefore not completely dependent on airfields. They were, for example, capable of operating from frozen lakes.

In the mobilization plans, it was assumed that the 6th Division's staff would split, with one part becoming the staff of the 6th Field Brigade and the other part the 6th District Command. The idea was that General Fleischer would take over as commander of the 6th Field Brigade and at the same time assume the role as overall commander in the war zone while the administrative functions outside the war zone would be the responsibility of 6th District Command.

The 6th Division regarded this as an unsuitable solution for North Norway. The reasons were that it was difficult to know in advance what would be a war zone, and because the 6th Field Brigade was viewed as a strategic reserve. In April 1937, the 6th Division proposed that the 6th District Command assume responsibility for the administrative functions in all of North Norway and that the division commander not be tied to any specific unit, such as the 6th Field Brigade.[4] This would facilitate his role as commander-in-chief in North Norway after the outbreak of war.

The proposal was never formally accepted but the District Command, located in Harstad, was established in January 1940 and augmented so that it would be able to function in the manner envisioned in the 6th Division proposal. It was responsible for the administrative, logistical, and support functions within the 6th Division's area of responsibility. Colonel Lars Mjelde, who reported to Fleischer, commanded this organization and had his own staff. Captain H. Løken was Colonel Mjelde's chief of staff. Among others on his staff was the chief quartermaster, chief medical officer, commander of the Hålogaland Engineer Bn, the district engineer, and the chief of sea transport. General Fleischer effectively separated the administrative and operational elements of his staff through this organizational setup. While some higher authorities looked upon this unique arrangement with disapproval, it appears to have worked satisfactorily.

General Fleischer

Major General Carl Gustav Fleischer (1883-1942) is one of the two key individuals in the Narvik Campaign, the other being his opponent General Dietl. Neither officer survived the war. While Fleischer was a controversial officer, many consider him the most competent Norwegian general of World War 2. While he had excellent General Staff credentials, he lacked the combat experience and extensive troop duty that characterized Dietl's career.

Fleischer is a well-known name in Norwegian society but Carl Gustav came from a modest and relatively unknown branch of that family. He was the son of a minister in the northern part of Trøndelag Province. His father was lost at sea when Carl Gustav was only two years old and his mother moved the family to Trondheim.

Carl Gustav grew up in a very religious home under tight economic conditions. The family moved from Trondheim to Oslo in 1899. Carl Gustav chose a military career despite opposition from his immediate family and he entered the military academy in 1902. This was a time when the Norwegian military was modernized and expanded in anticipation of a violent end to the country's union with Sweden. Carl Gustav graduated in 1905 when war with Sweden appeared inevitable. War was averted at the last moment, but the perception of Sweden as a potential military threat lingered for many years.

General Torkel Hovland, in his biography of Fleischer, gives an extensive and excellent depiction of the general's personality. It is important to keep these traits in mind since they assumed substantial importance during the Narvik Campaign. He appears to have been thoroughly honest and loyal to his followers. At times, he showed a reluctance to confront subordinates and superiors directly in disagreeable situations. Fleischer was a romantic, an ardent nationalist, had a feeling of destiny and a strong sense of duty and honor. He was stubborn, dogmatic, overly sensitive to actual or perceived affronts to his honor, and had a tendency to brood. The senior aristocratic British officers had little understanding for this unknown militia commander and his reaction to rather cavalier treatment by British military leaders affected the campaign. The Norwegian Government in exile shoved Fleischer aside and this serious affront to his sense of honor was undoubtedly a major factor in his suicide in Canada in 1942.

Fleischer spent many years on the General Staff but his command experience below regimental level was limited to a two-year tour in western Norway and three years with the Royal Guards. Fleischer was appointed Chief of Staff of the 6th Division in Harstad in 1919. He spent four years in this position and it was his first experience in the part of the country where he was to serve again 20 years later.

Fleischer was again posted to the General Staff in 1923 where he played an important role in the military reorganizations of the 1920s as Chief of the Mobilization and Readiness Division. The 1920s and 1930s were tough years for the Norwegian military. Pacifism, idealism, tough economic times, an anti-militaristic mood, and the lack of obvious threats combined to curtail severely the size and effectiveness of the military forces.

After three years (1926-1929) with the Royal Guards, Fleischer returned to the General Staff and continued there until 1934. He was also an instructor in tactics at the Military Academy at the same time as Otto Ruge, the future Commander-in-Chief. The lack of an amicable relationship between these two officers assumed some importance during the Narvik Campaign. Their careers crossed at various times in the years leading up to World War 2 and it appears that they grew to dislike each other. Most writers attribute this bad chemistry to the fact that they were on opposite sides in the bitter dispute over the 1933 army reorganization. Hovland believes that the problems were deeper. Ruge was a pragmatist by nature. Fleischer, on the other hand, was an idealist who abhorred compromise when it came to national defense. He had little understanding for or patience with the give and take that characterize the budgetary process and allocation of resources in a democracy. Ruge's view that military budget requests should be politically realistic and that the military should put the limited resources made available to the best use became the basis for the reorganization of 1933. Ruge made a distinction between what he called "peace defense," such as a military neutrality watch, and the sort of situation that would arise if the country became involved in a European war because of its strategic position. To accomplish this dual mission, Ruge argued that the military should give up its wishes for a large establishment, which would only exist on paper because of limited resources. He wanted a small, modern, and well-trained army. Fleischer and many fellow officers opposed the reorganization that Ruge pushed through in 1933. They considered it unsuitable for the defense problems confronting Norway and a sell-out of national security. General Roscher-Nielsen described Fleischer as Ruge's most incensed opponent.

Fleischer was promoted from major to colonel in 1934—skipping one rank —and assumed command of the 14th Inf Regt in Mosjøen. As commander of the 14th Inf, he was responsible for the defense of the area from Narvik to the Nord-Trøndelag provincial boundary. Fleischer was promoted to major general in January 1939, and given command of the 6th Division.

When the time came for the appointment of a new Minister of Defense in early 1940, Fleischer was one of three candidates under consideration. The other two were Colonels Ruge and Birger Ljungberg, the youngest of the three. Fleischer was not selected because it was judged unwise to make a command change in North Norway with hostilities just across the border in Finland. Ljungberg was eventually chosen because he was viewed as non-controversial and a person who could work well in a political setting.

The Town of Narvik

Narvik is located near the center of the area Fleischer and Hagerup were required to defend. At 68° 26' 8" N, it is 220 kilometers north of the Arctic Circle, near the same latitude as Barrow, Alaska (71° 18' 1" N). The distance from Narvik to Oslo is approximately 1,450 kilometers. Until 1902 Narvik was known as Victoriahavn. As late as 1883, it was an isolated community of a few farms, largely dependent on the Lofoten fisheries.

Narvik has an excellent ice–free harbor and this fact led to its selection as the western terminal of the Ofot Railway. Sweden and Norway had entered into a union in 1814 and the governments of the two countries decided, in the 1880s, to build a railroad to cross the 170km between the iron ore districts in Kiruna, Sweden and Narvik. The railroad would allow iron ore to be shipped during the winter months when the Gulf of Bothnia and parts of the Baltic froze. This immense, complicated construction project in a wild and inhospitable region took many years to complete, despite the involvement of thousands of laborers. The project included building harbor facilities to handle the iron ore and this caused a sharp increase in Narvik's permanent population from 300 in 1898 to 4,500 in 1903, the year after the railroad was completed.

By 1940, Narvik's population had grown to approximately 10,000 people, but the town remained very isolated. There were no road or railroad links to the southern areas of the country. A road or railroad through the mountainous wilderness between Narvik and Bodø was only in the planning stages. To reach Oslo or southern Norway from Narvik, a person had to take a coastal steamer to Trondheim or Bergen, and then catch a train for the remainder of the journey.

An alternate route was by train from Narvik to Luleå, and on to Oslo via Stockholm. There was a road leading north from Øyjord, across the Ofotfjord from Narvik; however, it was difficult to keep this road open for traffic during the winter and it could become impassable during the spring thaw.

Prior to the construction of the Ofot Railway, North Norway was more or less a military no-man's land. The railroad changed that and was the most important factor that caused the political and military leadership to plan a defense of the region. Russia was viewed as the main threat because of its well-known desire for ice-free harbors. A naval attack was viewed as the most likely form of Russian aggression and the plans to deal with this threat concentrated on naval and coastal artillery forces. Not much was accomplished, however, since in the period leading to the breakup of the Swedish-Norwegian Union in 1905, the southern and eastern parts of the country were viewed as the priority from a military perspective.

After 1905, Russia was still viewed as the main threat, but the possibility of a Swedish attack to secure the railroad and the harbor at Narvik had to be considered. The nationalistic movement that led to Finnish independence at the end of World War 1 posed another possible threat because of large Finnish settlements in North Norway. An expansionist movement for creation of a "greater" Finland could result in demands for parts of the two northernmost provinces, Finnmark and Troms. German naval maneuvers in northern waters in 1911 added a new potential danger and the period prior to and during World War 1 saw considerable activity with respect to Narvik's defenses.

Defense Plans for Narvik

Narvik is located on terrain that is not a very defensible. The military authorities demanded and received promises from the politicians that coastal fortresses would be constructed in the Narvik approaches as a condition for their blessing of the Ofot Railway project. The promise was only partially fulfilled, and after World War 1, it was ignored.

The early defense plans for Narvik focused primarily on a series of coastal artillery batteries supplemented by submarines and torpedo boats. Plans were set in motion to establish a naval base at Ramsund near the Ofotfjord entrance and for the construction of coastal artillery battery positions covering the fjord entrance from the north and west. A battery of 105mm guns was established at Forholten covering the northern entrances to Ramsund, which was dredged, and Tjeldsund. This battery was operational in 1916 but not activated in 1940. The battery at Ramnes, at the junction of Ramsund and Ofotfjord, was never completed. The three 6-inch guns for this battery were kept in storage for many years and in March 1940, they were sent to Bergen to be used in a planned gun battery on that city's northern approach. They were at the naval depot in Bergen on April 9 and were captured by the Germans.

The elaborate plans for a strong naval base at Ramsund never came to fruition and they were shelved in 1925 when Ramsund was designated as a naval depot rather than a naval base. The severe reduction in defense expenditures after World War I and the lack of any immediate threats were the primary reasons for the abandonment of these sensible plans. The navy did not resist the changed status for Ramsund and it did not see the same need as the army for a coastal battery at Ramnes. The navy viewed the battery as being part of the framework of the naval base, while the army viewed it as an important factor in the defense of Narvik and the Ofot Railway. After the 1933 defense reorganization, the coastal artillery came under the navy's jurisdiction.

Both General Fleischer and his predecessor requested repeatedly that the planned coastal fortifications at the Ofotfjord entrance be completed but they were turned down. Fleischer sought a promise from the navy for a three-hour early warning of an enemy attack on Narvik. The navy refused—with good reasons—to commit to such a promise.

Before and during World War 1, army plans for the defense of the railroad leading to the Swedish border were given a lower priority since the establishment of coastal artillery batteries and use of navy assets were viewed as the primary means of defense. However, since the defenses in the outer part of Ofotfjord were never completed, the army plans for the defense of the Ofot Railway took on added significance even during World War I.

Army plans called for the establishment of a blocking position in the Sildvik area, about 20 kilometers east of Narvik, and preparations for the destruction of the railroad if the defensive positions could not be held. The defenses in this blocking position consisted of bunkers for machineguns and artillery, and an armored railroad car with a 75mm gun. Searchlights, magazines, sidings, etc. to support the blocking position were installed. These projects were completed during World War I.

A reinforced company-size task force was initially designated to occupy these positions, and it was referred to as the "Narvik Detachment." The planners anticipated the need for a quick occupation of the defensive line and the troops were therefore located in Narvik where adequate quarters were available. From there, they would be able to occupy the defensive positions on short notice, something that would not be possible from the regimental base at Elvegårdsmoen.[5] The "Narvik Detachment" was a rapid reaction force, to be augmented as the situation dictated. It was not a force designed to defend the town of Narvik.

The plans for the defense of the railroad line to Sweden were rational. They recognized that the primary objective of any seaward attacker was Narvik *and* the railroad to the Swedish border. The capture of Narvik without also seizing the railroad would be meaningless, since the flow of Swedish iron ore would cease. The planners assumed that the attacker would have naval dominance before landing troops. A force defending Narvik would therefore be exposed to heavy naval gunfire and it could be cut off from a retreat along the railroad by an enemy landing at any point along the southern shore of Rombakfjord, possibly at Djupvik or Straumsnes. The plan to occupy a defensive line in the Sildvik area was therefore a sound solution. The positions would be less exposed to naval gunfire and more difficult to envelop.

The plan did have some weaknesses. The Sildvik position was difficult to reinforce from Elvegårdsmoen. With enemy control of the fjord, reinforcements had to come through the mountainous wilderness to the east of Elvegårdsmoen, a difficult and time-consuming operation. Moreover, it was prudent to anticipate that an attack on Narvik would also involve an attack on Elvegårdsmoen. It was therefore important to make the Sildvik blocking force as large and self-sustaining as resources would allow. The capture of Elvegårdsmoen would make it possible for the enemy to send a force through the mountains and reach the Ofot Railway behind the Norwegian blocking force, between Bjørnefjell and Nordal Bridge. A similar operation could also be launched from the village of Beisfjord, south of Narvik, but it was possible to block such a move without abandoning the Sildvik positions. The Norwegians in Sildvik, to avoid being isolated by forces moving east from Elvegårdsmoen, would have to retreat if other units were unable to block the enemy.

The failure to complete the coastal artillery batteries, and to establish a naval base with adequate forces meant that the army became the most important force in the defense plans for Narvik and the Ofot Railway. The political decision to rely on army forces rather than on coastal defense installations and the navy in the Narvik area went against all military recommendations since well before World War I.[6]

The German attack in 1940 was exactly the type of attack that had served as a basis for the military recommendations. The political leadership's reordering of military priorities, and the national military leadership's reluctant acceptance, had severe consequences. The government's failure to provide adequate resources forced local military leaders to improvise a defense in which they did not have much faith. In a recommendation on February 2, 1940 for completion and occupation of the coastal artillery batteries as soon as possible, General Fleischer notes that the failure to complete the coastal artillery batteries at the Ofotfjord entrance had forced the division to try to organize a harbor defense as means to thwart a surprise attack.[7]

Attempts to obtain heavy guns for use in Narvik failed. The intention was to use these guns in flanking positions against an attack from the sea. Those that were available, such as the 65mm mountain artillery pieces or 105mm guns, were unsuitable. In the end, only a single 75mm gun on an armored railroad car was made available.

The 6th Division's operational directive to the commander in Narvik dated February 19, 1937 instructed him to use two-thirds of his main force (the infantry battalion at Elvegårdsmoen) on the south side of the fjord, for the defense of Narvik and the Ofot Railway. The regiment's mission with respect to Narvik was to defend against air attacks and troop landings. The remaining third of the force was to stay on the north side of the fjord for use as security for Elevgårdsmoen. Differences in views between the division and the regiment on how to defend Narvik and the Ofot Railway surfaced because of this operational directive although they had probably been present for some time.

Colonel Sundlo conveyed the regimental views about the defense of Narvik to the Major General Carl Johan Erichsen, who was the divisional commander at the time, on several occasions following the issuance of the operational directive. The regiment believed that the most likely threats against Narvik were either a naval attack to destroy facilities to prevent the export of iron ore or a landing of troops from naval vessels to secure those facilities. The regiment felt it was imperative that some kind of defense measures be taken in the Ramsund area, such as a well-guarded minefield.

When the division threw cold water on this possibility, the regiment suggested that, as an interim measure, one reinforced company equipped with 65mm mountain artillery should be deployed to the fjord entrance. A reinforced infantry company, the train-mounted 75mm gun, some 65mm mountain artillery pieces, and one or two air defense batteries was considered the minimum force that should be stationed in Narvik. The regiment suggested that the force left at Elvegårdsmoen be reduced to one infantry platoon while the rest of the reinforced company be given the mission of defending the Ofot Railway (at the end of the fjord) and also used as a reserve for the force in Narvik.

The plan for the neutrality watch issued by the division at the end of 1937 dropped the idea of a forward deployed company at the fjord entrance, since the responsibility for guarding the coastline belonged to the navy based on an agreement between the commanders of the two services. The limit on the size of the force to be used on the south side of the fjord was retained.

The construction of bunkers and other defensive works in the Narvik area was, as Fleischer noted on February 2, 1940, a result of the government's failure to complete the long-promised fortifications at the fjord entrance. In the fall of 1939, divisional engineers constructed two reinforced concrete bunkers in Narvik and one for the defense of the largest of the railroad's bridges, known as the Nordal Bridge. The construction of bunkers in and around Narvik and Fleischer's order on February 17, 1940 for an absolute defense of the city signaled a major departure from the World War 1 plans.

The partial mobilization in late January 1940 included an engineer company that the division stationed in Narvik except for one platoon that was sent to East Finnmark. However, during the winter, the division pressed the regiment to use infantry units to construct the defensive works planned for the Narvik area, Elvegårdsmoen, and Øyjord. The construction in Narvik was delayed for several reasons. First, the regiment felt that the work was so technical in nature that it should be delayed until an experienced engineer officer became available. Second, the 1/15th Inf battalion that was stationed in the Narvik area at the time had been sent to East Finnmark. Finally, in addition to the difference of views between General Fleischer and Colonel Sundlo about the wisdom of defending Narvik relying primarily on infantry forces, they also differed on where the defense positions in Narvik should be located.

Sundlo considered it foolish to confront an attacker on the flat terrain in the harbor area where the defenders would be subject to the full fury of naval firepower. He wanted to establish the main defense line along the high ground in the eastern part of the town, with a covering force in the harbor area. This covering force was not expected to become involved in decisive combat but to delay and channel an enemy advance towards the main defensive line. It appears that Sundlo intended to use his forces in an offensive role and did not think elaborate defense works were called for. The division did not agree and Sundlo later clarified that when he had expressed the opinion that elaborate prepared defense positions were not needed, he referred to the covering force. Whatever the case, the difference in views between Fleischer and Sundlo apparently extended to precisely how that defense should be carried out.

It is difficult to determine the thinking behind the location of the first two bunkers. There was 3,000 meters between them and they were therefore not mutually supporting. The distances from the Fagernes and Framnes bunkers to the central harbor area were 1,800 and 1,000 meters, respectively. The central parts of the harbor were therefore outside the effective range of machineguns and small arms.

Major Sigurd Omdal, the regimental executive officer, recommended that a number of machinegun nests be built in the harbor area. The division plan for construction of defensive positions in Narvik, however, involved only the expansion and strengthening of the bunker system. It called for the construction of four additional reinforced concrete bunkers: one on the west side of the Framnes Peninsula, one near Vassvik, one at Ornes, and one at Ankenes on the west side of the harbor. The plan also called for supporting machinegun positions near at least two of these bunkers. The engineer company was tasked with building the bunkers. The regiment requested that the engineers also build the machinegun positions, but the division directed that infantry be used for that purpose. It appears that Colonel Sundlo also wanted to build machinegun positions along Rombakfjord. During his trial, Sundlo stated that he believed an enemy attack would come from the north side of town and he did not think a landing would take place directly in the harbor.[8]

Major Omdal's recommendation for the construction of machinegun positions in the harbor area was not acted on. Instead, infantry troops were to patrol or occupy posts along the 3-kilometer harbor area separating the two bunkers. There was only one prepared position between the two bunkers. This was a covered infantry position at the south end of the Iron Ore Pier. Infantry positions were also dug or blasted out of rocks along the north side of Framnes Peninsula, between Kvitvik and Lillevik.

There are differing reports on the general plan for defensive preparations. Colonel Sundlo still wanted to place the main defensive effort along the high ground on the city's northeastern side with a forward covering force, including machineguns, in the harbor area. General Fleischer did not agree. According to Sundlo, Fleischer wanted the defense to be concentrated on the western side of the city and as part of that decision, Sundlo was ordered to prepare positions for an infantry company along the northwestern slope of the Framnes Peninsula.

According to Sundlo, Fleischer confirmed this decision when he visited Narvik in early 1940. The division chief of staff, Major Odd Lindbäck-Larsen, stated later that the division did not tell the regimental commander how he should conduct the defense of the town and he found it unlikely that Fleischer would have ordered Sundlo to prepare infantry positions on Framnes Peninsula against the colonel's wishes and without telling the chief of staff. Lindbäck-Larsen stated that he was surprised to find defense works on that peninsula.

Fleischer inspected the Narvik defenses on March 7 and 8, 1940 and expressed his satisfaction with the progress. It seems strange that he would have approved the defense works on Framnes Peninsula if it were not his intention that they should be located there. According to his own testimony about the inspection, the chief of staff protested sharply the fact that there were no defensive positions in the harbor area. Fleischer did not support his arguments, stating that it was Sundlo's decision as to how he conducted the defense. According to Lindbäck-Larsen, this discussion led to a decision to place machineguns in the harbor area and to prepare a position at the southern end of the Iron Ore Pier.

The division directed the engineers to build bunkers at Vassvik and Ornes on March 18, and to construct an artillery bunker on Fagernes. The bunkers' exact locations were to be determined by Colonel Sundlo and the commander of 3rd Mountain Artillery Bn. Only the machinegun bunkers at Fagernes and Framnes were placed under the control of the regiment and occupied by infantry prior to April 8. The construction of the bunkers at Vassvik and Ornes had started. Those at Kvitvik and Ankenes were nearly complete but control had not been transferred to the regiment. Construction of the artillery bunker at Fagernes had not begun. The infantry positions in the Kvitvik-Lillevik area were to be completed by mid-April.

The defensive plans required that a reinforced infantry company maintain a state of readiness that would allow it to occupy all defensive positions in Narvik within three hours. The need for a higher readiness level was recognized after the navy announced that it could not provide three hours of early warning. The reinforced company earmarked for Narvik was located at Elvegårdsmoen in the inter-war period, not at Narvik. The tense situation after the *Altmark* incident and the need for a higher readiness level caused General Fleischer to move the reinforced company from Elvegårdsmoen to Narvik on February 17, 1940. He ordered Colonel Sundlo to prevent landings by foreign troops, regardless of nationality.

In hindsight it is easy to see where mistakes were made. The plan to mount the defense of the Ofot Railway in Narvik, particularly before all defensive works were completed, ignored a number of basic defensive principles.

An attacker would have dominance of the fjords and every part of the defense would be exposed to the devastating effects of close-range naval gunfire. The forces in Narvik were separated from the areas north of Ofotfjord and therefore from any reinforcements. There were no lines of communications through the mountain wilderness to the south. The positions in Narvik could easily be enveloped by enemy landings on the south side of Rombakfjord. These landing forces would isolate Narvik from the outside world. From the landing sites, an attacker could advance to the Swedish border virtually unopposed. He could also occupy the high ground east of Narvik, eliminating any realistic possibility of holding the town. If these military objections were not sufficient, there was the humanitarian factor. Why turn Narvik, with its 10,000 civilians, into a bloody battlefield when that was not necessary for defending the Ofot Railway?

The considerations enumerated above, along with the knowledge that the capture of Narvik was only important militarily to an enemy if it also included control of the railroad to the Swedish border, should have dictated a defense that did not involve trying to hold the town. It was not a prudent decision to meet an attack by an enemy with naval dominance at the water's edge. The attacker would have the advantage of selecting the point of attack, forcing the defender to spread his forces to meet threats from all directions. A fixed forward defense is usually unwise unless the defender has strong fortifications and sufficient reserves that can be moved quickly in response to a dangerous development. The inability of the Germans to move their reserves quickly to counter the landings in Normandy, because of Allied air dominance, virtually eliminated the value of their defensive works. In Narvik, there were neither strong defensive works nor any reserves.

A defense in the interior, along the railroad, would have had several obvious advantages. It would have spared the civilian population in Narvik, removed Norwegian forces from the reach of naval gunfire, made envelopment difficult, and forced an enemy to operate in a severe climate and unfamiliar terrain. From an interior position, contact could be established and maintained with Norwegian forces to the north.

Approximately 450 Norwegian troops were located in Narvik on April 8, but there were few infantry among them. The railroad gun had a crew of 8-10, the antiaircraft battery consisted of about 120 men, and the engineer company strength in Narvik was about 110. There was also a supply depot detachment of nine men. After making allowances for the skeleton regimental staff, Colonel Sundlo had approximately 190 infantry under his command in Narvik, but many of these were ordered away on April 8.

Naval Activities on April 8

April 8, 1940 was a busy and confusing day for the 3rd Naval District, as it was for the rest of the country's political and military leadership. The events started with British violations of Norwegian territorial waters early in the morning. The Norwegian patrol vessel *Syrian*, patrolling the outer area of Vestfjord, spotted several foreign warships on a southerly heading. These warships turned out to be eight British destroyers. Captain Kaaveland, *Syrian's* skipper, challenged the warships and demanded that they leave Norwegian territorial waters.

There was not much the 298-ton *Syrian*, with its crew of ten men armed with one 3-inch gun, could do to enforce its demands. The British destroyer *Hunter* answered the Norwegian challenge. The *Hunter's* signal read, "We will not leave territorial waters. You are heading towards a minefield. Stop immediately and await my further instructions."[9]

The British sent an officer aboard the patrol boat and the Norwegians were told that a minefield had been laid in the area and that British destroyers would remain in territorial waters for 48 hours to warn merchant vessels. Kaaveland received a map of the rectangular shaped minefield and a request to keep civilian vessels from approaching the minefield from the south. Kaaveland repeated his protest and stated that the mining operation would undoubtedly bring Norway into the war.

Syrian sent several messages to the 3rd Naval District about the British activities in Vestfjord and Captain Askim issued orders to stop all traffic in the area. The patrol boat *Svalbard II*, located in Bodø, was sent to guard the southern approaches to the minefield while the patrol boat *Kvitøy* was dispatched to Tjeldsund to stop southbound traffic. One ship stopped by *Kvitøy* was the German tanker *Jan Wellem*. The German plan called for this ship to sail from "Basis Nord" near Murmansk with fuel for the German destroyers. The ship was allowed to proceed to Narvik after the patrol boat skipper conferred with his superiors. Askim also directed that four patrol boats proceed to Ramsund Naval Depot to take aboard minesweeping equipment and prepare to sweep the British minefield.

The two coastal defense ships *Norge* and *Eidsvold* were anchored in Narvik on April 8. The submarines *B3* and *B1* were also in Narvik along with the submarine tender *Lyngen* and the patrol vessel *Senja*. The patrol boat *Kelt* was on patrol at the Ofotfjord entrance and the patrol vessel *Michael Sars* was in Lødingen, at the southern entrance to Tjelsund.

The British mining led Captain Askim to conclude that Norway would soon become involved in the war between Germany and Great Britain. He suspected that the British mining operation was only a first step and he expected a naval attack on the German ore ships in Narvik. Askim ordered his ships in Narvik to prepare for action. He also ordered Captain Brekke, the 3rd Submarine Division commander, to take his submarines and *Lyngen* to Liland on the north side of Ofotfjord. Brekke suggested that the submarines take their assigned positions in the fjord to launch torpedoes at any intruder. This suggestion was turned down and Brekke was later ordered to position the submarines inside Bogen to insure that they were not seen from the fjord.

The 3rd Naval District received the various intelligence reports discussed in Chapter 3. These reports were passed to subordinate units and to the 6th District Command. The report from the British Naval Staff that German naval forces were northbound and could reach Narvik by 2200 hours on April 8 had the greatest significance for Norwegian forces in North Norway. However, the report was passed to the 3rd Naval District with the comment that no one on the Norwegian Naval Staff believed it to be accurate.

Narvik was not a restricted area[10] and Askim contacted Admiral Diesen at 2345 hours to find out if there were any special instructions, particularly with respect to a possible British raid on the merchant ships in Narvik. Diesen's answer at midnight stated that force should be used to defend Narvik and the ships in the harbor. Askim sent this information to his subordinates. He also had a conference with Captain Odd Isachsen Willoch, *Eidsvold's* skipper.

The two captains decided that the coastal defense ships should meet an eventual attack on Narvik outside the harbor because of the many merchant ships located there.[11] This was a deviation from plans and the 3rd Naval District staff, 6th District Command, and Colonel Sundlo continued to assume that the two coastal defense ships were near the Ofotfjord entrance. The bad weather and very limited visibility appear to have been the reasons for this change in plans. *Eidsvold* took up a position outside the harbor entrance, about 500 meters from the Framnes shoreline, while *Norge* remained in the harbor. Both these senior naval officers realized that a fight between the two coastal defense ships and a substantial force of modern warships would be short.

Between 0130 and 0300 hours, the 3rd Naval District received several reports about shore batteries in the approaches to Oslo, Bergen, and Trondheim engaging foreign naval forces. The report from Bergen identified the warships as German. Captain Askim again called Admiral Diesen and asked if there were any instructions in case of a German attack on Narvik. It had finally become obvious to Diesen that such an attack was underway and, at 0420 hours, he amended his earlier instructions by ordering Askim to engage German warships but not to fire on British ships.

Askim increased the number of patrol craft at the Ofotfjord entrance from one to two after darkness on April 8. The patrol vessels had orders not to fire on foreign warships, only to report their sightings to the Ofot Division. At midnight, it was blowing a southwest breeze with frequent snow showers at the entrance to the fjord. Visibility was limited but the two patrol vessels maintained visual contact and had radio communications with *Norge*.

Army Activities on April 8

As already mentioned, General Fleischer and his chief of staff, Major Lindbäck-Larsen, were in East Finnmark, several hundred kilometers from Narvik on April 8. At about 1000 hours, the District Command notified the general by telephone that the British had mined Vestfjord. Fleischer took some tentative steps to prepare his command for possible war. He directed that quarters be requisitioned in Øyjord, which was across the fjord from Narvik, for a motorized mountain artillery battery. Øyjord was the planned position for an artillery battery to support the troops in Narvik. Fleischer also asked the District Command for an estimate of how soon the 2/15th Inf at Setermoen could be ready to move to Elvegårdsmoen.

Fleischer decided to remain in East Finnmark despite the gathering war clouds and the most serious breach to date of Norwegian neutrality. As previously planned, he went on maneuvers with the Varanger Battalion. In doing so, Fleischer removed himself from any means of communicating with his headquarters and subordinates during this crisis-filled day.

Major Lindbäck-Larsen left the maneuver in the afternoon and drove to Gornitak from where he was able to contact the District Command in Harstad. He was briefed on the situation, including the steps taken by the 3rd Naval District. Lindbäck-Larsen was informed that Askim had conferred with Colonel Sundlo.

The term "confer" may have given the recipients a false sense of security since it seemed to indicate that the army and navy were working closely together in Narvik. In fact, Askim was apparently not aware of what was happening in Narvik and Sundlo did not know that the coastal defense ships remained in or near the harbor instead of at the Ofotfjord entrance. Lindbäck-Larsen made several decisions on his own authority and communicated these to the District Command.

First, he directed the motorized artillery battery to move to Øyjord on April 9. It appears that this order did not reach the artillery battalion until 1750 hours. Second, he ordered the 2/15th Inf from Setermoen to Elvegårdsmoen as quickly as possible. It was assumed that this move would take place on April 9. Colonel Sundlo was not notified and learned about the order to reposition the battalion shortly before 0400 hours on April 9 when Colonel Løken called to coordinate the move.[12] Third, he ordered the deployment of sufficient machineguns and crews from Elvegårdsmoen to man all the bunkers in Narvik. Fourth, he gave a "be-prepared" order for the District Command to move from Harstad to Målselv. Finally, he requested an estimate on how quickly the Hålogaland Air Group could deploy to Bardufoss and ordered preparations for that move. General Fleischer arrived in Gornitak at 1800 hours and approved Lindbäck-Larsen's actions. The only change he made was to order the move of the District Command to Målselv on April 9. Thereupon, the general and his chief of staff drove to a hotel in Vadsø.

The District Command was informed around 1400 hours that German naval forces were northbound in the Kattegat and about the sinking of *Rio de Janeiro*. Lindbäck-Larsen does not mention receiving this intelligence when he talked to the District Command around 1600 hours. Captain Steen, in the official naval history, states that all important information received by the District Command from the 3rd Naval District, including the reports cited above, was forwarded immediately to General Fleischer and his principal subordinates. Furthermore, Captain Løken, the District Command's chief of staff, states that these reports were communicated to Major Lindbäck-Larsen in their telephone conversation at 1600 hours.

At 2000 hours, District Command gave Fleischer the British warning that German naval forces were on their way to Narvik and could be there as early as 2200 hours. The 3rd Naval District had received it by telephone from the naval staff at 1925 hours and, according to the naval history, forwarded it promptly to the District Command. Captain Løken claims that the report from the 3rd

Naval District was received at 2000 hours and a similar report from the General Staff arrived five minutes later.

Captain Løken also sent this report to Sundlo and asked what the colonel intended to do with respect to the defense of Narvik. Løken hinted that it might be a good idea to move the remainder of the 1/13th Inf into that city. Løken must have known that defense plans did not call for the move of the whole battalion to the south side of Ofotfjord. Colonel Sundlo answered that he still held the view that Narvik could not be defended by rifles against a naval force. Heavy guns were needed. Therefore, he did not plan to move the battalion to Narvik where it would be of no use.[13]

However, Colonel Sundlo did order Major Sverre Spjeldnæs, the commander of the 1/13th Inf, to send the machinegun company (Co 4) and the mortar platoon to Narvik. He also alerted Co 2, ordered that unit to send machinegun crews to the two bunkers, and directed its commander, Captain Langlo, to station an officer or senior NCO at each bunker. On his own initiative, Sundlo increased the strength of the guard detail at Nordal Bridge from 10 to 32 troops. This was done around 1800 hours, before the conversation with Captain Løken.

Lindbäck-Larsen's version is different. He writes that General Fleischer ordered the movement of the 1/13th Inf from Elvegårdsmoen to Narvik after the news he received at 2000 hours and that the above statement by Colonel Sundlo was made when the District Command forwarded that order. Under this version, Sundlo's statement was tantamount to a refusal to obey an order. Lindbäck-Larsen's version is suspect and must be viewed in the context of what he writes in the same report:

> It was the division's wish to provoke a disobedience, which would make the removal of Colonel Sundlo from his command justifiable since the division viewed him as not being up to the demands that the current situation would require. The division order was also given the colonel in the most ostentatious way by Colonel Mjelde …[14]

Lindbäck-Larsen's version of events and a distorted interpretation of Colonel Sundlo's reaction to a later directive about firing on Germans but not on the British, led—according to Fleischer's chief of staff—to a decision to remove the colonel from his command.

District Command passed Colonel Sundlo's views on bringing additional infantry to Narvik to General Fleischer. On receipt of this information, Fleischer ordered Sundlo, via the District Command, to move the battalion immediately from Elvegårdsmoen to Narvik. If possible, the machineguns and their crews were to move within one hour. This order was issued at 2050 hours. Sundlo had already directed the machinegun company and the mortar platoon to Narvik. Prior to this order, the war plans did not give him authority to move the whole battalion into Narvik, even if he wished to do so, since that would leave Elvegårdsmoen defenseless. Sundlo told Colonel Mjelde, who had conveyed Fleischer's order, that it was impossible to move the two machinegun platoons to Narvik in one hour. Colonel Mjelde answered that it was an order and as such had to be carried out as quickly as possible, if not feasible in one hour. Sundlo stated that he would comply.

At the same time as he ordered the battalion into Narvik, the division commander, again through Colonel Mjelde, asked for confirmation that Colonel Sundlo understood that his mission to defend Narvik was absolute. If Sundlo did not understand his mission clearly, General Fleischer requested that he state so immediately.[15]

It appears that General Fleischer used Colonel Mjelde as an intermediary in dealing with Colonel Sundlo. Fleischer's lack of direct contact with his subordinates during the most critical phase of Norway's modern history came up during Sundlo's trial in 1947. Lindbäck-Larsen explained that Fleischer was reluctant to deal directly with subordinate commanders when he was away from his headquarters and that this had become a "principle." As a result, the District Command functioned as a relay. It forwarded reports to the division commander and orders from the division to subordinate units. It is difficult to see any valid purpose in such an arrangement as long as the general and his chief of staff had means of communications at their disposal. Except for the afternoon of April 8, Fleischer could communicate directly with his subordinates as easily as he did with Mjelde. There appears to have been no direct contact between the general or his chief of staff and his two principal subordinates in the Troms/Ofoten region, Løken and Sundlo, before Narvik was captured.

At about 2050 hours and again through District Command, General Fleischer directed Colonel Løken to "Prepare the 2nd Battalion, 15th Infantry Regiment, including necessary trains, for transport by motor vehicles to the Narvik area. Orders for execution to follow."[16] This appears to be a repeat of directions Lindbäck-Larsen allegedly gave earlier that afternoon. Both Lindbäck-Larsen and Sandvik state that the move was to take place on April 9.

The District Command forwarded another order from General Fleischer at 2055 hours. This one directed the commander of the 3rd Artillery Bn, Lieutenant Colonel Hornslien, to move the motorized field artillery battery in Målselv to Øyjord that night, if possible. An advanced party was to leave for Øyjord at once. Colonel Sundlo was ordered to provide a work-detail to clear snow at the battery position. This work-detail came from Sundlo's resources in Narvik and proceeded to Øyjord before midnight. The battery of four 75mm guns was created specifically to provide artillery support for the troops in Narvik. The explanation for locating the battery in Målselv, more than 50 miles from its designated wartime position, is that it was a better location for training and maneuvers.

At around 2100 hours, Colonel Sundlo ordered Major Spjeldnæs to move the rest of his battalion to Narvik as quickly as possible and gave him a brief account of what was happening. The colonel also called a hurried staff meeting at his headquarters. He gave the staff a quick orientation on the situation, as he knew it, and ordered the preparations required to receive the battalion. This meeting took place between 2100 and 2130 hours.

Sundlo did not ask the commander of Co 2, Captain Langlo, to attend the meeting since that company was placed on full alert around 2000 hours and he felt that under these circumstances the commander's place was with his unit. The company executive officer, Captain Dalsve, attended the meeting and he was expected to brief Langlo. Some of Langlo's later statements to his subordinates indicate that he did not understand the situation.[17] The commanders of the engineer company, the railcar-mounted 75mm gun detachment, and the supply organization were not present at the meeting and Colonel Sundlo neglected to inform them about the events that were taking place. In addition, the chief of police and other civilian authorities were not notified.

Sundlo briefed Lieutenant Munthe-Kaas, the acting commander of the antiaircraft battery, about 2150 hours. He ordered Munthe-Kaas to insure that the guns were manned. The lieutenant pointed out that the battery did not have searchlights and it was impossible to pick out targets in the dark without them. Munthe-Kaas recommended that the personnel under his command be allowed to rest until morning and occupy the gun positions at first light. Sundlo agreed, provided that a skeleton crew was maintained at the battery during the night.[18] This detail was given to a sergeant and ten men.

The battery's primary mission was to engage enemy aircraft and the guns were therefore located on the high ground at Framnes. From that location, they could fire on targets in the fjord but not on targets in the harbor.

It took some time to move the battalion from Elvegårdsmoen to Narvik at night in a snowstorm. The ferry moved from Vassvik to Øyjord where it was ready to start loading at midnight. The distance from Elvegårdsmoen to Øyjord is 13 kilometers and the distance across the fjord is less than 5 kilometers. The ferry had to make several trips to bring the battalion to Vassvik and the turnaround time was about one hour. The battalion started its move from Elvegårdsmoen around midnight. It brought along the battle and kitchen trains. The pack train and trucks were left behind. Company 4 with two platoons (one platoon was already in Narvik) and the battalion commander with a small staff traveled to Øyjord by motor vehicles and made the first trip across the fjord. These troops arrived in Narvik between 0130 and 0200 hours. The second ferry carried Co 3 and part of the trains. The ferry captain refused to load the horses because of heavy seas in the fjord. Consequently, the sleds for the trains were loaded manually and unloaded in Vassvik in the same manner. Company 3 arrived in Narvik about 0300 hours. The ferry brought Co 1 to Vassvik on its third trip. The company had to wait in Øyjord for over one hour and arrived in Vassvik about 0445 hours.

In Sundlo's staff meeting at 2100 hours it was decided not to move the arriving units into defense positions immediately. Sundlo directed that the troops take up quarters in various locations in town to rest up and dry out from their rigorous travels. The troops were told to remain in battle gear and be prepared to move out on short notice. Officers were directed to remain with their units.

In view of what was known at the time, this was a logical decision. First, the only threat warning against Narvik came from the British and the Norwegian military authorities in Oslo passed it to General Fleischer and Captain Askim with the observation that it was not believable. Even Fleischer and his chief of staff concluded that the British report must have been false, since the authorities in Oslo did not order mobilization. They both expected a quiet night when they went to sleep. Second, Sundlo, the District Command and the 3rd Naval District believed that the two coastal defense ships had left the harbor to take up their planned positions at the Ofotfjord entrance. The distance from the early-warning patrol line at the Ofotfjord entrance to Narvik was approximately 60 kilometers (37 miles) and enemy warships, even if they traveled at maximum speed, would need more than one hour to reach the town. Even if he had known that the coastal defense ships had not taken up positions at the Ofotfjord entrance, it was reasonable for Sundlo to assume that the early-warning patrol vessels, with radios, would provide sufficient warning of an enemy approach to allow the troops in the city to take up defensive positions.

The decision not to deploy the forces immediately was sensible for yet another reason, although there is no evidence that it was an important factor in Sundlo's mind. The Norwegian forces were inadequate to defend a relatively long stretch of shoreline. It would be wise to keep relatively large reserves until the enemy's landing site was identified. If Sundlo deployed the forces as they arrived, he ran the risk of having only a small portion of his force covering the actual landing site and few, if any, reserves at his disposal. By retaining a sizable reserve and quickly moving it to the threatened location, it was possible for the Norwegians to muster sufficient combat power to frustrate an attacker.

Colonel Sundlo briefed Major Spjeldnæs when he arrived in Narvik. Apparently, both Major Spjeldnæs and Major Omdal, who was also present at the briefing, considered the decisions taken by Colonel Sundlo reasonable. At least they did not register any objections.[19]

Sundlo expected a mobilization order and he remained near a telephone in his headquarters all night. District Command had not informed him about the message it received from the General Staff at 2125 hours stating that a decision on mobilization would not be taken until the following morning. Sundlo was beginning to suspect that the warships approaching Bergen and Trondheim were the same ships that the report received at 2000 hours claimed were on their way to Narvik. Starting around 0300 hours, he tried to contact District Command by telephone but was unable to get through. Captain Dalsve, who was present, testified that the District Command had still not answered when he left the regimental headquarters at 0330 hours.

NOTES

1 Quoted in Trygve Sandvik, *Operasjonene til lands i Nord-Norge 1940* (2 vols; Oslo: Forsvarets Krigshistoriske Avdeling, 1965), vol. 1, p. 65.

2 Carl Gustav Fleischer, *Efterlatte papirer* (Tønsberg: Tønsbergs aktietrykkeris forlag i kommisjon hos T. Landberg, 1947), p.17.

3 The fact that a number of officers and NCOs in the units undergoing mobilization were in other parts of the country at the time of the German attack caused problems. Few of these individuals were able to reach their units. Some who did manage the long journey did so in fishing vessels or by traveling through Sweden.

4 Odd Lindbäck-Larsen, *Rapport om 6. Divisjons-kommandos virksomhet under nøytralitetvakten 1939-40 og felttoget 1940* Section 1, pp. 4-5.

5 Palle Ydstebø, *Geostrategi, trusselvurdering og operativ planlegging. Forsvaret av Nord-Norge 1880-1920* (Tromso: University of Tromso, 2000), p. 141.

6 Ydstebø, *Geostrategi*, p. 154.

7 Sandvik, *Operasjonene*, vol. 1, p. 80.

8 Sandvik, *Operasjonene*,, vol. 1, p. 83.

9 Steen, *Norges Sjøkrig 1940-1945*, vol. 4, p. 44.

10 At the outbreak of World War 2, Foreign Minister Koht suggested that Narvik be declared a restricted military zone. The 6th Division supported this suggestion but it met serious opposition from the permanent undersecretary at the Foreign Office and from the military authorities. Their argument was that to take such action after the outbreak of hostilities might be interpreted as provocative by the belligerents.

11 There were 27 merchant ships in Narvik on April 8. These included ten German iron ore freighters and the German tanker *Jan Wellem*. In addition, there were four Norwegian, six Swedish, one Dutch, and five British merchant ships in the harbor.

12 Colonel Løken's report on February 21, 1941 as quoted in Sandvik, *Operasjonene* , vol. 1, p. 93.

13 Report by Captain Løken on November 9, 1945 as quoted in Sandvik, *Operasjonene*, vol. 1, p. 94 and Colonel Sundlo's report on December 14, 1941 as quoted in Steen, *Norges Sjøkrig 1940-1945*, vol. 4, p.59.

14 Lindbäck-Larsen,, *Rapport* Section 4, p. 3.

15 Report by Captain Løken dated November 9, 1945 as quoted in Steen, *Norges Sjøkrig 1940-1945*, vol. 4, p. 59.

16 Steen, *Norges Sjøkrig 1940-1945*, vol. 4, p. 59.

17 In answer to questions from his subordinates about what was going on when he ordered the bunkers occupied, he allegedly told them that he did not know. Some subordinates thought the whole thing was one of the periodic alerts and not the real thing. See letters and reports from two lieutenants and one sergeant in 1940 and 1946 as quoted in Sandvik, *Operasjonene*, vol. 1, pp. 100-101. It is doubtful that this apparent lack of information stems from Captain Dalsve failing to brief Captain Langlo. Sundlo briefed Langlo and others on the developing situation at 1700 hours. Langlo spoke with Sundlo on several occasions that night and received orders to reinforce the guard detail at Nordal Bridge, to place his company on alert, to send a snow removal detail to Øyord, and to send an officer or NCO to each of two bunkers. It is very unlikely that the reasons for these orders were not mentioned or that Captain Langlo failed to ask the reasons for these actions.

18 Witness statement by Captain Munthe-Kaas on April 22, 1947 as quoted in Sandvik, *Operasjonene*, vol. 1, p. 98.

19 Report by Major Spjeldnæs on August 27, 1940 and report by Major Omdal on May 23, 1940 as quoted in Sandvik, *Operasjonene,* vol. 1, p. 102.

5

GERMAN ATTACK ON NARVIK

"Act with the greatest decisiveness in your approach
to the designated debarkation harbors and do not permit signals
to stop or other actions by military authorities, patrol vessels,
or fortresses to keep you from reaching your objectives."
ADMIRAL RAEDER'S INSTRUCTIONS TO HIS COMMANDERS
FOR THE PROSECUTION OF OPERATION WESERÜBUNG

The German Attack Force

Task Force 1 was approaching Narvik at high speed in the early morning hours of April 9, 1940. It consisted of three destroyer flotillas commanded by Captain Friedrich Bonte.[1]

The 1st Destroyer Flotilla, commanded by Commander Fritz Berger, consisted of two ships, *Wilhelm Heidkamp* and *Georg Thiele*. Berger was aboard *Georg Thiele* while the navy and army component commanders were aboard *Wilhelm Heidkamp*.

The 3rd Destroyer Flotilla, commanded by Commander Hans-Joachim Gadow, consisted of four ships: *Hans Lüdemann*, *Hermann Künne*, *Diether von Roeder*, and *Anton Schmitt*. Commander Gadow was aboard *Hans Lüdemann*.

The 4th Destroyer Flotilla, under Commander Erich Bey, also consisted of four ships: *Wolfgang Zenker*, *Bernd von Arnim*, *Erich Giese*, and *Erich Koellner*. Bey was aboard *Wolfgang Zenker*.

The German destroyers were modern warships, launched between 1935 and 1938. The destroyers *Wilhelm Heidkamp*, *Hans Lüdemann*, *Hermann Künne*, *Diether von Roeder*, and *Anton Schmitt* had a displacement of 2,411 tons. Their armament consisted of five 5-inch guns, four 37mm antiaircraft guns, and eight 21-inch torpedo tubes. They could reach a maximum speed of 38 knots and each had a crew of 315 men. The other five destroyers were somewhat smaller, with a displacement of 2,270 tons; however, they had the same armament, speed and crew as their larger brothers. There were about 3,150 naval personnel in Task Force 1.

The army component of TF 1 consisted of three battalions of the reinforced 139th Mountain Regiment of the 3rd Mountain Division.[2] The troops were for the most part Austrian. Colonel Alois Windisch was the regimental commander.[3] There were also advanced elements of the 3rd Mountain Division staff, a company of naval artillery, and intelligence and signal elements. Total strength was approximately 2,000 and the troops were divided equally among the 10 destroyers. Major General Dietl assumed command during and after the landing.

General Dietl

Eduard Wolrath Christian Dietl was born on July 21, 1890 in Oberbayern. He came from a middle class family of artisans and soldiers. Dietl's favorite hobbies were skiing and mountain climbing. He won numerous national and international sport awards and was captain of the German ski team at the 1936 Winter Olympics.

Dietl chose a military career, but his un-soldierly appearance kept him from being accepted in an infantry regiment from Bamberg. His second try resulted in an appointment, on October 1, 1909, in the 5th Bavarian Inf Regt. Dietl attended the Munich Military Academy and was commissioned a Lieutenant on October 26, 1911.

He began his service in World War I as a machinegun company commander. The courage and daring for which he became famous was quickly tested in the heavy fighting in Lorraine where he became the first German soldier in the war to receive the Iron Cross, 2nd Class. A couple of days later he was wounded and his two brothers killed. Dietl served as a company commander during the whole war, participated in the battles of Somme, Arras, and Flanders, and was wounded three times. The end of the war found him in a military hospital.

Dietl became a company commander in Freikorps Epp after the war and participated in the fighting against the communists. Later, he entered the Reichswehr and was assigned as company commander in the 3/19th Bavarian Inf. It was at this time that he became acquainted with Hitler. He and his company stood ready to support Hitler and his followers during the Beer Hall Putsch on November 9, 1923, but they were not called on to act. Subsequently, Dietl became an instructor in tactics at the Munich Infantry School and on October 1, 1928, he assumed command of the 3/19th Bavarian Inf. Dietl rose rapidly in rank. He was promoted to major on February 1, 1930, to lieutenant colonel on January 1, 1933, and to colonel exactly two years later. At the same time as he was promoted to colonel, he assumed command of the 99th Mountain Regiment in Füssen. Following the occupation of Austria, he was promoted to major general and assumed command of the 3rd Mountain Division. The division operated in the Carpathian Mountains during the Polish Campaign.

Dietl had some familiarity with Norway since he had undergone winter training in that country. He was in Norway for a two-month period in 1930 and 1931, attending the Infantry Winter School at Terningmoen in eastern Norway.

Dietl was respected and beloved by his soldiers. The loyalty and respect worked both ways as is illustrated by his concept of leadership:

> Soldiers must be led by the heart. Only then are they committed … He who has the soldier's heart can defy the devil in hell … Leadership calls for two separate things. The first is definitely, live with the man. Wish to have nothing but what he has. Go with him, listen to him, understand him, and help him in tough places. However, the second is, be better than the man. Never forgive yourself anything. Always know what you as a leader have to do. Be hard if necessary, demand the utmost, but first do the outmost yourself.[4]

Dietl's motto was "rules don't apply." This may in part explain some incidents that led the Norwegians to accuse the Germans of violating the recognized rules of war. Dietl was an ardent Nazi before the Beer Hall Putsch and he was one of Hitler's favorites. Dietl ventured everything on living up to Hitler's friendship and expectation. He faced the most difficult task in the German attack on Norway. Later in the war, he commanded the 20th Mountain Army in operations on the Murmansk front. He died in an airplane crash on June 23, 1944.

The German Plan

General von Falkenhorst issued a special directive for the attack on Narvik. In summary, it called for the 139th Mountain Regiment to capture Narvik, the army depot at Elvegårdsmoen, and the fortifications that the Germans mistakenly believed existed on both sides of Ofotfjord near Ramsund. Steen writes that the Germans had been informed, by Quisling among others, that shore batteries existed here. This information was allegedly given to Colonel Piekenbrock when he met Quisling in Copenhagen on April 4, 1940 (see Chapter 2, note 31). This is an unlikely scenario and Steen gives no source for his claim.[5] First, Quisling and his followers certainly had accurate information and if the intelligence had come from them, von Falkenhorst would have known that there were no coastal batteries covering the approaches to Narvik. Second, von Falkenhorst's operational directive for the occupation of Narvik is dated March 12, 1940, almost a month before the meeting between Quisling and Piekenbrock in Copenhagen.

Von Falkenhorst's overall goal in the Narvik operation was to secure the Norwegian part of the railroad to the Swedish iron district. After reaching the Swedish border, the troops were to be prepared to continue their advance to Kiruna. As far as possible, the operation was to have the character of a peaceful occupation. However, any resistance was to be met with all available resources. The communications and economy in this part of Norway were not be disrupted or interfered with unless necessary to accomplish the missions. The same applied to people's individual freedom and official duties. The fortifications near Ramsund were to be made ready for use by the German forces as quickly as possible. To strengthen the Norwegian coastal fortifications, antiaircraft weapons and a 6-inch battery were to arrive by transports. General Dietl was to establish contact with the German consul in Narvik and with the "reportedly pro-German" commandant, Colonel Sundlo.[6] The Norwegian Army depot at Elvegårdsmoen was to be occupied, peacefully if possible. Weapons and ammunitions at the depot were to be seized only if the loyalty of the Norwegian troops was suspect. The directive stressed that the honor and pride of the Norwegian defense forces should be respected and safeguarded. Norwegian troops were to be demobilized and allowed to return to their homes if they did not show hostile intent.

In case the destroyers could not force their way past the Norwegian fortifications, the landing was to take place at Elvenes, 18 miles north of Narvik, and the objectives were to be seized by overland movements, including the District Command headquarters in Harstad. Contact was to be established with the 6th Division in an attempt to secure its loyal support. Norwegian forces that threatened the area occupied by the Germans were to be neutralized or destroyed. Norwegian units along the Finnish and Soviet borders were to continue their missions. Tromsø was not to be seized until von Falkenhorst gave the order, but Bardufoss was to be captured and made operational for German aircraft as quickly as possible.

Units earmarked for reinforcements were first the two battalions of the 138th Mountain Regiment landed in Trondheim. They would be sent to Narvik by sea or air. The rest of the 3rd Mountain Division would move from Oslo to Trondheim by train. Transport from Trondheim would be by sea or air, unless transit through Sweden was permitted.

The naval operational orders, applicable to all task forces, also stipulated that the operation should be carried out by peaceful means, if possible. The orders emphasized that naval guns and other weapons were to be used only if the Norwegians fired the first shot. The German Navy's operational order left no doubt about this matter, stating that warning shots by Norwegians were not sufficient grounds to open fire. The destroyers in TF 1 were to depart Narvik for their return to Germany as quickly as the situation allowed. It was expected that they would rendezvous with the two battleships and the ships from TF 2.

The German Approach and Norwegian Reactions

Admiral Lütjens released TF 1 at 2000 hours on April 8 for its run up Vestfjord. A northwest gale was blowing, with snow squalls, and the ships had great difficulties in the turbulent seas. At times, the heavy seas virtually buried the German warships and washed overboard much of the weaponry and ammunition stored on deck. The high-speed run up the long and treacherous fjord under gale conditions in total darkness, relying mainly on dead reckoning, was a navigational feat of the first order. Captain Peter Dickens of the Royal Navy is not alone in his admiration for the German accomplishment:[7]

> Given the highest navigational skill it was still a courageous act to press on into evermore confined waters, and Bonte's heart must have been in his mouth. How could he be sure that the right allowances had been made for factors such as leeway, increased distance traveled when the gale had been astern and a reduction now that it was on the port bow and the ships were straining into it? There would also have been inaccuracies in steering and engine revolutions that were unavoidable in heavy weather and incalculable. Nevertheless he made for the entrance, as the British in no more difficult circumstances, did not.

The conditions improved as the destroyers came leeward of the Lofoten Islands, but it was still blowing a gale with heavy snow squalls and it was not until they had a sure fix on the land that the nightmarish navigational situation was somewhat alleviated. The fact that the navigational lights in Vestfjord remained lit was of considerable help as the German ships neared the entrance to

Ofotfjord. Nevertheless, there were times when violent evasive maneuvers were necessary to avoid colliding with cliffs along the route.

Task Force 1 entered Ofotfjord at 0310 hours on April 9. The ships were traveling in column at 30 knots with Captain Bonte's flagship, *Wilhelm Heidkamp*, in the lead. Dawn was breaking but visibility was still severely limited by snow squalls. Both *Michael Sars* and *Kelt*, patrolling the waters between Barøy and Tjeldøy, observed the lead German warship and informed Captain Askim by radio. In the span of ten minutes, another eight German destroyers passed the patrol boats. This information, along with the observation that the warships were German, was also reported to the Ofot Division. The two patrol boats sent separate messages and this caused some unfortunate confusion. *Kelt* identified the ships as German while *Michael Sars* referred to them only as foreign warships.

Kelt gave an accurate report when it identified nine German destroyers. The *Erich Giese* became separated from the rest before the encounter with *Glowworm*. The toppling waves had flooded her gyro room and navigation was by a magnetic compass that gyrated violently as the ship was tossed around in the violent seas. In the afternoon of April 8, Lieutenant Commander Karl Smidt, *Erich Giese's* skipper, brought his ship around to pick up a soldier who had washed overboard. The soldier was saved but the rescue operation caused *Erich Giese* to fall even further behind the rest of the task force. The destroyer was running low on fuel and the ship's violent movements in the northwesterly gale caused the pumps to lose suction sporadically. Speed was reduced to conserve fuel and *Erich Giese* had fallen about 50 miles behind when the rest of the task force entered Ofotfjord.

The reports from the two patrol vessels at the entrance to Ofotfjord reached Captain Askim at 0310 hours, with the last message from *Kelt* coming in at 0320 hours, and he ordered battle stations on *Norge*. Askim also alerted Captain Willoch in the other coastal defense ship. The 3rd Naval District was informed by radio via the communications center in Tromsø at 0320 hours. The message from *Norge* to the communications center identified the force simply as "foreign warships." The 3rd Naval District informed District Command in Harstad at 0337 hours. The message to District Command read, "From the commanding officer *Norge*. *Michael Sars* reports foreign warships entering Ofotfjord. *Norge* and *Eidsvold* are casting off."[8]

Captain Askim, located about two kilometers from Colonel Sundlo, knew around 0310 hours that foreign warships had entered Ofotfjord. Askim reported that he tried to warn Sundlo but was unable to make contact since the telephone line from ship to shore was broken when the aft lines were cut loose. He did ask a harbor official to warn Norwegian ships in the harbor but neglected to ask him to warn the army.[9] Captain Steen observes,

> As a result of this [failure to notify Colonel Sundlo directly], valuable time was lost. If the captain had managed to give this report, the colonel would have received it approximately 40 minutes earlier than he did, and he would also have received it in the correct version, that Germans ships were approaching in the fjord.[10]

The one-hour warning time the army expected was reduced to 10–20 minutes.

The exact time Colonel Sundlo learned that foreign warships were approaching is somewhat uncertain. Steen and Hovland give the time as about 0400 hours. Sandvik writes that Sundlo was informed at 0337 hours. It was probably later, since the District Command received the message from the 3rd Naval District at 0337. Sandvik writes that the 6th Division was informed at 0400 hours, although Lindbäck-Larsen claims it was 0345 hours, and it is logical to assume that Sundlo received the information about that time. Whatever the exact hour, the slow pace of passing information cost the forces in Narvik valuable preparation time.

Shortly after 0430 hours, Colonel Sundlo received another message that caused uncertainty and that gives some insight into the intrigues going on in the 6th Division. Lindbäck-Larsen writes that the District Command reported that it had received an order from the General Staff at 0330 hours not to fire on British and French warships. The same report stated that when informed about the order, Sundlo had commented, "in other words, the Germans are to be fired on but not the British." Sandvik writes that Colonel Mjelde reported this conversation to General Fleischer "in view of Colonel Sundlo's well-known attitude towards the Germans." According to Lindbäck-Larsen, the decision was made to relieve Sundlo of his command after this comment. Lindbäck-Larsen writes that before they were able to contact Narvik to carry out the decision, the report arrived (0345 hours according to him) that foreign warships had entered Ofotfjord. This made it too late to make a command change.

Some claims in Lindbäck-Larsen's report on this event fail to stand up to close scrutiny. Sundlo admitted having made the above statement when Captain

Knudsen at the District Command relayed the General Staff message, but only for the sake of repeating the order to make sure he understood it correctly. Navy Captain Siem, Chief of Sea Transport at District Command, who was present when the conversation took place, also concluded that Sundlo was only trying to clarify the order.[11] The naval history and a report by the District Command, backed by telephone logs, show that the order from the General Staff arrived at 0430, not at 0330. This time is undoubtedly correct since the Commander-in-Chief of the Navy sent out a similar order to the 3rd Naval District, where it arrived at 0420 hours.[12] If Fleischer decided to relieve Colonel Sundlo prior to 0430 hours, he could not base or justify that decision on Sundlo's reaction to a General Staff order that had not yet arrived.

Fleischer and his chief of staff assumed they would have a quiet night at their hotel in Vadsø after receiving a message from the General Staff around 2200 hours. District Command received the message at 2125 hours. It announced that a decision on mobilization would not be taken until the following morning.[13] Based on what Lindbäck-Larsen writes, both he and Fleischer concluded that this message from the General Staff meant that the earlier British warning about Germans reaching Narvik by 2200 hours was false. District Command did not forward this message to Sundlo.

Lindbäck-Larsen was awakened around 0300 hours (0315 according to Sandvik) by a telephone call from District Command, which related that foreign warships were attacking Oslo, Bergen, and Trondheim. Lindbäck-Larsen requested District Command to insure that the battalion from Elvegårdsmoen had reached Narvik and that all bunkers were occupied. He also directed that the movement of the 2/15th Inf and the motorized artillery battery from Setermoen be expedited.

The 3rd Naval District's chief of staff notified General Fleischer around 0345 hours that foreign warships had entered Ofotfjord. This message was followed 15 minutes later by a similar report from the District Command. At the same time, District Command reported that all was ready in Narvik. This statement was apparently in answer to Lindbäck-Larsen's request 45 minutes earlier for confirmation that the battalion from Elvegårdsmoen had reached Narvik and that the bunkers were occupied. What the District Command used as a basis for the claim that all was ready in Narvik is not known. Colonel Sundlo tried unsuccessfully to contact District Command from 0300 until at least 0330 hours. It is true that the machinegun crews had occupied the bunkers the previous evening but the movement of the battalion was not completed.

Fleischer decided to return to his headquarters and two naval aircraft were placed at his disposal for transport from Vadsø to Tromsø.

The patrol vessel *Senja* left Narvik at 0135 hours to escort merchant ships past the British minefield in Vestfjord. At 0340 hours, the patrol boat sighted a warship, believed to be a British destroyer, near Ramnes. This report reached Captain Askim but it was interpreted as a British cruiser. His reaction, according to Steen, was, *"Thank God, there are also British ships in the Fjord."* As *Senja* approached to challenge the warship, it turned out to be German. A second German destroyer was also sighted. This information was transmitted to Captain Askim by radio but, for unknown reasons, he did not receive the report. The Germans sent an armed boarding party aboard the Norwegian ship, put its radio out of commission, removed critical parts from the 76mm gun, and ordered the skipper to proceed to Narvik. Captain Askim had ordered the patrol vessels at the Ofotfjord entrance not to engage foreign warships. This was a sensible order in view of the disparity in size and armaments between these small vessels and destroyers. *Senja* arrived in Narvik at 0630 hours.

Search for Shore Batteries

The German forces approaching Narvik were divided into three groups: Group West, Group Narvik, and Group Elvegårdsmoen. These groups were to carry out nearly simultaneous attacks on the three main objectives.

Group West consisted of the 3rd Destroyer Flotilla (*Hans Lüdemann, Anton Schmitt*, and *Diether von Roeder*) and the troops aboard these destroyers. Captain Bonte detached the 3rd Destroyer Flotilla at 0340 hours. Group West's mission was to land two infantry companies to capture the non-existent Norwegian shore batteries at Ramnes and Hamnnes. *Anton Schmitt* was to land the reinforced Co 1 on the south side of Ofotfjord, in a small side fjord called Vargfjord. The plan called for the company to advance across the narrow peninsula and attack the imaginary Hamnnes battery from the rear. Thereafter, the company would continue along the north shore of Vargfjord and attack a battery the Germans believed was located at Jevik. Company 1 belonged to the 1st Battalion, which landed at Bjerkvik.

Hans Lüdemann was to land the reinforced Co 6 at Skarvik, just east of Ramnes. The company would advance westward and attack the Ramnes battery from the rear. Company 6 belonged to the 2nd Battalion, which landed in Narvik. The two destroyers remained in the fjord, prepared to support the operation with naval gunfire. These were the two destroyers encountered by

Senja. The reserve for these two landings was aboard *Diether von Roeder.* This destroyer positioned itself near Barøy where it would be near enough to the landing sites quickly to land the reserve and at the same time be in position to assist *Erich Giese* when she arrived, should that be necessary.

The German troops exhausted themselves in a fruitless search in six feet of snow for the non-existent guns. They reembarked on destroyers around 0700 hours and landed in Narvik.

Capture of Elvegårdsmoen

Elvegårdsmoen was a major mobilization center as well as the training area for the 15th Infantry Regiment, the Hålogaland Engineer Battalion, and several smaller units. It was a major weapons, ammunition, and supply depot. Among the items at the depot were 4,000 rifles, 2,000 carbines, 600 handguns, 222 machineguns, 14 mortars, 1.5 million rounds of ammunition, and huge stores of uniforms, supplies, and food.

It was Group Elvegårdsmoen's mission to capture this depot. The group consisted of the 4th Destroyer Flotilla (*Wolfgang Zenker, Hermann Künne, Erich Koellner,* and *Erich Giese*) carrying 1st and 3rd Battalions of the 139th Mountain Regiment, commanded by Colonel Windisch. The 1st Battalion was short one company, which was part of Group West. The landing force was also short about 200 men who had embarked on *Erich Giese,* which had still not arrived. Bonte released the 4th Destroyer Flotilla at 0410 hours and the three destroyers proceeded on a northeasterly course. The troops were landed at a wooden pier in Bjerkvik from the destroyers' boats. The landing was unopposed and the troops advanced towards Elvegårdsmoen as soon as they came ashore.

When Major Spjeldnæs took his battalion to Narvik, he left a guard detail of 17 men from Co 3 at Elvegårdsmoen. In addition, there were about 150 non-combat personnel at the depot. It appears that Spjeldnæs failed to appoint a camp commander when he departed and the senior officer failed to assume command. Steen and Sandvik write that Spjeldnæs viewed the repositioning of the battalion as an administrative move and neglected to brief those left behind. The two authors claim that this behavior evidently stemmed from Colonel Sundlo not giving Spjeldnæs a reason for moving the battalion to Narvik.

However, it seems unlikely that Sundlo failed to give a reason for the move or that Spjeldnæs failed to ask why the colonel deployed his battalion with live ammunition and a battle train, on short notice, at night, and in a snowstorm. Spjeldnæs' own testimony fails to support the claim. Sundlo talked to Spjeldnæs at 2000 hours when he ordered the machinegun company and mortar platoon into Narvik and again around 2100 hours when he ordered the major to bring the rest of the battalion. While Spjeldnæs could not recall the details of the conversations, he was sure that the colonel gave the reason for the move during the second call.[14] Thus, he had no reasons to view the deployment as an administrative move.

The Norwegians at Elvegårdsmoen were warned about the approaching Germans 15 minutes before they arrived. The officers left behind at the depot spent those 15 minutes discussing whether they should issue live ammunition to the 17 troops. They could not reach a decision and the arrival of the German troops interrupted their discussion. Elvegårdsmoen was captured without a shot being fired. General Hovland writes that the depot commander surrendered the place after a telephone conference with Colonel Sundlo. This telephone call, which must have been made in the 15 minutes between the time Elvegårdsmoen learned about the approach of German troops and their arrival, a period when Sundlo was apparently away from his headquarters, is not mentioned in the official histories. In the end, it does not matter since there was little 17 soldiers could do against two battalions of elite troops.

Hurriedly moving the entire 1/13th Inf into Narvik only exacerbated the defense problems in the Narvik area. All the disadvantages of mounting a defense on the Narvik Peninsula were still valid and in the process, the depot was lost intact. Military planners must have realized that the seizure of military depots was an important supporting objective in securing Narvik and the railroad to Sweden. Their capture would prevent or disrupt any mobilization that might threaten the attackers hold on Narvik.

If it were General Fleischer's plan all along to bring the entire 1/13th Inf into Narvik in a crisis, it would have been prudent to plan for the defense or destruction of the depot at Elvegårdsmoen. To rely on the 2/15th Inf unit, which had to travel more than 40 miles over bad roads in wintertime was not a good solution. This is undoubtedly the reason the defense plan called for no less than one third of the battalion, at least a reinforced infantry company, to remain on the north side of Ofotfjord.

A reinforced infantry company could not hold Elvegårdsmoen, but it might have delayed the Germans long enough to permit the destruction of some of the valuable stores that fell into their hands. The captured food stores alone were sufficient to feed the German forces in the Narvik area for two to three weeks.[15] It is questionable whether they could have survived without them. There should have been standing operating procedures for moving or destroying the stores in the event of an emergency and the authority to execute these procedures should have been specified.

The Germans were surprised by the lack of resistance. Group Elvegårdsmoen consisted of almost two thirds of the German forces in the Narvik area. This attests to the fact that its capture was high on the list of German priorities and that they expected more resistance at Elvegårdsmoen than they did at Narvik.

The Sinking of the *Eidsvold*

Captain Bonte continued towards Narvik with the 1st Destroyer Flotilla, *Wilhelm Heidkamp*, *Bernd von Arnim*, and *Georg Thiele*, after detaching the 4th Destroyer Flotilla at 0410 hours. When they neared the harbor entrance at 0415 hours, the Norwegian coastal defense ship *Eidsvold* suddenly appeared through a snow squall. *Eidsvold* challenged the lead German destroyer, *Wilhelm Heidkamp*, with a signal light. A warning shot was fired when the German destroyer failed to respond and simultaneously the flags for the international signal, "Bring your ship to a stop" were hoisted. *Wilhelm Heidkamp* stopped about 200 meters off *Eidsvold's* port side and Captain Bonte signaled, "Sending boat with an officer." The other two destroyers continued towards Narvik.

Captain Willoch was perfectly within his right not to go through the formalities required by the neutrality regulations. The instructions from Admiral Diesen at 2345 hours stated that force be used against any attacker. The foreign warships that appeared at the harbor entrance were German and the ships attacking Bergen had been identified as German. These were more than sufficient reasons for Willoch to conclude that neutrality procedures no longer applied with respect to German ships. Instead of opening fire immediately, Willoch allowed a German destroyer to take up a position very close to his own ship, permitted Lieutenant Commander Gerlach to board *Eidsvold* and come to the quarterdeck, and allowed two German warships to proceed to Narvik.

It was well within *Eidsvold's* capability to destroy or severely damage the German destroyer. The destruction of *Wilhelm Heidkamp* might not have altered the eventual result in Narvik, but the possible elimination of General Dietl, Captain Bonte, 200 troops and over 300 naval personnel would most certainly have affected subsequent operations. Colonel Windisch would have succeeded to command of the German forces. He was a very capable officer but he did not enjoy Hitler's confidence in the same way as Dietl.

Commander Gerlach saluted the Norwegian captain when he stepped onto the bridge. With the military courtesies out of the way, Gerlach told Captain Willoch that the Germans had come as friends to defend Norwegian neutrality against the British. While appealing for cooperation, he demanded that Willoch surrender his ship. He stated that resistance was useless and that several Norwegian cities were already in German hands. Willoch asked for ten minutes in which to contact his superior for instructions. Askim's short answer was, "Open fire."

Captain Willoch's next action is even more difficult to understand. Gerlach had left the Norwegian warship and Willoch reportedly recalled the German officer and told him that he had orders to fire on the German destroyer. Gerlach saluted and left the Norwegian ship for a second time. *Wilhelm Heidkamp* had meanwhile changed its position and was now located 30° off *Eidsvold's* port bow at a distance of approximately 700 meters. Commander Gerlach fired a prearranged signal flare after leaving the Norwegian warship, which told his shipmates that the Norwegians had turned down the German demands. There was some quick soul searching among the officers on *Wilhelm Heidkamp's* bridge. Although old and outdated, the *Eidsvold* had a formidable armament. The two 8.3-inch, six 6-inch, and eight 3-inch guns could bring devastation to the German destroyer at this close range.

Eidsvold headed towards the German destroyer and the distance was quickly reduced to 300 meters before the destroyer skipper, Lieutenant Commander Hans Otto Erdmenger, ordered full speed ahead to take up another torpedo position. The Norwegian guns were aimed at the destroyer and Erdmenger was very concerned for the safety of his ship. He requested permission to open fire but Bonte was reluctant. The navy's operational order stated explicitly that German ships were not to fire the first shot. He was also concerned that an attack on the Norwegian warship would eliminate all chances for a peaceful occupation of Narvik. It was only after General Dietl, who was also on the bridge, demanded that he open fire that Bonte authorized Erdmenger to torpedo the coastal defense ship.

It is sometimes necessary in combat for a commander to deviate from plans and regulations when common sense dictates it in order to accomplish the mission. Such decisions are always risky and often heart wrenching. Captain Bonte faced such a dilemma when it became obvious that *Eidsvold* would use her big guns against his destroyer at close range. The directives from Admiral Raeder and General von Falkenhorst made it clear that German ships were to fire only after the Norwegians had opened fire. If Bonte waited for the Norwegians to open fire, he risked the destruction of his ship and put the accomplishment of the task force mission in jeopardy. He had to choose quickly between two parts of his order—"let nothing stop you from accomplishing your objective" and "the Norwegians must fire the first shot."

Four torpedoes were fired at the Norwegian warship from *Wilhelm Heidkamp's* aft torpedo tubes. Captain Willoch had meanwhile given the order to open fire on the German destroyer. The chief gunnery officer had just given the order, "Port battery, salvo, fire" when three of *Wilhelm Heidkamp's* torpedoes hit *Eidsvold*. The torpedoes hit along *Eidsvold's* port side and the effect was devastating. Their detonation set off the ammunition magazines and the enormous explosion broke the ship in two pieces. It sank within 15 seconds. The time was 0437 hours. Only six men from the crew of 181 were saved. Captain Willoch went down with his ship. Three survivors managed to swim to shore while the other three were rescued by the Germans. *Wilhelm Heidkamp* proceeded to Narvik.

The Sinking of the *Norge*

As soon as *Norge* cleared for action, she headed towards the harbor entrance. Around 0420 hours, the ship was in position about 300 meters from the Iron Ore Pier with the port battery aimed at the harbor entrance. Shortly after she took up her position, the two German destroyers, *Bernd von Arnim* and *Georg Thiele*, were seen through the snow squall at the harbor entrance. Because of the earlier report from the patrol boat *Senja* about a British cruiser near Ramnes and the sighting of numerous British warships in Vestfjord the previous day, Captain Askim was not sure about the nationality of the two warships. Admiral Diesen's message that British warships were not to be fired on had been received moments before the foreign warships appeared and Askim decided to challenge the ships with signal lights. The challenge went unanswered and the warships disappeared in a snow squall before he could open fire.

It was at this time that Captain Willoch radioed for instructions and Askim learned that the ships were German. Shortly thereafter, a muffled explosion was heard from the direction of the harbor entrance. Poor visibility prevented *Norge's* crew from witnessing the tragic fate of their sister ship.

On their way to the Steamship Pier, the two German destroyers were again observed passing between the many merchant ships in the harbor. Askim ordered his ship to commence fire and four or five 8.3-inch rounds and five salvos from the starboard 6-inch battery were fired at the German ships at a range estimated at 800 meters. It was almost impossible to see the targets through the telescopic sights. The first salvo fell short. Overcompensation caused the other salvoes to pass over the German destroyers and land ashore.

The German ships were in the process of docking on opposite sides of the pier and starting to disembark troops as *Norge* opened fire. *Bernd von Arnim* docked with the starboard side against the pier and its skipper, Lieutenant Commander Kurt Rechel, ordered the 5-inch guns as well as the machineguns to open fire on the Norwegian ship. Rechel was not in an enviable position. He had to fight a naval action on his port side from a stationary position while German mountain troops were scrambling ashore over the starboard side. The German fire was inaccurate and none of the 5-inch shells hit the Norwegian ship. *Bernd von Arnim* also fired seven torpedoes at the coastal defense ship.

The torpedoes were seen from *Norge's* bridge and an attempt was made to bring the ship parallel to their tracks. The first five torpedoes missed but the maneuver to bring *Norge* parallel to their track was not completed when the last two torpedoes hit their target, one aft and one amidships. As was the case with *Eidsvold*, the result was devastating. The ship capsized to starboard and sank with the bottom up in less than one minute. The ship had a crew of 191 and 101 of these went down with their ship. A boat from *Bernd von Arnim* saved nine sailors while merchant ships anchored in the harbor saved another 81. Captain Askim was brought ashore unconscious.

Within 23 minutes, the two largest ships in the Norwegian Navy were sent to the bottom with the loss of 276 lives, and without accomplishing anything against the enemy. The two coastal defense ships were floating coffins when pitted against modern warships. The prewar civilian and navy leadership in Norway must shoulder much of the responsibility for this disastrous event. These two ships were in Narvik in an attempt to compensate for the failure of successive governments over half a century to heed the pleas of the military to build coastal fortifications in the approaches to Narvik. By failing to provide adequate resources to the military in the interwar period, the labor government condemned Norwegian sailors to serve on ships that were antiquated and belonged to an earlier period of naval development.

The captains of the two ships must also share in the responsibility for what happened. They knew the severe limitations of their ships and had toyed with the idea of beaching one on each side of the relatively narrow entrance to Ofotfjord or Narvik's harbor, to use them as shore batteries. This was the only sensible course of action after the civilian leadership and naval authorities allowed these ships to be taken out of mothballs. As a witness during the court martial of Colonel Sundlo, Captain Askim stated that he would have beached the two ships on opposite sides of the harbor entrance if he had known how things were to unfold. However, he also stated that he could not do this without orders from Admiral Diesen.

To my knowledge, Captain Askim never requested conditional authority to beach the two ships if he deemed it necessary. By beaching the ships in preselected locations, those crewmembers not needed to operate the gun batteries could have been sent ashore. By the evening of April 8, conditions were such that beaching the ships at or near the harbor entrance would have been the wisest course of action. In his testimony at Sundlo's trial, Askim stated that he kept his ships in or near the harbor because it would have been idiotic to try to meet foreign warships in the fjord at night in conditions of near-zero visibility. If he had beached the two old ships, it is possible that they could have inflicted severe damage on some of the German destroyers. Whatever the outcome, such a course of action would have saved many Norwegian lives that morning.

There was not much left of the Norwegian Navy in the Narvik area after the two coastal defense ships were sunk. As already noted, the Germans captured the patrol boat *Senja*. The two patrol boats at the Ofotfjord entrance, *Michael Sars* and *Kelt*, were also intercepted by German destroyers and ordered to Narvik. When they hesitated, the Germans fired several close warning shots. Under the circumstances, these small vessels had no choice but to proceed to Narvik.

Now aware of the German attack, the 3rd Naval District ordered the two submarines and the tender *Lyngen* to the Lofoten Islands. *B1* and *Lyngen* were later instructed to remain in Liland because the Germans were reported to have mined the Ofotfjord entrance. *B1* remained in Ofotfjord without accomplishing anything and it was scuttled in 60 feet of water at 1020 hours on April 13 to keep it from falling into German hands. The timing was unfortunate since British naval forces took control of the fjord less than one hour later. *B3* managed to slip out of Ofotfjord on April 9 and continued to the Lofoten Islands. The 3rd Naval District ordered the submarine to remain in that location until further orders. The British asked the Norwegians not to employ this submarine in order to give them a free hand to attack any underwater contacts. By April 13, the Ofot Division was reduced to only *B3* and *Lyngen*, and ceased to be an operational organization.

The Comparative Strength and Condition of the Norwegian and German Forces

Some writers maintain that Colonel Sundlo, with over 1,000 troops at his disposal, could have driven approximately 400 seasick German soldiers out of Narvik without much difficulty. There are several points wrong with this assertion. First, the numbers are incorrect and misleading. Second, the Germans may have been seasick, but they had almost recovered in the seven hours that passed since the destroyers came leeward of the Lofoten Islands. The Norwegians themselves were not exactly well rested, fully organized, and ready for battle. Finally, numbers are seldom the determining factor in the outcome of a battle. More often than not, the numbers involved are much less important than other factors. These factors include leadership and the troops' faith in that leadership, training, equipment, battle experience, esprit de corps, and a strong sense of purpose. In all these categories, the Germans held a decisive advantage.

Company 2, commanded by Captain Langlo, was the primary combat unit at Colonel Sundlo's disposal before the arrival of the battalion from Elvegårdsmoen. A machinegun platoon from Co 4, commanded by Lieutenant Landrø, was attached to Captain Langlo's company. The full strength of an infantry company in the Norwegian Army was 182, including 12 non-combatants. It appears that the strength of Co 2 was about 150 on April 8. However, this was not the present for duty strength in Narvik when the Germans attacked. Twenty-one men had been sent to reinforce the guard detail at Nordal Bridge at 1800 hours on April 8. Another twenty-one men were sent to Øyjord around 2300 hours to prepare positions for the motorized artillery battery. One officer and six enlisted men were involved in preparing quarters for the battalion. The machinegun platoon had approximately 40 men. Thus, before the arrival of the battalion from Elvegårdsmoen, only about 150 troops in Narvik were trained to fight as infantrymen.

The first elements of the 1/13th Inf, two machinegun platoons from Co 4, arrived in Narvik about 0200 hours. The second group to arrive in Narvik consisted of Co 3. It arrived in Vassvik around 0300 and reached Narvik about 0330 hours. The company left behind a guard detail of 17 men in Elvegårdsmoen. In addition, the sled drivers were left behind in Øyjord when the ferry skipper refused to load the horses. Company 1, minus its sled drivers, arrived in Vassvik around 0415 hours and reached Narvik about 0445 hours, after the engagement between *Norge* and the German destroyers. The mortar platoon from the headquarters company arrived at the same time. Since no journals were kept, the above times are approximations based on the testimony of participants.

About 205 troops from the 1/13th Inf reached Narvik before the Germans landed. This brought Colonel Sundlo's infantry strength to about 355 and another 180 arrived while the Germans were landing. At the most, Colonel Sundlo had 535 infantry troops that could take up the fight with the Germans. Even if the combat support and service support personnel are added, the total is only 775.

The Germans landed about 600 infantry in Narvik, not 400. The 400 often referred to are no doubt the troops carried on the destroyers *Bernd von Arnim* and *Georg Thiele*. These were the first troops ashore but they were joined within minutes by the 200 troops aboard *Wilhelm Heidkamp*.

The German troops were relieved to disembark the destroyers. Most of them came from Austria and the interior parts of Germany and they had never been to sea. They had traveled crowded under deck in the destroyers as these headed into the storms they encountered from the time they left Germany until they arrived in Narvik. The destroyer captains welcomed the stormy weather since it would help conceal them from the British. The destroyers, heading north at high speed in order to stay on schedule and keep up with the battleships, were tossed around like toys in the heavy seas. The troops were also tossed around below deck and suffered not only from seasickness but also from broken bones and other injuries. Some, who ventured on deck to help secure equipment, were swept overboard.

Nils Ryeng, quoting a customs official who witnessed the landing, writes, "several hundred soldiers, running, walking, crawling, apathetic, indifferent and seasick. They looked like they were drunk and many fell into the water."[16] This observation deserves further scrutiny.

The two German destroyers were in the process of docking when a larger Norwegian warship opened fire on them at a range of only 800 meters. The German warships were stationary targets and it was imperative that they offload their troops quickly in order to get underway and start maneuvering. There was no time to put out gangplanks as *Bernd von Arnim* engaged the Norwegian warship with its main batteries, machineguns, and torpedo salvoes. It was imperative for the officers and NCOs to get the 400 troops off the warships as quickly as possible since Norwegian 8- and 6-inch shells were whistling overhead. The next puff of smoke from the Norwegian warship might well bring death. The troops scrambled over the railings and jumped onto the pier with no attempt at unit cohesion. Some may well have fallen into the water in the process. When ashore, unit cohesion had to be restored as quickly as possible because they expected fire from Norwegian troops at any moment. To an untrained observer, the scene must have looked like chaos as the German infantry companies scrambled ashore and reformed.

While the mountain troops endured great hardships during their passage, there is little to indicate that this reduced their combat effectiveness. German writers have not considered the effects of seasickness an important factor. The fact that the German troops seized the designated facilities in Narvik in a rapid and organized fashion is a further indication that seasickness had not demoralized them or impaired their combat effectiveness.

The adrenalin rush in soldiers going into battle helps them focus on their mission and survival and set everything else aside. Sometimes this phenomenon is so strong in battle that a soldier may not even notice an otherwise painful wound. Dietl's troops were among the best trained in Germany and they had been battle tested in the Carpathian Mountains in 1939. The soldiers likely spent the hours before landing with their NCOs and officers, going over the details of their mission for one last time. These intense activities probably helped them to forget their horrible experience at sea and calmed any fears they may have experienced in the minutes before landing.

How the available forces were used was far more important than the actual combat strength of the two sides. The Norwegians had to prepare to counter landings at any point along 10 kilometers of coastline from Fagernes to the east of Vassvik. The forward deployment of their forces guaranteed the Germans local superiority at any landing site and the consequent reduction in reserves impaired the Norwegians ability to launch counterattacks. It was impossible to establish an effective forward defense with the forces that were available. The harbor area alone stretched about three kilometers from Framnes to the Beisfjord entrance, covered by two bunkers that were not mutually supportive. A force landing in the middle of the harbor, while within the maximum range of the machineguns and small arms, would be outside their effective range. The prevailing heavy snow squalls and gale force winds in Narvik favored the Germans. The darkness and snow sometimes reduced visibility to only a few meters.

The Capture of Narvik

Colonel Sundlo held a meeting with his staff and principal subordinates after the arrival of Major Spjældnes and Co 4, about 0200 hours. Those present included

Major Spjældnes and his adjutant, Major Omdal, the commander of Co 4, Captain Brønstad, and Captain Dalsve, Co 2's executive officer. Sundlo explained what little he knew about the situation and announced that he would not deploy the arriving troops until first light. These units had come through a snowstorm on skis, were wet and cold, and had not slept for nearly 24 hours. The troops were to remain fully clothed and ready for immediate deployment. The officers were instructed to remain with their units.[17]

Those present recalled that Colonel Sundlo assumed that the patrol ships on the early warning line and the coastal defense ships, which he believed had deployed to the fjord entrance in accordance with plans, would provide sufficient warning for an orderly deployment of the troops. The staff and subordinate commanders were dismissed before 0330 hours. Sundlo remained at his headquarters. As on the previous evening, he failed to include the engineer company, the 75mm gun crew, and the civilian authorities in his briefing.

Company 3 had just arrived in Narvik and the troops were in the process of moving into the quarters when the meeting took place. Company 4, minus one machinegun platoon, was co-located with the battalion headquarters at the primary school, about 300 meters from the regimental headquarters. The antiaircraft battery personnel were in their quarters except for an alert detail of 11 men at the guns. The two platoons of the engineer company were in their quarters along the railroad tracks leading to the iron ore unloading facilities. An alert detail of three men was located with the 75mm railroad gun. The other four were in quarters near the engineers company. Thirteen men from the machinegun platoon attached to Co 2 occupied the two bunkers. The Fagernes bunker was occupied by one NCO and five men with two machineguns. The machinegun platoon's second in command, Sergeant Wesche, and six men were at the Framnes bunker. The remaining 30 soldiers of that platoon were on alert in their quarters, about one kilometer from the harbor area. The harbor defense force should have occupied posts along the waterfront from Fagernes to Framnes. Actually, some of them were at their quarters 200 meters from the Steamship Pier.[18]

Colonel Sundlo reacted to the news that foreign warships had entered Ofotfjord in a rather disorganized fashion. He alerted the battalion and directed Major Omdal, who was in his quarters, to notify all subordinate commanders to assemble at regimental headquarters as quickly as possible, and for Co 2 to deploy its reserve. Again, no one thought to alert the antiaircraft battery, the engineer company, the 75mm gun detachment, or the civilian authorities.

In the process of alerting the units, Major Omdal directed Captain Dalsve to assume command of Co 2. This change in command was apparently planned and had Colonel Sundlo's blessing, but it was nevertheless a strange thing to do as hostilities were about to begin. It was intended to use Langlo's familiarity with the local area to help deploy the arriving units since it was dark and snowing heavily. While Major Spjeldnæs was understandably annoyed at being left out of these arrangements, Sundlo and Omdal considered it proper to deal directly with the companies since time was crucial and they were more familiar with the town than Major Spjældnes who had just arrived. Sundlo decided to deploy Co 3, commanded by Captain Bjørnson, to the prepared positions between Lillevik and Kvitvik. A machinegun platoon was attached to the company as it passed the battalion headquarters.

Sundlo considered that stretch of shoreline and Vassvik the most likely enemy landing sites. He believed that Co 2 and its attached machinegun platoon covered the harbor area but there were no troops in the Lillevik-Kvitvik area. From that standpoint, the deployment is understandable. In retrospect, however, it was not a wise decision. Sundlo had insufficient forces to cover adequately all areas where an enemy could strike. It was therefore important to maintain a substantial reserve until the enemy had shown his hand.

The order not to fire on British forces but to fire on Germans was received about 0430 hours and it was relayed quickly to subordinate units without an explanation. As was the case in other areas of the country, this order was not helpful.

Both Major Spjeldnæs and Captain Bjørnson declared later that they were not properly briefed about the friendly situation. According to Sandvik, Bjørnson stated that he did not know how the machinegun company and Co 2 were deployed. This may well be true but a solution to part of the problem would have been for Captain Bjørnson to ask the machinegun company commander who was present at the battalion headquarters. In addition, the former commander of Co 2 was with Major Spjeldnæs and Captain Bjørnson for much of this time and could have explained that unit's deployment plans. A commander should use every means to obtain information he deems crucial and not wait to be spoon-fed that information. The lack of knowledge mentioned by Spjeldnæs and Bjørnson had little effect on the unfolding events.

Captain Dalsve had meanwhile deployed the rest of Co 2. He sent Lieutenant Bergli with 15–20 men to positions near the Fagernes bunker. Dalsve told Bergli that foreign warships were approaching Narvik. Lieutenant Skjefte commanded the Fagernes Bunker and Lieutenant Bergli assumed that his force would also come under Skjefte's command.

Captain Dalsve drove to the Framnes bunker with the rest of the company reserve, about 15–20 men. On the way, he stopped at the harbor guard force's quarters and ordered the senior NCO, Sergeant Sand, to occupy the prepared positions near the Iron Ore Pier. Dalsve apparently forgot that he had a machinegun platoon attached to his company. The platoon leader, Lieutenant Landrø, and 30 men were at their quarters and Captain Dalsve failed to give them any orders. Instead of requesting instructions from Captain Dalsve, Lieutenant Landrø assembled his platoon and marched it to the primary school to obtain instructions from Captain Brønstad, the machinegun company's commander.

Majors Omdal and Spjeldnæs were both in the school courtyard when they heard cannon fire from the direction of the harbor. The only uncommitted force available was a machinegun platoon. They decided to deploy this platoon to a position above the Iron Ore Pier from where it would be able to fire on targets in the harbor. The machinegun company commander and his executive officer accompanied the platoon. Though from the sounds an action was evidently underway, the darkness and heavy snowfall prevented observation of the harbor area. A temporary break in the weather revealed three warships in the harbor but since their nationality was unknown, they were not fired on because of the recent instructions not to fire on British forces.

Major Omdal recommended to Colonel Sundlo that Co 3 be recalled from the Lillevik-Kvitvik area since it was now obvious that an attack was in progress in the harbor. Sundlo agreed. He had just received a call from a customs official informing him that German troops were disembarking from warships at the Steamship Pier. This was the first message to give the attackers' nationality. Captain Bjørnson was in the process of deploying his company when a battalion runner appeared with an order directing him to return to the battalion headquarters area. It took most of an hour before this repositioning was completed.

Colonel Sundlo decided that they should try to drive the Germans out of town. This decision was wishful thinking at this stage. The Norwegian forces were spread throughout town in small groups and it was not possible to bring them to a central location in time to stop the Germans, who were advancing into town rapidly. There were no reserves available until the next unit arrived from Elvegårdsmoen.

Major Omdal proceeded to the school area and tried to scrape together whatever soldiers he could find at or near the school. Company 1, commanded by Captain Strømstad, and the mortar platoon arrived from Vassvik at this time. It was the only organized force available. Due to the seriousness of the situation, Omdal suggested that Sundlo come to the battalion headquarters. When Sundlo arrived, Omdal, who was in civilian clothes, ran home to put on a uniform.

Major Spjeldnæs ordered Co 1 to advance towards the market place and the harbor. It took only a few minutes for Captain Strømstad to brief his platoon leaders and ready the company for the advance. The machine gun platoon previously attached to Co 2 was ordered to support Strømstad's advance.

The Norwegians had advanced no more than a city block when they encountered a German force of at least equal size. Neither side opened fire. In addition to the force to his front, Captain Strømstad saw several groups of Germans on the north side of the railroad tracks. He tried to spread his force and reported to the battalion that he was in an untenable position if the Germans opened fire.

In 1947, Major Spjeldnæs testified that he had already started thinking about assembling his units for a withdrawal and therefore he had not given Strømstad orders to open fire. He reasoned that all hope of a withdrawal would be destroyed if hostilities were initiated. He only wanted the German advance stopped. Based on the testimony of one of the lead platoon leaders and the company executive officer, Major Spjeldnæs' involvement was more proactive. Both lieutenants stated that their platoons left the school area with orders to open fire. Before they confronted the Germans, new directives arrived directing them not to fire until further orders.[19]

Company 2's reserve had been located astride the route taken by the two German columns entering the town. When Major Omdal awakened Captains Langlo and Dalsve at Victoria Hospice, he ordered Dalsve to occupy the Framnes and Fagernes bunkers at once. It is uncertain what this order meant, since personnel from the machinegun platoon already occupied the bunkers. Captain Dalsve must have concluded that the order pertained to the 30-40 men of the reserve and, as noted earlier, these troops were sent to the two bunkers. This left no Norwegian infantry along the German routes into town.

Sergeant Wesche and his troops at the Framnes bunker had a few glimpses of warships around the harbor entrance but could not make out their nationality. It became obvious that they were not friendly when *Eidsvold* blew up a few hundred meters from the Framnes shoreline. Wesche found it useless to open fire on warships with rifles and machineguns. Captain Dalsve arrived at the Framnes bunker with part of the company reserve shortly after *Eidsvold* sank. The heavy snowfall prevented the Norwegians at or near the bunker from observing what was happening in the harbor. Three survivors from *Eidsvold* came ashore on Framnes and a large number of dead were floating near land. Captain Dalsve moved men from the reserve down to the water's edge to help bring the living and dead ashore.

Sand and his men witnessed the sinking of *Norge*, located only 300 meters from the Iron Ore Pier and they also saw what they believed was a foreign warship at the Steamship Pier. Sergeant Sand ran back to the quarters where they had come from earlier and warned both bunkers about these happenings. He also tried to contact the company commander for instructions. He was unable to reach Captain Dalsve, who was on his way to the Framnes bunker. Sand had just returned when German soldiers appeared and quickly disarmed his 20 men. They did not resist.

Lieutenant Skjefte and his men at the Fagernes bunker could hear cannon fire from the harbor and they received a call from the Framnes bunker that *Eidsvold* had been sunk. It was snowing heavily and the German warships could not be seen from the Fagernes bunker. Lieutenant Bergli arrived shortly after the firing in the harbor area started, with half of the company reserve. He passed Lieutenant Skjefte's position without talking to him and deployed his men on the hillside above, and out of sight from the bunker. Each officer related later that he assumed the other was in command.

When the snowfall eased momentarily, a warship was seen about 250-300 meters from shore. The Norwegians observed soldiers moving in their direction from the east and shortly thereafter, other soldiers, landed at the entrance to Beisfjord, were seen approaching from the west. The approaching soldiers called out in English and German for the Norwegians not to fire. Lieutenant Skjefte did not order his troops to fire and soon there were foreign soldiers all around his position. He explained later that he did not order his troops to open fire because he believed he was under Lieutenant Bergli's command and that officer had not given an order to fire. An officer told a runner sent to the bunker from Bergli's position that the troops should not fire until otherwise ordered. There was only one officer at the bunker, Lieutenant Skjefte. He testified later that he could not recall giving such an order. German and Norwegian troops ended up looking at each other on opposite sides of the barbed wire. Neither side opened fire.

The rapid German advance through town quickly neutralized most of the units that Colonel Sundlo and his staff had failed to alert. Captain Gundersen, the engineer company commander, and his men awoke to the sound of cannon fire. It took him a while to join his company since he was staying at one of the hotels.

Gundersen ordered his executive officer to prepare the company for movement while he drove to the harbor area to see what was happening. He drove straight into a unit of mountain troops. He was taken to the pier where German troops were disembarking from the destroyers and survivors from *Norge* were brought ashore.

The Germans believed Gundersen was Colonel Sundlo's representative. He denied this, but Dietl ordered Gundersen to accompany him in a taxi with eight troops standing on the running boards. Dietl asked Gundersen to arrange a meeting with Sundlo. Gundersen refused. After crossing the railroad, they were stopped by an excited lieutenant. He told Dietl that Colonel Sundlo threatened to open fire if the Germans did not withdraw within 30 minutes. Dietl exclaimed that this must not be allowed to happen and he asked Gundersen to accompany him to Sundlo. Gundersen refused, and in the confusion, he managed to slip away and rejoined his company. He took about 70 troops and moved towards the antiaircraft battery position, to act as a security force. Twelve engineers were assigned to help the gun crews. One squad was sent to the Framnes bunker and two squads to regimental headquarters. The company executive officer took the rest of the company to secure the railroad station in anticipation of a possible withdrawal. German troops surrounded and captured this force before it reached its destination.

The antiaircraft battery commander and his troops also awoke to gunfire in the harbor. He ordered his men to drive to the gun positions in cars parked near their quarters for that purpose. A German unit moving up the street at double-time surrounded the artillery troops before they could get out of the parking lot. The Norwegians were disarmed. A German lieutenant told Munthe-Kaas that the Germans had come as friends and, with the approval of the king, to protect the country against the British. He stated that all major Norwegian cities were in German hands and that Norwegian forces were directed to cooperate with the Germans.

Lieutenant Munthe-Kaas and his bugler managed to slip away and join the 11-man alert detail at the gun positions. The guns were positioned to fire against aircraft and they could not fire on targets in the harbor area. Each 40mm cannon weighed over two tons. With considerable difficulty, the men managed to move one gun through the deep snow, along with the machineguns, to a position where they could fire at targets in the harbor. The other three guns were not moved since there were insufficient personnel to operate them.

Munthe-Kaas was uncertain about the situation since he had not heard a single shot fired in the city. He was unable to get through to the regimental headquarters by telephone and decided to drive there for instructions. On the way, he met Major Omdal who was on his way home to change into a uniform. The lieutenant asked if the situation was such that he should destroy the 40mm guns. The major, who was in a hurry, asked, "Why, can't you fire them?" Munthe-Kaas answered that he could fire one gun and he turned around and drove back to the battery. The battery never opened fire, partly because of the limited visibility but mostly because of a sense of uncertainty since the city remained quiet.

Sergeant Eriksen and the off-duty crew for the 75mm railroad gun were also awakened by naval gunfire. They managed to move quickly to the gun position but this did not help much. The gun was positioned where it could fire on targets in the fjord and in the harbor entrance but a rock outcropping prevented the gun from firing on the harbor itself. A locomotive was necessary to move the gun and Eriksen tried to requisition one but the Germans had stopped all railroad traffic and posted sentries along the railroad.

It had become obvious to Colonel Sundlo, Major Omdal, and Major Spjeldnæs that they needed to concentrate all available forces as quickly as possible. Sundlo had agreed to Omdal's proposal to recall Co 3 and the attached machinegun platoon. It is claimed that Major Spjeldnæs ordered Co 3 and the machinegun platoon on Framnes back to the battalion headquarters on his own initiative. It was logical that orders to his subordinate units come through the battalion, but the action also suggests that the senior leaders had reached the same conclusion.

The mortar platoon had orders to take up positions on Framnes where it could fire on the German ships. Sundlo cancelled that mission at the last minute and ordered that all units in the Framnes area withdraw and assemble at the battalion headquarters. While Spjeldnæs may have thought about a withdrawal from Narvik, Sundlo had apparently not given up on the possibility of stopping the German advance. He ordered Spjeldnæs to prepare an advance against the Germans as soon as the recalled units reached the battalion area.

While Sundlo and Spjeldnæs were discussing the planned attack, a lieutenant arrived with a request from a German lieutenant colonel for a meeting with the Norwegian commander, apparently meaning the battalion commander. Colonel Sundlo decided to talk to the German officer himself, and he asked Major Spjeldnæs to accompany him. Spjeldnæs describes the meeting in a report he made on August 27, 1940:[20] 'The German officer stated, as soon as we met him: 'We will not fire if you don't fire.' Colonel Sundlo answered immediately: 'On the contrary, we will fire. If you don't withdraw immediately, we will open fire.'"

The German officer also told Sundlo that Denmark had surrendered without a fight and that the Norwegian Government had decided not to resist. Sundlo recommended a 15-minute cease-fire while he consulted his superiors. Spjeldnæs suggested that the cease-fire be extended to 30 minutes and the German agreed. Spjeldnæs hoped that the extra 15 minutes would allow the units withdrawing from Framnes to reach his location.

Colonel Sundlo proceeded to his headquarters, called the District Command at 0600 hours, and talked to Colonel Mjelde. Not surprisingly, we have two versions of the conversation that followed. First, Colonel Mjelde's version:[21]

Colonel Sundlo reported that the Germans are spread throughout the city and are handing out leaflets. He has talked to the German commander and they have agreed on a 30-minute cease-fire. The German commander will confer with his superiors. The colonel requested instructions. The colonel was reminded about his responsibilities and his earlier orders. The responsibility was his as the local commander in accordance with earlier orders.

Colonel Sundlo's version is that he first briefed Colonel Mjelde on the situation in Narvik. Then he told Mjelde that he intended to attack the German forces that were already in the city. Sundlo asked Mjelde for comments on the intended course of action. Mjelde answered: 'You are on the scene and fully responsible.'[22]

Although it is impossible to know which version is more accurate, it is worth noting that Colonel Sundlo had discussed mounting an attack with Majors Omdal and Spjeldnæs. The mad scramble to concentrate forces in a central location could also serve to facilitate a withdrawal, a course of action Spjeldnæs was considering. The German forces that had captured the railroad station had swung to the north and they were about to cut the Narvik-Vassvik road. The Norwegian forces would be trapped if the Germans captured that road as well as the railway.

Sundlo may have tried to find some moral support for the most difficult decision of his career. It was obvious that a decision to fight would lead to a high number of civilian casualties. While Mjelde was correct in pointing out that Sundlo was best qualified to make the decisions, his answer nevertheless strikes one as evasive and not very encouraging. Whatever happened, Mjelde was in the clear.

Colonel Sundlo headed back to the battalion headquarters after his telephone conversation with Mjelde. Outside the school that served as battalion headquarters, he encountered General Dietl, members of his staff, and the German Consul in Narvik. The general explained that the Germans had come as friends, to which Sundlo answered that the sinking of two Norwegian warships was not exactly an act of friendship.

General Dietl gave the colonel a short, inaccurate orientation of the overall situation, including his assertion that he had a full division at his disposal and that the major cities in southern Norway were occupied peacefully. He pointed out to Sundlo that powerful elements of his division were already ashore, that numerous German warships in the fjord were ready to bombard the town, and that Norwegian resistance would only lead to needless bloodshed. He demanded that the Norwegians surrender and that all units be disarmed and assembled in their quarters to await further orders.

Colonel Sundlo made a quick assessment of the situation. Despite an agreement that units would remain in their positions during the cease-fire, the Germans had used the period to secure key terrain and machineguns were set up at all critical junctions. From his headquarters, he had observed the German advance towards the town's municipal center and the railroad station. The Germans had passed to the left of the Norwegian troops, seized the high ground near the regimental headquarters, and set up machineguns that covered the area around the school where the battalion headquarters and assembly area were located. The Germans occupied the regimental headquarters shortly after Sundlo left.

Norwegian and German troops in Co 1's area had become intermingled, looking at each other with surprise and curiosity. Civilians had come into the streets to watch the drama unfold, not realizing the seriousness of the situation. Many, including women and children, were intermingled with German troops. It was obvious that a large number of civilians would be killed as soon as the first shots were fired. The Norwegian troops ordered to withdraw from Framnes had not arrived. The same was true for Co 3, ordered back from the Lillevik-Kvitvik area. Besides Co 1, the mortar platoon was the only force available to Colonel Sundlo. He concluded that the city was, for all practical purposes, already occupied.

Sundlo requested an extension of the cease-fire so that he could contact General Fleischer for instructions. General Dietl, fully aware of the untenable situation in which the Norwegians found themselves and Colonel Sundlo's hesitation and indecisiveness, refused to extend the cease-fire. After a tense period of silence, Colonel Sundlo informed Dietl in German, "Ich übergebe die Stadt" (I surrender the city). The time was approximately 0615 hours.[23]

General Dietl asked Sundlo to recall all units and insure that there were no incidents. Any incident would lead to immediate reprisals. Sundlo ordered Major Omdal to notify all units. He then proceeded to his headquarters under German guard. Sundlo informed District Command that he had surrendered the city. District Command notified General Fleischer at 0620 hours.

General Fleischer was convinced that Sundlo had failed to perform his duties. The fight that the general expected in Narvik had not developed. Fleischer finally called Narvik direct, but the call was not to Colonel Sundlo. He called Major Spjeldnæs and ordered him to place Sundlo under arrest and to drive the Germans out of Narvik. It is obvious from this order that the general did not understand the situation in Narvik. Spjeldnæs told Fleischer that Sundlo was a German prisoner of war. He also told the general that it was impossible to drive the Germans out of town since he had only about 100 troops at his disposal and these were surrounded by a much larger German force. Fleischer then changed his order. He directed Spjeldnæs to assemble as many units as possible, break through the German lines, and thereafter position the troops to defend the Ofot Railway. Major Omdal appeared while Spjeldnæs talked to Fleischer and Spjeldnæs pointed out that Omdal was his senior and the general then repeated his orders to Omdal.

The Germans had occupied the high ground around the school and the possibility of a fighting breakout was not promising. The two majors decided to try to bluff their way through the German lines. Company 3 had now arrived at the school. It was obvious that an attempt to leave Narvik would not succeed unless it was undertaken immediately. They could not wait for the other elements of the battalion to arrive.

Parts of Co 3, Co 1, and a machinegun platoon were ordered to form up in a column with weapons slung over the shoulder. The troops were told to bring only weapons and what ammunition they could carry. Skis and other equipment were left behind. The troops assembled within a few minutes and they marched out of the schoolyard with Major Spjeldnæs in the lead. As they approached a group of German troops blocking the street, a German officer ordered them to halt and asked their destination. Spjeldnæs stopped for a moment and answered truthfully that they were leaving town. The German officer stated that they would not be permitted to leave Narvik. Spjeldnæs gave the officer a smile and said calmly in German, "Doch wir marschieren. Guten Morgen." This brazen action caught the Germans off guard. While they hesitated, about 180 Norwegians marched through their position. They passed the railroad station, which was already in German hands, without interference.

Two messengers caught up with the formation as it approached the first railroad tunnel. They had a written message, purportedly from Colonel Sundlo, ordering them back to town. Another Norwegian officer, with a pistol to his head, had forged Sundlo's name. The two messengers joined the withdrawal. The Norwegians occupied positions near Djupvik where there was an exchange of fire with a German patrol that had followed them. The firefight lasted for less than 30 minutes and there were no losses among the Norwegians. The Norwegians remained near the Hundal railroad station until the morning of April 11. They then decided to continue the withdrawal to the Nordal Bridge, where the terrain was well suited for defense. The force grew to 210 with the addition of the bridge guard detail.

General Dietl had secured all first-day objectives by 0615 hours on April 9. The lack of shore batteries at the Ofotfjord entrance was his only major disappointment. In less than two hours, the Germans had captured the key town in North Norway, sunk two of the largest warships in the Norwegian Navy, captured three patrol vessels, secured a critically important mobilization depot, and captured nearly 600 Norwegian troops, all without sustaining a single casualty.

The Norwegian forces left in Narvik were disarmed and imprisoned. This included the headquarters company that had been the the last unit to move from Elvegårdsmoen. The troops in this company were welcomed by German troops as they came off the ferry at Vassvik. Many officers and men managed to slip out of town later and join Norwegian forces in the interior. About three-fourths of the engineer company managed to escape in this manner.

Colonel Sundlo's Performance

Finally, a few words about Colonel Sundlo and his actions on April 8 and 9 are necessary. Sundlo is mentioned in the German directives for Narvik. Admiral Raeder describes him as *"an officer with reportedly pro-German feelings,"* with whom they should establish contact at the earliest opportunity. Quisling provided information about Sundlo to the Germans but there is no indication that Sundlo was aware of this. Rosenberg mentions him in the memorandum he prepared for Hitler in preparation for his December 16 meeting with Quisling. Sundlo was not the only officer mentioned by Quisling, who was eager to convince the Germans that he had important connections within the Norwegian military establishment. There is no evidence that Sundlo provided any useful information to the Germans. The best indication of this is the fact that the Germans were unaware that there were no Norwegian shore batteries at the Ofotfjord entrance.

Despite this, Konrad Sundlo became Norway's Benedict Arnold. Word spread everywhere after April 9 that Colonel Sundlo was in German service and that he had betrayed his country by surrendering Narvik. For example, the very competent researcher Hans-Martin Ottmer, writing in 1994, refers to Sundlo as a betrayer of his country. He claims that he failed to carry out the orders from the division by not alerting his troops or occupying defensive positions, despite having adequate time to do so. Consequently, the Germans were able to land their troops at their leisure without any resistance.[24]

Sundlo's scapegoating began when General Fleischer sent out a communiqué after the loss of Narvik. The communiqué, while carefully worded, left no doubt that Fleischer meant to convey that Narvik fell to the enemy due to Colonel Sundlo's treason and several newspapers receiving the communiqué stated so without hesitation. The communiqué read, in part:[25]

> Colonel Sundlo initiated immediate negotiations for a cease-fire and withdrew the troops to Framnes. The Germans occupied the city and the Norwegian troops were surrounded between the Germans and the sea. The division commander, who was in East Finnmark, was notified about the situation by telephone and he ordered Colonel Sundlo's second in command, Major Omdal, to arrest Colonel Sundlo …

Hovland writes that on October 5, 1948 Sundlo was sentenced to life in prison at hard labor for failing to make the necessary dispositions and preparations to meet the expected German attack on Narvik, and for surrendering his troops to the enemy. It is true that Sundlo was sentenced to life in prison at hard labor in 1948, but the statement leaves the wrong impression with respect to why this sentenced was imposed. A military court of inquiry after the war cleared Sundlo of the charge of treason and did not reprimand him for surrendering the town.[26] With respect to Narvik, the court found Sundlo guilty of "negligence and incompetence." Sundlo was stripped of his commission and sentenced to life in prison for his actions as a province official during the war and his effort to secure Norwegian volunteers for the German army on the eastern front.

In General Fleischer's biography, Hovland refers to Colonel Sundlo as a "rotten apple." He denounces Sundlo's failure to follow orders and states that Sundlo was the direct reason why very weak German forces managed to capture Narvik through a bluff. He writes that Colonel Sundlo must bear the responsibility for the serious consequences the loss of Narvik had for the country and Norwegian and Allied forces.

Colonel Sundlo and his staff made inexcusable mistakes. He neglected to alert the engineer company and the 75mm railroad gun unit, or include them in two important meetings. The commander of the antiaircraft battery was not invited to the last commanders meeting at Sundlo's headquarters. Major Omdal failed to include these three units on his itinerary when he drove around alerting commanders shortly before 0400 hours. Elvegårdsmoen was not alerted. Finally, there were no efforts made to notify and seek the cooperation of the civilian authorities in town.

There were serious leadership problems in Narvik on April 8 and 9, especially in the 1/13th Infantry. The blame for the poor performance of this battalion cannot be placed on the soldiers. They would undoubtedly have performed as well as those in other battalions in the 6th Division if they had competent leadership. The leadership of both their officers and NCOs failed at virtually every level. There are examples of orders not carried out, breakdowns in the chain of command, troops not kept informed, a glaring lack of initiative, indecisiveness, failures to follow directives, and lack of plain common sense in the absence of orders. The remnants of the 1/13th Infantry battalion continued to turn in a poor performance after its withdrawal from Narvik.

Most of these failures can be traced to inadequate training, very limited periods of active duty in the 1930s, leaders well past what is considered an acceptable age for the rigorous physical and mental demands of combat at battalion and company level, and of course, to total lack of combat experience. Most units facing the shock of combat for the first time have problems, but strong leadership and extensive training can minimize these.

A conclusion repeated by several authors is that Colonel Sundlo failed to take the proper "military precautions" before the "expected German occupation of Narvik." The "military precautions" he failed to take are not spelled out. No military officer in North Norway expected a German attack before receipt of the British message around 2000 hours, and that message came with a note from the highest military authorities that it was not believable. On his own authority, Sundlo ordered the machinegun company and mortar platoon at Elvegårdsmoen into Narvik and reinforced the Nordal Bridge guard detail. He did not intend to move the other two rifle companies into Narvik but when the order came, he implemented it as quickly as possible.

The charge that Colonel Sundlo failed in his duties and surrendered his troops to the enemy applies to many Norwegian military officers on that eventful night or the weeks that followed. Admiral Smith-Johanssen, for example, surrendered Norway's main naval base at Horten, including all ships in the harbor, to a much smaller German force than that confronting Sundlo. Colonel Østbye in Bergen, when confronting a somewhat similar situation that would have caused a large number of civilian casualties, wisely chose not to take up the fight in the city, but withdrew his forces to defensive positions on its outskirts.

Carl Joachim Hambro, the leader of the conservative party and the Storting, tried to have Sundlo removed from his post because of his political views long before the German attack. The campaign for his removal even led to a police investigation, which concluded that Sundlo had not done anything wrong.

The intrigues within the 6th Division for Sundlo's removal and the activities of the conservative party leadership toward the same end may not have taken place in isolation from each other. The Allies posed the most serious threat to Narvik and no one seriously considered Germany capable of launching operations in North Norway. It is curious that individuals like Hambro and Fleischer considered it risky to have an officer with pro-German political views as the military commander in Narvik when all indications from 1939 on pointed to a British/French expedition being prepared against that city.

Colonel Sundlo could not mount a successful defense of Narvik with the forces located there and under the conditions that prevailed on 8 and 9 April. Combat in Narvik would not have changed the outcome of the German invasion, but would have caused a large number of civilian casualties. It would have been wiser to use these forces in the manner envisaged by the plans from an earlier generation.[27] Those who claim otherwise forget that General Dietl had enormous firepower and additional forces at his disposal. The failure to leave adequate forces at Elvegårdsmoen to destroy that depot if it could not be defended had more serious consequences for future operations than the loss of the town. Colonel Otto Jersing Munthe-Kaas, who was a battalion commander in the 6th Division and later the Norwegian Military Attaché to the U.S., wrote:[28]

> The campaign in Narvik area would have taken a different and for the Germans a less favorable course if the 1st Bn 13th Inf Regt at Elvegaardsmoen had not been moved, but instead had been given a chance to take up the defense against a German landing in Herjangen, a fjord-arm on the north side of Ofotfjord.
>
> A defense of Narvik requires long preparation and quite other military and maritime forces and auxiliaries than those that were available on the April night, and only a few hours' notice, to stand off a powerful and well-planned surprise attack by the Germans. It would have been better if Narvik had been declared an open city inasmuch as its adequate defense had no time to be organized. Instead, all available forces could have been used for isolating the Germans at Narvik by preventing them from pushing eastward along the Ofot railway and northward toward Troms province.

The facts that Sundlo was a member of Quisling's party and held positions in his administration during the war made the charges with regard to his conduct in Narvik stick, while leaving the conduct of others untarnished. Sundlo's subsequent behavior cannot be used as a basis for judging his conduct as military commander in Narvik or as an explanation for a spectacular German success that caught everyone in this part of the country by surprise.[29]

The failure of General Fleischer to curtail his inspection trip in East Finnmark was, in retrospect, a poor decision. The possibility of military action against Narvik should have been obvious to General Fleischer and it is difficult to understand why he did not head back to his headquarters as soon as the war clouds began to gather. The British mining operations on April 8 were clear signs of imminent hostilities, but even this failed to change Fleischer's itinerary. The start of one of the worst winter storms of the season prevented the general and his chief of staff from returning to the divisional headquarters for several days.

NOTES

1 The actual composition of the various flotillas changed from time to time when ships were attached or detached.

2 *XXIKTB*, No 3.279/16, reports that the strength and equipment of a mountain infantry battalion on leaving Wesermunde was: 25 officers, 528 non-commissioned officers and enlisted, nine motorcycles, 27 light machineguns, 10 heavy machineguns, nine light mortars, six heavy mortars, and two light infantry guns. Each of the three battalions consisted of a headquarters, a heavy weapons company, and three rifle companies. The heavy weapons company numbered 104 men and the armament consisted of six heavy mortars and two light antitank guns. The infantry companies also had 104 men and their crew-served weapons consisted of nine light machineguns, two heavy machineguns, and three light mortars. The companies in the German mountain divisions were numbered consecutively. That means that the first battalion in a regiment consisted of companies 1-5, the second battalion of companies 6-10, and the third battalion of companies 11-15. The next to the last company in each battalion (4, 9, and 14) were the heavy weapons companies while the last (5, 10, and 15) were headquarters companies.

3 Colonel Alois Windisch (1892–1958) was an Austrian and an exceedingly capable officer who proved to be a tough opponent for the Norwegians and French in the Narvik area. General Hovland calls him the most talented German officer in the Narvik Campaign and a dangerous opponent. He spent all of World War 1 at the front, was wounded three times, and highly decorated. He had a balanced career in troop command, combat, and general staff service. He organized the 139th Mountain Infantry Regiment in 1938 and commanded it during the Polish Campaign. His regiment participated in the attack on the Soviet Union on the arctic front. He was relieved of his command in March 1942 because he had launched a regimental attack without promised air support. For a while, he was in charge of the prisoner of war camp at Bezirk Kirowgrad. He was promoted to major general in 1943 and was later given command of the 285th Security Division in Yugoslavia. He became a Soviet prisoner of war in 1945, was handed over to Yugoslavia, tried, and sentenced to 20 years in prison. He was released in 1953.

4 Gerda-Luise Dietl and Kurt Hermann, *General Dietl* (Munich, 1951), p. 17.

5 Steen, *Norges Sjøkrig 1940-1945,* vol. 4, p. 28, second note and vol. 1, p. 136.

6 Colonel Sundlo is also mentioned in Admiral Raeder's operational directive of March 6, 1940. It states that the military commandant in Narvik, Colonel Sundlo, is friendly and that it was not expected that he would create any difficulties for the Germans.

7 Dickens, *Battles in the Fjords*, p. 32.

8 Captain Steen writes that the outgoing message from *Norge* identified the ships as German and implies that it somehow was muddled at the 3rd Naval District. General Sandvik writes (*Operasjonene*, vol. 1, p. 104 n. 52) that the message from *Norge* "was made to agree with the message" from *Michael Sars*, which simply identified the ships as "foreign". We will probably never know for sure where the mistake occurred since *Norge's* message log went down with the ship.

9 "Rapport fra sjefen for Norge og Ofotavdelingen til Kommanderende Admiral av 20 april 1940,' 4.

10 Steen, *Norges Sjøkrig 1940-1945*, vol. 4, p. 88.

11 Witness statement by Captain Siem on April 22, 1947, as quoted in Sandvik, *Operasjonene*, vol. 1, p. 107 n. 58.

12 Steen, *Norges Sjøkrig 1940-1945*, vol. 2, p. 124, vol. 4, p. 64, and 89. Torkel Hovland, *General*

Carl Gustaf Fleischer. Storhet og fall (Oslo: Forum-Aschehoug, 3rd edn, 2000), p. 78) reports that the General Staff order came at 0330 hours, the same time given by Lindbäck-Larsen.

13 Lindbäck-Larsen, *Rapport*, Section 4:3. It is likely that General Fleischer received this information 30 minutes earlier since he had a telephone conversation with Colonel Mjelde at 2130 hours, five minutes after Mjelde's headquarters received the message from the General Staff. See also Sandvik, *Operasjonene*, vol. 1, p. 99.

14 Spjeldnæs' testimony in Colonel Sundlo's trial on April 19, 1947, quoted in Sandvik, *Operasjonene*, vol. 1, p. 101.

15 Dietl and Hermann, *General Dietl*, p. 72.

16 Hovland, *Fleischer*, p. 79. The source given for this description is Nils Ryeng, *De fem trojanske hestene i 1940.*

17 Despite these instructions and the fact that their unit went on alert the previous evening, we find that Co 2's commander and executive officer spent the night at their quarters in Victoria Hospice, about one kilometer from their headquarters. Likewise, Major Spjeldnæs apparently stayed at his quarters in Bromsgård.

18 The sources give a confusing summary of how Co 2 was deployed. We know that it had an assigned strength of about 150. Forty-two soldiers were away from Narvik. Another six were involved in preparing the quarters for the units arriving from Elvegårdsmoen. The harbor defense force that was located in its quarters numbered about 20. The company reserve numbered 30-40 soldiers, depending on which source is used. That leaves 42-52 soldiers not accounted for. I believe these were also assigned to posts in the harbor area between Fagernes and Framnes. The NCO in charge of the harbor guards located in their quarters refers to them as "the remainder of the defense force." The explanation is probably that this force is in addition to 36 soldiers that Steen states were sent to occupy posts along the three kilometers long waterfront. These troops were probably deployed some time between 2000 hours when Colonel Sundlo placed Co 2 on alert and ordered the bunkers occupied and 2330 hours when he ordered that an officer be sent to each of the bunkers. This still leaves from 6 to 16 soldiers not accounted for. Some of those were probably cooks and runners. It is also possible that the detail preparing quarters for the arriving units involved more than six men.

19 Spjeldnæs testimony on April 19, 1947 as quoted in Sandvik, *Operasjonene*, vol. 1 p. 110 and n. 60.

20 Loc cit.

21 Quoted in Sandvik, *Operasjonene*, vol. 1, pp. 116-117.

22 Verbal report by Colonel Sundlo to the Military History Division on May 1, 1958 as reported in Steen, *Norges Sjøkrig 1940-1945*, vol. 4, p. 95.

23 The sequence of events that led to the surrender is that found in the official Norwegian histories of land and naval operations in North Norway in 1940 as well as in some German accounts. A number of the more popular and widely read accounts of these events deviate from the earlier histories without offering any new evidence.

24 Ottmer, *Weserübung*, p. 96. It seems obvious that Ottmer relied on secondary Norwegian sources to arrive at these conclusions.

25 Sandvik, *Operasjonene*, vol. 1, pp. 186-187.

26 The court decided unanimously "the defendant's [Sundlo's] actions pertaining to the surrender under the prevailing conditions can not be considered punishable. The conditions had reached a

point where a completely superior enemy surrounded the defendant and his troops. All defensive means must be viewed legally as taken, despite the fact that they were not activated, and every possibility of breakout or timely assistance had to be viewed as hopeless. The defendant had to make an immediate decision and weight the probable catastrophic results of resistance at that point against the duty to uphold the country's and own honor ... Accordingly, the accused is acquitted of point II of the prosecution's accusation and, similarly, he is found not guilty with respect to paragraph 83 of the penal code ..."

27 The Germans noted the failure of the Norwegian defense plans to use their troops to the best advantage and to exploit the difficulties presented by climate and geography. Karl Ruef writes "But also the natural advantages of the whole countryside around Narvik, the steep mountains, the flanking possibilities for infantry weapons, the lack of roads, the narrows and passes, the railroad tunnels, the knowledge of the terrain, the winter mobility of their own troops, the proximity of supply depots, all that the Norwegians failed to exploit." (*Odyssee einer Gebirgsdivision. Die 3. Geb. Div. im Einsatz* [Stuttgart: Leopold Stocker Verlag, 19760).

28 O. Munthe-Kaas, *The Campaign in Northern Norway. An Account of the Norwegian 6th Division's Advance Against the Germans in the Narvik Area April 9th – June 9th, 1940* (Washington, D.C.: The Royal Norwegian Information Service, 1944), p. 13.

29 One example of such despicable behavior took place in late May 1940 when, as a prisoner, he provided the Germans with the name of a person who could possibly serve as a guide for General Feurstein's forces in the wilderness area between Bodø and Narvik.

6

DESTROYER BATTLE

"Keep on engaging the enemy."

CAPTAIN WARBURTON-LEE'S LAST MESSAGE TO HIS DESTROYER

FLOTILLA MOMENTS BEFORE BEING MORTALLY WOUNDED.

The German Situation in Narvik

General Dietl and Captain Bonte had good reasons to congratulate themselves in the morning of April 9. They had sailed almost 1,500 miles through waters dominated by the British Navy and had captured Narvik without the loss of a ship, a sailor, or a soldier. They had inflicted a crippling blow on the Norwegian Navy, captured, without firing a shot, nearly 600 Norwegian soldiers and sailors, seized one of the largest Norwegian army depots, and captured five armed British merchant ships and their crews.

Despite these impressive successes, the German position in Narvik was not enviable. Dietl and Bonte each faced serious problems. Dietl's most immediate task was to consolidate his two beachheads against anticipated Norwegian and British attacks. Bonte's most urgent task was to return to Germany with his destroyers, a highly dangerous venture now that the British were fully alerted. Several factors complicated the situation for both Dietl and Bonte.

German planners had placed much reliance on the quick capture of the Norwegian shore batteries at the Ofotfjord entrance. It was one of three primary goals. They planned to use these batteries against any British attempt to enter Ofotfjord. The fact that these batteries did not exist increased the danger to the German forces. Dietl did not have the heavy weapons, equipment, and supplies on which he had planned. Most of the weapons and equipment carried on the destroyers washed overboard on the way to Narvik. The ships *Bärenfels*, *Rauenfels*, and *Alster* were scheduled to have arrived in Narvik before the destroyers. They carried weapons, equipment, and supplies. These three ships left Hamburg on April 3. They proceeded separately in order to give the appearance of innocent merchant ships. None reached their destination. *Bärenfels* fell so far behind schedule that she was redirected to Bergen, where she arrived on April 11. The British destroyer *Havock* crippled *Rauenfels* at the Ofotfjord entrance as the British warship returned from battle with the German destroyers on April 10. A British destroyer captured *Alster* north of Bodø on April 14. The loss of these three ships was a serious blow to Dietl since he could not count on receiving any further supplies by sea. This made the capture of the depot at Elvegårdsmoen all the more important.

Bonte's destroyers reached Narvik almost empty of fuel. They needed to refuel before they could start their return voyage to Germany but the two large tankers scheduled to be in Narvik when TF 1 arrived had not yet arrived. *Jan Wellem* sailed from Murmansk and reached Narvik on April 8. The *Kattegat* sailed from Germany and should also have reached Narvik on April 8. She stopped south of Bodø because of the British minefield and was intercepted by the Norwegian patrol boat *Nordkapp* and sunk in shallow water. The Norwegians later salvaged most of the cargo. German naval officers considered the loss of *Kattegat* the most serious blow to the Narvik operation since it prevented the German destroyers from departing Narvik on schedule.[1]

Bonte's problems were twofold. Each destroyer required about 600 tons of fuel for the return trip to Germany. With the loss of *Kattegat*, he had only half of the fuel called for in the operational plan. *Jan Wellem* could only provide this amount through the time-consuming procedure of mixing diesel oil with boiler oil.[2] The second problem involved the time required to refuel. With two tankers, he could have refueled four destroyers at a time and the time required would be much shorter since there would be no need to mix diesel oil and boiler oil. With one tanker, only two destroyers could refuel simultaneously, and each pair required seven to eight hours. Only three destroyers were refueled by 2400 hours, April 9.

The order in which Bonte refueled them presented a problem in itself. *Wilhelm Heidkamp*, Bonte's flagship, was one of the refueled destroyers. The other two were *Bernd von Arnim* and *Georg Thiele*. However, the last two destroyers also had minor engine troubles that needed to be fixed before they could undertake the voyage back to Germany. Only one destroyer was therefore fully ready to depart. At 1357 hours Captain Bonte sent a message to Admiral Saalwächter at Naval Command West and to Admiral Lütjens, who was waiting to link up with the destroyers. The message notified them that the destroyers could not depart Narvik on April 9 as planned, but Bonte intended to depart after dark on April 10, by which time all destroyers should be refueled. Saalwächter approved Bonte's decision and informed him that German submarines had taken up positions at the entrance to Norwegian fjords, including Vestfjord and Ofotfjord.

U-boat Group 1, consisting of *U25, U46, U51, U64* and *U65*, operated off North Norway. Some of these submarines were now patrolling Vestfjord and Ofotfjord along the approach any British force would have to follow. *U51* patrolled the inner part of Vestfjord; *U25* was in position off Barøy Lighthouse; and *U46* was in Ofotfjord, off Ramnes. Bonte's journal entries indicate that he had strong faith in the submarines' ability to warn him about approaching enemy ships. He was confident that the two submarines in the narrow straits near Barøy and Ramnes would detect any approaching enemy force. He even hoped that the submarines could prevent an enemy attempt to enter the fjord. This assessment was an overestimation of the submarines' capabilities in the low visibility caused by almost continuous snow squalls. Naval Command West informed Bonte about the submarines' positions and he in turn asked that command to impress upon the U-boat commanders the importance of their mission to report and hinder a British attack on Narvik.

The British would have been dismayed to know that the Germans had excellent and accurate intelligence about British naval operations. The information was obtained from intercepted and deciphered British radio traffic. Captain Bonte knew, for example, that a large naval force, thought to be the main body of the Home Fleet, was on its way north and that the force in or near Vestfjord included two battle cruisers. The most important intelligence passed to Bonte was that a British destroyer flotilla had orders to attack an unknown target.

Bonte may have feared air attacks more than a surface attack and this concern probably influenced how he deployed the ships that were not refueling in the evening of April 9. To some extent, his concern was unwarranted. Narvik was well beyond the reach of British land-based aircraft. The nearest British aircraft carrier was with the Home Fleet, still well out of range, but believed to be heading north. Bonte directed Commander Berger to send *George Thiele* and *Bernd von Arnim* into Ballangen Bay, about 15 miles southwest of Narvik. He ordered Commander Bey to take the destroyers *Wolfgang Zenker*, *Erich Giese*, and *Erich Koellner* into Herjangsfjord, about ten miles northeast of Narvik. Commander Hans-Joachim Gadow was to keep three of the 3rd Destroyer Flotilla's four destroyers in Narvik to refuel. The fourth destroyer was assigned patrol duty in Ofotfjord. This destroyer would be relieved, as required, by the refueling schedule. Bonte also kept his flagship, *Wilhelm Heidkamp*, in Narvik.

He planned initially to have the refueled *Wilhelm Heidkamp* join the three destroyers in Herjangsfjord. However, Dietl convinced him to remain in Narvik to facilitate consultations.

At 2200 hours on April 9, Captain Bonte received a radio message from Lieutenant Commander Knorr, the skipper of *U51*. This submarine patrolled the inner part of Vestfjord and reported sighting five British destroyers on a southwest course. This course took them away from Narvik and therefore the message did not cause Bonte to take any further precautions. As in the case of Admiral Forbes earlier with respect to Task Force 2, Captain Bonte placed too much reliance on the reported course of the British destroyers. These ships were waiting for dawn and high tide for their entry into Ofotfjord and the German submarine just happened to see the ships while they were heading southwestward.

Bonte is criticized for the actions he took or failed to take that fateful evening. Some of the criticism is justified, but not all. Bonte failed to be sufficiently on guard, despite knowing that superior British naval forces were in the Vestfjord area. However, it was logical for Bonte to assume that the three submarines at the entrance to Ofotfjord and one destroyer on patrol in the fjord outside the harbor entrance would provide adequate warning about a British attack. It was difficult for Bonte to increase the early warning patrols since seven of the ten destroyers were not refueled and did not have sufficient fuel to patrol. Nevertheless, he could have used his fully refueled flagship, despite Dietl's desire for it to remain in Narvik, and the two destroyers in Ballangen Bay to patrol further out in the fjord to provide earlier warning of approaching enemy forces.

He also kept too many destroyers in Narvik harbor, which was most likely to be the target of any surprise attack. There were five destroyers in the harbor when the British attacked but Bonte believed there were only four. Two had to be there in order to refuel. However, it would have been a good idea to move *Jan Wellem* to a side fjord to conduct the refueling operation. Refueling destroyers were vulnerable targets and the destruction of *Jan Wellem* would have ended all hopes of bringing the destroyers back to Germany. He could also have reduced the number of ships in Narvik by taking his flagship out of the immediate harbor area and by relocating the destroyer that was not actually involved in refueling operations. Bogen, on the north side of the fjord, or Rombaken would have been a good place for these two ships.

Captain Dickens is critical of Bonte for failing to issue orders to the destroyer captains about what actions to take in case of attack. With the exception of those in the harbor, the German ships were in excellent positions to respond to an attack. The three destroyers in Herjangsfjord threatened the flank of any force attacking Narvik. The two in Ballangen Bay could strike an attacking force from the rear. If instructions were in fact lacking, we can only conclude that the German destroyer captains responded in a professional manner and it is difficult to see how instructions could have improved on their actions.

General Dietl's main concern was a Norwegian counterattack and he placed his emphasis on improving and strengthening the defenses in the two beachheads. There were five armed British merchant ships in Narvik harbor when the Germans attacked. These were seized, the crews imprisoned, and attempts were begun to bring their guns ashore to support Dietl's troops. Bonte understood how exposed and ill equipped the German troops were, and he ordered all small arms and ammunition on the destroyers brought ashore for their use. The German operational plan called for Dietl to seize Bardufoss Airfield and the Setermoen depot and training area as quickly as possible after landing. The heavy snowfall blocked all roads leading north and it was therefore not possible to begin this part of the plan immediately.

The German dispositions at Narvik remained generally unchanged during April 9. The preponderance of the 139th Mountain Infantry Regiment (two battalions) remained near Elvegårdsmoen. This part of the 139th Regiment is later referred to as Group Windisch, after its commander, Colonel Windisch. Platoon and company-size security forces were positioned north of Bjerkvik and on both sides of Herjangsfjord. Dietl had to rely on Norwegian telephone facilities to communicate with Windisch since most of the division's communications equipment was lost on the stormy passage from Germany.

In retrospect, General Dietl's worries about a Norwegian counterattack were not well founded. The only Norwegian force near Narvik was the remnants of the 1/13th Inf that had managed to slip out of town. It was in no position to undertake offensive operations of any kind. The only other forces within a reasonable distance were the 2/15th Inf and the 3rd Mountain Artillery Bn. The 2/15 Inf, located at Setermoen, and a motorized artillery battery were ordered to Elvegårdsmoen late in the evening of April 8, but the heavy snowfall kept these units from making any appreciable progress.

General Fleischer remained in Vadsø on April 9 since the weather prevented a return to his headquarters. He kept in contact with District Command by telephone. Fleischer did not wait for the government to order mobilization. At 0445 hours on April 9 he ordered the mobilization of the remaining two line battalions of the 16th Infantry Regiment and later the same morning he expanded the mobilization to include the Alta Battalion and the remaining battalion of the 14th Infantry Regiment in Mosjøen. He also ordered all aircraft to Bardufoss where they could support operations near Narvik. Fleischer halted the move of the units from Setermoen to the Narvik area and these were instead concentrated in defensive positions in Salangsdal, south of Setermoen.

The British Reaction to the Capture of Narvik and Admiralty Intervention

It will be recalled that Admiral Whitworth finally dispatched his destroyers in the morning of April 9 to take up positions at the entrance to Vestfjord to prevent the Germans from reaching Narvik. The British were operating in an intelligence vacuum. The concentration of naval forces at the entrance to Vestfjord was based on the faulty assumption that the Germans were still to their south. When the 2nd Destroyer Flotilla, commanded by the 45-year old Captain Bernard Armitage Warburton-Lee, established a patrol line across the Vestfjord entrance at 0930 hours (GMT) on April 9, the Germans were already in firm control of Narvik.

Shortly after establishing the patrol line across Vestfjord, Captain Warburton-Lee began receiving a stream of contradictory orders and directives from his superiors. At 0952 hours (GMT) An order from Admiral Forbes, bypassing Admiral Whitworth, directed him to send destroyers to Narvik to ensure that no German troops landed in that city. Five minutes later, Warburton-Lee received an order from Admiral Whitworth to join him about 50 nautical miles southwest of Skomvær Lighthouse. Finally, at midday, the Admiralty intervened by sending the following message directly to Captain Warburton-Lee:

> Press reports state one German ship has arrived Narvik and landed a small force. Proceed Narvik and sink or capture enemy ship. It is at your discretion to land forces if you think you can recapture Narvik from number of enemy present. Try to get possession of battery if not already in enemy hands.[3]

This Admiralty message bypassed both Admirals Forbes and Whitworth. The Admiralty had no business in directing tactical operations in this way, but it is possible that Churchill was behind this order. While the Admiralty had now concluded that the Germans were already in Narvik, their intelligence was limited only to press reports, which were wildly inaccurate.

These messages must have both flattered and frustrated Warburton-Lee, but the conflicting orders gave him an opportunity to use his initiative and to follow his own instincts. The order from Forbes allowed Warburton-Lee to ignore the order from Whitworth to withdraw, since Admiral Forbes was the senior of the two. Warburton-Lee, the central actor in the coming events, is described as follows by Dickens:[4] "He was a man of integrity, honour and ambition; a dedicated man, intensely professional and although an excellent games-player, somewhat aloof and single-minded." This officer took his four destroyers, *Hardy, Hunter, Havock,* and *Hotspur,* and proceeded up Vestfjord to carry out the order of his Commander-in-Chief.

Warburton-Lee was more than a little skeptical about the information forwarded by the Admiralty. It appeared inconceivable that the Germans would have undertaken an expedition to Narvik with only one ship, and equally unlikely that they would have entrusted such an important operation to only a few troops. He was also concerned about the Norwegian shore batteries in the fjord. The general lack of intelligence led him to make an effort to gather whatever information he could on his own before taking any further action. He stopped at Tranøy Lighthouse (on the east side of Vestfjord, about 50 miles north of the British minefield) around 1600 hours (GMT) and sent two officers ashore to find out what the officials at the pilot station knew about the conditions in Ofotfjord and enemy strength in Narvik. While at Tranøy, a fifth destroyer, *Hostile,* joined the British force.[5]

The British party sent ashore did not speak Norwegian and the Norwegians they met did not speak English. The communications that followed boiled down to a mixture of a few words of English and gestures. The two officers came away from the encounter with the impression that there was some disagreement among the Norwegians whether four or five German warships had passed on their way to Narvik. For unknown reasons, the two officers reported that six German warships had headed for Narvik.

It appears likely that the Norwegians were trying to tell the British that two groups of German warships had passed, one consisting of five vessels and the other of four. This is logical since one German destroyer, *Erich Giese,* had fallen 50 miles behind the others. The remaining nine destroyers passed Tranøy around 0300 hours (local). *Erich Giese* passed several hours later and may not have been observed in the midst of heavy snow squalls.

The two British officers concluded from their conversation with the Norwegians that a submarine had also passed on its way to Narvik, that the Norwegians believed the Ofotfjord narrows were mined, that the German warships were much larger than the British ships that were now at Tranøy, and that strong German forces had occupied Narvik. Finally, the Norwegians warned them not to attack until they had twice as many warships.

Captain Warburton-Lee's task was now altered drastically. He was no longer dealing with a lone German transport, but with six warships reported to be twice as large as his own as well as with at least one submarine. He could not ignore the possibility that the Germans had mined the narrows behind them and he still had to worry about the imaginary shore batteries. He had received a message from the Admiralty about 1300 hours (GMT) that read: "Battery at Narvik reported to consist of three 12 or 18 pounders mounted on Framnes and facing northwest [first mention of a shore battery in Narvik harbor]. Guns 4-inch or less may be in position on both sides of Ofotfjord near Ramnes." Finally, he had to consider the possibility that the Norwegian coastal defense ships were in German hands.

Warburton-Lee was well aware that the odds against him were considerable and he spent some time pondering what to do. If he launched an attack in the knowledge that he was facing superior enemy forces and it led to failure or disaster, he would bear the responsibility and his superiors could determine his action foolhardy. Heavy reinforcements were available and could join him at the entrance to Ofotfjord before morning. The battle cruiser *Repulse*, the cruiser *Penelope*, and four destroyers had arrived at the entrance to Vestfjord as Warburton-Lee's destroyers departed their patrol station. The *Renown* was also within striking distance, although it was doubtful that the Admiralty would risk either of the two battle cruisers in the restricted waters of Ofotfjord. Furthermore, two German battleships were still prowling the northern seas. On the other hand, Warburton-Lee may have feared that failure to proceed aggressively after receiving orders to attack from both the Commander-in-Chief and the Admiralty could be interpreted as timidity that would damage his ambitions.

Captain Warburton-Lee's officers reported that he spent about 30 minutes by himself agonizing about the decision he had to make. In the end, he told his men that they would attack and sent a message to the Admiralty at 1751 hours (GMT) that read: "Norwegians report Germans holding Narvik in force, also six destroyers and one U-Boat are there and channel is possibly mined. Intend attacking at dawn high water." It may be as Dickens writes that Warburton-Lee opted to follow the well-established naval custom of "Never 'propose' when you can 'intend', and never, never, ask for guidance."[6] Tactically, it made sense to attack at dawn and at high tide. High tide might allow the British warships to pass safely over the reported minefield. Dawn was viewed as the most likely time to achieve surprise.

Most British accounts place emphasis on the famous last sentence of Warburton-Lee's message and neglect to consider why the captain began his message with an alarming report of the obstacles in his way. It may well be that this young officer had found a way to avoid being labeled either timid or foolhardy. He may have hoped that on receipt of this new intelligence, either Whitworth, Forbes, or the Admiralty would intervene and tell him to wait for reinforcements. This would keep him from being considered too cautious. On the other hand, if they did not intervene and the attack was unsuccessful, his superiors would not be able to label him a dangerous risk-taker since their silence indicated their acquiescence.

Warburton-Lee's message made Admiral Whitworth concerned about the wisdom of the planned attack. The five British destroyers were not only outnumbered but the German ships were much larger and better armed. The responsibility for the operation now underway would have been his had it not been for the Admiralty's earlier intervention. He knew that every ship in his powerful force could reach Narvik before dawn but how would the Admiralty react to his entrance in what had now become their operation? He decided to intervene and sent the following visual signal to the ships in his vicinity at 1959 hours (GMT):

> To *Penelope*, repeat to Warburton-Lee. Take *Bedouin, Punjabi, Eskimo, Kimberley* under your orders and proceed to support of Captain (D) 2 in dawn attack on Narvik as directed by him. Unless otherwise ordered by him you should pass through position 20 miles southwest of Tranøy at 0100 tomorrow, 10th.

Before the message could be encoded and sent by radio, Whitworth changed his mind and at 2038 hours (GMT), he signaled his ships, "Cancel my 1959".[7] The assessment and decision reflected in Whitworth's original message was obviously correct and it was unfortunate that he reconsidered and sent the second message. Whitworth, Forbes, and the Admiralty received Captain Warburton-Lee's original message simultaneously at about 1830 hours (GMT). Admiral Whitworth had not ordered the Narvik attack. Admiral Forbes had ordered Warburton-Lee to proceed to Narvik almost nine hours earlier and about seven hours earlier, the Admiralty had ordered him to go on to Narvik and sink or capture the lone German transport they believed to be in that city. Both the Admiralty and the Commander-in-Chief left Whitworth out of the loop. Knowing that both Forbes and the Admiralty had received Warburton-Lee's message giving the latest intelligence and intention, Whitworth no doubt expected them to amend their previous orders. This is probably the reason he waited one and a half hours before intervening.

If Whitworth had stuck with his original plan as reflected in his visual message, it may well have changed the outcome of the upcoming battle and perhaps alleviated the need for another attack three days later. In the 39 minutes that passed between his initial order and its cancellation, Admiral Whitworth may have decided that it was not his prerogative to amend or change the earlier orders of his superiors that they had left standing by their silence.

Whitworth did have the authority and prerogative to reinforce, from his own resources, a unit under his own command about to engage the enemy. It is possible that Admiral Whitworth simply decided not to run the risk of offending his superiors by interfering in actions they had commenced.

Derry and MacIntyre conclude that Admiral Whitworth decided not to reinforce the 2nd Destroyer Flotilla because such action could delay the attack and that the element of surprise would therefore be lost. Derry writes that the *Repulse*, *Penelope*, and the four destroyers had not joined Admiral Whitworth's forces at the time when he contemplated reinforcing Warburton-Lee. This is not correct, as is demonstrated by the fact that Whitworth used visual signals to communicate his orders to *Penelope*. In fact, the *Hotspur* made visual contact with *Repulse* when it departed its patrol line to enter Vestfjord around 1300 hours (GMT).

Churchill takes note of Admiral Whitworth's consideration to reinforce Captain Warburton-Lee and writes, " … but the time seemed too short and he felt that intervention by him at this stage might cause a delay. In fact, we in the Admiralty were not prepared to risk the *Renown*—one of our only two battle cruisers—in such an enterprise."[8] This is misleading. Admiral Whitworth did not intend to use the *Renown* or *Repulse* to reinforce Warburton-Lee. Moreover, Whitworth and his staff had calculated that *Penelope* and the four destroyers could be at the pass through position southwest of Tranøy at 0100 hours (GMT) and the distance from there to the Ofotfjord entrance is about 30 miles. The fact that the *Penelope* and the four destroyers did not depart immediately upon receiving Admiral Whitworth's first message indicates that they did not think that the time factor was critical. They were about 40 miles from the pass through position designated in Whitworth's first message and they could reach that point at the designated time by leaving as late as 2300 hours (GMT). In fact, the 2nd Destroyer Flotilla was still to the south of Tranøy at midnight and the flotilla navigation officer sighted Tranøy Light at 0030 hours (GMT). Warburton-Lee's destroyers entered Ofotfjord at 0130 hours and it is therefore true that *Penelope* and its escorts could not have made it from the designated pass-through position to the Ofotfjord entrance in time unless a more northerly pass-through position or an earlier pass-through time was designated. There are no obvious reasons why this could not have been done.

The silence from Admirals Whitworth and Forbes must have served as a reminder to the Admiralty that they had ordered the operation and that they should therefore reply to Captain Warburton-Lee. A message sent to the destroyer flotilla commander at 2100 hours (GMT) directed him to patrol east of Ramnes to keep the German warships from slipping out through channels leading to the north. MacIntyre concludes that the Admiralty worried that the Germans would escape to Vågsfjord through Tjelsund. It is more likely that they worried about escape through Ramsund since Tjelsund can be blocked without entering Ofotfjord.

Churchill and the Admiralty were obviously concerned that the German destroyers could slip out of Narvik during the night. This had in fact been the original plan but the loss of *Kattegat* made its implementation impossible. The Admiralty was not aware of Bonte's problems and was determined not to allow him to add insult to injury by slipping past them twice.

The Admiralty message ended with, "Attack at dawn: all good luck". This was the green light that Captain Warburton-Lee needed and must have come as a relief. He had reported what he believed he was up against and the Admiralty's blessing on his intention to attack meant that he would not be responsible for a foolhardy action in case things went wrong.

The British chain of command above Warburton-Lee took a major and unwarranted risk in not providing reinforcements. This failure is not attributable solely to the lack of intelligence. A German force of one battleship, two cruisers and ten destroyers was sighted on a northbound course in the North Sea late on April 7, and a large part of this force was known to be north of Trondheim on April 8. The Admiralty, Admiral Forbes, and Admiral Whitworth should have asked themselves what happened to the ten destroyers. The *Renown* had encountered the *Scharnhorst* and *Gneisenau* without their destroyers on April 9. This, combined with the report received from the Norwegians at the Tranøy Pilot Station, should have led to the conclusion that the residue of the German force sighted in the North Sea on April 7 and 8 had in fact headed for Narvik.

German Fatigue and Complacency

Captain Bonte retired to his cabin on *Wilhelm Heidkamp* before midnight on April 9 after having made the earlier described deployment of his forces. The fact that the weather and visibility worsened dramatically during the evening undoubtedly gave the German captain a false sense of security. He should have remembered that the dismal weather had worked to his advantage in achieving surprise less than 24 hours earlier. The weather made it more difficult for the British to navigate the narrow fjord but it also made it more difficult for the German submarines to spot the British ships.

The 3rd Destroyer Flotilla was refueling and Commander Gadow, the flotilla commander, was responsible for securing the harbor entrance. He initiated the harbor patrol at 1900 hours with the destroyer *Hermann Künne*, one of the warships not yet refueled. The lack of fuel contributed to frequent relief of the patrolling destroyers. *Hermann Künne's* skipper, Lieutenant Commander Friedrich Kothe, interpreted his order as allowing him to use his own initiative in cruising between Bogen Bay on the north side of Ofotfjord, directly opposite Ballangen Bay, and Ramnes. Lieutenant Commander F. Böhme took his ship, *Anton Schmitt*, out of the harbor to relieve *Hermann Künne* at midnight. Bitter cold and continuous snowstorms reduced the visibility to only a few hundred feet.

Fatigue on the part of the Germans may have helped the British achieve surprise at Narvik on April 10. Most of the German destroyer crews had been at their stations for 48 hours. Some were able to rest for a few hours in the afternoon of April 9, but the refueling operations kept most busy. Consideration for the exhaustion of his officers and men may have played a role in Bonte's decision not to further disperse his destroyers, keeping more than he should in the harbor.

Anton Schmitt was relieved of its patrol duty at 0400 hours (local) by *Diether von Roeder*. Lieutenant Commander Erich Holtorf, the *Dieter von Roeder's* skipper, had received the following order from Commander Gadow via radio: "At 0400 [local] hours relieve 'Anton Schmitt.' Anti-submarine defense of harbor entrance until dawn."[9] *Anton Schmitt* anchored near *Jan Wellem* in anticipation of going alongside the latter to refuel. Lieutenant Commander Böhme retired to his cabin for a rest, but the fact that he remained fully clothed and kept his life jacket on are indications that he did not feel at ease with the situation.

The Attack by British Destroyers

Meanwhile, the 2nd British Destroyer Flotilla proceeded up Vestfjord at 20 knots. It was a nerve-wracking passage in the severely reduced visibility. There were several near misses, not only with the shoreline but also between the destroyers trying to keep within sight of each other in the heavy snow squalls. Skill and the quick reactions of the destroyer crews kept disasters from happening and the line of ships made the starboard turn into Ofotfjord at 0130 hours (GMT) without reducing speed and without being sighted by *U51*. *U25* also failed to see the British warships. Warburton-Lee reduced speed to 12 knots as he neared the narrow part of the fjord between Finnvika and Tjeldøy. Luck was again with the British. They were not sighted by *U46*, patrolling the narrows near Ramnes.

The Admiralty, in session throughout the operation, had time to consider the hazardous nature of Warburton-Lee's undertaking and have second thoughts about its wisdom. However, they could not bring themselves to take the responsibility to call off the attack or delay it until the 2nd Destroyer Flotilla could be sufficiently reinforced. Instead, they sent a cautionary message to Warburton-Lee just as the British warships were entering Ofotfjord (0136 hours GMT):[10] "Norwegian defense ships *Eidsvold* and *Norge* may be in German hands. You alone can judge whether in these circumstances attack should be made. We shall support whatever decision you make."

The Admiralty knew that there were six German destroyers in Narvik, along with one submarine. They suspected that the Norwegian shore batteries and the two coastal defense ships were in German hands. Finally, they were told that the fjord entrance might be mined. This intelligence about the situation in Narvik should have caused the Admiralty sufficient concern about sending five relatively small destroyers into what could be a hornet's nest. Warburton-Lee was already in Ofotfjord when the Admiralty threw the ball back into his court. The cautionary message had no effect on his plans. The problem of looking too cautious was still there but the danger of being labeled foolhardy was removed by the last sentence in the Admiralty message.

The British destroyers were now approaching Narvik. Their navigational difficulties and near misses with the shoreline and each other resulted in the exchange of numerous radio signals between the destroyers as they proceeded into the fjord. The signals were sent in the clear. Navigational problems, as they were approaching their target, warranted taking this otherwise unacceptable risk. The British were again lucky. The German radio operators were obviously not searching various frequencies for enemy tactical information.

Diether von Roeder headed for the entrance to Narvik harbor at 0330 hours (GMT), after only 30 minutes on patrol. Lieutenant Commander Holtorf calculated that this would bring him into the harbor at first light, about 0420 hours (GMT). Bonte's journal notes that Gadow was to arrange for *Diether von Roeder* to remain on guard until relieved by *Hans Lüdemann*, Gadow's flagship. It is obvious that there was some miscommunication, because it is difficult to understand why Holtorf left his post without notifying the flotilla commander. Holtorf could not help but notice that *Hans Lüdemann* was still alongside *Jan Wellem* when he entered the harbor and dropped anchor. The Germans claim that *Diether von Roeder* did not wait to be relieved due to a misunderstanding of orders.[11]

Diether von Roeder's navigation officer plotted the ship's position and it happened to coincide exactly with a plot made by the navigation officer on the British destroyer *Hardy* at precisely the same time. The British navigation officer appears to have made a slight mistake in the ship's dead-reckoning position, due perhaps to over-compensation for current and wind. However, the ships were probably not much over one mile apart. Captain Warburton-Lee signaled his ships at 0343 hours (GMT), "I am steering for the entrance of Narvik Harbour."[12] The British destroyers headed for the harbor entrance at eight knots, on the same course as *Diether von Roeder*. Both sides were unaware that the enemy was so close to hand.

The first light of dawn was beginning to break when land appeared off the lead British destroyer's port bow. It should have been the Framnes Peninsula if navigation had been on the mark. However, it turned out to be Emmenes, on the other side of the harbor entrance. This three kilometer mistake in navigation turned out to be very fortunate for the British, since it prevented them from running into *Diether von Roeder* and giving the German destroyers some warning of the impending attack.

The British made a course adjustment towards the harbor and despite an increase in speed to 12 knots, the fortuitous delay resulted in *Diether von Roeder* entering the harbor just moments before the British. It took the British six minutes to reach the harbor entrance. By this time, it was light enough to see a large number of ships anchored in the harbor, but the enemy destroyers were not yet detected.

Warburton-Lee dispatched the destroyers *Hotspur* and *Hostile* to the northeast to prevent any enemy ships that could be outside the harbor from interfering with the attack and to cover any possible shore batteries on Framnes. He entered the harbor alone with the *Hardy*, telling *Hunter* and *Havock* to await their turn to attack. The visibility had now improved to almost one mile, but the haze of the breaking dawn kept the British from immediately seeing the German destroyers. Two of these, *Hermann Künne* and *Hans Lüdemann*, were refueling on opposite sides of *Jan Wellem*. *Anton Schmitt* was behind the tanker, waiting its turn to refuel. *Diether von Roeder* had just dropped anchor west of the city pier, and the German flagship, *Wilhelm Heidkamp*, was further to the south.

Hardy slid quietly by some of the merchant ships and sighted *Anton Schmitt* and *Wilhelm Heidkamp* through a gap between the merchant ships. Bonte's ensign was observed flying from *Wilhelm Heidkamp's* mast.

The alarm had not sounded as the British broke out their battle flags. Warburton-Lee ordered the engine engaged slightly in order to maneuver into torpedo position. The two German ships were stationary and it was difficult to miss them at this short range. Torpedoes were launched and Warburton-Lee instinctively swung *Hardy* around and headed back for the harbor entrance at 20 knots. The time was 0430 hours (GMT). The first torpedo missed its target and hit a merchant ship. The second found its mark. The violent explosion detonated the aft magazine on the *Wilhelm Heidkamp*, blowing off the ship's stern. The massive explosion tore off the three aft guns and munitions continued to explode for several minutes. Captain Bonte never knew what happened. He and 81 of his crew died instantly. *Wilhelm Heidkamp's* skipper, Lieutenant Commander Hans Erdmenger, miraculously escaped death and he managed to secure his wrecked ship to the Swedish transport *Oxelösund* in order to save the wounded and some of the valuable equipment. *Wilhelm Heidkamp* remained afloat until April 11.

Two additional German destroyers were sighted as *Hardy* exited the harbor at high speed, the *Hermann Künne* refueling alongside *Jan Wellem*, and *Diether von Roeder*. *Hardy* fired a salvo of three torpedoes at the German warships but they missed and detonated against the piers in the northeast corner of the harbor.

Hunter now entered the harbor. Lieutenant Commander Lindsay de Villiers, *Hunter's* skipper, was less discriminating in picking his targets. He fired the ship's torpedoes into the crowded harbor at the same time as he opened up with his guns. The resulting chaos was indescribable. *Anton Schmitt's* crew came on deck thinking they were under air attack. This thought was quickly dispelled when a shell hit the forward part of the ship. Lieutenant Commander Böhme was trying to leave his cabin when a torpedo from *Hunter* hit the ship's forward turbine room. The explosion jammed the cabin door, trapping him inside. The German warships were now returning fire and *Hunter* laid smoke as she exited the harbor. *Havock* entered the harbor as *Hunter* exited. Her task was more difficult than that of her predecessors. The Germans were now aware that they were under a surface attack and the visibility that had been tolerable 15 minutes earlier was again very limited because of all the smoke from gunfire and burning ships. *Havock's* skipper, Lieutenant Commander Rafe E. Courage, spotted *Hermann Künne* alongside *Jan Wellem* and opened fire on these two ships. No hits were scored. *Hermann Künne* had sufficient steam pressure to maneuver away from the tanker. This was done with a great sense of urgency and without taking time to detach the wires and hoses connecting it to *Jan Wellem*. Commander Courage now turned his attention to *Anton Schmitt* and gave that ship his full attention. A salvo of three torpedoes was fired at the German warship. The first two torpedoes hit two merchant ships. The third torpedo hit *Anton Schmitt* in the aft boiler room just after Böhme had managed to open the jammed door to his cabin and was on his way to the quarterdeck. Böhme was thrown overboard by the explosion. He was wearing a life jacket and this saved his life. German and Norwegian sources report that two torpedoes hit *Anton Schmitt* amidships and that the destroyer broke in two and sank almost immediately.

Hermann Künne had managed to back away from *Jan Wellem* and it was located less than 50 meters from *Anton Schmitt* when the latter received the second torpedo hit. The tremendous explosion sent shock waves through *Hermann Künne* and temporarily made its engines inoperable. As the forward part of *Anton Schmitt* rolled over, her mast settled on *Hermann Künne's* deck and the two ships became entangled and remained immobilized for the next 40 minutes.

There is some dispute as to what happened during this first phase of the attack and that is understandable in such a violent and sudden encounter. Captain MacIntyre writes that torpedoes from *Hardy* caused the destruction of both *Wilhelm Heidkamp* and *Anton Schmitt* and that while both *Hunter* and

Havock fired torpedoes, these appeared to have missed. Moulton appears to accept the same reasoning but this may be because he seems to have relied heavily on what Captain MacIntyre wrote about this event. Dickens and Harvey, however, maintain that torpedoes fired by *Havock* sank *Anton Schmitt*. German sources and the sequence of events leading to Commander Böhme reaching the quarterdeck at the same time as the torpedo struck the ship, support Dickens and Harvey's version.

The German gunfire became increasingly effective as the men began to recover from their surprise, and Courage decided to break off his attack. *Havock* received fire from *Hans Lüdemann*, which was now loose from *Jan Wellem*, and *Diether von Roeder* as she exited the harbor. *Havock* was not hit, but *Hans Lüdemann* sustained two damaging hits. One shell put one of her forward guns out of action while a second shell started a fire in the aft part of the ship, making it necessary to flood the rear magazine to keep it from exploding. *Havock* was also subjected to a hail of rifle and machinegun fire from German troops on shore. The battle had lasted 30 minutes and the crowded harbor was a terrible scene of destruction.

Hotspur, skippered by Commander Herbert F. N. Layman, and *Hostile*, skippered by Commander J. P. Wright now joined the battle, as they had returned from their mission to check any shore batteries at Framnes. *Hostile* became engaged in a gun battle with *Diether von Roeder*, still at anchor and immobile. The battle was intense but the visibility was so reduced by smoke that the gunnery was not very effective. *Hostile* took no hits, but *Diether von Roeder* sustained two damaging hits. *Hunter* fired four torpedoes into the harbor and hit two merchant ships, one being the British *Blythmoor*. The British had fired 22 torpedoes into the harbor. All five British destroyers were now steaming in a rough counter-clockwise formation outside the harbor, engaging targets as they came abreast of the entrance.

Due to the reduced visibility caused by the smoke from the fires and guns, the three surviving German destroyers and their five opponents were aiming their fire at observed gun flashes. Commander Wright was trying to get into a position to launch a torpedo attack against *Diether von Roeder*, but Commander Holtorf beat him to the draw. *Diether von Roeder* had taken a punishing pounding from the British fire. Two shells from *Hostile* penetrated her port side below the bridge, rupturing a fuel tank, and damaging the steering controls. The fire from the broken fuel tank set the aft boiler room ablaze. The ship was still immobile but Holtorf feared that the spreading fire would reach the magazines and he decided to launch his torpedoes before it was too late. He sent a spread of eight torpedoes between the merchant ships towards the harbor entrance. *Hans Lüdemann* and *Hermann Künne* also sent torpedo salvos towards the entrance.

The British destroyers were now engaged in desperate maneuvers to avoid the many torpedo tracks coming towards them. They managed to avoid most of them, but the after-action reports indicate that three destroyers would have been hit if the German torpedoes had functioned properly by staying at the preset depth. *Hardy*, *Hunter*, and *Havock* reported that torpedoes passed under them and would have been hits if they had traveled at the correct depth.

Diether von Roeder continued to defend itself in a fierce duel against the five British attackers. The German destroyer had dropped its anchor after returning from patrol and the anchor could not be lifted because the power supply to the electrically operated windlass was severed. The warship was a stationary target on which the British concentrated their fire. The boiler room was ablaze, the fire direction system was inoperable, and a shell struck the mess killing eight men and starting a fire that turned the forward part of the ship into an inferno.

A British shell hit and destroyed gun number 3, killing six of its crew. Another shell ignited an ammunition locker and one penetrated the ship near the aft magazine. This made it necessary to flood the magazine. *Diether von Roeder's* guns kept firing, directed locally since the central fire control system was down. The ship's engine still functioned and Commander Holtorf backed his ship to safety between the fiery wrecks of merchant ships, dragging the anchor. He managed to reach the Steamship Pier and there the ship remained with its bow facing the harbor entrance. The fires were extinguished with the help of shore-based fire-fighting equipment. Despite the crew being full of fight, Commander Holtorf decided that his ship had sustained so much damage and its fighting ability was so reduced that it would be folly to keep the crew aboard. He ordered all unnecessary personnel to leave the ship.

Warburton-Lee made a quick assessment of the situation. There was no fire coming from the harbor. The British had counted at least four or five German destroyers in the harbor out of the six that they believed the Norwegians at Tranøy had reported entering Ofotfjord. Warburton-Lee decided, after he was told the ships had 16 torpedoes left, that there was little risk in completing the work he had started and he ordered the destroyers to reenter the harbor and finish off the enemy.

The British destroyers entered the harbor in a line-ahead formation at 20 knots in order to be better able to avoid enemy torpedoes, and circled in a counter-clockwise direction while raking all observed targets in the harbor with their guns. The British ships exited at high speed about 0530 hours (GMT).

Warburton-Lee led his five destroyers westward at moderate speed to a point northeast of Skomsnes and held a council of war on the bridge. Everyone favored making another run into the harbor to ensure that all enemy ships were destroyed. It is an understandable emotion by men flushed with at the prospect of complete victory. Warburton-Lee accepted the views of his officers and even ordered landing parties readied. This was a strange order since the landing parties consisted of no more than one lightly armed platoon on each ship and the British had received a hail of small arms and machinegun fire from the shoreline, an indication that the shore was held in force. The fateful decision to make a third foray into the harbor spelled the end to the amazing run of British luck.

Dickens claims that the Germans finally alerted their five destroyers located outside the harbor about 0530 hours, one hour after the action began. The outlaying destroyers no doubt received word late about the British attack on Narvik, but probably not quite as late as indicated by Dickens.

Warburton-Lee took his flotilla back into the harbor at 20 knots. The mist and smoke was heavy as the destroyers weaved their way past the graveyard of sunken or sinking hulls of merchant ships in their path. They met gunfire from *Hans Lüdemann* and *Hermann Künne*. Those ships were not visible but the British fired at the point of the gun flashes. *Hans Lüdemann* also fired a salvo of four torpedoes at the attacking British destroyers but they all missed, one passing under *Hostile*. *Hostile* ventured a little too close to the enemy in launching its torpedoes and received the first large caliber hit by a British ship so far in the action. The damage from the 5-inch shell was not serious. *Hardy*, leading the line of British warships, turned west as she exited Narvik's harbor.

Jan Wellem had so far escaped the carnage but its captain now felt that her time had come and ordered the ship abandoned. *Jan Wellem* carried a number of British prisoners and the captain and his crew remained aboard until the prisoners were lowered safely away.

The distance from the three German destroyers in Herjangsfjord to Narvik was approximately 10 miles, and the distance to Ballangen Bay was about 15 miles. From the time these destroyers received word about the British attack, they needed to weigh anchors, get underway, and cover the distances mentioned above.

The official Norwegian naval history agrees with Dickens that the destroyers in Herjangsfjord were notified about the action in Narvik in a message from *Hans Lüdemann*. However, it states that this message was sent at 0515 hours, at the same time as Warburton-Lee's destroyers were beginning their second run into the harbor. This seems a more realistic timeline although it is still probably too tight.

There are therefore reasons to believe that the message may have been sent even before the time indicated by the Norwegian history, possibly after the three British destroyers had completed their first run. It took the German destroyers in Herjangsfjord at least 15 minutes to weigh anchor and they set out for Narvik at the maximum speed allowable by their scant fuel supplies. The British destroyer flotilla exited Narvik harbor after its third run around 0550 hours, about 35 minutes after the German destroyers in Herjangsfjord were alerted if we accept the sequence of events reported by the Norwegians.

The German Counterattack

One can well imagine the surprise on *Hardy's* bridge when, as the British flotilla turned westward from the harbor entrance, they observed an enemy force steering in their direction from the northeast at a distance estimated to be 7,500 meters. Warburton-Lee was the first to see the enemy force and he estimated that it consisted of one cruiser and three destroyers. He is reported to have told those present on the bridge, "This is our moment to get out," and as he sent the following message to his superiors at 0551 hours, "One cruiser, three destroyers off Narvik. Am withdrawing to westward,"[13] he increased speed to 30 knots and fired the emergency withdrawal signal.

Warburton-Lee was mistaken as to both the composition and number of enemy ships but the German destroyers were large ships and it is understandable that one could be identified as a cruiser. It was also undoubtedly difficult to ascertain the exact number in the hazy morning light.

Commander Bey's destroyers were in an oblique formation that allowed all ships to open fire with their forward guns without endangering each other. They opened fire shortly after they were sighted and the battle developed into a running engagement on a westerly course. The British ships, with the exception of *Hostile* that lingered behind still looking for targets in the harbor, were able to reply to the German fire with full broadsides as the enemy was off their starboard beam. The fire by both sides was ineffective and all shells fell far short of their targets. The reason was undoubtedly a mistake in range estimation. The British estimated that the enemy ships were 7,000 to 7,500 meters away when they opened fire. German reports state that the distance was over 10,000 meters.[14]

Commander Erich Bey, the commander of the 4th Destroyer Flotilla, became the senior German naval officer when Captain Bonte was killed. He was an experienced and respected destroyer officer, but tended to err on the side of caution.[15] He was not fully aware of what had happened in Narvik or of the size of the opposing enemy force. The only message he received from Narvik after being alerted stated that *Wilhelm Heidkamp* was sunk, that Bonte was killed, and that three destroyers were prepared to serve as floating batteries.

This sounded rather ominous to the new naval commander, who placed heavy emphasis on that part of Admiral Raeder's operational order that called for the preservation of the ships and their early and safe return to Germany. It was natural for him to conclude that a much superior enemy force caused what appeared to be a disaster and he saw it as his first duty to salvage what was left. It may be, as stated by Dickens, that Bey assumed his three destroyers were trapped, that he intended to fight it out, but that he wanted the two refueled destroyers in Ballangen Bay, *Georg Thiele* and *Bernd von Arnim*, to save themselves by breaking out to the west. Dickens goes on to say that Bey actually signaled these destroyers to break out.

The British destroyers, in the order *Hardy, Havock, Hunter, Hotspur,* and *Hostile,* laid smoke as they sped westward at maximum speed. The smoke helped shield the British ships from their three pursuers, but was of little help in meeting the next surprise sprung on Warburton-Lee. When he observed two big warships approaching from the west at high speed, he assumed initially that they were British cruisers coming to his aid. It was only when Commander Wolf turned *Georg Thiele* to port in order to bring all its armaments to bear on the British, that it became obvious to the officers on *Hardy's* bridge that the ships were German.

Georg Thiele, commanded by Lieutenant Commander Max-Eckhart Wolf, and *Bernd von Arnim*, commanded by Lieutenant Commander Kurt Rechel, were anchored in Ballangen Bay when the British attacked Narvik. They were alerted at the same time as Commander Bey but very dense fog and heavy snowfall kept them from reaching Ofotfjord until 0540 hours. Wolf and Rechel must have ignored Commander Bey's order to break out as related by Dickens. They turned eastward as soon as they reached the open waters of Ofotfjord, intent on giving battle. They flew large recognition signals to prevent being fired on by other German ships which they assumed were converging on the British from the northeast.

The British were now caught in a pincer between the two German destroyers from Ballangen Bay and the three destroyers from Herjangsfjord. The British were in a precarious position. The number of ships involved was equal, but the German ships were considerably larger and they now had the tactical initiative. *Georg Thiele* and *Bernd von Arnim* were closing on the British destroyer column at an effective speed of 60 knots and this left precious little time for decision-making.

The two aggressive German destroyer captains knew that a tragedy had befallen their comrades in Narvik and they were now bent on revenge. By turning to port and opening fire at a range of approximately 4,000 meters, Commander Wolf achieved the classic crossing of the "T" and brought all his guns to bear on *Hardy*, the lead British destroyer. Warburton-Lee, approaching the German ships head on, could only use his two forward guns and when he finally turned to port to bring the rest of the armament to bear on his opponents, he had lost precious time. The smoke screen prevented the destroyers behind *Hardy*, with the exception of *Havock*, from observing what was happening. The three pursuing German destroyers were delayed at this critical moment by the evasive actions they took to avoid the torpedoes and gunfire from their comrades in Narvik. Warburton-Lee's immediate problem was therefore only the destroyers coming at him from the west and these were not only outnumbered five to two but the British had a gun advantage of 21 to 10. However, the British commander had to assume that the three German destroyers from Herjangsfjord were hot on his heels and that his ships were caught in a vise.

Bernd von Arnim, seeing that *Georg Thiele* was engaging *Hardy*, concentrated its efforts on the second destroyer in the British line, *Havock*. Warburton-Lee signaled his ships at 0555 hours, "Keep on engaging the enemy." This message took on a legendary quality in the British Navy since it was believed that Captain Warburton-Lee issued this order after he was mortally wounded. However, based on testimony of the only surviving officer on *Hardy's* bridge, this message was sent before the ship was hit and was meant as a tactical instruction to the three rearmost destroyers in the British line to keep engaging the German warships coming up from behind.[16]

Georg Thiele found the range with its fourth salvo. Two shell struck *Hardy's* bridge and wheelhouse and other shells destroyed her forward guns. Everyone on the bridge was either killed or wounded. The only officer alive and not mortally wounded on the bridge was Paymaster Lieutenant Geoffrey Stanning, and his leg was shattered. *Hardy* was out of control, and heading towards the rocky shore at 30 knots. Stanning ordered the helmsman to change course but the wheelhouse was destroyed and there was no one at the helm.

The rest of the British line, not knowing that *Hardy* was out of control, followed in her wake. Stanning, in an amazing feat of bravery and determination, climbed down the ladder to the wheelhouse despite a shattered leg. Here he found that the helm was partially destroyed, but that it still functioned when he turned what was left of the wheel. He altered course away from the shore, but initially he could not see out of the wheelhouse, overcorrected, and found himself heading towards the enemy. He was able to correct the course and found a seaman who took the wheel while he made the painful climb back to the bridge. He saw two German destroyers off his starboard bow firing rapid salvoes. His first thought was to ram one of his antagonists but then a shell hit the boiler room, sending out billowing columns of steam. The ship was losing power and would soon become a stationary target at the mercy of the enemy. He decided to beach *Hardy* in order to save the crew. The ship almost came to a stop before reaching shore but she eventually slid gently onto the rocky beach at Virek.

Stanning, who was ineligible for command because of a physical disability, performed a heroic act in bringing the wrecked ship ashore. Nineteen sailors died on the *Hardy* and there were more than a dozen seriously wounded. The losses would have been far worse had it not been for Lieutenant Stanning's actions. Warburton-Lee was mortally wounded and died shortly after being brought ashore. He was the first recipient of the Victoria Cross in World War 2.

While the *Hardy* was being beached, the furious battle in the fjord continued. Commander Wolf assumed that the 4th Destroyer Flotilla was pursuing the British from the east. In order to keep the British ships in the trap, he turned *Georg Thiele* around and stayed ahead of the British ships, off their starboard bows. *Bernd von Arnim* followed suit.

The 4th Destroyer Flotilla was in fact well to the rear and this could have subjected the two German ships to the full fury of the four remaining British destroyers. However, the smoke kept both sides from knowing the exact situation. This worked to the advantage of the two aggressive German destroyer captains and they were able to maintain the initiative. There may have been two factors explaining Bey's apparent lack of aggressiveness in the pursuit. First, the three ships of the 4th Destroyer Flotilla had not refueled and their fuel levels were so low that a prolonged engagement with the British ships could cause them to run dry and become immobile targets. The second factor was related to the first. The German Navy's operational order stressed the importance of avoiding combat, especially decisive combat. The objective was the preservation and early return of the destroyers to Germany. The burden of ensuring compliance with the operational order fell on Bey after Bonte was killed.

In Bey's defense, it should be kept in mind that the two sides opened fire on each other at a range that may have been as much as 10,000 meters. The British were heading west at maximum speed and the chance that Bey could close the distance was not great unless the British westward progress could somehow be slowed. The difficulty in catching up with the British was further complicated when the 4th Destroyer Flotilla took evasive actions when it was engaged by its own ships in Narvik.

This left *Georg Thiele* and *Bernd von Arnim* to battle the British alone. The smoke was not helpful to the British at this point. Since it also obscured the enemy, they did not realize at first that their two opponents had changed to a parallel course. They kept up the smoke in the belief that Commander Bey was closing fast on their rear.

Havock was now the lead ship in the British column. The British commanders may have been unaware of the German course change, but the gunners kept engaging whenever they saw a target through the smoke. They finally began to register hits. A 4.7-inch shell made *Georg Thiele's* forward boiler inoperable and another started a fire that required flooding the aft magazine. A torpedo salvo from *Hostile* passed harmlessly between the German ships.

While the British gunners were beginning to find their targets, the Germans continued to inflict damaging hits on their opponents. *Havock* escaped serious damage, but both *Hunter* and *Hotspur* were hit at this time. Commander Courage did not see any enemy ships to his front because the British smoke apparently shielded *Georg Thiele* and *Bernd von Arnim*. He concluded that all the pressure was from the rear. To alleviate this pressure, Courage made a 180° turn. It speaks volumes about the confusion in this battle that the other British ships did not notice *Havock's* maneuver. The Germans, however, did notice the turnabout.

What Courage saw as he raced down the line of his own ships at a relative speed of 60 knots, was not encouraging. It appeared that *Hotspur* was out of control and *Hunter* was burning from bow to stern and losing speed. As he reached the rear of the British line and exited the smoke, he saw what he believed to be four enemy warships coming up fast at a range he estimated to be about

10,000 meters. He planned to engage them in order to slow their pursuit, but changed his mind when informed that the two forward guns were out of commission. He turned his ship around and engaged the enemy with his two aft guns. The German fire was in the process of bracketing *Havock* when the latter re-entered the smokescreen on *Hostile's* port quarter. Several fragments from near misses hit the British ship.

Georg Thiele was now ahead of the British line. Commander Wolf assumed that the British had slowed to protect their damaged ships and he concluded that the time was right to press the attack. He turned *Georg Thiele* to starboard but in doing so the ship sustained several damaging hits. One shell hit one of the forward guns, killing nine of its crew. Another shell passed through the forward funnel and exploded above deck. Finally, as *Georg Thiele* was completing her starboard turn, an armor-piercing shell exploded in the fire control room. Wolf did not let these hits deter him from closing on the British line now led by *Hunter* and followed by *Hotspur*, *Hostile*, and *Havock*, in that order. The British ships were still heading west at maximum speed, but not for long. *Hunter* was ablaze and with the range reduced to about 1,700 meters, *Georg Thiele* provided the finishing blows to the crippled British warship. The range was so short that *Georg Thiele* could employ her secondary as well as her main armaments. *Hunter*, a flaming wreck, lost power and made an unintended turn towards the enemy ship. She quickly became motionless and Wolf fired a torpedo salvo at her as he passed on an easterly course to the north of the British line. At least one torpedo hit *Hunter* amidships.

Hotspur followed closely no more than 1,000 meters behind *Hunter* but those on the bridge were unable to make out what was happening due to smoke. *Hostile* and *Havock* were also enveloped in the smoke screen, but in their case the screen served a useful purpose by shielding them from the three German destroyers approaching from the east. *Hotspur* fired torpedoes at *Georg Thiele* as the German ship passed to its starboard but both torpedoes missed their target. Two shells from *Georg Thiele* hit *Hotspur*.

The German shells caused total communications failure on *Hotspur* and put her hydraulic steering mechanism out of commission. The ship took an uncontrollable turn to starboard and sliced into *Hunter's* amidships engine room. The result was devastating, adding significantly to the already existing carnage on that ship. The two ships were motionless and subjected to a withering fire from the two German destroyers. *Hostile* then took violent evasive action that prevented a further pile-up.

Hotspur was still pushing against *Hunter* with its 34,000 horsepower engines at full throttle. Lieutenant Commander Layman could not communicate with the engine room and left the bridge to establish verbal communications. He was successful in ordering the engines reversed, but in his absence a German shell struck the bridge and killed most of those present. *Hunter* righted itself as *Hotspur* backed away, but only for a moment. *Hunter's* one remaining functioning gun was still firing as the ship slowly rolled over on its starboard side and sank.

Georg Thiele was forced to withdraw from the battle at this crucial moment. The ship had sustained at least seven major hits: she was ablaze, two magazines were flooded, and her fire fighting ability had been severely reduced. Commander Wolf had sighted the three destroyers from Herjangsfjord coming up fast behind the British column and he decided it was time to exit the battle to save his ship and leave the cleanup to others.

Bernd von Arnim tried to finish off *Hotspur*. Layman was able to establish a double human chain of communications between the shattered bridge and the engine room. With the ship's communications system destroyed, the guns operated under local control to good effect. The gunners calmly kept up a relentless rapid fire directed at *Bernd von Arnim* as she passed to the north. The German destroyer sustained at least five hits, and as the three other German destroyers were approaching, she also left the battle to lick her wounds.

The two remaining British destroyers, *Hostile* and *Havock*, continued westward after their near collision with their stricken friends. From two miles to the west, they saw *Hotspur*, badly damaged from the collision and enemy fire, still making headway to the west. The two British destroyer captains decided instinctively, and independently, to turn around and help the stricken ship. At this critical moment, the initiative swung to the British.

The Germans, believing that the battle was over except for completing the destruction of *Hotspur*, were somewhat dismayed at the sight of the two British destroyers turning around and coming at them at high speed, firing as they came. *Hostile* and *Havock* reached *Hotspur* and took up protective positions to her rear. The three ships continued westward to safety.

The three ships of the 4th German Destroyer Flotilla were unable to prevent the British escape, and Bey appeared satisfied with having driven the enemy from the fjord. His ships were less than 5,000 meters off the British warships as *Hostile* and *Havock* swung in behind *Hotspur*. At that range, the Germans should have been able to bring a devastating fire to bear on their enemies. However, Bey approached the enemy while continually zigzagging across the fjord. The danger of British torpedoes was minimal if the Germans had pressed their attack directly, as they would have combed their tracks. The fuel levels in the German ships were dangerously low, but more fuel was expanded in the zigzag course than in a direct approach. The constant course changes delayed closing with the British and caused the German fire to be ineffective. Wolf and Rechel were probably dismayed at how the enemy escaped the battlefield they had prepared so well. Bey missed an opportunity to inflict a severe blow on the Royal Navy.

The beached *Hardy* fired at the German destroyers with its one remaining serviceable gun. *Erich Giese* fired a torpedo at *Hardy* but it malfunctioned. *Erich Giese* was so low on fuel that the fuel pumps were expected to start sucking air at any moment and the ship was in no position to continue the pursuit. *Wolfgang Zenker*, Bey's flagship, also gave up the chase for unknown reasons, but probably because of dangerously low fuel levels. *Erich Koellner* continued as far as Djupvik before it also turned back. She joined *Wolfgang Zenker* and *Erich Giese* in searching for survivors in the area where *Hunter* had sunk. As Dickens writes, the 48 survivors (10 later died from wounds and exposure) bore testimony to the gallant help and care given them by the officers and men of the German destroyers.

The Germans suffered another mishap of considerable importance before the British warships cleared the fjord. Unknown to the Germans in Narvik, the supply ship *Rauenfels* entered Ofotfjord as the three British destroyers were exiting. The *U25*, which was patrolling east of Barøy, was the first warship to see *Rauenfels*. The submarine commander, Lieutenant Commander Viktor Schütze, had heard gunfire from the direction of Narvik and although not sure, considered it possible that the ship was a British transport. Despite his doubts, he decided to attack. One torpedo was fired at *Rauenfels*. Either it missed its target or, more probably, malfunctioned, as did so many German torpedoes during the Norwegian campaign.

The *U46*, commanded by Lieutenant Herbert Sohler, patrolled the waters near Ramnes and her crew also heard gunfire from the direction of Narvik. Sohler did not know what was happening until he saw three British destroyers heading directly towards him from the east. The *U46* managed to dive before being spotted. Sohler tried to get into position to fire torpedoes, but before he could do so, the British destroyers had passed.

Lieutenant Commander Layman was the senior of the three British destroyer captains but since his communications were destroyed, he turned over tactical command to Lieutenant Commander Wright on *Hostile*. As the British reached the fjord entrance, they spotted *Rauenfels* entering. They did not know the ship's nationality, but this doubt was removed when she refused signals to stop. This had been a bad day for the captain of the supply ship. One German submarine had already attacked the ship and now he confronted three British destroyers.

Commander Wright ordered two high explosive shells fired into *Rauenfels* when she failed to obey the heave-to orders. The German ship began to burn and the crew abandoned ship. Wright continued to escort the crippled *Hotspur* out of the fjord and ordered Lieutenant Commander Courage in the *Havock* to take care of the German ship. A boarding party was sent aboard *Rauenfels* but they decided to leave because they feared an explosion. The British were also worried that German destroyers could reach them from the east at any moment. Bey, although he did not know it, missed another opportunity to punish the British. If the two German destroyers with some fuel left had continued their pursuit another few miles, they may have saved the *Rauenfels*, caught up with *Havock*, and perhaps destroyed her. Courage ordered two more rounds fired at the German ship as soon as the boarding party returned. Dickens describes the event:[17]

> The result must have been one of the most shattering explosions of those good old days before nuclear weapons. Mr. Leslie Millns, Torpedo Gunner, saw a bright flash in the center of the ship which expanded until she shone from end to end, it seemed that it was not just the cargo which detonated but the whole ship … Wright in the *Hostile*, now well around Barøy and separated from the *Rauenfels* by the 500 foot contour or higher, saw what he swore was her funnel gyrating in the sky …

The British account of *Rauenfels'* end has also found its way into some German sources. However, there are serious differences between that account and the events described in the Norwegian naval history. While *Rauenfels* was damaged severely, she did not explode. In fact, the German crew reboarded the ship after the British departed, managed to bring the fires under control, and beached their ship to keep it from sinking. The Norwegians captured the crew of 48 (one was killed in the encounter with the British). The Norwegians eventually salvaged most of the cargo but much was badly damaged by exposure to seawater.[18]

With the departure of *Havock* from the vicinity of *Rauenfels*, the First Naval Battle of Narvik was over. In terms of damage and losses, it was a tossup. Each side lost two destroyers and all that participated, except three German ships, were damaged. The British had 147 dead and the Germans 176. From both a tactical and strategic view, the battle was a British victory. The Germans were surprised, their refueling operation was interrupted, they sustained heavy losses, six German iron ore ships were sunk (along with one British), and a supply ship was badly damaged and its salvageable cargo fell into Norwegian hands. While the British also sustained heavy losses and their ships barely escaped destruction, they could sustain naval losses to a much greater degree than their opponents.

In retrospect, both sides made serious mistakes. The Germans, in view of their own successful surprise operation 24 hours earlier, should have been more alert to a similar operation by their opponents, particularly since they were fully aware that large British naval forces were in the general area. It would have been wise for Captain Bonte to keep one or two of the three refueled destroyers, *Wilhelm Heidkamp*, *Georg Thiele* and *Bernd von Arnim*, on continuous patrol near the Ofotfjord entrance. Only those destroyers actually refueling should have remained in Narvik while the rest were moved to nearby bays and fjords to present a multi-directional threat to an attacker. The German reliance on submarines was misplaced, as they accomplished nothing.

Two events during the battle could have changed the outcome in German favor. An earlier warning to the outlaying destroyers could have trapped the British between the three surviving destroyers in Narvik and the five that were located outside the harbor. An earlier warning may have resulted in the destruction of the 2nd Destroyer Flotilla. Second, when the outlying destroyers were finally alerted, Commander Bey's failure to close aggressively with his opponents may have saved the remaining British destroyers.

The British took a great risk in launching the operation without waiting for reinforcements. They were fully aware that they were going against superior enemy forces and that the suspected shore batteries could be in German hands, as could the two Norwegian coastal defense ships. This risk-taking is attributable to Admiralty interference in tactical operations. However, Admirals Forbes and Whitworth are not without blame.

The British had large naval forces in the area and more on their way. They could easily have bottled up the German ships at their only exit routes from Narvik, Vestfjord and Vågsfjord, and disposed of them at their leisure. However, even if the sense of urgency is accepted, the British could have added a cruiser and another destroyer flotilla to the attacking force. This may well have removed the necessity for a second battle. Warburton-Lee and his men fought the battle in the best tradition of the Royal Navy, assisted by what began to look like an unbelievable run of luck. The stage was now set for a final naval showdown.

NOTES

1 Dietl and Hermann, *General Dietl*, p. 70, report the following entry in Commander Erdmenger's (*Wilhelm Heidkamp's* skipper) journal: "The absence of the ship was of decisive significance for the future development of the Narvik undertaking."

2 *Jan Wellem* also served as a submarine tender and carried a cargo that consisted of a mixture of diesel oil for submarine and boiler oil for destroyers.

3 As quoted by Dickens, *Battles in the* Fjords, p. 42.

4 Dickens,, *Battles in the* Fjords, p. 46.

5 This destroyer belonged to Captain Warburton-Lee's destroyer flotilla but it was detached earlier to serve as an escort for the cruiser *Birmingham*. When this cruiser was sent back to England, *Hostile* hurried back to join its flotilla.

6 Dickens, *Battles in the Fjords*, p. 46.

7 Dickens, *Battles in the Fjords*, p. 47.

8 Churchill, *The Gathering Storm*, p. 597.

9 Hubatsch, p. 113, n.ote 13.

10 Donald MacIntyre, *Narvik* (London: Evans Brothers Limited, 1959), p.75.

11 Alex Büchner, *Narvik. Die Kämpfe der Gruppe Dietl im Frühjahr 1940* (Nechargemünd-Heidelberg: Scharnhorst Buchkameradschaft GmbH, 1958), p. 24.

12 Dickens, *Battles in the Fjords*, pp. 56-57.

13 Dickens, *Battles in the Fjords*, p. 75.

14 Steen, *Norges Sjøkrig 1940-1945*, vol. 4, p. 113, second note.

15 Bey advanced in rank to Rear Admiral. He went down with the battleship *Scharnhorst* on December 26, 1943.

16 Dickens, *Battles in the Fjords*, p. 78.

17 Dickens, *Battles in the Fjords*, pp. 94-95.

18 Steen, *Norges Sjøkrig 1940-1945*, vol. 4, pp. 171 and 222. The salvaged equipment included 96 aerial bombs, about 320,000 rounds of machinegun and small-arms ammunition, 30,000 boxes of hermetically sealed food, 20-mm guns, cars, and motorcycles.

7

CONFUSION AND DISSARAY

"Against Whom?."

KING HÅKON VII's REACTION WHEN AWAKENED
BY HIS ADJUTANT AND TOLD NORWAY WAS AT WAR.

Myths of Treason and Sabotage

I have shown that Quisling and his party had little effect on German operational planning. The Germans used the organization as a source of information on political conditions in the country but Quisling was not informed about the forthcoming attack and his organization had no part in the operations. The Germans had come to realize that Quisling and his followers were not held in high regard in Norway.

Despite this fact, the writings during and immediately after the war accredited many of the German successes and Norwegian-Allied failures to treachery, sabotage, espionage, and fifth column operations. Politicians and historians alike, contributed to these myths. Even Winston Churchill added to these misconceptions. He writes in 1948:

> German lecturers, actors, singers, and men of science had visited Norway in the promotion of a common culture. All this had been woven into the texture of the Hitlerite military plan, and a widely scattered internal pro-German conspiracy set on foot ... The deed of infamy and treachery now performed may take its place with the Sicilian Vespers and the massacre of St. Bartholomew. [1]

While historians have now debunked most of the myths, there are people on both sides of the Atlantic who cling to the view that the Germans used deceit, espionage, and treachery in their attack on Norway and that Norwegians betrayed their own country. Many of the most outrageous claims came from British soldiers returning from their abortive efforts to stop the Germans.

In his excellent analysis of the Norwegian and Allied rationale for defeat,

Richard Petrow writes that such stories served to make an otherwise incomprehensible defeat understandable.[2] He could have added that the stories also served as convenient shields for the mistakes by civilian and military officials in both Norway and Great Britain.

The facts are that the political and military leaders in Norway and Great Britain were asleep at the wheel and ignored the loud wake-up calls that came in for two weeks prior to the invasion. Most ignored clear indications that a military storm was gathering just over the horizon. That fantasy evaporated at 2315 hours on April 8 when foreign warships entered the restricted zone in Oslofjord. Thirty-five minutes later a short message from the 1st Naval District reported that the outer forts were engaging foreign warships. Norway's 126 years of continuous peace had ended.

The Landings

The German pre-dawn attacks in southern and central Norway must be viewed as an unparalleled success. By the end of the day on April 9, all major Norwegian population centers and ports were in German hands. The success did not come without losses but these were judged acceptable by the Germans. About 1,500 men in the invasion force perished by April 10 and the material losses to the German Navy were considerable. These losses point to the high risks the Germans were willing to assume and to the fact that the invasion could have been a costly affair if the Norwegians had heeded the many warnings received during the week leading up to the attack.

The Germans were correct in their assumption that the Norwegian Navy posed no serious obstacle, even to the lighter units of the invasion force. They also assumed that the coastal fortresses were no serious obstacles because they had only a caretaker, or small complement, present for duty. This underestimation caused considerable losses to the ships in the task forces.

The manning of the coastal forts was inadequate and the minefields covering the approaches to the main harbors were not laid. Only about 30% of authorized strength was present for duty and some of the personnel had not served since 1918. A number of gun batteries were therefore not manned and some guns had not fired a live round since the 1890s. The failure to provide infantry protection led to the quick capture of the forts and the Germans hastily prepared them to contest expected British attacks. While a full discussion of the landings is outside the scope of this book, a short summary of the landing operations is in order.

Task Force 5 entered Oslofjord shortly before midnight on April 8. The Germans were able to pass the outer line of forts without sustaining damage because of heavy fog and Norwegian adherence to neutrality procedures, which called for firing warning shots. The TF approached the inner line of forts (Oscarborg) at slow speed (12 knots) with the flagship, the heavy cruiser *Blücher*, in the lead, followed by the heavy cruiser *Lützow* and the light cruiser *Emden*. The Germans hoped to pass the fort without receiving fire and to capture the capital and the Norwegian Government by surprise.

With Colonel Birger Eriksen in command, the Norwegian fort opened a devastating fire on *Blücher* at a range of only 1,800 meters as dawn was breaking. *Blücher*, which had been commissioned only seven months earlier and was the most modern of the large units in the German Navy, sustained numerous hits from heavy caliber shells and torpedoes. Within a short time, the ship capsized and sank with the loss of about 1,000 soldiers and sailors. The German naval and land component commanders passed temporarily into Norwegian captivity. The shore batteries then shifted their fires to the other major German units, and the heavy cruiser *Lützow* sustained substantial damage before the task force withdrew. This action disrupted the German timetable and allowed the Norwegian government and royal family to leave the capital. After withdrawing outside the range of the Norwegian guns, the Germans landed troops on the east side of the fjord, and the unprotected Oscarborg surrendered at 0900 hours on April 10.

German plans called for the capture of Fornebu Airport outside Oslo by parachute troops followed by air-landing two infantry battalions. The parachute drop was aborted due to heavy fog. The seven operational Norwegian Gladiators took to the air and engaged the German aircraft in a spirited fight. They were able to destroy five German aircraft before they exhausted their fuel and ammunition. Three of the Norwegian aircraft were destroyed while the remaining four landed on lakes in the country's interior. The German fighters that were to provide cover for the parachute operation ran out of fuel and had to land at Fornebu despite the fact that the airfield had not been secured. The transport aircraft, which had now arrived on the scene, saw the fighters land and followed suit. Two German aircraft were destroyed and five severely damaged by fire from the three Norwegian machinegun positions on the airfield. Despite losses, the Germans quickly overcame the defenders. The transports brought in about 900 troops and these were dispatched towards Oslo. The virtually defenseless capital was surrendered at 1400 hours.

Task Force 5 also had the mission of capturing the main Norwegian naval base at the nearby town of Horten. There were only two operational Norwegian warships, one minelayer and one minesweeper, in the harbor and 40% of their crews were on shore leave. These two ships put up a determined fight, sinking one German minesweeper and damaging a torpedo boat. Another minesweeper sank later because of damage it sustained. In a daring operation, a force of about 50 Germans managed to capture the naval district headquarters and this led to the surrender of Horten and the ships in its harbor. Over the next week, the outer forts, which were increasingly cut off from friendly forces as the Germans advanced along both sides of the fjord, were captured or surrendered. In the process, the Germans lost one torpedo boat.

Lützow was the only ship in TF 5 that returned to Germany immediately after the landing. She was hit by a torpedo from the British submarine *Spearfish* while in international waters, and towed home for repair. She was out of commission for about a year.

The towns of Arendal and Egersund, both terminals for overseas cables were captured without resistance by company-size German forces. The attack on the city of Kristiansand was repelled twice by its forts despite heavy shelling and air bombardment. The Norwegians believed that Allied assistance was on its way and a German signal flag was misread as the French tricolor during the third attack. The Germans were able to slip into the harbor and they quickly captured the city, forts, and naval units. The German light cruiser *Karlsruhe* was sunk by a British submarine on its return to Germany during the night of April 9-10.

The city of Stavanger, with its important airfield at Sola, was to be captured by parachute troops. Only two platoons of Norwegian troops were on the airfield at the time of the attack and it was captured quickly, although the paratroopers suffered a number of killed and wounded. Two battalions of German infantry arrived in transports in the course of the day. A Norwegian destroyer was able to sink one of the German supply ships before it was itself destroyed by German aircraft. Another Norwegian destroyer captured a second German supply ship but it was scuttled by its crew as the Norwegian warship tried to bring it to England. A large number of German bombers, fighters, and reconnaissance aircraft had arrived at Sola already by April 9. Their presence became a decisive factor in British naval operations off the Norwegian coast. The Norwegian forces abandoned the city of Stavanger and withdrew into the interior to complete their mobilization.

Bergen, Norway's second largest city, was securely in German hands by the end of April 9 but not without losses. The Norwegian torpedo battery was not activated but the guns at the two inner forts caused considerable damage to the German artillery training ship *Bremse*. The light cruiser *Königsberg* was so severely damaged that it was not seaworthy. Fifteen British aircraft attacked Bergen after dawn on April 10 and two bombs hit *Köningsberg*, which was abandoned.

Unlike the task forces destined for Oslo and Bergen, TF 2 approached the mouth of Trondheimfjord at high speed and in tight formation. The strong searchlights from the heavy cruiser *Admiral Hipper* blinded the Norwegian gunners and the ships were able to pass the forts without sustaining any damage. The city, army depots, and the naval headquarters were captured by the Germans without resistance. The forts were captured later in the day after some sharp fighting. Værnes Airfield, 22 miles east of Trondheim was captured without resistance on April 10. The loss of this important facility had a significant effect on subsequent Norwegian and Allied operations since its possession extended the reach of the Luftwaffe by several hundred miles.

Norwegian Reactions during the April 8–9 Crisis

The Germans placed great hopes in a quick capture of the Norwegian capital, since a success in Oslo could be expected to result in a peaceful occupation of Norway. The Germans hoped to capture the government, the royal family, the ministry of defense, and possibly both the army and navy staff. The Germans believed that with the royal family and government in their hands, the Norwegians would accept the German ultimatum.

The date and time of the German attack was revealed to the German naval and air attachés in Oslo four days before the attack. Both attachés were instructed not to reveal this information to the German Ambassador in Oslo, Dr. Bräuer. He was not informed until the evening of April 8 when he was given a note for delivery to the Norwegian Foreign Minister early in the morning of April 9. The ambitious German timetable was disrupted when TF 5 failed to reach the capital on April 9.

The Norwegian Government had grappled all the day of April 8 with massive Allied violations of Norwegian neutrality. There was a distinct possibility that Norway would soon find itself at war with Great Britain. At the same time, alarming reports were received about German naval movements through the Skagerrak and Kattegat. British violations of Norwegian waters, reports of German naval movements and even the sinking of *Rio de Janeiro* whose rescued German troops admitted they were on their way to Bergen, failed to alarm the government sufficiently to take prudent defensive measures.

The government met in continuing sessions in the evening of April 8 and throughout the night. A decision to mobilize was postponed until the following morning, but the sudden events of that day and the looming threat of attack from both the English and the Germans seem to have paralyzed the Norwegian Government.

The government assembled again in the Foreign Ministry at 0130 hours on April 9. This meeting followed an air raid alarm and blackout in Oslo at 0015 hours. The government had not requested that the two service chiefs attend their meeting and this had serious consequences. The cabinet ministers were told that something was happening in the Oslofjord but that the situation was unclear. All doubts were removed at 0150 hours when the 2nd Naval District reported that German warships had entered the restricted area around Bergen.

Prime Minister Nygaardsvold made a telephone call to the palace and talked to King Haakon VII. The king's reaction to the news that the country was at war was, "Against whom?", a fitting expression of the confusion and uncertainty that had prevailed for the past 24 hours. The Norwegians decided to ask Great Britain for assistance. Foreign Minister Koht made a wakeup call to the British Ambassador, Sir Cecil Dormer. Koht met with Dormer at 0220 hours and Dormer sent a query to London at 0236 hours: "MOST IMMEDIATE. Norwegian Government stresses the need for strong and quick assistance before Germans establish firm footing on Norwegian soil. Please reply by 6 p.m. whether strong assistance can be (immediately) forthcoming."[3] The British answer, which promised their full assistance "forthwith," was received at 1255 hours. This message gave the Norwegians, who did not know the confused state of affairs in Great Britain, unrealistically high expectations.

Irrational Mobilization Decision

The government finally decided to mobilize, and Defense Minister Ljungberg passed this order to General Kristian Laake. When questioned by Laake, Ljungberg confirmed that the order dealt with the forces that the military had recommended for mobilization on April 5: the 1st, 2nd, 3rd, and 4th Field Brigades. This decision would have serious consequences.

Ljungberg (1884–1967) was a career army officer who started his service in 1906. He was a colonel commanding an infantry regiment when he received his appointment as Defense Minister on December 22, 1939. He was not the government's first choice. The prime minister favored General Fleischer but it was considered unwise to move him from his sensitive assignment in North Norway. Most of the cabinet favored Colonel Ruge but the defense minister he would replace, Fredrik Monsen, was adamantly opposed and threatened to withdraw his resignation. Ruge was viewed by some as stubborn and difficult to work with and many officers in the army had a negative view of him because of his involvement in the 1933 military reorganization.[4]

The army staff was confused about the orders received from Minister Ljungberg. The order called for only a partial mobilization of units in southern Norway. The order did not include the 5th Division in Trøndelag or the 6th Division in North Norway. Full mobilization called for the activation of 66 infantry battalions, at least on paper. The procedures for full mobilization called for notification by all available means, including radio. In a partial mobilization, on the other hand, the 18 infantry battalions (plus artillery, cavalry, engineers, and support units) in the four divisions in South Norway would be notified about the call-up by mail.

Those who wrote the procedures felt that a partial mobilization would be in response to a growing threat. Full mobilization, on the other hand, was a response to an immediate crisis or attack. The reserves, outside the six field brigades, were not trained and, in many cases, did not have the required equipment. All decision makers knew that this state of affairs would take several years to rectify. The distinction between full mobilization and the mobilization of only six field brigades had become blurred. Many, who felt that full mobilization, as originally envisioned, was impractical, viewed mobilization of six field brigades and supporting units as full mobilization.

General Laake decided to wait until Ljungberg determined the method of notification before sending out mobilization orders. Colonel Rasmus Hatledal, the chief of the general staff, protested to no avail. Valuable time was wasted in this absurd argument. Ljungberg eventually arrived at army headquarters and Hatledal pressed him for an order for full mobilization, but Ljungberg decided to leave the order for partial mobilization in force until he could discuss the issue with the cabinet.

The delivery of the German ultimatum delayed this discussion. There are those who claim that Ljungberg assumed that the mobilization of the four field brigades would be handled as an immediate action and others claim that he was the victim of the government's failure to pay attention to the many military warnings about the possibility of a surprise attack.[5] His decision is not justified by either of these two explanations and it is hard to believe that Ljungberg, having just come from the command of a regiment, did not know the difference in procedures for partial and full mobilization. The decision was made to mobilize by mail, giving a date of April 12.

Hatledal protested and pointed out that mobilization had to be announced over the radio since it was too late to mobilize via the postal system. Laake, who apparently still did not believe that an invasion was in progress, did not support him. The order for mobilization by letter remained in force.

Colonel Hatledal, on his own responsibility, moved the first day of mobilization from 12 to 11 April, increased the number of troops called to the colors from 24,000 to 38,000, and included the 5th Division in Trøndelag. There were also many units in North Norway that required mobilization despite the fact that the 6th Division was on a partial war footing. Hatledal did not dare take the final and most important step, sending the mobilization order by radio. Such action would probably result in his relief and a countermand of his order, resulting in even more confusion.

It is certainly true that full mobilization included individuals who were not trained and who lacked some of the required equipment. However, to justify the decision to mobilize by mail by claiming that full mobilization was an unrealistic option that would lead to more chaos demonstrates the rigidity that characterized the Norwegian military and civilian leadership in 1940. Hatledal was not arguing for full mobilization, only that the notification by radio and telegram applicable to full mobilization should be used in the current situation. Whatever additional chaos may have resulted was certainly preferable to giving the Germans three days to consolidate their bridgeheads.

The German Ultimatum and Negotiations

Minister Bräuer's instructions called for the presentation of the German note to the Norwegian Foreign Minister between 0400 and 0500 hours on April 9. The Germans believed that if the ultimatum was delivered to the Norwegian Government before the start of hostilities, there was a good chance that the Norwegians would accept the German demands. They assumed that German attack groups would not meet any resistance before 0400 hours at the earliest. This assumption was unrealistic since hostilities had started as early as 2300 hours on April 8. By 0400 hours, the Norwegians were aware that there were German attacks taking place against Oslo, Bergen, and Trondheim. At 0414 hours, the naval headquarters in Oslo also learned that an attack was in progress against Narvik and at 0500 hours that Kristiansand was under attack.

Curt Bräuer met with Mr. Koht in the Foreign Ministry library at 0430, while the second air raid alarm of the night took place. Bräuer presented the German note immediately. It announced that Germany had found it necessary to occupy parts of Norway as a preemptive operation to forestall British plans against Norway. Norwegian unwillingness or inability to defend its neutrality against British violations also necessitated the German operation. The note stated that the German occupation would only be for the duration of the war, and that the integrity and sovereignty of Norway would be respected. If the Norwegians resisted, the resistance would be broken with all means at Germany's disposal. To prevent unnecessary bloodshed, the Norwegian Government should take the necessary political and military steps to cooperate with the German authorities. The note had an enclosure detailing the steps that were necessary. These included a demand for the Norwegian Government to announce to the Norwegian people that all resistance should cease. All military installations were to be turned over to the Germans. The Germans were to take control of all communication facilities, the press, radio, and postal system. Norwegian military units should be ordered to contact and cooperate with the German armed forces.

Koht listened silently as Bräuer read the German ultimatum. When the German had finished, Koht stated that he needed to consult the cabinet. Bräuer insisted on an immediate answer. Koht replied that the cabinet was in the next room and a quick answer should therefore not be a problem. It took the government only a couple of minutes to decide unanimously to reject the German ultimatum. Koht returned to the library and informed Bräuer that Norway would not submit to the German demands. Bräuer stated that this meant war and that nothing could save Norway. Koht replied that the war had already started. Bräuer reported the Norwegian reply in a telegram to General von Falkenhorst at 0618 hours.

The Norwegian Government and the royal family left Oslo for Hamar by a special train at 0723 hours. Koht had an interview with the Norwegian Broadcasting System at the railway station in Oslo and reported what had transpired and that general mobilization had been ordered. While this was not exactly what had been decided, it is how news about mobilization first reached thousands of Norwegians and they began showing up at mobilization centers all over the country.

The Norwegian Parliament was able to convene in the afternoon of April 9 at Hamar, a town located 76 miles north of Oslo. Despite the confusion that reigned that day, only five of the 150 members were absent. The members of the government, with the exception of Defense Minister Ljungberg, were all from the Labor Party. Prime Minister Nygaardsvold offered the government's resignation in order that a new government, with all parties represented, could be formed. However, at the urging of Hambro, the leader of the conservatives, it was agreed unanimously that the government should remain in power and that three members from the opposition parties be added as ministers without portfolio.

The government also received a request from Ambassador Bräuer for negotiations and a meeting with the Norwegian Government and King. While most of those present felt that to negotiate with the Germans was meaningless, Foreign Minister Koht, who was skeptical about the extent and timeliness of Allied assistance, convinced them that they should at least listen to their proposal. A message sent to the Germans stated that the proposal would be submitted to the Parliament provided the Germans did not make any offensive military moves. The parliamentary session adjourned at 1930 hours when it was learned that a German force was approaching Hamar. For the second time in a day, the government was forced to move. Their new destination was the town of Elverum, about 20 miles from Hamar and 50 miles from the Swedish border.

The government meeting in Hamar, as the ones on the previous day, is hard to understand. It was time for action, not for discussions, and particularly not for discussions involving the Parliament. Odd-Bjørn Fure writes, "In a situation that demanded observations, analysis, and action, the government became tied up in an endless and purposeless debate in the Parliament."[6] The fact that the military chiefs were not represented at the most important meetings on April 9 was a major blunder. The cabinet ministers had little understanding of the military issues involved as the country went from peace to war. They did not understand how the war would be fought and therefore they made decisions without appreciating their military consequences.

Captain Spiller's "Private War" Ends Negotiations

The event that caused the Norwegian Government and the royal family to flee to Elverum was a daring raid organized by the German air attaché to Norway, Captain Eberhard Spiller. Spiller and Captain Erich Walther, the commander of the two airborne companies that landed at Fornebu earlier in the day, had quickly organized an expedition using one company of German paratroopers. These troops were loaded on requisitioned buses and trucks and headed north, intermingled with the stream of civilians fleeing the capital. It was an independent attempt to capture the Norwegian Government and royal family in a lightning raid on Hamar. In 1945 von Falkenhorst referred to the raid as "Spiller's private war,"[7] and it seems that neither he nor Bräuer knew about or sanctioned Spiller's action.

The Germans arrived in Hamar only to learn that the Norwegian authorities had continued their flight to Elverum and Spiller continued on towards that town. Major O. Helset, a Norwegian officer scraped together some Royal Guard recruits, officers attending a chemical warfare course, and local gun club members. This improvised force of 93 men met the Germans at Midtskogen, a narrow passage on the road between Hamar and Elverum. The defenders hoped to catch the Germans in a deadly crossfire but the plan could not be executed because the German column was intermingled with civilian vehicles fleeing Oslo. The Germans encountered the Norwegian defenses around 0230 hours on April 10 and withdrew after a sharp engagement. Nine Norwegians were wounded. The exact number of German casualties is not known, but Captain Spiller was fatally wounded.

The Norwegian Government and royal family were saved from capture for a second time in a 24-hour period, first by Colonel Eriksen's guns at Oscarborg and then by a motley and hastily assembled group at Midtskogen. After the loss of Captain Spiller, Captain Walther abandoned the deep penetration and returned to Oslo.

The ability of the Germans to make such a deep penetration into Norway served to illustrate the weaknesses of the Norwegian defenses at this stage but it also had political fallout that worked against German interests. It demonstrated that the Germans could not be trusted since they had undertaken offensive moves despite a Norwegian stipulation to the contrary in their reply to the German request for a meeting. Furthermore, although it was only a minor skirmish, the action at Midtskogen boosted Norwegian morale in the same way as Colonel Eriksen's action at Oscarborg. In their mind, a scratch force of trainees and gun club members had stopped and driven back a force of German paratroopers of equal size.

The Germans were still hoping for a political solution. Minister Bräuer broadcast an appeal to the Norwegians to cease all resistance. This took place at about the same time as he requested the meeting with the Norwegian Government and King. The parliament, when it reconvened at Elverum, gave the government full powers to take the decisions necessary to ensure the country's security. It also designated a delegation to negotiate with the Germans. The officials also learned that Quisling had formed a government in Oslo.

Quisling met Hans Wilhelm Scheidt, Rosenberg's personal representative in Norway, in the morning of April 9 and claimed that he was the only person who could fill the political vacuum created when the Norwegian Government fled. Scheidt passed the question to Berlin and Hitler agreed that same afternoon, disregarding Foreign Minister Ribbentrop's reservations. Bräuer was instructed to cooperate with Quisling and to demand that the Norwegian king accept Quisling as Prime Minister. Quisling also made a broadcast at 1930 hours. He announced that he had seized the reins of government and ordered the people to cease all resistance.

The news of Quisling's coup in Oslo and the German raid to capture the government and the king served to stiffen the Norwegians resolution to resist, not only among those assembled at Elverum but also among a public that had long looked upon Quisling with disdain. Dr. Bräuer traveled to Elverum on April 10. He demanded a one-on-one meeting with the king. The king declared that he would only negotiate if his foreign minister was present and this was agreed.

The German envoy repeated the earlier demands with the addition that the king should accept Quisling as his prime minister. For their part, the Germans guaranteed Norwegian sovereignty and the continuation of the monarchy. If the Norwegians refused these demands, the full power of the German armed forces would be used to break all resistance, causing needless bloodshed. The king told Bräuer that he could not, under his constitutional responsibilities, answer without conferring with the government. The German Ambassador returned to Oslo while the king met with the government.

In the meeting with his government, the king stated that he saw it as a breach of his constitutional duties to accept a government that did not have the people's support. If the government felt it necessary to accept the German conditions, he would abdicate. The government decided unanimously to reject the German demands and this decision was telephoned to Bräuer while he was on his way back to Oslo.

The Germans changed their approach from persuasion to force. An air attack on Elverum, with the obvious goal of eliminating the government and the royal family, destroyed the town's central district and caused 32 fatalities. While no officials were killed, the government and the royal family were forced to move to Otta and later to the town of Molde on the west coast. As in the case of Spiller's raid and the appointment of Quisling as prime minister, the bombing only served to galvanize the Norwegian resolve to resist.

A New Norwegian Commander-in-Chief

Justice Minister Terje Wold met General Laake and his staff at the army headquarters on April 10 in what he describes as a defeatist setting. In this heated meeting, the officers accused the government of bringing on a catastrophe by its neglect of the defense establishment and its failure to heed earlier calls for mobilization. Laake, who did not have faith in Allied promises of timely support is alleged to have stated that the only choices open to the government were those of negotiation or capitulation. It was obvious that there had to be a change in the military leadership to energize defense measures after the rejection of Germany's demands for a second time on April 10. The exhausted and sickly Laake understood the situation and offered his resignation, which was quickly accepted.

Colonel Otto Ruge, Inspector General of Infantry, had argued for resistance and he was now promoted to Major General and given the daunting task of trying to organize a defense to stop the Germans. Ruge accepted the appointment and his first priority was to orient himself on the exceedingly confused situation. He discovered that General Hvinden-Haug had ordered the mobilized parts of the 2nd Division to withdraw from its main defensive line along the Nittedal River north of Oslo. Ruge made it clear that he did not believe it possible to save eastern Norway.

The Germans were not pressing the 2nd Division and there was no apparent reason for it to give up the advantageous forward defensive positions. Spiller's deep penetration in the division area had given rise to wild and unfounded rumors of other German units operating behind the Norwegian lines, which had precipitated this unfortunate withdrawal. In the process, two mobilization depots were left defenseless and one cavalry and one infantry regiment lost more than 50% of their personnel and equipment.

Before General Ruge could make any plans on how to cope with the Germans, he needed to get an overview of the military situation in South Norway. First, he needed to know what forces he had at his disposal. He also moved the army headquarters from its location in Rena, Østerdal to the more central location at Øyer in Gudbrandsdal.

Norwegian Mobilization Efforts

Many individuals designated for mobilization who lived in the country's population centers awoke on April 9 to find that the Germans had taken control of their area and had captured the nearby mobilization centers. This threw mobilization into a state of chaos. Many of those who were liable for military service in the cities and towns captured by the Germans managed to slip away but ended up reporting for duty at mobilization centers other than those designated in the mobilization plans.

The Norwegian Government had a very liberal policy in granting exemptions from military service in the 1920s and 1930s. Untrained and sometimes medically unfit individuals now showed up at mobilization centers to offer their services, but they had no unit assignments and were not included on any mobilization rolls. While this feeling of duty to country was a laudable and positive development at the outset, problems developed. Since these men reported of their own volition, they felt no obligation to remain if they chose otherwise. Many came from social groups and families with strong anti-military views and a strong skepticism of military authorities.

A large number did not understand the reason for the chaos that accompanied an emergency mobilization under conditions where many population and mobilization centers were already under enemy control and others under threat of capture. They saw the confusion and disorder as proof of treason and sabotage and these rumors spread like wildfire. Lindbäck-Larsen writes that, in some units, the rumor-mongering tendencies began to disappear as units became organized but in others they lingered below the surface as "poisonous wells" that reappeared in times of hardships and reverses and contributed to the breakdown of esprit de corps, discipline, and the will to resist.

In North Norway, either most units were mobilized at the time of the attack with several months of active duty and some training behind them or they were able to complete mobilization almost according to plans. The units in the western part of the country and in Nord-Trøndelag were also able to mobilize in a somewhat orderly manner, but the greater cohesion and training found in North Norway were lacking. In other areas of the country, the fight was initiated after a very disorderly and improvised mobilization that resulted in under strength units with little cohesion.

Those mobilization depots not captured at the outset were located by the Germans and bombed heavily. While this was further disruptive to Norwegian mobilization, it did not halt the effort. The extent of disruption due to the surprise capture of population centers and mobilization depots is illustrated by the fact that only about 55,000 saw service during the campaign, despite the fact that many who had no training or mobilization assignments showed up for service. This number constituted half of the planned mobilization strength and the effective fighting force at any one time probably did not exceed 30,000.

The greatest need was for infantry units and many who showed up for mobilization from other arms were used as infantry. Those with no military training were in some cases assigned to units sent to the front but for the most part, they were assigned to training units that supported and served as a replacement pool for the fighting units. There was a serious shortage of artillery and a total lack of tanks or antitank weapons. Most of the aircraft that could have been effective against the Germans were lost the first day. German air superiority was a decisive factor in most parts of the country.

Other factors also contributed to the confusion and uncertainties in the days following the German attack. Quisling took to the airwaves in the evening of April 9, announcing that he had taken over as prime minister. He ordered that resistance cease and he followed up this order by threats against those who did not obey. The legal government responded in a communiqué the following day but the answer lacked firmness and persuasion and was not a ringing appeal to arms. There was no confirmation that mobilization should continue. The government simply expressed confidence that the people would do everything to resurrect the freedom and sovereignty that a foreign power wanted to destroy by force.

General von Falkenhorst, on the other hand, communicated to the people in straightforward and unmistakable terms on April 13 what a refusal to follow Quisling's demands would mean. Those who followed the bidding of the "former government" and obeyed its order to mobilize would face military tribunals that would most likely lead to executions. This communiqué was sent out over the state radio, published in proclamations that were displayed prominently, and through leaflets dropped in virtually all areas of the country. While most disregarded the admonitions and threats from Quisling and the Germans, they caused a number of breakdowns in the will to resist among both military and civilian authorities.

The German Breakout from Oslo

The Germans were temporarily thrown off balance by their failure to capture Oslo quickly and by the unexpected determination by the Norwegians to resist. Reports of Norwegian mobilization were flowing into von Falkenhorst's headquarters and he adopted a more cautious approach than that envisioned in the original plan, which called for sending a battalion to Bergen and one to Trondheim by rail. For now, he took a guarded attitude pending the arrival of sufficient forces to undertake major offensive operations. Only local operations, primarily to the southeast, were undertaken. In the two days following the landing, the main elements of the 163rd and 196th Divisions were brought to Oslo by the 1st and 2nd Sea Transport Echelons and by air.

Having failed to bring about a Norwegian surrender, the Germans needed to move into the interior quickly, disrupt Norwegian mobilization efforts, prevent them from organizing a defense, and link up as quickly as possible with the other isolated beachheads. Von Falkenhorst impressed on his subordinates the absolute need for speed and relentless pressure in order to keep the staggering Norwegian defense from regaining its balance. German forces in Stavanger, Bergen, and Trondheim were directed to limit themselves to local offensive operations until reinforced.

Group XXI's orders for the breakout from the beachhead were issued on April 12 and 13. The major units for the offensive from Oslo were the reinforced 163rd and 196th Infantry Divisions. The 196th Division, commanded by Major General Richard Pellengahr, would drive through the two great north-south valleys of Gudbrandsdal and Østerdal with the ultimate mission of linking up with the forces in Trondheim. This division was also assigned the sector east and southeast of Oslo. One battalion was to advance south along the east side of Oslofjord to capture Sarpsborg, Fredrikstad, and Halden. Another battalion operated further to the east, towards Mysen and the Swedish border.

The 163rd Division, commanded by Major General Erwin Engelbrecht, operated further west with the ultimate goal of opening land communications with the forces in Kristiansand and Bergen. Since it consisted of four regiments, two of its own and one each from the 69th and 181st Divisions, it had the secondary mission of securing the area around Oslo and to the southwest of that city. There were no serious threats in this area and large forces were not required to carry out this additional task. The immediate missions were to capture the rail junction at Hønefoss and the weapons and ammunition-manufacturing town of Kongsberg along the Oslo-Kristiansand railroad.

The Germans adopted a flexible approach, a method that was to prove very effective not only in Norway but also in their later campaigns in other parts of Europe. They did not operate as battalions and regiments but switched to a system of tactical groupings, known as battle groups, which were named either after their commanders or in relation to their operational areas. These battle groups varied in strength and composition, as dictated by the terrain and Norwegian opposition, almost on a daily basis. For maximum speed, the battle groups were motorized with the help of requisitioned vehicles. The Norwegians, primarily due to the disruption of their mobilization effort, eventually adopted similar tactical groupings.

The German advance was rapid and relentless. The southeastern thrust disrupted the mobilization of the 1st Division and captured Fredrikstad, Sarpsborg, and Halden by April 14. By the same date, the eastern drive captured the border fortresses with their skeleton crews. These multiple drives captured over 1,000 Norwegian troops. Major General Erichsen and the remnants of the 1st Division, about 3,000 men, were driven across the border into Swedish internment. Southeastern Norway was in German hands five days after they landed in Oslo.

The 163rd Division captured Kongsberg on April 14 and the 3rd Norwegian Infantry Regiment surrendered the following day. Hønefoss was also captured on April 14 and a motorized column reached the southern end of Lake Mjøsa.

These drives, in all directions from Oslo, secured the beachhead and set the stage for further German advances into the interior, bringing them into areas where General Ruge intended to make his major delaying efforts. The Germans were reinforced for the next stage of operations by the arrival of a tank battalion, three motorized machinegun battalions, and a motorized infantry battalion.

The Germans in Kristiansand advanced north through the Setesdal Valley. The Norwegians gave up their forward positions without engaging the Germans and a panic developed in units of the 3rd Division as it withdrew. The Norwegians regrouped but German units appeared in front of their positions on April 12. Neither side opened fire. General Liljedahl agreed to a cease-fire and a demarcation line was established north of Evjemoen. A German parliamentarian appeared on April 13 and demanded that hostilities cease. Liljedahl agreed to a 24-hour extension of the cease-fire. He explained the situation to General Ruge and stated that his units were "depressed," combat ineffective, and the valley was full of hungry refugees. In his reply, Ruge stated that complete capitulation would be very detrimental to the army's morale and defeat and captivity was better for the country than willing capitulation. If the fight could not continue, Ruge directed Liljedahl to allow those who were willing to carry on the fight to join units in other areas.

Liljedahl held a conference with his officers and it was agreed not to continue the fight. At the same time, Liljedahl was notified that the soldiers in position at the line of demarcation had given notice that they would cease hostilities within 20 minutes. The only word to describe this is "mutiny," and that by a unit that had seen little or no combat. General Liljedahl initiated negotiations with the Germans and surrendered his forces on April 15.

General Ruge's Dilemma

On April 15, the future looked bleak for the new Norwegian Commander-in-Chief. The Germans were well into their breakout from Oslo. Almost half the Norwegian forces in the area south of Trondheim were already lost because of disrupted mobilization, the internment of the remnants of the 1st Division in Sweden, the surrender of Colonel Einar Steen's 3rd Infantry Regiment near Kongsvinger, and General Liljedahl's surrender in Setesdal. The 8th Infantry Regiment was isolated east of Stavanger, as was the 4th Field Brigade at Voss. Except for some scattered and ad hoc units, the 2nd Division was the only force at General Ruge's disposal, but it had withdrawn precipitously from its main defensive line along the Nittedal River, north of Oslo. The mobilization apparatus was still functioning, but in total disorder in some places.

Any thoughts of recapturing the capital were out of the question. There were about 5,000 German troops in Oslo by the end of April 9. By April 14, German forces in and around the city had grown to two divisions, major elements of a third division, and several separate battalions. General Ruge realized that he could not undertake offensive operations with the meager and disorganized troops at his disposal.

Ruge recommended to the government that the highest priority be given to the recapture of Trondheim. The recapture of the country's ancient capital would have an important and positive psychological effect on the Norwegian people. Furthermore, the city had an excellent harbor suitable for Allied reinforcements and a good airfield of vital importance in contesting German air superiority. The recapture of the airfield would also remove any possibility of the Germans providing air support for their forces in Narvik.

Ambassador Dormer managed to link up with the Norwegian Government on April 12. The ambassador passed on Ruge's urgent appeal for assistance, especially the recapture of Trondheim, to London. Mr Foley from the British Embassy reached General Ruge's headquarters on April 13. Neither the French nor the British had army attaches living in Norway. Officers designated as attachés, Commandant Bertrand Vigne and Lieutenant Colonel King Salter, arrived on April 15.

On the morning of April 9, the British Government had promised the Norwegians full assistance "forthwith." There was still no evidence of this assistance. In a message to the British Prime Minister on April 13, Ruge stated that Norway had decided to resist based on the British Government's promise that it would send assistance quickly. Unless immediate assistance was received, primarily in the form of air assets and limited ground forces, Ruge warned bluntly that the Germans could secure the country within a week. He had placed his trust in the British promise and he must not be let down. This was followed by messages from the Allied military representatives at Ruge's headquarters on April 14 that stressed the need for assistance and the urgent necessity of recapturing Trondheim. These messages also vouched for the new commander-in-chief's determination and steadfastness. The numerous appeals and warnings from Norway about a possible collapse if aid was not received quickly resulted in a message from Neville Chamberlain on April 14 that read, "We are coming as fast as possible and in great strength. Further details later." [8]

General Ruge's plan, outlined in a directive he issued on April 15, was to delay the German advance in the south while the Allies, in conjunction with Norwegian forces, eliminated the German bridgehead in Trondheim. From there, General Ruge intended to build up his forces for a continuation of the war with Allied help. The operational directive laid out the objective for his forces. "Assistance [from the Allies] is in preparation and promised soonest. In these circumstances, our task in East Norway is to win time." [9] Ruge intended to fight successive delaying actions and to destroy lines of communication in order to allow time for the arrival of Allied assistance.

General Ruge intended to establish a defensive line at the southern entrance to the three great valleys of Østerdal, Gudbrandsdal, and Valdres. Since the recapture of Bergen with Allied help did not seem likely, Ruge directed the 4th Field Brigade, mobilizing at Voss, to move to eastern Norway.

Some recent writers, among them General Hovland, question the wisdom of Ruge's decision to conduct delaying actions. The disadvantages of delaying actions in a situation where the enemy is able to build up his strength quickly are obvious but no alternatives are suggested. Offensive operations were out of the question until the Norwegian Army could mobilize sufficient forces. The problem, however, was that the German buildup was much quicker than Norwegian mobilization and the discrepancy in combat power had become decisive by April 15. The German consolidation and expansion of their bridgehead in the first five days disrupted mobilization and led to the loss of major Norwegian combat formations. A rigid defense would no doubt have led to the destruction of the 2nd Division and this would have opened wide the road to Trondheim and Bergen.

Allied Reactions on April 9—Confusion and Discord

News about events in Norway began to filter into the various government offices in London in the early hours of April 9, but the information was fragmentary and confusing. That there would be a German reaction to the mining of Norwegian waters was fully expected, but it was believed that it would take the Germans considerable time to mount effective countermeasures. The fact that the Germans had a simultaneous operation underway against Norway came as a surprise. The British Admiralty was convinced that the German naval movements underway since April 6 were attempts to break out into the Atlantic, not an invasion of Norway.

The British command authorities had blind faith in the supremacy of their sea power and concluded that a German attack on the western Norwegian shoreline was impractical. The suddenness and scale of German naval operations in these areas dealt a hard blow to their earlier preconceptions. However, the British continued to believe that the British Navy could deal with the attackers, even after receiving news of the German invasion on April 9.

A hastily convened meeting of the Chiefs of Staff Committee (CSC)[10] assembled at 0600 hours. Information about the unfolding events in Norway was fragmentary and there was great uncertainty about how much credence should be accorded the various reports. Nevertheless, it was clear that German naval operations and landings north of Stavanger, hitherto considered extremely unlikely, had become a reality. It appeared to those assembled that attacks were in progress against Oslo, Bergen, and Trondheim and that some of these cities had been occupied. The chiefs did not believe that the Germans had reached Narvik, despite the Admiralty's warning to the Norwegians on the previous day that German forces could reach that city as early as 2200 hours on April 8, and they decided to dispatch a battalion to that city immediately. The military leaders in Great Britain did not yet appreciate the size and scope of the German operations. They also agreed that the recapture of Trondheim should be a primary objective.[11]

The inadequacy of the military plans developed to support the mining operations now came back to haunt the Allies as they began to grapple with the question of what to do about the German invasion. In a meeting of the British

War Cabinet at 0830 hours, General Ironside presented the results of the deliberations by the CSC. He stated that it was the view of the committee that the priority task was the seizure of Bergen and Trondheim so that the Allies could use those excellent harbors. The chiefs considered the occupation of Narvik a secondary goal. Churchill pressed for immediate action against Narvik and maintained that this was within their capabilities since only small forces would be required at Bergen and Trondheim in the initial stages. Cyril Newall, the Chief of the Air Staff, argued for operations against Stavanger. He was the only one who had a true appreciation for the advantages that would accrue to the Germans from the capture of Sola Airfield.

It was decided that the main effort should be directed at the recapture of Bergen and Trondheim. However, this decision rested on the very tenuous assumption that Narvik was still in Norwegian hands and that large forces would therefore not be required in that area. There was still no definite information on what kind of resistance the Germans were encountering from Norwegian forces. However, it was agreed that the early recapture of these cities would encourage the Norwegians to continue their struggle.

The War Cabinet directed the Chiefs of Staff to prepare expeditions to wrest Bergen and Trondheim from the Germans at the same time as a force was dispatched to occupy Narvik. First, however, the naval situation needed to be brought under control. These discussions serve to explain both the earlier mentioned instructions to Admiral Forbes, and the background for Admiralty direct involvement in the tactical operations at Narvik. According to Moulton, neither Ismay nor Ironside came away from the meeting with a clear understanding of what had to be done and for what purpose.

The War Cabinet reconvened at noon—after a second CSC meeting—and it now appeared that their earlier assumption about Narvik being in Norwegian hands had fallen by the wayside. Unconfirmed news reports from Norway indicated that the Germans had occupied Narvik. Allied plans now became totally reactive and continued to illustrate a lack of understanding and logic. It was decided to send a few destroyers in the direction of Narvik to determine what was going on and to make a battalion available to support the destroyer operation. The chiefs informed the cabinet that a further seven battalions would be ready to sail by April 12. However, there was no decision made on how and where to use these additional battalions when they were ready!

The mood was still very optimistic since most of those in attendance expected that the use of overwhelming naval power would turn the German enterprise into a great Allied victory. This optimism—like the plans—was devoid of realism and logic. Churchill, who had access to the latest information from the Admiralty, optimistically told his colleagues that operations against Bergen and Trondheim were underway and he predicted that the application of British sea power would lead to the end of the landings in a week or two.

The telegram from Lord Halifax to his ambassador in Norway, Cecil Dormer, should be viewed in the light of this optimism. The message stated that the British Government was taking immediate action against the Germans in Bergen and Trondheim. This information was passed to the Norwegians and created false expectations. In fact, the members of the War Cabinet were already shifting their attention away from south and central Norway to Narvik.

Admiral Pound briefed Churchill after the War Cabinet meeting. Pound considered the operation against Bergen too risky after discovering that there were two German cruisers in that city. Churchill agreed and this led to the cancellation of the attack. By the time the telegram from Halifax to Dormer was on its way, telling the Norwegians that the British were moving immediately against the Germans in Bergen, Churchill and the Admiralty were canceling that operation. In retrospect, Churchill concluded that the Admiralty had interfered too much in operational matters and that the decision on whether or not to attack Bergen should have been left to Admiral Forbes.

A meeting of the Supreme War Council was convened at 10 Downing Street around 1730 hours on April 9, with the French represented by Reynaud, Daladier, and Admiral Darlan. The discussion focused on what could be done to thwart the Germans in Norway. The British pointed out that the two divisions held back in England for use in Scandinavia had been sent to France after the conclusion of peace between the Soviet Union and Finland. Consequently, there were only eleven battalions in Great Britain available for operations in Norway. The council was told that two of these battalions were embarked and sailing that night. Another five battalions would be available in three days, earmarked for Bergen and Trondheim according to Secretary of State for War Oliver Stanley, and the remaining four would not be ready for another two weeks. Some of the battalions were short of equipment and supplies left behind on the warships when *R4* was cancelled and the fleet readied for naval action.

If additional British forces were required, they had to be withdrawn from those deployed in France. The French offered an alpine division that they claimed would be ready to embark in 40 hours. Even now, after the Admiralty's cancellation of an attack on Bergen and heavy attacks on the Home Fleet by

German aircraft operating from Sola Airfield, the highest level of the government continued to operate as if all would turn out well. Chamberlain informed the French that he hoped to recapture not only Narvik, but also the west coast ports of Bergen and Trondheim.

The War Council was not in agreement over the action that should be taken in Norway. Whereas the French preferred to concentrate on resecuring Narvik, Stanley advocated the capture of Trondheim and Bergen, which would shore up Norwegian resistance. Churchill remained confident that this could easily be achieved and that the Allied troops would be able to push as far as the Swedish border. In the end, no decisions were taken on how to handle the situation in Norway. The meeting concluded with a very vague reference to the employment of forces at ports on the Norwegian coast, with particular emphasis on Narvik.

There was a meeting of the Military Coordination Committee (MCC),[12] chaired by Churchill, at 2130 hours on April 9. Churchill proposed that no action be taken against Trondheim and that the focus should be on Narvik. Ironside and the others present agreed. Their fixation with the old question of iron ore meant that they failed to change their thinking in response to the new situation created by the German invasion. Even a successful local operation in Narvik would be of limited use if the Germans held the rest of the country.

The successful conquest of southern and central Norway by the Germans would eventually make the Allied presence in northern Norway untenable. The German forces in Narvik were isolated almost 500 miles from their nearest comrades in Trondheim. They could not receive reinforcements on a meaningful scale and supply by air presented enormous problems, particularly if actions were taken to make the Værnes Airfield near Trondheim unusable. The greatest blow against the Germans in Narvik could best be struck by contesting the German conquest of central Norway. Some at the meeting must have thought along these lines since the committee's directive to the Chiefs of Staff to prepare plans for the capture of Narvik included a provision for establishing footholds in central Norway, at Åndalsnes and Namsos.

Chamberlain, addressing the House of Commons, was greeted by loud applause as he concluded that the events in Norway would prove to be catastrophic for the Germans. He, like his French counterpart, believed that the references to Narvik in the dispatches were mistakes. He believed they meant the town of Larvik, about 900 miles to the south.[13]

Kersaudy's summary of the Allies' response during the first day of the German invasion is on point:[14]

… the Allies, after six major gatherings in seventeen hours, had covered considerable ground—on paper at least: at 6:30 a.m., top priority given to Bergen and Trondheim, with a progressive drift towards Narvik in the course of the morning: confirmation of Narvik's new-found predominance during the afternoon, under insistent pressure from the French: "definite" shelving of Trondheim in the evening, with the surprise appearance in the late-evening conclusions of the Military Co-ordination Committee of the small ports of Namsos and Aandalsnes … some 500 miles south of Narvik.

Realities Set In

After the series of confusing meetings in Great Britain on April 9, the War Office faced the task of earmarking and assembling the force required to implement the decisions, a task made very difficult by the Admiralty order to debark the forces planned for *R4*. The planners began to realize that the Allies had been caught napping and that the German operations in Norway were on a much larger scale than they had anticipated. However, they were also operating in an intelligence vacuum. Because the Allied representatives became separated from the Norwegian government due to the German thrusts, there was no reliable information on what was happening in that country, on where the government was now located, what it intended to do, or on whether the Norwegian forces were actively opposing the Germans. They could only guess at the strength of the German beachheads.

The lackluster planning that had gone into the Allied plans for occupation of certain points on the Norwegian coast now became very apparent. The planners were unable to locate reliable information on landing sites and they ended up scraping together information and photographs of various harbors in Norway. The forces previously intended for Norway had been chosen on the assumption that they would face unopposed landings. They were not trained or equipped for the opposed landings that now appeared certain. They had no artillery, very limited transport capability, and no air support. In the afternoon of April 10 the planners informed General Ironside that an immediate recapture of Narvik was not feasible with the available forces.

The results of naval operations filtering back to London were not encouraging. The German Luftwaffe, which was now operating from recently captured Norwegian airfields, made naval operations along the Norwegian coast risky. Admiral Forbes' reaction was to withdraw the Home Fleet northward and out to sea. The Narvik situation was uncertain and it looked like the naval action there that morning had ended in a draw.

The meeting of the War Cabinet made it clear that Narvik was the priority objective. The policy makers were still preoccupied with the iron ore issue and failed to consider the larger strategic picture. There was even discussion of pressing on to the Swedish iron ore areas after Narvik was recaptured, or if that was not possible, to attack German shipping in the Swedish port of Luleå!

It seemed clear that the Allies had already sustained a crushing defeat, and some of the discussions centered on how to deflect the storm of criticism that was sure to follow. Since this setback came on top of the Allied failure to give aid to the Finns, it was necessary politically to launch a concerted effort to shift the blame. Churchill blamed Norway's "strict observance of neutrality" in a speech delivered to the House of Commons the following day.[15]

> It is not the slightest use blaming the Allies for not being able to give substantial help and protection to neutral countries if we are held at arm's length until these neutrals are actually attacked on a scientifically prepared plan by Germany. The strict observance of neutrality by Norway has been a contributory cause to the sufferings to which she is now exposed and to the limits of the aid which we can give her.

Even now, on April 11, Churchill sounded full of optimism and predicted a catastrophe for the Germans as he spoke to the House of Commons:

> In the upshot, it is the considered view of the Admiralty that we have greatly gained by what has occurred in Scandinavia and in northern waters in a strategic and military sense. For myself, I consider that Hitler's action in invading Scandinavia is as great a strategic and political error as that which was committed by Napoleon in 1807, when he invaded Spain.[16]

Disorganized Forces, an Untidy Command Structure, and Bewildering Orders

As a result of their hurried debarkation in *R4*, the eight battalions available for disposition were in a state of confusion. Derry states that the list of forces available was "not numerically unimpressive." This is a strange statement. The British had only 11 battalions available for operations in Norway and it would take up to two weeks for all of these to be ready to deploy. In the first week, the German forces in Norway had grown to over 45 battalions.

The 24th Guards Brigade was to figure prominently in the early efforts by the Allies to offer a riposte to the German capture of Narvik. This brigade of regulars had existed since the end of 1939, but the headquarters staff assembled hurriedly in the first days of April. It had never trained together as a unit. The 1st Battalion Irish Guards and the 1st Battalion Scots Guards were moved north from the London area on April 6. The Scots Guards were loaded on the *Batory*, a Polish transport, in the Clyde. The two remaining battalions were not yet at their embarkation points. The Irish Guards embarked in the liner *Monarch of Bermuda* in the morning of April 11. The third battalion of the brigade, the 2nd Battalion South Wales Borderers, had recently returned from India, not exactly a good training ground for arctic operations. This battalion embarked on the *Reino de Pacifica*.

Unfortunately, little thought was given to how equipment was loaded. Those items most essential for landing on a hostile shore were loaded deep in the holds while there was so many unnecessary "comfort" items for headquarters operations that it ended up cluttering the piers. Tactical loading was ignored.

The 146th Infantry Brigade, consisting of three territorial battalions, was added to these forces. One battalion of the 146th Infantry Brigade had Trondheim as its destination under *R4* and it was ready in the Clyde. The other two battalions of this brigade, previously destined for Bergen, had gone through the hurried debarkation five days earlier and much of their equipment remained on the ships in the mass confusion associated with that embarkation.

Two territorial battalions from the 148th Infantry Brigade also required several days to replace equipment left behind on the ships. The six battalions of French alpine troops that had been part of the forces for *R4* were scheduled to deploy a week after the first British forces.

The 49th Infantry Division was designated headquarters for the force at Narvik with Major General Pierce C. Mackesy as its commander. No plan had yet been formulated, not even in conceptual terms. The possibility of copying the German method of landing troops directly in the target area was not realistic since the troops were embarked in large merchant vessels with little thought given to their tactical employment without first disembarking, and then being organized and equipped.

The most frantic efforts were made to get the forces underway as quickly as possible. The 24th Guards Brigade lacked artillery, vehicles, and engineers and was therefore not in a position to advance overland against organized opposition, particularly in the wintry wilderness around Narvik. The 146th was hurried on its way on April 12, without taking time to re-equip. As pointed out by Moulton, it appeared that in their haste to take some action, the command authorities mistook another hasty embarkation as signs of drive and energy.

The selection of commanders was equally confusing and the failure to designate a clear-cut chain of command violated sound operational principles. Admiral Sir Edward Evans had been designated to lead British forces against Narvik before the German attack. However, he was dispatched as a member of the Allied delegation to Sweden and Admiral of the Fleet Lord Cork and Orrery was appointed commander of the naval forces for the Narvik operation. Since Admiral Cork was senior to Admiral Forbes, his nominal superior as Commander-in-Chief of the Home Fleet, the Admiralty put the control of naval operations within 100 miles of Vågsfjord in the hands of Admiral Cork. General Mackesy was sent to Scapa Flow in a hurry to accompany the Scots Guards. Mackesy, the 24th Guards Brigade commander, and two companies of the Scots Guards sailed on the same warship.

The British had only the vaguest ideas as to those two most important elements in coming up with a workable operational plan: the enemy and the terrain. A few lines from General Ironside's written notes accompanying General Mackesy instructions are illustrative:[17]

> Latest information is that there are 3,000 Germans in Narvik. They must have been knocked about by naval action . . . You may be able to work up the Norwegians, if they still exist in any formed body in or around Harstad. Tell them that a large force is coming. There should be considerable numbers of ponies in the village and neighbouring ones. Let no question of paying trouble you. Issue payment vouchers and we will see that you get a paymaster as soon as possible. Don't allow any haggling over prices.

The departing troops were told that there was little or no snow in the Narvik area. One can well imagine their dismay upon arrival in Harstad, seeing snow several feet deep all the way to the water's edge. General Ironside had drafted General Mackesy's instructions but neglected to coordinate or discuss these with the other service chiefs of staff. Ironside directed Mackesy to secure a foothold in Harstad, establish contact with Norwegian forces in the area if they existed, prepare the area for the arrival of additional forces, and then to proceed against the enemy in a deliberate manner. However, Ironside's notes were themselves contradictory. In one place, Mackesy is urged to take bold advantage of naval action but in another place he is told, "It is not intended that you should land in the face of opposition."[18]

Admiral Cork had no written instructions, but he received verbal briefings from Admiral Pound, the Military Coordination Committee, and finally from Churchill. There was no doubt in Cork's mind that he should seize Narvik as quickly as possible and that he should not hesitate to take risks in doing so. Churchill writes that neither he nor the Admiralty received copies of the instructions given to General Mackesy. In an obvious understatement, Churchill admits that the instructions given to Cork and Mackesy "were somewhat different in tone and emphasis."[19]

Unity of command was completely disregarded. General Ismay, one of the participants, has summarized neatly what transpired:[20]

> The Chief of the Naval Staff and the Chief of the Imperial General Staff acted with sturdy independence. They appointed their respective commanders without consultations with each other; and worse still, they gave directives to those commanders without harmonizing them. Thereafter they continued to issue separate orders to them. Thus was confusion worse confounded.

Since there was no theater commander, decisions that would normally have fallen to him, were relegated to a large number of committees in London. What was even worse, there was no single commander for all services in the three areas of Norway where the Allies eventually operated. Since the army commanders in the three areas did not command any air or naval forces, they relied on cooperation from those services. The Germans also struggled with unity of command because of service rivalries, but their problems were largely overcome at the operational levels by subordinate commanders who worked together as professionals.

Admiral Cork and General Mackesy did not even meet before they set out for Narvik by separate conveyance on April 12. Cork departed from Rosyth on the cruiser *Aurora* while Mackesy departed from Scapa Flow on the cruiser *Southampton*. The remainder of the 24th Guards Brigade (two companies accompanied General Mackesy and the brigade commander on the

Southampton) and the three battalions of the 146th Infantry Brigade left for Narvik on April 12 with a strong naval escort consisting of the battleship *Valiant*, cruisers *Manchester*, *Birmingham* and *Cairo*, and eleven destroyers.

Changing Allied Strategy and Plans

When we last looked at the confusing scene of Allied decision-making with respect to Norway, it appeared that they had settled firmly late on April 9 on making the recapture of Narvik—codenamed Rupert—the top priority while examining the possibility of landings at Namsos and Åndalsnes. However, the consensus was weak and open to outside influences that soon made themselves felt.

Prime Minister Reynaud was dubious about the early ability of the Allies to land sufficient forces in Norway. He was still preoccupied with the iron ore question and decided to send a diplomatic-military delegation to Sweden to try to convince that country to enter the war on the Allied side. The mission stopped in London on April 11 on its way to Sweden, and Chamberlain, who liked the French idea, decided a British delegation should join the venture.

The Swedes told the delegations that they would remain neutral under all eventualities but they did give advice as evidenced by a telegram from the French ambassador in Sweden on April 13: "The Allied missions here, and also the Swedes, are unanimous in their opinion that the most effective Allied help would be the recapture of Trondheim." Admiral Evans, who headed the British delegation, expressed similar views in a telegram to the Foreign Office: "Most urgent is Trondhjem be re-captured forthwith, or both Norway and Sweden will completely lose faith in us. . . . Narvik could wait anyway a fortnight."[21]

The confusion in Allied ranks during these early days of the Norwegian campaign was not entirely due to lack of intelligence, as some British authors claim. The Allies had had no contacts with the Norwegian government since the German attack, and they made no concerted attempt in those early days to get in touch with the Norwegian military authorities. Contact was reestablished on April 12 when Ambassador Dormer linked up with the Norwegian government near the Swedish border.

Dormer sent a message to the British Foreign Office via Stockholm in which he confirmed Norwegian resolve to carry on the war against the Germans. However, the message also stated that the Norwegians would only be able to cope with the Germans militarily if aid from the Allies arrived quickly, and it carried an urgent appeal from General Ruge for the recapture of Trondheim.

Dormer wrote, "I venture to urge that military assistance at Trondheim is first necessity. Seizure of Narvik was of little assistance to Norwegian government."[22]

The political and strategic reassessment caused by these messages now resulted in a change in plans with further confusion. For reasons that should have been obvious to all before April 12, Trondheim assumed a new importance. It was not only an ancient capital but it was also the third largest metropolitan area in Norway, and it formed the country's main communications hub. Both Germans and Norwegians considered the city the key military objective.

The only strategic importance of Narvik, in Norwegian view, was as a shipping port for iron ore. Narvik is located over 400 miles north of Trondheim. The German forces in Narvik were isolated and the only realistic hope of reinforcements was overland from Trondheim. The recapture of that city and Værnes Airfield would place Narvik beyond the range of any supporting German aircraft. The Norwegian forces mobilizing in North Norway were capable of isolating the Germans and then going on the offensive. Their greatest need was air and naval support. Some Allied forces were welcomed but the Norwegians felt that they could be put to far better use for both the overall campaign and the effort in Narvik if they were used to recapture Trondheim, removing any chance of German reinforcements and eliminating their air threat.

Some within the MCC—particularly Sir Cyril Newall, Chief of the Air Staff —had recognized the importance of Trondheim as early as April 9. He resurfaced the idea at a meeting of the committee on April 11 but it was reluctant to undo the planning and preparations undertaken the past two days. Churchill, while agreeing that the recapture of Trondheim should be studied, stressed that no decision be made until it was known what was required at Narvik. The MCC adjourned without making any changes to the plans and preparations.

Moulton writes that Churchill, Admiral Pound and Air Chief Marshal Newall went to see General Ironside at 0100 hours on April 12. Churchill and the others who have written about the Norwegian campaign do not mention this meeting. The visitors suggested that part of the force on its way to Narvik be diverted to Namsos as part of a drive on Trondheim. Ironside reportedly argued vehemently against this solution on dubious practical grounds. His reasoning was that it was not possible to divert an invasion force destined for one location to another. This would be true under normal circumstances, but in this case the force was not ready for immediate action at either destination.

The War Cabinet met the following morning and the messages from the political/military mission to Sweden and from Sir Cecil Dormer had arrived.

Churchill argued for no action against Trondheim that would threaten the success in the operation against Narvik. He conceded that if that city was recaptured quickly, the French alpine troops could be diverted for operations against Trondheim. Chamberlain was impressed with the views expressed by the Swedes and Norwegians and suggested that forces to recapture Trondheim should be put ashore in Namsos. Churchill was quick to point to the lack of information on the military situation in that part of the country and that such information was vital before undertaking any operations. Apparently, none of those present had the courage to point out to Churchill that there was an equal scarcity of information about the military situation in the Narvik area. The decision to make Narvik the priority target was left standing, but not for long.

The War Cabinet met again in the afternoon. This time both Chamberlain and Halifax argued for the political necessity of retaking Trondheim. Ironside objected initially because the expedition would require troops that were now in France, but then he qualified his position by stating that diversion of some troops destined for Narvik would not imperil that operation. Most cabinet members now threw their support behind Chamberlain and it was decided that operations to retake Trondheim be undertaken while allowing the operation against Narvik to proceed. While Churchill and Ironside's insistence on Narvik was strategically fallacious, no one had the wisdom or moral courage to go after the logical objective—Trondheim—with all available forces. This division of effort almost guaranteed failure of both undertakings.

We are getting a little ahead of ourselves, but when the news of the naval action on April 13 reached London, the decision makers became overconfident. They felt that the capture of Narvik would be relatively easy and only a few days away. They decided to divert the 146th Brigade—now only hours from Harstad —to Namsos to form the northern prong of the pincer movement envisioned against Trondheim. This caused additional problems and further confusion. The 146th Brigade had no maps of its new area of operation, much of its equipment was loaded on ships carrying the 24th Guards Brigade to Harstad, and the brigade commander and his staff had already landed in Harstad, over 300 miles from the brigade's new destination.

The selection of the unit sent to Namsos also seems strange. If operations against Narvik were viewed as easy, it would make better sense to send the best troops—the 24th Guards Brigade—to Namsos instead of the poorly trained and equipped territorial brigade. As matters developed, the Guards sat in the Narvik area for weeks without taking part in operations.

Churchill intervened again. In a visit to Ironside at 0200 hours on April 14, he proposed yet another alternation to plans. He suggested a direct attack on Trondheim by landing a small force to seize the city in conjunction with landings at Namsos and Åndalsnes. Ironside, who had earlier agreed reluctantly to the diversion of the 146th Brigade, now had second thoughts about the wisdom of that agreement. He relented when Churchill pointed out that the suggestion was made in his capacity as Chairman of the MCC; in other words, as Ironside's superior in the British wartime chain of command. The order from the Chiefs of Staff was sent out on the 14th. It covered the landings of the 146th Brigade at Namsos and called for reinforcement of that force with a half-brigade of Chasseurs Alpines (CA) that the French had reluctantly agreed to divert from Narvik.

The MCC considered Churchill's suggestion to land inside the fjord near Trondheim on April 13. The naval staff's assessment of the feasibility of such an operation was positive. They believed that the shore batteries at the fjord entrance could be dealt with easily, and plans for the operation were prepared. These plans envisioned the use of three battleships and two aircraft carriers with eighty aircraft. Bomber Command would make nightly attacks on Værnes Airfield, and the airfields at Sola and Fornebu would be given special attention just before and during the operational phase.

The plan—code-named Hammer—called for a landing near Værnes, at a village called Hell, by the 15th Infantry Brigade. This unit was part of the 5th Division located in France. A force of two Canadian battalions would land near the fjord entrance and capture the shore batteries. The 147th Infantry Brigade would serve as a reserve. Major General Hotblack, with a divisional head-quarters, was designated the force commander.

In its larger scope, the plan called for the 146th Brigade and French alpine troops to advance from Namsos and link up with the 15th Brigade near Værnes. Simultaneously, the 148th Infantry Brigade would land at Åndalsnes and advance towards Dombås. Its mission was two-fold. First, it would block any push towards Trondheim by German forces in the south in case these were able to break through the Norwegian lines. Secondly, it was hoped that the Germans in Trondheim would send forces to meet this southern threat. Except for the rosy assumption that two battalions of poorly trained territorial troops, without artillery, air support, winter training, or winter equipment could traverse the 190 miles between Åndalsnes and Trondheim across snow-clad mountains, it was a good plan—the best the Allies had developed so far.

NOTES

1 Churchill, *The Gathering Storm*, pp. 590 and 606.

2 Richard Petrow, *The Bitter Years: The Invasion and Occupation of Denmark and Norway April 1940–May 1945* (New York: William Morrow and Company, Inc.), 1974, p. 1.

3 PRO, *FO* 371, 24829, N4101.

4 Chr. Christensen, *De som heiste flagget*, pp. 74-75.

5 Tamelander and Zetterling, *Niende april*, vol. 3, p. 271.

6 Odd-Bjørn Fure, *Norsk uterikspolitiske historie.* Vol 3. *Mellomkrigstid 1920–1940* (Oslo: 1996), p. 378.

7 Nicholaus von Falkenhorst, *Bericht und Vernehmung des Generalobersten von Falkenhorst* p. 84. "That was absolutely von Spiller's private war. I knew nothing about it. It was in no way anticipated."

8 PRO, *FO* 371, 24834, N4326, April 13, 1940; Otto Ruge, *Felttoget. General Otto Ruges erindringer fra kampene april–juni 1940* (Olav Riste,ed.; Oslo: Aschenhoug, 1989), pp. 29, 37, 43, 53, and 55; and PRO *FO* 371, 24834 N4339 and N4579, April 14, 1940.

9 O. Lindbäck-Larsen, *Krigen i Norge 1940* (Oslo: Forsvarets Krigshistoriske Avdeling, 1965), p. 77.

10 This committee had been in existence since 1923 and in April 1940, it consisted of Admiral Sir Dudley Pound, First Sea Lord, General Sir Edmund Ironside, Chief of the Imperial General Staff, and Air Chief Marshal Sir Cyrice Newall, the Chief of the Air Staff.

11 PRO, *CAB* 79/3 C.O.S.C. 9.4.1940 and Lord Ismay, *The Memoirs of Lord Ismay* (London: Heinemann, 1950), p. 120.

12 This committee was formed at the outbreak of war in 1939 and consisted of the three service ministers along with their chiefs of staff. The Prime Minister was the chair and Churchill was the deputy chair.

13 United Kingdom, *Parliamentary Debates. House of Commons*, vol. 359, col.511.

14 Kersaudy, *Norway*, p. 86.

17, "Copy of a message written out in Manuscript by C.I.G.S. for General Mackesy 2330 hours 10th April, taken by Brigadier Lund," (Derry, *The Campaign in Norway*, Appendix A, pp. 247-248).

18 Loc cit.

19 Churchill, *The Gathering Storm*, p. 612.

20 Ismay, *Memoirs*, p. 111.

21 Kersaudy, *Norway*, p. 91 and PRO, *FO* 371, 24834, N4317, April 13, 1940.

22 As quoted in Kersaudy, *Norway*, p. 92.

8

BEACHHEAD CONSOLIDATION AND SECOND NAVAL BATTLE

"I do not believe that soldiers were ever, in the history
of warfare, sent against an enemy with such a useless weapon."
ADMIRAL KARL DÖNITZ ON THE GERMAN TORPEDO PROBLEMS.

Admiralty Eagerness to Follow up on First Naval Battle

After receiving Warburton-Lee's last message that one enemy cruiser and three destroyers were attacking him, Admiral Whitworth finally took action. He sent the cruiser *Penelope*, commanded by Captain Yates, and four destroyers to Warburton-Lee's aid. They arrived too late to participate in the battle and did not enter Ofotfjord. The Admiralty sent a message directly to Captain Yates in the *Penelope* at 2012 hours on April 11: "If in light of experience this morning you consider it a justifiable operation, take available destroyers in Narvik area and attack enemy in Narvik tonight or tomorrow morning."[1]

Whitworth apparently had his fill of the Admiralty dealing directly with his subordinates. He sent a message that did not mention the breach of the chain of command but complained that he had received three tasks, and they appeared incompatible. He mentioned that he had orders to prevent the Germans from leaving Narvik, to prevent reinforcements from reaching Narvik, and to attack the Germans in Narvik. He asked for some clarification and added that he considered an attack on Narvik risky and that it would interfere with what he saw as his primary mission of keeping reinforcements from reaching Narvik. Admiral Forbes adopted an attitude of diplomatic silence by not sending a message supporting Whitworth. The Admiralty simply ignored Whitworth's pique.

Captain Yates appears to have had doubts about his orders. Warburton-Lee's message about an enemy cruiser in the Narvik area worried him, and the destroyer *Bedouin* had reported the presence of electrically controlled mines in the fjord and possible German shore defenses on Barøy. The explosions that *Bedouin* reported as mines were actually torpedoes fired at it by *U25*. The torpedoes were not observed from the destroyer, missed their target and exploded nearby without causing any damage. So far, the British had not observed any submarines, so this threat did not add to the total of Yates's concerns.

The Admiralty had waited over 13 hours after receipt of the message from *Hostile* before prodding Captain Yates to attack Narvik. Despite their own sluggishness, they were asking him to make an immediate attack, either that night or early in the morning. Yates sent a diplomatic response about three hours after he had received their suggestion:[2]

> I consider attack justifiable although element of surprise has been lost. Navigational dangers from ships sunk today eliminate chances of a successful night attack. Propose attacking at dawn on 12th since operation orders cannot be got and issued for tomorrow in view of escorting ships' dispositions and destroyers on patrol.

On April 12, he would face the same navigational obstacles, the same enemy, and they would have had time to make repairs and prepare their defenses in the interim. Yates may have shared the views of his superior, Admiral Whitworth, about the risks involved in an immediate attack. He used the speculative and inaccurate assessment by Lieutenant Commander McCoy in the *Bedouin* to end any possibility of a quick attack on Narvik. At 0930 hours on April 11, he signaled the Admiralty: "*Bedouin* is of the opinion that the operation on the lines of yesterday's attack could not be carried out successfully. In light of this report I concur and regret that I must reverse my decision given in my 2310/10th."[3]

The German Naval Situation

Commander Bey's report to Naval Command West was received with dismay, despite the fact that significant losses had been expected and ruled acceptable. The operational status of the German destroyers in Narvik after the naval battle on April 10 was as follows:

Wilhelm Heidkamp. In the process of sinking. Eighty-one dead.
Dieter von Roeder. Immobile after five hits. Forward guns were still operable and the ship could be used as a floating battery. Not refueled. Thirteen dead.
Anton Schmitt. Sunk. Fifteen killed.
Hermann Künne. Undamaged but not refueled.

Hans Lüdemann. Sustained two hits. One gun destroyed and aft magazine flooded. Not refueled. Two killed.

Georg Thiele. Badly damaged by seven hits. Severe damage to hull and engines. Two guns and fire control system not reparable. Magazines flooded. Not refueled. Thirteen killed.

Bernd von Arnim. Badly damaged by five hits. Un-seaworthy because of hull damage and one boiler out of action. Refueled. Fifty-two killed.

Wolfgang Zenker. Undamaged but not refueled.

Erich Giese. Undamaged but not refueled.

Erich Koellner. Undamaged but not refueled.

The German Naval Staff realized its worst fears. The quick return of the destroyers was thwarted by the failure of one tanker to reach Narvik. It is surprising that the Germans had not made allowances for one or two additional tankers to be at Narvik. This would have increased the probability that more than one tanker would be in position when required. Furthermore, it would have permitted quicker refueling and allowed the destroyers to head back home while the enemy was still in a state of confusion. Now, almost half of Germany's destroyer force appeared trapped. The Luftwaffe facilitated the return of warships from ports in western and southern Norway by keeping British surface units at a distance, but there was little help from the Luftwaffe in the Narvik area.

Jan Wellem had miraculously escaped the carnage in Narvik harbor on April 10. Refueling could therefore continue but at the same slow rate as on April 9. Shortage of ammunition was also a serious concern for Commander Bey. The destroyers had used over half of their ammunition supply. German hopes for resupply by sea were dealt a final blow on April 11 when the British destroyer *Icarus* captured the supply ship *Alster* in Vestfjord.

Commander Bey reported to Naval Command West in the afternoon of April 10 that none of his damaged destroyers would be ready to attempt a breakout in time to link up with the two battleships that evening. Only two of the surviving destroyers would be refueled by dark, *Wolfgang Zenker* and *Erich Giese*.

Commander Bey did not appear anxious to attempt a breakout with the two refueled destroyers. Naval Command West believed that he failed to appreciate the deadly trap in which he found himself. They finally resorted to an unusual procedure for a command that normally left tactical decisions to the senior commander at sea. They sent Bey a curt message at 1712 hours on April 10 to leave with *Wolfgang Zenker* and *Erich Giese* as soon as it was dark. If he needed further persuasion, Naval Command West transmitted, two hours later the very precise intelligence that in addition to the *Renown* and *Repulse*, three more British battleships were headed for the Lofoten area. The second message may not have served its intended purpose. Instead, it may have convinced Bey that a breakout was futile.

The two German destroyers ordered to break out departed Narvik at 2040 hours. They proceeded westward at high speed at about the same time as *U25*, whose commander did not know that a breakout was in progress, confronted two British destroyers on patrol near Barøy. The British destroyers withdrew when they began to suspect that they were near a minefield. This left an unintended opening for the two German destroyers, which passed through the area about one hour later and turned south through Vestfjord. Within a few minutes of entering the fjord, the Germans sighted the silhouettes of three warships, one identified as a cruiser. The visibility was excellent despite the onset of darkness and Commander Bey decided that a breakout was not achievable. The German destroyers turned around within 7,000 meters of the British ships and headed back to Narvik while laying smoke. The British ships, which were probably the cruiser *Penelope* and the destroyers *Bedouin* and *Eskimo*, did not see the German destroyers.

German Torpedo Problems

U25, when she confronted *Bedouin* and *Eskimo* prior to Bey's unsuccessful breakout attempt, fired four torpedoes at the British warships at a range of no more than 1,200 meters. Lieutenant Commander Schütze, the *U25* commander, heard explosions and assumed his torpedoes had found their targets at that very close range. They had not. Two exploded in the vicinity of the British ships and one detonated against the shore. The two destroyer captains became sufficiently concerned that they withdrew from the area. The British apparently did not considered that there could be a submarine in the area and *Bedouin's* skipper, Lieutenant Commander McCoy, sent a message suggesting that the explosions were mines or torpedoes fired from shore batteries on Barøy. This message had—as we have seen in the case of Captain Yates on the *Penelope*—considerable impact on British plans.

The German destroyer crews were extremely dissatisfied with the service provided by their submarines, and the submariners were especially upset with their research and development services. No provisions were made for direct communications between the destroyers in Narvik and the German submarines operating in the area. This problem was finally overcome when Commander Bey contacted Naval Command West and arranged for a personal meeting with Lieutenant Herbert Sohler, captain of the submarine *U46*, on April 11.

Arrangements were made for direct communications between the destroyers and the submarines to include radio warnings transmitted in the clear of an enemy approach. Sohler assured Bey that the submarines would provide better support to the destroyers in the future. The fact that this was not to be cannot be blamed on the submarine commanders' lack of effort.

Another submarine, *U51*, attacked a British destroyer near Tranøy about 0200 hours on April 11. The torpedoes either missed or failed to function. *U51* had another opportunity within half an hour, but the result was the same. The *U47*, commanded by Lieutenant Günther Prien, fired two salvos of four torpedoes each against a large transport and cruiser at anchor near Bygden in Vågsfjord between 2200 and 2400 hours on April 15, but scored no hits. She then developed engine troubles and had to return to Germany. Southwest of Vestfjord, she encountered the battleship *Warspite* and two escorting destroyers. Prien fired two torpedoes at a distance of only 900 meters, again without results.

These are only a few examples of the 31 submarine attacks carried out against British warships during these critical days. The German Navy concluded that 20 of these attacks would certainly have hit their targets, which included one battleship, seven cruisers, seven destroyers, and five transports, but for the malfunctioning of the torpedoes.

It was discovered later that the new magnetic pistols that allowed the torpedo to be detonated by the magnetic field of a ship's hull when it passed underneath, without requiring a direct impact, were ineffective at these northern latitudes. It was also discovered that the depth-regulator mechanism did not function as intended. This also applied to the destroyer torpedoes as shown by their failure against British destroyers on April 10. The failure of the submarine torpedoes to function properly had a serious effect on operations around Narvik, and certainly on the psychological confidence of the submarine crews. On his return to Germany, Prien summed up succinctly the confidence crisis in the torpedoes among submarine commanders: "One cannot again expect him [submarine commander] to fight with an air gun."[4]

German Destroyers Trapped

By noon on April 11, *Wolfgang Zenker*, *Erich Koellner*, *Hermann Künne*, and *Hans Lüdemann* were ready to sail from Narvik. *Erich Giese* was also ready but developed a minor engine problem. However, Commander Bey continued to maintain that conditions for a breakout were unfavorable. Some writers have suggested that the lives of his sailors were uppermost in his mind and that he felt they had a better chance to survive if the ships remained in Narvik. However, he also knew that he was expected to uphold the honor of the German Navy by fighting to the end.

Naval Command West was becoming impatient at what they must have viewed as Commander Bey's procrastinations. They issued Bey an order in the afternoon of April 12 to make use of the first opportunity of reduced visibility and bad weather to break out. However, Bey maintained that any attempt to break out was futile in view of the overwhelming British naval presence at the entrance to Ofotfjord. This may have been his view all along.

All discussions of a breakout at this time appear to have focused on a southwest passage through Vestfjord, an area heavily guarded by the Royal Navy. There was another possible route that the destroyers could have used to reach the open sea without the danger of running the British gauntlet in Vestfjord. The narrow strait of Ramsund, between Tjeldøy and the mainland, leads to the broader Tjeldsund, and that strait exits into the Vågsfjord just southeast of Harstad. The entrance to Ramsund is inside Ofotfjord and at least ten miles from the British patrol line. The distance from where Tjeldsund intersects with Vågsfjord to the open sea is not more than five miles. The British Navy did not reach Vågsfjord in force until April 14, and the route to the open sea would therefore be relatively clear for the German destroyers. The *U49* in Vågsfjord could provide intelligence on British naval activities.

After the German destroyers had reached open sea on a southwesterly course, it would have been very difficult for the British to intercept them. The destroyers, in moderate weather, were capable of speed of 36 knots and the British did not have heavy units capable of that speed. It seems strange therefore, that Bey and Naval Command West appear not to have considered this escape route. Navigation through Ramsund or Tjeldsund at night would be very tricky, but possible.[5]

A series of events after April 11 made it considerably more difficult for the Germans to make a successful breakout. Two destroyers—*Erich Koellner* and *Wolfgang Zenker*—ran aground in Ofotfjord while on patrol during the night between April 11 and 12. *Erich Koellner* was so badly damaged when it hit an underwater reef that it was no longer seaworthy. *Wolfgang Zenker's* propellers were damaged, limiting its speed.

Commander Bey reported to Naval Command West in the afternoon of April 12 that two destroyers—*Hans Lüdemann* and *Hermann Künne* – were operational, that three destroyers—*Erich Giese*, *Bernd von Arnim*, and *Georg Thiele*—could operate at a maximum speed of 28 knots, and that *Wolfgang Zenker* could travel at a maximum speed of only 20 knots. The remaining two destroyers—*Erich Koellner* and *Diether von Roeder*—were so heavily damaged that they were not seaworthy. Bey planned to use *Erich Koellner* as a floating battery on the north side of Ofotfjord, just east of Ramnes. He planned to use *Diether von Roeder* in a similar capacity in Narvik harbor.

The German Situation Ashore

The Germans quickly brought ashore all recoverable weapons, equipment, and supplies from those destroyers damaged beyond repair in the destroyer battle on April 10. Survivors from *Wilhelm Heidkamp* and *Anton Schmitt* were organized into a naval infantry battalion, armed mostly with weapons from the Norwegian depot at Elvegårdsmoen. Lieutenant Commander Erdmenger, the skipper of the sinking *Wilhelm Heidkamp*, was placed in command of this force. The Germans also continued to bring ashore and set up the heavy guns from the armed British merchant ships in the harbor.

General Dietl's situation looked precarious to General von Falkenhorst and the OKW. He was isolated in an area over 400 miles from the nearest friendly forces. He had lost many of his supplies and equipment and was faced by a Norwegian army in the process of mobilizing superior forces and with the distinct prospect that the Allies would land troops either directly in Narvik or nearby. Dietl was directed to find a suitable place for a temporary airfield pending the capture of Bardufoss. This was a tall order in the mountainous area around Narvik and resulted in a request from Dietl that long-range seaplanes and bombers be used for resupply. He was promised that seaplanes carrying supplies would arrive on April 11, but only one appeared, and it did not land. A German unit discovered that the ice on Lake Hartvigvann was more than three feet thick and Dietl directed that it be examined to determine if it could be used as an airfield.

Dietl still had to accomplish two critically important parts of his mission, securing the railway from Narvik to the border and capturing Bardufoss Airfield and Setermoen. Control of Narvik would be meaningless unless the railroad connection to Sweden was secured. Securing the northward advance to Bardufoss was also important, but the ability to accomplish it with the available resources was questionable. No immediate move was made towards the Swedish border and only a reinforced company from one of the two battalions available to Colonel Windisch saw any appreciable combat on the northern front before the last week in April. The weather played a role as the month of April witnessed some of the worst conditions in many years. The fear of Allied landings and stiffening Norwegian resistance were undoubtedly other factors that led to the somewhat hesitant German attitude.

General Fleischer's Assessment

The return of General Fleischer and his chief of staff from eastern Finnmark was delayed because of snowstorms. They managed to get to Tromsø after a harrowing five-hour flight on April 10 and by April 12, Fleischer was at his headquarters at Moen in Målselv.

Since the northern part of the country was now isolated from southern and central Norway, General Fleischer assumed the mantle of Commander-in-Chief in North Norway. This gave him control of the civil administration and naval forces in the area. Both the mobilization and assumption of overall command were taken on his own initiative. The right to order mobilization was reserved for the government and although he was designated as wartime commander-in-chief, no orders were received to execute that contingency plan. It is to Fleischer's credit that he took these important decisions without waiting for orders from a government that appeared incapable of taking immediate effective action in this chaotic situation.

Fleischer's area of responsibility stretched about 600 miles as the crow flies, from north to south. An enemy bridgehead now cut that area in two. The southern portion was relatively safe for now since the Germans were located in the Trondheim area, over 100 miles from the southern border of his command. However, he had to keep an eye on the situation in the south since it would be logical for the Germans to try hard to establish land communications with their forces in Narvik. Furthermore, he could not neglect the border with the Soviet Union. Soviet actions in Poland while the Germans were invading that country from the west were still fresh in everyone's mind. That danger was somewhat alleviated with the arrival of Allied forces in North Norway since it was unlikely that the Soviets would risk hostilities with the British and French. Even as he kept these threats in mind, Fleischer had to contend with an expanding German bridgehead in Narvik and assemble sufficient forces to commence offensive operations.

Fleischer's first task was to bring the German advances to a halt, particularly their northern thrust towards Bardufoss Airfield. German capture of this airfield would significantly alter the situation in their favor and put any Allied assistance in jeopardy. The German northward thrust also posed a threat to Setermoen, the other major Norwegian mobilization depot and training area. The Norwegians knew that a German battalion was advancing northward with the mission of capturing these two objectives. The total strength of the Germans in Narvik was not known, but General Fleischer assumed that they numbered several thousand of Germany's most elite troops.

Fleischer reasoned that it was not sufficient merely to isolate the Germans in Narvik. Such an approach would tie down his forces, give the Germans time to organize and build up their strength for continued attacks at points of their choosing while waiting for a link-up. He believed that a defensive strategy would not be successful since he had to assume that German forces from the south would drive aggressively towards Narvik and he had no forces to halt such an attack as long as Dietl's 3rd Mountain Division tied him down.

The only clear alternative in Fleischer's mind was to attack and destroy the German forces in Narvik or drive them over the border to Sweden. This would allow him to move substantial forces south to meet an eventual German drive from Trondheim. He viewed his soldiers as the hardiest in the world and felt certain that they would acquit themselves well when pitted against the German mountain troops.

In order to achieve local superiority for an attack, Fleischer found it necessary to risk reducing troop strength along the Soviet Border. He ordered the 1/12th Inf to the Narvik front as quickly as possible. He also decided to bring the Alta Bn south as soon as its mobilization was completed. These forces had to be transported by sea, which would take some time. Fleischer had only the 1/14th Inf battalion in Mosjøen in the southern part of his area. This force was inadequate to cope with a German advance from the Trondheim area and Fleischer decided that the best use of this unit was to move it south and attach it to Colonel Getz' 5th Field Brigade in the Steinkjer area. Halfdan Sundlo, the brother of the regimental commander in Narvik, commanded this battalion.

Fleischer's plan had as its goal the gradual reduction of the German ability to fight by first taking their base area at Bjerkvik and Elvegårdsmoen, prevent them from establishing a connection to Sweden, and finally of capturing Narvik. Fleischer concluded that the experienced German elite troops were professionally superior to his own units but he planned to compensate for this drawback by relying on what he saw as Norwegian superior mobility in the wild and snow-covered terrain around Narvik.

The partial destruction of the 1/13th Inf on April 9 was a serious setback for the Norwegians. It was doubtful that the remnants of the 1/13th could successfully resist a strong German advance to the border. It was hoped that the threat of Allied landings and Norwegian attacks from the north would prevent the Germans from undertaking offensive operations towards the border.

The loss of Elvegårdsmoen was most serious. It was the mobilization center for the 15th Infantry Regiment and a number of other units. Their valuable stores of equipment and supplies were now lost and this made it difficult or impossible for these units to carry out an orderly mobilization. In addition to acquiring a bridgehead on the north side of Ofotfjord for their northward drive, the Germans obtained stores that proved of immense importance and made the Norwegian task of eliminating the German bridgehead more problematic.

The Defense of the Ofot Railway

The remnants of the 1/13th Inf that withdrew from Narvik on April 9 were located along the railway leading to Sweden. Majors Spjeldnæs and Omdal decided to establish defensive positions and hold Nordal Bridge until they received more definite orders. Captain Bjørnson's company went into positions at the bridge while the rest of the troops moved to Bjørnefjell railroad station, about three kilometers to the northeast.

Major Omdal had to prepare against a German advance from Elvegårdsmoen as well as along the railroad from Narvik. A platoon from Co 3 was sent to take up defensive positions near a chain of small lakes northwest of Bjørnefjell. This platoon surprised and captured a 13-man German patrol on April 11. According to Buchner, the patrol was a German attempt to establish a link between German forces in Elvegårdsmoen and Narvik.

The 16th Infantry Regiment established contact with Major Omdal's forces on April 11 via a ski patrol. Omdal informed the general that he intended to prevent the Germans from pushing through to the Swedish border but his troops were in great need of supplies. Fleischer ordered Omdal to hold the Nordal Bridge as long as possible and authorized its destruction in case it could not be held. He also ordered the tunnels at the west end of the bridge destroyed. The rails west of the bridge were removed on April 13 and two iron ore cars were demolished within the tunnel.

The Norwegian troops that escaped from Narvik had only brought with them weapons, what ammunition they could carry, and a few rations. Skis were left behind and this made mobility in the snow-covered mountains difficult and exhausting. In the days immediately following their arrival in the Bjørnefjell area, the Norwegians were able to obtain skis, winter camouflage clothing, rifle ammunition, and some provisions from Swedish military units across the border. These Swedish supplies eventually dried up, due to German pressure on the Swedish Government, and assistance became limited to humanitarian help in the form of provisions and the evacuation of seriously ill or wounded soldiers.

The Norwegians had hoped for Swedish weapons and ammunition, but the Swedes were maintaining their neutrality. As a result, the Swedes at the border confiscated ammunition sent by the shortest route from the Norwegian forces in East Finnmark to their forces in the Narvik area.

The commander of the Hålogaland Air Group, Major L. Feiring, who had just arrived from southern Norway via Sweden, suggested that Major Omdal's forces be supplied by air. The first supply drop took place on April 14 and then four aircraft were able to land on a frozen lake on April 15. In this manner, ammunition and provisions for eight days were brought to the troops at Bjørnefjell.

The German Northward Advance

The German push north from Elvegårdsmoen was undertaken by the 1/139th Regiment, commanded by Major Stautner. General Dietl may have already decided that his forces were insufficient to secure Bardufoss and Setermoen, the final objectives in his directive. The goal of his northward advance was therefore limited to seizing more defensible terrain by pushing through the Gratangen Valley to seize the Oalgge Pass, immediately west of Lapphaugen. Control of that high ground would leave Colonel Windisch's troops less exposed to Norwegian counterattacks and would allow the Germans to trade space for time.

Major Stautner's troops seized Elvenes, 17 kilometers north of Bjerkvik, late on April 10 without encountering Norwegian resistance. Heavy snowfall slowed the German advance and they were too exhausted to push further without a rest. They continued their advance on April 12 through the Gratang Valley towards Lapphaugen.

The Norwegian forces from Setermoen were caught in a vicious snowstorm as they tried to make their way to the Narvik area on April 9. The motorized battery from the 3rd Mountain Artillery Bn made it to the Gratangen Tourist Station by 1100 hours when it had to stop because of blizzard conditions. It later withdrew to the Fossbakken area. The main force of the 2/15th Inf was ordered to take up positions at Lund in Salangsdal, with a platoon-size security force near Lapphaugen. Colonel Løken, commander of the 6th Field Brigade, decided, however, to stop the Germans in the defile near Lapphaugen. The position near Lund (Brattli) was more defensible, but to let the Germans advance that far would reduce the Norwegians' ability to carry out mobile operations in the wild and roadless terrain to the south. The Gratang/Fossbakken area had to be held in order to cover Setermoen and Bardufoss and for mobilization of units in that area.

Sixty-six students from the 6th Division command and leadership school, commanded by Captain O. Forseth, were on their way from Tromsø to their training area near Setermoen on April 8. They learned about the German attack when they landed at Sjøvegan at 0800 hours on April 9. After arriving in the Setermoen area, Captain Forseth was ordered to organize his students and personnel at the training area into a field company. This 170-strong force was organized on April 10. At noon on April 11, Forseth was directed to take up defensive positions at the Gratangen Tourist Station and delay the German battalion moving north from Bjerkvik. This was necessary to provide time for the 2/15th Inf and the 3rd Mountain Artillery Bn to prepare defensive positions near Lapphaugen. Forseth's unit was in defensive positions at the Gratang Tourist Station shortly after midnight on April 11.

The first contact with the enemy was made at 0630 hours on April 12. The fighting lasted most of the day. The Norwegians were forced to destroy the tourist station and make a hasty withdrawal to Lapphaugen when a double German envelopment threatened to cut their line of retreat. The southern German envelopment was within 400 meters of cutting the Norwegian route of withdrawal but they managed to slip through since visibility was severely reduced by a heavy snowfall.

The fighting around Gratangen Tourist Station was a minor engagement with light casualties. The Norwegians had no losses while the Germans had two killed and three wounded. However, this small engagement had a substantial impact on future operations. It gave the Norwegians another 24 hours to organize and prepare. The Germans noted the stiffening resistance and realized that any attempt to push past Oalgge Pass with the limited forces at their disposal would be very hazardous as their flanks became increasingly exposed.

Forseth's company reached Lapphaugen about 2100 hours on April 12 where it linked up with a platoon from Co 5 and a mountain howitzer from Battery 8. Captain Forseth received a report from brigade at 0430 hours on April

13 that a large German force was advancing on Fossbakken from Vassdal. Forseth considered it possible that this was the same force reported at 0100 by a security patrol but he was unable to confirm this by reconnaissance since it was dark and near blizzard conditions. There were no Norwegian forces at the important road junction at Fossbakken and Captain Forseth decided to withdraw from Lapphaugen and occupy the road junction before the Germans captured it.

Lapphaugen and the mountain pass immediately to the west (Oalgge) are located along the most elevated part of the road leading north from Gratangen—Route 50. Faulty intelligence caused Forseth's company to abandon this excellent defensive position, an important objective in the German plans. Forseth's men had operated continually for 72 hours in severe weather and it was beginning to tell. The exhausted troops were beginning to hallucinate, heavy fire was opened several times during the night at imaginary targets, and one soldier was killed by friendly fire. The company was finally relieved by the 2/15th Inf on April 14 but remained attached to that battalion until April 30.

By April 14 the Germans had not managed to secure the railroad to the Swedish border. The capture of Narvik would lose its value unless this was achieved. The German northern thrust had reached a point about 30 kilometers north of Bjerkvik against stiffening Norwegian resistance. They were still 30 and 57 kilometers respectively from their objectives at Setermoen and Bardufoss.

The Second Naval Battle

The Admiralty, operating on the assumption that there could be one or possibly two German cruisers and five to six destroyers in Narvik, decided on April 12 to launch a far heavier attack on those forces. Forbes' main force was concentrated south of the Lofoten Islands, knowing that the German battleships had returned safely to Germany. The Admiralty ordered Forbes "to clean up enemy naval forces and batteries in Narvik by using a battleship heavily escorted by destroyers, with synchronized dive-bombing attacks from Furious."[6] No mention was made about landing forces to capture the city.

The detailed order issued by Admiral Forbes also makes no mention of a landing in Narvik although Forbes knew that the recapture of that city was a high British priority. It was to be purely a naval operation, a continuation of the action begun on April 10. The decision to send in a battleship may not have been taken so lightly had the British known that five German submarines were present in the area. Some writers point out that it would have made more sense to delay the operation until a suitable landing force could take advantage of the naval bombardment to capture the town. The same critics maintain that it made little sense to risk a battleship in these restricted waters solely to eliminate the German destroyers since they could be bottled up until a landing force was available.

However, the problems associated with carrying out immediate landing operations were more difficult to overcome than the critics would lead us to believe. First, the troops headed for Harstad were not ready to make a landing on a hostile shore and it would take weeks before they were operational. Second, the inter-service coordination and cooperation was entirely lacking and the service component commanders were responding to uncoordinated orders and directives. Admiral Cork and General Mackesy were still operating independently.

In the meantime, the British launched air attacks against Narvik. Nine British aircraft from the carrier *Furious* conducted a bombing raid on Narvik between 1800 and 1900 hours on April 12. They launched from the carrier in bad weather while the ship was 150 miles from Narvik. The British were apparently impressed with the German dive-bombing of their fleet in the North Sea and decided to try this method after the failure of torpedo attacks in Trondheim. The slow double-decker Swordfish aircraft were unsuitable and their crews untrained for this type attack. Despite releasing some bombs from an altitude of only 400 feet, the German destroyers were not hit. The captured Norwegian patrol vessel *Senja* was sunk and another captured Norwegian patrol boat, *Michael Sars*, was damaged and sank the following day. The British pilots reported intense and accurate antiaircraft fire and two aircraft were lost in the attack. A third aircraft was lost in the night landing on the aircraft carrier.

A second wave of nine British aircraft from the *Furious* ran into a snowstorm and forced to return to the carrier. The attack did slow the repairs on *Erich Koellner* and prevented it from taking up its floating battery position that day. *U64* arrived in Narvik in the evening of April 12 and reported hectic British naval activity in the Vestfjord.

German naval intelligence again proved to be excellent, but it was not much help to the trapped German destroyers. By listening to British radio signals, the Germans concluded that the British would attack in the afternoon of April 13. Two messages from Naval Command West to Commander Bey at 0044 hours and 0900 hours on April 13 gave a rather accurate order of battle for the British forces assembling off Narvik.[7] The 0044 message read, "German aircraft report the following warships in the Vestfjord near Tranøy on the afternoon of April 12. One large ship with two smokestacks, a smaller ship with one smokestack, four torpedo boats and three destroyers further out." The 0900 hours message related that an enemy attack on Narvik was expected in the afternoon of April 13. It reported that the battleships *Warspite* and *Repulse*, nine destroyers and one aircraft carrier would take part in the attack.

The report from Naval Command West was wrong in only one detail. *Repulse* did not take part in the attack. Admiral Forbes' heavy units south of Lofoten consisted at this time of the battleships *Rodney* and *Warspite*, the aircraft carrier *Furious*, and the battle cruisers *Repulse* and *Renown*. He had detached a part of the Home Fleet to provide security for the troop transports on their way to Harstad.

There was no longer any doubt in Commander Bey's mind that a major attack was imminent and he issued the following orders, but apparently failed to insure that they were carried out in a timely manner:

1. All seaworthy destroyers are to be disposed in such a manner that they can surround the lighter British naval forces as was done on April 10.

2. The destroyers that are not seaworthy are to be at battle stations by 1200 hours.

3. *Erich Koellner* is to proceed immediately to Tårstad (east of Ramnes) and placed in position as a floating battery.

Admiral Forbes ordered Whitworth to carry out the Admiralty orders in the afternoon of April 13 with a force consisting of the battleship *Warspite* and nine destroyers. Whitworth transferred his flag to *Warspite* and assembled his force in Vestfjord that morning. The weather was squally but the visibility was good.

The April 13 operation made no attempt at surprise and relied instead on massive force. The passage through Vestfjord took place in full daylight, within easy observation from shore. The aircraft from the carrier were ordered to bomb the coastal fortifications that the British still believed existed in Ofotfjord as well as targets in Narvik harbor.

A reconnaissance aircraft launched from *Warspite* managed to provide exceptionally good service for the approaching fleet. It not only reported two German destroyers behind a small island near Hamnes but managed to dive-bomb and sink *U64* at the mouth of Herjangsfjord with a 100-lb bomb. This was the first sinking of a German submarine by aircraft during World War II. Eight German sailors died in the attack.

The British fleet narrowly escaped what could have been a disaster at the entrance to Ofotfjord. *U46*, commanded by Lieutenant Herbert Sohler, spotted the British armada as it entered its patrol sector east of Barøy. Sohler had promised Bey on April 11 that the submarines would provide better service to the destroyers in the future and he now had an opportunity to make good on his promise. Sohler managed to slip in behind the British destroyer screen and was in a perfect position to launch torpedoes against *Warspite*. The range was approximately 700 meters as the giant 32,000-ton battleship appeared in Sohler's periscope. *Warspite* had a deep draft and the problem with the depth-seeking mechanism on the German torpedoes was therefore not as crucial as in the case of attacks on destroyers. *U46* was ready to launch its deadly salvo of torpedoes when the submarine collided with an underwater ridge. The impact interrupted the firing and forced the submarine to surface. It managed to dive before being spotted. It was not until after the war that the British learned how close they came to possibly losing a battleship.

The German destroyer *Erich Koellner*, which was capable of a speed of only seven knots and carrying only enough personnel to operate the ship as a floating gun platform, was escorted by *Hermann Künne* in Ofotfjord on its way to Tårstad when it spotted a British aircraft to its west. The destroyers were still three miles short of their goal. A short time thereafter, *Hermann Künne* spotted nine British destroyers near Barøy and reported to Commander Bey that the British were entering the fjord.

The German destroyer turned around immediately and headed for Narvik. The British opened fire but the shells fell considerably short of their target. The 1913-vintage *Warspite* also opened fire with its 15-inch guns, but the slow firing guns were ineffective against a fast moving destroyer steering a zigzag course.

Commander Alfred Schulze-Hinrichs, *Erich Koellner's* skipper, realized immediately that it was too late to reach his designated location and decided to take his ship to Djupvik, on the southern shore of the fjord. He picked an excellent flanking position that was hidden in view from the fjord. Schulze-Hinrichs' intention was to open a surprise barrage against the British destroyers with guns and torpedoes as they passed his position.

Erich Koellner opened fire at a range of only 1,500 meters as the first British destroyer came into view. The British were not surprised since they had been warned about the ambush by *Warspite's* reconnaissance aircraft. The German destroyer also fired torpedoes against the British ships but those failed to hit their targets or malfunctioned. *Bedouin*, *Punjabi*, and *Eskimo* had their guns and torpedoes trained to starboard as they rounded the Djupvik Peninsula and concentrated their fire on the lone German ship. Many hits were registered but the Germans continued to fire and it was not until *Warspite* fired several 15-inch salvos that the enemy was silenced. *Erich Koellner* sank at 1215 hours after a number of devastating hits. Thirty-one crewmembers were killed and 35 wounded. Norwegian forces captured the survivors.

Hermann Künne had meanwhile continued towards Narvik on a zigzag course at 24 knots. She laid smoke in an effort to shield those German destroyers exiting Narvik harbor to meet the British but the fresh wind quickly removed the smoke. Kohte, seeing the size of the approaching enemy force, must have realized there was little he or his friends could do to save the situation. The German destroyers had not taken their designated defensive positions in the side fjords, despite intelligence warnings of an imminent attack. Bey's orders came too late or were not executed swiftly.

Commander Bey exited Narvik on a westerly course at 1215 hours to meet the British. His force consisted of *Hans Lüdemann*, *Wolfgang Zenker*, and *Bernd von Arnim*. *Hermann Künne* also reversed course to join its friends in their futile attempt to halt the British advance. *Georg Thiele* and *Erich Giese* remained in Narvik since they were not ready to get underway.

Knowing that the attacking force included a battleship, Commander Bey would have been wise not to meet the British in the relatively open waters of Ofotfjord where *Warspite's* massive guns could be used. A withdrawal into one or more of the narrow side fjords where *Warspite* could not follow would have reduced the odds and made German fire, especially the torpedoes, more effective since the enemy's maneuver room would be restricted.

The British force was within range when the three German destroyers came abreast of Ballangen Bay and *Hans Lüdemann* opened fire at a distance of 17,000 meters against the British destroyers that were preceding *Warspite* by three miles. The long-range gun battle that followed was generally ineffective on both sides. Commander Rechel tried to carry out a torpedo attack against *Warspite* but was driven back by overwhelming firepower.

The engagement in Ofotfjord lasted approximately one hour, and five of the German destroyers—*Hermann Künne*, *Hans Lüdemann*, *Wolfgang Zenker*, *Bernd von Arnim*, and *Georg Thiele*—eventually participated. The results of this relatively long engagement were surprisingly minor. The British fire did not hit the German destroyers. The aircraft from *Furious* were even less effective. They dropped more than 100 bombs but these fell in the sea without doing any damage to the German ships. Two British aircraft were shot down.

The German destroyers were slowly forced further into the fjord and soon found themselves near the junction of Herjangsfjord and Rombakfjord. By 1315 hours, they had exhausted almost all their ammunition. Their main objective became one of saving the lives of the crews and preventing their ships from falling into British hands. Bey ordered the destroyers to withdraw into Rombakfjord. Four destroyers withdrew as ordered under a smokescreen. *Hermann Künne* failed to receive Bey's order and withdrew under pressure into Herjangsfjord. According to Assmann, the Germans scuttled the destroyer after it had fired its last rounds.

Erich Giese exited Narvik harbor at the same time as the other destroyers were withdrawing into Rombakfjord. She met the concentrated fire of six British destroyers and was attacked aggressively by *Bedouin* and *Punjabi*. The intense bombardment resulted in 22 heavy caliber hits, which caused uncontrollable fires aboard the German ship, and she began to sink. Lieutenant Commander Karl Smidt, *Erich Giese's* captain, ordered the ship abandoned at 1430 hours. The destroyer sank quickly in deep water, taking 85 of its crew with it. There were many wounded and nine were captured. Before she sank, *Erich Giese* managed to score a torpedo hit on *Punjabi*, forcing that warship to withdraw from the battle.

Diether von Roeder had engine problems and remained tied up to a pier in Narvik. *Warspite* and a group of British destroyers approached the harbor while *Erich Giese* was sinking and were fired on by *Diether von Roeder*. The British destroyers *Cossack*, *Foxhound*, and *Kimberley* entered the harbor and opened fire on the immobile German destroyer at distances that varied from 2,000 to 8,000 meters. Shells from the three destroyers and *Warspite* struck the German ship repeatedly. *Diether von Roeder* continued to fight despite the many hits and managed to place seven shells into *Cossack*, forcing that ship to beach. It was only after her crew had exhausted all ammunition that *Diether von Roeder* was scuttled with demolition mines. *Foxhound*, who was coming alongside for boarding, narrowly escaped the explosion.

Two of the four German destroyers retiring into Rombakfjord, *Wolfgang Zenker* and *Bernd von Arnim*, had exhausted their ammunition and continued southeastward to the end of the fjord, called Rombaksbotn. There the ships were scuttled. *Georg Thiele* and *Hans Lüdemann* still had some ammunition and torpedoes left and took up good positions immediately east of a narrow strait, to use their last ammunition to inflict a final blow against the British as they tried to enter through the narrow strait. This delay also allowed their comrades in *Wolfgang Zenker* and *Bernd von Arnim* to make their escape up the cliff-like side of the inner part of the fjord. *Warspite* did not follow the German destroyers into Rombakfjord.

Eskimo, Forester, Hero, Icarus, and *Bedouin* followed the German ships, with *Eskimo* in the lead. *Warspite's* reconnaissance aircraft informed the attacking British destroyers that *Hans Lüdemann* and *Georg Thiele* were waiting for them just inside the narrow strait. *Hans Lüdemann's* bow faced east and it was in position for a rapid departure in case the ambush failed. The fire control system on both German destroyers was damaged and the guns were operated under local control. After firing its last shells against the approaching British warships, *Hans Lüdemann* followed *Wolfgang Zenker* and *Bernd von Arnim.* Friedrichs fired his last torpedoes at the British destroyers as he headed eastward. *Hans Lüdemann* was abandoned and scuttled when it reached the end of the fjord.

Lt. Commander Wolf, so instrumental in the destruction of *Hardy* and *Hunter* on April 10, again played a key role in the last minutes of this battle. *Georg Thiele* remained behind to confront the five British destroyers by herself when *Hans Lüdemann* retired. This gave the other destroyers time to scuttle their ships and the crewmembers time to escape capture. *Eskimo,* under Commander Micklethwait, was the first British destroyer to make the daring dash through the narrow strait, followed closely by the *Forester,* under Lt. Commander Tancock.

Georg Thiele took repeated hits and she had almost exhausted her ammunition. However, she continued to fight as the British were closing. Micklethwait tried to position his ship for a torpedo attack on its stubborn foe, but had to take a sudden evasive maneuver to avoid one of the torpedoes fired by the departing *Hans Lüdemann.* The maneuver resulted in *Eskimo* presenting its broadside to *Georg Thiele* at a very short range. Wolf seized the chance and fired his last torpedo. The torpedo hit the forward part of the British destroyer and the explosion tore off *Eskimo's* forecastle, killing 15 sailors. Micklethwait reversed engines and managed to retire through the narrow strait where the destroyer was grounded in rather deep water because the sunken wreckage of its forecastle was still attached. The path of the destroyers following *Eskimo* was temporarily blocked.

Georg Thiele had received numerous hits by British shells and everyone on the bridge was killed except Commander Wolf. Without more shells or torpedoes to fire, Wolf signaled full speed ahead on the engine room telegraph and beached the destroyer at high speed near Sildvik. The ship capsized and the aft portion sank at 1500 hours while the forward part remained beached. Fourteen crewmembers were killed and 28 wounded.

The actions of Commander Wolf throughout the fighting in Narvik—admired by friend and foe alike—had a fitting ending. Commanders Rechel in *Bernd von Arnim* and Smidt in *Erich Giese* were also singled out for praise by their opponents for their daring and determination. The British concluded that the German destroyers acquitted themselves as well as could be expected under the circumstances. The ineffectiveness of their submarines, torpedoes, and their shortage of ammunition doomed their efforts from the start. The British destroyer commanders also showed their traditional daring and aggressiveness.

The crews from the German destroyers assembled ashore and headed up the hillsides on the south side of Rombaksbotn, towards the railway line. This was not an easy task on the steep hillsides in deep snow and under fire from the British destroyers. According to the 3rd Division journal, the British fired after the escaping German destroyer crews with both their main armaments and machineguns. The crews were later transported to Narvik. When they entered the inner part of the fjord, the British found *Hans Lüdemann* still afloat and she was sunk by a torpedo from *Hero*.

The British Consider Landing

Admiral Whitworth reported to Admiral Forbes at 1742 hours that a German submarine and all destroyers were sunk. He considered the idea of a landing in Narvik, but concluded that his exhausted men were in no state to face the 2,000 or so German troops he believed to be in the city.

The British naval bombardment caused no fatalities among German troops and the material damage was minor, even though many buildings in and around the city were destroyed. Whitworth's assumption that German morale was low may well be correct. They had watched helplessly as their warships were destroyed. The German troops occupied positions along Rombakfjord and the troops in Narvik were in their positions with orders to repel any landing attempts.

Some British writers leveled mild criticism against Admiral Whitworth for not seizing the opportunity to capture Narvik. Norwegian writers have been more direct. They point out that Dietl's forces in Narvik numbered only 800 spread along the shoreline from Fagernes to Vassvik as well as along the Rombakfjord, and that they knew it was hopeless to engage an enemy with overwhelming naval artillery with only individual or crew-served weapons. Colonel Munthe-Kaas concludes that "There is no doubt that Narvik would have fallen if a determined amphibious commander had understood to exploit the demoralizing state of mind in which the Germans, for a second time, found themselves, particularly after witnessing their destroyer fleet shattered."[8] He points out that Whitworth had 2,700 men at his disposal and that two companies from the 24th Guards could have augmented this force if the admiral had only waited in the fjord for another half day. The 2,700 were not Royal Marines but the crews of the British battleship and the nine destroyers. Munthe-Kaas fails to consider that the two Guard companies embarked on the cruiser *Southampton* were prepared for an administrative landing. They carried only individual and a few crew-served weapons and were not ready for combat operations.

Norwegian conclusions that German morale was broken are based primarily on the observations of civilian observers, whose judgment of discipline in the German units is at least debatable. Railroad traffic inspector, Johan Olsen, stated that "Both the Germans and we civilians expected that the British would land in Narvik. The Germans were panic-stricken. Crowds of them threw away their weapons, asked for the way to Sweden, and left the city."[9]

The fact that the German troops did not sustain any fatalities and only a few wounded calls into question the accuracy of reports about disintegration of discipline and unit cohesion. There is no reliable information that the German mountain troops were in a state of panic. They were battle-experienced and professionally led troops and their performance against numerically superior Norwegian forces two days later indicates that reports of their demoralization and panic are much exaggerated.

Admiral Whitworth does not deserve criticism for not landing shore parties in Narvik on April 13. Such action would likely have resulted in a severe setback and the possible loss of the inadequate landing parties carried on the warships. Moulton reports that the marines available on the heavy ships of the Home Fleet amounted to two or three companies and that many of these ships were not in the Ofotfjord area. The lead elements of the 24th Guards Brigade were still 24-36 hours away and were unprepared for immediate combat operations. A failed landing would have been an undesirable ending to an otherwise successful operation. Whitworth also feared that enemy submarines and aircraft would attack *Warspite* if she remained in the fjord. He withdrew *Warspite* and most of the destroyers from Ofotfjord around 1830 hours.

The 140 survivors from the destroyer *Hardy* were moved from the immediate vicinity of the wrecked ship to the village of Balangen where they were cared for by local Norwegians. Here they joined 47 merchant seamen who had been prisoners aboard *Jan Wellem*. Admiral Whitworth returned with the battleship and destroyers after dark and remained in the fjord during the night taking aboard wounded sailors. Norwegians brought the survivors from *Hardy* and the British merchant seamen who had joined them, to a place where they were taken aboard two British destroyers. All British ships withdrew from the fjord by daylight on April 14.

The German problems with their torpedoes again saved the British from potentially heavy losses. Lieutenant Commander Viktor Schütze in *U25*, positioned in Vestfjord, made two attempts to torpedo *Warspite* as she left the fjord the first time. The destroyer *Foxhound* drove off one attack while the second attack failed, probably because of faulty torpedoes. Schütze tried again on the battleship's second visit to the fjord. The single torpedo again missed, or malfunctioned. The ability of both *U25* and *U46* to penetrate the destroyer screens with relative ease demonstrates the inordinate risk the British were taking by sending a battleship into these restricted waters. The Second Naval Battle of Narvik could have been a costly affair if the German torpedoes had functioned properly.

At 2115 hours the Admiralty urged Admiral Forbes to occupy Narvik in order to prevent later opposition to a landing. They apparently believed that the German troops were driven out of town because of the naval bombardment. Derry writes that it is unknown if Admiral Whitworth was aware of this message since the reception conditions in the fjord were poor. He did send a message later that evening reporting that he believed "the enemy forces in Narvik were thoroughly frightened" and recommended that the main landing force should occupy Narvik as quickly as possible.[10] Whitworth followed up this message the following morning with one recommending that a small landing force could secure the city if he could support such a landing with the naval forces under his command.[11] However, Forbes soon ordered Whitworth to take *Warspite* out of Vestfjord for fear of submarine and air attacks. The Home Fleet's experience with the Luftwaffe in the North Sea may have influenced this decision.

The British losses in the Second Naval Battle of Narvik were 41 killed (15 on *Eskimo*, 14 on *Punjabi*, 11 on *Cossack*, and 1 on *Foxhound*) and over 60 wounded. No British destroyers were sunk but most sustained some minor damage from German shells. The destroyers *Eskimo*, *Cossack,* and *Punjabi* were heavily damaged, and they were brought to the improvised naval depot in Skjellfjord for repairs. In the three naval engagements as a whole, 276 Norwegians, at least 316 Germans, and 188 British were killed.

The Home Fleet departed for Scapa Flow on April 15, but British naval operations in the area continued. The First Cruiser Squadron under Admiral Cunningham stayed behind in the Troms/Finnmark area as did all the ships involved in the transport and escort of the troops that were beginning to arrive.

The loss of ten German destroyers in the two battles was a hard blow to the German Navy. It represented 45% of their destroyer force. However, the survivors from the destroyers enabled Dietl to add about 2,100 men to his force, doubling its size. The crews from the four destroyers sunk in the inner part of Rombakfjord were organized into a regiment commanded by Commander Fritz Berger, which was used initially as a security force for the railroad east of Narvik.

The crew of *Hermann Künne* was organized into a battalion under the command of Lieutenant Commander Kohte and assigned to Colonel Windisch. The survivors from *Wilhelm Heidkamp* and *Anton Schmitt* were organized into a battalion commanded by Lieutenant Commander Erdmenger and given the mission of local defense in Narvik. This allowed Dietl to move soldiers from the 3rd Mountain Division inland to take part in ground operations. Technical personnel from the destroyers were used to maintain and repair the railroad line. The destroyer crews were issued uniforms, weapons, and supplies from Norwegian stores captured at Elvegårdsmoen.

NOTES

1 Derry, *The Campaign in Norway*, p. 104.

2 Ibid, p. 105.

3 Ibid, p. 106.

4 As quoted in Hubatsch, p. 128.

5 Information received from knowledgeable individuals in Norway – including long-time residents – indicate that Ramsund had a depth of 10–15 meters and that ships with a length of 120 meters could not transit safely without the use of a knowledgeable pilot. The German destroyers were about 120 meters in length and had a draught of approximately 12 meters. Others have written that the Ramsund-Kjeldsundet-Vågsfjord route can take civilian cargo ships up to 40,000 tons. The fact that the Norwegians established a coastal artillery battery of two 105mm guns at the northern entrance to Ramsund – Forholten during World War II is a further indication that the strait was navigable for warships. Even if Ramsund was not sufficiently dredged or the service of reliable pilots could not be obtained, there was the option of turning right just west of Barøy, into the more navigable Tjelsund and from there north to Vågsfjord. Large ships, such as *Jan Wellem*, used this route on a regular basis.

6 Dickens, *Battles in the Fjords*, p. 108.

7 Kurt Assmann, *The German Campaign in Norway* (Admiralty: Naval Staff, 1948), p. 41.

8 Munthe-Kaas, *Krigen i Narviksavsnittet 1940*, p. 66.

9 As quoted in ibid, p. 64.

10 Message from Admiral Whitworth to Admiral Forbes at 2210 hours on April 13 and forwarded by Admiral Forbes to the Admiralty in Derry, *The Campaign in Norway*, p. 51.

11 Message from Whitworth, loc cit.

9

THE NARVIK FRONT, APRIL 13–26

"One should give something up as lost only when it is lost."
GENERAL ALFRED JODL'S RESPONSE TO HITLER ON APRIL 14, 1940
WHEN THE LATTER PLANNED TO GIVE UP NARVIK.

"The British are coming"—Unprepared for Operations

As the Second Naval Battle of Narvik was fought, a convoy of British troops was on its way to Harstad carrying most of the 24th Guards Brigade and the 146th Brigade. The two transports carrying the 146th Brigade were diverted to Namsos shortly before they reached Harstad. General Mackesy, in the cruiser *Southampton*, arrived in Harstad on April 14 with two companies of the Scots Guards.

Admiral Cork, in the cruiser *Aurora*, had intended to proceed directly to Harstad but a message from Admiral Whitworth caused him to change his plans and proceed to Skjellfjord. He arrived there before noon on April 14. The message from Whitworth to the Admiralty and copied to Admirals Forbes and Cork gave Whitworth's assessment of the situation in Narvik. He estimated that there were 1,500 to 2,000 German troops in Narvik and was convinced that the city could be taken by direct assault without serious opposition, provided a naval force on the same scale as that used in the battle on the previous day supported the landing.

In view of this assessment, Cork decided to carry out a combined attack on Narvik in the morning of April 15 using the two companies embarked on the *Southampton* and about 200 Royal Marines from the ships in Skjellfjord. He sent an order to *Southampton* to proceed to Skjellfjord, to arrive there by 2000 hours on April 14. Because of poor radio communications, the message was not received until after *Southampton* arrived in Harstad and had landed the troops at Sjøvegan.

General Mackesy was dubious about Admiral Cork's planned operation and said as much in a message to the admiral. He went on to state that if the operation were to be carried out, the troops would have to come from the transports bringing the main force of the 24th Brigade, and they would not arrive until April 15. Cork also received a message from the British Admiralty at about the same time that put another brake on the operation: "We think it imperative that you and the General should be together and act together and that no attack should be made except in concert."[1] These two messages put an end to the plan for an immediate attack on Narvik, and Cork proceeded to Harstad, where he arrived on April 15.

General Mackesy established contact with the Norwegian civil authorities in Harstad soon after he arrived on April 14. Through these contacts, he learned that there were no Germans in the area and that the British would be well received by the population. Mackesy also wished to establish contact with the Norwegian military authorities as quickly as possible. He learned that the Norwegian military headquarters was located in Moen, Målselv. This was the reason he landed the two companies of the Scots Guards at Sjøvegan. These troops established contact with Norwegian ground forces before evening.

Aurora entered Andfjord in the morning of April 15, at the same time as the convoy carrying the 24th Brigade arrived. The battleship *Valiant* and nine destroyers escorted the three troop transports. There were now a number of German submarines in the Vågsfjord area. Admiral Dönitz, at the request of the German Naval Staff after the British attack on the German destroyers in Narvik on April 10, had ordered four boats from the 5th Submarine Group (*U38*, *U47*, *U48*, and *U49*), patrolling the waters between the Shetlands and the Norwegian coast, to patrol Vågsfjord and adjacent areas.

A Norwegian naval observation station warned the British about the presence of German submarines. The British destroyers *Fearless* and *Brazen*, escorts for *Aurora*, attacked and sank *U49*. One German from a crew of 42 was killed. Admiral Maund writes that the British were aware when they left Scapa Flow that the Germans had four submarines on patrol in the Lofoten-Narvik area and that all four had been accounted for with the sinking of *U49*, three sunk by destroyers and one by aircraft from *Warspite*. He is mistaken. The Germans had five submarines in Group 1, which operated along the Narvik approaches, and they lost only one, to *Warspite's* aircraft. *U49* belonged to Group 5. However, the loss of *U64* and *U49* as well as the torpedo problems caused the Germans to redeploy the submarines to the vicinity of the Shetlands on April 19 and 20.

The 1st Irish Guards and 1st Scots Guards battalions and the brigade headquarters arrived in Harstad on April 15. The 1st Irish Guards were moved to Bogen, on the north side of Ofotfjord, on April 19. The 34th Light Anti-Aircraft Battery was also landed in Harstad, but it had no guns. The brigade's third battalion, 2nd South Wales Borderers, landed on April 16 and moved to Bogen to join the 1st Irish Guards on April 21. Various support troops more than equal to the combat forces in numbers, were also landed on April 16.

Harstad had a population of about 4,000 in 1940 and the pier, transport, and storage facilities were limited. The unloading and clearing of the harbor was completed on April 17 and 18 and the transports returned to Great Britain. Derry reports that confusion caused by conditions and decisions that marked the expedition's inception was great. The lack of tactical loading required that everything be sorted after landing and much had to be reloaded and sent to Namsos since it belonged to the 146th Brigade.

François Kersaudy is more graphic in his description of conditions in Harstad. He describes the arrival of several convoys, without warning, over a five-day period, "1,000 administrators, office clerks and accountants, together with huge amounts of office furniture." He also notes that General Mackesy discovered that "His brigade had practically no mortar shells, very few grenades, no spare ammunition, no artillery, no anti-aircraft guns, no skis, no snow shoes, no trucks, no landing craft ... "[2]

The British found Harstad unsuitable as a naval base, and Admiral Cork decided to establish a base for the naval forces at Skånland, at the northern end of Tjeldsund. This place is located approximately 15 miles southeast of Harstad. A Royal Marine Fortress Unit prepared positions for placing shore batteries; however, the work was not finished. The British also started work on a large airfield near Skånland but it was never completed to the point where it could be used.

The Debate about an Immediate Attack on Narvik

There has been much speculation about the possible success of an attack on Narvik after the destruction of the German destroyers on April 13. Churchill charged General Mackesy with tardy and negligent behavior not warranted by the tactical situation. While Derry finds little to support Churchill's conclusion, Ziemke takes the opposite view. He writes:

> In view of present knowledge it seems that a landing during the first days would have had a good chance of success since Dietl had only one battalion of mountain troops in Narvik to oppose two British battalions at hand on the 15th and an additional battalion that arrived on the 16th.[3]

However, the British units were not prepared to deal with opposition immediately after landing. They required a period in a relatively secure area to organize and receive their equipment, to compensate for their hurried deployment. This delay cannot be attributed to Mackesy.

The first meeting between Admiral Cork and General Mackesy took place on April 15. While no records are available, it was described as a heated encounter. Cork was surprised to find that the troops were embarked in anticipation of a peaceful landing and not ready for immediate operations. He was equally surprised to learn that Mackesy's orders also precluded the landing of troops against organized opposition.

While the general viewed his instructions as not forbidding an immediate move against Narvik if a favorable situation presented itself, there were serious practical impediments. The primary ones had to do with the loading of the transports and the lack of certain necessary equipment. The troops of the 24th Guards Brigade had never operated in the Arctic and the deep snow made movement practically impossible. Faced with Mackesy's determined conclusion that a direct attack at this time was "sheer bloody murder," Cork gave up his plan for an immediate attack on Narvik and informed the Admiralty accordingly.

Almost all principles pertaining to command were violated at the outset of the Narvik operation. The British had developed an excellent set of principles in their Combined Operations Manual, based on many years of experience. It is incredulous therefore, that most of these principles were discarded.

1. No unity of command—no single individual was in charge of the whole operation.

2. Commanders had contradictory and uncoordinated orders – one written and one verbal.

3. Mackesy reported to the War Office while Cork dealt with Churchill via private code.

4. The two commanders sailed independently and never met until April 15.

5. The ships were loaded for an administrative landing – not tactically loaded.

6. Some equipment was on ships re-directed to Namsos at the last moment, and most of the equipment for the troops sent to Namsos arrived in Harstad.

7. The troops were not equipped or trained for operating in mountainous terrain under Arctic winter conditions. For example, they had no skis or snowshoes. However, since they did not know how to use them, it made little difference.

8. The troops had no transport, no artillery, very little mortar ammunition, no antiaircraft guns, and no landing craft.

Not only were the two component commanders independent of each other at the outset, but there was a vast difference in rank, age, and personalities. Mackesy was a relatively young Major General, an engineer with limited experience in field command, while Admiral Cork was the most senior naval officer on active duty. He was appointed commander of Allied operations in North Norway on April 20.

This was an unfortunate choice. Cork was undoubtedly a courageous officer with unusual connections and influence among Allied political leaders. However, he represented the generation that fought the Battle of Jutland and had not kept up with the advances in technology, particularly airpower, which had transformed naval warfare. He also lacked understanding of land operations, particularly in the arctic wilderness, did not have the right temperament to lead combined operations, and displayed indifference for Norwegian military and civilian authorities. Even British naval officers recognized that the Narvik expedition was predominantly an army affair and that the commander should have been an army officer.[4]

Ziemke and others who believe that the chances of a successful attack immediately after April 13 were good have not given sufficient weight to the condition of the three British battalions. The British units—as noted earlier—were not loaded tactically and they needed a period in a relatively secure area to organize and receive their equipment. The fault for this does not rest with General Mackesy but with the unrealistic planning involved in *R4*, the mass confusion caused when the Admiralty ordered disembarkation on the 8th, and with Churchill and the military services. They were so eager to do something after their humiliation on April 9 that they embarked on enterprises without any thoughts to either strategy or preparations.

The fact is that the Guards were neither trained nor equipped for Arctic warfare. The conditions are summed up in General Mackesy's official report.

Although nobody without personal experience of Arctic winter conditions can possibly picture the climatic difficulties we experienced in the early days, a word or two of description may not be out of place. The country was covered by snow up to 4 feet or more in depth. Even at sea level, there were several feet of snow. Blizzards, heavy snowstorms,

The town of Narvik in 1940.

Narvik on April 8, 1940. The two coastal defense ships are at center and left.

The German supply ship *Altmark,* which was also carrying British prisoners.

Narvik in 1940 (with author's annotations).

The British destroyer *Cossack*.

The German battleship *Gneisenau* (*Scharnhorst* was of the same class).

The German heavy cruiser *Admiral Hipper*.

Summer 2007 view of the Gratang Valley looking generally to the west-northwest, with Gratangsbotn Fjord in the distance. The ridgline to the right is where the Alta Battalion was located during the battle.
(Courtesy of Magnor Kr. Fjellheim)

A 1984 photo of Bjerkvik from the west. (Courtesy of Magnor Kr. Fjellheim)

German Admiral Günther Lütjens.

Admiral Dudley Pound, First Sea Lord.

The town of Elverum in ruins.

German seaplane transport in Norwegian fjord.

The British destroyer *Glowworm* on fire as seen from the bridge of the German heavy cruiser *Admiral Hipper*.

German airborne drop near Narvik.

Narvik harbor after British attack on April 10 with two German destroyers at the pier.

German troops advancing through a burning Norwegian town.

German paratroopers landing at Bjørnefjell, near Narvik.

Adolf Hitler and Major General Eduard Dietl, commander of German mountain troops.

Brigadier General Marie Emilie Béthouart, commander of French forces at Narvik.

French Alpine troops in the Narvik area.

German troops landing from seaplane.

The British battleship *Warspite* and escorts entering Ofotfjord on April 13, 1940.

Wreck of the German destroyer *Hans Ludemann*.

The German destroyer *Erich Giese* on fire and sinking.

The British destroyer HMS *Cossack*.

German mountain troops and naval personnel in the Ankenes Mountains with Narvik in the background.

Allied troop convoy in Norway.

French tank stuck in the mud a short distance from the beach in Narvik.

Photo of Narvik Harbor taken from a German aircraft.

Norwegian patrol in the Narvik area.

Major General Zygmunt Bohusz-Szyszko, commander of Polish troops at Narvik.

German Ju-52s on Hartvigvann (Hartvig Lake).

Destruction of ships and railroad stock in Narvik following a British attack.

bitter winds and very low night temperatures were normal. Indeed until the middle of May even those magnificent mountain soldiers, the French Chasseurs Alpines, suffered severely from frostbite and snow blindness. Troops who were not equipped with and skilled in the use of skis or snowshoes were absolutely incapable of operating tactically at all. I had no such troops at my disposal when I first landed.[5]

Unless landed from destroyers or Norwegian fishing/coastal vessels directly in the harbor, British units would have to land under fire and advance against German positions through snow up to six feet deep. The two companies of Scots Guards landed behind the Norwegian lines in Sjøvegan were incapable of taking part in an offensive operation ten days after they arrived and the Norwegians gave them a symbolic defensive role.

Dietl's forces in Narvik at this time were controlled by Major Arthur Haussels, the commander of the 2/139th Regiment. A reinforced company, not part of the 2nd Battalion, provided railroad security and it would soon be used against the Norwegians in the Bjørnefjell area. Haussels also had at his disposal the crews of the destroyers *Anton Schmitt* and *Wilhelm Heidkamp*, organized into a battalion commanded by Lieutenant Commander Erdmenger. The quality of naval personnel as infantry is questionable, but the combined German force operating from previously prepared Norwegian trenches and pillboxes presented a tough obstacle for a British landing force.

German sources give no indication that their troops were in a state of panic. The 3rd Division's journal, which does not hide the fact that panic set in among the naval infantry during the landing at Bjerkvik about one month later, fails to mention any problems on April 13. The German losses were minor and not a single soldier was killed. Furthermore, Dietl did not consider it necessary to bring in additional forces from the two battalions in Group Windisch to shore up the defenses in Narvik. On the contrary, the following morning (April 14) he sent a reinforced company to clear out the Norwegians holding the railroad between Nordal Bridge and the Swedish border. This indicates that Dietl was not worried about the morale of his troops or their reliability.

Initial British/Norwegian Meeting

The British had still not contacted the Norwegian Army at the command level five days after the Germans captured Narvik. This is extraordinary in view of their knowledge that General Fleischer was in charge of both military and civilian functions in a 1,000 kilometer stretch of the country. Both Mackesy and Cork were apparently busy trying to bring some semblance of order to their activities in and around Harstad. Fleischer and his staff were in total darkness with respect to Allied plans. This changed somewhat on April 14 when he was asked to meet a British representative, Admiral John Cunningham. The meeting took place aboard the cruiser *Devonshire* in Tromsø. Cunningham, who operated directly under Admiral Forbes, had no authority over Allied operations in the Narvik area. His mission was to patrol the coast between Tromsø and Kirkenes. Cunningham was therefore primarily interested in discussing practical naval issues as they pertained to his own mission. He was unable to clarify for the Norwegians what the Allies were up to or to enlighten Fleischer about planned operations. The Norwegians came to the meeting with rather high expectations and Fleischer was both disappointed and annoyed at being called to a meeting with a British flag officer with no coordinating authority for future operations.

When Fleischer returned to his headquarters in the evening of April 14, his chief of staff, Major Lindbäck-Larsen, briefed him. The major told him about the British landing in Sjøvegan and that he had met Mackesy's chief of staff, Colonel Dowler. Dowler and Lindbäck-Larsen had agreed that the major should come to Harstad on April 15 to meet the commander of British land forces in North Norway. Fleischer chose not to attend this meeting, in all likelihood because his honor was slighted by the meeting with Cunningham. Both sides would have benefited from the meeting, despite the fact that there was only a slim chance that Cork and Fleischer would get along. As it was, relations between the British and Norwegian militaries got off to a bad start.

Cork and Mackesy were now involved in a hot debate among themselves and with the Admiralty about whether or not to undertake an immediate attack on Narvik. Norwegian officers had seen the two companies of Scots Guards in Sjøvegan. While they were duly impressed with the professional bearings of these troops, they realized quickly that they were not experienced, trained, or equipped for arctic warfare. Fleischer had detailed knowledge of the terrain and climate and a better appreciation for enemy strengths and capabilities. While the same is true for his chief of staff, a personal briefing by Fleischer would have had a much more favorable impact on the reserved and tradition-bound British flag officers. It would have given them better arguments in their debate with the Admiralty about the wisdom of an immediate direct attack on Narvik.

Lindbäck-Larsen met a rather demoralized Mackesy in Harstad. Mackesy was obviously overwhelmed by the disorganized state of his own forces, the weather, terrain, the inconsistency in his orders, and doubts about what Admiral Cork and the Admiralty were urging on him. Lindbäck-Larsen concluded quickly that it would be difficult to arrange any agreements for operational cooperation with Mackesy under the conditions in which he and his forces found themselves. He gave the general an orientation on the situation and outlined Fleischer's plans for offensive operations. The orientation included a detailed description of the Narvik defenses now in German hands. He pointed out to Mackesy that even though the road conditions in the area were poor, they would become much worse in a few weeks because of the spring thaw. Operations that depended on road travel would be even more impeded by the thaw conditions.

General Mackesy gave some vague hints that he planned an advance on Narvik along both sides of Ofotfjord. The Norwegian major pointed out, tactfully, that the wild and roadless terrain, intersected by deep fjords and inlets, presented great obstacles to such an advance and suggested, in line with instructions from Fleischer, that an advance in close cooperation with the 6th Division held out greater promise of success. If, on the other hand, the British wanted to stick to their plan for an advance on Narvik from the west, a direct approach was better since amphibious landings would be required in any case. Lindbäck-Larsen's overall impression was that the British did not have any clear objectives and were not operationally ready. In the end, the only positive result of the meeting was the exchange of liaison officers.

General Mackesy sent a message to the War Office on April 16 that included a description of the Norwegian military situation and the defensive installations in Narvik. Lindbäck-Larsen's briefing undoubtedly influenced Admiral Cork to join in reporting to the War Office later in the day that a landing at Narvik was not feasible at this time.

The British Again Consider Landing in Narvik

Churchill and the Admiralty found it difficult to accept Cork's message on April 16 that ruled out an immediate attack on Narvik. A message from the Admiralty in the afternoon of April 17 pleaded with both Cork and Mackesy to reconsider. The message explained that *Warspite* would only be available for the next two or three days and that the French alpine troops, planned as reinforcements for Mackesy, should not be expected for some time since they were held in Scapa Flow as reinforcements for Namsos. Cork, who probably did not want to disappoint Churchill, held a conference with Mackesy on April 18. Derry writes that he urged the general to take a "gamble on the chance" that the enemy's morale would break under an overwhelming bombardment from a battleship, two cruisers, and eight destroyers. Mackesy agreed reluctantly to have a force ready for landing if the situation after the bombardment made the success of such an operation possible in his estimation.

Mackesy made a reconnaissance of the Narvik area in the cruiser *Aurora* on April 20 and his opinion had changed radically when he returned. He informed Cork that he was convinced that the operation could not succeed and that it would lead to the destruction of the 24th Brigade. He maintained that a bombardment of Narvik would only be successful if it led to a German surrender of the city *before* British troops landed. To achieve such a lofty goal it was necessary to bombard the city itself. This, in his view, would destroy future Norwegian cooperation and was a direct violation of the British Government's instruction governing bombardment of shore targets. This directive could only be changed by a governmental order. The Admiral and General agreed to restrict the bombardment targets.

The final plan was based on the hope that the Germans would surrender the city after a powerful bombardment by British warships. Troops were not to be landed as long as German opposition could be expected, but only when the Germans hoisted the white flag. The bombardment was scheduled for April 24 and the radio station in Tromsø directed the civilian population in Narvik to evacuate the city.

Low cloud cover, a snowstorm, and poor visibility characterized the weather in Ofotfjord on April 24. These conditions precluded the participation of aircraft from the *Furious* but they also prevented the Luftwaffe from attacking the warships. The bombarding force consisted of the battleship *Warspite*, the cruisers *Effingham*, *Aurora*, and *Enterprise*, and the destroyer *Zulu*. The 1st Battalion, Irish Guards embarked on the old cruiser *Vindictive*, prepared to land in Narvik if the Germans surrendered the city.

The British warships bombarded targets in the Narvik area for about three hours but the results were disappointing. One pier in Narvik was heavily damaged and a ship tied up to that pier sank. Some railroad rolling stock was also damaged. Enemy defensive positions were not observed and the British concluded that they had not been neutralized. The Germans displayed no signs of broken morale or that they intended to surrender the city. In fact, they suffered no fatalities from the bombardment. In a report dated July 17, 1940,

Admiral Cork states that the weather conditions on April 24 precluded any assessment of the bombardment's effectiveness and this led to the decision not to land.

The 1st Battalion, Irish Guards, was put ashore in Bogen in the afternoon of April 24. Most British warships returned to Scapa Flow. Only ten destroyers remained in North Norway to support operations. By April 25, 11 days after the first British troops landed, they had not fired a shot in anger. In fact, they had not even seen a German soldier.

The First Crisis in the German High Command

The critical situation in Norway, particularly in Trondheim and Narvik, brought on a crisis in the German high command. German troops in those two cities were isolated because Operation *Weserübung* had failed to achieve a Norwegian surrender that would have given the Germans control of the interior lines of communications. Hitler was well aware that the responsibility for a defeat in Norway would fall on him personally since the political decision, the military planning, and the execution were carried out by the OKW under his direct supervision. The German Army had deliberately refrained from involving itself in the planning for and conduct of this operation. Its participation was limited to providing officers for the planning staffs and meeting the requirements for troops, supplies, and equipment that emanated from the OKW. A defeat in Norway could deal a fatal blow to Hitler's prestige and could provide the army with the moral courage to depose him.

Hitler became agitated before he learned the fate of the destroyers in Narvik. By the evening of April 12, it became clear that the forces in Narvik were isolated and that the hoped-for link to the Swedish border and the capture of an airfield had not been achieved. It also appeared that similar situations were developing in Trondheim and Bergen and von Falkenhorst's full-scale breakout from the Oslo bridgehead had not started.

It was decided at a strategy conference on April 13 not to force the issue in Norway by pouring in more troops in case of further deterioration. Instead, the Halder Diary notes that a decision was made to examine the possibility of launching the attack in the west within a week or two, in order to reduce Allied pressure in Norway. This, however, was a very problematic solution because of inclement weather forecasts and since units could not move into attack positions on short notice without alerting Allied intelligence.

The diaries of the participants depict Hitler in a state of near panic when word of the naval catastrophe in Narvik arrived in the afternoon of April 13. In what is described as "a state of frightful agitation," Hitler proposed that Dietl be ordered to give up Narvik and withdraw southward. General Jodl tried desperately to persuade Hitler on April 14 not to give up on Narvik and not to order Dietl to break out to the south. The diary notes that he told Hitler, " … one should give something up as lost only when it is lost."

General Keitel told Brauchitsch the following day that Narvik would be evacuated. The OKH was not about to be drawn into what they probably viewed as a trap by Hitler and the OKW. If they ordered, or acquiesced in an order, to give up Narvik, they suspected that the responsibility for this debacle would be shifted to their shoulders. Brauchitsch decided that they should not agree to an evacuation and he ordered Halder to talk to Jodl. Jodl answered that Narvik could not be held, that the troops were to withdraw to the surrounding mountains, but that the question of the complete evacuation of the area was not yet decided. The OKW sent a message to Dietl discussing the possibility of evacuating Narvik and withdrawing into strong points in the mountains near the Swedish border.

The problem came to a boil again on April 17, despite the news that Dietl's forces had reached the Swedish border. Hitler now insisted that Dietl's forces evacuate by air or withdraw into Sweden. Jodl insisted that the mountains south of Narvik barred any possibility of retreat in that direction. He even brought along a professor from Innsbruck who vouched for the facts that the mountains between Narvik and Bodø were impenetrable even for mountain troops. With respect to air evacuation, Jodl pointed out that there were not enough long-range aircraft. Some German forces had to remain behind and the losses in aircraft would be heavy. He warned that any evacuation would have a shattering effect on German troop morale.

Despite Jodl's efforts, a document showed up in OKW that afternoon giving Dietl discretionary authority to evacuate Narvik, cross into Sweden, and be interned. A gutsy young staff officer, Lieutenant Colonel Bernhard von Lossberg, delayed the dispatch of the document while Jodl reasoned with Hitler.[6]

OKH was concerned about how a withdrawal would affect the army but Brauchitsch avoided a direct intervention. The German situation in Narvik was not as dire as viewed from Berlin and General Dietl remained generally optimistic. He had been promoted to Lieutenant General and Brauchitsch used the opportunity to send a congratulatory message to Dietl that he hoped would counteract any idea of evacuation. The message read, "Congratulations on your promotion. I am certain that you will defend Narvik, even against superior enemies."7

Jodl meanwhile argued his case strenuously. He finally convinced Hitler to issue a revised directive. The new document directed Dietl to hold Narvik as long as possible before withdrawing into the mountains along the Swedish border after extensive destruction of facilities in Narvik and the railroad between Narvik and Sweden. The written instructions were signed by Hitler on April 18 and sent by an air courier, Captain Schenk von Sternberg. They did not reach Dietl until April 22.

The aircraft bringing Captain Sternberg to Narvik also brought a demolition expert, Captain Oberndorfer. He began immediate preparations for demolitions in the harbor and railroad. The storage facilities at the iron ore pier were burned on April 22 and trains with numerous iron ore carriers were driven over the side of the pier to prevent ships from coming alongside. The pier was demolished on April 23. Further demolitions were delayed because explosives were lacking.

The 3rd Division Headquarters, which had occupied the top three floors of the Hotel Royal in Narvik, was relocated in the evening of April 24. It became operational in Strømsnes on April 25. The move had been planned for some time because of the concentration of Norwegian forces against Group Windisch. Dietl expected that the main enemy effort would be in that area and he wanted to be closer to that part of the front.

Another event of some importance took place on April 18. General Dietl had thus far operated under General von Falkenhorst, who had his headquarters in Oslo. There was little von Falkenhorst could do to affect the situation in Narvik, about 700 miles from his headquarters. The forces in Narvik were placed directly under OKW, which meant that for all practical purposes, Dietl now reported directly to Hitler.

The Norwegian Defeat at Bjørnefjell

The Norwegians were having problems of their own trying to cope with the German drives to the north and east. In the north, the Germans had occupied Lapphaugen on April 13 and were expected to continue their drive with an attack on Fossbakken. In the east, the remnants of the 1/13th Inf were positioned around Nordal Bridge and the Bjørnefjell Railway Station near the Swedish border. The Germans did not launch immediate operations to secure the railway to Sweden. The naval actions on April 10 and 13 no doubt delayed an advance because the required forces might be sorely needed in Narvik. Prior to April 14, the only contacts between Norwegian and German forces in the area to the east of Narvik were through patrol action. This was soon to change.

Co 1, 139th Regiment, under Major von Schleebrügge, had the mission to capture the Norwegian coastal battery that the Germans believed existed at Hamnes on April 9. Rather than rejoining its parent battalion at Elevgårdsmoen, this company was brought to Narvik and Dietl deployed it to secure the railroad as far as Hundal. It operated as an independent company and was not part of Major Haussels' 2nd Battalion in Narvik. On April 14, the day after the alleged panic of his troops, Dietl ordered von Schleebrügge to drive the Norwegians from the Bjørnefjell area and secure the railroad to Sweden. The company, reinforced by 20 naval personnel, assembled in Hundal on April 15.

Norwegian patrols reported increased German activities in Hundal on April 13 and a decision was made to destroy the Nordal Bridge the following day. Lack of dynamite and expertise in demolition resulted in only a partial destruction but the Norwegians believed it was sufficient and that a strong wind would bring the bridge down. This proved wrong and the Germans repaired the bridge to where a light locomotive was able to use it within three weeks.

Major Omdal withdrew the security detail from the bridge to the Bjørnefjell area in the evening of April 14 because the position was dominated by the Katterat Mountains to the south and the troops were exhausted from lack of sleep and exposure to the elements. Omdal also asked permission to withdraw his force northward to link up with other Norwegian units because of the critical supply situation. General Fleischer denied this request.

After withdrawing from Nordal Bridge, the Norwegian forces were positioned to cover further stretches of the railroad. Company 3, commanded by Captain Bjørnson, had one machinegun platoon attached but was short one rifle platoon The company was located on the high ground above a railroad tunnel a short distance south of Nordstrømvann. There were security elements to the west and northwest of the main positions. The troops were quartered in cabins and railroad guard facilities during the night of 15–16 April. The planned line of retreat, if that should become necessary, was in a northerly direction between two mountain peaks, Rundfjell and Bjørnfjell.

Company 1, commanded by Captain Strømstad, was located at the Bjørnefjell railroad complex. The troops were divided between the two main buildings. There was also a small guard detail at the tourist hotel, located between the two main buildings, to guard the 13 Germans captured on April 11. The company had a four-man outpost in the Katterat Mountains. The danger from

Elvegårdsmoen was considered most acute since the Norwegians believed they would have adequate warnings of a German advance along the railroad. The main German force set out from Hundal across the rough Katterat Mountains in the afternoon of April 15 while a smaller force (21 men plus the company trains), commanded by Lieutenant Trautner, advanced along the railroad towards Nordal Bridge. The Germans hoped the Norwegians would focus their attention on Trautner's men, allowing the main force to execute a successful envelopment.

A 12-man German patrol encountered the Norwegian outpost on the Katterat Mountains on April 15. In the short encounter, one Norwegian was killed and another captured. The remaining two men made their way to Co 1. A larger force was sent out to recover the body of the fallen Norwegian and it did not encounter any Germans. For unknown reasons, the outpost was not reconstituted. This left the approach through the Katterat Mountains unguarded during the night of 15–16 April.

The Germans had accurate information about the location of the Norwegian units, obtained either from patrols or perhaps from prisoners. The German launched almost simultaneous surprise attacks on the two Norwegian companies. Members of the machinegun platoon were the first to see the Germans around 0400 hours. Co 3 was unable to reoccupy its positions since the Germans had seized them and the company fought from the vicinity of their quarters. Attempts to assemble proved futile because the Germans had infiltrated some of the areas that separated their quarters. The positions of the scattered Norwegian units became untenable when the Germans began using mortars. Those who were able to do so withdrew to the north, linked up with the northwest security force, and continued the fight from a position north of Nordstrømvann.

Captain Bjørnson became separated from his men and the company executive officer, Lieutenant Torgersen, assumed command. The withdrawal continued when the enemy threatened to envelop the Norwegian positions. The Norwegians heard firing from the direction of the Bjørnefjell Railroad Station. Rather than following the planned line of retreat, Torgersen decided to go to Co 1's assistance. The Norwegians made a mistake in the route and when they eventually came within sight of the railroad station, they saw smoke rising from it and realized that it had fallen to the enemy. This was confirmed by a Swedish border post. The company turned north, intending to join Norwegian forces in Salangsdal, but the weather turned bad with heavy snowfall. The inclement weather and the exhausted condition of the troops caused Torgersen to cross into Sweden where the troops were interned.

The Germans also launched a surprise attack around 0400 hours on Co 1. The Norwegians fought from windows in the two main buildings and the Germans did not press the attack. The firing lasted for about two hours and then the area fell quiet. The Norwegians assumed that the Germans had withdrawn but they attacked in greater force around 0800 hours.

The second attack was supported by heavy weapons, probably the antitank weapons found in each heavy weapons company. The fire forced the defenders away from the windows in the two buildings and this allowed German infantry to approach the western of the two buildings. They blew open the door, stormed into the building, throwing hand grenades and opening fire with sub-machineguns. A few Norwegians jumped from the back windows and some eventually made their way to Sweden. Major Spjældnes and a number of his men were trapped on the second floor and captured. Major Omdal and his troops in the eastern building were captured soon after the first building was rushed.

The fighting in and around Bjørnefjell resulted in six Norwegian dead, 16 seriously wounded and 45 prisoners. The rest managed to slip over the border to Sweden. Some evaded capture and were able to join Norwegian forces further north and others escaped from German captivity.[8]

A Norwegian humanitarian group had established a relief station in Kiruna in Sweden and personnel from this station, with German permission, fetched the 16 seriously wounded Norwegians on April 16 and brought them to their relief station. Two days later, the same organization brought the six fallen soldiers to Kiruna where they were buried on April 24 with full military honors. Occasionally, the Germans allowed seriously wounded or sick Norwegians transferred to Swedish hospitals. Major Spjældnes became seriously ill on May 5 and he was sent to a Swedish hospital after giving his word of honor that he would return to German captivity when well. Spjældnes was released from the Swedish hospital on July 20 and he turned himself in to the Germans in Halden the following day.

The Germans captured whatever supplies the Norwegians had at Bjørnefjell, including 12 machineguns and 150 pairs of skis that would prove very useful later in their operations. According to Buchner, the German losses at Bjørnefjell were one killed and seven wounded. The German success at Bjørnefjell must be viewed as a remarkable achievement. They were outnumbered almost 2 to 1, operated in unfamiliar terrain, and attacked an enemy in defensive positions.

There are several reasons for the Norwegian failure. They may have seriously underestimated German abilities to operate in the mountains to the east of the railway and rumors of German "demoralization" after the naval battle may have reached them and given a false sense of security. Major Omdal placed too much reliance on civilian warnings of any German move against Bjørnefjell. The Germans were quick to seize all communications facilities in Hundal, thus preventing any telephonic warning. It was noted in chapter 5 that the 1/13th Inf displayed serious leadership problems at virtually all levels. This was again apparent at Bjørnefjell.

The Norwegian lack of adequate early warning measures was a serious mistake for which the majors and the company commanders are primarily responsible. Placing all of Co 1 in the two main buildings without any outposts or forward positions to keep the Germans away was not wise. In addition, Co 3 should have kept about one third of the men in the defensive positions at all times. This defensive force could have been relieved periodically to give the personnel rest and shelter from the elements. These are elementary and routine precautions for properly trained, disciplined, and well led units. While the weather conditions were miserable, they were no more so for the Norwegians than the Germans.

The German Situation in Mid-April and Early Supply Efforts

The loss of Bjørnefjell was a serious Norwegian setback and an encouraging development for the Germans. By securing the railroad from Narvik to the Swedish border, Dietl had accomplished all immediate objectives spelled out in his operational order except for capturing Bardufoss Airfield. The seizure of Bjørnefjell could alleviate the acute supply and reinforcement problems if the Swedes were prevailed upon to allow trans-shipments.

After securing the railroad to Sweden and the occupation of good defensive positions along the northern front, Dietl decided that was all he could do with the resources at his disposal in face of stiffening Norwegian resistance. The Germans were aware that Norwegian mobilization was proceeding rapidly and that the forces confronting them in the north were growing in strength daily. At the same time, they worried about Allied landings on the coast.

Dietl's troops did not have much heavy equipment and weapons when they landed. Most of their artillery washed overboard on the stormy passage and the supply ships destined for Narvik never reached their destination. The Germans were helped immeasurably by the early capture of Elvegårdsmoen, with its ample supplies of weapons and provisions. However, the mountain troops were not clothed and equipped for operations in the terrain and climate in the Narvik area. Instead of their usual winter gear, their clothing and equipment were more suitable for spring conditions. Things such as sleds, skis, and winter bivouac and camouflage equipment were lacking. One can only conclude that the Germans, like the British, misjudged the climate in Narvik at this time of the year or that they did not expect the Norwegians to offer any serious opposition after the capture of their main cities.

The destroyer crews more than doubled the forces available to Dietl. While these men were armed and provisioned from captured Norwegian stocks at Elvegårdsmoen, their usefulness in land operations was questionable. However, they constituted valuable assets for the close protection of Narvik and other installations captured by the Germans. This allowed Dietl to send most mountain troops to the front. The naval personnel were instrumental in bringing ashore guns and ammunition from the sunken destroyers. The five British armed merchantmen in Narvik harbor on April 9 each carried two 105mm guns. These were brought ashore and two were mounted on rail cars. The sailors were also active in getting the railroad back into operation. The fact that some were dressed in captured Norwegian uniforms, a breach of conventions, was the source of much criticism.

The Germans made a concerted effort to supply the Narvik forces by air. The first aircraft to arrive was a Ju-90 that dropped ammunition at 1130 hours on April 12. A Do-24 (seaplane) landed in Narvik around 1230 on April 13 with ammunition for the destroyers, but this was too little and too late.

Eleven Ju-52s, commanded by Colonel Bauer, landed on the frozen Hartvig Lake in the evening of April 13. The aircraft brought the 2nd Battery, 112th Mountain Artillery Regiment, commanded by Captain Lochmann, from Berlin. The unit consisted of about 100 men who brought with them four 75mm guns.

The Germans had similar misfortune in using frozen lakes as landing fields as the British did in central Norway. Three aircraft were damaged while landing and one was destroyed by Norwegian aircraft. There was a sudden thaw in the weather creating a layer of water on top of the soft ice. The aircraft froze into the ice as the weather again turned cold, and this prevented all but one from taking off. The remaining aircraft on Hartvigvann were eventually captured by the Norwegians, but then unfortunately destroyed by British bombing.

After their ill-fated experience on the lake, the Germans turned to airdrop and the use of seaplanes. Three Ju-52 transports appeared over Hartvigvann at 1030 hours on April 14. They did not attempt to land but dropped their loads of medical supplies over the lake. Two Do-28s landed near Narvik in the afternoon of April 15, carrying mortar ammunition and medical supplies. Both aircraft took off later that evening. A message from Oslo at 1215 hours on April 16 stated that a flight of He-11s was on its way to attack enemy naval forces in Narvik. The 3rd Mountain Division journal notes sarcastically, "the announced flight—two planes—arrived at about 1400 hours and one dropped bombs over Narvik harbor, now empty of enemy forces."

Attempts by the German Navy to bring supplies to Narvik by submarines did not succeed. On April 10, SKL ordered three submarines in homeports (*U26*, *U29*, and *U43*) readied for a re-supply mission to Narvik. The submarines left Germany between 12 to 16 April, each carrying 40 to 50 tons, mostly ammunition. Because of the uncertain situation in Narvik, these boats were redirected to Trondheim.

The seizure of the Bjørnefjell area improved General Dietl's supply situation. After the German troops reached the border, the German Government demanded permission from Sweden to send supplies to Dietl's troops through that country. The Swedish Government agreed, on April 17, to permit the transshipment of supplies of "a humanitarian nature."[9] The following day, Sweden granted permission for the transit of Red Cross personnel. The first shipment reached Sweden on April 19. It consisted of 34 railroad cars with 25 tons of medicines and medical equipment, 20 tons of clothing, and 350 tons of provisions. The train arrived in Bjørnefjell on April 26. It is estimated that the provisions on the train were sufficient to sustain 4,000 troops for three months. The train also brought 30 intelligence personnel, apparently disguised as Red Cross workers.[10] The Germans were also allowed to send personnel to Germany and the first transport consisted of 514 personnel. These were primarily crews from German merchant ships sunk in Narvik as well as naval specialists that the SKL required back in Germany.

Fleischer's Offensive Plan

While Fleischer had no precise knowledge of the German order of battle, he knew that it was possible to achieve local superiority since a large portion of the German force had to defend Narvik and the railway to Sweden. It was important to keep the Germans guessing as to the location of the attacks and to present them with multiple threats that would make it difficult for them to switch forces on interior lines to meet Norwegian thrusts.

General Fleischer's original offensive plan, after halting the German advance along the road at Lapphaugen, involved launching attacks along multiple axes.

Gratangen was the brigade's immediate objective. The 2/15th Inf, supported by the 3rd Mountain Artillery Bn and reinforced by Co Forseth, would engage the Germans at Lapphaugen and drive them south along the road to Gratangen (Route 50) while the 1/16th Inf moved west from Bones through the wilderness in Vassdal, Gressdal, and Raudal. The 1/12th Inf would attack across Fjordbotneidet from the north. The Alta Bn would constitute the Brigade reserve from a location near Levangen, behind the advancing 1/12th Inf. The Norwegians hoped that the Germans would concentrate their defense along Route 50. The force advancing through Fjordbotneidet would threaten the German left flank and their line of retreat along Route 50. The force moving from Bones could bring about two possible successes: the destruction of the main German force by cutting their line of retreat or the early capture of Bjerkvik and Elvegårdsmoen by the force moving northwest through Raudal.

The two sides spent the time after April 13 consolidating their positions and preparing for future operations. Both sides, particularly the Norwegians, engaged in heavy patrol activities. The Norwegians needed information about German strengths and positions in preparing their offensive. From the patrol activities, the Norwegians concluded that the enemy had two battalions in the Bjerkvik-Gratangen area, with about 300-400 troops in Gratangen. They estimated correctly that the Germans had one reinforced company at Lapphaugen. German ski patrol, from 15 to 60 men in size, operated regularly to the east in the Hartvigvann-Gressdal area but a move against Bones or Lund was not attempted.

Mobilization and Deployments

The forces called for in General Fleischer's plan were not yet available. The units envisioned for the drive through Fjordbotneidet against the German left flank, the 1/12th Infantry and the Alta Bn, were still in Finnmark, more than 300 miles from where they were needed. The distance itself fails to tell the whole story. Road communications were virtually non-existant at this time of the year, and the troops had to be transported to their new operational area by sea. Most Norwegian naval forces in Fleischer's area of responsibility were destroyed or captured and this presented a problem. The 1/12th Inf, commanded by Major Nils Bøckman, was transported from Kirkenes to Sjøvegan in two echelons, arriving there on April 17 and 20. British warships escorted the transports. The Alta Bn, commanded by Lieutenant Colonel Arne D. Dahl and consisting of 830 officers and men and 112 horses, was transported in two coastal passenger ships and one cargo ship, without naval escorts, and disembarked in Sjøvegan on April 21. The battalion arrived in the Tennevoll area in Levangen in the evening of April 23. The 2/15th Inf was located in the Fossbakken area. The 3rd Mountain Artillery Bn was also ordered to that area. The road through Salangsdal was impassable and it was not until April 22 that the 9th Battery (motorized) of the battalion reached its destination. The plan called for half of Battery 8 to support the advance of the 1/12th Inf while the other half was located in Fossbakken along with Batteries 7 and 9.

Except for the 15th Regiment and some smaller units that had their depot at Elvegårdsmoen fall into enemy hands on the first day of the German attack, the mobilization in North Norway proceeded in an orderly manner. The 1/15th Inf had problems mobilizing. Most of the weapons, equipment, and supplies required had to come from reserve depots located some distance from the new place of mobilization near Setermoen. Mobilization day was April 18 but due to equipment and personnel problems, the battalion was not fully mobilized until May 20. Major Omdal assumed command on April 24 and the partially mobilized battalion moved to Bardufoss Airfield for security on May 5. One ski platoon acted as security for the British and Polish troops in Bogen. The Reserve Battalion, 15th Inf had the same problems as the 1/15th since Elvegårdsmoen was also its mobilization depot. Attempts were made to mobilize, with a planned completion date of June 10.

The 1/16th Inf (less one company), commanded by Major Nils Hunstad, departed its mobilization depot at Setermoen on April 15 for the Lund-Bones area in Salangsdal. Nevertheless, the unit was not fully mobilized until April 21, when it numbered 720 officers and men. Co 3 was ordered to Fossbakken where it was attached to the 2/15th Inf. It reverted to the control of its parent battalion in the morning of April 22. The 1/16th Infantry's missions were to secure the valley between Lund and Bones and prepare to take part in the upcoming offensive by moving against the German right flank through Gressdal and Raudal.

The 2/16th Inf completed mobilization on April 20 when it had 802 officers and men present for duty. This battalion had not participated in the neutrality watch and it was therefore necessary to give it some training before it was committed. The Reserve Battalion of the 16th Inf assembled at Setermoen on April 18 and it remained there until April 30.

Lieutenant Colonel Nummedal was acting commander of the 14th Infantry Regiment in the area south of Narvik. The commander of this regiment, Colonel Løken, was detached to command the 6th Field Brigade and the executive officer, Major Halfdan Sundlo, commanded the 1/14th Inf on neutrality duty in

East Finnmark. This battalion returned to Mosjøen after the middle of March and was demobilized. The battalion was remobilized and ready on April 13. Fleischer, as already noted, attached this battalion to Colonel Getz' forces in Trøndelag. The Reserve Battalion of the 14th Inf completed its mobilization on April 21. Many of its personnel participated in the Lofoten fisheries and their absence slowed the mobilization effort. The battalion, with units both south and north of Mosjøen, needed training. Nummedal was left as the local commander with orders to prepare for a possible German northward drive if the defenses in Trøndelag failed.

The Hålogaland Air Group was ordered to concentrate its aircraft at Bardufoss Airfield. One Fokker aircraft, with the group commander aboard, was captured at Bjørnefjell on April 16 and two Fokker aircraft were wrecked on April 20 and 25. Except for the 22-lb type, the availability of bombs was very limited as was ammunition for aircraft and antiaircraft machineguns. An airfield in Salagen was later expanded to support combat operations.

The 6th Brigade was partially reorganized to make it more suitable for mobile operations. Some organizations were modified for operations in the roadless wilderness on both sides of Route 50. Parts of the heavier supply organizations were transferred to District Command where they served a useful purpose as additional combat groups were organized.

Except for what was in the depots, weapons and ammunition were not available in North Norway. Ammunition for the mountain howitzers was in particular short supply; the whole inventory was limited to about 6,500 rounds. The 75mm ammunition was more plentiful. Ammunition for machineguns and individual weapons became a serious problem as the campaign progressed.

Modifications to the Offensive Plans

The final directive for the offensive was issued on April 17. Fleischer worried about the effects of the spring thaw and wanted to start the operations as quickly as possible. The 1/12th Inf was in position in Levangen on April 20 and the Alta Bn arrived shortly thereafter. From Levangen, these two units were in position for an advance through Fjordbotneidet. The 2/15th Inf was located in the Fossbakken area, prepared to attack Lapphaugen. The 1/16th Inf (minus one company) was in Salangsdal between Lund and Bones, ready to begin the envelopment through the mountains southeast of Route 50.

The deteriorating weather compelled the Norwegians to modify their earlier plan. The revised plan increased the weight of the direct drive against Lapphaugen by making it a two-battalion operation, with the 2/15th Inf on the right and most of the 1/16th Inf on the left. These battalions were to drive the Germans from their positions by frontal attack and local envelopments. Having driven the Germans from their positions, the plan called for cutting their retreat by advancing to Hill 509.

The battalion-size envelopment from the south was scrapped and the forces operating in this area were reduced, first to two and later to one company. The 1/16th Inf, minus one reinforced company, left Bones for Fossbakken at 2300 hours on April 23. The weather was so bad that even local guides did not know where on the road the battalion was located at any one time. Thoroughly exhausted, the battalion reached the woods near Fossbakken early in the morning of April 24. The revised plan made no changes to the right envelopment over Fjordbotneidet, and the Alta Bn remained as the brigade reserve. Another reserve, Co Forseth, was located behind the brigade's left flank. The two companies from the Scots Guards landed in Sjøvegan on April 14 were placed at General Fleischer's disposal, but only for defensive operations. More or less as a symbolic gesture, they were positioned behind the Norwegian lines at Fossbakken.

General Fleischer decided on April 22 to launch the offensive at midnight on April 23, but the launch was delayed. The brigade commander briefed his subordinates on April 22. For security reasons, the order to the companies was delayed as long as possible. This secrecy resulted in little time for the companies to prepare for action. The commander of Co 5, 2/15th Inf received his order at 2330 hours on April 23, and he was not able to brief his platoon leaders until midnight. The battery commanders in the 3rd Mountain Artillery Bn did not receive their orders until 0040 hours on April 24.

Company 1 from the 1/16th Inf still remained in Raudal and at 1910 hours on April 23, it was ordered to advance cross-country towards Lapphaugen and establish contact with its parent battalion. A blizzard prevented it from making its way through the mountains and at 1230 hours on April 24, it was ordered to remain in its position to provide security in the Raudal/Stordal area. However, that same evening the company was ordered back to Bones and the following morning it was directed to join its battalion in Fossbakken. It arrived in Fossbakken, totally exhausted, at 1400 hours.

The Envelopment

The 1/12th Inf started its move from Levangen in the afternoon of April 23. The troops labored incredibly hard to ascend Fjordbotneidet at night, in a raging snowstorm on the steep roadless incline that rose 1,200 to 1,500 feet from the valley bottom. They carried loads of 60 lbs as they struggled forward in snow that was chest deep at times. The wind blowing in their faces made it difficult to see and a large number suffered from snow blindness. It was particularly difficult to bring the artillery forward. Major Bøckman moved the battalion with two companies forward in order to maximize his firepower if he should encounter the enemy. This meant that numerous tracks had to be made through the snow over a relatively broad area. Local guides noted that the winter storm was one of the worst they had experienced in an area where snowstorms are frequent and severe.

There was a misinterpretation of orders from the very start within the right envelopment force. The 1/12th Inf had no contact with the Alta Bn after leaving Tennevoll. The brigade order directed the Alta Bn to provide security for the 1/12th's right flank and rear. Bøckman interpreted this to mean that the two battalions should advance together across Fjordbotneidet. The brigade commander also understood the division's directive to mean that the force advancing over Fjordbotneidet consisted of the 1/12th Infantry, the Alta Bn, and half of a mountain artillery battery.

The snowstorm became so bad during the day that Fleischer considered calling off the attack. However, he allowed the operation to proceed since he concluded that it would be more difficult to bring the 1/12th back over the mountains than to allow it to proceed. Fleischer, his chief of staff, and the British liaison officer arrived in Levangen by car in the afternoon of April 23 and Lieutenant Colonel Dahl briefed them. Fleischer planned to spend the night at the 6th Brigade's CP and left the Alta Bn around 0200 hours on April 24. The weather had turned vicious, the general and his party were snowed in at Levangen, and the house of a merchant in Soløy became the division CP for the rest of the operation. The 1/12th Inf had left a communication relay station in Soløy and this allowed Fleischer to communicate with the Alta Bn, the 1/12th Inf, and the 6th Brigade CP.

Communications problems plagued the operation from the beginning, as did the lack of maps. The radio communication equipment promised the 1/12th Inf in the operational order failed to materialize and the detachment laying landlines as the unit advanced failed to keep up in the storm. Major Bøckman sent his adjutant to the rear to inform the brigade that the battalion, because of the weather and limited visibility, could not accomplish its mission of preventing traffic on Route 50 from Gratangen to Lapphaugen. Brøckman's orders called for blocking Route 50 by fire from the hills to the north. He was not permitted to enter the valley. Hovland's explanation for Fleischer's decision that the 1/12th should not enter the valley but should cut the German line of retreat and reinforcement by blocking-fire from afar is that he wanted to give the battalion a "careful baptism of fire."

Bøckman now requested brigade permission to enter the valley and physically cut Route 50. This request came to Fleischer's attention and he concluded that it was inappropriate for Colonel Løken to direct the operation over Fjordbotneidet since the brigade no longer had reliable communications with the 1/12th. After a short telephone call to the brigade, Fleischer assumed direct control of the two battalions in the envelopment. The frontal attack on Lapphaugen and the envelopment were two parts of the same operation but now those two parts answered to two commanders.

It appears that the brigade CP had no great difficulties communicating with the 1/12th Infantry's communications relay station since Fleischer, who was located near that station, communicated regularly with the brigade by telephone. The difficulty was with communications between that station and the battalion. Therefore, Fleischer's assumption of control failed to solve the communications problem.

General Fleischer approved Major Bøckman's request to cross into the Gratang Valley to the Fjellhøgda Farm and ordered him to send security into the south mountains, including Hill 509, if that was possible. The lead elements of the battalion cut Route 50 around 0600 hours on April 24. This severed the road between the reinforced German company at Lapphaugen and the rest of the battalion in the Gratangen area. The half battery of mountain artillery supporting the 1/12th remained on Fjordbotneidet, in a position where it could fire into the valley.

No German units were sighted except for a three-man patrol that was captured. Major Bøckman concluded that the German battalion had withdrawn its forward line to the high ground in the pass between Gratangen and Bjerkvik. He planned to send reconnaissance into the mountains south of Route 50 but the soldiers were too exhausted after their overnight advance in the blizzard.

The troops needed shelter and food and the adjutant skied back to the communications relay to brief the division and ask for permission to go into quarters on the farms near Route 50. This request was approved provided the battalion employed strong local security. According to the adjutant, Major Lindbäck-Larsen told him that the Alta Bn was advancing across Fjordbotneidet to secure the 1/12th Infantry's flank and rear and that a conclusion of operations at Lapphaugen was expected within a couple of hours. This indicates that the division was aware of the movement of the Alta Bn despite later claims that the battalion had moved without authorization prior to the order to do so that evening.

The 1/12th took up quarters in the valley between 1700 and 1800 hours, with the rifle companies in the built-up area north of the river and the battalion CP and headquarters' company in the area between the river and Route 50. The machinegun platoons were attached to the rifle companies. The positions astride Route 50 that the battalion had spent the day preparing were abandoned with the intention of reoccupying them at 0600 hours on April 25. As at Bjørnefjell, no security forces were left in the defensive positions. This was an indefensible breach of elementary rules for military units in proximity of the enemy.

The unit's 15-hour march over mountains in a howling blizzard and a further 12 hours preparing defensive positions stretched the soldiers' physical and mental capabilities to their limits. It would have been wise to rest the troops in shifts as soon as they reached the valley. However, physical exhaustion does not explain why Majors Omdal and Spjældnes allowed a similar thing to happen at Bjørnefjell.

Because of the storm and limited visibility, the companies were ordered to establish only close-in security and to maintain unit cohesion as they took quarters. It is obvious, based on subsequent events, that the security measures were inadequate. The Germans noted, 'The Norwegians did not figure on any German counterattack because of the storm and the deep snow and were so negligent that hardly any sentries secured their nightly rest area."[11]

The Frontal Attack

Another reason for Fleischer assuming direct command of the enveloping force and for allowing the 1/12th to take quarters in the valley may have been his belief that the attack against Lapphaugen was going well. In fact, it was not launched according to plan and was not going well. The heavy snowstorm was the primary factor for the faltering attack, but the way it was executed and the determination by which it was pursued by the brigade contributed to its failure.

The 2/15th Inf advanced with two companies forward, but in a rather disorganized fashion due to the blizzard. Company 5 advanced along Route 50 while Co 6 tried to make a curve-like advance to the right of Co 5, allowing it to approach the German positions from the northeast near the eastern point of Lake Lapphaugvannet. Company 5 had to shift to the left in order to give room for Co 6. The battalion reserve, Co 7 with an attached machinegun platoon, followed behind and slightly to the north of Co 6.

The attack started shortly before 1000 hours on April 24, ten hours later than planned, after Battery 7 fired a 20-minute preparation. The heavy weapons company's mortars and machineguns fired on the German positions for five minutes during a momentary clearing in the weather. The advancing Norwegian troops had snow driven by gale force winds in their faces, resulting in near-zero visibility. The German defenders had the wind at their backs, making it much easier to observe to their front. The Norwegians struggled to make headway through heavy snow. Their skis sank into the loose snow up to their knees. The attack came to a halt in the bad weather, and the forward troops dug in and fired at the Germans during the brief moments of visibility.

It was much the same story with Co 6. Its attack was stopped by German fire and the troops sought concealment by digging into the snow. One soldier was killed. Company 7 attempted a flanking movement, approaching the German positions from the north, but was caught in the open by German machinegun fire and two of its soldiers were killed before the unit withdrew into the wood line. The 2/15th Infantry's attack came to a halt by noon.

The Norwegians made the mistake of not maintaining contact with the enemy. They even failed to keep the German positions under observation after the initial attack failed. Consequently, they were unaware that the Germans withdrew from Lapphaugen around 1500 hours.

Colonel Løken had a significant superiority in numbers with almost two battalions supported by two and a half batteries of artillery and heavy mortars. However, he used his resources in a piecemeal and hesitant manner. The 1/16th, minus one company, was scheduled to advance on the left flank of the 2/15th. That battalion arrived in Fossbakken at 2300 hours the previous night after a tortuous march from Bones. It went into bivouac in the woods a short distance south of Fossbakken. For reasons that are not obvious, the 1/16th did not participate in the initial attack.

Around 1300 hours, the brigade tried to get the attack going again by sending the 1/16th along the southern hillside where it could approach the German positions from the southeast. The heavy snowfall prevented the 1/16th from reaching its attack position during the day, despite enormous efforts. The snow was so deep that it was impossible to bring heavy weapons forward even with the use of sleds. Major Hunstad, the battalion commander, finally reported to Løken around 2000 hours that his battalion was in position about one kilometer east of Lapphaugen and was ready to attack.

The brigade, however, concluded that a continuation of the attack at night in a snowstorm was pointless. The 1/16th was ordered into bivouac positions between Lapphaugen and Fossbakken and it arrived there around midnight. We do not know why Colonel Løken did not order the 1/16th to proceed westward another two kilometers and take up positions in Oalgge Pass instead of withdrawing two kilometers eastward to its bivouac area. While the 1/16th could not trap the Germans because they withdrew around 1500 hours, the Norwegians did not know this and occupation of the pass would have cut the line of retreat for the German company the Norwegians still believed was at Lapphaugen. The companies from the 2/15th were also withdrawn a short distance and went into bivouac in the same general area as the 1/16th. The brigade notified division that blizzard conditions made a continuation of the attack on Lapphaugen impossible.

The termination of the frontal attack left the 1/12th Inf in position behind the enemy force withdrawing from Lapphaugen. The battalion therefore sat astride the line of retreat of a smaller German force. However, the division worried that the 1/12th would be caught between German forces at Lapphaugen and other units further south and decided to make deployment changes. The Alta Bn was ordered to break out of its bivouac in Levangen and proceed through Fjordbotneidet to secure 1/12th Infantry's right flank. The Alta Bn was in fact already in positions on the south side of Fjordbotneidet, behind the 1/12th.

Lindbäck-Larsen writes that the early movement of the Alta Bn was contrary to operational plans. Lieutenant Colonel Dahl maintains that he received orders to move forward earlier than claimed by Lindbäck-Larsen otherwise he would not have taken his battalion on a 15-hour, 1,200 feet ascent in the most difficult weather conditions imaginable. Dahl's adjutant reported later that his commander received orders to move forward around 0500 hours on April 24 because the 1/12th Inf had entered the Gratang Valley.[12] Whatever the case, the early move was fortunate since Dahl's battaliion was already in the position to which the division now ordered it.

However, the division limited the Alta Battalion's role to protecting the right flank of the 1/12th and supporting it by fire. It was ordered not to enter the valley. The Alta Bn had no contact with the 1/12th after midnight. The supporting unit was responsible for maintaining contact with the supported unit. This was apparently not done.

Fleischer's second action dealt with the 1/16th Inf, a unit already worn down from moving around in a winter blizzard for two days without much rest. The general directed the brigade to send this battalion to Tennevoll in Levangen where it would come under the division commander's direct control. The battalion received the movement order at 0230 hours on April 25, two and a half hours after it had reached its bivouac.

This action changed the very nature of the offensive since the northern pincer over Fjordbotneidet now became the main effort. Colonel Løken's original command of four infantry battalions was reduced to one, with the other three now under Fleischer's direct command. There was no obvious need for a third battalion on the northern flank and certainly no need for it to make another exhausting night move in a snowstorm. Over three feet of new snow had fallen and the battalion commander stated that he was uncertain when he could reach his destination. The battalion was then ordered to rest in a bivouac at Fossbakken before making the move.

The 1/16th Inf began its move at 1900 hours on April 25. The companies, in relays, had to clear the road as they moved since it was impossible for horses and sleds to move in the deep snow. The snow clearing was hard work but the battalion arrived at its destination around 0800 hours on April 26. It remained in Levangen for four days after which it was ordered back to Fossbakken. The 1/16th reached its destination at midnight on the 29th and went into bivouac between Fossbakken and Lapphaugen, alongside the 2nd Battalion of the same regiment, which had also been directed to that location.

The German Counterattack

The German 2nd Battalion, 139th Regiment commanded by Major Ludwig Stautner was deployed in depth from Lapphaugen to Elvenes in Gratangen. The reinforced Co 2 was at Lapphaugen. The battalion's heavy weapons were located near Elvenes with the primary mission of supporting Co 2 and covering its possible withdrawal. Company 13 was in battalion reserve. This unit and the battalion CP were located near Storvann. One platoon from Co 13 provided flank security at Foldvik.

German patrols sent towards Fjordbotneidet and Fossbakken prior to April 24 were unable to carry out proper reconnaissance because they encountered Norwegian troops. The Norwegian attack, while expected, came as a surprise as far as timing was concerned. The daily heavy snowfall also caused severe problems for the Germans. It was difficult to bring supplies and provisions forward from Bjerkvik and impossible to conduct air reconnaissance. Except for patrols and a small number of other units, the German troops were not equipped with skis. They bought all the skis they could lay their hands on and improvised by using white bed sheets, drapes, and later white parachutes as winter camouflage cover.

Major Stautner received a radio message around 0900 hours on April 24 from Lieutenant Bauer, the commander of Co 2 at Lapphaugen, reporting that the unit had been under heavy artillery fire since 0830 hours and that the enemy was attacking. There were no further contacts with Co 2. Reports from two reconnaissance patrols reported enemy forces numbering 100-200 men advancing from the north and northeast. Stautner believed these to be part of the force that had attacked Co 2 and he concluded that the unit at Lapphaugen was cut off by the Norwegian advance. He sent a message to Colonel Windisch at Elvegårdsmoen around 1600 hours reporting his situation and asking for reinforcements. The request for reinforcements was denied.

Windisch had good reasons for denying the major's request. The Norwegian offensive was launched on the same day the British carried out the heavy bombardment of Narvik with a battleship and several cruisers. The Germans did not know that this was just a coincidence and they had every reason to assume that the two operations were coordinated. They knew that there were two British battalions in Bogen, to the west of Bjerkvik, and it was reasonable to expect that they might advance on Bjerkvik and Elvegårdsmoen as part of a joint operation with the Norwegians. Major Lindbäck-Larsen had suggested this kind of cooperation to General Mackesy when they met on April 15.

Major Stautner decided to concentrate his forces and ordered those near Elvenes to withdraw to Storvann where Co 13 and the battalion CP were located. Reconnaissance reported that a strong enemy force had occupied the built-up area east of Elvenes in the evening but that it was not moving towards Elvenes.

Radio contact was reestablished with Co 2 around 2200 hours. Under the cover of the snowstorm, it had managed to withdraw from Lapphaugen, leaving behind the wounded and both mortars. With great effort in deep snow, the company had moved slowly southward for seven kilometers and Lieutenant Bauer reported that his men were still withdrawing and located east of the former tourist station. Another message from the company was received about 30 minutes later. It reported that the enemy had not pursued them through Oalgge Pass. The report also stated that, while they had no contact with the enemy, the Norwegians in the Gratang Valley were resting in buildings at the Moen, Nylund, and Dalsletten areas with hardly any sentries posted.

Stautner saw an opportunity and grabbed it. He did not waste time in discussing the situation with Colonel Windisch, or even ask permission to undertake his planned operation. His actions provide an excellent example of the advantages of decentralized control.

Stautner ordered Co 2 to take up blocking positions along Route 50, southwest of the former tourist station from where it could use all its weapons against the area occupied by the Norwegians. One platoon was located where it could defend against a possible enemy approach from the east. The company was ordered to hold its positions at all costs in order to prevent an enemy breakout to the south. Two platoons from Co 13 and one ski platoon were to quietly approach the Norwegian positions in three columns from the west, overrun the Moen and Nylund farms and continue to the end of the valley. The heavy weapons company occupied positions at the road junction near Storfossen to provide fire support for Co 13. The attack force assembled at Elvenes School at 0440 hours and the attack was launched at 0550 hours. The two infantry platoons advanced along Route 50 while the ski platoon paralleled the road along the hillside to the east.

While the German attack came as a surprise to the 1/12th Infantry, there were indications in the early morning hours that something was afoot. There were reports during the night of enemy patrol activity and between 0400 and 0600 hours reports of enemy forces along Route 50. The final report, shortly after 0600 hours, indicated that the Germans had occupied the empty Norwegian defensive positions. It was obvious that the security measures taken by the Norwegians had been inadequate.

The Norwegians apparently had no plans to meet an attack other than to reoccupy the defensive positions they had abandoned the night before. They made the initial move in this direction when they came under intense fire, direct and indirect, from the high ground on the south side of the valley. At the same time, the Germans launched their ground attack from the west. Company 2, located on the Moen farms, was the first Norwegian unit to feel the brunt of the German attack. The troops exited their quarters and fought from various positions around the farmhouses. It was still blowing a gale with heavy snow squalls and the visibility varied from good to almost zero. The German center column engaged Co 2 frontally while the other two slipped around its flanks. The Norwegians were under fire from several directions and the company commander, Captain Nils Øvreaas, was among the first to be killed.

After the fight had lasted for a while, the Norwegian company fragmented into small groups. Some continued the fight while others surrendered. Still others tried to withdraw up the hill towards Fjordbotneidet but heavy enemy machinegun fire made this difficult. A number of troops escaped by following creek beds that gave them some cover. Forward elements of the Alta Bn on Fjordbotneidet tried to help by opening fire but it is possible, in the limited visibility where it was difficult to discern friend from foe, that the fire caused more harm to their comrades than to the enemy. Companies 1 and 3 believed they received fire from the Alta Bn on Fjordbotneidet during the fighting and Captain Mitlid sent a messenger to Lieutenant Colonel Dahl in the morning of April 26 asking that all firing into the valley stop.

Company 1, located at the eastern farms and to the north of the tourist station, tried to retake its defensive positions, now in German hands. The troops were under heavy fire as they tried to work their way up the steep hillside and the commander, Captain Thormod Casper Mitlid, was wounded and evacuated. The Norwegian attack faltered. Some of the troops dug in while others withdrew back into the valley.

Major Bøckman had not noticed any efforts by the Alta Bn, which was supposed to protect his right flank, to come to his assistance. He sent his adjutant to the telephone station to try to establish contact. He did not locate his CP where he could communicate with both the Alta Bn and General Fleischer. The adjutant reached the house where the telephone was located but the telephone connection was severed by German fire.

The hillside leading to Fjordbotneidet was swept by German machinegun fire and the lieutenant had to give up trying to contact the Alta Bn. He gave Co 3's commander, Captain Hilmar Mjøen, an order from Bøckman to attack and drive the Germans from Route 50. The adjutant was wounded on his way back to the battalion CP.

Major Bøckman had meanwhile ordered Captain Otto Ludvig Nyquist, the commander of Co 4 to support Co 3 in its attack and to place fire on the Germans attacking from the west. Captain Nyquist was wounded on his way back to his unit but continued to coordinate the fire support with Captain Mjøen. He had just sat down to dress his wound when a mortar shell killed him. Norwegian machinegun fire succeeded in temporarily stopping the Germans near the eastern Moen farms.

Company 3, minus one platoon, advanced towards its old positions along

Route 50, now occupied by Germans from Co 2, 139th Regiment. The going was slow as the attackers were under continued direct and indirect fire. A flank attack by one platoon made good progress until it reached open terrain and was stopped by enemy fire from three directions.

The Norwegian attack on Co 2's position caused a critical situation for the Germans. They were exhausted from fighting at Lapphaugen and a night withdrawal in a snowstorm. Every man was committed to bring the Norwegian attack to a halt. The fighting was vicious and at close quarters. The attack faltered under heavy crossfire, and the Norwegians withdrew.

Under cover of a heavy snow squall, the Germans in the Moen area managed to close in on some of the farm buildings still occupied by Norwegian troops. Some were captured and the Norwegians claimed that the Germans used these captives and civilians as shields in their advance against Co 4. There were other reports of prisoners and civilians used as shields. The Germans denied the charge but admitted that prisoners were brought forward behind the attacking forces since moving them to the rear was impossible.

The fighting began to subside around noon. German medics, under white flags, moved onto the battlefield to remove the dead and wounded. Through a returned prisoner, the Germans requested Norwegian medical assistance. Later, Norwegian medical personnel received permission to evacuate wounded soldiers through Gratangen. Four fishing vessels with medical personnel were dispatched from Sjøvegan to Gratangen. From there, medics and litter bearers moved east through the German lines, picked up the wounded, brought them back through German lines to Gratangen, and evacuated them to Harstad.

There were two reasons the fighting died out around noon. The determined attack by Co 3, 1/12th Inf came close to overwhelming the Germans in Co 2, 139th. The unit needed rest. The second, and probably more important reason, was that Major Stautner learned from prisoner interrogation and from what the Germans had observed in the direction of Fjordbotneidet, that a fresh Norwegian battalion was located on those heights, threatening their flank and rear. In fact, if the Alta Bn had moved forward into the valley during the morning, most of the German forces would have had to break contact quickly or be isolated.

An operational plan seldom survives long past the first shot and Fleischer made a serious mistake when he did not alter the plan and order the Alta Bn forward. While the centralized philosophy of the Norwegian military frowned on the kind of individual initiative displayed by Major Stautner, it is nevertheless difficult to understand why Dahl did not question the wisdom of remaining inactive on the forward slope of Fjordbotneidet where all he could do was be a witness to what happened in the valley. His primary mission was to protect the right flank of the 1/12th. After the 1/12th moved into the valley, the Alta Bn could no longer provide effective flank cover from the location specified in the orders. Dahl should also have made a concerted effort to reestablish communications with the 1/12th when that communication was lost around midnight.

Having confirmed that there was a fresh Norwegian battalion in the area and knowing that an additional battalion or two were located about 8 kilometers to the north, Stautner made the prudent decision to terminate the attack and withdraw from the valley. In order to maintain strict control of the troops as they withdrew, Stautner directed the units to assemble in their attack positions. The ski platoon covered the withdrawal, accomplished without losses despite artillery shelling from Fjordbotneidet. Company 13 and the heavy weapons company took up defensive positions at the entrance to the pass across the Gratangen Isthmus. Company 2, worn out after several days of fighting and moving in snowstorms, moved further east.

Major Bøckman was able to assemble the various subordinate units during the afternoon and decided to withdraw and reorganize the battalion after nightfall. The medics were left behind to care for the wounded. All heavy equipment was hidden, to be retrieved later. The Germans took note of low Norwegian morale. A message from the 139th Regiment to General Dietl's at 1240 hours on April 26 states that prisoners expressed great bitterness against the British. The message suggested that the time was right for leaflet drops.

While the offensive resulted in a German withdrawal from their forward positions at Lapphaugen and within a few days, a withdrawal from Gratangen to new defensive positions in the defile on the Gratangen Isthmus, the price paid by the Norwegians was high. Their attack was in fact a costly failure. They had nearly 2,500 troops to throw into the attack against 300–400 Germans, and only about 150 of these were in forward positions at Lapphaugen. According to the Germans, only 230 Germans participated in the attack on the 1/12th. The two platoons from Co 13, for example, had a strength of only 74 men.[13]

The 1/12th was combat ineffective because of the losses it sustained and General Fleischer decided to pull the battalion back to Levangen to reorganize. The losses were so great that when it again took part in operations at the beginning of May, the 1/12th had only two rifle companies, a machinegun platoon, and a mortar platoon.

The final tally of Norwegian losses was 34 killed, 64 wounded, and 180 captured. Initial reports after a battle are often inaccurate and this is illustrated in the 3rd Division's war diary. The entry for 1900 hours on April 25 gives the Norwegian losses as 200 killed, including a battalion commander, at least as many wounded, and 114 prisoners. German losses were listed as 16 killed and about 40 wounded. The numbers are corrected in an entry three hours later when their own losses are placed at eight killed, 15 wounded, and six missing.

The Norwegian Offensive in Retrospect

The fighting in Gratangen demonstrated that the individual Norwegian soldier could fight well when properly led and it was only a matter of time and experience until he was equal to the German mountain troops. Company 3's attack against Co 2, 139th nearly succeeded. The fact that three company commanders were killed shows that they did not hesitate to expose themselves in trying to rally their troops. The higher leadership, from General Fleischer down to the battalion commanders proved weak. The Norwegian plan looked good on a map, but it was something else to put into operation on the ground in a violent blizzard with inadequate communications between units. The result was an uncoordinated, piecemeal effort and less than one quarter of Fleischer's attacking force was involved at any one time. Only the 2/15th participated in the attack on Lapphaugen while the plan called for a two-battalion attack. On the second day, only the 1/12th was involved in fighting. The troops in the Alta Bn were passive onlookers. No orders were given for the 2/15th to resume its attack that day and the 1/16th was sent on a useless march to Levangen.

The 1/12th made glaring mistakes, not unlike those made by the 1/13th in Narvik and Bjørnefjell. Whole units were allowed to seek the comfort of shelter at the same time while at least one third of each company should have remained in the prepared positions. This is all the more remarkable since the Norwegians were the ones used to the severe climate found in this area and should have been able to endure the weather conditions in the open better than their opponents. This very fact may have led to an underestimation of enemy capabilities. Norwegian security was lax in Narvik, at Bjørnefjell, and in the Gratang Valley. General Hovland notes that the main reason for the failure of Major Bøckman and others who made glaring mistakes was lack of experience. There is no doubt that lack of experience was a major factor in many of the mistakes, but the errors at Bjørnefjell and Gratangen weer so elementary to the military profession that the "lack of experience" explanation falls short.

The three failures—Narvik, Bjørnefjell, and Gratang Valley—led the Norwegians—like Admiral Forbes after the German bombing attacks on the Home Fleet—to become overly cautious and methodical, as we will see in subsequent chapters. The Germans noted the Norwegian display of hesitancy and caution after the reverse in Gratangen and also noted the importance of Stautner's daring attack for future operations around Narvik.[14]

Hovland does not exempt General Fleischer from criticism but places the major blame for the debacle in Gratangen on the general's subordinates.[15] The military commanders may have been weak but the general's own mistakes cannot be ignored. Fleischer's attack plan was good but the multiple envelopments originally envisioned were too complicated for units that had not worked together and were going into combat for the first time. The lack of adequate communications exacerbated the problem. It is puzzling that he should have opted for such a complicated operation in the worst possible weather conditions in view of his own assessment that his units were hardly able to undertake missions involving maneuver in war until they had undergone extended training under favorable conditions. It would have been wise to keep the envelopments tighter and simpler since the Germans were deployed on a narrow front.

The constant shifting of units in atrocious weather conditions before and during the fighting exhausted the troops. The frequent incremental changes to the attack plan and the exhausting movements of units to accommodate these changes point to a sense of doubt and hesitancy at brigade and division. It is debatable whether the attack should have been launched at all in those deplorable weather conditions. There may have been an unstated feeling that the Germans would be incapable of mounting a defense under such circumstances. The blizzard had raged for 24 hours when the 1/12th was ordered forward and it is strange that the effect of weather on the operation was not seriously considered before sending that unit across Fjordbotneidet.

Colonel Løken and Lieutenant Colonel Hyldmo failed to insure that the forward units kept contact with the enemy after the attack ground to a halt. With their superior mobility, the Norwegians could have harassed the withdrawing Germans and possibly inflicted severe losses on them. If the Norwegian troops near Lapphaugen knew the Germans had withdrawn, they could have informed the 1/12th that a German unit was heading in its direction. This may have averted the calamity that followed the next morning.

While the wisdom of Fleischer's decision to take personal command of the envelopment force can be questioned, the results would undoubtedly not have been different if Løken was left in command. The prohibition against the two enveloping battalions descending into the Gratang Valley is difficult to understand. If both battalions were allowed to enter the valley, one could have pushed towards Elvenes, and thereby fixed the German forces in that area. The other battalion could have served as a blocking force against the reinforced company at Lapphaugen, which had to withdraw if the pressure was maintained. Under these circumstances, it would have been a good idea to appoint an overall commander for the enveloping force. Dahl was the senior of the two battalion commanders and therefore the logical choice.

Rather than redeploying the 1/16th from Fossbakken to the Tennevoll area, Fleischer should have ordered the 6th Brigade to resume its attack on Lapphaugen with two battalions. The 1/12th was sitting astride the German withdrawal route and it was the right time to pry the Germans out of their Lapphaugen position. A resumed advance would have revealed that the Germans had already withdrawn and this would have rectified, to some extent, the failure to maintain contact with the enemy.

General Hovland is right in identifying the wartime leadership quality among the officers as the most serious problem within the 6th Division in April 1940. The actions in Narvik, Bjørnefjell and Gratangen all support this conclusion, but I believe that the problem went down to the company level, at least in the case of Narvik and Bjørnefjell.

There is no evidence that General Fleischer came down hard on his subordinates for their failures and this may be because he was fully aware of his own mistakes. The reverse in the Gratang Valley did not affect the careers of his battalion commanders adversely. Bøckman and Hyldmo retired as colonels and Hunstad and Dahl as major generals.

NOTES

1 Despatch by Lord Cork, Section I, (6), as quoted in Derry, *The Campaign in Norway*, p. 147.

2 Kersaudy, *Norway*, p. 125.

3 Ziemke, *The German Northern Theater*, p. 90.

4 See, for example, L. E. Maund, *Assault from the Sea*, 29-30.

5 Report found in Despatch by Lord Cork, Appendix A, Section 6, as quoted in Derry, *The Campaign in Norway*, p. 151.

6 Bernhard von Lossberg, *Im Wehrmachtführungs-stab. Bericht eines Generalstabsoffiziers*

(Hamburg: H. H. Nölke, 1949), p. 70.

7 *3. Gebirgsdivision Kriegstagesbuch* (hereinafter *3GDKTB*), April 17, 1940.

8 Major Omdal, one lieutenant, one sergeant, and seven soldiers managed to escape on May 19. Two soldiers were caught trying to cross into Sweden. Major Omdal rejoined Norwegian forces further north on May 20 and took command of the 1/15th Infantry on May 24. The other seven apparently made good their escape to Sweden.

9 Olof Sundell, *9. april* (Stockholm: Sohlmans, 1949), p. 227.

10 *3GDKTB*, 04261130. These, and later specialists, were mostly camouflaged military personnel. A message from Group XXI (Nr. 298 dated May 22, 1940 at 1900 hours) reads, "40 machinegun and mortars specialists are leaving Berlin for Narvik via Sweden at 1000 hours on May 23. A further 80 specialists will follow in about 3 days. Appropriate attire will be worn for the purpose concealment."

11 Büchner, *Narvik*, p. 52.

12 Reports by Major General Dahl in 1946 and Captain Olav Løvland in 1941 as quoted in Sandvik, *Operasjonene*, vol. 1, p. 240.

13 Arne Dagfin Dahl, *Med Alta bataljon mot tyskerne* (Oslo: H. Aschehoug & Co., 1945), p. 60.

14 Ibid, p. 53. He writes, ". . . A determined advance by the hitherto un-noticed concentration of three rested enemy battalions in the Elvenes area would have encountered a precarious Group Windisch and could have opened the road to Bjerkvik. It is thanks to the determined attack by the 1/139, under the command of Major Stautner that this did not happen. Because of his surprise attack, the Norwegians were forced into a more careful tactical mode that was noticeable repeatedly until the end of the fighting and thereby he secured for Group Narvik a gain of decisive significance."

15 Hovland, *Fleischer*, p. 126.

10

CAMPAIGNS IN THE SOUTH

"... shocking inaction of the Navy at Trondheim, for which you
and your pusillanimous, self-satisfied, short-sighted naval advisers
must bear full responsibility."

APRIL 29, 1940 LETTER FROM ADMIRAL OF THE FLEET
SIR ROGER KEYES TO CHURCHILL.

In order to understand the unfolding operations in North Norway it is necessary
to examine the campaigns in eastern and central Norway. These operations and
the strategy dictating them had profound effects on events in the Narvik area
and they created ill feelings between the Norwegians and the Allies, feelings that
took on added importance as the focus shifted to Narvik. The operations in
western Norway are not included in this summary since they had little effect on
what transpired in the north.

The German Buildup

The German assault elements landing at various points on the Norwegian coast
were lightly armed and it was anticipated that they would need immediate
reinforcements, equipment, and supplies. These were provided for in the
operational plans.

In general, the German sea transport operations must be viewed as a
success. During the campaign, about 370 merchant ships brought in 107,581
troops, 109,400 tons of supplies, 20,339 vehicles, and 16,102 horses. While the
Germans lost 21 merchant ships, 15 escort vessels, and about 2,000 men, these
losses were judged acceptable from their point of view. The Allies lost six
submarines—four British, one French, and one Polish.

The Luftwaffe also made a significant contribution to the reinforcement
and supply effort. It carried out successfully the largest air transport operation
in military history up to that time. Five-hundred-eighty-two transport aircraft
flew 13,018 sorties. These brought in 29,280 troops and 2,376 tons of supplies.

The rapid German buildup in southern Norway contributed greatly to their success. The disrupted and cumbersome Norwegian mobilization machinery and the confused and hesitant efforts by the Allies were no match for the rapid pace at which German forces were reinforced and supplied.

The German Offensive Begins

The German offensive into the interior to link up with their beachheads in Trondheim and Bergen began in earnest on April 13.

The northward advance of General Richard Pellengahr's 196th Division was divided into two groups. Colonel Hermann Fischer, commander of the 340th Inf Regiment, commanded one group. His task was to advance north through Østerdal towards Trondheim. Colonel Ländle, commander of the 345th Inf Regiment, led the second group. His mission was to advance north through Gudbrandsdal along the east shore of Lake Mjøsa.

Two German battle groups drove northward towards Gjøvik and Dokka. Colonel Zanthier was commander of the 349th Inf Regiment, 181st Division, and his battle group consisted of two infantry battalions from the 349th Regiment as well as the motorized portion of the 1/324th Inf. Artillery and engineers supported this group, as they did the others. Its mission was to advance along the railroad towards Gjøvik. The forces on both sides of Mjøsa Lake were to converge in the Lillehammer area. Groups Ländle and Zanthier sent out side columns for mutual support and these became Group Nickelmann, under Colonel Helmuth Nickelmann commander of the 324th Inf Regiment, 163rd Division. It eventually consisted of three infantry battalions, artillery, engineers, a tank detachment, and two separate infantry companies. This group advanced along the west shore of Lake Mjøsa.

One, Group Adlhoch, under Colonel Xaver Adlhoch, commander of the 236th Inf Regiment, 69th Division, consisted of four infantry battalions and two separate companies as well as artillery, engineer and tank elements. Its mission was to advance north on both sides of Randsfjord to capture Fluberg, Dokka, and Bagn. From there, the group would press on in a northwest direction and establish contact with the German forces moving east from Bergen. Adlhoch decided to subdivide his forces on April 14.

Group Adlhoch consisted of two infantry battalions and an engineer company. This group advanced north along the east shore of Randsfjord towards Fluberg and Dokka. Major Daubert had command of two battalions for an advance towards Bagn along Sperillen Lake. Group Ritzmann consisted of one infantry battalion with supporting elements. It advanced in the direction of Gulsvik. The 163rd Division also had smaller groups operating to the west and southwest with the mission of securing the coastal areas between Oslo and Kristiansand and capturing the remaining Norwegian mobilization centers in that part of the country.

The Norwegian forces contesting the German advance were primarily elements of four regiments of the 2nd Division. The forces to the east of Lake Mjøsa consisted of the Kongsvinger Battalion, Colonel Hiorth's 5th Inf Regiment, and Colonel Jørgen Jensen's 2nd Cavalry Regiment. Colonel T. H. Dahl's 4th Inf Regiment and Colonel Carl Mork's 6th Inf Regiment covered the area between Lake Mjøsa and Randsfjord. Colonel Østbye's 4th Field Brigade, redeploying from western Norway, was moving into the area northwest of Sperillen Lake.

The Germans encountered stiff resistance as they reached the 2nd Division's defense line south of Mjøsa, Randsfjord, and Sperillen. Fighting was heavy and the Germans sustained considerable losses. As they moved into the interior, they also encountered deep snow that made movement off the roads very difficult. Norwegian defenses fell into a pattern that would characterize the rest of the campaign in central Norway. They were based on a series of barricades and cuts in lines of communications, supported by flanking fire that made German clearing actions difficult. The Germans adapted quickly to the conditions confronting them and their tactics were quite effective. They organized their columns into combined arms teams of infantry, artillery, engineers, and armor. These attempted to break the Norwegian lines under heavy supporting fires while ski troops worked around the defenders' flanks.

The various attacking columns operated in near flawless cooperation. When the advance in one sector reached a point where it was behind Norwegian defenders in the next sector, smaller groups would peel off from the more advanced column. These became threats to Norwegian flanks and rear, often forcing precipitous withdrawals. The innovative tactics and German superiority in artillery, tanks, and complete dominance in the air soon made themselves felt. The Norwegians had no tanks, no effective antitank weapons, and no air support.

Group Fischer captured Kongsvinger on April 16 and turned north to the opening of Østerdal. It had to fight hard as it made its way northward against stubborn Norwegian resistance. Group Ländle advanced along the east side of Lake Mjøsa while the Norwegian troops withdrew slowly to a strong defensive position at Strandlykkja where the German attack was stopped temporarily. There were no obvious ways to turn the Norwegian flanks. Lake Mjøsa was partially covered with ice and the Germans gambled that it was thick enough to send a force across the southern end from the west shore, threatening the Norwegian right flank and rear. One infantry battalion was sent across the lake and the operation was successful. The Norwegians made a hasty retreat towards Hamar, which fell to the Germans on April 18.

This event had far-reaching consequences. The Germans sent a group east towards Elverum that made rapid progress and linked up with Group Fischer on April 20. Colonel Hiorth's forces in Østerdal found its right flank and rear exposed by the German group advancing from Hamar and was forced to withdraw. The last railroad connection to Sweden was severed. The Hamar broadcasting facilities, through which the Norwegian Government had communicated with the occupied areas, were captured.

General Pellenghar began a relentless pursuit of the Norwegian forces withdrawing north from Hamar. He took personal command of the offensive in Gudbrandsdal as troops from the 163rd Division, advancing north along the west shore of Lake Mjøsa, came under his command. The Norwegians succeeded in withdrawing to Lundehøgda on April 18 and 19.

The German advance west of Mjøsa also met stubborn resistance in the early days of the offensive. Group Zanthier's advance encountered an ad hoc Norwegian unit at Hakadal and the fight raged all night of April 14–15. The Norwegians withdrew in the morning. The Germans encountered a better-prepared defense near Bjørgeseter (about 25 kilometers southeast of Brandbu) the following day. The first German attack was repulsed. The German commander wanted to wait for more artillery before resuming the attack but he was overruled by the division commander. The second attack also failed after heavy German losses, mostly caused by Norwegian ski troops operating against the German flanks.

Group Adlhoch started its attack at dawn on April 15 with two battalions along the road that led north from Hønefoss. The attack was stopped by the 1/5th Inf after heavy fighting. Colonel Adlhoch's report to the division that evening reads in part: "Both battalions have suffered heavy losses. The position is unfavorable since the enemy dominates the terrain with their heavy weapons. Have committed the last regimental reserve. The attack will be continued in the morning."[1] The message went on to request artillery, air, and tank support. Six tanks and some mountain troops were provided overnight.

The Norwegian 1/5th was relieved by the 2/5th during the night. The German attack resumed on April 16 after a 30-minute mortar bombardment. The two battalions again attacked along the road but this time they had tank support. The Norwegians, with two companies forward, had no effective weapons against tanks and these were able to drive into the Norwegian positions. The right flank company was able to disengage before it was overrun but was overwhelmed in its new positions 500 meters further back. At that point, the position of the left flank company became untenable. Tanks appeared in its rear and forced a withdrawal. The unit was scattered and only a few soldiers reached friendly lines. A counterattack by the battalion reserve failed. The battalion commander was killed and the unit was scattered. The destruction of the 2/5th Infantry made the positions of other units opposing Group Zanthier untenable and forced a general withdrawal.

Group Adlhoch captured Fluberg on April 19. One battalion turned east on April 20, along the road to Gjøvik. Group Zanthier advanced north through the middle of the area between Randsfjord and Lake Mjøsa and captured Tobru, about halfway between Fluberg and Gjøvik. Group Nickelmann continued along the west shore of Lake Mjøsa and captured Gjøvik on April 19. One battalion continued north in the direction of Vingnes the next day.

The Germans were stopped temporarily at Bråstad, about six kilometers north of Gjøvik. Heavy fighting took place from Bråstad westward on April 20 and 21. Several Norwegian units were isolated, but the Germans were held in check by committing every available reserve, including staff and support personnel. Colonel Dahl, who commanded Norwegian forces between Lake Mjøsa and Randsfjord, decided to retire to new defensive positions near Fåberg on April 21.

In the area between Sperillen Lake and Randsfjord, Major Daubert's forces made progress against the reserve battalion of the 6th Inf Regiment after capturing Hallingby at the southern end of Sperillen on April 14. Bjørnevika, near the northern end of the lake, was captured on April 16. Group Daubert reached the vicinity of Bagn on April 18. There followed three days of hard fighting with Norwegian forces, reinforced by units from the 4th Field Brigade that had arrived in the area to the west of Bagn.

The reserve battalion of the Norwegian 6th Inf had marched and fought for nine days and the 1/10th of the 4th Brigade relieved it on April 18. The Norwegians overwhelmed a German company on April 21 after heavy fighting. The Germans lost 13 killed, 19 wounded, and 65 prisoners. Major Daubert concluded on April 20 that his two battalions could not break Norwegian resistance and he withdrew his forces to Hønefoss where they arrived in the evening of April 21. From there they joined Group Adlhoch in the Fluberg area.

The Failed German Airborne Assault on Dombås

The Germans realized soon after their landings that the link-up with other bridgeheads in south and central Norway would not be as easy and quick as they had hoped. Von Falkenhorst was frustrated at the inability of his two divisions to trap and destroy major elements of the 2nd Norwegian Division. Rumors of planned Allied landings at Åndalsnes and Namsos reached the Germans on April 13. To speed the link-up with the forces in Trondheim and trap Norwegian units in Gudbrandsdal, the Germans attempted an airborne operation in the Norwegian rear at Dombås. This was an important road and railroad junction, where the routes from Oslo to Trondheim intersected with those leading west to Åndalsnes.

The airborne operation was launched on April 14 in haste, without adequate intelligence, no time for planning, in unfavorable weather, and with inadequate forces. Fifteen German aircraft carried the reinforced Co 1, 1st Airborne Regiment (185 men). The company commander had the only map of the Dombås area, which was at a scale of 1:100,000. Dombås is located in the mountains but the German paratroopers had no winter or camouflage clothing. The soldiers had provisions for only three days and ammunition was limited to what they carried. The element of surprise was lost when one aircraft was shot down near Lillehammer by Norwegian antiaircraft fire.

The German aircraft had little time to find suitable drop zones since they had to return to Oslo before dark and because they were receiving heavy fire from Norwegian forces. The paratroopers were dropped in six different locations over a 30-kilometer area around Dombås. Not a single platoon was able to assemble all its personnel. The return of the German aircraft turned into a catastrophe. Only seven aircraft returned to Oslo. The rest were shot down or forced to make emergency landings as they ran out of fuel.

Unfortunately for the Germans, the operation took place near the location of the 2/11th Inf. The Norwegians had moved this unit to Dombås to take part in the planned Allied operation against Trondheim. The German commander, Lieutenant Herbert Schmidt, assembled 63 paratroopers who entrenched themselves south of Dombås. The rest were killed, captured, or missing. Schmidt's men managed to block the road and railroad from Oslo to Trondheim for five days. They repelled two Norwegian attacks before the badly wounded Schmidt surrendered on April 19 when his men ran out of ammunition and supplies. Göring had refused to reinforce the paratroopers despite urgent requests. He was incensed because a court martial was ordered for one of his top generals in Norway for having launched the poorly planned and ill-prepared operation. The charges were eventually dropped due to Göring's intervention.

While the Dombås operation was a German failure, it had a profound psychological effect on Norwegian and Allied commanders. A number of units that could have been used more productively in other tasks were employed to guard against the threat posed by this new tactical innovation.

Still hoping for an early link-up with forces in Trondheim, von Falkenhorst planned a second airborne operation on April 16 in order to bypass the Norwegian defenses in the Lake Mjøsa area. An infantry battalion and an airborne company were to land on the ice at the northern end of Lake Mjøsa, capture Lillehammer, and advance to Dombås. The operation was cancelled after the Luftwaffe refused to participate because of "technical difficulties."[2]

Operation *Hammer* Is Abandoned

The MCC decided on April 13 to make Trondheim the priority objective in central Norway while at the same time keeping Narvik as a high priority. The plan called for attacks from north and south in conjunction with a direct attack in the fjord. Two Canadian battalions would land near Agdenes and capture the coastal batteries. The 15th Infantry Brigade (withdrawn from the 5th Division in France) would land at the village of Hell, near Værnes Airfield, on April 22. The 147th Brigade constituted the reserve for the operation. The 15th Brigade (*Hammerforce*) would link up with British and French forces moving south from Namsos (*Mauriceforce*). The 148th Brigade would land at Åndalsnes (*Sickleforce*) and move to Dombås. It had a dual mission. First, by threatening Trondheim from the south it was hoped that German forces would be drawn from that city at the same time as the direct attack was carried out. Second, the 148th would be in a position to assist the Norwegians in the south. The overall Allied operation against Trondheim, codenamed *Hammer*, was to be commanded by Major General F. E. Hotblack.

Problems plagued the planned operation from the start. General Hotblack suffered a heart attack in London on April 17. The commander of the 15th Brigade, Brigadier General Berney-Ficklin, was promoted and designated as Hotblack's replacement. Simultaneously, the main attack in Trondheimfjord was delayed until April 24. Berney-Ficklin and most of his staff were injured in an airplane crash at Scapa Flow on April 19. Major General Paget took Berney-Ficklin's place but the attack in Trondheimfjord was cancelled by the end of the day.

The British naval staff believed that the shore batteries at the fjord entrance could be dealt with easily. Admiral Forbes was informed about the planned operation on April 14 and asked for his opinion. Forbes warned the Admiralty that they should expect heavy losses in ships and troops from German air attacks. Churchill asked him to reconsider. Forbes replied that he saw no serious difficulties if, among other things, he was given sufficient forces, the troops were carried on warships, and he was given a large number of landing craft. Forbes was surely aware that there were only ten landing craft in Great Britain.[3]

The Joint Planning Committee (JPC), which had viewed Trondheim as the key to Allied operations in Norway, prepared a paper on April 15 at the request of the chiefs of staff. It argued against a direct attack and recommended that the main efforts to capture Trondheim be made by the forces landed at Namsos and Åndalsnes. The JPC met all day on April 16 and produced a new version of the paper. The JCP members now concluded that Trondheim, if recaptured, could not be held because of German air power.

The chiefs of staff initially overruled the JCP but on April 19, they advised the MCC against a direct attack on Trondheim. Admiral Forbes' views were now known and these weighed heavily on the JPC. There can be no doubt that the only serious objection to the operation was the exposure of the Home Fleet to German air power. However, the potential rewards of a direct attack were great and it is not obvious why the British concluded that the danger to the navy in an attack on Trondheim, after seizing the shore batteries, was greater than the danger faced in the waters around Namsos and Åndalsnes. The air staff was against all operations in Norway. They felt that any ground operations in that country were doomed to fail unless they had adequate air support and they viewed the diversion of air assets from France and Britain as an unjustified squandering of precious resources.

The effectual abandonment of the operation against Trondheim doomed operations in southern and central Norway to failure. Those who maintain that Ruge was responsible for the abandonment of *Hammer* because he diverted the forces intended as the southern pincer to shore up the front to the south, fail to consider the discussions in Great Britain that led to its abandonment. The operations from Namsos and Åndalsnes were designed to draw German forces away from Trondheim, thereby facilitating the quick capture of the city and Værnes Airfield by a direct attack. The two pincer movements lost their rationale when the direct attack was abandoned. The direct approach was abandoned *before* Ruge requested that the forces landed in Åndalsnes be used in the south.

This is demonstrated by the order Brigadier Morgan received from General Ironside while at sea on April 17 (see later in this chapter).

There was virtually no chance that the Allies would be able to cover the long distances from the landing sites at Namsos and Åndalsnes to Trondheim through a snow-covered landscape against eight German infantry battalions. If the two battalions of the 148th Brigade had turned north at Dombås, they would most likely have been trapped by the northward German advance, which would have cut them off from their base at Åndalsnes.

The Second Crisis in the German High Command

The Allied landings in central Norway that began on April 14, the slow progress of the German drives from Oslo, and the failure to come up with a political solution acceptable to the Norwegians threw the German leadership into a second command crisis. For his failure, Ambassador Bräuer was recalled on April 17 and retired from the diplomatic service. Göring painted a picture of widespread guerrilla warfare in Norway, argued for strong measures against the population, and complained that the navy was not doing its part in transporting troops to Norway. A close friend of Göring, Josef Terboven, came to Berlin on April 19 and Hitler appointed him Reich Commissioner in Norway.

The OKW wanted to avoid repressions against the civilian population that could bring on an extended campaign against the Norwegians. Keitel and Jodl were interested in limiting Terboven's powers and sharply delineating von Falkenhorst and Terboven's respective spheres of authority. This led to an argument between Hitler and Keitel on April 19 that became so heated that Keitel stomped out of the room. Jodl notes in his diary, "We are again confronted with complete chaos in the command system. Hitler insists on issuing orders on every detail; any coordinated effort within the existing military command structure is impossible." The military's worries about the delineation of authority between von Falkenhorst and Terboven continued, as did worries that the latter could take actions that would stiffen Norwegian resistance. Jodl writes on April 20 that, "We must do nothing to cause the Norwegians to offer passive, still less active resistance. That would simply be to play the game of the English … "

The OKW planned to transfer the 11th Motorized Brigade to Norway from Denmark. Hitler cancelled the transfer of the 11th Brigade on April 21 and instead ordered the 2nd Mountain Division to Norway. He also planned to send the 1st Mountain Division but the transfer of the latter was cancelled when a linkup with the forces in Trondheim was achieved.

Still very apprehensive about the forces in Trondheim, Hitler proposed on April 22 to send a division to that city using the two ocean liners *Bremen* and *Europa*. Raeder regarded this as completely out of the question. The whole fleet would be required to escort the two ships and the likely outcome would be the loss of the ocean liners, the fleet, and the division. Raeder's arguments convinced Hitler to give up on the idea. Instead, he directed the employment of all means to open the land route between Oslo and Trondheim. The Germans had established an air-bridge from Oslo to Trondheim on April 14. In addition to needed supplies, the airlift brought one engineer and five infantry battalions to Trondheim by April 20.

The British Arrive

By April 20, the Germans had reached the approximate line between Rena and Dokka where General Ruge planned to mount his main defense. The situation, however, was not to the general's liking. The delaying actions had not been as effective as hoped and had failed to inflict heavy losses on the attacker or win the necessary time to organize a proper defense. However, they provided the delay necessary for Allied assistance to arrive. This assistance, however, was inadequate, not well planned, and carried out hesitantly.

The fighting that took place in a large number of hard-fought small-scale delaying actions in eastern Norway is largely ignored in the English literature. While the Germans suffered higher numbers of killed and wounded than the Norwegians, the latter had far more troops captured and missing. This was primarily due to German use of tanks and their air dominance. German armor quickly penetrated and overwhelmed Norwegian defensive positions before an orderly withdrawal was possible. The scattered defenders were captured, had great difficulties rejoining their units, or failed to do so. Ruge's forces were badly depleted, exhausted, and demoralized by their helplessness against German armor and air power.

Ruge's greatest disappointment had to do with the lack of Allied assistance. His operational directive of April 15 assumed quick and effective Allied assistance and stated as much at the outset. This assumption, in turn, was based on the personal promise received from the British Prime Minister on April 14. This promise was not kept. Furthermore, the Allies never informed him where they intended to land and what their plans were. He would have been far more dismayed if he had known the true state of Allied confusion and lack of preparedness.

The "great strength" that Chamberlain had promised turned out to be about 1,000 troops from the 148th Territorial Brigade, commanded by Brigadier General Morgan. This brigade consisted of two battalions, the 1/5th Leicestershire and the 1/8th Sherwood Foresters. It was embarked on two cruisers destined for Stavanger on April 6. The troops were offloaded in a hurry on April 7 and lost much of their equipment in the process.

On April 13, the brigade was ordered to Namsos and was already embarked on the transport *Orion* in the evening of April 16 when new orders arrived. The 146th Brigade was now underway to Namsos and the 148th was ordered to disembark from *Orion*, board five warships, and proceed to Åndalsnes. The order to disembark was carried out at night in great confusion. Colonel Dudley Clarke, who took part in the operation, describes the scene:[4]

> In the original haste to get off to a quick start, goods of every kind had been stowed in the holds in the order in which they arrived, with each following consignment piled in on top. Now reserves of food and ammunition were mixed with unit equipment and skis for the Norwegians; bicycles and sappers' tools lay with medical provisions, while such things as the long-range wireless equipment as often as not was split between two holds. There was never a chance of sorting this out in the dark and getting it into the right ships in time, so the plan was being adopted of skimming the top layers from every hold and loading them in turn into each warship as she came alongside.

The results were simply disastrous for this poorly trained militia force. One-half of the Leicestershire battalion and other essential units were left behind because of space limitation. These troops, about 600 men, followed two days later and arrived in Åndalsnes on April 21. When the warships reached open sea, it was realized that most of the brigade's communications equipment, mortar ammunition, vehicles, as well as essential antiaircraft equipment were left behind. There was no artillery and no provisions for air support. When the maps were unfolded, they were all for the Namsos area.

Morgan's operational orders were equally confusing. His instructions dated April 16 read, "Your role to land Aandalsnes area secure Dombaas then operate northwards and take offensive action against Germans in Trondheim area."[5] If this was not ambitious enough, Morgan received additional orders from Ironside while en route to Norway. The emphasis seemed to have switched from an offensive to a defensive role and required him to face south as well as north. More baffling, Morgan was ordered to contact the Norwegian high command "and avoid isolating Norwegian forces operating towards Oslo."[6] Morgan's orders were now contradictory, ambiguous, and unrealistic.

Ruge was forced to change his earlier strategic plan. He still considered the capture of Trondheim the highest priority, but forces operating against that city from the south would find their rear threatened and their line of communication to Åndalsnes cut if Norwegian defenses in the south collapsed. He considered it necessary to abandon the southern pincer against Trondheim in order to shore up the defenses in the south. King-Salter and Bertrand Vigne agreed with his assessment when they met Brigadier Morgan at Dombås in the afternoon of April 19. They described the situation in the south and pressed Morgan to help prevent a collapse of Norwegian resistance. King-Salter pointed out that Ruge had received a message from the War Office giving him authority to call on British forces. Morgan felt that he had to refer the issue to London since Allied operations that far south were not envisaged. In the meantime, he accompanied the attachés to meet General Ruge around midnight.

After expressing his displeasure at not being informed about Allied plans and disappointment at the size and composition of the British force, Ruge came right to the point. He expected all troops in Norway, no matter what nationality, to conform to his strategy, which he briefly explained. Morgan promised to give whatever help he could wherever needed. Ruge insisted that he needed the two British battalions in the area south of Lillehammer to bolster the Norwegian forces, consisting of two infantry battalions and a battery of artillery on east side of Lake Mjøsa under General Hvinden-Haug and two reduced battalions and a number of improvised units on the west side under Colonel Dahl.

Morgan ordered his units at Dombås to Lillehammer and this decision was endorsed by Ironside on April 20. Since *Hammer* has been cancelled the previous day, there was no longer an urgent need for Morgan's troops to move north. The British planners had reached the conclusion that Trondheim could not be held, even if captured, without a significant increase in the resources the Allies had made available. The dispatch of the best troops to Narvik contributed to this state of affairs.

Ruge accompanied Morgan to the railroad station at about 0300 hours on April 20 to greet the British troops. One of Ruge's officers, Lieutenant Colonel (later Major General) Roscher-Nielsen, remembers the disappointment: "These were not regular troops ... and we were alarmed to see that they were only armed with rifles and light machineguns ... No antiaircraft guns, no heavy antitank weapons, no artillery, no vehicles ... "[7]

Morgan not only agreed to place the 148th Brigade under Norwegian command, he allowed the two battalions to be spread out among Norwegian units. This was an unorthodox step and the issue was raised at a conference at midday on April 20. It was a tense meeting because Ruge was angered by a suggestion from the British that there was an intelligence leak at his headquarters. According to Derry, Ruge presented a written document demanding that all British units comply with his orders or he would resign.

King-Salter had decoded a message from Ironside to Ruge less than two hours earlier. This message told Ruge that Morgan had instructions to cooperate but would not come under Ruge's command. In this delicate situation, King-Salter decided to delay the message to Ruge. The conference ended on a positive note with Morgan promising cooperation and Ruge stating that he would try to hold the front near Lillehammer until Trondheim had fallen. His new allies had failed to tell him that the attack on Trondheim had been cancelled a day earlier.

Ruge's decision to spread the British units among the Norwegian troops would be unwise under normal circumstances, but these were far from normal. After seeing that the British troops were not regulars and lacked all types of necessary weapons and equipment, Ruge was probably uneasy about their ability to hold a major sector against the Germans. The British infantrymen, with limited training, found themselves in completely unfamiliar surroundings, waist-deep in snow, and without equipment for winter warfare. They had no maps of the area, no artillery, no radio communications, no means of transport, and no supply organization. They relied on Norwegians for support in these areas. It was also hoped that the appearance of British troops in the major units would serve to stiffen Norwegian resolve and boost their morale. In the end, it had the opposite effect.

The German Breakthrough

A half battalion of Foresters, commanded by Major Roberts, was attached to Task Force Dahl with the mission of protecting its right flank. Lieutenant Colonel Ford, with the rest of the Foresters, was positioned behind the Torkilsen Battalion at Lundehøgda on the east side of Lake Mjøsa. Two companies of the Leicester's, commanded by Lieutenant Colonel Garman, were given a reserve mission behind the 2nd Cavalry Regiment near Åsmarka.

Major Roberts' troops were recalled from their flank security mission and ordered to Biri. The Norwegian front in that area, under attack from battle groups Adlholch, Zanthier, and Nickelmann, was in danger of collapsing after hard fighting, including several Norwegian counterattacks. Colonel Dahl decided on April 21 to pull his line back to the area near Fåberg since his left flank was exposed after the Germans broke through Norwegian lines east of Lake Mjøsa. The withdrawal went well, covered by the two companies of Foresters and a Norwegian ski company and engineers. The covering force had difficulties extracting. It sustained a number of casualties, and many troops became separated from their units.

There were approximately 2,000 Norwegian soldiers contesting the German advance to the east of Lake Mjøsa but they were exhausted after ten days of continuous delaying actions. The 7-kilometer long Norwegian front was held by the Torkilsen Bn on the right with an approximate strength of 575. The left was held by units of the 2nd Cavalry Regiment. The Germans opened their attack on April 20 with one infantry battalion and a machinegun battalion along the road and railroad against the Norwegian positions on Lundehøgda, and one infantry battalion along the Moelv-Arneberg-Lillehammer road against the 2nd Cavalry Regiment.

The German attacks on the Norwegian positions at Lundehøgda were repelled all day but part of the defending force withdrew in the evening to Biskopåsen, about four kilometers behind the line. A British mortar section and two light antitank squads were sent forward to strengthen the Norwegian line. The Germans resumed their attack on April 21, with heavy artillery, mortar, and air support. The British mortars were silenced quickly. This was the first ground action between German and British forces in World War II. The Norwegian lines held until after 1400 hours when the right flank was driven back. The Norwegians counterattacked but the commander was badly wounded, the executive officer was killed, and the Germans were able to roll up the Norwegian positions. Despite problems in disengaging, the Norwegians eventually brought most forces to Biskopåsen but that position was abandoned in the evening. More than half of the Torkilsen Bn was captured or missing during the disengagement and withdrawal. By the end of the second day of fighting, it consisted of only 216 men.

A motorized machinegun company from the 2nd Cavalry Regiment held the German attack in check until noon on the 21st when it withdrew to the main positions at Arneberg. The Germans quickly attacked this position and the pressure increased during the afternoon. The 2nd Cavalry Regiment retreated during the evening to Fåberg. Lieutenant Colonel Garman's two companies followed. Between 60 and 80 Norwegians were missing after the withdrawal. Some of these later rejoined their regiment.

The two British half-battalions on the east side of Lake Mjøsa withdrew during the night, mostly on foot in deep snow because some of the Norwegian trucks did not show up. One group of six officers and 50 men was captured by the Germans. The German losses in the two-day attack were 35 killed and 50 critically wounded.

On the evening of April 18, Task Force Hiorth in Østerdal withdrew from Elverum to the Åsta-Rena area for reorganization, but this was hampered by relentless attacks by the Luftwaffe on the following day, which resulted in near destruction of the village of Rena. Group Fischer attacked Åsta on April 21. They broke into the Norwegian positions in the afternoon after heavy fighting and there were no reserves left for a counterattack. The Norwegians managed to withdraw but one company on the left flank was lost in the process. A delaying position was organized at Rena and the forward troops withdrew through this position during the night and organized in new positions at Deset and Kroken.

The British Defeat at Balberskamp

German forces were regrouped on April 21, primarily because of the threat posed by the Norwegian 4th Field Brigade that had crossed the mountains from the west. The northward advance of the 163rd Division was terminated and it was turned westward to protect the German left flank. Group Zanthier, west of Lake Mjøsa, which had been part of the 163rd Division, came under the command of the 196th Division when it reached the northern end of that lake. Group Nickelmann's mission was limited to clearing actions. The reinforced 196th Division, with one column in Gudbrandsdal and another in Østerdal, was tasked to link up with the forces in Trondheim.

The strength of Norwegian forces withdrawing from Lundehøgda and Åsmarka had fallen to only 1,400 men. General Hvinden-Haug insisted that they needed rest and reorganization before they could again take part in operations. General Ruge reluctantly agreed since the Norwegian units were so reduced in strength that they were almost combat ineffective. He had no choice but to ask General Morgan to use his troops to buy sorely needed time to rest and reorganize the Norwegian remnants. The Torkilsen Bn was assembled near Fåberg and the 2nd Cavalry Regiment in the Øyer area, about 12 kilometers north of Fåberg.

After their difficult retreat, the four British companies under Lieutenant Colonels Ford and Garman, regrouped and decided to make a stand at the southern end of the defile at Balberskamp. The British formed their traditional two lines, with the two companies of Foresters in front and the Leicesters in the second line. The terrain rises steeply from the river east of Fåberg to the top of Balberskamp, a height of about 2,000 feet. This was the first time the British faced the Germans alone. They worried about their left flank since they had great difficulties moving a security force up the steep western side of Balberskamp. Morgan requested some ski troops from Ruge to protect the flank but none were available. The Germans were not about to give the British any respite. The four British companies came under intense mortar fire and air attack as they began occupying their defensive positions. With British attention fixed on the German approach along the road from Lillehammer, the Germans sent ski troops around and over Balberskamp, thus turning the British left flank.

The British made a rapid and disorganized withdrawal to escape the trap. Part of the German encirclement force overran the British headquarters with a surprise attack. Among the papers captured by the Germans were documents dealing with Allied plans to occupy Norwegian cities before April 9. It has never been explained what such documents were doing at a forward tactical headquarters. These documents, frequently referred to by Hitler, were used effectively by the Germans to justify their attack on Norway.

The two Forrester companies apparently did not receive the order to withdraw and most ended up surrendering to the Germans. The retreating British were subjected to continual attacks from the air, by tanks, and by armored reconnaissance vehicles. They abandoned most of their supplies along with 25 machineguns and 15 antitank rifles.[8]

General Hvinden-Haug described the loss of the Balberskamp defile as the "first serious defeat of the war," and a loss that resulted in severe consequences for Norwegian units.[9] This is an unfair statement. If he deemed the Balberskamp position so important, its defense should not have been left in the hands of untried troops unfamiliar with the terrain and unable to maneuver off the roads. He should have provided ski units to secure the British flank despite his troops' exhaustion after 12 days of continuous fighting.

The British and Norwegian Defeat at Tretten

The 148th Brigade stopped temporarily at Øyer, about ten kilometers north of Balberskamp. Here, it was joined by the two companies of Leicesters previously left behind in Great Britain. The British came under heavy enemy fire and abandoned their positions by 1900 hours on April 22. A new delaying position at Tolstad, another five kilometers further north, was held until noon the following day when the retreat continued for another five kilometers to Tretten. Here, the British were joined by Major Roberts' two companies of Foresters, earlier attached to TF Dahl.

The 148th Brigade began its final two days of existence as a fighting force. The British intended to stand at Tretten and Morgan insisted on Norwegian troops to secure their left flank. Ruge directed the 2nd Cavalry Regiment to make troops available for this purpose and three under-strength companies were sent forward and placed under Morgan's command. The combined force confronting the advancing Germans consisted of eight British and three Norwegian companies, 700 and 300 troops respectively.

General Ruge reportedly considered it essential to hold Tretten for at least one full day. Other than winning time for reorganizing his forces north of Tretten, it is not clear why holding the place for the specified time was important. Some writers contend that Ruge had decided to bring TF Dahl into Gudbrandsdal and Tretten was the last crossing point over the Lågen River for over 50 kilometers.[10]

While Ruge had toyed with this idea, he had decided to leave Dahl on the west side of the river to present a flank threat to the Germans. While TF Dahl was under the operational control of General Hvinden-Haug in Gudbrandsdal, on April 23 Ruge directed that it stay on the west side of Lågen and later make its way either to the 4th Field Brigade in Valdres or rejoin the 2nd Division further north.[11] Therefore, there was no reason to hold the bridge for the use of TF Dahl. Norwegian engineers had in fact prepared it for destruction. This would prevent the Germans from using it to strike at TF Dahl's rear.

The British established a defense in depth with the equivalent of six companies near the village of Rindheim. The forward line consisted of two companies of Foresters with one company of Leicesters higher up the hillside. The Foresters occupied prepared positions. The three under-strength Norwegian dragoon companies were placed behind the British left flank on a plateau formed by the saddle between Hills 616 and 526. There were no prepared positions for the Leicester company and the dragoons, and their visibility was severely reduced in the heavily wooded terrain. A company of Foresters was in reserve along the road leading to Tretten and another company moved to the west side of Lågen. The rest of the Leicesters formed the second British line.

The British expected that the main German effort would be directed at their mountainous left flank so they placed a company of Leicesters and the Norwegian dragoons in this area. The Germans did not attack as the British expected. At about 1300 hours, their main attack, led by tanks, commenced along the road against the two Forester companies, with a secondary effort along the west side of the river. The British antitank rifles proved ineffective against the tanks. The reserve company was committed, but within one hour the British defenses disintegrated and the Germans continued towards Tretten.

The Norwegian dragoons, their route of withdrawal threatened by the German breach of the British line, started a retreat to Tretten. Fifteen to 20 British officers and NCOs offered to serve as a delaying force and most were killed or captured. The German advance was so rapid that the dragoons found their line of retreat cut. After a short engagement, the dragoons withdrew into the mountains and, after failing to reach friendly lines, were demobilized.

The fighting had now reached Tretten. The German force advancing on the west side of the river was able to get guns into position where they could fire on the bridge and the village. Tretten and the bridge were held until early evening. In the confused withdrawal of British forces west of Lågen, the lines connecting the prepared charges were disconnected and the Norwegian engineers, caught up in the panicky withdrawal, did not stay around to reconnect the charges. The Germans captured the bridge intact. A rear guard held a final position about two kilometers north of the village until 2130 hours. The remnants of the brigade dispersed and, using trucks and busses, they headed for Heidal. A Danish officer, a volunteer in the Winter War and now serving as a volunteer in the Norwegian forces, gives a rather uncomplimentary description of the British retreat to Heidal:

> Truck after truck of hysterical British soldiers drove past me. When I reached Fåvang, there was wild confusion on the road. British officers had managed to stop the trucks and tried unsuccessfully to restore order. They refused to follow orders and drove on, yelling and screaming. It had a depressing effect on the Norwegian soldiers who witnessed the behavior.[12]

British authors describe Tretten as an unmitigated disaster. Derry writes that the brigade, after regrouping, was reduced to nine officers and 300 men. A few dozen survivors managed to reach Sweden or the coast in the days that followed.

The Germans captured about 250 British soldiers, including Lieutenant Colonel Ford and a severely wounded Lieutenant Colonel King-Salter, the British Military Attaché.

Moulton blames the Norwegians for the defeat at Tretten. He claims that the confusion over the withdrawal of TF Dahl from Gausdal was the immediate cause for the defeat. This conclusion is highly questionable and shows reliance on British accounts, to the exclusion of Norwegian and German sources. It is not obvious that the withdrawal of TF Dahl from Gausdal would have altered the outcome. This was the fourth action by the 148th Brigade and it is extremely doubtful that the outcome would have been any different if it had engaged the Germans further north. The fault lies with the British authorities who rushed an untrained and poorly equipped militia force into the snow-clad mountains of eastern Norway without air support, artillery, or effective antitank weapons while their best troops sat on their hands in the Narvik area.

Norwegian Delaying Actions at Tromsa and Vinstra

Encouraged by their success against the British at Tretten, General von Falkenhorst altered the mission of the 196th Division. Group Fischer was put under von Falkenhorst's direct command with the mission of linking up with German forces moving south from Trondheim. The rest of the division was ordered to conduct a relentless pursuit in Gudbrandsdal towards Åndalsnes, to destroy or capture the British forces in central Norway.

The Norwegian 11th Infantry Regiment carried out a near normal mobilization in the Møre and Romsdal Province and two line battalions were brought to the Dombås area to join the British in their southern drive to Trondheim. After the defeat at Tretten, the regiment was moved into Gudbrandsdal and the 1st Bn was placed under the command of Major Torkildsen near Tromsa, about ten kilometers north of Tretten. These troops witnessed the British retreat, and it certainly had a negative effect on their morale. If Ruge had known that operation *Hammer* was cancelled, he may have moved the 11th Regiment into Gudbrandsdal earlier.

The Germans attacked the 1/11th Inf with tanks and infantry in the morning of April 24. With the arrival of additional armor and seeing how helpless the Norwegians and British were against this weapon, the Germans changed their tactics. Rather than immediately initiating flanking maneuvers, they made frontal attacks led by armor. This tactic was successful at Tretten and at Tromsa. While their armor broke into the positions at Tromsa, the

Norwegians succeeded in making an orderly withdrawal to another delaying position. The Germans followed and broke through the Norwegian lines with tanks that same afternoon. A number of Norwegians were driven into the mountains. The battalion, reduced to 550 troops, withdrew to an assembly area north of Otta, about 40 kilometers to the north. The Torkildsen Battalion was not attacked and managed to withdraw to Ringebu (15 kilometers to the north) in the evening but only after losing 50 men, who were cut off by the Germans.

Meanwhile, the 2/11th Inf had occupied a hasty delaying position north of Vinstra, about 12 kilometers from Ringebu. The roadblocks were held open for retreating units but the Germans were in such hot pursuit that it was not possible to close them after the last retreating units came through late on April 24. The German armor drove through the Norwegian frontlines, driving some of the defenders into the mountains. The Norwegian reserves managed, with great difficulty, to stop the Germans, who withdrew to Vinstra for the night. That same night the Norwegians were ordered withdrawn to Otta. The 2/11th was badly mauled. It had lost one infantry company, most of the machinegun company, and another infantry company had lost 30 men. The 2nd Cavalry Regiment was reduced to two squadrons. German armor and air power were major factors in the inability of the Norwegians and British to halt the relentless German pursuit, a pursuit that repeatedly scattered and isolated the defenders.

British Reinforcements

Lieutenant General H. R. C. Massy was appointed commander of all British forces in Norway, except those in the Narvik area, on April 20, but he never left London. Major General P. G. T. Paget was appointed commander of forces operating in southern Norway on April 20, now that this was about to become a multi-brigade operation with the diversion of the 15th Brigade to Åndalsnes from its original mission against Trondheim. Brigadier General H. E. F. Smyth commanded the 15th Brigade and this unit began landing in Åndalsnes and Molde from cruisers and destroyers on April 23. The 15th Brigade, unlike the 148th, consisted of regular soldiers, withdrawn from the western front with great secrecy. The original plan called for this brigade to enter Østerdal and assist TF Hiorth. However, the disaster at Tretten made it necessary to move the brigade into Gudbrandsdal to shore up the crumbling defense there.

The British tried to remedy their mistake in not providing air support. They were reluctant to bring aircraft carriers sufficiently close to the coast to be effective and decided to counter the German air threat by bringing in fighter aircraft and more antiaircraft guns. However, half the antiaircraft guns were lost when a German submarine sank the transport *Cedarbank*.

The British could not find a suitable airfield in this mountainous terrain and decided to base their operations from the frozen Lake Lesjaskog, between Dombås and Åndalsnes. Despite objections by their own officers sent to reconnoiter, the British Air Staff decided to use Lake Lesjaskog since it was closer to the operational area than the larger lake near Vang in the Valdres Mountains, which was used by the Norwegians.

Ground personnel arrived in Lesjaskog on April 23 where Norwegians had cleared enough snow to make one landing strip. The British set up operations the following day when 18 Gladiators from the 263rd Squadron flew in from the aircraft carrier *Glorious*. The problems started the next day when some of the carburetors and controls had frozen, making it difficult to get the motors started.

The Germans reacted quickly to this threat to their air dominance. Only one Gladiator managed to take off before the Luftwaffe appeared. The first visit caused little damage and the Germans lost one aircraft. The Germans reappeared in greater force around 0830 hours. In the interim, a further two Gladiators had become airborne and were flying air cover in Gudbrandsdal. The other 15 Gladiators were still on the ice. Although a couple managed to become airborne, ten were destroyed in the course of the morning.

The bombing caused panic among the ground personnel and they fled into the woods along the lake. This caused a severe slowdown in operations since it took the pilots over one hour to replenish their ammunition and fuel. Those aircraft able to take off shot down two German aircraft. By evening, there were only four operational Gladiators left. These flew to Åndalsnes next morning, where the parade ground of a Norwegian training camp was used as a landing strip. Since these aircraft ran out of fuel the following day, all were destroyed.

British Actions at Kvam, Kjørem, and Otta

General Smyth reported to General Ruge in the morning of April 24 and was directed to occupy positions at Kvam, about eight kilometers north of Vinstra. Smyth occupied the Kvam positions with the battalion of the King's Own York and Lancaster Infantry, an antitank company, and some engineers. Norwegian engineers delayed the German advance sufficiently to give Smyth five to six hours to organize his defense. These professional soldiers proved more difficult for the Germans to defeat. They also had effective antitank weapons.

General Pellengahr's forces in the area had grown to six infantry battalions, a mountain battalion, a motorized machinegun battalion, several batteries of artillery, and a number of tanks. The narrowness of the valley allowed for only a part of this force in the forward area. Most German units were deployed in depth all the way to Ringebu. The first German attack at 1130 hours on April 25 was repelled despite considerable British losses to an intense enemy artillery bombardment. The forward British company was forced to withdraw by 1600 hours after having lost 89 men. The Germans tried to envelop the defending force but the British managed to extend their left flank and frustrate the flanking movement. General Smyth was wounded early in the engagement and Lieutenant Colonel Kent-Lemon assumed command of the brigade. The York and Lancaster Battalion occupied a position behind the village through which the forward units could withdraw.

The Germans resumed their attack at 0630 on April 26. This time they sent a whole battalion around the British left flank and the companies there became heavily engaged. The Germans also attacked in the center with heavy air and artillery support. While the French-made British antitank guns proved effective, some were neutralized by enemy artillery fire. Despite supporting attacks by Norwegian ski troops sent by General Hvinden-Haug, the British were in danger of having the road behind their positions cut by the German envelopment. The situation was becoming precarious for the British, not only because of the envelopment, but also from groups of Germans who infiltrated gaps between the companies.

General Paget ordered withdrawal from Kvam at 2300 hours. The York and Lancasters, and one company from the Green Howards, were to set up a position at Kjørem, five kilometers to the north, and the British were to withdraw through these positions. Two companies on the far left of the British line were not informed about the withdrawal and had to make a perilous escape through the hills.

Generals Paget and Ruge met on April 26, and a new command arrangement was worked out. The British now had the preponderance of forces in Gudbrandsdal and it was therefore natural that all forces in that area should be under British command since British forces had operated under Norwegian command when the situation was reversed. Paget, who was worried about a German breakthrough in Østerdal presenting a threat to his rear, had suggested a withdrawal to the rugged terrain south of Dombås but this was not acceptable to Ruge. To do so would mean sacrificing TF Dahl, now on the offensive against the German left flank at Fåberg.

Both Paget and Ruge reported back to their respective governments around this time. Paget's report on April 26 refers to the 148th having "had a dusting," and it fed the flames of ill feeling among the Norwegians by calling some of their units "unreliable." He also gave a greatly exaggerated estimate of German strength when he reported that the 15th Brigade faced two or three German divisions.[13]

General Massy's reply on April 27 emphasized the importance of holding a bridgehead that included Dombås and a 70-kilometer stretch to the north as far as Opdal in order that a second base could be developed in Sunndalsfjord. It is difficult to understand Massy's message in view of what was going on in London and Paris. Chamberlain had ordered plans finalized for an evacuation of Åndalsnes and Namsos on April 26 and Massy received permission from the Prime Minister and the War Office to evacuate Åndalsnes the following day, the very day on which he sent the message to Paget.

General Ruge's report to the government on April 25 was bleak. He stated that his troops were exhausted after over two weeks of continued fighting and he expected the Norwegian and British forces to be swept aside within a day or two. He concluded that future operations had to be based in Trøndelag and North Norway.[16] Ruge was apparently in the dark as to the situation in Trøndelag. On the day prior to Ruge's report the Allies, rather than advancing on Trondheim, were in full retreat.

Kjørem was only a temporary delaying position. The British were preparing positions at Otta, 12 kilometers to the north. Kjørem was held by the York and Lancaster battalion. The Germans launched their attack shortly after 0800 in the morning of April 27. They repeated their tactics of frontal attack supported by heavy artillery at the same time as they worked on the British flanks. The front company in the British defenses was driven out of its positions when the woods around it were set on fire. Attempts to recapture the position failed.

The British had sent security well into the hills on both flanks but when the order was given to withdraw, they discovered that a German flanking movement over the mountains had succeeded in cutting the road behind their positions. The British managed to escape the trap, but sustained heavy losses. One company became separated and made its way back to Dombås after a 24-hour march through snow-covered mountains. The battalion lost about half of its original strength of 600. The Germans had only ten killed and 42 wounded.

At Otta, it was the Green Howards' turn to try to slow the German advance. The battalion was short one company. The area southeast of Otta was excellent defensive terrain. The Germans softened up the British positions by air attacks and artillery fire before launching a ground attack. The Green Howards were well dug in and they suffered only minor losses from these attacks. The British antitank weapons again proved effective and the ground fighting, which began around 1030 hours, ebbed back and forth most of the day until the British company on the west side of the river was forced back towards the town and across the railroad bridge, which was destroyed around 2200 hours. The order to withdraw from Otta was issued about this time. Again, one of the forward companies did not get the message but it managed to disengage.

Norwegian Operations in Gausdal, Østerdal, and Valdres

After it was decided not to pull TF Dahl into Gudbrandsdal, Colonel Dahl considered two possibilities: 1) link up with Colonel Østbye's forces fighting in Valdres; or 2) conduct delaying actions in Gausdal south of Vinstra. A reconnaissance proved that it was not possible to link up with Østbye in Valdres because the roads could not be opened. It was possible to move to Vinstra but the move would take three to four days and it was uncertain where the forces in Gudbrandsdal would be at the end of that period.

Dahl's forces consisted of the 1/6th Inf, the 1/4th Inf, and a number of company-size improvised units, some of an independent mindset or questionable quality. The enemy consisted of the three battalions from Group Nickelmann and a battalion that crossed the river at Fåberg on April 26.

When the Germans captured the bridge at Tretten intact in the evening of April 23, Colonel Dahl decided to withdraw into Vestre Gausdal since his rear was now exposed. The decision was accelerated by a false report that German armor had crossed the bridge in force. Dahl realized later that his withdrawal had been unnecessary and he ordered his troops forward again late on April 26.

Dahl's force was divided into two groups. the 1/4th Inf, a cavalry training company, and an under-strength ski company, commanded by Major Broch, advanced southward against Follebu, located west of Lågen River on the road to Fåberg. The second group, consisting of the 1/6th Inf and an improvised 3/6th Inf under Major Abildgaard, was sent northward towards Tretten. Task Force Broch soon faced the German battalion that had crossed Lågen at Fåberg that same day. The Norwegian battalion attacked frontally while the cavalry troop and ski company began an envelopment. The German battalion commander reported he was surrounded and requested help.

The flank threat against the Germans that Ruge had hoped for was now realized and it caused immediate German reactions. The battalion facing TF

Broch was reinforced, primarily with artillery, while three battalions, with five tanks, were pulled from their advance in Gudbrandsdal and crossed the bridge at Tretten on April 27.

Major Broch was killed and the reinforced German battalion halted the Norwegian advance at Follebu. Task Force Abildgaard reached as far as Svingvoll, about six kilometers west of Tretten without meeting any appreciable opposition.

The German advance of three battalions from Tretten encountered a Norwegian company at Svingvoll and it withdrew slowly northward in the direction of Åmot, followed by a German battalion. Reinforcements from 1/6th Inf stopped the other two battalions at a bridge near Svingvoll. In a pause in the fighting that occurred with the appearance of a German negotiator under white flag, the German tanks crossed the bridge and the Norwegians were compelled to withdraw. They made a stand near Østre Gausdal where heavy fighting continued throughout the day until German armor enveloped the Norwegian right flank.

Because of increased enemy pressure against both his task forces, Colonel Dahl stopped his offensive and pulled his forces back to Vestre Gausdal. Norwegian units managed to halt the German advance in a defile about four kilometers east of Vestre Gausdal and on April 28, Ruge asked Dahl to stay in that area and tie down as many German units as possible.

However, Dahl's troops were exhausted, running short of ammunition and provisions, and it was no longer possible to reach friendly units near Dombås. Under these circumstances, Colonel Dahl decided to accept a German offer to negotiate that led to surrender terms that allowed Norwegian troops to demobilize rather than become prisoners. The final arrangements were made in person between General von Falkenhorst and Colonel Dahl. The surrender on April 29 included about 200 officers and 3,000 soldiers.

Group Fischer was tasked with linking up with German forces south of Trondheim. It consisted of three infantry battalions, two artillery battalions, one engineer battalion, two motorized companies, and two platoons of 10 tanks. These forces broke through the Norwegian defenses in the Rena area after three days of fighting.

Task Force Hiorth no longer had the strength to contest the German advance through Østerdal. With his main force of about 600 men Colonel Hiorth planned to make a stand in the Rasta area on the east of Glåma River. The Germans attacked in the morning of April 23. They were held in check until evening when German armor broke through the Norwegian left flank.

Hiorth did not have many resources left after the fighting at Rasta. The last defensive operations in Østerdal took place between Kvikne and Nåverdal.

While heavy fighting took place for three days along the Kvikne-Nåverdal road without a Germans breakthrough, the eventual outcome was a foregone conclusion. The last Norwegian position in Nåverdal capitulated on April 28 and Group Fischer linked up with forces moving south from Trondheim near Berkåk at noon on April 30. The remnants of TF Hiorth crossed into Sweden and were interned.

We saw earlier that General von Falkenhorst turned the 163rd Division westward to deal with the flank threat posed by the 4th Field Brigade, which had crossed the mountains from western Norway. The fighting between the 163rd Division and the 4th Field Brigade in Valdres and Hallingdal was among the heaviest in Norway. The Germans committed eight infantry battalions, two artillery battalions and 17 tanks in these areas.

The Norwegians conducted tough delaying actions in the hope that the Allies would land forces in Sognefjord. The brigade was still fighting at Fossheim in Valdres on April 30, but the situation had become precarious as various units were splintered and beginning to dissolve. With no prospect of assistance, Colonel Østbye decided to accept German demands and surrendered his 2,000 men at Fagernes. The Norwegians had lost 46 killed, 240 wounded, and about 800 missing and captured since April 25. The total German casualties are not known but their lead regiment had 157 killed and about 360 wounded.

Allied Decisions

The Supreme War Council met in Paris on April 22 and all major actors, political and military, attended. Reynaud found himself in a dilemma similar to that faced by his predecessor concerning Finland. If operations in Norway proved unsuccessful, he might share the same fate. He saw a way out of the dilemma by insisting on increased efforts in Norway. If things turned out well, he would get much of the credit. On the other hand, if things did not go well, he could blame the outcome on the British for not prosecuting the war vigorously. This was probably the main French motive for arguing that nothing should stand in the way of a successful conclusion in Norway. However, there was still a strong feeling that the commitment of more Germans in far-off Norway would reduce the threat to the French homeland. He argued for strong efforts against Trondheim and talked about sufficient troops in the Narvik area to occupy the Swedish iron ore fields after eliminating Dietl.

Chamberlain expressed complete agreement with Reynaud and explained that the recapture of Narvik was postponed only because forces were redirected to Trondheim. His explanation caused the French to believe that Operation *Hammer* was still alive and well. The French were not told that it had been cancelled several days before this meeting. While Chamberlain may not have known that the northern pincer against Trondheim was in full retreat through the burning town of Steinkjer, and that the 148th Brigade had been decimated in Gudbrandsdal, he was not honest with his ally. That the fog of war was even thicker at the highest counsels than on the battlefield is illustrated by Reynaud congratulating the British Army on "not hesitating to march on Oslo immediately after landing in Norway." Reynaud concluded the meeting by summarizing that they had agreed on winning the battle for Trondheim and establishing a strong base there for future offensive operations. The British did not object despite having already cancelled operations against Trondheim.[14]

The British political and military apparatus was again in a state of confusion. Reports of defeats around Steinkjer and in Gudbrandsdal were arriving in London. Other problems were also obvious. After the landing of the 15th Brigade, Åndalsnes and Namsos had become primary targets for the Luftwaffe. The antiaircraft fire from both land-based guns and the guns on the antiaircraft cruisers proved ineffective. It was not long before the harbor facilities and the town were reduced to ashes. The Luftwaffe also rained destruction on the subsidiary base at Molde, Ålesund, and the city of Kristiansund.

Brigadier General Hogg, who was in charge of the garrison and port facilities in Åndalsnes, concluded in the evening of April 26 that unless the air situation was brought under control, the base would become unusable. General Paget agreed, pointing to his own precarious position. Paget may have intended this as a form of pressure on London to send additional forces, particularly air and antiaircraft assets. If this was his intention, it had the opposite effect after Hogg sent an urgent message next morning to General Massy calling for immediate evacuation. On the previous day, the MCC had already recommended that plans be readied for an evacuation from Åndalsnes and Namsos. Chamberlain and other cabinet members hoped the evacuation could be delayed long enough to announce Narvik's recapture. The effect of an evacuation on the Norwegians was not discussed, but the British were rightly fearful of reactions in France.

The news of a planned evacuation from southern and central Norway caused tempers to explode in Paris. An enraged Reynaud sent a personal letter to Chamberlain, which caused consternation because of its unusually frank language. One sentence, "One must think big or stop making war, one must act fast or lose the war" was typical of the letter's flavor.[15] General Gamelin came to London and insisted that the Allies hold a sizable bridgehead in central Norway and occupy as many points as possible on the coast between Namsos and Narvik.

On April 27, the two messages from General Hogg supplemented by a memorandum from General Massy, decided the issue. General Massy reminded the government that General Ironside had given him a free hand regarding the timing of any evacuation and he rejected the MCC's conclusion that an evacuation should be delayed as incompatible with his prerogatives. In a second memorandum on the same day, General Massy requested authority to evacuate both Åndalsnes and Namsos. The request was considered at the meeting of the War Cabinet the following morning and Ironside stated that there were enormous difficulties in carrying out General Gamelin's proposal and that a disaster was a real possibility unless an immediate evacuation was ordered.

Only Churchill spoke against the evacuation and recommended that forces be left in Norway to do the best they could. He even suggested reconsideration of a *Hammer* type operation. His colleagues were not willing to face the political fallout of a military disaster, and although the minutes of the meeting are vague it is likely that the participants were fully aware that a decision for immediate evacuation had been made. A message to General Carton de Wiart, the commander in Namsos, sent immediately after the meeting, as well as Ironside's diary confirm this conclusion.[16]

The British were less than candid with their allies at the meeting of the Supreme War Council and did not reveal the fact that the decision to evacuate had been made. Chamberlain stated that Gamelin's suggestions from the previous day were under study. In fact, they had been rejected. While he noted that the situation in Norway had deteriorated and it was no longer possible to take Trondheim, he assured the French "this was not tantamount to a decision to evacuate," only a recognition that "it could not long be delayed.[17]

Reynaud stressed that a complete withdrawal from central Norway would be a moral and political disaster. He argued that some sort of foothold be kept north and south of Trondheim along the lines proposed by Gamelin. Chamberlain concurred and the French came away believing the British had agreed to Gamelin's proposals. Two hours after the meeting, the British ordered the immediate evacuation of south and central Norway. This was nothing short of an open defiance of the Supreme War Council and an insult to their allies.

The French did not learn about the evacuation until the afternoon of April

29. They also learned that the order to evacuate had been issued two hours after the Supreme War Council meeting that led them to believe that the British had agreed to General Gamelin's proposal. The French made every effort to reverse the evacuation order. Reynaud wrote a letter to Chamberlain asking that it be cancelled "in the name of friendship between our two peoples."[18]

There were also pressures within Great Britain to make a more aggressive effort in Norway. Admiral of the Fleet Sir Roger Keyes, the hero of Zeebrugge, even addressed the House of Commons on the matter, after repeated letters to Churchill evoked neither action nor response.

The Norwegians were even less well informed than the French. They still believed that the Allies would launch their long promised attack on Trondheim. General Ruge was regrouping and reorganizing his forces, about 4,000 men, near Dombås for the anticipated attack against Trondheim.

The British Evacuation

General Paget received orders to evacuate in the early morning hours of April 28. The order stated that he should not inform the Norwegians. Paget found this part of the order completely impractical since he had to rely on Norwegians for road and rail transport as well as flank protection as he withdrew his forces 180 kilometers through Romsdal to Åndalsnes. He decided to ignore that part of the order and proceeded to General Ruge's headquarters at about 0500 hours.

It was a painful meeting. The news was devastating to General Ruge who remarked, "So Norway is to share the fate of Czechoslovakia and Poland."[19] As his anger grew, he left the room. A few minutes later, he returned and stated that these things were not for soldiers to debate. He asked how he could help the British in their task. An agreement was reached whereby a British battalion would stay in positions at Dombås to cover the withdrawal of the Norwegians. The Norwegians, for their part, would provide transport for the withdrawing British, means to evacuate the wounded, and ski detachments for security. Ruge hoped that his troops would be evacuated and brought to North Norway, but this was not to be.

The Norwegian King and his government were in Molde. The British sent the cruiser *Glasgow* and destroyer escorts to bring them to safety. They were concerned that the Norwegians might throw in the towel and the captain of the *Glasgow* had orders to bring them along by force, if needed. This proved unnecessary as the Norwegians decided on Tromsø as their destination. Ruge followed on May 1 after first refusing to board British ships bound for Scapa

Flow before proceeding to North Norway. As the Norwegian Army commander, he refused to go to Great Britain, even temporarily, since it would appear he was fleeing the country. In the end, Ruge and his staff were transported to Tromsø in a British destroyer.

Since the British did not attempt to evacuate the Norwegian troops, reportedly because they lacked adequate shipping, Ruge ordered the 11th Infantry Regiment demobilized and turned over the command of all forces in the Åndalsnes area to General Hvinden-Haug, along with an authorization to surrender. The surrender took place on May 3. Conditions were lenient. The troops were allowed to proceed to their homes if they gave assurance that they would not participate in any further hostilities against the Germans.

The Operations in Trøndelag and the Evacuation of Namsos

The 2/13th Inf battalion was in Nord-Trøndelag on April 9. The 1/13th Inf was in Narvik. An improvised third battalion was mobilized and organized within a couple of days after the attack, while the reserve battalion was organized into a territorial command. The 3rd Cavalry Regiment was in the process of mobilizing on April 9. Three squadrons were ready on April 11 and the remaining four a few days later. The 12th Infantry Regiment in Sør-Trøndelag also had a battalion on duty in North Norway, which later took heavy casualties at Gratangen. The mobilization depots for the 12th Regiment and the 3rd Artillery Regiment were located in Trondheim and captured by the Germans on April 9. It was therefore only possible to raise improvised units of a small battalion and one independent company.

There were about 180 Norwegians, mostly 5th Division's school personnel, at Værnes Airfield on April 9. They prepared to defend the airfield and prevented German attempts to land on April 9. The executive officer of the 3rd Artillery Regiment, Major R. Holtermann, was at Værnes to receive troops reporting for duty with the regiment on April 9. He moved about 250 of these troops to the old fortress at Hegra. The 2/13th Inf moved south towards Trondheim after the German attack and was located at Åsen, only about 20 kilometers from Værnes. Instead of moving forward to the airfield, the unit was ordered back to Verdal in the evening of April 9 because German warships were reported in the fjord. The 5th Division school personnel were also ordered to Verdal. The front line was established north of Steinkjer with one motorized machinegun company at Verdalsøra to secure the bridge.

The Germans sent about 500 troops towards the airfield on April 10. Before their arrival, a German officer showed up in a taxi and demanded surrender. The

Norwegian officer in charge contacted General Laurantzon who ordered him to comply with the German demand. Failure to defend Værnes was a major blunder that made Norwegian and Allied operations extremely difficult. The capture of the airfield ended the isolation of Colonel Weiss' forces in the Trondheim area. Værnes was also the only airfield in relative proximity to Narvik and played a decisive role in the transport of supplies and reinforcements in May and June. Aircraft from Værnes provided essential close ground support and resupply during the 2nd Mountain Division's drive through Nordland Province to relieve Dietl's forces. Finally, German aircraft based at Værnes influenced the British decision to abandon Operation *Hammer*. The airfield had a limited capacity but was quickly expanded using Norwegian labor.

Operation *Maurice*, the northern pincer against Trondheim, involved both British and French forces. The British contingent consisted of the 146th Infantry Brigade with three territorial battalions. The French 5th Half-Brigade of alpine troops also had three battalions. Major General Carton de Wiart commanded the Allied forces with Brigadier General C. G. Phillips commanding the 146th and General Audet the French contingent.

Carton de Wiart was promised forces that he never received. In addition to the 146th Brigade he was pledged the 148th Brigade, to arrive on April 17, French forces on April 18, and the 147th Brigade with artillery on April 20 or 21. The 147th and the artillery never arrived and the 148th was diverted to Åndalsnes.

The landing of British forces in Namsos, as in the other areas of the country, took place amid considerable confusion. The 146th Brigade was destined for the Narvik area when diverted to Namsos at the last moment. The brigade commander landed in Harstad and it took some time for him to rejoin his command. There were no maps of the area, only of Narvik. This brigade, like the 148th, was separated from some of its critical equipment in the confusing period after April 7 and the transports were not loaded tactically. To make matters worse, much equipment ended up in Narvik and had to be reshipped to Namsos. There was no artillery, no air support, and the skis had no bindings.[20] In the hurry to get the transports out of the Luftwaffe's reach, at least 130 tons of valuable supplies and equipment sailed away in the returning transports.

Colonel Ole Berg Getz, commanding the 5th Field Brigade, was in charge of all Norwegian troops in this part of the country as of April 16. His forces did not come under General Carton de Wiart's authority, but as soon as the Allies landed, Getz reported to Carton de Wiart and offered whatever help and cooperation was needed. He placed all his forces at the disposal of the British and he undertook a major reorganization of his command in order to create as many ski detachments as possible. The 2/13th Inf provided one ski company and two were formed by the 3rd Cavalry.

General Fleischer, as mentioned earlier, transferred the 1/14th Inf from his control to that of Getz on April 14. This force arrived in the Namsos area on April 18–19 and was organized as a ski battalion. Getz explained to Carton de Wiart that Norwegian forces were pulled back to Steinkjer because of the amphibious threat posed by the Germans who controlled the fjord and because his troops had only a one-day supply of ammunition.[21]

Carton de Wiart decided to establish himself in the Steinkjer area initially, with forward security at Verdal, near the Norwegian security force. The French forces remained in the Namsos area while waiting for the arrival of equipment and supplies. The Norwegian forces assumed the mission of protecting the British eastern flank. Carton de Wiart placed strict limitations on the operational information shared with Getz because he feared leaks. Consequently, the Norwegians were unsuccessful in their attempts to coordinate their activities with the British forces. The British troops were assembled at Steinkjer on April 19 with one battalion south of that town and a one-company security force at Stiklestad. The Allied troops now numbered about 4,700.

Colonel Getz urged them to move forward and secure a defile south of Åsen and about 50 kilometers from Trondheim, before the Germans seized it. The number of Norwegian troops at Trøndelag was about equal to that of the Allies and together they had a clear numerical superiority over the Germans. The defile south of Åsen was an excellent defensive position, could be supported by the Norwegian forces at Hegra, and served as a good starting point for an offensive against Trondheim. However, it appears that the Allies felt there was no urgency.

Major General Woytasch, commander of the 181st Infantry Division, arrived in Trondheim on April 20 and he immediately initiated operations to secure his northern front. His first goal was to secure the area between Steinkjer and Snåsa, to protect Trondheim from the threat of a Norwegian–Allied offensive. He sent an infantry battalion, two companies of mountain troops, and some artillery into that area. Some of these troops advanced along the road from Trondheim while others carried out amphibious landings at Innerøya and Trones, in the right rear of the Norwegian and British forces at Verdal and Stiklestad. The landings were made from armed trawlers and seized Norwegian fishing vessels.

The Norwegian motorized machinegun troop at Verdalsøra repelled frontal attacks in the morning of April 20. After about one hour of fighting, the German unit that landed at Trones attacked the Norwegians from behind. The Norwegians lost one platoon and the rest of the troop withdrew to Stiklestad where it linked up with the British company. The British were trying to regroup their forces to defend against the German landing at Inderøy by pulling the company at Stiklestad back to the northern end of Lake Leksdal. The Norwegian troops also withdrew and, at the request of the British, most were sent to the Ogndal area to provide the British with flank protection.

The Germans infiltrated the British lines, forcing a withdrawal to Ogndal in the afternoon of April 20. That night, the Germans also made an amphibious landing near Steinkjer. General Phillips decided to withdraw his brigade to the Beistad area on the road from Steinkjer to Namsos. Getz also withdrew his forces and positioned his forward units at Stod and at another line along Lake Snåsa, in the Valøy-Øksnes area. In the short span of 24 hours, the Germans had captured the area between Åsen and Steinkjer and forced the Allies to abandon Steinkjer.

The Luftwaffe conducted continuous attacks against Steinkjer and Namsos and the Allies lost much of their supplies in these attacks. Carton de Wiart, who witnessed the destruction of Namsos, sent a message to the War Office on April 21 in which he pointed out that it would not be possible to carry out his mission as long as the enemy had air dominance. He followed this up two days later with a message recommending withdrawal. Carton de Wiart was directed to assemble his forces and remain on the defensive. On April 28, he received the order to evacuate but was told to keep this information from the Norwegians.

Colonel Getz reached agreement with the Allies on April 27 for an offensive against Steinkjer. The Norwegians were to advance on the left with Allied forces in the center and on the right. The Germans had remained inactive in the Steinkjer area for several days, waiting for reinforcements before continuing their advance. The Norwegian advance began on April 28 and there were only sporadic contacts with the enemy.

Unknown to the Norwegians, who continued their advance towards Steinkjer, the Allies began thinning out their frontline forces. By April 28, they had withdrawn most of their troops to a location near Namsos from where they could reach the harbor within a few hours. This left the Norwegian right flank exposed. The Norwegians noticed the withdrawal but were told that only some forces were withdrawn to take part in a direct operation against Trondheim.[22]

The Allied evacuation was successful, embarking about 4,200 troops in four hours. The Luftwaffe did not attack until the ships were at sea. The air attacks caused the loss of two destroyers carrying the Allied rear guard, the French *Bison* and the British *Afridi*, with the loss of more than 250 men. This was in addition to the loss of the British antiaircraft sloop *Bittern* on April 30.

The Norwegians were still involved in operations against Steinkjer in the evening of May 2 when Colonel Getz received a curt letter from General Carton de Wiart regretfully announcing the withdrawal. He received a more personal letter from General Audet apologizing for the necessity imposed on him. A part of this letter read, "Be assured that the situation in which I find myself is very painful because I am afraid you will conclude that I have not been loyal to you. I am a victim of war's necessity, and can do nothing but follow orders."[23]

Getz found himself in a difficult situation. His right flank was wide open and the Germans were pouring through that opening and moving into his rear. Despite a severe shortage of ammunition, he managed to extricate his forces and withdraw towards Namsos. Knowing that a capitulation was probable, he sent the battalion belonging to General Fleischer northward so that it would not be included in the surrender. Whether Getz should have attempted a northward withdrawal will be discussed later.

In his letter announcing the withdrawal, Carton de Wiart had written, "We are leaving a quantity of material here, which I hope you can come and take, and know it will be of value to you and your gallant forces."[24] Instead, the Allies destroyed most of what they left behind. Upon entering the destroyed town of Namsos, the Norwegians found the promised supplies: a dozen burned out trucks, some antiaircraft guns damaged beyond repair, 300 rifles without ammunition, and a few crates of food.[25] Getz surrendered his forces on May 3.

Hegra Fort held against repeated German attacks but lack of food after Getz' surrender made defense of the fort meaningless. Major Holtermann assembled his troops on May 4 and announced, "Today, each man will receive 10 kroner and one pack of tourist rations. And what this means, everyone understands."[26] He and his 200 troops surrendered on May 5.

NOTES

1 Lindback-Larsen, *Kriegen*, p. 66.
2 Ziemke, *The German Northern Theater*, p. 70.
3 Bernard Fergusson, *The Watery Maze* (London: Collins, 1961), p. 44.
4 Dudley Clarke, *Seven Assignments* (London: Jonathan Cape, 1948), p. 88.

5 Derry, *The Campaign in Norway*, Appendix A, p. 251.

6 Ibid, p. 99.

7 Kersuady, *Norway*, p. 116.

8 Tamelander and Zetterling, *Niende april*, p. 164.

9 Jørgen Jensen, *Krigen på Hedemark* (Oslo: Tanum, 1947), p. 138.

10 See, for example, Tamelander and Zetterling, *Niende april*, p. 165 and Derry, *The Campaign in Norway*, p.111. Morgan was not present when the Germans attacked. He had traveled to Åndalsnes where the 15th Brigade was landing the following day.

11 Gudbrand Østbye, *Krigen i Norge 1940. Operasjonene på Vestsiden av Mjøsa – Follebu-Gausdal* (Oslo: Forsvarets Krigshistoriske Avdeling, 1960), pp. 231-233, 250-251 and Lindbäck-Larsen, *Krigen*, p. 95.

12 Tage Ellinger, *Den Forunderlige Krig* (Oslo: Gyldendal Norsk Forlag, 1960), pp. 27-28

13 As quoted in Derry, *The Campaign in Norway*, p. 122.

14 Lindbäck-Larsen, *Krigen,* p. 94.

15 Kersuady, *Norway*, p. 154.

16 As quoted in Tamelander and Zetterling, *Niende april,* p. 165.

17 MacLeod and Kelly, *Time Unguarded*, p. 287.

18 As quoted in Kersuady, *Norway*, p. 167.

19 Ibid, p. 176.

20 Norwegian Broadcasting System (NRK) interview with Major General Roscher-Nielsen on January 18, 1965 as quoted in Kersuady, *Norway*, p. 170.

21 Ash, *Norway 1940*, p. 100, after describing the troops' lack of essential equipment, notes how they were issued lavish personal kits "to make up for everything…" which they had to carry due to lack of transportation and "General Carton de Wiart declared with some heat that the men could not carry all their kit, while if they put it on they looked like paralysed bears and were unable to move."

22 Since ammunition for Norwegian weapons was not produced outside Norway and because they were cut off from their source in southern Norway, the solution was to supply them with British weapons. About 7,000 rifles and 250 Bren guns with ammunition finally arrived in the transport *Chobry* on April 28 but off-loading priority was given to French antiaircraft batteries (despite that day's evacuation order). The Norwegian weapons and ammunition sailed away on the transport. This may have been deliberate since the British did not want these weapons to fall into German hands.

23 Ole Berg Getz, *Fra krigen i Nord-Trøndelag 1940* (. Oslo: Aschehoug & Co., 1940), p.139.

24 Ibid, p. 144.

25 Kersuady, *Norway*, p. 181.

26 As quoted in Kersuady, *Norway*, p. 125.

11

NORWEGIAN-FRENCH OFFENSIVE, APRIL 29–MAY 12

"Group Narvik's mission can only be accomplished if
reinforcements are received. . . . Nothing else possible."
GENERAL DIETL'S JOURNAL ENTRY FOR MAY 4, 1940.

The Norwegian Reorganization and Allied Buildup

The Germans withdrew to positions on the high ground in the defile between Gratangen and Bjerkvik within a few days after the engagement in Gratang Valley. The valley was in Norwegian hands and the capture of Elvenes and Gratangen made it possible to resupply forces by sea since it proved very difficult to open the roads after the heavy snowfall. However, there was still a German force at Foldevik. Norwegian patrol boats bombarded the German positions two nights, starting on April 28 and this caused the Germans to withdraw. A reinforced Norwegian company was brought from Sjøvegan to Gratangen to secure the area after the second bombardment.

Norwegian forces were reorganized into two light brigades after the fiasco at Gratangen, with a combat strength of about 4,800 troops. The reorganization became effective on April 30. Colonel Løken retained command of the 6th Brigade, which consisted of three infantry battalions (1/16th, 2/16th, and 1/12th), the 8th Mountain Artillery Battery, and a medical company. Colonel Faye was designated commander of the newly created 7th Brigade but Lieutenant Colonel Dahl commanded it pending his arrival. The Brigade consisted of two infantry battalions (Alta and 2/15th), the Mountain Artillery Battalion minus one battery, the 9th Motorized Artillery Battery, an engineer platoon, part of a medical company, and a reinforced company from the Reserve Battalion of the 16th Infantry Regiment. The remainder of that battalion was under division control.

There was no significant increase in Allied ground force strength in the two weeks following the landing of the 24th Guards Brigade on April 15 and 16. The three battalions of that brigade had not participated in any combat operations since their arrival. The flow of Allied combat troops into the Narvik area started again in late April and early May.

The 27th Half-Brigade of Chasseurs Alpins (CA) arrived on April 28. This unit consisted of the 6th, 12th and 14th Battalions. This Half-Brigade was held initially in Scapa Flow as a reserve for the operations in southern and central Norway. It was relieved of its reserve mission and sent to North Norway on April 24. Brigadier General Marie Emilie Béthouart, who had commanded the French ground forces under General Audet in Namsos, received a telegram from General Gamelin on April 26 ordering him to Harstad to take command of French forces in North Norway. He arrived there on the destroyer *Acasta* at about the same time the 27th Half-Brigade under Lieutenant Colonel Valentini was disembarking. British authorities ordered the 6th and 14th Battalions to land behind the Norwegian front at Sjøvegan and Salangen, respectively. The 12th Battalion landed at Bogen, on the north side of Ofotfjord, and came under the operational control of Brig. General Fraser, the commander of the 24th Brigade. The first shots fired by Allied ground forces at Germans took place in the morning of April 29, when a German ski patrol approached Bogen from the east.

The disposition of the three battalions of the 24th Guards Brigade at this time was as follows: The two companies of 1st Scots Guards were moved from the Fossbakken area to Harstad. The 1st Irish Guards along with headquarter elements of the 24th Brigade were moved to Bogen on April 19. General Fraser later moved his forward headquarters to Ballangen, on the south side of Ofotfjord. The 2nd South Wales Borderers were moved to Skånland initially and to Ballangen between 26 and 28 April.

The 203rd British Field Artillery Regiment finally received its guns on April 29. The French also brought 12 75mm guns. Some amphibious assault craft from the limited British resources were made available to support the planned operations. These consisted of four Assault Landing Craft (ALC) able to carry 40 infantry troops each and four 20-ton Mechanized Landing Craft (MLC) capable of carrying vehicles, equipment, and supplies.

A convoy carrying the 13th Half-Brigade, consisting of two battalions of the Foreign Legion, and support elements of the 1st Light Division arrived in Harstad on May 6. Two companies were kept near Harstad to protect that town against threats from the west. The rest of the 13th Half-Brigade landed at Kjeldebotn, on the south side of Ofotfjord, across from Ramnes. The divisional support and supply organizations were moved to Ballangen.

A convoy carrying 4,778 troops of the Polish brigade, organized into two half-brigades of two battalions each, arrived off Tromsø on May 5.[1] The Allies planned to land the brigade in Tromsø and move it to East Finnmark. Norwegian authorities opposed its planned use in East Finnmark because the deployment of Polish troops on the border could be viewed as a provocative move by the Soviets. The convoy remained at sea for two days pending the selection of a new landing site. In the end, the Polish troops were landed in Harstad in the evening of May 7.

The facilities in Harstad were limited and the buildup had reached a saturation point. The lack of an effective liaison with Norwegian authorities and a very rudimentary civil affairs program led to friction between the civilian population and the Allied troops. The brigade staff, the 1st Half-Brigade, and support troops were camped outside Harstad. The staff and 4th Battalion of the 2nd Half-Brigade were moved to Salangen as reinforcement for the 27th Half-Brigade. The 3rd Battalion was moved to Ballangen where it was to be used as a security force towards the south and southeast.

With the landing of the two Polish half-brigades on May 7, the Allies had achieved a decisive superiority in combat troops in the Narvik area. There were three battalions of British regulars, three battalions of French Chasseurs Alpins, two battalions of the French Foreign Legion, and four Polish battalions. In addition, there were six Norwegian battalions. The German forces consisted of three battalions of mountain troops and the destroyer crews organized into seven small battalions.

The Allied naval presence continued to be impressive. The battleship *Resolution* replaced *Warspite* and aircraft from the carrier *Furious* provided air support throughout the second half of April and early May. The aircraft carrier *Ark Royal* replaced her in early May after her engines were damaged from a near miss by a German bomb. Requirements for the evacuations in central Norway reduced the number of cruisers but, on average, 15 destroyers were available to Admiral Cork. While German air attacks caused damage to Allied ships, only the Polish destroyer *Grom* was sunk during this period.

Continued Allied Caution

General Mackesy still viewed a direct landing in Narvik as too risky. He planned to begin an advance on Narvik on both sides of Ofotfjord with French and British troops. The southern advance would start from Ballangen towards Ankenes and the northern advance from Bogen towards Bjerkvik. The problem with this scenario was that half the Allied ground forces, four battalions, were located over 50 kilometers to the north, behind the Norwegian front with roads that were almost impassable. This was pointed out to Cork and Mackesy when General Béthouart had his first meeting with them a few hours after arriving in Harstad on April 28.[2]

Admiral Cork recommended that Béthouart make a reconnaissance in the fjord aboard a destroyer. Béthouart concluded that the Germans occupied only part of the coastline near Narvik in force and he felt it was possible to land both at Øyjord and to the east of Narvik. Capturing Øyjord would threaten the rear of the Germans in the Bjerkvik area and provide a starting point for an amphibious operation against Narvik.

Admiral Cork appeared to agree with the recommendation but General Mackesy did not approve when General Béthouart briefed him after returning to Harstad. Instead, he ordered General Béthouart to take command of the two French battalions in the Salangen area and advance on Bjerkvik in coordination with the Norwegians.

Béthouart proceeded to Salangen on April 29 and made contact with Lieutenant Colonel Valentini and with General Fleischer. This was the first meeting between the two generals. They established a good working relationship. From Fleischer, Béthouart learned that the Norwegians had recaptured the Gratangen area and that it was possible to move his battalions from Sjøvegan to Gratangen by sea. The 6th Battalion CA and the brigade CP were moved to Gratangen on April 30 in Norwegian fishing vessels. Valentini co-located his headquarters with that of the 7th Brigade. Béthouart established his headquarters at Straumsnes, on the south side of the fjord.

Mackesy's planned advance along both sides of Ofotfjord began on April 29 when the South Wales Borderers, reinforced by the ski reconnaissance platoon (Section d'Éclaireurs Skieurs, SES) from the 12th Bn CA, made an unopposed landing at Skjomnes, on the northwest side of Ankenes Peninsula. The main British force advanced towards Ankenes along the coastal road while one company and the French reconnaissance platoon were sent into Håvikdal as a screen for the British right flank.

At this time, there were only weak German outposts on the Ankenes side of Narvik harbor. However, German artillery and heavy machineguns from Narvik could fire on the coastal road west of Ankenes and this fire stopped the South Wales Borderers and forced them to fall back to positions near Båtberget. General Fraser was lightly wounded while carrying out a reconnaissance and

Lieutenant Colonel T. B. Trappes-Lomax, the commander of the Scots Guards, assumed command of the brigade.

The Germans increased their forces on Ankenes Peninsula after the British landing at Skjomnes. A detachment of skiers, reinforced by naval personnel, was sent across the bay with orders to occupy Hill 606 between Håviksdal and Beisfjord. This force, commanded by Lieutenant Mungai, conducted an active defense and moved into Håviksdal where it encountered the British and French flank security force and drove it back to Mattisjord.

Company 6 of the 139th Regiment, commanded by First Lieutenant Obersteiner, was moved across Beisfjord to Ankenes Peninsula on the night of May 1–2. In a surprise attack, the German company threw the advance elements of the South Wales Borderers back from Båtberget to a rear position at Emmenes. The German company was preparing to attack the new position when it came under fire from British warships and suffered considerable casualties, including the company commander. It withdrew to Ankenes and by May 6, its strength was down to about 50 men. The South Wales Borderers suffered three killed and several wounded. Another three soldiers were killed and an equal number wounded on May 2, when German aircraft bombed the battalion CP.

This was the first and last employment of British ground forces in the Narvik area. The South Wales Borderers could make little progress off roads in the deep snow and it was decided to withdraw them and turn the operations on the south side of Ofotfjord over to the 12th Bn CA.

The Allies failed to inform General Fleischer about their operation on the south side of Ofotfjord before it began. The Norwegians viewed the activities on Ankenes Peninsula as inconsequential for the operation against Narvik. Fleischer sent Major Lindbäck-Larsen to Harstad to confer with the Allied commanders and to convince them that decisive results could be achieved on the north side of the fjord. Two alternatives were suggested: landings in Rombaken east of Øyjord followed by an advance through the valleys leading to Jernvannene (Iron Lakes) or landings on the west side of Herjangsfjord, followed by an advance on Bjerkvik. Lindbäck-Larsen was unable to reach accord with the British.

The Norwegians provided the British liaison officer with an operational draft the following day, May 7. This draft stated that the division's primary effort would be directed against Bjørnefjell. The plan assumed that an Allied operation against the Bjerkvik area could be undertaken with relative ease while the Norwegians attacked from the north.

There was a second reason for sending Lindbäck-Larsen to the British headquarters. The Allied withdrawal from Namsos gave the Germans an opportunity to come to Dietl's assistance through Nordland Province where there were only weak Norwegian forces. Reports had reached Fleischer that a small British force had landed in Mosjøen but the situation was unclear. Lindbäck-Larsen failed to obtain an agreement for joint operations in Nordland Province since the forces there were not under General Mackesy's command.

Lindbäck-Larsen points out that coordination with the Allies was exceedingly bad and it was difficult to understand their operational goals. Fleischer's headquarters requested that the Norwegian Army High Command (HOK) assist in bringing about regular cooperation with the Allies. Norway's interests would be best served, in Fleischer's view, if the Allies devoted their main effort at stopping the German advance from Namsos.

Norwegian-French Offensive Plans

General Fleischer issued orders for the continuation of the offensive on April 29. While the 7th Brigade, supported by one battalion of French CA, attacked towards Bjerkvik and Elvegårdsmoen through Gratangseidet and Labergsdal, the 6th Brigade would advance through Gressdal and Vassdal and thereby threaten Elvegårdsmoen and Bjerkvik from the east. The plan called for the main force of the 6th Bn, 27th CA to advance south through Labergsdal while one company of that battalion advanced along Route 50 from Elvenes to Bjerkvik. The operation was assisted by the Norwegian capture of Hill 509 on April 27. This height dominated the road and the area around Storfossen and its capture forced the Germans to fall back and establish their defenses with the western flank along the chain of lakes on the east side of the Route 50. The German withdrawal allowed the Norwegians to move forward and occupy the area around Fjelldal, Holtås, and Kvernemoen.

The Germans needed to protect themselves against a possible drive against their right flank over the mountains from Lortvann. The area did not lend itself to a continuous front and the Germans did not believe the Norwegians would be able to conduct large-scale operations in this roadless wilderness. Furthermore, it would be extremely difficult to keep large German forces supplied in this area. The Germans elected to base their defense on patrols and a few observation points. These had radios that enabled them to report any threatening activities. The plan called for the Norwegian 7th Brigade to advance towards Bjerkvik on the east side of Route 50 with the Alta Battalion on the right and the 2/15th on the left. The forces on the two flanks would make the main effort: the French advance through Labergsdal on the right and the units of the 6th Brigade operating in the east. The 7th Brigade expected to move forward as the pressure on the German flanks forced them to withdraw.

According to French sources, Fleischer gave Béthouart command on April 30 of the forces operating along both sides of Route 50 between Gratangen and Bjerkvik, including one Norwegian battalion. They allegedly agreed to an operational boundary between the French and Norwegian commands along a line from Durmåsfjell over Hills 1150, 1118, and 1009. The same sources claim that Béthouart delegated command of French and Norwegian forces in this area to Lieutenant Colonel Valentini, commander of the 27th Chasseurs Alpins.[3]

There are no indications in Norwegian records that such a command agreement was ever put into operation. The actual arrangements were apparently based on close coordination between Lieutenant Colonels Dahl and Valentini. The Norwegians placed one company from 2/15th Inf at the disposal of the French for security missions in Labergsdal, since the French had only a limited number of ski troops. Only one SES and ten men in each company had skis. The rest used snowshoes.

The 6th Brigade's immediate objective was the Vasshaugen-Elvemo area east of Hartvigvann. Fleischer expected the brigade to reach this area by May 5. The division order of April 29 required that the 6th Brigade be prepared to start its offensive within 24 hours. It was allowed to send the reinforced Co 6, 2/16th to Gressvann early in the evening of April 29 and the reinforced Co 7, 2/16th to Brattbakken. The mission of Co 6, 2/16th was to clear the Germans from the area north of Gressvann while Co 7, 2/16 provided flank security and patrolled towards Storfossen, behind the German defensive positions at the southern end of Gressvann. Norwegian aircraft stationed at Bardufoss and naval aircraft operating from Tromsø were to support the attack.

German forces contesting the Norwegian-French offensive consisted of the 1st and 3rd Battalions of the 139th Regiment. The 1st Bn, commanded by Major Stautner, consisted of 2nd, 4th, 5th, and 13th companies. Company 1 of this battalion was detached, as earlier related, to Bjørnefjell. The 1/139th covered the Gratangen-Bjerkvik road. Patrols from both battalions covered the approaches in the mountainous area in the east for about eight kilometers, to the vicinity of Lortvann and Høgtind. Since the Germans did not believe it possible for major enemy units to operate in the eastern wilderness, it was weakly defended when the Norwegian offensive began. For example, a 16-men detachment with only one machinegun had the mission of securing the Gressvann area.

The bulk of the 3/139th (Co 12 and parts of Cos 14 and 15), commanded by Major Hagemann, was co-located with the regimental headquarters in the Hartvigvann area. Company 11 of this battalion defended Bjerkvik against possible enemy landings in Herjangsfjord. The road leading west from Bjerkvik was secured by only one platoon. The coastline south of Bjerkvik was covered by three companies from Naval Battalion Kothe. The Øyjord area was occupied by Co 3, 139th. The operational boundary between the two German battalions was a line over Hills 785, 842, and 856 with the mountain tops assigned to the 1st Battalion.

6th Brigade's Attack

The 6th Brigade ordered 1/16th Bn commanded by Major Hunstad and 2/16th Bn commanded by Major Munthe-Kaas, to prepare to execute the attack on a one-hour notice after midnight on April 30. The 1/12th Inf, now assigned to the brigade, did not participate since it was still undergoing reorganization because of its heavy losses in Gratangen on April 24. The advance was divided into three phases. The first phase line was near Hill 437, a ridgeline that separated Gressdal from the Stormyra area. The second phase line ran from Hill 1009 across Gressvann to Hill 1013. The valley in this area is actually a defile with almost vertical walls that are 1200 to 1500 feet in height. An advance through this defile was only possible if the western mountains were in friendly hands. The final phase line ran from Læigastind (Hill 1335) to Hill 1146 (Bukkefjell). The broken mountainous terrain, and their superior cross-country mobility, offered the Norwegians an opportunity to outmaneuver the Germans. The 8th Mountain Artillery Battery was to follow 1/16th Inf and set up in firing positions on Hill 437.

A platoon from Co 6, 2/16, on a security mission at the southern end of Stormyra, made the first contact with the Germans during the night of April 29. Two machinegun sections sent towards a cabin at the southern end of Gressvann ran into a German unit. This German squad-size unit had an observation mission at the southern end of the Stormyr area and withdrew as the Norwegians approached. The sergeant who commanded the Norwegian unit was wounded and he and two machine gunners were captured. The rest of the platoon took up positions on Hill 437.

The early and piecemeal forward movement of Norwegian forces in the east alerted Colonel Windisch to the fact that his troops faced a major threat in that area. He made an urgent request to General Dietl for reinforcements. Dietl had expected the main Norwegian-French effort along Route 50 because of extensive shipping activities in the Sjøvegan and Gratangen areas since the last week in April. However, he now viewed the threat through the Gressdal-Vassdal area as the most dangerous. In this respect, Generals Fleischer and Dietl were thinking alike. A successful Norwegian advance through Gressdal, Raudal, and Vassdal, slipping behind the Germans occupying the high ground to the north, would pose a direct threat to the rear of Group Windisch. The Norwegians could not only sever its supply but cut its line of retreat.

The Germans had, as already mentioned, only a 16-man detachment at the southern end of Gressvann, which served as a supply point for forward observation posts. Dietl agreed with Windisch that it was imperative to reinforce Group Windisch's right flank quickly. He immediately stripped three companies from forces located in other areas and sent them by forced marches to the threatened area. He ordered Major Schleebrügge, who had commanded the successful attack on Bjørnefjell in mid-April, to take Co 1, 1/139th to the threatened area on the right flank of the German northern front. The company started its march at 1300 hours on April 30. At Windisch's request, the division had ordered one platoon from this company to Elvegårdsmoen on April 28. The mission of Co 1 in the Bjørnefjell area was taken over by naval Co Zenker. By an exhausting forced march, one platoon from Co 1 reinforced the detachment at the southern end of Gressvann while the rest of the company occupied Britatind on May 1 and caused much difficulty for the 6th Brigade. [4]

The other two German companies rushed in as reinforcements were a mixture of mountain troops and naval personnel from Narvik, Cos Brucker and Erdmenger. These units started their move in the evening of April 30 via a difficult route in order to avoid fire from British warships. They marched from Narvik along the southern shore of Beisfjord, climbed and crossed the mountains at the southern end of this fjord to Sildvik from where they were brought by train to Nordal Bridge. From there, they undertook an arduous 29-hour march through mountains covered by 3-6 feet of loose snow to the area east of Hartvigvann. Company Müller (1st Lieutenant Müller from the division staff took over command when Captain Brucker became ill) arrived at its destination at 0330 hours on May 2 followed by Co Erdmenger at 0230 hours the following day. Company Erdmenger relieved Co 11, 3/139th of its coastal defense mission in the Bjerkvik area and that company was attached to 1/139th. Company

Müller occupied the area from Storebalak northeastward during the night of May 4. The 3rd Division directed Group Windisch to relieve Co 3 at Øyjord with naval personnel in order that this full-strength company of mountain troops could be used for other missions. The regimental reserve was reduced to Co 12, 3/139th.[5]

The 2/16th Inf began its advance at 0500 hours on May 1. It took place in difficult terrain with deep snow. The battalion commander noted in his report that his unit had been severely reduced by the time the operation began and consisted of only one reinforced rifle company, one under-strength rifle company, a machinegun platoon, and a mortar section. Two squads from this force were also sent into the mountains on the west side of Gressdal as security. To make matters worse, the battalion had never operated as a unit and the troops had not even tested their weapons.[6]

There appears to have been some confusion about the operational boundary between the 7th and 6th Brigades and this became a factor in the failure of the 6th Brigade to reach its objective in Vassdalen. Major Munthe-Kaas, the commander of the 2/16th Inf, assumed that the 7th Brigade was responsible for securing the high ground west of Gressdal. The 6th Brigade order appears to recognize a responsibility for the western high ground since it directed the 2/16th Inf to protect the brigade's right flank and clear the mountainous area north of Læigasvann. The confusion was increased by a report from division that there were no German forces in the Britatind (Hill 1009) area. Munthe-Kaas probably assumed that this report was based on the 7th Brigade having captured this area or determined that it was clear of German forces.[7]

The 2/16th Inf reached the first phase line at 0800 on May 1 and sent Co 6 forward to take up positions at the northern end of Gressvann, near the second phase line. At 1035 hours, the battalion was ordered to attack the German forces located at the southern end of Gressvann. This was a deviation from the planned two-battalion drive, one on each side of the lake, after the 1/16th Inf had passed through the 2/16th Inf. The 1/16 was still at the first phase line and the advance became a single battalion action. Whatever the reasons for the change, it became very difficult to deploy two battalions in the narrow valley after the Germans secured Britatind.

The 2/16th, with Co 6 in the lead, progressed steadily but rather slowly because of difficult snow conditions. The Norwegians continued forward even after they met heavy German fire from the heights west of Gressvann, heights they had assumed were clear of enemy forces. The great difference in altitude made the German fire inaccurate and only a few soldiers were wounded, one seriously. The battalion was well supported by mortar and artillery fire as long as there was landline connection but when they ran out of communication wire and ammunition for the mortars, the advance came to a halt. The lead company was withdrawn after a large German force was reported southeast of Hill 1009.

The lead company of the 1/16th Inf reached phase line two at 1530 hours on May 1. The battalion continued its advance along the east side of the lake but received heavy fire from German positions at the southern end of the lake and from Britatind. The Norwegians placed effective mortar and artillery fire on the enemy positions near the cabin located at the southern end of the lake and the 16-man German detachment withdrew to positions on the northwest slope of Bukkefjell (Hill 1146). Unfortunately, the Norwegians did not press the attack. They undoubtedly did not know the actual strength of the German defenders but the fact that the Germans had only one machinegun should have told them that the force was small. Instead of pursuing, the 1/16th Inf went into night positions and sent security patrols into the mountains to the east. One patrol drove a German outpost from Rivtind (Hill 1458).

The 6th Division was concerned that the troops would soon be exhausted in the winter wilderness. The division estimated that the troops could only tolerate two nights of operations in the mountains. In the division's view, the 6th Brigade had to reach Vassdal by the morning of May 5 or the brigades would have to retire to positions where the troops could rest. Lindbäck-Larsen wrote later that the troops demonstrated they could endure far more than the division anticipated.

In the evening of May 2, after a delay of nearly 24 hours, the 6th Bde ordered the 1/16th Inf to resume its advance along the east side of Gressvann towards the area to the northeast of Storfossen. The battalion was reinforced by Co 5 from the 2/16th. Major Hunstad began his advance at 0400 hours on May 3 with two companies forward, the 1st on the left and the 3rd on the right. While Co 3 followed the east shore of the lake, Co 1 worked itself diagonally up the steep mountainside into a flanking position between Hills 1013 and 1146. Despite continued fire from German positions on the high ground to the west and on the northwest slope of Bukkefjell, the battalion reached its initial objective at the southern end of the lake.

The German positions southeast of the cabin, on the northwest slope of Bukkefjell, were the battalion's next objective. Company 1 worked its way along the foot of Hill 1146 towards the German right flank. The company eventually reached an avalanche within 400 meters of the Germans. Company 3 occupied the high ground east of the cabin. Both companies found themselves in open terrain under heavy German fire that the artillery and mortars failed to silence. Around 2000 hours, Hunstad ordered the companies to dig in for the night. It took quite an effort to keep the troops, soaked from the wet snow, from falling asleep.

There were good reasons for the stiffened German resistance. The 16-man detachment, driven back on May 1, was reinforced that evening by a platoon from Schleebrügge's force. The defenses in the Sorebalak-Gressvann area were taken over by Lieutenant Müller's company in the early evening of May 3. Dietl and Windisch were sufficiently concerned about the Norwegian threat in the east to order Co 11 commanded by Captain Lömberger to move into the area between Læigastind (Hill 1335) and Britatind (Hill 1009). Company 11 had just arrived in the Storfossen area from Bjerkvik and Co Erdmenger took over its positions in that area.

The left prong of the Norwegian advance ran out of steam at the line reached by Major Hunstad's battalion. This was five kilometers short of the 6th Brigade's objective for the offensive. The 1/16th Inf remained in these positions until May 5 when the battalion was relieved by the 2/16th Inf and given another mission. The 1/16th was first moved to a rest area north of Hill 437 but after a couple of hours in that position, it was alerted for an advance via Lortvann to the lake on the east side of Læigastind (Hill 1335). At that point, the battalion would come under the operational control of the 7th Brigade. The withdrawal of 1/16th Inf from the Gressdal front was compensated for by the movement of 1/12th Inf to the north end of Gressvann where it became the brigade reserve.

The 2/16th Inf continued the pressure on the German positions on the ridgeline between Bukkefjell and Gressdalselven (Gressdal River), placing these positions under heavy direct and indirect fire. Because of this pressure, the Germans withdrew and the Norwegians promptly occupied their positions. The Germans carried out a series of air attacks against the 2/16th on May 7 without inflicting any serious casualties. The Norwegians continued to probe towards Storfossen and the north side of Storebalak where the Germans had now established a number of defensive positions. The Gressdal River had thawed below Storfossen and it was not possible to move ammunition, supplies, and heavy weapons forward using sleds. The Norwegians examined alternate routes over the mountain plateau east of Storebalak.

The Germans concluded that the Norwegian advance in Gressdal had ended and that they were preparing an operation to bypass Gressdal with an advance through Bukkedal and against Storebalak. These conclusions were undoubtedly based on the failure of 2/16th to resume the attack in force and observations of Norwegian activities associated with the examination of alternate routes.

There are several reasons for the failure of General Fleischer's main effort to reach its objective. The Norwegians neglected to secure Britatind overlooking the route of advance through Gressdal. The division reported the mountain clear of German units, but the Norwegians failed to send forces to occupy it. The early and piecemeal beginning of the 6th Brigade's offensive tipped their hand and Colonel Windisch's quick recognition of the dangers posed by the Norwegian advance in Gressdal and Dietl's quick dispatch of three companies to this flank averted a serious problem.

Major Schleebrügge's grasp that Britatind was the key to the operation and his quick occupation of that objective enabled the Germans to place flanking fire on the advancing Norwegian troops. At the same time, his quick reinforcement of the German defenders in Gressdal reduced the chance of a Norwegian breakthrough.

The 6th Brigade attacked with two battalions but, as noted, the 2/16th Inf had been reduced to little more than a reinforced company when it began its advance. The weakest battalion was given the lead and there was insufficient space in the valley to deploy more the one battalion at a time.

General Dietl noted that Norwegian marksmanship was outstanding and their winter equipment and cross-country mobility was superior. However, their lack of aggressiveness when faced with obstacles demonstrated that they had still not achieved the required experience to eliminate quickly even a few determined defenders.[8]

There was a change in command of the 6th Brigade on May 8. Colonel Løken was reassigned to command the 6th District Command when Colonel Mjelde fell ill. Lieutenant Colonel Ole Berg, who had been a member of General Ruge's staff, became the new 6th Brigade's commander. This change of command came after the left prong of the Norwegian offensive ran out of steam and it could therefore not have contributed to the abandonment of the Gressdal attack.

The Germans were experiencing problems of their own. They were outnumbered by more than 6 to 1 on the northern front and they lacked some key equipment for winter warfare. There are repeated references in the 3rd Division journal to requests for such things as sunglasses and snowshoes. These were slow in arriving and General Dietl finally sent a curt message to General

Jodl on May 4 stating that despite repeated requests, equipment needed badly by Group Windisch had not arrived. The 3rd Division was informed within four hours that sunglasses and snowshoes were on their way. The first parachute drop to Group Windisch on May 6 resulted in a mess of broken sunglasses.

The Germans also had difficulties obtaining ground support from the Luftwaffe. There are repeated references in the 3rd Division journal to requests for air support that was not provided, to requested aircraft arriving in the area but not dropping bombs, and to the Luftwaffe bombing German positions. One such incident resulted in six killed and four wounded. The problem was twofold. The Luftwaffe had not provided liaison to Dietl's forces, not even a transmitter/receiver by which they could communicate with the aircraft. Radio equipment was finally delivered on May 6.

The second problem with air support was that pilots used maps with a scale of 1:1,000,000, rendering accurate air support an impossibility. Major Schleebrügge's forces were bombed by their own aircraft on May 7 and he sent a blunt message that was relayed to Group XXI and the air support center in Trondheim. The major pointed out that effective close air support was impossible without a direct radio link between the troops and supporting aircraft. The maps carried by pilots made it impossible to distinguish between friendly and enemy positions in the mountainous terrain. Under these conditions, calling for air support often made a bad situation worse.

Attack by the Chasseurs Alpins

The dispositions of the 7th Brigade and the 6th Bn, 27th CA were discussed earlier in this chapter. There was still some movement of forces on April 30 in preparation for the planned offensive. The reinforced Co 2 from the Reserve Battalion, 16th Inf arrived by sea from Salangen and deployed to Foldevik and Laberget as rear security. The 6th Reserve Medical Company was also on its way by sea to the same location.

Lieutenant Colonel Dahl issued the attack order on May 1. The French forces were to attack that same day towards the southern end of Storevann with three companies driving south through Labergsdal while the fourth company and the mortars advanced along Route 50. These forces would converge at the southern end of Storevann. The Alta Bn remained in its positions in the Fjelldal-Holtås area during this initial phase of the attack and awaited further orders. The 2/15th Inf was in an assembly area in the woods southeast of Kvernmoen, while the 7th Mountain Artillery Battery was in position in the Fjellhøgda area. The

9th Motorized Artillery Battery did not reach the area until May 7 because the roads had to be cleared of snow.

Aerial reconnaissance indicated that the Germans had abandoned their positions north of Hestevann, the northernmost lake in the string of lakes on the east side of Route 50. The reconnaissance also showed that there were German defensive positions in the valley between Hills 513 and 785.

Reconnaissance by Co 5, 2/15th Inf in Labergdal revealed that the Germans had a strong blocking position in Nedre Labergdal. A German platoon-size force occupied the blocking position in an area consisting of large boulders from which they dominated the flat valley below. Major Celerier, commander of the 6th Bn CA, conducted a personal reconnaissance with Captain Hanekamhaug, commander of Co 5, 2/15th. In the afternoon of April 30, Celerier ordered Hanekamhaug's company, reinforced by the battalion's SES, to seize the German positions on May 1.

Hanekamhaug's plan involved sending two platoons towards the German positions along the valley bottom, one on each side of the river. The two platoons were to approach the German positions frontally and halt at a distance where fire directed towards them would be ineffective. Hanekamhaug with the other two platoons and the French SES constituted the main attack. This force would advance along the western slopes of Snaufjell, approaching the German flank from the northeast.

The advance began at 0500 hours. The two platoons in the valley moved to within 500 meters of the German positions and dug in without receiving fire. The Germans were so preoccupied with this direct approach that they did not notice the advance of the main attacking force along the west slope of Snaufjell. When Captain Hanekamhaug came even with the Germans, he ordered the French Lieutenant Blin, commander of the SES, to close on the enemy positions. Hanekamhaug sent one platoon and the machineguns forward another 300 meters as security against an expected German counterattack.

Lieutenant Blin and his men were able to approach the Germans unnoticed and when his men were in a good location to storm the positions, they opened a devastating volley. After about two minutes of intense fire, the Germans displayed the white flag of surrender and 18 of them with six machineguns passed into captivity. The Norwegian reports are full of praise for the conduct of their French allies in this operation. The two Norwegian platoons in the valley occupied the German positions quickly and prepared for a counterattack. The counterattack came in less than 30 minutes against the Norwegian left flank and some of the Norwegian troops in the 1st Platoon were driven temporarily from their positions. The German attack was eventually repulsed but not before the 1st Platoon commander was fatally wounded.

A three-man Norwegian patrol sent out shortly before the German counterattack to establish contact with the French unit advancing along Route 50 was lost. Another squad size patrol was sent out on the morning of May 2. It worked its way past the German machinegun nests, established contact with the French unit, returned without losses, and provided important information on German dispositions.

While the Norwegians and French had successfully eliminated the German blocking position between Nedre and Øvre Labergsdal, the Germans succeeded not only in blocking further French advances through Labergsdal and along Route 50, but also occupied the Snaufjell mountain between the two axes of advance. From this high ground, small German ski detachments harassed the French units constantly and made it impossible to establish any reliable contact between the two axes of advance. The German ski platoon on Snaufjell was small, only about 20 men. Lieutenant Colonel Valentini finally requested that Lieutenant Colonel Dahl clear the Snaufjell plateau with Norwegian ski troops. Captain Hanekamhaug was given this mission.

Major Celerier opposed the operation because he believed the Norwegians would take heavy casualties. Consequently, Hanekamhaug's order was changed to a reconnaissance in force of the western, northern, and eastern approaches to Snaufjell. The company, with SES attached, carried out the reconnaissance, often under fire, in an exhaustive 25-hour march that brought them back to Labergsdal through Elvenes. In the process, Hanekamhaug's troops drove the Germans from Hill 513, and this allowed the French in Labergsdal to establish contact with their company on Route 50. The reconnaissance resulted in a sketch map of the German positions, but this proved of little help as the Germans kept shifting their men from position to position, giving the impression that the mountain was held by a much larger force than they actually had.

French attempts to clear the Germans from Snaufjell were slow and methodical against stiff German opposition. The German forces in this isolated position were resupplied by air and General Béthouart reported that they displayed "extraordinary endurance."[9] The slow French progress was due to their lack of training in winter conditions and their shortage of appropriate equipment. Béthouart was well aware of the difficulties his troops faced. He ordered that all operations take place at night in order to minimize exposure to

German air attack and to take advantage of the improved mobility provided by the night frost. Béthouart concluded that it would take a long time to reach Narvik from the north. Admiral Cork eventually ordered that French troops on the northern front limit themselves to keeping the Germans tied down until the planned landing in the Bjerkvik area drew German forces in that direction.[10]

The Norwegians were not informed about this decision. The result was that the hopes in the original plan of bypassing the German positions on Gratangseidet by the advance through Labergsdal never came to fruition. The Norwegians demanded better operational coordination, which was one of the reasons for Lindbäck-Larsen's visit to the British headquarters in Harstad on May 6, discussed earlier in this chapter.

The Germans committed considerable air assets against the French-Norwegian attack through Labergsdal and along the Bjerkvik road. The coastal steamer *Dronning Maud*, carrying the 6th Reserve Medical Company from Sørreisa was attacked by German aircraft in the evening of May 1, as it was about to dock in Foldvik, despite clearly displayed large Red Cross markings. Nineteen were killed and 31 seriously wounded.

The 14th Bn CA relieved the 6th Bn CA in the evening of May 8. The 6th was pulled back to a rest area in Gratangen. According to Béthouart, 65% of the troops in this battalion were combat ineffective because of frostbite and snow blindness. The French troops received increased indirect fire resources when the French 75mm battery finally showed up in the period 6-9 May. The Norwegian 9th Motorized Artillery Battery, in positions near Hestvann, also provided support for the French troops.

The 14th Bn CA resumed its advance on May 9. The battalion cleared the Germans from Snaufjell that same day. Its lead elements reached Storevann where it was stopped by flanking fire from the western slopes of Roasme (Hill 856). The battalion spent the following days clearing Labergsdal. The battalion's SES later reached the eastern slopes of Hill 1013, but the French advance was stopped by strong German positions astride Route 50.

7th Brigade's Attack

The original offensive plan did not call for the 7th Brigade to undertake any major attacks, but to follow up the expected German withdrawal caused by the pressures exerted by the advance of the 6th Brigade and the 27th CA. The partial failure of the CA's part of the operation forced some changes in the original concept.

The beginning of operations found the 7th Brigade at the foot of the Lægastind Massif on which the Germans had positions with excellent observation and fields of fire to the north and west. The Germans occupied both heights east of Reisevann, Hill 785 and Roasme (Hill 856) and the 6th Brigade reported that a German company had occupied the high ground around Britatind. Dahl viewed the capture of the heights east of Reisevann and Hill 785 as the objectives of most immediate importance. It was decided that the Alta Bn should remain in its current positions for the time being while the 2/15th Inf, commanded by Major Hyldmo, attacked to secure the high ground around Hill 785. One company from the Alta Bn would cover the left flank of the attacking battalion against the German force reported to be on or near Britatind.

The 2/15th began its attack at 0230 hours on May 2. The attacking companies began the ascent to Hill 785 in thick fog. The fog lifted as the units neared the top and the advance was halted by heavy German fire. Nevertheless, Co 7 managed to get close enough to the German positions to storm and secure the objective. Heavy German fire from Hill 842 prevented a pursuit. Company 7 occupied Hill 785, with one platoon about 400 meters to the south of the summit. Company 6 occupied some heights to the east with its front facing Roasme (Hill 856), southwest of Hill 785. The two companies remained in these positions for several days while the Alta Bn and the French tried to work their way forward in the valley.

Company 2, Alta Bn occupied Hill 559 (to the northeast of Hill 785) on May 2 without opposition. A security detachment was sent towards Lortvann. This detachment was later moved to the area between Britatind and Stortind (Hill 1150). The Norwegians kept Hill 559 occupied by one company until May 6. Company 2, Alta Bn and Co 2, 1/16th, the latter sent via Lortvann from the 6th Brigade to secure the 7th Brigade's left flank, relieved each other in 24-hour intervals and conducted extensive patrolling to their front between Britatind and Lægastind. These patrols reported considerable German activity that pointed to a counterattack.

The counterattack came against Hill 785 during the night between May 4 and 5. The most forward Norwegian platoon was driven out of its position but it was recaptured in a counterattack the same day. Fourteen German soldiers, including one officer, were captured along with a number of weapons including machineguns and mortars. Five of those captured were wounded. The Germans admit losing a platoon to Norwegian ski troops in this attack and blame the loss on the unit's lack of mobility in the deep snow.

Company 3, Alta Bn had the difficult task of trying to eliminate German positions, including a number of well-concealed machinegun nests, from the very broken and difficult terrain between the mountains and Route 50. The company moved from Fjelldal, where it had been the battalion reserve, on May 3 and occupied the high ground about one kilometer east of Reisevann. The company resumed its advance at 2330 hours but it soon ran into heavy German fire and the attack was called off after a fight that lasted over three hours. Norwegian casualties were one killed and six wounded. The company continued to patrol and probe the German positions on May 5 and 6. There were frequent clashes, with losses on both sides. The Germans withdrew to new positions between Reisevann and Storevann on May 6.

Norwegian army and naval aircraft provided valuable support for the ground operations by flying numerous reconnaissance and ground support missions. Attacks by Norwegian aircraft are mentioned frequently in the 3rd Division's war journal. The Luftwaffe was also active, despite problems mentioned earlier. One Norwegian aircraft was shot down and four others were wrecked. Two pilots were captured.

The Germans were well armed with automatic weapons and were able to establish a belt of interlocking fire along the valley and Route 50. The same applied to the mountain massif where the placement of machineguns on key terrain covered not only the approaches to the heights but also the valleys between those heights. The German positions reduced the possibility of bypassing and flanking maneuvers and it became necessary for the Norwegians to drive the Germans from their mountain strong points by frontal attacks. This proved both tough and time-consuming in difficult terrain with deep snow against very competent and obstinate German defenders.

Orders from the division on May 5 called for a continuation of the offensive by both brigades. The division saw the clearing of the area north and northeast of Læigastind as the most important mission for the 7th Brigade. Dahl viewed Hill 842 as the key German defensive position. He decided that Hills 698 and 684 had to be captured before an attack could be carried out against Hill 842. The Norwegian attack on these hills was carried out during the night between May 5 and 6. The attack against Hill 698 succeeded but the attack against Hill 684 was repelled.

Dahl decided to attack along his whole front from Hill 785 to Britatind. Two companies on the Brigade's left flank were to attack the high ground near the lake to the east of Læigastind while two companies attacked Hill 842.

Another two companies were kept back as brigade reserve. The attacks were supported by all available artillery and mortar resources and by air attacks against Hills 842 and 780.

The Norwegian attack proceeded according to plans. Company 1, Alta Bn successfully stormed the well-fortified Hill 842 at 0600 hours on May 7. Company 7, 2/15th Inf passed through Co 1 quickly and proceeded against Roasme (Hill 856). The Germans were driven from this important height and the Norwegians now had a clear view of Herjangsfjord and could see the Narvik Peninsula in the distance. They were less than eight kilometers from Colonel Windisch's headquarters. The distance is misleading since some very rough terrain still separated the Norwegians from that location.

The Germans mounted a determined defense against the attack by the 7th Brigade's left flank units and they succeeded in keeping Norwegian reconnaissance patrols at a distance. The reinforced Co 2, Alta Bn, carried out the attack. It did not start out well since the platoon that was to secure the company's right flank was bombed by friendly aircraft and had to withdraw temporarily. German fire intensified as the company neared its objective and the attack stalled despite the commitment of an additional platoon from Co 2, 1/16th. Another platoon was added to the attacking force in the morning of May 7, but the Germans were able to keep the attack from progressing despite heavy artillery support from the 8th Mountain Artillery Battery.

The Norwegians learned that Britatind was unoccupied. The relatively short distance from Britatind would allow effective fire to be placed on the German positions from that location, especially by snipers. A platoon from Co 2, 1/16th quickly occupied Britatind. It appears that neither the 139th Regiment nor the 3rd Division knew that Britatind was unoccupied since the 3rd Division journal states that a message from the 139th reported that Britatind was lost after it was attacked by a Norwegian battalion with heavy artillery support. The Norwegian platoon on Britatind placed effective fire on the enemy positions and the German company withdrew in some disorder. When the Norwegians occupied the abandoned positions, they found weapons, ammunition, hand grenades, and rucksacks discarded in the hasty withdrawal. The Norwegians, who had suffered five badly wounded, captured five Germans, one wearing a Norwegian uniform.

Dietl and Windisch concluded that the situation on the northern front had reached a crisis stage. They decided to withdraw to a line Storfoss-Læigasvann-Ørnefjell-Skogfjell. Dietl's concerns are illustrated by the fact that at 1745 hours on May 7, he ordered Major Haussels in Narvik to send another company of mountain troops to Bjørnefjell. This order was cancelled at 1900 hours after the 3rd Division was notified by Group XXI that a 60-men company of mountain troops would arrive by air the next day.

General Dietl put on his skis, and in the company of two NCOs, made a personal visit to Colonel Windisch's headquarters. The meeting between the two commanders resulted in the conclusion that it would be impossible to hold positions at both ends of Læigasvann if reinforcements were not received. A message to Group XXI after Dietl's return to his headquarters on May 8 stated that two companies were needed immediately.

In a draft of future operations provided to the brigades and also to the British liaison officer on May 7, General Fleischer emphasized the importance of reaching a line where the brigades could rest before continuing offensive operations. This involved securing a line running roughly from Storfossen in the east via Læigasvann and Ørnefjell to the Bjerkvik road on the southern Snaufjell slopes. Occupation of this line would also place the Norwegians within a short distance of the Hartvigvann area, an objective for the continued offensive. The advance to the proposed line would, in the opinion of the division, draw German forces away from the planned Allied landing areas near Bjerkvik. The plan made it clear that the goal of future operations was the capture of the Bjørnefjell area on the Swedish border.

The 7th Brigade gave 1/16th Inf the mission of clearing any German forces from the area between Britatind and Læigastind, including the eastern and southern slopes of these mountains. This would secure the brigade's left flank and facilitate the 6th Brigade's advance in Gressdal. The Alta Bn held Roasme (Hill 856). It and the 2/15th Inf, in cooperation with the French forces, were to be prepared to clear the Germans from the east side of Route 50, as far as the northern slopes of Snaufjellene. The next brigade objectives were Ørnefjell (Hills 667 and 664) and Vassdalsfjell (Hill 894). The successful capture of these mountains would bring the brigade into positions just north of Hartvigvann and less than five kilometers from Elvegårdsmoen.

The 1/16th attacked the German positions in the area between Britatind and Læigastind on May 8 and the Germans were cleared from the area after some sharp fighting. They left a considerable amount of supplies and ammunition when abandoning their positions. Germans losses were five killed, five wounded, and four captured. The Norwegian had only one wounded.

The 1/16th was ordered forward and established itself in positions at the eastern end of Læigasvann. Except for supporting the French in their efforts to reach the area near Snaufjellene, Lieutenant Colonel Dahl recommended to division that the rest of the brigade remain in its positions until the units on the flanks had reached their objectives. Supplying the forces in forward positions required enormous effort and the number of personnel in these positions was kept to a minimum to ease this task.

The 1/16th continued its attack with two companies on May 9 against the east side of Læigas Lake and Hill 697. The attack failed in the open terrain in front of the mountain heights (Vassdalfjell and Storebalak). The Norwegians encountered intense direct and indirect fire from these locations. Fortuitous showers and fog helped the Norwegians to disengage and withdraw, by providing some concealment in the open terrain.

Dahl reorganized the units on his right in preparation for a continuation of the attack from Roasme against Vassdalsfjell and Ørnefjell. Two companies from Alta Bn (2 and 4) were in positions north of Hill 842. These units, while providing flank protection against the Germans in the Storevann area, were prepared to take part in the forthcoming attack. Company 3 of the same battalion would attack the plateau about 700 meters east of Storevann. This planned attack was later cancelled and the company took up positions on Roasme, where it remained until May 13. Company 1 remained in defensive positions on Roasme. The 2/15th occupied positions between Roasme and Læigastind. It was responsible for maintaining contact with 1/16th Inf on its left.

The operation, which should have begun any time after 2000 hours on May 7, was postponed. The postponement was due to a Norwegian-French plan for a joint attack from Roasme in support of the 27th CA along Route 50. Parts of the 6th Bn CA, which had been in a rest area near Gratangen, were moved to Roasme, to the right of the Alta Bn. The plan for the attack was worked out between Lieutenant Colonel Dahl and Major Celerier. A one-hour artillery preparation against Hills 676 and 664 by Norwegian and French artillery and mortars was to begin at 2200 hours and thereafter switch to Ørnefjell. Reinforced Company 7, 2/15th would begin its movement towards Hill 676 at 2230 hours, supported by ten mortars located at Roasme. A French company was to advance and occupy Ørnefjell in conjunction with the Norwegian seizure of Hill 676.

The Norwegian attack began in the evening of May 9. The forward movement was assisted by snow and fog but when the company closed on the initial objective, it came under heavy fire from Hill 676, Hill 664, and Ørnefjell. The attack faltered and stopped. Friendly supporting fire did not work out as anticipated because of poor visibility and poor cooperation between the two nationalities. A misunderstanding of the attack plan may have contributed to the failure of the attack. The French unit refused to advance, insisting that they were in reserve, and despite repeated requests for fire support, their six mortars failed to open fire until late in the day.

The weather prevented effective artillery support and the four Norwegian mortars failed to silence or dampen the enemy fire. Norwegian machineguns that could have provided covering fire for the attack were not leapfrogged forward and found themselves 2,000 to 2,500 meters from their targets. Consequently, the attacking company was pinned down the whole day, unable to move either forward or fall back. It managed to disengage and withdraw to Roasme after darkness.

A mountain howitzer was brought forward to Roasme during the night of May 11. In a remarkable achievement, the horses were outfitted with snowshoes and managed to pull the howitzer to the top of Roasme, an 1800 feet difference in elevation from their start point. The 7th Mountain Artillery Battery and the 9th Motorized Artillery Battery were brought forward to new positions at the north end of Storevann to provide better support for a planned French attack on Ørnefjell from Roasme. This attack was cancelled due to changes in plans for Allied operations in the Narvik area.

The Norwegian-French Offensive in Retrospect

The Norwegian-French attacks on the northern front took place during a period of continued Allied inactivity except for the French operations on Ankenes Peninsula. It was a grueling experience for the troops, especially the French. They were not trained or equipped for the conditions that existed in the Narvik area. They were unable to conduct effective off-road operations and the troops suffered enormously. The Norwegians were better equipped for winter warfare and most had lived under these climatic conditions. Nevertheless, as Major Hunstad's report illustrates, the units suffered many hardships: "The days and nights were cold and wet up there, with little food and no heat. In the beginning, the battalion had nothing but holes dug into snow-banks for shelters since the tents had to be left behind in Gressdal because of their weight." The situation was the same in Major Hydlmo's battalion (2/15th) in the Roasme area:[11]

> The operations in this sector were very stressful for the soldiers and their leaders. All supplies—ammunition, firewood, provisions—had to be carried on the backs up into the high mountains. The trains with the

field-kitchen were near Storfossen in Gratangen, where dinners and dried meals had to be fetched. These trips took 5 to 6 hours.

The offensive operations were carried out in a roadless winter wilderness where survival alone was a major challenge. The enormous effort required to keep men and machines of two brigades functioning under these conditions cannot be overstated. The supply operation was a daunting task and a major accomplishment. It took 12–14 hours to bring provisions and ammunition to the 1/16th Inf during the fighting around Britatind from the battalion trains located near Hill 437. Each man carried a load of 90 lbs up the steep mountainsides in deep snow.

Prior to resuming their offensive on April 29, the Norwegians could look back on a series of disastrous defeats at the hands of the Germans: Narvik, Bjørnefjell, and Gratangen. While these defeats had instilled in them a sense of caution, they had not broken the morale of the leadership or the troops. The two brigades had become veterans by the second week in May. The leaders had learned not to underestimate the Germans and they and the troops had learned the hard way the price paid for disregarding basic military principles and by neglecting security for personal comfort. Two weeks of operations in the mountains northwest of Narvik restored much of their self-confidence and did much to boost their morale. They discovered that they could operate successfully against German mountain troops and were able to drive a well-trained, battle-hardened, and determined enemy from excellent defensive positions.

The primary British writers about the fighting in and around Narvik—Derry, Moulton, and Ash—devote little space to the enormous effort undertaken by the French and Norwegians on the northern front. Derry writes that, "It had taken ten painful days to advance five miles towards Narvik." This statement is not only dismissive of the actual achievement in the mountain wilderness, but it fails to mention the crisis the advance caused for the German command and its commitment of forces that could otherwise have been used against the forthcoming Allied amphibious assault. Derry, in describing the ascent of Fjordbotneidet by the 1/12th Inf in a snowstorm on April 23, writes ". . . a Norwegian battalion native to the country and expert on skis, not cumbered with heavy equipment, took eight hours to move two miles with a rise in height of about 300 feet."[12]

The unit making the ascent, the 1/12th Inf, came from Trøndelag, not North Norway and the troops were not all expert skiers. The men carried loads of 60 lbs as they struggled forward at night in blizzard conditions in snow that was chest deep at times. They brought with them not only mortars and artillery but basic loads for those weapons. The ascent was not 300 feet but 1,200 to 1,500 feet.

The German sources, as we have seen, give a far better appreciation of the difficulties facing them on the northern front, and the extraordinary effort required to overcome them. In its situation report to OKW on May 4, Dietl stated that reconnaissance and experience led him to conclude that defense of the mountains in the north would not be possible with the forces he had at his disposal in the face of a numerical superior enemy.[13]

Group XXI, to which Dietl's forces had again been transferred, concluded on May 6 that the situation for the troops in the Narvik area had become critical and was not surprised by a message from Dietl two days later stating that his forces could not hold the northern front without immediate reinforcements and strong support from the Luftwaffe.

The Government and General Ruge Arrive

The Norwegian King and Government arrived in Tromsø on May 1. The defense and foreign ministers continued on to England in the cruiser and from there to France. The campaigns in southern and central Norway had caused a deep skepticism within the Norwegian Government about Allied plans and intentions. These two ministers had the task of finding out how the Allies viewed the situation in Norway and what their plans were for the future. They were to demand official assurances that the Allies would continue the campaign in Norway and guarantees of immediate and effective assistance. The prime minister made it clear that, without such assurances, he would be compelled to recommend to the king that negotiations be initiated with the Germans for a cease-fire.[14]

The government members were spread throughout the area near Tromsø at first but found that arrangement unworkable and by the middle of May, all major governmental offices were moved to Tromsø. General Ruge and HOK (Army High Command) arrived on May 3, with a reduced staff of about 30 officers and civilians.

Ruge had written a memorandum for the government on his way to North Norway. The memorandum laid out Ruge's view of the situation and recommendations for the future and became the basis for governmental policy for the remainder of the campaign. It assumed that the Allies would soon evacuate

Nord-Trøndelag and that this would compel the government to make the vital decision of whether or not to continue the war. Ruge pointed out that the war would not end until the great powers concluded peace. His personal views, political as well as moral, were that the Norwegians should continue the war.

Providing the government decided to continue the war, General Ruge made a series of proposals that he considered imperative for success. He identified German air superiority as the single-most important factor in the defeat in southern and central Norway. It was therefore imperative that the Allies bring in sufficient fighter aircraft to neutralize the German air threat that would become serious after the Luftwaffe had a chance to become fully operational in Trøndelag. The expected German drive from Trøndelag had to be met and this required the early elimination of General Dietl's forces. He emphasized that it would not be possible to hold a line south of Bodø without a significant increase in forces in that area. The size of the Norwegian Army had to be increased and they needed to be better equipped. He realized that a significant increase in size was not possible before Trøndelag was recaptured and that equipment had to come from Allied sources. All recommendations were based on the assumption of continued Allied assistance.

General Fleischer was not overjoyed by the arrival of the government and General Ruge. Up to then, he had been the commander-in-chief in North Norway, with full authority over both military and civilian affairs. He had to expect that this situation would now change, that the government would take over the civil administration, and that Ruge would become his military superior in fact as well as in name. His greatest concern was that he would lose control of military operations.

Fleischer was therefore both anxious and skeptical when Ruge showed up at his headquarters for their first meeting on May 6. His anxiety was relieved after Ruge presented his views on how he saw their division of responsibilities. Ruge stated that he had no intention of becoming involved in Fleischer's command of operations against Narvik. The role of HOK would be to take over coordination with the Allied military authorities and acquire supplies and matériel for current and future operations. In addition, the operation of airfields, mobilization, and organizing and equipping additional forces would remain the prerogative of HOK. Fleischer was authorized to continue operational coordination with Allied military leaders. Ruge's decision on these points was laid out in a paper prepared by HOK that same day. The British command in Harstad was informed about the new arrangements.[15]

Fleischer was relieved and pleased by the results of his meeting with Ruge. Ruge had also decided that HOK did not need all the general staff officers it had assigned and some of these were placed at the disposal of the 6th Division. Among those were Lieutenant Colonel Berg who became the 6th Brigade commander and Lieutenant Colonel R. Roscher-Nielsen, the General Staff's chief of operations, who took over as local commander in Mosjøen on May 13 from Lieutenant Colonel Nummedal.

Hovland writes that, "Fleischer's happiness would soon turn to dismay and bitterness. Ruge did not keep his promises, and Fleischer's position as commander-in-chief in this part of the country was systematically undermined in the following weeks until he no longer even had control of his own division."[16] As examples, Hovland mentions the fact that Fleischer lost command of the naval forces as well as the army air corps. While Fleischer would undoubtedly have preferred to retain his position as civilian and military leader in North Norway, that preference was unrealistic. The government was entitled to pick up civil leadership and it was sheer fantasy to expect that General Ruge or Admiral Diesen (who arrived on May 4) had come to North Norway to sit on their hands.

Hovland's contention that Fleischer no longer had control over army aircraft and his statement that "From the end of May the division again commanded the Hålogaland Air Group after having had to manage without Norwegian air support from May 7," are misleading.[17] What Hovland fails to mention is that Ruge turned all air resources, except for Captain Reistad and two other individuals, over to Hålogaland Air Group on May 8, an organization that remained under Fleischer's operational control. The 6th Division directive of May 11 ordered Norwegian naval and army aircraft to support Norwegian troops attacking from the north during the Bjerkvik landing. Norwegian aircraft also supported the French attack on Hill 220 on May 13/14. The air resources available consisted of 12 aircraft and personnel that escaped from south and central Norway.[18] These were later joined by other aircraft from the southern part of the country.

Ruge wrote later that his meeting with Fleischer reinforced his decision not to make any immediate changes in the command structure, since Fleischer seemed to have his affairs in order and because of the latter's obvious disappointment at no longer being the senior commander in the area. He goes on to note that Fleischer's personal feelings and resentment played an important role in the weeks that followed. [19]

NOTES

1 Karol Zbyszewski, *The Fight for Narvik: Impressions of the Polish Campaign in Norway* (London: L. Drummond, 1041), p. 3. While styled Chasseurs de Montagne or Chasseurs du Nord, many of the troops had never seen any mountains and they were definitely not trained for arctic winter warfare.

2 Raymond Sereau, *L'Expedition de Norvège 1940* (Baden-Baden: Regie Autonome des Publications Officielles, 1949),p. 48.

3 Ibid, p. 51 and an 11-page manuscript in Norwegian titled "Rapport – General Bethouart," p. 3.

4 *3GDKTB*, 04281945, 04300930, and 05011900.

5 Ibid, 05020330, 05030230, and 05031420.

6 Munthe-Kaas, *Kriegent*, p. 109, note.

7 Ibid, p. 109 and Johan Helge Berg and Olav Vollan, *Fjellkrigen 1940. Lapphaugen-Bjørnefjell* (Trondheim: Wennbergs Trykkeri A.S., 1999), pp. 142-143.

8 *3GDKTB*, 04290930.

9 "Rapport – General Bethouart", p. 3.

10 Sereau, *L'Expedition*, p. 54 and "Rapport – General Bethouart", p. 3.

11 As quoted in Sandvik, *Operasjonene*, vol. 2, p. 54.

13 *3GDKTB*, 05042010.

14 Trygve Lie, *Leve eller dø. Norge i Krig* (Oslo: Tiden norsk forlag, 1955), p. 206.

15 Quoted in Sandvik, *Operasjonene* , vol. 2, p. 67.

16 Hovland, *Fleischer*, p.157.

17 Ibid, p. 227.

18 Sandvik, *Operasjonene*, vol. 2, pp. 114, 69.

19 Ruge, *Felttoget*, p. 130.

12

2ND MOUNTAIN DIVISION
TO THE RESCUE

"It was [seemed] evident that if the French Chasseurs could not retire along this route, the Germans could not advance along it."

GENERAL MASSY'S DISPATCH AS QUOTED BY CHURCHILL.

The Way North

The news coming from southern and central Norway in late April caused Fleischer to be concerned. The possibility of German forces moving north from Oslo linking up with those in Trondheim was real and information about the operations in the Steinkjer area was disheartening. It was becoming more and more obvious that a threat was looming in the form of a German advance that could bring them into the southern part of Nordland Province.

The straight-line distance between Namsos and Narvik is about 480 kilometers. Much of the sparsely populated Nordland Province consists of a relatively narrow sliver of land between the Norwegian Sea and the Swedish border. The terrain is difficult. It is mountainous, was covered with snow, and the north-south route is cut by a number of fjords. Namdal, the area between Grong and Mosjøen, was especially tough to traverse. There are numerous islands off the coast and in the fjords. The Arctic Circle cuts through the province and the differences between high and low tides are very pronounced at these latitudes. Fjords with narrow entrances have treacherous currents. The north-south road, Route 50, was in poor condition. Ferries were required at several points along the route and there was no road at all for the last 140 kilometers before reaching Narvik. Most of this area was a mountain wilderness. There was no railroad north of Mosjøen and the portion between the southern provincial boundary and Mosjøen was not completed. To make matters worse, there were hundreds of lakes of various sizes and the terrain was heavily forested in some parts.

Bickering Between Norwegian Commanders

To make difficulties for a German advance in the southern part of Nordland Province, Fleischer issued orders for destruction of lines of communications in that area. On April 27, he ordered the destruction of the railroad in the Namdal area north of Grong. While the railroad was not open for use, it was believed that the railroad bed would provide the Germans with an additional line of advance to the north. The Directorate of Roads in Mosjøen was also ordered to prepare the first 30 kilometers of roads north of the provincial boundary for destruction.

While events proved General Fleischer correct in his assessment of the military situation, it is important to look at these events from the standpoint of what the commanders knew at the time. While the situation in southern Norway looked bleak, Fleischer had no indications of an imminent collapse in South Norway or that the Allies were about to evacuate either Åndalsnes or Namsos. His order was issued three days before the Germans established an overland connection between their forces in southern Norway and those in Trøndelag. Under these circumstances, an order to destroy lines of communications in Nordland Province immediately was bound to have a depressing effect on the morale of the troops fighting in Trøndelag.

Fleischer had placed 1/14th Inf at Colonel Getz's disposal for his operations in the Steinkjer area as well as the responsibility for Nordland Province south of Bodø on April 20. Getz, as the Norwegian field commander in Trøndelag, reported directly to General Ruge. He also assumed the duties as commander of the 5th Division when General Laurantzon received a medical discharge. Fleischer had no authority to issue orders directly to Getz, or to the civil authorities within his area of responsibility. Fleischer's orders led to serious recriminations between him and Getz.

Getz received copies of the orders to the Directorate of Roads and Chief of Railroads on April 27. An earlier forgery of an important message from General Fleischer made the 5th Brigade uneasy on this subject.[1] Getz provided copies of the telegrams to General de Wiart since he assumed that the orders, if not falsified, were issued because of an imminent threat of enemy landings in the north that would menace the Allied rear and make the situation in Namsos critical. Since this possibility seemed rather remote, Getz sent a message to Fleischer asking for confirmation of the order. The following day he requested that the British undertake aerial reconnaissance of the fjords between Mosjøen and Mo in order to determine if there were any enemy activities in these areas.

It was natural for Colonel Getz to be concerned about the orders since the road from Mosjøen to Grong was not only his supply route but also a logical line of retreat if that should become necessary. Fleischer, rather than consulting with Getz, issued an order on April 28 to Lieutenant Colonel Nummedal, the military commander in Nordland, to carry out the orders conveyed in the previous day's messages to the civilian authorities.

On the same day that Nummedal received his directive from the 6th Division, Getz was told that the order (for destruction) was to be carried out and that his authority over Nordland Province would be rescinded if he created any further difficulties. Getz answered the same day, explaining the military situation in Trøndelag and stating that if it became necessary for his forces to withdraw, they would do so towards Mosjøen and destroy the railroad and road behind them.[2] In view of this, Getz asked for immediate confirmation that the 6th Division wanted the lines of communications destroyed between Mosjøen and Grong. Getz kept the Allies informed about the messages between himself and Fleischer and he claims they were equally convinced that the orders were false.[3]

Colonel Getz also sent a message to General Ruge asking if the Army High Command had any knowledge about what he described as "an incomprehensible message" from General Fleischer to Lieutenant Colonel Nummedal. He also stated that he viewed the message as a forgery and that he would not carry out the destruction called for before he had an answer from Fleischer giving the reasons for the order. Based on a report in June 1940, Nummedal, appears to have been equally confused about what was required by the 6th Division since the order was not implemented.[4]

Subsequently, Getz had a telephone conversation with Fleischer, in which he claimed that Fleischer admitted that the intention of the order was to prepare the lines of communications for destruction.[5] Lindbäck-Larsen denies Getz's version vehemently although he states that he had no part in the matter since Fleischer handled it personally.[6] Lindbäck-Larsen goes on to allege that Getz tried to obtain authority from the British to sabotage the order in the morning of May 2. He does not explain this serious accusation. It is probably a reference to a letter from Getz to General Carton de Wiart on that day where Getz explains that Fleischer's order only pertained to preparations for destruction and where he mentions that a letter from the British general to Fleischer about the affair would be helpful.[7]

Hovland writes that Fleischer was furious when he learned on May 2 that the Allies had evacuated Namsos without prior notification to Colonel Getz. He viewed their action as nothing short of abandoning their comrades on the field of battle. Getz was equally bitter towards the Allies. He demonstrated his anger by giving a copy of Carton de Wiart's letter to a Swedish newspaper, *Svenska Dagbladet*. General Feurstein writes in his book that he met Colonel Getz on his way north and the colonel gave him a copy of the British notification of evacuation while they had breakfast together.[8] Hovland also maintains that Getz tried to sabotage Fleischer's order and that he sought Allied support for this action:

> As untidy as the command relationships were, General Fleischer's authority for the order is open for discussion. What is not open for discussion is the fact that his assessment of the situation was correct, and that Getz failure to follow orders from the only superior he had contact with at this time, had disastrous consequences for later operations in Nordland.[9]

Whatever the facts, it is very unlikely that successful destruction of lines of communications would have prevented the "disastrous consequences." The Germans were prepared for heavy destruction of communications lines. This was the pattern withdrawing Norwegian forces had established in southern Norway. The Germans committed large resources to repairing and improving the road and railroad between Nord-Trøndelag and Mosjøen. Five engineer companies and a large work force were employed in opening and maintaining the Grong-Mosjøen road.

While roadblocks and blown bridges required much effort to repair, those repairs were carried out speedily. Many of the breaks were repaired within 24 hours and larger projects such as railroad bridges were opened for traffic within 48 hours.[10] The composition and organization of Feurstein's lead battle groups, Sorko and Schratz, were such that they could by-pass any lines of communications breaches and be supplied by airdrop or by seaplanes. The destruction of lines of communications was therefore only a small hindrance as long as German air superiority remained unchallenged. In their withdrawal from Mo to Posthus, the British destroyed about 30 bridges behind them. This had little effect on the speed of the German advance and goes a long way to deflate the arguments of those who claimed that Getz and Nummedal's failure to carry out destruction of the lines of communication in the southern part of the province had catastrophic consequences. However, it was unfortunate that such relations existed between two commanders who shared a common goal and it is puzzling what motives Getz and Nummedal could have had in allegedly "sabotaging" Fleischer's order. One explanation is that they considered it illogical to destroy lines of communications that were also their supply lines after April 26, ahead rather than behind withdrawing troops.

Colonel Getz informed General Fleischer on May 2 that he was relinquishing his authority in Nordland and that he had sent the 1/14th Inf back into that province. Getz's remaining cavalry and infantry units covered the disengagement and withdrawal of the 1/14th. It is debatable whether Getz's two infantry battalions could have disengaged and withdrawn via Grong after the surprise Allied evacuation. The Germans were quick to move north and occupy Grong. However, Getz should have tried. While his troops were almost out of ammunition and rations, it should have been possible for them to follow in the footsteps of the 1/14th in the hope that they would be supplied along their route of withdrawal. An order to that effect from General Ruge arrived on May 3, after the surrender and while Getz's forces were in the process of demobilizing.[11]

The morale in Sundlo's 1/14th Inf battalion was high prior to Getz's surrender. The battalion was in position on the east side of Snåsvann and had repelled several strong German probes in that area. The news of the Allied evacuation and the subsequent surrender of Getz's forces came as a shock to the battalion from which it never recovered. A train accident at the outset of the battalion's transportation northward, resulting in seven killed and over 30 wounded, did not help. From just north of Grong, the battalion made its way on skis and by motor vehicles over the stretch where railroad tracks had not been laid, and arrived in Mosjøen on May 5.

The low morale among the Norwegian troops in the 1/14th, which resulted in a number of desertions as the battalion withdrew through its home area, almost became a mutiny. A soldier's committee sent a telegram to General Fleischer on May 5 suggesting that the area not be made a war zone since the means available to the battalion were so inadequate that its position was untenable. Fleischer's answer pointed out the importance for the operations against Narvik of a tough defense as far south in Nordland Province as possible. His message concluded, "A more important mission has never been given to a Norwegian battalion."[12]

Allied Finger-Pointing

The British had considered it extremely improbable that the Germans would advance from Namsos to Narvik, and consequently they were presented with a situation for which they had not planned. However, by the end of April, some in the Allied camp understood that the evacuation of Namsos gave the Germans an opportunity to advance north to relieve their hard-pressed forces in Narvik. Both Paris and London urged that part of the forces evacuated should do so overland while some should proceed to Mosjøen by sea.

The news that Carton de Wiart did not plan to leave forces in the area north of Namsos apparently came as a surprise to General Ironside. After a midnight call on April 29 from a French admiral, a hurried meeting with the French Military Attaché, and a visit to General Massy's home before 0300 hours, Ironside discovered that his "orders issued about the occupation of various points on the fiords to the north of Namsos had not been obeyed."[13] A message from Massy to Carton de Wiart stressed the importance of holding Mosjøen and suggested that part of the force in Namsos be moved there by sea while other forces were used to delay the Germans along the road from Grong.

Generals Carton de Wiart and Audet argued that they did not have sufficient ski troops to cover the evacuation, that the road north was impassable because of the thaw, and that the troops would be exposed to heavy German air attacks.[14] If the Allies had adequate liaison with Norwegian forces they would have learned that the railroad bed across the mountains had been cleared of snow prior to April 19 and that as of April 26, the 5th Brigade was supplied from Mosjøen by using both the railroad and road. At the time that local Allied commanders declared the route impassable, the 1/14th Inf was withdrawing over it.

General Gamelin, surprised by both the evacuation and the fact that forces were not left behind to hinder the German northward advance, sent instructions directly to General Audet on May 2, directing French forces to take up positions near Grong.[15] While this led to a hurried meeting between Audet and Carton de Wiart, it came too late and was not sufficient to convince the two commanders. They argued that the force would be trapped since it could not withdraw overland.

It was unfortunate that the decision on how to withdraw from Namsos was left to the local commanders since it had a direct effect on the operations in Narvik over which neither they nor General Massy had any authority. Allowing the two battalions of 5th Demi-Brigade CA to fight a rearguard action along the Grong-Mosjøen road and railroad may have been to Allied benefit. It is quite possible that Getz, encouraged by the fact that some Allies were still at his side, would have withdrawn his remaining two battalions by the same route and the presence of French forces may have prevented the demoralization of the 1/14th

Inf. The Allies did send a small French force of about 100 men with two British light anti-aircraft guns by sea to secure Mosjøen against airborne attack.

By a quick decision and decisive action it should have been possible to keep the forces fighting north of Grong supplied through the small port of Mosjøen. The German air threat mentioned by Derry did not present greater problems for the delaying force than it later posed to the piecemeal and ineffectual British attempts to insert troops along the coastline to stem the German advance. In fact, as the Allies were wrangling about how to withdraw their forces from Namsos, on April 29, General Mackesy was directed to send forces from the Narvik front to Nordland Province.

Generals Gamelin and Ironside insisted that part of the evacuating force conduct an effective delaying action between Grong and Mosjøen. The authors of Ironside's diaries write:

> Now that Namsos was on the point of being lost, it was imperative to stop the Germans moving up the coast and relieving their garrison at Narvik before we had captured it ourselves. Ironside [and Gamelin] accordingly wanted his only ski-troops, the Chasseurs Alpins, to retire, not by sea, but slowly up the road to the north, via Grong and Mosjoën, being supplied from the several small ports on the Norwegian coast, delaying the enemy as long as possible and eventually joining the British at Narvik.[16]

Gamelin's and Ironside's views are confirmed by the message Gamelin sent to the French commander in Namsos on May 2 and General Massy's message to Carton de Wiart on April 29 after what Ironside describes as a stormy meeting in the early morning hours. Hovland places the blame on the British, more specifically on Churchill. Churchill, however, writes:

> I was most anxious that a small part of the Namsos force should make their way in whatever vehicles were available along the coastal road to Grong. Even a couple of hundred would have sufficed to fight small rear-guard actions. From Grong they would have to find their way on foot to Mosjoen ... I was repeatedly assured that the road was impassable. General Massy from London sent insistent requests. It was replied that even a small party of French Chasseurs, with their skis, could not traverse this route. "It was [seemed] evident," wrote General

Massy a few days later in his dispatch, "that if the French Chasseurs could not retire along this route, the Germans could not advance along it … "[17]

British authors appear to place the blame on the local commanders, especially the commander of the French contingent. Moulton writes that General Audet considered the road from Grong to Mosjøen impassable and that Carton de Wiart accepted his opinion. Derry writes that Generals Audet and Carton de Wiart were equally opposed to the idea of an overland withdrawal of some forces.

However, General Béthouart relates a different story:

One could have evacuated all or parts of the troops along this road [Namsos to Mosjøen] with all equipment and thereby delayed the enemy's advance and established a front that with ease and effectiveness could have stopped the enemy … My half-brigade of alpines together with the Norwegian brigade under Colonel Getz were especially well suited for this mission.[18]

A Supreme Allied War Council decision in early April gave the British command of and responsibility for operations in Scandinavia. We know that General Carton de Wiart's views on operations in Nord-Trøndelag were heavily influenced by the massive German air attacks on Steinkjer and Namsos. He may well have concluded that any operations in this area were futile unless he received effective air support. General Audet probably shared these views. However, the decision on what to do with the forces in Namsos was a strategic decision that affected what now had become the main Allied operation to recapture Narvik, and it was therefore a decision that should have been made in London, and insisted on.

Feurstein Begins his Advance

The Germans wasted no time in exploiting the vacuum left by the Allied evacuation and the surrender of the 5th Brigade. They entered the ruins of Namsos on May 4 and General von Falkenhorst issued orders that same day for the 2nd Mountain Division, commanded by Lieutenant General Valentin Feurstein, to begin its overland drive to establish contact with Dietl's forces in Narvik.[19]

The 2nd Mountain Division was not part of the forces originally earmarked for the invasion of Norway. This elite unit was added when Hitler became concerned in late April about the situation in Norway and particularly about a link-up with Dietl in Narvik. The 2nd Mountain Division was located in the Eifel area when it was ordered to Oslo via Denmark. There were several difficulties and mishaps during its deployment.

Since the division had not been part of the original invasion force and therefore not part of the movement plans, there was a scramble to find transport and much of the heavy equipment was left behind. In addition, there were serious losses in equipment during the transport from Denmark to Norway. Finally, Group XXI detached the division's engineer battalion for service in southern Norway.[20]

The 2/137th Inf, reinforced by one mountain artillery battery and one engineer company, moved by air to Værnes Airfield on May 2. Lieutenant Colonel August Sorko commanded this group. While the bulk of the division was underway to Trondheim on foot or by railroad, Sorko's forces were rushed to Grong to begin the advance towards Narvik.

General Feurstein and his staff ran into some of the same problems that plagued other Germans in Norway. For example, they could not put their hands on adequate maps and were forced, like the pilots over Narvik, to rely on maps on a scale of 1:1,000,000 or road maps. Feuerstein met with General von Falkenhorst and his chief-of-staff, Colonel von Buschenhagen, in Trondheim on May 4 and received his marching order.

While Von Falkenhorst may have expected that any resistance north of Namsos would be minimal after the Allied withdrawal and the surrender of the 5th Norwegian Brigade, he also wanted to light a fire under his subordinate. His order emphasized the need for haste and made light of any possible opposition. Feurstein was less exuberant than his superior and answered, "We will do everything, but please do not expect the impossible."[21] Feurstein knew that there were still elements of the 14th Norwegian Regiment in the area north of Grong. Furthermore, he anticipated that the Allies would make every effort to impede his advance, an advance that threatened their stranglehold on Narvik and Dietl's forces.

Feurstein and a small staff set out the following day from Trondheim in three taxis to make contact with Sorko. Group XXI's evening situation report for May 5 stated that Group Feurstein was on its way from Grong to Mosjøen with all available motorized forces. Was this a sarcastic reference to the three taxis? The motorized transport for the two mountain divisions was still in southern Norway waiting for the opening of the road to Trondheim or in Denmark awaiting shipping to Norway. In his history of World War 2, General von Tippelskirch writes that an army corps consisting of one mountain division and one infantry division pressed forward into North Norway after the Allied evacuation of Namsos. Feurstein notes sarcastically that his "army corps" consisted of six and a half companies of mountain troops, one artillery battery, and a staff of six. The 181st Division under General Woytasch had conducted the operations against the Allies and Norwegians north of Trondheim but this unit was only used to repair the lines of communications behind the 2nd Division, assist in the supply effort, and later help clear the offshore islands. The major forces eventually available to General Feurstein for his mission consisted of the 136th and 137th Mountain Infantry Regiments, Colonel Weiss' 138th Mountain Infantry Regiment (belonging to the 3rd Mountain Division), 83rd Engineer Battalion from the 3rd Division, 1st and 2nd Bns of the 730th Artillery, and the 40th Anti-tank detachment.

The forces available to General Feurstein for the first phase of his daunting task, the 200 kilometer advance from Grong to Mosjøen, consisted of only two mountain infantry battalions (2/137 and 3/138), a battery of mountain artillery and one engineer platoon. This is a far cry from General von Tippelskirch's claim that Feurstein began his advance with a mountain corps consisting of what amounted to two reinforced divisions.

Scissorforce

Fleischer and Ruge were concerned about Narvik's southern flank and had argued repeatedly that Allied units be moved to Nordland to bolster the weak Norwegian forces in that area. Cork and Mackesy were also concerned and one company of the Scots Guards was sent to Bodø from Harstad during the night of April 29–30. Its mission was to prevent the seizure of the town by a German airborne operation. This did not satisfy the Norwegians or Mackesy. He wanted sizable forces to stop the Germans in the Mosjøen area and General Gamelin in Paris was arguing for a similar strategy.

The British, having become reluctant to expose major naval surface units in areas of German air superiority, now adopted a similar attitude when it came to larger ground units. Since air protection was not forthcoming, they decided to use smaller units to try to stop the German advance through Nordland Province. Derry explains the logic behind this decision:

The Germans were to be stopped by demolitions along the road, by guerrilla activities on their flanks, by raising the countryside against them, and by preparing to deal firmly with whatever small parties they might land from the sea or the air. This was to be the work of the Independent Companies, which were so organized as to need air defence neither for themselves nor for their base.[22]

The decision to use five Independent Cos, who collectively became known as *Scissorforce*, in Norway was made on April 18 but they were not ready until the end of the month. Before they were deployed, the command relationships were further muddled on April 27. Admiral Cork was given command of all forces from Bodø north while General Massy, still operating from London, commanded all forces south of Bodø. It was bad enough to have these forces commanded from far-away London, but the decision failed to recognize that the operation in Nordland was very much a part of the Narvik Campaign and, as such, should have fallen within the same command structure. Cork's concerns and confusion are made clear in a message he sent to the Admiralty on May 4.

Request I may be informed of the general policy regarding Bodø, Mo and Mosjöen. It seems most important to hold in force the Mo road leading north. From Admiralty messages it appears the forces being sent are hardly adequate for this purpose and with such weak detachments in the air another naval commitment comes into being. These areas do not, I presume, come under Narvik. Are there any Allied forces to the south of me?[23]

This shortcoming in the command structure was rectified on May 7 when the Independent Cos were placed under Admiral Cork.

The Independent Cos were the forerunners of the famous Commandos of later years. However, in April 1940, they fell far short in quality and training of those highly professional and well-trained units. These companies were large, numbering 20 officers and 270 enlisted. The officers came for the most part from the territorial forces, but included a sprinkling of regulars and members of the Indian Army. The enlisted were all volunteers from the territorial forces. The units, which included some engineers, communicators, and medical personnel, had not worked and trained together for any length of time, even less than the normal territorial forces. Furthermore, while they had some winter gear, such as snowshoes, winter boots, and sheepskin coats, they had no transport to carry provisions and ammunition and no training in winter and arctic warfare.

The British decision to revert to small-scale units rested on conclusions that proved erroneous. The units were organized and equipped to operate with and in support of an organized local guerrilla resistance movement. The sparsely populated Nordland Province could not support a large and effective guerrilla movement and the Norwegians were unprepared for this type of warfare in 1940. If the British were not aware of these facts, they would have learned them if they had consulted Norwegian authorities. Secondly, these companies were actually light infantry units and it should have been rather obvious that they could not succeed against well-trained and battle-hardened German troops with artillery and air support. Finally, these units were designed to work against the enemy's flanks with hit-and-run type operations. However, they lacked the mobility for such operations in the snow-covered terrain of Nordland Province.

The Independent Cos (named *Scissorforce*) were commanded by Lieutenant Colonel (brevet Colonel) Colin McVean Gubbins with a brigade-size staff. An entry in Ironside's diaries on May 9 shows that he had a high opinion of Gubbins: "Gubbins has arrived at Mosjöen, thank goodness. Only just in time perhaps. Always confusion and delay in these improvised operations. Unavoidable, I suppose. It now depends upon the guts that Gubbins has. He ought to be good." [24]

The *Scissorforce* headquarters was established at Hopen, about 18 kilometers east of Bodø and some 330 kilometers by road from Mosjøen. The 1st Independent Co landed at Mo, about 90 kilometers north of Mosjøen, on May 4. Independent Co 2, landed at Bodø on May 9, some 240 kilometers by road north of Mo. Independent Co 3 joined this unit on May 13. Independent Cos 4 and 5 landed at Mosjøen on May 8 and the Chasseurs Alpins located there since April 30 were withdrawn to Scotland.

The piecemeal deployment of *Scissorforce* along a 300-kilometer stretch of coastline in Nordland Province revealed their strategy not only to the Germans but also to the Norwegians. It was obvious that the British intended only to slow the German advance, not to halt it. This realization dismayed not only General Mackesy and the Norwegian High Command but was obvious to the troops in the 14th Inf, fighting and withdrawing through their home areas. The realization that the Allies did not intend to stop the Germans and eventually go on the offensive did much to weaken the already shaken morale of these troops.

Loss of Mosjøen

The British expected the nearest Germans to be at least 160 kilometers from Mosjøen when they landed. One can imagine Colonel Gubbins' surprise and dismay when he learned that the Norwegians had been fighting the Germans since May 7 only 40 kilometers from Mosjøen. Lieutenant Colonel Sorko and his men had lived up to von Falkenhorst's demands and covered 160 kilometers in two days, through terrain that Generals Carton de Wiart and Audet had declared impassable for their own mountain troops.

Nummedal planned to establish a delaying position with the retreating 1/14th Inf and the reserve battalion of the same regiment in the Vefsa area near Fjellingfors. After a conference with Major Sundlo and his company commanders in the evening of May 4, it was realized that the 1/14th was demoralized and needed rest and reorganization. The battalion was moved to a reserve position near Mosjøen. It appears from Nummedal's reports that the demoralized condition of the 1/14th had also infected the reserve battalion.

Nummedal gave Sundlo command of the Norwegian forces in the Mosjøen area. He also ordered Sundlo to send one company to Korgen to cover the eastern approach. Company 1 of the battalion was still shaken from the railroad accident a few days earlier and Co 2's strength had fallen to 120 men. It was decided to send both companies north since they needed rest and reorganization. These detachments left Major Sundlo with only one rifle company, a reduced strength machinegun company, and the mortar platoon. These forces occupied defensive positions in a defile south of Mosjøen.

The reserve battalion of the 14th Inf, commanded by Captain Sundby, occupied positions about 40 kilometers south of Mosjøen. The British planned to send one of their companies to reinforce the under-strength Norwegian battalion. It caused some bitterness among the Norwegians when the British decided to join this company with the Norwegians located in the defile further to the rear.

The Norwegians fought two delaying actions in this area over the next three days but were unable to halt the German advance. They planned to occupy a third delaying position but before that could be carried out the battalion commander received orders from Nummedal to withdraw through the 1/14th Inf to Mosjøen where the battalion would embark on ships for Mo. The battalion's low morale was the primary reason for its withdrawal. Nummedal was dissatisfied with its performance, confirmed by reports that the withdrawal was carried out in stages. The withdrawing troops witnessed the hectic rear area activities involved in evacuating supply depots and this probably did not help their low morale.

Colonel Gubbins left Independent Co 4 for seaward protection of Mosjøen and for security of the road leading to Mo. He held a conference with Major Sundlo the following evening, May 9. Two platoons from Independent Co 5 were made available to secure the Norwegian flanks in the defile south of Mosjøen while a third platoon occupied a rear position.

The Germans attacked early in the morning of May 10. The lead German bicycle troops were caught in a deadly crossfire from the defenders and suffered a number of casualties. British reports place the German losses at about 50 killed and wounded. Major Sundlo, in his report, states that the British claim was exaggerated.[25] The Germans soon mounted organized attacks along the railroad against the Norwegian right flank and the British platoon in that area and frontally along the main road. The fighting lasted for about four hours but around noon, the Norwegians and British were forced from their positions and withdrew to Mosjøen.

There were no other suitable defensive positions south of Mosjøen. Gubbins and Sundlo decided to continue the retreat past Mosjøen to Mo and to delay the Germans as much as possible in the process. The British abandoned this plan when the Germans made an amphibious landing in their rear. Sandvik writes that the withdrawal order came from the War Office. Colonel Finne, the Norwegian liaison officer at the British headquarters in Harstad informed General Ruge on May 10 that Gubbins had received instructions from the War Office to leave Mosjøen. Ruge sent Minister of Defense Ljungberg (who was in London) a telegram the same day, stating that the British in Mosjøen had War Office orders to evacuate. It reads in part "A small English force in Mosjøen, which operates directly under the War Office, has received orders to evacuate Mosjøen under certain circumstances. Based on experience from the south, it is feared that the opportunity will be used."[26]

Since all Allied forces south of Narvik were placed under Admiral Cork as of May 7, it is odd that part of that force came directly under the War Office. Both Derry and Moulton imply that Gubbins made the withdrawal decision without orders. However, the fact that Gubbins' forces were transported on destroyers indicates that the Admiralty agreed with his decision.

Other British writers, such as Adams, maintain that Gubbins had no alternative but to make his escape by sea. However, the Independent Cos were organized and equipped to operate in a guerilla environment behind enemy lines, if necessary. The 600 British troops along with Major Sundlo's forces had an opportunity to delay Sorko long enough for British and Norwegian forces in the Mo area to eliminate the German amphibious landing. This, in turn, would have opened the line of retreat from Mosjøen.

Colonel Gubbins withdrew his forces from Mosjøen by sea aboard Norwegian fishing vessels to waiting destroyers in the evening of May 10 and the morning of May 11 that took them to Bodø. The British destroyed their heavy weapons but a considerable amount of supplies and equipment fell into German hands.

The Norwegian troops were left to make their way north overland, knowing that a German force had landed in their rear. They viewed the British withdrawal as another example of treachery and were exceedingly bitter. Major Sundlo testified that he was not informed about the withdrawal and that some of his vehicles were confiscated by the British for use in their retreat. Most Norwegian supplies in Mosjøen were evacuated by fishing vessels, but the Germans captured some. Nummedal and his staff evacuated by sea while Sundlo and his troops began an exhaustive march to Elsfjord where they arrived in the evening of May 11. From there, the troops were transported by boats to Valla on May 12.

The Germans entered Mosjøen on May 11 but did not linger long in that town. They reached Elsfjord shortly after the Norwegians had departed, but found no means to cross the fjord. Most set out across the mountains to Korgen. While the lead elements of the 2nd Division had covered nearly 250 kilometers in six days, von Falkenhorst pressed for a continuation of the rapid pace. It appeared that the Germans were temporarily halted at Elsfjord and Korgen and he hinted that Feurstein, whose headquarters was in Mosjøen, should spend more time at the front to insure a relentless pursuit. This elicited a quick and sharp response from Feurstein, stating that he knew his place in battle.

Operation *Wildente* (Wild Duck)

While Feurstein's initial advance was rapid, Group XXI had noted with concern that resistance had stiffened on April 7 and that it took Feurstein's forces four days to cover the remaining 40 kilometers to Mosjøen. This was too slow for von Falkenhorst, who was well aware of Dietl's desperate situation. Group XXI also worried about reported Allied landings along the coast.

A daring, small-scale amphibious operation, which won the admiration and respect of both British and Norwegians, was undertaken to regain the speed of the northward advance. The operation involved Co 1 from the 138th Regiment, a reinforced mortar platoon from Co 4 of the same regiment, two mountain howitzers from the 112th Mountain Artillery Regiment (part of the 3rd Division), and two 20mm antiaircraft guns. The task force numbered about 300 troops and Captain Holzinger was in command. The Germans commandeered a 1,000-ton Norwegian coastal steamer, *Nord-Norge*, and replaced its crew with naval personnel under the command of Lieutenant Vogelsang. One gun and a couple of machineguns were mounted on the steamer. The Germans began their hazardous 500-kilometer journey through enemy infested waters in the evening of May 9, escorted by German aircraft.

Holzinger's mission was to land his troops at Hemnesberg, about 20 kilometers southwest of Mo and 10 kilometers north of Elsfjord. He was then to seize the road junction at Finneid, and hold it against all attacks until the arrival of the lead elements of the 2nd Division, which would then mount its attack against Mo. It was hoped that any Norwegian or Allied forces south of Hemnesberg would be caught in a trap. The plan called for landing an additional 70 troops by seaplane near the town to assist the German landing.

The director of the shipping line to which *Nord-Norge* belonged warned the Norwegian military authorities as soon as the ship had departed. He did not know the ship's destination. This report was passed to the British. Another message, reporting the ship passing Rørvik, a coastal town a short distance south of the Nordland provincial boundary, escorted by two aircraft, reached the 3rd Sea Defense District in the morning of May 10. The report was forwarded immediately to the British naval headquarters in Harstad along with a request for the dispatch of naval units to capture or sink the ship. It was not until one hour and 40 minutes later that orders were given to the two nearest ships, the antiaircraft cruiser *Calcutta* 50 miles west of Skomvær Lighthouse and the destroyer *Zulu* in Skjelfjord. *Calcutta* waited two hours for a second message that gave the transport's destination as Mo, before she set out to intercept. Finally, she waited for escort from the destroyer *Zulu* and that link-up did not take place until 1700 hours, 40 miles from the approach to Mo. The Germans were thus able to slip into the fjord unmolested before the British ships arrived.

The staff at the British headquarters in Harstad, as well as the Norwegians, were well aware of the dangers of German amphibious operations under air cover along the Nordland coastline. The Admiralty had suggested to Admiral Forbes that a destroyer flotilla be made available to patrol the coast from Namsos to Bodø but Admiral Cork notes that this was unfortunately not acted on.

Lieutenant Colonel Nummedal had ordered the reserve battalion of the 14th Inf to Mo to rest and reorganize. This unit arrived in Mo by sea on May 10 but it was in a state of disintegration and needed time before it could again become an effective combat unit. The only other Norwegian forces in Mo on May 10 consisted of Co 2, 1/14th Inf and a security force from a training unit. Company 1, 1/14 and a company from the reserve battalion of the same regiment were at Korgen facing south and the 1/14th Inf was at Mosjøen. The Norwegian troops at Korgen and Mosjøen would have their line of retreat cut if the Germans seized Hemnesberg and cut the road to Mo. Also in Mo at the time of the German landing at Hemnesberg was Independent Co 1, commanded by Major May. It had a platoon at Hemnesberg.

Nord-Norge hoisted the German flag as it came within sight of Hemnesberg, where it docked at 1900 hours on May 10. However, the German attack had started shortly before then when two Do-26 seaplanes landed a small group of men from Co 7 of the 138th Regiment, commanded by Lieutenant Rudlof, at Sund, a short distance east of Hemnesberg. Another five seaplanes bringing in additional troops from Co 7, about 70 in all, followed shortly. The seven seaplanes made multiple trips to Hemnesøy, bringing in equipment and supplies.

There was a Norwegian squad-size security force in the Hemnesberg harbor area along with approximately 30-35 British troops from the 1st Independent Co. These forces opened fire on the Germans before the ship reached the pier. The mountain troops stormed ashore, covered by fire from the machineguns on the steamer, and they launched a full-scale attack on the small British/Norwegian force when German aircraft appeared overhead and dropped bombs. The fighting was sharp and at close quarters but the British and Norwegians were eventually driven out of the village, leaving most of their heavier equipment behind. Five Germans and eight British soldiers were killed and a larger number were wounded.

The Germans were meanwhile unloading their equipment, ammunition, and mountain howitzers from *Nord-Norge*. They also brought their own and British and Norwegian wounded aboard the ship. The two British warships, *Calcutta* and *Zulu*, appeared at 2015 hours and sank *Nord-Norge* with gunfire. Most of the German supplies were already unloaded but a number of wounded aboard perished when the ship sank.

The British and Norwegians who withdrew from Hemnesberg found the road blocked by the Germans who had landed by air. Holzinger and his troops linked up with the men from Co 7 during the night after some further fighting with the retreating British and Norwegian troops. These withdrew to the north side of the island and made their escape by boats. German losses had increased to eight killed.

A Danish officer, Tage Ellinger, who had seen service in Finland and volunteered for service in the Norwegian Army had made his way to North Norway and was given command of a company in the Mo area on May 10. The 120 troops in the company were all from the 14th Inf. This company was sent to Hemnesberg to take care of 14 Germans reported to have landed from a seaplane. The company crossed the isthmus to Hemnesøy in the evening of May 10. Major May decided to follow the Norwegians with his troops. They reached the peninsula south of Sund around 0300 hours on May 11.

The first Germans encountered and captured were three naval personnel. Ellinger and May learned from the prisoners that 400 Germans had landed, not 14 as originally reported. The prisoners also told their captors where the German troops were deployed and it was decided to try a surprise attack on the Germans in positions on the road to Sund. The Germans discovered their presence and the operation failed before there was any serious fighting.

Major May decided to withdraw his forces to protect the isthmus between Hemnesøy and Finneid. Ellinger's troops followed in the afternoon of May 11. The British and Norwegians quartered their troops in abandoned homes just north of Finneid, along the road to Mo. Ellinger took his company back to Hemnesøy on May 12, but they were forced to withdraw to the mainland during the night.

The 6th Division remained in the dark about developments in the southern part of Nordland Province. It had hoped for a tough delaying action south of Mosjøen but news indicated that the Germans had reached Mosjøen without meeting any resistance. It was obvious from all reports that the morale in the 1/14th Inf had reached a point where the unit was no longer fit for operations. Hovland blames Major Sundlo for his "miserable leadership."[27]

While it can certainly be argued that a more effective commander could have produced better results, that same is true for other units in General Fleischer's command. As we have seen, some unusual demands were placed on this militia battalion. The unannounced withdrawal of the Allies from Namsos, the surrender of the 5th Brigade, the train accident, and the sudden British withdrawal from Mosjøen did much to break its morale. The northward withdrawal past the homes of many of its members, the men privately believing that the British could not, or did not intend to, halt the Germans, did not help.

Many of the leaders in the two battalions in Nordland were located outside the province. In many cases, these leaders were unable to join their units because of the nature of the German invasion. The Reserve Battalion, 14th Inf, for example, lacked a battalion commander and three company commanders. Fleischer was aware of this situation but he was unable to rectify it in any meaningful way. Nevertheless, the delaying actions by the 1/14th Inf slowed the German advance and it may have continued to do so except for Colonel Gubbins' sudden withdrawal from Mosjøen, leaving the Norwegians to make an exhaustive overland withdrawal.

General Fleischer obviously recognized the threat to his southern flank but he did not have many resources at his disposal to meet that threat. It was only through effective Allied action that the German advance could be stopped. Their actions were not only muddled and piecemeal, but lacked in resolve and overall strategy. However, as of May 15 Fleischer had not even bothered to meet with his Allied counterpart. Whatever the shortcomings in Major Sundlo's leadership abilities, the blame for the failure to stop Feurstein's forces cannot be placed on a single battalion commander.

When news arrived about the German amphibious operation at Hemnesberg and the British evacuation of Mosjøen, Fleischer concluded that the line of withdrawal for the two battalions of the 14th Inf was cut. He considered it imperative to recapture Hemnesberg in order to save these two battalions. A General Staff officer, Captain Ø. Dahl, was sent south on May 8 to become Nummedal's chief of staff. Dahl arrived in Mo in the morning of May 10 and discovered that the reserve battalion had already reached that town but was in a state of dissolution. Dahl reported the situation to the 6th Division on May 11. In answer to the division's desire to establish a defensive line in the Hemnesberg-Korgen area, Dahl answered that an additional 200 German troops had arrived on Hemnesøy by air and that it was not possible to recapture Hemnesberg with the available Norwegian troops. The recapture of Hemnesøy required British ground and naval support.

On the same day, General Ruge sent a sharply worded message to Admiral Cork, the gist of which is reported by General Sandvik:

> The Commander-in-Chief pointed out that the German "bluff maneuver" at Hemnes and the resulting re-embarkation of the British companies at Mosjøen has not only changed the situation on our

southern front but has broken the confidence in our allies among our troops in that area. In this regard, the destructive effects for the defense of South Norway of the unexpected earlier withdrawals from Åndalsnes and Namsos were pointed out ... The Commander-in-Chief stressed the need to re-establish the southern front. This was, in his view, possible with minor means and without complicating the situation in Narvik. He pointed out that there were, at the moment, more troops in the Narvik-Harstad area than could be used on the Narvik front.

Another message from Ruge to Cork, also on May 11, announced that his chief of operations, Lieutenant Colonel Roscher-Nielsen, had assumed command in Nordland Province. Ruge wrote "I hope you agree that in the prevailing crisis, there must be one commander there and that you will order the British troops to act in accordance with the orders issued by Colonel Roscher Nielsen."[28] The British ignored this suggestion.

General Mackesy, who was also very concerned about developments in the south, decided to send the 1st Bn, Scots Guards to Mo. He also sent along a half-battery of 25-pounders, four antiaircraft guns, and engineers. This force, under the command of Lieutenant Colonel Trappes-Lomax, landed in Mo early on May 12. Mackesy viewed the defense of Mo as important since it was the terminal of the last road connection to Sweden and the airfield located just north of that town had to be kept out of German hands. Mackesy also prepared to reinforce the Scots Guards in Mo with the 1st Bn of the Irish Guards.

German Supply Problems

The Germans were having difficulties in supplying their forward units. Von Falkenhorst's order on May 4 had specified that the 2nd Mountain Division would pass through General Woytasch's 181st Division in the Grong area. The 181st Division would expand its area of responsibility northward behind the rearmost elements of Feurstein's forces and assume responsibility for the movement of supplies in those areas. The north-south road was in terrible shape after the thaw set in and it was unsuitable for transport of supplies on a large scale before May 20. Until then, most supplies were brought in by air but the weather conditions made even this effort unpredictable. The capture of the British supplies in Mosjøen on May 11 alleviated the precarious supply situation for five to six days.[29]

The Germans attempted unsuccessfully to bring supplies to the 2nd Division by sea. Their failure was attributable to Norwegian patrol boats operating from bases on the islands along the coast. This forced the Germans to undertake operations to secure the sea route by occupying a number of larger islands along the coast in order to prevent Norwegian patrol vessels from operating in the fjords and forcing them out to sea.

This mission was given to the 181st Division and carried out systematically during the rest of May and early June, assisted by a task force from the 2nd Mountain Division. Only small groups of Norwegian volunteers opposed them. Nevertheless, the last island was not captured until May 31. The route along the coast on the inland side of the islands was now open and the Germans began using this on a regular basis; but it was still necessary to plan a large-scale German naval operation for early June.

The Fight at Finneid

Captain Dahl met Lieutenant Colonel Trappes-Lomax soon after the 1st Bn, Scots Guards landed early on May 12. He tried to persuade the British commander to attempt to recapture Hemnes while the Germans were suffering from a lack of supplies. Trappes-Lomax replied that he would await the arrival of reinforcements and that night the British battalion went into positions at Dalselv, approximately midway between Mo and Finneid, a position he considered very strong. This left the defense of Finneid, which was the most defensible position south of Mo, to the 1st Independent Co, without artillery support, and Captain Ellinger's weak company.[30]

Roscher-Nielsen and Nummedal arrived in Mo on May 13. Roscher-Nielsen took command of the Norwegian forces in the area while Nummedal retained his responsibilities for mobilization and training. Roscher-Nielsen's initial thoughts were for the 1/14th Inf to hold or delay the German northward advance from Elsfjord and Korgen. However, Trappes-Lomax informed him in the evening of May 13 that he had given orders for the 1st Independent Co to withdraw, since the road leading north from Finneid was under German mortar fire from Hemnesøy. Roscher-Nielsen prevailed on his counterpart to delay the withdrawal long enough to assist Captain Ellinger in his effort to cover the withdrawal of the 1/14th through Finneid.

Ellinger's men occupied positions along the road from Sund to Finneid and remained there while the soldiers in the 1/14th withdrew through Finneid to

Mo. A company from the reserve battalion of the 14th Inf was the last unit to withdraw from Korgen in the morning of May 14. Ellinger's men withdrew from Hemnesøy and British engineers destroyed the road behind them.

The 6th Division was still somewhat in the dark about the situation in Nordland. Roscher-Nielsen sent a message to the division at midnight on May 13, reporting the steps taken, including the withdrawal from Korgen. He also reported that another British battalion was expected on May 14 and that naval gunfire support was required. A message from the division on May 14 requested detailed information about force deployment, to include the exact location of each company in preparation for a meeting with the new British commander, General Auchinleck. Fleischer also wanted to know if the withdrawal from Korgen was due to enemy pressure.

In a message at 2300 hours on May 14, Roscher-Nielsen tried to explain the difficult and serious situation in the Mo area to General Fleischer:

> The expected British battalion was yesterday ordered to Bodø instead of Mo. Simultaneously, the British battalion in this area was ordered to concentrate on the defense of Mo. Despite repeated protests, the defense of Finneid will be abandoned tomorrow at 2200 hours. Consequently, the reduced combat effective Sundlo battalion could not be left in Korgen. The Germans have not pressed their attack and it is my belief that Hemnesøy could be recaptured if there was help from the sea but this appears hopeless … Both battalions have lost most of their transport and have no horse-drawn trains. They can only be used for stationary missions.[31]

Both Major May and Captain Ellinger expected to be attacked by the Germans on Hemnesøy as well as by the Germans approaching from the south. It was obvious that they did not have sufficient forces to meet attacks from two directions. The German attack across the isthmus from Hemnesøy began at 1700 hours on May 14. The attack was well supported by mortar and artillery fire and the Germans quickly drove back the British outposts and established themselves on the isthmus. Two British warships appeared in the fjord and bombarded the village of Hemnesberg but the bombardment did nothing to help the units fighting at Finneid.

The fighting in some sectors was intense. The units facing south were switched to face west because no attack from the south materialized. However, the Germans had now driven the British and Norwegian troops from the isthmus and crossed to the mainland. May informed Ellinger at 2100 hours that he was withdrawing his forces and suggested that Ellinger do likewise. Ellinger's machineguns were still effective and they continued to contest the German advance until 2300 hours when both direct and indirect fire became so intense that Ellinger disengaged and withdrew towards Mo.

Tamelander and Zetterling, referencing Captain Holzinger's after-action report, state that the Germans only had two wounded and that they captured seven of their opponents. However, Ellinger, quoting from Lieutenant General Paul Klatt's book *Die 3. Gebirgs-Division 1939-1945*, writes that the number of Germans killed in the engagement is not reported but 46 wounded were evacuated by air. Similarly, Ruef writes, "The price [for capturing Finneid] was a row of fallen, almost 50 wounded and two exhausted task forces."[32] The fact that two of the ten Knight Crosses to the Iron Cross awarded to the 3rd Mountain Division in the Norwegian operation were awarded for actions at Hemnes and Finneid attest to the intensity of the fight.

British-Norwegian Conference on May 16

Generals Ruge and Fleischer requested a conference with General Auchinleck to discuss the situation on the southern front. This conference took place in Harstad on May 16. It was Fleischer's first meeting with a British general. Ruge gave Auchinleck a memorandum setting forth his own estimate of the situation. The memorandum stressed the importance of holding the Mosjøen area as a base for future offensive operations and it recommended the Allies land troops in this area as soon as possible and that these forces be augmented as quickly as the situation in the Mo area permitted. The German air threat was also a major part of Ruge's concern. German aircraft operating from Værnes Airfield near Trondheim could spend less than one hour over their targets in Narvik area. The time-over-target factor would increase significantly if the Germans were able to make fields further north operational. They would be able to quickly gain air superiority and make both land and sea operations very difficult. It was therefore of great importance to halt the German advance as far south as possible.

Hovland criticizes Ruge for devoting a large part of his memorandum to future plans and operations at the expense of immediate concerns. Although events on the Continent would soon present the Allies with a situation where any thoughts of future offensive operations in Norway were unrealistic, developments had not reached that stage at the time of the conference. It was realistic to expect the British to strike effectively at the Germans behind their forward units and thus disrupt their advance. So far, only the Germans had taken such action, in Trondheimfjord and at Hemnesberg.

Both Ruge and Fleischer stressed the absolute necessity of holding Mo, with its airfield. Fleischer was already sending whatever units he could spare to shore up the southern front. The newly mobilized 1/15th Inf, which had provided security at Bardufoss Airfield, would be sent south as soon as a French battalion relieved it. Auchinleck stated that he would do all in his power to stop the Germans and he intended to send reinforcements to Mo.

Other questions that were discussed at the conference led to some agreements. The Norwegians were promised that Colonel Finne, the Norwegian liaison officer at the Allied headquarters, would get copies of all orders to the British commander in the Bodø area. This promise was soon violated. To Ruge's suggestion that some French battalions from Narvik be sent to Mo and Bodø, Auchinleck answered that this was under consideration. For his part, Auchinleck requested improved administrative support from local authorities and better control of the civilian population within the operational areas.

General Fleischer stated that his troops were running low on ammunition and stressed the need for new weapons using the same ammunition as Allied forces. Fleischer was told that a supply of weapons and ammunition for his troops had arrived from Great Britain. These weapons were never issued to the Norwegians since they were used to reequip the Irish Guards and South Wales Borderers after their losses in their abortive efforts to reach Bodø on May 14 and 17.

It is obvious that Auchinleck began to take a slightly more aggressive attitude with respect to Mo than was demonstrated in his briefing to Brigadier Fraser on May 13. He sent a message to Colonel Gubbins on May 16 telling him not to abandon Mo. This came on the heel of a message from Brigadier Fraser on May 15 stating that it was militarily unsound to hold Mo. Auchinleck's amplifying instructions were sent with the ill-fated South Wales Borderers on May 17.[33]

Auchinleck received a note from Admiral Cork late in the afternoon on May 15 about moving the South Wales Borderers to Mo. This probably influenced Auchinleck to try to hang on to Mo as long as possible more than the visit the following day by the two Norwegian generals. The admiral told him that they had to hold Mo for six more days until the squadron of aircraft at Bardufoss became operational.

The Norwegian generals came away from the conference on May 16 with some mixed emotions. While some administrative matters were cleared up and Auchinleck had expressed understanding and agreement with their desire to hold the Germans as far south as possible, the promises were no more definite than those made by the British Government and commanders shortly before the sudden withdrawals from Åndalsnes, Namsos, and Mosjøen. An arrangement for coordinated operations in the southern area was not achieved, only a promise that the Norwegians would get copies of British operational directives.

British Strategy Changes and Mishaps

General Feurstein's troops had advanced 270 kilometers in nine days over terrain that Allied commanders had considered impassable. They had covered about half the distance to their beleaguered comrades in Narvik and there was no indication that their forward progress would slow. The British authorities had finally become alarmed. Churchill writes, "It would be a disgrace if the Germans made themselves masters of the whole of this stretch of the Norwegian coast with practically no opposition from us in the course of the next few weeks or even days."[36] This was written before the Germans captured Mosjøen. Since then, they had captured another 70 kilometers of coastline and the British commander at Mo reported that it was militarily unsound to hold that town. According to Ironside, Churchill's own feelings about further commitment of significant ground forces in Norway without adequate air support is partially to blame for this situation. He writes on May 2:

> We had a peaceable Chiefs of Staff meeting and Cabinet too. So far Winston has not troubled us very much. He delivered a long tirade and then said that we had been right in recommending that we did not put ashore a large army in Norway. He forgets what he felt so passionately a week or so ago.[34]

Allied operations in Norway were hamstrung by lack of air power from the very beginning. One aircraft carrier was kept on duty in the Narvik area but it proved inadequate for the task. The British began the construction of an airfield at Skånland but it never became usable. There were Norwegian airfields at Bardufoss and at Bodø but the British were slow in making them operational. They had been in the country almost a month before they decided to use Bardufoss. It took some time to clear the snow from the runway and it was not in operation until the end of May. Survey teams were sent around to other airfields such as the ones at Bodø and Mo. Although quick actions were called for, reports were submitted and decided on in a fashion more appropriate to a peacetime environment. This was no way to counter the tempo of German operations.

The Germans captured Værnes on April 10 and employed a large Norwegian work force to clear the snow. The airfield was operational by April 12 and reinforcements began landing the following day. OKW stressed the need to establish landing fields along the route of advance to support operations. An airfield at Hattfjelldal, southeast of Mosjøen, was ready for use by late May as a refueling point for aircraft returning from Narvik and the nearly completed airfield north of Mo was captured when Mo was evacuated.

Colonel Dowler and Brigadier Fraser discussed the problems of reinforcing the Mo area with General Auchinleck and they described the situation there as becoming critical. Auchinleck decided to change Mackesy's plan to send the 1st Irish Guards to Mo. Instead, Brigadier Fraser was ordered to take the battalion to Bodø. He also announced that he would send South Wales Borderers to the same location. He reasoned that it was not possible to supply the force by the mountain road over Saltfjell since it was still closed by snow. Mo was at the end of a long fjord and Admiral Cork was reluctant to supply the forces there since ships would be exposed to air attacks in confined waters. Auchinleck directed Fraser to hold the Bodø area "permanently" and to try to establish contact with the forces in Mo "if he could."[35] Moulton's statement that the intent was to send the 1st Irish Guards and 2nd South Wales Borderers by road from Bodø to Mo is therefore somewhat misleading.

In a letter to General Dill on May 13, Auchinleck announced that he intended to give up on the use of the Independent Cos in a guerrilla role. This is an interesting statement since he had never used them in that role. He stated that he intended to coalesce them into a light infantry unit under Gubbins and place the whole force under Brigadier Fraser's command. The inevitable outcome of the decision to send Fraser to Bodø was to give up Mo and to surrender another 150 kilometers of excellent defensive terrain to the enemy. The decision left no British combat forces in the Narvik area. Operations in that area became a joint Norwegian-French-Polish effort. Operations in the south became a British-Norwegian effort. There continued to be no unity of command in either area.

Misfortunes continued to plague the British. They decided to send the 1st

Irish Guards to Bodø in the Polish transport *Chobry*. The Norwegians had suggested that the troops be transported in fishing vessels to reduce the exposure to German air attacks and to avoid navigational mishaps in the treacherous approach to Bodø. This advice was rejected according to Kersaudy. The ship was attacked by a German aircraft when it reached the southern tip of the Lofoten Islands at 0015 hours on May 15. The regimental history states that three Heinkel aircraft carried out the attack and Moulton implies that there was more than one aircraft. It has since been established that only one aircraft was involved in the attack and that it dropped its bombs during its second pass over the ship. Auchinleck's biographer writes, "There was more than a suspicion that there had been a leakage of information before the ship sailed."[39] This is another example of the unfounded accusations that did so much to poison the relations between the British and Norwegians. The Germans would surely have sent more than a single aircraft if they had known about the ship and its cargo.

The bombs hit the transport amidships. The explosion killed the battalion commander and most of the senior officers. The ship was on fire and began to sink. In an outstanding example of the discipline in the British Navy and among the Guards, 694 men were successfully transferred from the sinking ship to the escorting destroyer *Wolverine* while another escort, the sloop *Stork*, remained nearby to protect against further air attacks. The transfer was accomplished in 16 minutes. The battalion lost all its equipment along with the only three British tanks in the country. Adams and Derry write that the soldiers brought along their weapons as they were transferred, but Auchinleck, in a letter to General Dill, wrote 'They had no rifles, machine-guns or anything.'[36] The escorts transported the troops back to Harstad. Here they were reorganized and reequipped.

The next disaster was not long in coming. It was decided to send the 2nd Bn, South Wales Borders to Bodø in the cruiser *Effingham*, commanded by Captain J. M. Howson. The cruiser was part of a five-ship task force that also consisted of two antiaircraft cruisers, and two destroyers. All troops were embarked on *Effingham*. The ships departed Harstad at 0400 hours on May 17. The warships proceeded west of the Lofoten Islands at top speed. Rather than following the normal approach to Bodø, it was decided to make a shorter back-door approach in order to minimize the submarine threat.

The first ship to hit the Flesene shoals about 12 miles from Bodø was the destroyer *Matable*, which struck only a glancing blow, losing its starboard propeller but remaining afloat. The antiaircraft cruiser *Coventry* also touched bottom but the damage was minor. *Effingham*, traveling at 23 knots, hit the shoal hard, tearing open its bottom. By great good fortune, there were no casualties. The troops were transferred rapidly and in an orderly way from the sinking cruiser to the destroyer *Echo*. All equipment, except that carried by the troops, was lost, including the Bren-gun carriers. Even some individual weapons were abandoned. *Echo* transferred the troops to *Coventry* and went back to rescue the *Effingham's* crew. It was not possible to salvage the cruiser and it was sunk by torpedoes.

There was again an attempt to place blame where it did not belong. Adams writes:

> Within hours of boarding the *Coventry* a strong rumour spread throughout the ship that a Norwegian was at the helm when the ship struck the reef. It was alleged that he was a follower of Quisling and that the sinking of the *Effingham* was a deliberate, traitorous act. One version of the story was emphatic that the Captain of the *Effingham* executed the "traitor" on the bridge by shooting him in the head. This rumour, like many others of its kind, seems completely without foundation.[37]

There was no Norwegian pilot on the cruiser. The British had a Norwegian navigational chart, and the report of the cruiser's loss admits that the chosen channel was "more foul of navigational dangers than the normal approach." It also notes that it carried a remark that vessels with local knowledge could make the passage, implying that it should not be attempted without such knowledge. The report states, however, that the qualification concerning local knowledge is commonplace on Norwegian navigational charts outside the main shipping lane and that "hitherto, experience had shown that no extreme regard need be paid to it, provided normal pilotage precautions were observed."[38]

The Germans claimed they sank the British cruiser. A photograph in *Signal*, Hitler's wartime picture magazine, shows the wreck of *Effingham*. The caption claims that the cruiser, damaged by German bombs, was beached, and finally capsized.

NOTES

1 Sandvik, *Operasjonene*, vol. 2, pp. 60-61, n. 4.

2 Lindbäck-Larsen, *Rapport*, Section 8:3-4 and Getz, *Nord-Trøndelag 1940*, pp. 115-116, entries for 1225 hours on April 28 (Message 329 from 6th Division) and 1330 hours same day (letter Nr.

125 from Getz to Fleischer).

3 Getz, *Nord-Trøndelag 1940*, pp. 122-123, entry 1130 hours April 29.

4 Ibid, p. 116, entry for 1300 hours April 28 and Sandvik, *Operasjonene*, vol. 2, pp. 60-61, n. 4. Ruge was in the process of relocating his headquarters from Åndalsnes to North Norway and had no communications with Colonel Getz until May 3, by which time the situation had changed.

5 Getz, *Nord-Trøndelag 1940*, pp. 117 and 122. Getz notes that he sent messages to the 6th Division direct, via Sweden, and through the Allied headquarters but received no explanation for the orders. Sandvik relates that General Fleischer sent a letter to Getz on April 30 confirming that the order was genuine but that Getz never received the letter (*Operasjonene*, vol. 2, p.61).

6 Lindbäck-Larsen, *Rapport*, Section 8:4.

7 Getz, *Nord-Trøndelag 1940*, p. 140, entry for 0850 hours May 2.

8 Valentin Feurstein, *Irrwege der Pflicht 1938-1945* (Munich, Verlag Welsermühl, 1963),p. 73.

9 Hovland, *Fleischer*, p. 150. He points out that the military investigating committee, in its review of Colonel Getz' surrender, gave special weight to the fact that road connection to the north was severed by Fleischer. He goes on to state that Getz should have been the first to know that the destruction of the road northward had not been carried out. Getz, however, claims that the destruction had already started and this is why the 1/14th Inf left the battalion trains behind when it began its retreat into Nordland Province.

10 Sandvik, *Operasjonene*, vol. 2, pp. 100, 106.

11 Quoted in Lindbäck-Larsen, *Krigen*, p. 124. The order read: "Send as many troops as possible back to Mosjøen. Seek connection with units of the 6th Division in that area. The forces will thereafter come under General Fleischer. Destroy the roads thoroughly as the troops withdraw. Roadblocks must be defended."

12 Quoted in Sandvik, *Operasjonene*, vol. 2, p. 63.

13 Macleod and Kelly, *Time Unguarded*, p. 289.

14 Derry, *The Campaign in Norway*, p. 178 and Moulton, *A Study of Warfare*, p. 235.

15 Maurice Gustave Gamelin, *Servir*, (3 vols; Paris: Plon, 1946-47), vol. 3, pp. 366-367.

16 Macleod and Kelly, *Time Unguarded*, p. 292.

17 Churchill, *The Gathering Storm*, p. 648.

18 Marie Emile Béthouart, *Cinq années d'espérance. Mémoires de guerre, 1939-1945*. (Paris: Plon, 1968), pp. 31-32.

19 The 2nd Mountain Division, like the 3nd, was formed from units in the Austrian army after the incorporation of Austria into the Third Reich. The 2nd was formed from units of the 6th Austrian Mountain Division and German mountain troops in April 1938 and mobilized on August 26, 1939. Like the 3rd, it participated in the Polish Campaign as part of Army Group South. It was transferred to Germany at the conclusion of that campaign.

20 Karl Ruef, *Odyssee*, p. 54.

21 Feurstein, *Irrwege der Pflicht*, p. 71.

22 Derry, *The Campaign in Norway*, p. 167.

23 *London Gazette* Supplement, 10 July 1947, 3173 as quoted in Jack Adams, *The Doomed Expedition. The Norwegian Campaign of 1940* (London: Leo Cooper, 1989), p. 71.

24 Macleod and Kelly, *Time Unguarded*, p. 297.

25 Derry, *The Campaign in Norway*, p. 180; Moulton, *Study of Warfare*, p. 237; Adams, *The Doomed Expedition*, p. 73; and Sandvik, *Operasjonene*, vol. 2,p. 84, n. 74.

26 HOK 916/40 quoted in Sandvik, *Operasjonene*, vol. 2, p. 88.

27 Hovland, *Fleischer*, p. 150.

28 Sandvik, *Operasjonene*, vol. 2, pp. 88-89.

29 Hubatsch, 215.

30 Ellinger, *Den Forunderlige Krig*, pp. 65-66. The morale in Ellinger's company had deteriorated and some of the troops tried to leave on May 13. Ellinger decided it was better to operate with people who wanted to fight. He spoke to each platoon and told those who wished to leave to step forward and turn in their weapons. In the end, he had only 52 men left. The disarmed soldiers were sent to Mo where Roscher-Nielsen put them to work on a road-gang.

31 Lindbäck-Larsen, *6. division* (Oslo: Gyldendal, 1946), p. 118.

32 Ruef, *Odyssee*, p. 63.

33 John Connell, *Auchinleck* (London: Cassell, 1959), pp.119-120. The instructions read, in part: "You will have had my telegram telling you that I wish the detachment at Mo to hold on to its position, and not withdraw. I think it most important that we should give up no more ground. I know the detachment is somewhat isolated at present, and I know the Germans may be in superior force to the south of you, but I am pretty sure that they are groping in the dark very much as we are, and I hope that when they come up against really determined opposition they will sit back and think about it."

34 Macleod and Kelly, *Time Unguarded*, p. 292.

35 Connell, *Auchinleck*, p. 115.

36 Connell, *Auchinleck*, p. 119; Derry, *The Campaign in Norway*, p. 184; and Adams, *The Doomed Expedition*, p. 69.

37 Adams, *The Doomed Expedition*, p. 70.

38 Report to the Naval Court of Inquiry, D.3A Reports of Losses of H.M. Ships. Effingham 17/5. Prepared on H.M. Transport *Sobieski* at Sea on May 20, 1940, paragraph 6.

13

THE BJERKVIK LANDING AND THE MOUNTAIN OFFENSIVE

"Ah, it is all very difficult. We are used to traveling on camels across the desert, and here you give us boats, and we have to cross the water. It is very difficult but it will be all right. I think so."

REACTION BY AN OFFICER OF THE FRENCH FOREIGN LEGION WHEN TOLD THAT HIS UNIT WOULD MAKE THE FIRST AMPHIBIOUS LANDING OF WORLD WAR II.

Pressures on the Allied Commanders to Act

Churchill and his colleagues in London were understandably exasperated by the lack of initiative displayed by their military commanders at Narvik. The Norwegians were also baffled by the unwillingness of the Allies to use their enormous firepower and clear numerical advantage. London continued to exert pressure on the field commanders to get them to act but some of the messages reveal that the officials in London were out of touch with realities on the ground. On April 28, Churchill sent a message to Admiral Cork in which he maintained that the focus of effort must be on Narvik and the Gallivare ore fields.

Churchill was still thinking of advancing 250 kilometers through a winter wilderness at a time when a brigade of British professionals had great difficulties operating along a coastal road. The following comments by Professor Hubatsch, while directed primarily at the Germans, apply to the Allies to an even greater degree, "In the Norwegian Campaign more than in any other theatre of war, we see the fascinating problem of how different the impressions gained by the men at the front could be from those held by the High Command."[2]

Churchill kept up the pressure on Admiral Cork.

Admiral Cork and General Mackesy had been engaged in a debate about strategy since they arrived in Norway. Some of the blame must be placed on those who issued instructions that were conflicting and not coordinated at the highest levels.

The possible window of opportunity for a landing in Narvik closed rather quickly and the Norwegians never suggested that the Allies should attempt a direct landing in Narvik. Lindbäck-Larsen concluded that a direct attack on Narvik was impractical within a few days after the destruction of the German destroyers on April 13.

Mackesy's reluctance to launch an attack against Narvik in the first week or two after his arrival has considerable validity as long as the 24th Guards was the only force at his disposal. His arguments quickly lost their soundness after the Norwegians began their offensive in late April and with the arrival of significant reinforcements. He appears haunted by fears of a disaster long before committing his forces to battle. In one dispatch quoted by Derry, he talks about the "snows of Narvik being turned into another version of the mud of Passchendaele." Moulton observes that this was, "… strange and hysterical language for a military commander, and symptomatic of long-suppressed fears and doubts of the ability of traditional infantry to attack at all … British soldiers were helpless to act, and in the end left the fighting to others." Mackesy was not a lone holdout. A number of army and navy officers supported his arguments. Cork, for his part was unwilling to overrule Mackesy on land operations, especially after he experienced personally how difficult it was to move in snow up to his waist.

Allied warships carried out a number of shore bombardments in late April and early May. Some caused damage, particularly at Elvegårdsmoen, where on April 27 several barracks and a considerable amount of supplies and equipment were destroyed. German casualties were five killed and six wounded. Naval gunfire against targets in Narvik on May 3 resulted in four Germans killed and several wounded.

General Fleischer had recommended a landing near Bjerkvik and General Béthouart had suggested landings at either Øyjord or east of Narvik after his reconnaissance on April 28. The British had promised to study Fleischer's suggestion; Béthouart's suggestion was turned down by General Mackesy the same day it was made.

Béthouart came to see Mackesy in Harstad on May 2. He explained the difficulties experienced by his troops in Labergsdal and concluded that the operation would not yield timely results because of very stiff German resistance, difficult terrain and his troops' lack of mobility in the deep snow. Béthouart stated that it was folly to press the attack under conditions where only the Norwegians and Germans were qualified to operate. He warned that his battalions would melt away from exhaustion and losses. This time he insisted that an amphibious landing be made in Bjerkvik in order to relieve the pressures on his troops.[5]

General Mackesy was not moved. He met Béthouart again the following day and told him that after a reconnaissance by officers, he had concluded that a landing in Bjerkvik or on the east shore of Herjangsfjord was impossible. The western shore of the fjord offered better possibilities but the homes in this area were filled with civilian refugees including many women and children. A landing there was therefore out of the question. Béthouart suggested an overland move from Bogen and offered a battalion of the Foreign Legion, expected to arrive in Harstad within a few days, for this mission.

There was another meeting on May 4 at Cork's headquarters. At this meeting the decision was made for French troops on the northern front not to press their attack but only tie down the Germans. This decision was taken without consulting or informing the Norwegians. The 7th Brigade found itself pressing forward alone, increasingly disappointed in the weak support provided by the French. The 7th Brigade's advance pulled the French forces along as the Germans opposing them withdrew because of worries about their right flank. Nevertheless, the bulk of the French forces were still two miles behind, at the north end of Storevann on May 9 as the 7th Brigade was attacking the high ground on both sides of Læigastind.

Under pressure from London, Admiral Cork decided on a direct attack against Narvik and gave orders for Mackesy to carry it out. The admiral had made a reconnaissance on May 1 and come to the conclusion that the snow had thawed sufficiently that it no longer presented the kind of obstacle it had earlier. The operation was scheduled for May 8 and Mackesy planned to land two battalions on the northern shore, a few kilometers from the city.

However, this was not the end of the British Army's attempts to delay the attack. Senior army officers, including Brigadier Fraser, the commander of the 24th Guards Brigade, protested to Cork about the planned operation. Their objections fell into three general categories. First, there was an acute shortage of ALCs. Local fishing vessels and ships' boats would therefore have to be used and their deeper draft limited the areas where landings could be made. Second, continual daylight and a lack of smoke shells eliminated the element of surprise and provided no concealment during the approach to the beaches and the initial period ashore. Finally, the troops in the open boats would be exposed to German air attacks. Even some naval officers, including Cork's chief of staff, Captain

Loben E. H. Maund, argued against the operation.[6] It is interesting that the same objections were not raised five days later when it was decided to send the Foreign Legionnaires ashore in Bjerkvik under similar conditions.

Allied intelligence about the situation in Narvik and the surrounding area was woefully inadequate at this stage. The Norwegians had a much better knowledge of the German order of battle but no formal machinery existed for sharing vital intelligence information. The British commanders did not know that Dietl had sent the preponderance of his mountain troops to shore up the northern front or that he had removed some of the naval personnel from Narvik for the same purpose. Von Falkenhorst's situation report on May 6 termed the situation in Narvik critical, a term used sparingly by German commanders. It is debatable whether better intelligence would have altered the Allied decision.

It may be that Cork was reluctant to overrule his army subordinates or that he had himself become somewhat infected by their caution. In any event, he sent a list of the army objections to his proposed attack on Narvik to London on May 6 for consideration. Before receiving a reply, Cork decided to adopt an alternate operation recommended by General Mackesy and postpone the attack on Narvik until a new army commander arrived.

After the arrival of the French Foreign Legionnaires and the Polish brigade, Admiral Cork had 12 infantry battalions under his command. There were about 25,000 Allied troops when support and service support personnel were included. The British Government decided that the size of the ground forces in North Norway was so large that it warranted the appointment of a corps commander. The ground forces were named the North Western Expeditionary Force and Lieutenant General Claude Auchinleck was appointed as commander, on April 28.

Auchinleck was an officer with considerable experience in mountain warfare in India but no experience in amphibious or arctic operations. While the growing size of the international force in the Narvik area undoubtedly warranted a higher ranking ground commander, it was also a convenient way for Churchill and his colleagues to rid themselves of the cautious and recalcitrant Mackesy.

Mackesy was rushed to North Norway on short notice in early April. General Auchinleck, on the other hand, was in no hurry. He arrived in Harstad on May 11. Auchinleck's "secret instructions," according to his biographer, were to assume command immediately upon arrival in Norway. His official instructions, signed by Oliver Stanley on May 5, were apparently a watered down version since they told him not to interfere with existing plans "until they have either achieved success or been abandoned."[7]

The British Chiefs of Staff wanted to send a message to Admiral Cork encouraging him to launch the attack on Narvik but instead it was decided to ask Cork for his personal views. This may have been a way for Churchill to put pressure Cork, who had written that he would do his best to justify the trust Churchill had placed in him. Cork replied that he favored the attack, although there was no certainty of success, but he had decided to await the arrival of Auchinleck. The Chiefs of Staff, with the approval of the War Cabinet, answered that strong action was favored, that risk-taking would be supported, and that "Auchinleck's coming should be left out of his calculations."[8] Cork's answer stated that he had committed himself to the alternate operation recommended by Mackesy. Ironside notes that Churchill appeared to be weighted down by events in Narvik, wanted the city taken, "yet doesn't dare to give a direct order to Cork."[9]

Despite having considered a landing at Bjerkvik out of the question only a few days earlier, Mackesy now ordered General Béthouart to do just that. Some consider that the addition of the Polish troops, now just arriving, gave him more confidence but this is not very likely since he and Cork were already considering sending the 24th Guards Brigade south to meet the German drive from Namsos. It is more likely that he saw that his attempts to delay operations would no longer work and that he settled on what he considered the least dangerous of two courses of action, landing at Narvik or landing at Bjerkvik. The operation against Bjerkvik was also in accordance with an earlier recommendation by General Fleischer and the wishes of his French allies.

The Bjerkvik Landing

General Béthouart was charged with the planning and execution of the landing. He decided to use the two battalions of the 13th Half-Brigade of the Foreign Legion for the landing. The reaction of a legionnaire officer to this mission was probably typical:[10] "Ah, it is all very difficult. We are used to traveling on camels across the desert, and here you give us boats, and we have to cross the water. It is very difficult but it will be all right. I think so." Béthouart also intended to use one of the newly arrived Polish battalions for an overland approach against Bjerkvik from Bogen.

Simultaneously, he planned that the troops on Ankenes Peninsula undertake operations to tie down German forces in that area. Finally, he sought and received General Fleischer's agreement on May 8 for an attack by the 7th Brigade and the 6th and 14th Battalions of the 27th CA towards Bjerkvik from the north against the 1/139th. The 6th Brigade would attack on the left against the 3/139th on the Kuberg Plateau.

The plan called for the 27th CA to advance along Route 50 to secure the ridgeline from Hill 409 to Hill 416. Having secured Hill 416, the 27th would proceed towards Kvandal, link up with the Foreign Legion at Hill 336 (Skogfjell), continue eastward in the area north of Hartvigvann and make contact on their left with the 7th Brigade and on their right with units of the Foreign Legion advancing eastward from Elvegårdsmoen. The Norwegians were asked to secure the high ground from Hills 664 to 842 and thereafter cut the German line of retreat. Béthouart's original plan called for the amphibious operation and the Norwegian and French attacks from the north to take place simultaneously during the night of May 10-11. The Norwegians were to launch their attacks at the sound of the heavy guns in Ofotfjord.

The lack of amphibious resources forced Béthouart's legionnaires to attack the shore in two waves. The 1/13th Half-Brigade constituted the first wave to be landed directly in Bjerkvik while the 2nd Bn, in the second wave, landed at Melby, on the eastern shore of Herjangsfjord. Difficulties in loading the five light tanks that were to support the landings caused one MLC to be damaged beyond repair and this, along with the delay in transporting the Polish battalion from Harstad to Bogen, caused the attack to be delayed for 24 hours. The Polish troops lacked all their medical equipment and much of their means of transportation since these items had been loaded on an unknown ship in Brest.

The operation was postponed yet another day because of transportation difficulties, caused primarily by efforts to shore up the defenses in Nordland Province. The assault force assembled in Ballagen on May 12. The battleship *Resolution*, the cruisers *Effingham* and *Aurora*, and five destroyers constituted the bombardment part of the force. The 1,620 assault troops were embarked on warships, ALCs, and open boats. Cork, Auchinleck, and Béthouart were on the cruiser *Effingham*. Mackesy was ill on May 13.

The naval bombardment began at midnight and lasted intermittently for two hours. It was already so late in the year that there was only partial darkness in the Narvik area and a night landing had little concealment from enemy observation. However, darkness still prevailed in central Norway and it was hoped that the night landing would complicate German air operations from that part of the country.

The bombardment did little to improve relations between the Allies and the Norwegians. General Béthouart wrote later that no movements ashore were observed and he assumed that the Germans had sought shelter in the many homes along the shore. He states that he had received General Fleischer's assurances that the civilian population had been evacuated.[11] The bombardment and subsequent fighting devastated the village, killing 17 civilians and gravely wounding many more. Kersuady quotes a dramatic account by a Corporal Favrel of the Foreign Legion, "Then the assault began and a frightful butchery ensued, in the course of which we slaughtered more civilians than Germans..." He goes on to write that after its capture, Bjerkvik was systematically plundered, just like Namsos, but this time without British participation.

Hovland writes that General Fleischer had repeatedly warned the population via the radio station in Tromsø to evacuate by Saturday, despite the fact that the message might alert the Germans to the forthcoming landing. Most heeded the warning and evacuated, but when nothing happened on either Saturday or Sunday, many returned and suffered in the battle. This unfortunate incident is yet another example of inadequate coordination and cooperation between Norwegian and Allied forces.

The landing went generally according to plans. It took some time to transfer the light tanks from *Resolution* to the MLCs but Co 1 of the 1st Bn landed at 0100 hours. It was planned to land directly in Bjerkvik but machinegun fire convinced the commander to land about one kilometer further west, at the Haugen farm.

The covering fire from British warships became more effective after the Germans opened fire and revealed their positions. The relentless fire from so many naval guns forced the Germans to retire into the hills. Colonel Windisch, who had been alerted to the forthcoming landings by the heavy traffic of warships and smaller craft in Ofotfjord, had planned just such a retirement. The three light tanks brought ashore by the French proved very effective initially and the lead legionnaires were able to clear the shoreline quickly with only light casualties, allowing the rest of the battalion to land and begin its northward advance to link up with the 27th CA. It was intended that the two forces should meet near Tverelven, but the advance from the north was stopped by the 1/139th in the area west of Skogfjell. The tanks became stuck in the deep snow and flanking fire from the heights west of Hartvigvann made movement very difficult for the Legionnaires.

The 2/13th Half-Brigade, supported by two light tanks, landed on the eastern side of Herjangsfjord. This landing was delayed until the 1st Bn had landed and sufficient small craft became available. The area from Bjerkvik to

Øyjord was held by naval battalion Kothe, consisting of three weak companies from the crews of the sunken destroyers. There were doubts among the German officers about the ability of naval personnel to fight effectively as infantry and they were now put to the test.

The French planned to land the 2nd Bn at a point on the coastline close to Elvegårdsmoen but heavy machinegun fire forced the Legionnaires to land on an alternate beach several hundred meters to the south. Kothe's naval personnel, badly demoralized by the bombardment, offered little resistance and abandoned their positions, leaving behind nearly all machineguns.

The 2nd Bn divided into two forces after securing the beach. One headed for Elvegårdsmoen, which was secured after some sharp fighting with a small screening force of mountain troops. The camp had been heavily struck in the naval bombardment. The second force headed south towards Øyjord. A company of naval personnel, commanded by Lieutenant Kühlenkamp, abandoned its positions at Gjeisvik after coming under naval gunfire but before a ground attack.

The 3rd Division journal tells about the disintegrated and panic-stricken German naval units arriving at the division base at Bjørnefjell, including all of Company Kühlenkamp. The troops that showed up at Bjørnefjell included a few mountain troops, but these were sent back to the front immediately. The fleeing naval personnel were assembled and kept at Bjørnefjell. Company Kühlenkamp's abandonment of its positions opened the way to Øyjord and a French motorcycle platoon captured the place within a few hours without resistance.

The 2nd Polish battalion began its advance from Bogen (Lenvik) at 2200 hours on May 12. Their front and flank were secured by Norwegian ski troops. The battalion reached Bjerkvik after an arduous 12-hour march. The platoon-size German security force in this area made a hasty withdrawal. It found its line of retreat through Bjerkvik blocked and withdrew into the mountains to the north. The unit lost its way in the unfamiliar terrain, ended up in Gratangsbotn on May 16, and was promptly captured by French forces. A small element of the Polish battalion was sent northward to secure the Legionnaires' left flank near Skoglund while two companies were sent to relieve the French motorcyclists at Øyjoro.

The first opposed amphibious operation of World War II proceeded generally according to plans. There were only 36 French casualties but Moulton notes that it was not a great day for the British:

Of all soldiers, British soldiers should have been most willing to attack from the sea, should have been experts trained and equipped to make such attacks. Yet they left it to men from the desert to show how it could be done. That they should have lacked the skill and equipment was perhaps no worse than that the Chasseurs Alpins came to Norway inadequately trained and equipped to fight in the snow mountains. But at least the Chasseurs made the attempt, and in making it could retain some pride.[13]

General Hovland's assessment is that "Béthouart and his Foreign Legionnaires have received most of the honor for the liberation of Bjerkvik. There is little reason to believe that this operation would have succeeded if Fleischer had not simultaneously attacked from the north."[14] It was not so much Fleischer's simultaneous attack that made the landing a success, but his offensive that had been underway since April 23. These operations had necessitated the commitment of nearly all mountain troops available to Colonel Windisch as well as other units from Bjørnefjell and Narvik. Consequently, the Germans had virtually no reserves left when Béthouart landed his Legionnaires. The German sources attest to this conclusion: "The defense of Herjangsfjord's east shore was left to three companies of Naval Battalion Kothe alone. All other parts of Group Windisch stood with their fronts to the north, in heavy defensive fighting against continual attacks by superior Norwegian forces."[11]

The loss of Elvegårdsmoen was a blow to the Germans. Some magazines, although considerably reduced from April 9, fell into French hands. The Germans left behind three doctors and 45 seriously wounded at their field hospital, all of whom were captured. Group Windisch was now entirely dependent on supplies from the base at Bjørnefjell and the spring thaw made the route to that location very difficult.

Group Windisch Escapes

The Norwegian part of the operations against the Germans involved an attack by the 7th Brigade on the right to seize the Vassdalsfjell area north of Hartvigvann. This attack was expected to result in a link up with the Legionnaires who were moving northeast from Elvegårdsmoen, thereby trapping the 1/139th in its defensive positions astride Route 50. The 6th Brigade on the left was to seize a foothold on the Kuberg Plateau before the Germans could settle into new defensive positions.

Group Windisch was in danger of having its line of retreat severed. Windisch also had to establish a new front, one that faced north as well as west against the forces landed in Herjangsfjord. He had to delay the French advance northeast of Elvegårdsmoen and prevent a link-up with an anticipated advance by the 7th Brigade while shoring up the front facing the 6th Brigade. Failing to do so would prevent the withdrawing forces from occupying and preparing new defensive positions.

Windisch issued orders at 0500 hours on May 13 for his dangerously exposed forces on the German left to withdraw eastward to the area south of Hartvigvann and for the establishment of new defensive line from Storebalak to Fiskeløsvann. Units had orders to destroy heavy weapons and equipment that could not be brought along. Several factors came into play to allow Group Windisch to extricate itself successfully.

The advance of the 1/13th Half-Brigade halted on a line running from Skoglund to Skogfjell while the 1/139th was able to halt the southward drive of the 14/27th CA before it reached the planned link-up point at Tverelven. The two French units were therefore unable to join on May 13 as planned. The advance of the 2/13 Half-Brigade from Elvegårdsmoen was slowed by some very effective, but costly, German rear-guard actions. Lieutenant Bauer, the commander of Co 2 1/139, led a 30-man platoon from his company and tried to halt the French advance. The platoon was driven back after some vicious close-quarter fighting and Bauer was killed. Many of his men were also killed, wounded, or captured.

Elements from Co 13 were ordered to counterattack and try to throw the French back to the coast. The attack failed and the unit took up positions in the hills facing west. This allowed them to keep the Hartvigvann road as well as Route 50 under observation and fire. This fire contributed to halting the northward drive of the 1/13 Half-Brigade.

The fighting now switched to Hill 220 northeast of Elvegårdsmoen. This knoll was held by a weak detachment from Co 11 under the command of Lieutenant Tollschein. His mission was to cover the German withdrawal. The French eastward drive was stopped and the Legionnaires suffered a considerable number of casualties. Tollschein and his men repelled repeated attacks supported by naval gunfire and attacks by Norwegian aircraft. The two tanks supporting the second French attempt to take Hill 220 were stopped by mines that blew off their treads. Tollschein and his men managed to hold the Legionnaires of the 2nd Bn for 24 hours, allowing their comrades to make an orderly, but very difficult, retreat to the east. The position fell on May 14 after a French multi-directional attack. Only five of Tollschein's men escaped by climbing down the hill's 180-foot cliff-like backside. Buchner writes that it is difficult to understand why the French did not try to bypass the detachment by advancing south of Hartvigvann where there were no German defenders.

The German divisional reserve consisted of Lieutenant Ploder's Co 3, 138th Regiment: two officers and 65 men who were landed in Rombakfjord between May 8 and 10. Early in the morning of May 13, this unit was ordered to move forward, occupy Mebyfjell from Hill 482 to Hill 548, and cover the withdrawal of Group Windisch. Hill 482 was secured by only two squads until 0600 hours when the company, ignorant of the actual situation, tried to return to its previous location. It ran into Colonel Windisch who turned it around. French detachments, probing eastward from the landing areas, found no Germans in their path but instead of continuing their advance, they settled in on the plateau and were subsequently driven back by Co 3/138th.

It was of the greatest importance for the Germans to secure and hold open the bridge over the Vassdal River near Gamberg for the withdrawing units, in case the enemy was able to brush aside the delaying forces or descended into the valley from Vassdalsfjell. The river was in flood because of the spring thaw and there was no other crossing point. The regimental engineer platoon was ordered to hold the bridge. Strong Norwegian forces in Gressdal also posed an acute danger to the regiment's right flank and the weak remnants of naval company Erdmenger had the mission of blocking this threat.

The 1/139th, on the German far left, faced the most difficult withdrawal. The battalion had to disengage while under pressure from French and Norwegians forces from two directions. By leapfrogging from position to position and under the cover of well-selected machinegun emplacements, the remnants of the four companies withdrew successfully. Two mountain howitzers at the east end of Hartvigvann provided continuous support for the withdrawing units. The withdrawal of Group Windisch was mostly completed by 0700 hours on May 14 and the regimental headquarters, the last unit to cross the bridge at Gamberg, was established at the northeastern corner of Fiskeløsvann by 0900 hours.

There was precious little General Dietl and his staff could do to assist Colonel Windisch from their location at Bjørnefjell. Radio communications with Group Windisch were only sporadic after 2145 hours on May 12 and the situation remained unclear until the morning of May 14. Messengers took a long time to cover the distance to Bjørnefjell.

The only unit available after Dietl ordered the divisional reserve, Co 3/138th, forward to cover Windisch's withdrawal was a platoon of engineers under the command of Lieutenant von Brandt. This unit was sent forward to the hills immediately west of Cirkelvann but it was not expected to arrive until the next day because of difficult snow conditions. The arrival of fleeing and demoralized naval personnel did little to improve the expectations of Dietl and his staff. Communications were also lost between Colonel Windisch and Major Schleebrügge's task force on the far right.

The 3rd Division expected at any time to receive news of catastrophic events on the northern front. The entry in the division journal for 0700 on May 13 offers a concise summary of the prevailing sentiment: "It is doubtful that Gruppe Windisch will succeed in withdrawing its units since the enemy has made deep advances in its left flank." Group XXI's report to the OKW in the evening of May 13 is equally pessimistic: "Success [of Group Windisch's withdrawal] in view of its current battle worthiness is questionable."

Messages to Group XXI and the air support center in Trondheim called for immediate reinforcements and strong Luftwaffe support. The weather prevented effective air support and the only reinforcement received was Co 1, 1st Parachute Regiment commanded by Lieutenant Becker. Sixty-six men of this unit parachuted into the Bjørnefjell area around noon on May 14. The 3rd Division journal notes that the paratroopers arrived without rucksacks, overcoats, snowshoes and equipment needed for mountain operations. Clothing and equipment had to be scraped together to make these troops capable of operating in the mountains. However, within six hours of their arrival, the paratroopers were sent northward to reinforce Major Schleebrügge's hard-pressed troops where the situation had become critical because of 6th Brigade's attacks.

Dietl must have uttered a sigh of relief when Windisch reported at 0700 hours on May 14 that his exhausted mountain troops had managed to occupy new defensive positions running generally from Hill 548 in the west (Melbyfjell) to Storebalak in the east. The situation was still critical and it was doubtful if the Germans could hold Storebalak and Neverfjell.

We have seen why the Foreign Legionnaires advancing from Elvegårdsmoen failed to close the trap on Group Windisch in the Hartvigvann area. Let us now examine why the French 6th Battalion CA and the Norwegian 7th Brigade failed to do so from the north. The two postponements of the amphibious assaults made things difficult for General Fleischer. The deteriorating conditions for supplying his left wing due to the spring thaw, led him to allow the 6th Brigade to ignore the second postponement.

Fleischer visited Lieutenant Colonel Dahl and the men of the Alta Bn on Roasme on May 12. After the visit, he issued an addendum to the order for the forthcoming operation. The addition was clear and to the point, "The attack tonight will only begin, as far as the 7th Brigade is concerned, when it is determined indisputably that the French advance has actually begun."[12] Hovland suggests that this more cautious approach was a result of the events in Gratangen on 24 April.

More recent events may also have influenced Fleischer. The French advance along Route 50 had fallen almost two miles behind that of the 7th Brigade and exposed that unit's right flank to possible German counterattacks. Then there was the refusal of the French company from the 6th Bn CA to advance from Roasme against Ørnefjell in support of the Norwegian attack on Hills 676 and 664, or even to provide mortar support for the Norwegians pinned down in front of those two objectives. Dahl and Major Hyldmo are likely to have brought these examples to Fleischer's attention.

Regardless of whether or not the addendum was justified, it was also unfortunately open to interpretation by his subordinates as a lack of faith in his allies. An openly expressed attitude of that nature has a tendency to spread rapidly. Some have used the order as an illustration that Fleischer had become too cautious and that his excessive concern for the welfare of his own units led to a lack of initiative and a failure to exploit opportunities. General Ruge wrote later "The circumstances were that the German forces in Narvik could indisputably have been liquidated earlier if we and the allies had pressed harder."[13] Hovland writes that this is a serious accusation. However, the conclusion drawn by Ruge is similar to views expressed by German writers.

There also appear to have been some difficulties with respect to the operational boundaries between French and Norwegian forces. This caused Fleischer to send a written message to the French commander (Béthouart?) in the evening of May 12 to clarify the boundaries and to insure " ... that the French units in this operation occupy the terrain to and including Ørnefjell *on the assumption that the attack is actually carried out tonight* ... " Fleischer states that if the attack was postponed again "then the terrain east of Storevann-Kvandal will be occupied by the 7th Brigade tomorrow before noon."[14]

This clarification was sent to the French only hours before the Bjerkvik landing. It is not known when it reached the French but it is unlikely that it filtered down to subordinate units before they landed. The 27th Half-Brigade may have received it directly from the division or the 7th Brigade. It is, in any case, a rather muddled and belated clarification to an operation that was about to begin. While the word "attack" in the highlighted portion of the message is probably a reference to the French landing in Bjerkvik, not to the attack by the 6th Bn, 27th CA on Ørnefjell, this last minute amendment should have been clearer. The failure of the 7th Brigade to move forward until May 14 is probably due to Fleischer's earlier order that it not move forward until it was "determined indisputably that the French advance has actually begun," meaning the 6th Bn CA's attack on Ørnefjell. This delay and the French failure to seize Ørnefjell until late on May 14 facilitated Windisch's escape.

The 14th CA was unable to link up with the Legionnaires moving north from Bjerkvik on May 13 and it was not until around 1300 hours on May 14 that contact was established with the Poles and Legionnaires near Skoglund. The 6th CA captured Ørnefjell late on May 14, despite considerable losses to German air attacks. The battalion reached a position from which the troops could observe their compatriots in the Skogfjell area, but the attack was not pressed. Instead, the French battalion was withdrawn to an area near Gratang (Fjellhøgda) to rest and treat the large number of troops suffering from frostbite.

The Alta Battalion did not begin its advance until May 14. Part of the battalion advanced over Hills 676 and 664. Other parts advanced in the area east of Storevann and made contact with units of the 1/13th Half-Brigade southeast of Kvandal. The rifle companies were sent forward to the area north of Hartvigvann while the machinegun company took positions two kilometers southeast of Kvandal. From that position, the machineguns were able to cover the southern shore of Hartvigvann. By then, the Germans had made good their escape. They were not fired on as they withdrew in full view from Vassdalfjell since the 6th Brigade did not secure that area until May 14.

It is uncertain whether an earlier advance by the 6/27th CA and the Alta Bn would have trapped the withdrawing Germans, but the possibilities of closing the escape route for a major portion of the 1/139th were promising. Instead of timing their advance to coincide with the amphibious assault, as planned, the 6th Bn CA did not move against Ørnefjell until the following day. Fleischer's amended orders to the 7th Brigade kept that unit from advancing until the French began their forward move. The planned coordinated attack against the Germans north of Bjerkvik from two directions failed and this greatly facilitated Colonel Windisch's ability to extricate his forces.

The German account of the operation credits Group Windisch's escape to effective delaying actions, poor cooperation between the allies, failures by the French and Norwegians to attack weak covering forces aggressively, and ineffective naval fire support.[15]

The Norwegians Seize Footholds on the High Plateau

General Fleischer allowed the 6th Brigade to begin its operations one day before the Bjerkvik landing. It was directed to seize Hill 697 (south of Læigasvann's eastern end) and to be ready to launch the attack after 0100 hours on May 12. Unless otherwise directed, the brigade commander was to set the time of attack. As of May 9 when the 1/16th Inf reverted to its control, the 6th Brigade consisted of three battalions. The under-strength 1/12th Inf relieved the 1/16th Inf in the area around Lake 780 on May 11. The 2/16th Inf was located at the southern end of Gressdal. The 1/16th (minus one company under Brigade control) was moved to the vicinity of Hill 437. The battalion received orders in the afternoon of May 11 to attack Hill 697. The 1/12th and 2/16th were to support this attack by fire.

The attack against Hill 697 was cancelled at 2200 hours on May 11 by orders from the division, who wanted the attack to take place at the same time as the Allied landing in Bjerkvik. The slow progress of the French advance from Bjerkvik so delayed the move of the 7th Brigade against the Vassdal Mountains that the Germans had managed to establish a new defensive line in the mountains south of Vassdal. This may be one reason why the attacks by the 6th Brigade were never carried out as planned.

However, the views of the new 6th Brigade commander, Lieutenant Colonel Berg, may have been the primary factor. He took command of the 6th Brigade on May 9 and he visited the units at Lake 780 the following day. This personal reconnaissance convinced him that a main attack from the Læigastind-Gressvann area would not succeed because the terrain was characterized by level mountainsides that gave troops little cover from German fire. In his view, the opening of Gressdal was best accomplished by capturing Vassdalsfjell or by first seizing Storebalak. He saw better maneuvering possibilities in the area from Nævertind eastward and suggested that the 1/16th Inf advance through Raudal to Nævertind and from there to Storebalak. This opened the possibilities of a drive southward between Nævertind and the Swedish border or into the Jernvann area.[16] Unless Gressdal was opened in the near future by an attack from the west by the 7th Brigade, Berg suggested that the 6th Brigade hold the

Læigastid-Bukkefjell area while the 1/16th conducted its operation to the east. General Fleischer disagreed with Berg's suggestion.

Despite Fleischer's rejection, Berg was apparently able to carry out part of the plan outlined in his May 12 proposal. The sources are silent on this issue and the archives are missing. It is unlikely that Berg disobeyed Fleischer's orders and got away with it. It is more likely that the two officers worked out a compromise solution. Berg, for his part, must have agreed to drop his more ambitious suggestion of a southward drive between Næverfjell and the Swedish border and agreed to have the 1/12th Inf conduct the attack against Hill 697. Fleischer, in turn, probably agreed to allow Berg to move the 1/16th Inf eastward to attack the Kuberg Plateau and Storebalak from Bukkedal.

In retrospect, we know that the German right flank was wide open until forces were rushed there in the period 17-19 May. The greatest worry for the Germans in early May was the possibility that the Norwegians would undertake a quick drive, parallel to the Swedish border, against Bjørnefjell. Colonel Windisch was thinking along the same lines as Lieutenant Colonel Berg. It was this worry that caused Colonel Windisch to send a long-range reconnaissance patrol, under the command of Lieutenant Tollschein, into this area on May 4. Tollschein returned in the evening of May 6 and reported considerable Norwegian activities in Bukkedalen, ski tracks leading to the east, and an encampment at Brattbakken. Colonel Windisch concluded that the Norwegians intended to advance through Raudal and then westward through Bukkedal or a decisive drive southward to Bjørnefjell. He wrote that this report had immense importance for future operations and the very survival of the 3rd Mountain Division.[17]

However, the Germans did not have forces available to secure the eastern flank near the Swedish border before the withdrawal following the Bjerkvik landing. Colonel Windisch decided to move Major von Schleebrügge's rein-forced company from the vicinity of Hartvigvann to the Kuberg Plateau. This move was executed on May 7–8, though the new positions were not fully prepared until May 11. Occupation of the Kuberg Plateau gave protection against a possible Norwegian drive across those mountains to cut Group Wind-isch's lines of communications to Bjørnefjell in the area east of Jernvannene.

As noted earlier, Co 7 from the 2/16th Inf occupied Brattbakken on April 30 and remained there for more than two weeks. In addition to patrolling towards Storfoss, it sent patrols into the high plateau to its south. These patrols reported that the Germans had not occupied Nævertind and Storebalak. Colonel

Løken (the 6th Brigade commander at the time) made a serious and costly mistake when he did not order the company to occupy the Kuberg Plateau and send additional reinforcements into that area. Over May 7-8, the Germans occupied the high plateau, so that when Berg sent Co 1 there from Hill 437 at 0430 hours on May 13, the Germans were already in place. Company 1 reached Brattebakken at 1800 hours after an exhausting 11-hour move around Rivting and Snetind. Berg later moved the rest of the battalion (minus one company) to that area to be in position to gain a foothold on the plateau south of Bukkedal in a combined effort with the 2/16th Inf from Gressdal.

Berg wanted his force at Brattbakken (Cos 7 and 1) to reconnoiter and probe to the south and west. His message at 0345 hours on May 14 stated that it was very important that an operation against Næverfjell be undertaken since 2/16th Inf would attack Storebalak that evening, before the remainder of 1/16th reached Brattebakken. Two platoons from Cos 1 and 7 seized Hills 875 and 860 in the morning of May 14. They reported that Kuberg and the north slope of Nævertind were occupied by the Germans. Major Hunstad arrived in Brattebakken shortly after noon on May 14 with Co 1 and the mortars. The machinegun company did not arrive until 0200 the following day and it took the trains two full days in the very difficult terrain.

It was decided to attack Næverfjell as quickly as possible before the Germans could prepare their defenses. Two companies attacked that same afternoon, with heavy artillery support, and captured Hill 769 without losses. They proceeded against Hill 870. Fog on the top of the mountains facilitated the Norwegian advance and they stormed the German positions at 2100 hours. The Germans fled westward, leaving behind two killed and four wounded. They ran into a flank security force for the 2/16th's attack on Storebalak and withdrew in an easterly direction, pursued by the Norwegian security force. Twenty-seven Germans surrendered the following morning (15 May) but a few slipped away from their captors later.

The 2/16th Infantry was ordered to begin its advance against Storebalak at 1750 hours on May 13. The order to attack Storebalak was issued shortly after midnight and Hill 717 was secured by 1740 hours on May 14. The higher part of Storebalak, Hill 763, was still in German hands. The Germans had committed two companies in this area with orders to fall back to Kobberfjell if Storebalak could not be held. The terrain between these hills was open and dominated by German automatic weapons on the higher ground.

The 1/12th Infantry sent one platoon towards Vassdalfjell on May 13 where

Germans were reported withdrawing. The rest of the battalion moved to the southern end of Læigasvann. It resumed its advance the next day and occupied Vassdalfjell and Hill 697 by 0130 hours. From here, the battalion provided fire support for the 2/16th attack against Storebalak. If Vassdalfjell and Hill 697 had been occupied earlier, the Norwegians would have been in a position to harry Colonel Windisch's withdrawal.

As of May 15, the Alta Bn was on the north side of Hartvigvann and the 6th Brigade in positions on Vassdalfjell, Hill 717 on Storebalak, and Hill 870 on Næverfjell. They had established a foothold on the Kuberg Plateau, which served as a starting point for a continuation of the advance in the days that followed.

The Bjerkvik landing deprived Group Windisch of its operating base and the southward drive by the French and Norwegians had opened Route 50 between Gratang and Bjerkvik. The Germans were forced into the mountain massif south of Bukkedal-Vassdal and the Norwegians had gained a precious foothold on the south side of both valleys. The French were pressing Group Windisch's left flank. Two German companies holding Hills 548 and 482 facing west on Group Windisch's left flank were driven out of their positions in the early evening of May 15 and barely managed to withdraw. The mountain plateau represented the last defensible area north of Rombakfjord and its loss would threaten the German headquarters and base complex at Bjørnefjell. Dietl considered the situation critical and did not believe Windisch could hold the new positions without reinforcements.

A Question of Strategy

General Dietl viewed a direct attack on Narvik as the logical next step by the Allies after his forces were expelled from Bjerkvik and had withdrawn to the mountains north of Rombaksfjord. While he assumed that the large Allied buildup was for the purpose of a direct attack on Narvik, he still viewed the threat from the north as the most dangerous. A Norwegian breakthrough resulting in the loss of Bjørnefjell would seal the fate of his command. His reports and frequent requests for immediate reinforcements in the following days painted a picture of a dire situation on the northern front. Dietl had concluded that unless that front was stabilized he would be forced to withdraw from Narvik, even if a direct attack against that city did not develop. He made it clear that the only avenue open to his exhausted forces if the northern front did not hold was a retreat to the mountains in the Bjørnefjell area.

Dietl, however, was in desperate need of reinforcements to stem Norwegian pressures in order to carry out such a withdrawal successfully. Even if a withdrawal succeeded, lack of timely reinforcement would probably result in a retreat into Sweden. In a message sent on May 13, Group XXI requested OKW approval for such a move if it became necessary. The lead elements of Feurstein's forces were still about 300 kilometers from Narvik and no one seriously believed that they would reach Narvik in time to save the situation.

For the Norwegians, the stage was set to secure the key terrain on the high plateau. However, the German defense line had been shortened considerably and if their losses in personnel and equipment could be replaced, they would be able to occupy the remaining defensive positions with stronger forces.

Generals Fleischer and Béthouart felt the troops needed some time to rest before tackling the difficult tasks ahead. The attack on Narvik was expected within a few days and as soon as the city was taken, the offensive against Bjørnefjell would be launched. The timing of these attacks was unfortunate since it spared the Germans from having to face simultaneous offensives against both Narvik and Bjørnefjell.

Béthouart assumed command of all Allied ground forces in the Narvik area when the British units moved south to stop General Feurstein's advance. On May 14 he met with Fleischer at the 6th Division headquarters to discuss the offensive and establish a boundary between the French and Norwegian troops. It was agreed that the initial boundary would run from just northwest of Hartvigvann to the southwest portion of Fiskeløsvann. It was also decided that one Norwegian infantry battalion and a motorized field artillery battery would participate in the direct attack on Narvik. Fleischer selected the 2/15th Inf since many troops in this unit were recruited from the town and surrounding area. This battalion and the 9th Motorized Artillery Battery were removed from the front to Setermoen. They sat idle at Setermoen for almost two weeks because of repeated postponements of the Narvik attack. The newly mobilized 1/15th Inf was at Bardufoss preparing to move to the Bodø area. The Reserve Battalion, 16th Inf had completed its training period at Setermoen on April 30 but was not deployed to the front as a unit. By pulling the 1/15th out of the line, Fleischer reduced his forward-deployed forces to the equivalent of three and one half battalions since the 1/12th Inf was still recovering from its losses in Gratangen.

At this time, the Allied forces were positioned as follows:

1. The two French Foreign Legion battalions were located in the Bjerkvik-Øyjord area with 1st Bn occupying Hills 509 and 589, the high ground east of Herjangsfjord; 2nd Bn was at Elvegårdsmoen with forward units west and south

of Hartvigvann.

2. The 27th Half-Brigade CA had its battalions spread throughout the area. The 6th Bn was relocated to Gratangen (later to Sjøvegan) since 65% of its personnel suffered from frostbite. The 12th Bn on Ankenes Peninsula was relieved by the 1st Polish Bn in the evening of May 17 and moved across Ofotfjord to Lenvik as a reserve. The 14th Bn was located in the Øyjord area and plans were to move east from that area but frostbite problems ruled out an overland move. The battalion was moved in ALCs and a British destroyer to Liljedal during the night of 18-19 May with the mission of establishing a bridgehead in the Aasen area.

3. The entire Polish Brigade was located on Ankenes Peninsula, or to its west, by May 19.

The Foreign Legion moved into the area around Fiskeløsvann on May 16 but heavy air attacks and German artillery fire brought the advance to a halt. The French forces withdrew on May 19 after the Norwegians assumed responsibility for this area. The Germans bombed the headquarters of the French half-brigade in Bjerkvik on May 17 and eight soldiers, including the battalion commander, were killed. General Ruge, who was visiting, was not hurt.

Fleischer had made it clear in his directives since late April that Bjørnefjell was his main objective and the 6th Brigade was expected to carry out the main burden of the attack. However, the 6th Brigade was deployed on a wide front from just east of Lillebalak to the Swedish border with no apparent main effort, despite Lieutenant Colonel Berg's earlier suggestion that better possibilities for maneuver existed in the east, between Nævertind and the Swedish border.

Would the outcome have been more favorable if Berg's suggestion had been taken up? There were no German forces deployed in that area on May 14. General Dietl and Colonel Windisch became very concerned about their right flank after reports of Norwegian troop movements, their seizure of the Nævertind area, and a buildup against Kuberget. These actions on the part of the Norwegians resulted in a scramble by the Germans to make forces available to plug the gaping hole in their right flank. It was not until May 19 that the flank was covered, by relatively weak forces. If Berg had been allowed to move significant forces into the area between Nævertind and the Swedish border, he may have found no German defenses to speak of between that area and Bjørnefjell.

A two-battalion attack in the area from Kuberget to the Swedish border, conducted at the same time as the rest of the Norwegian and French forces tied down the remainder of Group Windisch, could have led to a quick termination of the campaign. It would have posed a direct threat to what was a rather defenseless base area in the middle of May. Only a quick withdrawal of Group Windisch would have produced sufficient forces to blunt such a drive. Failure to do so in a timely manner would have isolated Group Windisch and caused the loss of the Bjørnefjell base. Its loss would spell the end to any possibility of Dietl's forces surviving for more than a few days. If successful, a thrust along the Swedish border would give the Norwegians ample time to eliminate the last pocket of German resistance before the situation in Narvik was overtaken by events.

A breakthrough drive by the 6th Brigade in the east would have involved minimal risks to its right flank, if the other Norwegian and French forces had maintained pressure on Group Windisch as it withdrew. The risk would have been more than offset by the turmoil such an advance would cause for the 3rd Division and the avoidance of a three-week slugging match that resulted from the set-piece broad front approach. German reinforcements were beginning to trickle into the Narvik area and it was important to conclude the operation successfully before this became a significant flow. It was also important for General Fleischer to move forces to the south to confront General Feurstein.

There are differences of opinion with regard to who was at fault for not exploiting an excellent opportunity to conclude the campaign. General Hovland maintains that Fleischer intended to conduct "maneuver warfare" and blames Berg for either misunderstanding or ignoring Fleischer's instructions.[18] Hovland refers to the 6th Division's operational directive on May 15 as proof of Fleischer's intentions. This directive calls for the advance to Bjørnefjell to start *after* Narvik was recaptured and the troops had had an opportunity to rest in positions suitable as starting points for future operations.

The 6th Brigade did not stop for a rest and it was due to its initiative on the high plateau that the Norwegians were able to capture this area before the Germans built up their defenses and brought in reinforcements. There was no pressure from the division to hurry the attack. With respect to future operations, the brigades were encouraged to send reconnaissance detachments into the Cirklevann and Kuberg areas and to maintain strong combat patrols there.[19]

The Norwegians had good intelligence about German dispositions that indicated that the bulk of their forces were in the west and center of their sector.[20] Berg had the lack of German troops between Nævertind and the

Swedish border in mind when he suggested shifting the weight of his attack eastward on May 12. He pointed to the difficulties involved in an attack from Læigastind and Gressvann and the obvious defensive preparations the Germans had made on the plateau south of these locations. He saw maneuver possibilities in the area from Nævertind to Isvann and the Swedish border. A concentration of forces in the east would still allow for an offensive against Jernvannene. Berg anticipated that supplying an easterly offensive would be more difficult but concluded that it was possible.

It may well be that Fleischer intended to avoid the German strongpoint on the plateau as much as possible, and it may have been his intention to push through the center and cut off the German retreat near Jernvannene. However, there is no convincing evidence of "maneuver warfare" in the Norwegian operations after May 1. There is no evidence of a main effort or of attempts to out-flank the Germans. The operations can be characterized as an effort to drive the Germans back on a broad front. Fleischer was familiar with the positioning of the various units along his front. He also had copies of the brigade orders for their operations and objectives. These should have told him that the Norwegians were engaged on an systematic assault on and capture of key terrain all along the front, with little thought given to bypassing the enemy. There were no units positioned to widen a breakthrough and push into the enemy rear. Dietl had ordered the Kuberg-Kobberfjell area held "unconditionally" and it was against these strong defenses that the 6th Brigade was ordered to launch its operations.

The next division directive was issued on May 19, as the fighting for the key objectives on the high plateau was already in progress. Again, there is no expressed sense of urgency.[21]

Ø.K. [Fleischer] finds no grounds to force [hasten] the advance. Ø.K. would prefer that the units first expand their supply lines. However, if the Allied troops advance, it is the responsibility of the advance security force [6th Brigade] to insure that Norwegian troops reach the line Spionkop-international border first. And, the 6th Brigade may initiate this advance on its own initiative along a line of advance it finds most suitable.

However, we must give credit to Fleischer who appears to have been the only general officer who considered Bjørnefjell the main objective. The Allies—from Churchill down—continued their fixation with the town of Narvik, a town that had lost whatever importance it may have had as a military objective. It had only a symbolic importance. The objective of an offensive is the destruction of enemy forces or placing these forces in an untenable situation. The capture of Bjørnefjell would do that since Dietl would be forced to defend his last link to the outside world and would withdraw—as he indicated—from Narvik to defend his base area if that became necessary.

If all available forces were committed on the northern front and the Allies concentrated their efforts on supplying these forces, there was an excellent possibility of concluding the campaign. Fleischer was also correct in placing the weight of his effort on the left flank and his order on May 19 appears to give great latitude to Berg as to the timing and direction of attack. His failure, as I see it, was not to exploit the opportunity of the open German right flank quickly and vigorously. The claim that Berg misunderstood or willfully ignored Fleischer's wishes must be viewed in the context of several events:

1. The exchange of views that took place between Fleischer and Berg from May 12.

2. The 6th Division's directives of 15, 19, and 22 May.

3. Fleischer's apparent acquiescence in the 6th Brigade's final operational concept developed after May 12, which did not include slipping around the enemy's still open right flank.

4. The statement made by Colonel Berg at the end of the campaign.

The Norwegians Capture the High Plateau

The rest that Fleischer anticipated before resuming the offensive did not materialize, as both unit commanders and troops were eager to clear the high plateau. The fighting over the next week was concentrated around the high grounds: Kuberget (Hill 820), Kobberfjell (Hill 914), and Lillebalak (Hill 572). Four Norwegian infantry battalions participated in the attack on the mountain massif. The 6th Brigade was in the east with the 1/16th closest to the Swedish border and facing the Germans on Hill 860 and Kuberget. The 2/16th in the center faced the Germans on Hill 914 and Hill 648. The 1/12th faced the Germans west of Storebalak, including at Hill 648, while the Alta Bn faced the Germans on Lillebalak and Hill 482. Only a passing reference to this achievement is made by British authors.

The fighting for the high plateau in the week from May 15 to 22 was the heaviest and most demanding of the campaign. It brought Group Windisch to a state of near collapse. The Germans suffered serious casualties and with troops approaching complete exhaustion, they were forced to withdraw to a last defensive line north of their base at Bjørnefjell.

The Norwegian plan called for an attack by two battalions of the 6th Brigade, to seize the Kuberg-Koberfjell area at the same time as the 7th Brigade attacked further west. The Alta Bn was to secure Hill 336 and the 1/12th would begin its advance up the very steep river valley between Lillebalak and Storebalak when its neighbor to the west moved against Hill 336. The two battalions of Legionnaires would attack the Germans in their sector from Hill 648 to Rombakfjord.

At the outset of the fighting, the Germans were deployed with the 1/139th on their left and the 3rd Bn on the right. The far right later became the responsibility of Group von Schleebrügge. The German companies were switched around frequently during the fighting to reinforce certain parts of the front and prevent breakthroughs. However, at the outset we find Co 1 in the Kuberg area (Hills 860 and 820), Co 2 in the Holmevann area, Cos 3, 4, and 5 north of Fiskeløsvann, Co 11 on Hill 648 (to the west of Kobberfjell), Co 12, on Kobberfjell, and parts of Cos 14 and 15 on Lillebalak. Co Müller was located south of Jernvannene as Group Windisch's reserve, and later as reserve for the 1st Bn. Company 13 was located south of Kobberfjell as the 3rd Bn's reserve. Company 3/138th was pulled out of the front as divisional reserve on May 15 but had to be committed as reinforcement for Schleebrügge already on May 17. As a replacement for Co 3, Group Windisch received a platoon from the reorganized Naval Battalion Kothe.

Kuberget is the most easterly of the prominent heights south of the Nævertind-Næverfjell area. The 1/16th Inf, commanded by Major Hunstad, was ordered to seize it on May 15. Schleebrügge's Co 1/139th occupied the Kuberg area. This reinforced company became part of Group Schleebrügge by divisional order on May 18 when it became responsible for the German right flank. Norwegian reconnaissance established that the Germans occupied strong defensive positions on Hills 860, 820, and 794 and they concluded that a frontal attack would be difficult and costly. A couple of attempts on May 14 and early on May 15 failed to drive the Germans from Hill 860.

The battalion commander decided to strike at the German flanks with the main attack consisting of Cos 1 and 7 from the east, while Co 2 attacked from the north to seize Hill 794 and the ridge between it and Kuberget. One machinegun platoon supported Co 2 while the rest of the machinegun Co supported the two-company attack from the east. The Norwegian maneuver made the German position on Hill 860 untenable and it was abandoned around

1800 hours on May 15.

Company 2 started its advance at 1430 hours. The plans called for one platoon to seize Hill 794 while two platoons captured the western part of Kuberget as well as the ridge between it and Hill 794. The resistance was heavy and by 2000 hours, the company was still well short of its objectives.

Companies 1 and 7 began their advance at 1400 hours but the attack faltered after the commander of Co 7, Lieutenant Liljedahl, was seriously wounded around 2100 hours. The question of pulling back from Kuberget was under discussion at Dietl's headquarters and the Germans had already started withdrawing from some of their positions under Norwegian pressure, but reoccupied them quickly when the Norwegian attack began to waver.

A reshuffling of forces took place within the 1/16th Inf during the fighting for Kuberget that is difficult to understand. It appears that Co 1 was pulled out of the line on May 16 and used to bring provisions forward. The company, reinforced with a machinegun platoon from the 1/12th Inf, was directed to relieve Co 7 and prepare to attack Kuberget. Company 1, instead of attacking Kuberget, was moved to the high ground south and east of Lake 796. It remained in this area until the Germans withdrew during the night of May 22. Company 7 was also pulled back and assigned a security mission between Hill 796 and Hill 1097 on the Swedish border.

The redeployment of the two companies, which reduced Norwegian combat power in the Kuberg area, was apparently not connected to any planned offensive operations in this area. It seems that they were sent into the long mountainous stretch between Kuberget and the Swedish border for security reasons. This movement was one reason why the Germans rushed forces to fill the vacuum on their right flank.

The Norwegians made several unsuccessful attacks against Kuberget over the next few days. A determined German defense, periods of fog, and German close air support frustrated all attempts until Co 2 captured Hill 794 around 2200 hours on May 16, after bitter close-quarter fighting. A small German force had held this hill earlier until Lieutenant Trautner's ski platoon rejoined its parent unit on May 15. This ski platoon was down to 14 men. The Norwegian losses were light. Lieutenant Trautner was among the fallen Germans. From Hill 794, the Norwegians placed effective fire on the southern slopes of Kuberget and this made it extremely difficult for the Germans to supply their forces. It was therefore important for the Germans to retake Hill 794 quickly. Von Schleebrügge ordered Lieutenant Hans Rohr to recapture the hill with his own men and the remnants of Lieutenant Stautner's ski platoon.

Rohr managed to drive the Norwegians off the summit but failed to secure the hill completely. The fighting continued during the unusually bright night and the Germans were particularly exposed to Norwegian sharpshooters. Hovland quotes from Rohr's journal:

> We managed to occupy the old positions, but we were pinned down by well-placed Norwegian snipers. We constantly heard shots but could not locate the snipers. Corporal Ogris and I crawled up on a small mound in order to observe the surrounding terrain. Then, a single shot rings out and Ogris falls off the mountain … He was hit between the eyes, the cerebral matter flowed out … Sleep was out of the question that night, I had to rush around the perimeter because the Norwegians repeatedly tried to break in at different locations. We managed to hold the position primarily through the use of hand grenades.[22]

Company 13, commanded by Captain Schönbeck, was ordered to join Rohr's men and clear Hill 794 in the morning of May 17. This was Norway's Independence Day and the Norwegians were able to exact some revenge on the German company that had inflicted so much damage on the 1/12th Inf in Gratangen more than three weeks earlier. The German attack was repelled with seven killed and another seven seriously wounded. The bitterness of the fighting is attested to by the fact that among the original 23 men in Rohr's unit, six were killed, 12 wounded, and three captured.

The Germans rushed reinforcements into the area southeast of Kuberget for fear of a Norwegian breakthrough on the German right flank that would threaten their base at Bjørnefjell and the railroad connection to Sweden. The division reserve, Co 3/138th, was sent towards the right flank at 0100 hours on May 17. This unit occupied Hill 529 in the afternoon, after driving off a small Norwegian security force, and Hill 620 on the night of May 18-19. Two naval companies occupied Rundfjell and Haugfell, the two mountains immediately north of Bjørnefjell.

Three officers and 63 men of the German 1st Para Co, under the command of Lieutenant Becker, were parachuted into the Bjørnefjell area around noon on May 14. Six hours later, General Dietl ordered these paratroopers to Kuberget. They were assigned to the right flank on Kuberget, with their front curving southward to meet the Norwegian threat from the east. A second part of the 1st

Para Co, under Lieutenant Mösinger, arrived at 0100 hours on May 19 and was sent off quickly to join the rest of the company on Kuberget. These paratroopers were well armed with at least 12 light machineguns but they were not dressed or equipped for the climate and had no experience in mountain warfare.

The Germans withdrew from Kuberget in the early morning of May 21 and the Norwegians quickly occupied the hill. The decision to withdraw was due to events further west and in accordance with a decision to retire to a new defensive line. The Germans had taken considerable losses in the fighting around Kuberget. The Norwegians found a mass grave and several German dead were found on the southwestern slope of Hill 794, leading to Skitdalsvann. Major Schleebrügge's report to the 3rd Division on May 18 lists the casualties for the last three days as 13 killed, 25 wounded, 27 missing, and six cases of frostbite. This was almost half of the German troops involved in the fighting.[23] The 1/16th remained in position from Kuberget to the Swedish border until friendly units to the west reached Jernvannene.

The 2/16th Inf, commanded by Major Munthe-Kaas, spent May 15 clearing German snipers from the area west of Storebalak. Subsequently, the battalion attacked with three companies forward: Co 5 on the right with Storebalak (Hill 763) as its objective, Co 6 in the center with Kobberfjell as its objective, and Co 8 and the heavy weapons remaining, for the time being, in positions on Hill 717. Company 3 became the brigade reserve, and along with a mortar squad from the 1/12th Inf was placed at the disposal of 2/16th and located on the left flank near Co 8.

Storebalak fell to the Norwegians around 2100 hours on May 15. One Norwegian and five Germans fell in the fighting. The German defenders retired to Hill 648. Company 6 attacked Kobberfjell in the morning of May 17 while the reinforced Co 5 made a supporting attack against Hill 648. The attacks met heavy resistance and were repelled. By nightfall, Co 5 was located on the southern slopes of Storebalak and in contact with enemy units on or near Hill 648. Company 6, supported now by Co 8, was located on Kobberfjell's northern slope while Co 3 was located on the northeast slopes of that same mountain.

It had become obvious that the best way to secure Kobberfjell itself was by threatening the defenders' line of retreat, since the very steep mountainsides would make a frontal assault very costly. Lieutenant Colonel Berg ordered the attacks delayed pending the outcome of "negotiations at higher levels" about a large-scale joint action, apparently with the 7th Brigade and the French. Munthe-Kaas writes, "As many times before during the campaign, nothing came of the coordinated attack. "24

Major Munthe-Kaas and his men used the pause to bring additional fire-support into place. They hoped to bring two of the four howitzers in the 8th Field Artillery Battery across the Vassdal River, now in flood. They managed to bring one howitzer across a snow-bridge before it collapsed. The howitzer was disassembled and a 72-man workforce managed, with the use of ropes and pulleys, to bring it up the precipitous 1500-foot north side of Storebalak within a period of two hours. The howitzer was quickly reassembled and firing on the surprised Germans on Kobberfjell.

A coordinated battalion attack was launched at 1100 hours on May 18. When the forces on the right flank began to stall, the battalion commander switched all but one platoon of Co 3 to that flank to bolster the attack. The fighting subsided around midnight because of a heavy fog. The Norwegians succeeded in seizing a hill about 300 meters northwest and across a small lake from the German positions on Hill 648. Major Munthe-Kaas writes in his report to the brigade on May 19:

> The enemy has excellent prepared positions with stone front and side protection. The fire is especially heavy from Hill 648, from the south side of Kobberfjellvann, from three places on Kobberfjell, and from the high ground between Næverfjellvannene ... The last four days have been exhausting with little sleep, little chance for hot meals, cold nights, continual combat, and strenuous transports. The fog today is welcomed since it makes large-scale fighting impossible. I have no reports about contact with the Alta Battalion or the French.25

Berg had a meeting with the Alta Bn commander on the same day, to coordinate their operations. They decided that the 6th Brigade would continue its two-battalion attack against Kuberget and Kobberfjell while the 1/12th advanced through the steep valley between Storebalak and Lillebalak and attacked Hill 648. Simultaneously, the Alta Bn would attack and seize Lillebalak (Hill 572) and Hill 482. It was anticipated that the French would attack towards Fiskeløsvann and Hill 482 from their positions west and south of Hartvigvann. According to Norwegian sources, one company made this attack on the night of May 17-18 but was stopped by heavy German air attacks. This attack is not mentioned in French sources.

The Alta Bn's attack order issued in the evening of May 19 stated that it would attack southward that night while a French battalion attacked in the direction of Nedre Jernvann from Trældal. This was apparently the 14th Bn CA, which had arrived in Liljedal by ALCs and a destroyer that morning. The Alta Bn's attack was to be carried out by three companies. Company 1, on the left, would cross the river and seize Lillebalak. It would dig in and support the attacks on German positions near Kobberfjellvann and Hill 336 with its heavy weapons. Company 2, in the center would attack one hour after Co 1 and seize Hill 336. Company 3, on the right, would make a concealed approach one hour after Co 1 began its advance, to attack positions northwest of Hill 482.

The brigade notified Major Munthe-Kaas at 2350 hours on May 19 that the attacks by the 1/12th Inf against Hill 648 and by Alta Bn against Lillebalak and Hill 482, were in progress. The 2/16th was unable to participate in or witness the attacks because a heavy fog blanketed the areas above 500 meters. Contact between the two 2/16th and 1/12th was established at noon on May 20. The 2/16th began its attack at 1500 hours, after the fog had lifted. It continued its attacks against Kobberfjell and Hill 648 in the evening of May 20 but encountered heavy resistance from both objectives.

Company 1, Alta Bn seized Lillebalak and Co 2 also captured its objective, Hill 336. There was contact between Co 2, Alta Bn and the right flank company of the 1/12th Inf. A little over three hours after securing Lillebalak, the Norwegians came under heavy artillery fire and withdrew from the hill. Two soldiers were killed and another three wounded. Soon thereafter, Co 2 on Hill 336 came under heavy mortar fire from the hills south of Hartvigvann. It appears that French artillery and mortar fire caused both incidents. The French had difficulties in differentiating between the grey-green uniforms worn by both Germans and Norwegians. Sometimes, even Germans and Norwegians experienced this difficulty. Special markings were agreed on between the Norwegians and the French, but these were apparently misunderstood or not seen. There was a direct telephone line between the French forces and the Alta Bn and the latter had notified the French at 1300 hours that Norwegian forces had occupied Lillebalak, but word did not filter down to the gun batteries.

The results of the Alta Bn's attacks were disappointing. The Norwegian troops withdrew back across the river to rest while only a picket line was left on the northern slope of Lillebalak and Hill 336. The Germans reoccupied Lillebalak and their machineguns put a stop to the advance of the 1/12th Inf in the valley between Lillebalak and Storebalak.

The two battalions of the 6th Brigade had so far been almost solely responsible for the high plateau operation. Except for the abortive effort against Lillebalak and Hill 336 in the morning of May 20, the 7th Brigade remained relatively inactive. The advance of the 1/12th Inf was brought to a halt and the major combat elements of the Alta Bn were either withdrawn back to their starting positions or remained passive on the northern slopes of their objectives. The French had not undertaken any offensive operations. Nothing came of the coordinated attack on the high plateau supposedly worked out between Generals Fleischer and Béthouart on May 14. There is no evidence of attempts to carry out "maneuver warfare."

The troops in the 6th Brigade had reached almost the limits of their endurance, as noted in an extract from Major Munthe-Kaas' report to the brigade in the evening of May 21:

> The enemy's unusual obstinate defense yesterday and last night against our repeated attacks has tired our units heavily after days of continual combat under the most unfavorable conditions for care, rest, and personal hygiene. All forces are committed and must remain so until we are secured against counterattacks and the loss of the territory captured. Tactically, we need relief from the pressure through attacks by forces on our right flank. Materially, we need help to get our supplies, particularly ammunition up to the front … The capture of the heavily occupied and bravely defended Hill 648 presents many possibilities for continual advances but first we must consolidate, rest, and be re-supplied …[26]

The Norwegian units operating on the high plateau captured prisoners from several German units. From these and some captured documents they concluded that they faced six enemy companies that had orders to defend their positions against all odds. The severity of the fighting attested to the fact that these orders were followed.

Group Windisch's losses in the three-day period 17-19 May amounted to 32 killed, 57 wounded, and 45 missing. Such losses could not be sustained much longer, and Windisch and Dietl agreed that the group needed to retire to a shorter defensive line.

In addition to the threat from the northeast, the Germans were also concerned about the French battalion that landed at Liljedal on May 19. If it advanced northeast over Aasen (Hill 332) in conjunction with an attack by the Legionnaires against Hill 488 from Hill 621, Group Windisch's southern flank would be threatened. One officer and 15 men from Co 3, 138th, who had landed by seaplane on May 20, were reinforced by 36 naval personnel and rushed across the Rombakfjord in small boats to the area south of the French landing site to secure Group Windisch's flank. Hergot, south of Liljedal, was occupied by the French in the morning of May 21 but was retaken by the Germans the following evening.

A German withdrawal from the high plateau had been under discussion for several days. Positions were reconnoitered and bridges over the swollen rivers prepared for demolition. Group Windisch was near collapse, pressure was mounting along the whole front, its line of retreat was threatened, the supply situation was in chaos, and the flow of reinforcements noted below was not sufficient to replace losses or turn the tide of battle:

May 14—66 troops from the Co 1, 1st Parachute Regiment parachuted into the Bjørnefjell area.

May 15—22 paratroopers arrived.

May 16—76 additional airborne troops parachuted into the Bjørnefjell area.

May 18—Two seaplanes brought in 16 mountain troops from Co 2, 138th Regiment.

May 20—Two seaplanes brought in 19 mountain troops with one anti-tank gun from Co 2, 138th. Forty specialists also arrived by train through Sweden.

May 22—Six seaplanes brought in 63 troops and an antitank gun from Co 2, 138th.

The decisive moment for Dietl and Windisch came on May 21 when Munthe-Kaas' men stormed Hill 648. The Germans lost 50 troops killed or captured. Both officers commanding the troops on that hill died in the fighting. A breakthrough in the center, leading to heavy losses, was now a distinct possibility. Dietl decided to carry out the planned withdrawal, which would shorten and strengthen the front. The timing and conduct of the withdrawal was left to Colonel Windisch. Light infantry and engineer units covered the withdrawal, which began at 2100 hours on May 21. The withdrawal was carried out according to plans and without interference from Norwegians and French forces.

The Norwegians attacked Lillebalak during the night of the withdrawal and occupied that key terrain as well as Hill 482 in the morning of May 22. The 6th Brigade had continued its pressure around Kobberfjell, trying to isolate that dominating terrain. The German withdrawal allowed it to occupy Kobberfjell by the middle of the day on May 22. Munthe-Kaas notes with regret that the

Germans managed to withdraw without being pursued:[27]

> The withdrawal took place without interference; it caused despair but there was nothing that could be done at that time. The 6th Brigade lacked the fresh and rested troops required for an effective pursuit that could have ended in trapping or destroying the withdrawing enemy or, more likely, in their flight into Sweden. It [the brigade] could not squeeze more from its combat units that had, day and night, for four weeks fought their way forward, without relief or hope of relief, in unusually difficult, completely roadless, and snowed-under mountain terrain against the battle-experienced troops of a great power. Exhausted units – despite a glowing desire for the fatherland's freedom, good discipline, and eagerness to fight – can not be used in such demanding operations as the pursuit of an enemy retiring in good order.

By the evening of May 22, most of the German units were in their new defensive positions behind the watercourse formed by Storeelven, Jernvannene, and Holmeelven. The paratroopers on Group Schleebrügge's far right failed to get the withdrawal order because Norwegian units prevented the messenger from reaching them in time. They managed to disengage eventually and withdrew to Hills 620 and 698. The covering forces along the front succeeded in retiring behind the new front after carrying out the planned destructions.

NOTES

1 As quoted by Adams, *The Doomed Expedition*, p.17.

2 General Béthouart's Journal de Marche, chapter 3, p. 38, as quoted in Sandvik, *Operasjonene*, vol. 2, p. 30.

3 Sandvik, *Operasjonene*, vol. 2, p. 31 and Loben E. H. Maund *Assault from the Sea* (London: Methuen, 1949), pp. 52, 58.

4 Instructions from the Secretary of State for War to Lieutenant General Auchinlek, found in Derry, *The Campaign in Norway*, Appendix A , pp. 259-260.

5 Derry, *The Campaign in Norway*, pp. 169-170.

6 Macleod and Kelly, *Time Unguarded*, p. 295.

7 Maund, *Assault from the Sea*, p. 40.

8 Béthouart, *Cinq années d'espérance*, p. 51.

9 Moulton, *Study of Warfare*, p. 225.

10 Hovland, *Fleischer*, p. 162.

11 Büchner, *Narvik*, p. 93.

12 Sandvik, *Operasjonene*, vol. 2, p. 116.

13 Ruge, *Felttoget*, p. 209.

14 Sandvik, *Operasjonene*, vol. 2, p.116.

15 Büchner, *Narvik*, p. 103.

16 In his letter of May 12, Lieutenant Colonel Berg wrote, *"An attack to the south is difficult from Læigastind-Gressvann. The mountain area is even without the possibility of cover and is under effective fire from German machinegun positions. . . . The brigade still has maneuver possibilities in the area Nævertind-Isvann-Swedish border, provided we don't lose our chance as the Germans move their positions eastward."* Berg and Vollan, *Fjellkrigen*, p. 257.

17 Berg and Vollan, *Fjellkrigen*, p. 241.

18 Hovland, *Fleischer*, p. 175.

19 Sandvik, *Operasjonene*, vol. 2, pp. 124-125.

20 See, for example, extracts of reports dated 10, 12, and 21 May, in ibid, pp. 52, 124, and 140.

21 Sandvik, *Operasjonene*, vol. 2, p. 30.

22 Hovland, *Fleischer*, p. 173.

23 A report by the German war correspondent Karl Springenschmid is quoted in Berg and Vollan, *Fjellkrigen*, p. 314: "it was customary for the Norwegians to attack in inclement weather. They now fought harder than at any time. The mountain troops had already learned that they [Norwegians] were outstanding skiers, could fight on skis, and that there were excellent sharpshooters among them. However, the fact that they launched direct assault on fortified positions came as a surprise. Driven back, the reassembled, and time after time assaulted over their own fallen and forced their way into the positions. These stubborn Norwegian 'peace soldiers' had in the course of a short time, accustomed themselves to war and had become dangerous opponents."

24 Munthe-Kaas, *Krigen*, p. 154.

25 Sandvik, *Operasjonene*, vol. 2, pp. 134-135.

26 As quoted in ibid, p.140.

27 Munthe-Kaas, *Krigen*, p. 151.

14

THE LOSS OF NORDLAND PROVINCE

'In this Norwegian encounter, our finest troops, the
Scots and Irish Guards, were baffled by the vigour,
enterprise, and training of Hitler's young men."
CHURCHILL'S COMMENTS IN *THE GATHERING STORM* ABOUT
THE OPERATIONS IN NORDLAND PROVINCE.

The Battle of Stien and the Loss of Mo

When the Germans reached Elsfjord early on May 14, they found that the retreating Norwegians had destroyed or taken with them all boats that could be used for crossing the fjord. With General Feurstein's approval, Lieutenant Colonel Sorko prepared to cross the roadless mountains between Elsfjord and Korgen. The grueling march across the snow-clad mountains to Korgen took 16 hours. The troops were so exhausted when they reached their destination that Sorko was compelled to give them a short rest before continuing to Finneid along the east shore of the fjord. Holzinger's units had already cleared the Norwegians and British from Finneid by the time Sorko reached that location from the south. Sorko continued the advance while Holzinger's units remained to secure Hemnesøy and Finneid.

Derry writes that 1,750 Germans attacked the 1st Scots Guards at Stien on May 17.[1] This estimate is probably more than double the number of Germans involved. While Feurstein's forces had grown to four infantry battalions (2/136, 3/136, 2/137, and 3/138), a reconnaissance battalion, an engineer battalion, an independent company of mountaineers, a bicycle company, a tank company, and four artillery batteries, most of these forces were spread from Namsos to Mosjøen and did not participate in the action at Stien. Ziemke claims that Feurstein had six infantry battalions but this is not in accordance with reports to Group XXI on May 13 and 15. Only Sorko's group, consisting of one reinforced battalion, took part in the fighting at Stien. Since the strength of a mountain infantry battalion was approximately 500, the size of Sorko's force was probably between 700-800 men.

The British forces at Stien were deployed in two defensive lines. The first line was located north of the River Dalselv, covering the defile in the road to Mo between the Veten-Kobbernaglen Mountains and the fjord. Two companies from the 1st Scots Guards, the 1st Independent Co, and a supporting artillery battery occupied the first line. The two Scots Guards companies were located to the east of the Finneid-Mo road while the Independent Co and the artillery battery were located astride the road a little further to the north. The battalion battle trains and one company occupied a second line about four kilometers to the north. One company from the battalion was on its way from Bodø.

Lieutenant Colonel Roscher-Nielsen was reorganizing the Norwegian forces in the Mo area. He considered neither of his two battalions combat effective. They were demoralized and there was a critical shortage of young NCOs and officers. He sent an urgent request to the 6th Division on May 16 for young and energetic leaders. The 1/14th was less than half strength, with only about 300 effective. Both battalions had lost most of their trains.

Lieutenant Colonels Trapes-Lomax and Roscher-Nielsen had reached an understanding on how to divide the responsibilities for the defense of Mo. The British would undertake the defense of the Finneid-Mo road as described above. The Reserve Battalion of the 14th Inf would defend Mo along the Ranaelv (Rana River). The 1/14th Inf and a company from the 1st Scots Guards, with the machinegun company from the reserve battalion of the 14th attached, were positioned at Ytteren for the defense of the north end of Ranafjord. The 1/14th had one company deployed forward on the north side of the fjord. Captain Ellinger's company, which was reduced to a machinegun platoon after the near mutiny at Finneid, was now part of the 1/14th and located in this area.

Two ski detachments of approximately 60 men each from the 1/14th Inf were sent into the mountains between the British positions and Umbukta as security. There was already a security detachment from the Reserve Battalion located north of Store Akers Vann. A group of approximately 40 returned volunteers from the Winter War was located on the southern outskirts of Mo. Despite Norwegian warnings the British failed to secure the high ground to the east and rear of their defense lines.

The Germans learned from prisoners that a British battalion was located at Stien. They also expected the units withdrawn from Finneid to join that battalion. Furthermore, they knew that there were additional Norwegian forces in the Mo area. Sorko decided to attack as quickly as possible. He sent one company from his own battalion and a platoon outfitted with skis from

Holzinger's group on a difficult flanking movement through Bjerkadalen. It was intended that this force would seize the heights of Kobbernaglen and Veten and from there move west to attack the British flank and rear at the same time as Sorko attacked frontally along the road. The enveloping force, facing a march of 50 kilometers in roadless snow-covered terrain, set out in the evening of May 16. To give these units adequate time to get into position, Sorko delayed the battle group's advance until noon on May 17. Group XXI had toyed with the idea of a simultaneous airborne operation to cut the road north of Mo, thereby trapping all forces located in or south of that town. It was not carried out.[2]

The Norwegian security detachments at Bjerkmoen and Lille Akersvann spotted the German enveloping force. They reported about 150 German soldiers moving in a northerly direction in the area southeast of Bjerkemoen. The British concluded that these were German paratroopers and their sources make frequent references to them. This faulty information even became part of the official history,[3] but there were no German parachute troops involved in the action at Stien.

The Norwegians had urged the British to occupy the close-in hills and ridgelines overlooking the British positions. While the recommendation envisioned establishing early warning outposts on the ridgeline from Hills 717 to 996, the most critical terrain was the ridgeline from Hills 441 to 796 as well as Hill 481. These heights dominated both British defensive lines, and their occupation by the enemy could trap the forces in the forward line. The British had not learned yet to respect the mountain warfare maxim: "Go high and wide."

The two westerly Norwegian ski detachments, numbering about 120 men and fighting in familiar terrain and weather, should have been able to stop or seriously delay the German envelopment force. The detachment at Bjerkemoen withdrew without offering resistance except for some long-range rifle fire. The detachment at Lille Akersvann resisted and held its position. The Germans bypassed the Norwegian detachment without attempting to eliminate it. The Norwegians failed to prevent the continued northward movement of the German force.

Sorko's main force approached the British positions along the Finneid-Mo road. He started probing the British positions at 1830 hours while waiting for the expected flank attack of the enveloping force. Artillery on both sides was involved. British artillery fire became ineffective after German artillery fire severed the wire communications between the guns and the forward units. The

Germans were unable to cross the river near the destroyed bridge because of intense British fire and they suffered a number of casualties.

Meanwhile, there was no news from the envelopment force and Sorko concluded that the difficult terrain had prevented it from reaching its attack positions. The enveloping force finally reached Kobbernagel at 2030 hours, two hours after Sorko began his probing attacks, and its commander sent a messenger to the battalion in order to insure that their attack would coincide with Sorko's main attack. The messenger did not reach his destination until the following morning and by then the German main force had broken into the British positions. The enveloping force commander heard sounds of heavy fighting during the night but remained confused about the situation and decided to wait until morning. Fortunately for the British, he also decided not to carry out the planned advance to the road to cut their line of retreat.[4]

After his probing attacks were repulsed and with no news from his enveloping force, Sorko decided to carry out a more limited envelopment with Cos 6 and 8 of his main force. He moved this force eastward and managed to make an unopposed crossing of the river east of Hjelmedal. This enabled the Germans to launch a full-scale attack on the British left flank around 0200 hours. Some intense close-quarter fighting followed but within one hour, the Germans broke into the British positions. Lieutenant Colonel Trappes-Lomax tried to reinforce his left-flank company from his other forces but his men were slowly driven back over Hill 441. This forced a general withdrawal through the second defensive line.

The wider of the two German flanking forces divided into two elements after passing the Norwegian positions west of Lille Akersvann. One company proceeded to Kobbernaglen where it remained rather inactive. The ski platoon from Captain Holzinger's company continued eastward towards its objective west of Mofjell. It reached the built-up area in the rear of the British forces around 1700 hours on May 17. The British assumed that this force included the German paratroopers believed to have landed to their east and this threat may have contributed to their decision to abandon their second defensive line.

At 2100 hours, Roscher-Nielsen ordered the Winter War volunteers located on the southern outskirts of Mo to attack and eliminate the German unit that had reached the main road in the rear of the British positions. About 40 volunteers had arrived in Mo on May 16 and were commanded by a Swede, Captain Björkman, who had previously participated in the fighting near the Swedish border in central Norway.

Captain Björkman and his men encountered the Germans and attacked them frontally and in the flank and drove them back into the mountains. British sources make no mention of the counterattack by the Winter War volunteers. They do give considerable praise to another Swedish volunteer, Captain Count Erik Lewenhaupt, who helped bring the company that failed to get the withdrawal order to safety.

Trappes-Lomax informed Roscher-Nielsen at 0230 hours on May 18 that his position at Stien was enveloped and that he had to withdraw from Mo since there were no hopes of reinforcements. Roscher-Nielsen asked General Fleischer if he wanted the Norwegians to continue the defense of the Mo area alone. Fleischer ordered him to withdraw.

Roscher-Nielsen and Trappes-Lomax worked out a plan and timetable for the retreat. They agreed that the British would cover the Norwegian battalions as they withdrew to Storfoshei, about ten kilometers northeast of Mo. From there, the Reserve Battalion, 14th Inf was to be withdrawn during the night of 18–19 May and the 1/14th Inf the following night.

Sorko pressed his attack, but it was not until the evening of May 18 that the area around Hill 481 was cleared. The withdrawing British companies lost men who became separated from their units during the withdrawal. Company B, occupying the second line, apparently failed to get the withdrawal order and found its line of retreat to Mo blocked by German forces. If that is correct, either the German ski unit must have returned to the road after its engagement with the volunteers, or other units from Sorko's group had managed to slip behind the second line. The battalion commander assumed that Co B was lost. However, it disengaged and made an exhaustive retreat through the mountains in deep snow and across the Rana River. It reached the main road a few miles north of Mo. The Germans reached Mo in the evening of May 18.

Buchner reports the German losses as 14 killed and 26 wounded. This is about the same numbers given by Breckan. The British had at least seven killed and 40 were captured by the Germans. Adams puts the number of British killed, wounded, and missing at over 70 while the regimental history states that they suffered between 70 and 80 casualties of whom three were killed. The Germans report that they captured 14 machineguns, 6 mortars, and one 40mm antiaircraft gun. Three Norwegians and one Swedish volunteer died in the fighting.

Gubbins, who had received another brevet promotion, this time to brigadier, arrived at Trappes-Lomax's headquarters, a couple of kilometers north of

Storfoshei, on May 19. General Auchinleck had given Gubbins command of all forces in the Bodø-Mo area after Brigadier Fraser had been invalided back to England. While there are differences in British and Norwegian accounts of what transpired, it appears it was Lieutenant Colonel Roscher-Nielsen's turn to experience Gubbins' inconsiderate behavior, much as Major Sundlo had done at Mosjøen. Gubbins ordered the withdrawal speeded up without informing the Norwegians.

British sources note that Trappes-Lomax told the Norwegians about the withdrawal but they fail to mention that the withdrawal plans were changed later without informing the Norwegians. Adams writes that after Trappes-Lomax announced the withdrawal to the Norwegians, they "promptly commandeered most of the civilian transport, leaving the Guards to march to Mo." Roscher-Nielsen reported that he learned about the change in plans by accident and, as a result, much of the Norwegian equipment and supplies being evacuated found itself between the withdrawing British and the pursuing Germans.[5] The British withdrew quickly to Krokstrand (about 25 kilometers from Mo).

Roscher-Nielsen was forced to make some quick adjustments to the withdrawal plans. A company from the 1/14th Inf and Ellinger's men were moved to positions north and northeast of Mo during the night, to keep the Germans from cutting the Norwegian line of retreat. These two units covered the withdrawal of the remaining Norwegian forces from Mo.

Auchinleck's Force-Level Request

While the Scots Guards and the Norwegians were attacked at Stien on May 17, General Auchinleck prepared a message to London setting out his force requirements. As far as naval forces were concerned, he stated that he needed four cruisers and six destroyers. He also requested a ground force of 17 infantry battalions, 200 anti-aircraft guns, seven batteries of field artillery, and some armor. His request for air assets included four squadrons.

That same evening, before the request was sent, a message arrived from the Chiefs of Staff in London stating that the situation had been changed by the happenings in France and that his force would be limited to the 1st French Light Division (French and Poles), the 24th Guards Brigade, ten independent companies, a proportionate amount of artillery, 68 antiaircraft guns, and two squadrons of aircraft.

The Chiefs of Staff's message also requested that efforts at "galvanization of Norwegians to take part in defence must be pushed firmly."[6] This statement illustrates how out of touch the military leaders in London were with events on the ground in Norway.

General Auchinleck replied in a message that probably served only to reinforce the prevailing view among the Chiefs-of-Staff: "No galvanization of the Norwegians, few in number and not proving of great value, can compensate for deficiencies in these two prime essentials [air support and anti-aircraft guns]."[7] London was either unaware of, or chose to ignore, the fact that Norwegians forces had so far carried the heaviest burden of ground fighting in the Narvik area, while British land forces remained inactive for a month after their arrival. The Norwegian and French pressure on the northern front was the primary cause for Dietl's desperate situation. In fact, the Norwegians had tried to galvanize the British into action in Nordland Province for the past three weeks.

A full reply to the Chiefs of Staff request was provided on May 21. Auchinleck had concluded that he could do with the land forces promised in the Chiefs of Staff message. This is not surprising since the infantry forces already under his command or promised by the Chiefs of Staff were numerically equal to what he had requested. Auchinleck already had three British, five French, and four Polish infantry battalions, along with five independent companies at his disposal. The five additional independent companies promised by London were large units and made up for the difference between the 17 battalions requested and what the Chiefs of Staff proposed. Auchinleck's agreement that the suggested ground forces would suffice was contingent on the assumption that there would be a proper mix of artillery and other supporting units, including one machinegun battalion.

Auchinleck took a dimmer view of the air and antiaircraft resources proposed by the Chiefs of Staff. He pointed out that the number of antiaircraft guns he requested had been cut in half and that his earlier request represented only 2/3 of what the General Staff had considered necessary before he departed London. He concluded that it was unreasonable to expect him to accomplish his missions with this reduction if the enemy began to make heavy attacks on air bases and ports, which could quickly make the Allied position in North Norway untenable.

He noted that the morale of his forces was undermined on an accelerated scale by German air superiority. The range of the Gladiators was very limited and he stressed the need for a minimum of two Hurricane squadrons and one bomber squadron. With respect to his ability to hold North Norway with the means proposed by the Chiefs of Staff, he made the rather convoluted statement that it depended on the German ability to attack. If the Germans were able to attack, he declined to accept responsibility for the safety of his forces.

Retreat from Mo to Posthus

The road distance from Mo to Fauske, where the road bends westward to Bodø, is approximately 140 kilometers. The provincial capital of Bodø, one of the largest towns in North Norway, is located about 35 kilometers west of Fauske. Considerable forces were available to Brigadier Gubbins for the defense of this area. The Irish Guards and South Wales Borderers who had lost all their equipment in earlier attempts to reach Bodø were now reequipped and brought to Bodø in destroyers and Norwegian fishing vessels on May 20 and 21, without loss. This gave Gubbins a force of two infantry battalions, four independent companies, and two artillery batteries in the Bodø area. He also had one infantry battalion and one independent company between Mo and Bodø. The numerical strength of his forces was around 4,500.

The demoralized remnants of two Norwegian infantry battalions, a company from the reserve battalion of the 16th Inf, and the 11th Motorized Artillery Battery were located between Mo and Bodø. The final Norwegian reinforcement, the 1/15th Inf reached Røsvik (north of Fauske) from Bardufoss on May 25.

Trappes-Lomax and Roscher-Nielsen met during the night of 19-20 May at Krokestrand. They agreed to hold a rear guard position at Messingsletten to allow a quick withdrawal of their main forces over the barren Saltfjell mountain plateau and to organize an effective defense in the area between Storjord and Posthus. At this time, Trappes-Lomax received a message from General Auchinleck, quoted by Connell, saying, "You have now reached a good position for defence. Essential to stand and fight ... I rely on Scots Guards to stop the enemy."

Trappes-Lomax pointed out that to fight a decisive action at Messingsletten, with the barren mountains at their backs, was tantamount to squandering the only battalion in the area. A telephone conversation with Brigadier Gubbins led to a slight modification in the orders. Trappes-Lomax was to fight hard and only retire when necessary to save his battalion. Based on Norwegian sources, it appears that the overall plan was for Trappes-Lomax to hold the Krokestrand area as long as possible and thereafter withdraw to the Viskiskoia area, which was to be held for at least three days to give the Irish Guards and two independent companies time to prepare defensive positions at Posthus.

The advance elements of General Feurstein's division underwent a slight reorganization after the fighting at Stien. The two leading battle groups, Sorko and Schratz (commander of the 3rd Battalion, 138th Regiment) were placed under the command of Lieutenant Colonel Nake, the new commander of the 138th Regiment. The first German objective after capturing Mo on May 18 was to secure the Saltfjell plateau. Group XXI's order to Feurstein on May 19 called for a relentless pursuit, even if it had to be undertaken with weak and lightly armed detachments.

The defense of the Krokestrand area was based on three delaying positions behind destroyed bridges. The German advance was delayed by the destruction but the fight at each position was short. Contemporary news reports of actions between Mo and Posthus were wildly inaccurate, citing German losses of 1,000 men.[8] In fact, the 2nd Mountain Division suffered only 467 casualties (200 killed, 234 wounded, and 33 missing) during the campaign in Norway.[9]

The first delaying position, covering a blown bridge at Messingsletten, was held by one company of the Scots Guards and Captain Ellinger's detachment. The British and Norwegians were tired and depressed after days of fighting and withdrawing under continued German air attacks. The British held the left side of the road while the Norwegians held the more broken terrain on the right. Ellinger describes what occurred after the first German probe:

> Then something strange happened. From my command post, I saw one of the guards stand up on the other side of the road, throw away everything and vanish to the rear. One more did likewise, then others, and at the end, the whole company disappeared while the field was strewn with rifles, pouches, and lambskin overcoats. I did not understand what had happened … It was never established what caused the panic. Fear is an acute evil and very infectious. But it was strange that anything like this was possible in one of the world's best-trained and disciplined regiments.[10]

Ellinger and his men collected a truck-full of discarded equipment and delivered it to Trappes-Lomax the following morning.

The next delaying position was behind the blown bridge at Krokestrand. Trappes-Lomax met Captain Ellinger on May 21 and showed him a written order he had received stating that this was the place where he should be able to stop the Germans. Ellinger reports that they both smiled sarcastically since it was hard to imagine terrain less suitable for defense. While reconnoitering a final delaying position south of Saltfjell, Trappes-Lomax asked Ellinger what they were lacking. Without hesitation, Ellinger answered "One thousand Finnish soldiers." The Germans attacked the British position at Krokestrand and Trappes-Lomax ordered a retreat when a German envelopment threatened the British line of withdrawal.

In the last position south of Saltfjell, the Guards had their backs to the mountains, figuratively speaking. It was held until the evening of May 22 since German air superiority made a retreat over the narrow road on the desolate mountain plateau during daytime impossible. Norwegian troops had cleared the road to make the retreat possible and Ellinger describes the snow as several meters high on both sides. The Germans repaired the bridge at Krokestrand within 24 hours and they soon applied strong pressure on the Scots Guards' position. The British battalion and the Norwegian detachment withdrew from this last position south of Saltfjell after darkness on May 22 and covered the 30-some kilometers of mountains before daylight.

The British military leadership in Harstad appears to have placed great reliance on Gubbins, who called Colonel Dowler, Auchinleck's chief of staff, in the evening of May 19. Gubbins told Dowler he had spent the day with Trappes-Lomax and was quite happy about the situation. Dowler briefed him on the exchange that had taken place between Trappes-Lomax and Auchinleck and the latter's insistence on a stubborn defense. This caused a quick change in Brigadier Gubbins' view of the situation. He told Dowler that he understood and concurred with Auchinleck's desires and related that during his meeting with Trappes-Lomax he had expressed some disagreement with his plan. Gubbins received a call from Auchinleck at midnight to confirm what his chief of staff had said earlier. Gubbins again voiced understanding and agreement and said he would travel south to see Trappes-Lomax. Auchinleck told Gubbins not to hesitate to remove any officer unfit for command.

Dowler saw Gubbins in Bodø on May 22 and sent a glowing report back to his superior saying, "I feel that the operations about Bodo could not be in better hands." Auchinleck gave Cork a summary of Dowler's report on the situation, concluding, "Gubbins has whole situation well in hand, and is doing very well. He has his plans to stop enemy well laid."[11]

The Scots Guards went into position at Viskiskoia on May 23. Gubbins intended to hold this position until May 27. The Scots Guards were reinforced by the 3rd Independent Co, which had marched south from Rognan, and two

Norwegian ski detachments, each numbering about 40 men. The morale of the battalion had deteriorated considerably.

The pursuing Germans gave the Guards precious little time to rest. They attacked the Viskiskoia positions at 1600 hours on May 23, only a few hours after the British arrived. Adams writes that it was during the heat of the resulting battle that the Guards learned that their popular commander had been relieved. Lieutenant Colonel Trappes-Lomax was ordered back to Harstad. The battalion war diary describes the effect on the troops:

> This crushing blow took place in the middle of an enemy attack, and it is hardly to be wondered at that the morale of both officers and men was still further shaken by the loss of a Commanding Officer for whose personality and ability everyone had the highest respect, and in whom everyone had the greatest confidence.[12]

While his career was damaged, Trappes-Lomax was exonerated, promoted to colonel in 1944, and retired as a brigadier in 1948. When he died in 1962, an old comrade wrote the following about his actions in Norway in *The Times*: "Trappes appreciated every situation during that enforced retreat with calmness, patience and accuracy. He was right where others were wrong time and time again."[13] The removal of Trappes-Lomax was also a disappointment to the Norwegians. He had worked well with Roscher-Nielsen and other Norwegian officers.

Trappes-Lomax's relief did not alter the British situation. The independent company was driven back and this allowed the Germans to enfilade the Scots Guards' main position. It was ironic that Brigadier Gubbins, who had arrived at the battalion, had to cancel his earlier demand that Viskiskoia be held until May 27. He ordered a withdrawal at 1800 hours to a new position behind a blown bridge at Storjord.

One British and one Norwegian company, along with a Norwegian ski detachment occupied the Storjord position before the arrival of the Scots Guards. This position was given up without a fight when Gubbins ordered the withdrawal to continue through Posthus, which was 20 kilometers further back and now occupied by fresh troops. The Scots Guards were evacuated to Bodø by sea from Rognan on May 25.

The disposition of British forces in the Bodø area should have aroused Norwegian suspicions that another unannounced evacuation was imminent.

Gubbins had decided not to hold Posthus, only to fight another rear guard action. He spread most of his forces along the Bodø Peninsula, supposedly to prevent amphibious and/or airborne landings. This was undoubtedly a genuine concern and it shows the long-term psychological effects of German amphibious operations in Trondheimfjord and at Hemnesberg.

Roscher-Nielsen pointed out to General Fleischer on May 22 that the British force disposition north of Saltfjord included only one company between Fauske and Finneid. The route to Narvik led through Finneid and Fauske. While Gubbins had assured the Norwegians that this area would be defended, the positioning of the British forces may have led Roscher-Nielsen to suspect that the British were no longer preoccupied with halting Feurstein's advance in the direction of Narvik. A defense of the Bodø Peninsula west of Fauske would not impede the German drive to the north. It was possible that the Germans would have halted to eliminate the Bodø bridgehead but it was more likely that they would leave a covering force to protect their flank while continuing their advance. Follow-up forces could then deal with Bodø.

The Norwegians were desperately trying to reorganize and reconstitute their own forces in the area, knowing that these forces alone had no chance of contesting Feurstein's advance. The trouble-plagued 1/14th Inf was dissolved and parts of it were organized into ski detachments, while other members still fit for duty were distributed among the companies in 1/15th Inf when that unit arrived in the Bodø area. An infantry company from the reserve battalion of the 16th Inf and the 11th Motorized Artillery Battery had already arrived. Company 3, 1/15th Inf arrived in Finneid aboard fishing vessels on May 21. Roscher-Nielsen sent this company immediately into the Sulitjelma area to prevent an enemy envelopment of the Saltdal front.

Despite their enormous setbacks, a strange optimism prevailed among the British leaders in Harstad, even after the Germans had crossed Saltfjell. Auchinleck prepared a Special Order of the Day for May 24, Empire Day. It was apparently so well liked that all service commanders signed it. This was the day before the order to evacuate Bodø. A couple of excerpts are illustrative:

> It is our firm intention to stop the further advance northwards of the enemy and to round up their forces in the Narvik area ... Our brave allies, the French, had already carried out a brilliant landing operation from boats near Narvik and bundled the enemy out of their forward positions; they are pressing forward steadily in the most difficult country

and have the upper hand … Man for man you are more than a match for the Germans so give them what they deserve.

While the order may have reflected the new mood at the British headquarters, it was also undoubtedly intended to lift the spirit of soldiers who were tired and whose morale was declining. A more accurate reflection of Auchinleck's view of the situation is contained in a letter he wrote to General Dill, the new Chief of the Imperial General Staff, a few days later:

> It is lamentable that in this wild underdeveloped country where we, with all our wealth of experience, should be at our best, are outmaneuvered and outfought every time. It makes me *sick* with shame. The French are all right, real soldiers. As I said, our new armies will have to be very different from our old if we are going to recover our lost ascendancy in battle.[14]

The Guards, especially the Scots, and some of the independent companies were well aware that the campaign in Nordland Province had been an unmitigated disaster. They could look back on nearly three weeks of continuous setbacks and retreats. They had never seen a British aircraft and their experience with the navy was one that they would rather forget. They were told repeatedly that the Germans were operating at the end of a very vulnerable supply line, but still they kept coming and the destruction of roads and bridges did not slow them down. The enemy appeared to be suffering less from a shortage of weapons and ammunition than their own units.

The proclamation was intended primarily for the British troops but it inevitably found its way to forces from other nations. It mentions the French success at Narvik but fails to mention the contributions of the Norwegian and Polish soldiers who carried so much of the burden and losses in the fighting around Narvik. The proclamation did nothing to enhance the reputation of the British among those troops.

The optimistic mood among the British leaders also infected the Norwegians. The Norwegian leadership was fully aware of the disastrous events in France and continued to be haunted by the fear that the rug could be pulled from underneath them at any time. The 6th Division, however, anticipated optimistically that the operations against Dietl in Narvik and the Bjørnefjell area would end within a few days in his surrender or internment in Sweden. Plans were already prepared to bring the main elements of the division by sea to Sonja (north of Hemnesberg) for operations against Mo from the west, in conjunction with an attack from Bodø. The Norwegians were assured that the Bodø area would be held. Even if most Allied ground forces were later withdrawn, Fleischer and Ruge hoped that their forces would continue to be supplied from Allied resources and would be provided naval and air support.

The Battle of Posthus and the Retreat to Fauske

Posthus was a good defensive position. The British forces in this position included four companies of the Irish Guards, three independent companies, and a platoon of field artillery. Norwegian forces included one infantry company, a mortar platoon, Captain Ellinger's unit, and a ski detachment. The British had decided to fight a tough delaying action rather than a prolonged defense. The object was to gain time for the preparations of defensive positions on the Bodø Peninsula.

Posthus is a small village located about 15 kilometers inland from the southern arm of Skjerstadfjord. Saltelva (Salt River) runs through the village and is of considerable width at this point. There were several bridges in the area. The main bridge brought the road from the east to the west shore of the river. There was a suspension bridge spanning the Vatselva tributary that comes into Saltelva from the east, and another bridge across Saltelva about four kilometers north of the village. The area was characterized by dense woods that limited fields of fire and by steep hillsides leading to rugged mountains and ridgelines. It was a good defensive position provided fields of fire were cleared and adequate flank security existed to counter the German preference for flanking operations.

The British occupied the Posthus positions in their customary double line of defense, primarily along the west side of the river. This time they sent out an outpost line and right flank security. These forces came from Independent Co 2, part of which had still not arrived in the area at the beginning of the engagement. Independent Co 1, which had preceded the retiring Scots Guards, was also involved in the fighting according to most sources but if so, it is not clear where they were positioned. They may have augmented the outposts and flank security detachments. The first line of defense consisted of three companies from the Irish Guards, echeloned to the right. Company 1 was posted on a wooded ridgeline on the east side of the river, just to the south of the village. Companies 3 and 4 covered the road on the west side of the river but their location also allowed coverage of the east shore. A Norwegian ski detachment augmented the security of the right flank and another security detachment and the mortars were located on the hillside off the British right flank. Captain Ellinger's detachment was located immediately behind the British first line of defense. One company from the Irish Guards and Independent Co 3 occupied the British second line of defense, about three kilometers to the north. A platoon of artillery was located along the road, about one kilometer from the infantry. Lieutenant Colonel Hugh Stockwell, the former commander of Independent Co 2, commanded all British forces at Posthus.[15]

The exhausted Scots Guards withdrew through the positions of the Irish Guards at midnight on May 24. Fitzgerald notes that the two units passed each other in silence, without the customary jeering and exchange of good-humored insults. The bridge across Saltelva was blown behind them, leaving Co 1 of the Irish Guards rather isolated on the east side of the river except for a long detour over Vatselva into the village and across another bridge further downstream. Posthus was, along with Stien, the sharpest encounter between British and Germans forces in Nordland Province. The fighting raged for the better part of two days.

The German attack began in the morning of May 25 on the east side of the river. The lead element consisted of bicycle troops. They rode directly into Norwegian machinegun fire from the west side of the river as they rounded the bend in front of Co 1 of the Guards, and suffered a number of casualties. The attack followed the now familiar and effective pattern of probing and the build-up of pressure along the front to fix the defenders while other units fanned out to search for openings or weak spots in the flanks. In the meantime, supporting mountain howitzers, mortars, and machineguns went into positions to support the attack. The German forces involved in the fighting on the first day consisted of Lieutenant Colonel Sorko's reinforced 2/137th Bn, well supported by the Luftwaffe.

There was a lull of several hours while the German infantry deployed after the bicycle troops were ambushed. The initial phase of the German attack drove back the British outposts but was halted by heavy fire from British artillery and Norwegian mortars. An attempt to storm the positions of Co 1 of the Irish Guards around 1400 hours on the heels of a strafing attack by five German aircraft against the mortars and artillery failed, but the company soon found its left flank enveloped. The lull that followed the German attack gave Co 1 a chance to disengage before its line of retreat was cut. The company commander, Captain Eugster, sent two platoons off the ridgeline with orders to cross Vatselva via the suspension bridge. He remained with one platoon to cover their withdrawal for half an hour. When the time came for the last platoon to withdraw, it found that the bridge had been destroyed prematurely. The river was too swift and deep to ford and, with the Germans hot on their heels, the troops linked rifle straps and sent a good swimmer across to fasten one end to the opposite shore. The platoon was able to cross with only minutes to spare before the Germans reached the riverbank. The company moved north along the east side of Saltelva and crossed to the west side via the suspension bridge located a short distance north of the British second line of defense.

German air attacks had forced the battalion commander to relocate his CP. Because of the movement of the CP, the battalion commander did not learn about the withdrawal of Co 1 until about 1800 hours. He sent Co 2 and Independent Co 3 to the east side of the river to shore up that flank by occupying the dominant high ground between the two rivers. These units were in position on the high ground between the two rivers by 0430 hours on May 26.

The Germans, however, did not press the attack on the east side of Saltelva. During the night, while the British commander moved almost half of his combat power to the east side of Saltelva, German combat engineers constructed a pontoon bridge about a kilometer south of the main bridge at Posthus. Sorko's command, now reinforced by units from Schratz' group, crossed the pontoon bridge in a steady stream. By early morning, the Germans had successfully switched their main attack to the west side of the river at the same time as the British had moved half of their combat power to the east side of the river. They were also trying to secure the log bridge over the river at Posthus. The destruction of this bridge had been only partly successful. Company 4 and the Norwegian detachment were able to keep the Germans from crossing the remnants of the bridge and inflicted a number of casualties on the attackers.

The Germans drove back the British outposts on the west side of the river and began a flanking movement via the high ground to the southwest of Posthus Bridge. Stockwell committed his last reserve, part of Independent Co 2, in a vain attempt to counter the envelopment. The second line of defense was now empty. As happens so often in an engagement, the initiative was with the attacker. The two companies on the east side of the river were mere onlookers to the main event on the other side of the river.

Brigadier Gubbins gave the order to retreat around 1130 hours but the order was not carried out until about 1900 hours. Independent Co 2 withdrew after its unsuccessful attempt to counter the German envelopment and took up a delaying position near the suspension bridge in order to allow the two companies on the east side of the river to cross back to the west side and the road leading to Rognan. Independent Co 3 received the order to cross the river but could not reach the bridge before it was destroyed. Company 2 of the Guards did not receive the order to withdraw until a Norwegian liaison officer arrived and told them. This happened after the bridge had been destroyed. The two companies were left to make their retreat on the roadless east side of the river.

The disengagement of Cos 3 and 4 was helped by the unexpected appearance of a lone British aircraft that strafed the German troops. Three aircraft had flown from Bardufoss and landed at Bodø Airfield to refuel. They took off again as the Germans were bombing the airfield. One crashed, one returned, and the third is the one that made its appearance above the withdrawing Irish Guards. In the history of the Irish Guards, it is claimed that this lone aircraft shot down three Heinkels. Derry and Ash claim that the two Gladiators that remained after the third crashed shot down two German aircraft and damaged two more. German sources do not mention the loss of any fighters or bombers but they do record the loss in this area of two transports on their way to Narvik.

The Norwegian volunteers under Captain Ellinger occupied two delay positions along the route of withdrawal, one at Sundby and one at Meby. These delays provided the Irish Guards with the time they needed to embark on ferries and fishing boats that brought them across the fjord to Langset, from where the road continued to Finneid and Fauske. The German pursuit was slowed because at that time there was no road between Rognan and Langset. Later that year, in London, Colonel Stockwell introduced Captain Ellinger at the Irish Guards Officer Mess as the man who saved their lives in Norway.

Of the two British companies that made their withdrawal on the east side of the river, Independent Co 3 managed to re-cross the river and board the last ferry. Company 2 of the Irish Guards was unable to cross the river and made a 30-kilometer march through very difficult terrain to Langset.

The Irish Guards and the Independent Cos reached Finneid early on May 27. The unit history relates that those unaccounted for at Rognan arrived throughout the day in twos and threes. By evening, all were accounted for except 20 members of the battalion staff. One eventually reached Fauske alone. The British remained in Fauske until the following night when they moved eight kilometers further west.

The advance of the 2nd Mountain Division through Nordland Province won the forthright admiration of their enemies. Churchill writes:

At Bodo and Mo, during the retreat of Gubbins' force to the north, we were each time just too late, and the enemy, although they had to overcome hundreds of miles of rugged, snow-clogged country, drove us back in spite of gallant episodes. We, who had the command of the sea and could pounce anywhere on an undefended coast, were outpaced by the enemy moving by land across very large distances in the face of every obstacle. In this Norwegian encounter, our finest troops, the Scots and Irish Guards, were baffled by the vigour, enterprise, and training of Hitler's young men.[16]

The Evacuation of Bodø

As the British and Norwegians were fighting at Posthus, the Germans made their breakthrough to the Channel Coast in France and the desperate British evacuation from Dunkirk was about to start. Churchill decided that all available resources had to be concentrated on the defense of Great Britain. Part of this decision involved the evacuation of Bodø, which was ordered on May 25, the first day of the fighting at Posthus. The British were still reinforcing Bodø that day with the arrival of the last company of the South Wales Borderers. It is rather ironic that the destroyer bringing this company to Bodø also brought Colonel Dowler from Harstad carrying the evacuation order for all British forces.

The original plan was to bring the German northward advance to a halt at Finneid. As pointed out by Ash, this was the best defensive position during the whole campaign with water in front and on the flanks, anchored against high mountains in the east, stretching to the Swedish border, about 30 kilometers away. The Norwegians considered it imperative to halt the German drive in this location in order to provide General Fleischer time to eliminate the Germans in the Narvik area and thereafter switch his forces against General Feurstein. For that reason, Lieutenant Colonel Roscher-Nielsen had concentrated the remnants of the withdrawing Norwegian forces and the newly arrived battalion from Bardufoss in this area.

The Norwegians were therefore dismayed to see the British forces withdraw westward to positions that were less suitable for defense and did not cover the route to Narvik. To the Norwegians, who were again not informed about the evacuation, the westward movement of the British forces was, in the words of Sandvik, "incomprehensible and ominous." General Fleischer was notified by a telegram, copied to General Ruge, late in the evening of May 28. Gubbins made no mention to Roscher-Nielsen about the British evacuation decision, taken three days earlier. The same applies to a conference Major Lindbäck-Larsen had with Colonel Dowler at Harstad after the latter's return from Bodø on May 26.

Lindbäck-Larsen reported his conversation with Dowler to Roscher-Nielsen on May 28, and to Fleischer, and Ruge the following day. Dowler had promised that British fighters would operate from Bodø, a lengthy deployment of British aircraft carriers to the Bodø area, eight Bofors guns for the Norwegians to use at Finneid, additional reinforcements, and that the Finneid line would be held.

The Norwegians redeployed their forces when the British moved their defense line to the Fauske area. A Norwegian force was sent towards Langset to delay the German advance. One company that had been sent to Sulitjelma earlier, to block the eastern and more mountainous route into the Finneid area, was ordered back to Fauske in order not to be isolated by the German advance, now that Finneid was not to be defended. The commander was told that Norwegian forces would attempt to hold the road through Finneid open until the following day (May 29).

The German advance was more rapid than anticipated and the Norwegians were forced back across the bridge at Finneid in the evening of May 28, after which the bridge was destroyed. The forces at Sulitjelma were isolated and Roscher-Nielsen ordered them to withdraw over the mountains and the glacier of Blåmannsisen to Røsvik.

Defensive positions south of Djupvik were prepared and occupied by two infantry companies from the 1/15th Inf, an artillery battery, two mortar platoons, and an engineer platoon. Brigadier Gubbins had promised Roscher-Nielsen that he would send his chief of staff to the latter's headquarters to arrange details of future cooperation. The chief of staff never appeared.

The Luftwaffe attacked Bodø in strength on May 27, in a continuation of a series of bombing raids that began on May 20. The Germans began by dropping heavy explosive bombs and thereafter a large number of incendiary bombs. The attack lasted for two hours. The two remaining Gladiators were quickly put out of operation and the Germans reduced the town to rubble. Fortunately, most of the civilian population had evacuated when German air raids began a week earlier, and as a result, only 15 civilians were killed. Nothing was spared, including the hospital where a large number of wounded Scots Guards were located.

Roscher-Nielsen had a telephone conversation with Brigadier Gubbins after the German raid and when asked about the situation, Gubbins gave an ambiguous answer. Roscher-Nielsen came away from the conversation with the understanding that the British were still holding their positions in Fauske but he noted that Gubbins also made it clear that the Norwegians should remove their own units as quickly as possible.

Colonel Finne, the Norwegian liaison officer at the British headquarters in Harstad, was finally told on May 29 that the British were about to evacuate Bodø. General Ruge sent an immediate message to Colonel Finne directing him to appeal the evacuation decision, since a German occupation of Bodø meant that German fighters would soon dominate the skies over Narvik. He also pointed out that the surrender of the Bodø area to the enemy would have a detrimental impact on Norwegian morale after the operations there had resulted in the destruction of the city.

Roscher-Nielsen asked Fleischer to prevail on the British to delay their evacuation by three days to allow him to withdraw his troops safely. Fleischer did this through General Ruge's headquarters on May 29. Derry and Hovland write that the request to delay the evacuation from Bodø for three days was accepted. This is misleading. The final evacuation took place in the evening of May 31, two days after the request. Furthermore, the withdrawal from Fauske was completed before May 30, when Roscher-Nielsen reported that he was alone on the isthmus.

The Irish Guards and the two independent companies had actually departed the isthmus in the morning of May 29. To the Norwegians, it was not important when the British evacuated the town of Bodø but when they evacuated the Fauske area. This would leave the Norwegians in the untenable position of facing the Germans alone. Ash agrees, writing that Gubbins withdrew his forces during the promised three-day delay and that the Norwegians were cut off long before the time was up.

The Norwegian Navy assembled over 100 fishing vessels and these were sent to Røsvik to evacuate the Norwegian troops. Roscher-Nielsen decided to hold the Djupvik positions with units from 1/15th Inf while the Reserve Battalion, 14th Inf was sent to Røsvik for evacuation. This battalion was successfully evacuated to the Lofoten Islands on May 30. Only one platoon from the company at Sulitjelma reached Røsvik. The rest of the company found its route of withdrawal to Røsvik blocked by German detachments and it was demobilized.

General Feurstein had to make a quick decision as his lead elements approached Fauske. He was presented with the same dilemma as had faced Admiral Lütjens, almost two months earlier. It was tempting to let battle groups Sorko and Schrantz aggressively pursue the retiring British troops. There is little doubt that large elements of the British brigade-size force would have been destroyed or captured if he had selected that course of action. However, Feurstein did not lose sight of the main objective, the relief of General Dietl's forces in Narvik.

Feurstein split his forces when he reached Fauske. The forces approaching that location consisted of two and one-half mountain infantry battalions, two companies of bicycle troops, and one mountain artillery battery. Lieutenant Colonel Nake commanded these forces. Feurstein allowed one part of this force, under Nake, to follow the British while the remainder, under Sorko, continued its trek northward to Røsvik. The forces sent westward did not press their pursuit and there were no significant engagements between them and the retreating Guards. Between May 28 and 31, the British successfully evacuated their forces in two destroyers and the old cruiser *Vindictive*, under the cover of aircraft operating from Bardufoss. They faced little German interference. Two of the independent companies were taken directly to Great Britain aboard *Vindictive*, while the other forces were brought to Harstad. The British destroyed most of their heavy weapons, vehicles, and the oil storage facilities in the harbor.

British operations in Nordland Province, which had begun with considerable optimism three weeks earlier, ended as the last destroyer pulled away from Bodø. British losses in the Nordland Campaign, according to Derry, amounted to 506 killed, wounded, and captured. This included a small number from the South Wales Borderer's on Ankenes Peninsula at Narvik.

The 1/15th Inf, under Major Omdal, fought an effective delaying action from their position at Djupvik. The first German attack was repelled. The position held until the early afternoon of May 31 when a withdrawal was ordered, covered by the machinegun company. The last engagement took place three kilometers south of Røsvik. The evacuation was carried out during a period of fog that prevented German air operations. Horses and vehicles were left behind but the floating depot was towed away. The rear guard managed to hold the Germans at a distance until the last unit had embarked at 1800 hours on May 31.

Operation *Büffel (Buffalo)*

With the British and Norwegian forces out of his way, Feurstein could begin what was perhaps the most difficult part of his effort to relieve Narvik. His forces had covered about 700 kilometers under difficult conditions in 27 days. These forces were still over 150 kilometers from Narvik and ahead of them lay a roadless mountain wilderness that the OKW had declared impassable even by mountain troops. There were several efforts underway to bring assistance to Narvik but the connection through the mountains was viewed by some as the only effective way.

Planning and preparations for the last leg of the advance began when the Germans were still between Mo and Posthus. Three battalions of specially selected individuals were created by selecting a platoon of the best soldiers from each company in the division. These three platoons from each battalion would form a company. The three companies thus formed became a "Narvik Battalion." Each battalion was reinforced with three heavy machineguns, one infantry gun, and two mountain howitzers. The battalions consisted of about 600 men. Special equipment for high-mountain operations was ordered and delivered to Fauske.

Lieutenant Colonel Ritter von Hengl, commander of the 137th Regiment and a future commander of the 2nd Mountain Division, was selected to command the "Narvik Battalions." He established his headquarters in Mo and began the detailed planning for the operation, code-named *Büffel* (*Buffalo*). According to Major Zorn, the 2nd Division's operation officer, he selected this name because it used to be the battle cry of Dietl's downhill skiers when Dietl was a company commander in Munich.

The route selected for the battalions avoided places where the troops could come under fire from British warships and any violation of the Swedish frontier was strictly forbidden. The advance would take place at night and the troops would rest during the day. Hengl selected the camps along the route during an aerial reconnaissance on May 29. He planned to complete the march to Narvik in nine to ten days, with the troops covering about 15 to 20 kilometers each night. The total force of about 2,500 men was to assemble when the Germans reached the Fauske area. Some of the troops would come from the lead units while others needed to be brought forward.

The soldiers were instructed to leave sub-machineguns behind and to carry only rifles and pistols. Hand grenades, helmets, and gas masks were also left behind. Each man carried 30 rounds of rifle ammunition. Four boxes of ammunition for each machinegun and 15 rounds for each light mortar were brought along. Supply was entirely by airdrop at designated rest areas and the heavy weapons and their ammunition were to be air dropped to the advancing troops when they reached a point close to Narvik. Each man carried rations for four days but these were not to be used unless the planned airdrops did not materialize. Essential Alpine equipment was brought along, such as ropes, iron climbers, ice picks, about 50 skis per battalion, and snowshoes. The men carried light sleeping bags and an additional 10 sleeping bags and five 10-man tents were to be air dropped at each rest area. These were to be left behind and new ones dropped at the next area.

The Luftwaffe was asked not to make advance airdrops since the Germans believed that a force of 500 Norwegian troops had taken the same route northward. Each company was assigned special medical personnel and litter carriers. In addition, one doctor and 25 litter carriers were to be stationed at the rest areas as these were reached, with five carriers at each location. The battalions were equipped with radios.

The *Büffel* force of 10 companies was assembled in the Fauske area in the evening of June 2. The June 1 evening situation report from General Dietl described the situation in the Narvik area as extremely serious. Sorko's battalion, which was the lead element of the *Büffel* force, had already started on its way to Narvik, led by a special advance party of mountaineers. Inclement weather prevented Sorko's unit from receiving the special equipment planned for the advance in time, and those units with a later starting time gave up some of their equipment to insure that the lead elements were properly equipped.

Feurstein was not optimistic about operation *Büffel's* chances of success but Dietl was in dire straits and it seemed like the best of all alternatives for coming to his aid. He was not alone in his skepticism. Both Group XXI and the OKW had written off Dietl and his forces, despite all the various attempts to bring help. In fact, a force reorganization plan was prepared in early June for carrying out the conquest of North Norway after the anticipated loss of the 3rd Mountain Division. This involved the creation of a Mountain Corps under Feurstein's command, consisting of the 2nd and 5th Mountain Divisions commanded respectively by Colonels Nake and Weiss.

In defiance of chronology, this may be the place to describe the end of Operation *Büffel*. By June 8, the forward elements of Sorko's unit had reached only as far as Hellmoboten and were ready to continue to the next camp. That night, a message was received announcing the armistice and canceling the operation. Hengl considered that the most difficult part of the route was over and he stated later that there was no doubt in his mind that his regiment could have reached Narvik in a battle-worthy condition by the middle of June.[17]

A symbolic picked force of 20 men under Lt. Gressel was sent to Narvik over the planned route. Gressel and his men reached Skjommen and proceeded from there to their destination by boats. He reported to General Dietl on June 16.

General Feurstein did not share Hengl's optimism about the ability of the 2,500-man force to reach Narvik and he writes that both Lieutenant Gressel, whom he discussed the issue with in Narvik, and Lieutenant Colonel Sorko shared his view.[22]

NOTES

1 Derry, *The Campaign in Norway*, p. 185. Adams (*The Dooomed Expedition*, p. 76) states that the Germans attacked with 1,700 men. David Erskine (*The Scots Guards 1919-1955* [(London: William Clowes and Sons, Limited, 1956]), p. 38,) gives 1,750 as the estimated strength of the German force.

2 Sandvik, *Operasjonene*, vol. 2, p. 108, n. 137.

3 Derry, *The Campaign in Norway*, p. 186. He writes: "The Germans also dropped paratroops on the mountainside nearer Mo, who developed a subsidiary flank attack at Lundenget." Steen, *Norges Sjøkrig 1940-1945*, vol. 4, p. 198 also refers mistakenly to German paratroopers landing between Stien and Mo.

4 Alex Büchner, *Kampf im Gebirge* (München-Lochhausen: Schild-Verlag, 1957), pp. 22-23. Tamelander and Zetterling, however, claim that the Germans on Kobbernaglen engaged the British at midnight and this caused Sorko to attack frontally. They cite as their source M. Kräutler and K. Springen-Schmidt, *Es war ein Edelweiss, Schicksal und Weg er zweiten Gebirgsdivision*, pp. 53ff (*Niende april*, p. 250). Hans Breckan, *Tapte skanser. IR 14 i april, mai, juni 1940* (Brønnøysund: Eget forlag, 1986), p. 45 also alludes to the fact that the flanking maneuver succeeded and that Sorko attacked after the enveloping force went into action. This is contrary to what Büchner, Sandvik, and Ruef write.

5 Lieutenant Colonel Roscher-Nielsen's report on June 3, 1940, as quoted in Sandvik, *Operasjone*, vol. 2, p. 103.

6 As quoted in Connell, *Auchinleck*, p. 121.

7 Ibid, p. 126.

8 Norwegian News Company, *Norway* (Brooklyn: Arnesen Press, Inc. 1941), p. 2.

9 Feurstein, *Irrwege der Pflicht* , p. 85.

10 Ellinger, *Den Forunderlige Krig* , pp. 84-85.

11 Connell, Auchinleck, p. 129.

12 Loc. cit.

13 As quoted in Ash, *Norway 1940*, p. 268.

14 As quoted in Connell, *Auchinleck*, pp. 130-131 and 141.

15 Desmond J. L. Fitzgerald, *History of the Irish Guards in the Second World War* (Aldershot: Gale & Polden Ltd, 1952), pp. 55-57 and Sandvik, *Operasjone*, vol. 2, pp. 233-234. Stockwell was a major who held the brevet rank of Lieutenant Colonel. He was later promoted to full general, knighted, and commanded ground forces in the 1956 Suez operation.

16 Churchill, *The Gathering Storm*, p. 649.

17 Hubatsch, p. 218.

15

THE WEEK THAT LOST THE CAMPAIGN – STRAINED RELATIONS

'The commander finds no reason to push the advance.
The commander prefers that the units first expand
their supply service."

EXTRACT FROM GENERAL FLEISCHER'S DIRECTIVE
TO THE BRIGADES ON MAY 19.

Inactivity

It can be argued that a successful conclusion to the Narvik Campaign was lost in the ten-day period beginning on May 22. The delays, procrastinations, and failures of the Allies and Norwegians to coordinate their operations gave General Dietl the respite he so desperately needed to bring in additional reinforcements and to organize his new defensive line. The planned attack on Narvik, initially scheduled for May 21, suffered several postponements that delayed the operation by one week. The Norwegian and French forces on the northern front took a breather after May 22 and did not re-start offensive operations until May 30, after the operation against Narvik was completed. This failure to orchestrate their operations had ruinous consequences at a time when the flow of reinforcements to Dietl tripled, the German air activity increased, and when the Allies suffered devastating defeats in France.

Béthouart and the British Navy planned the Narvik attack. The first of several postponements took place on May 19 after a meeting at British headquarters. The reasons were that landing craft were not available because they were supporting the construction at Bardufoss Airfield and land-based air support was not available. The new date was the night of 23–24 May, or the first favorable opportunity after that date. A "favorable opportunity" depended on weather that would prevent German air operations during the landing as well as the availability of sufficient Allied land-based air support to make air cover effective.

German air activity increased significantly after the Bjerkvik landing. In addition to ground support operations, numerous attacks were carried out against lines of communications, harbor facilities in the rear areas, the town of Harstad, and naval forces. Carrier-based aircraft were not able to neutralize enemy air operations despite energetic attempts. It became obvious that land-based aircraft with the ability to remain over the target area for a considerable period was a prerequisite for any amphibious operation. The Bjerkvik landing earlier in the month was carried out in favorable weather and during a period when German air operations over Narvik were on a much-reduced scale.

At a meeting between General Béthouart and the British around noon on May 23, it was decided to postpone the attack on Narvik until the night of May 25–26, May 26–27, or May 27–28. Weather played a role in which night was selected but the deciding element was the availability of sufficient air cover. General Auchinleck had decided that it would be reckless to undertake the operation with only one fighter squadron in support. He decided, with Admiral Cork's approval, to postpone the operation until the Hurricane squadron was available.[1]

The Norwegians were informed that the attack had been postponed indefinitely but they were not given the reasons. They believed the delay was caused by a leak through the national broadcasting system. A report from the front by a reporter was read over the radio at 2000 hours on May 23. The reporter stated that all civilians in Øyjord were ordered to move, as the Allied and Norwegian forces were preparing to take Narvik within a couple of days.

The Allies were furious and the Norwegians launched an investigation. It revealed that the report had been aired through a misunderstanding at the station. In a distortion of the sequence of events, Derry writes that this leak not only caused the postponement of the attack but was also a factor in the decision to keep the Norwegians in the dark about their planned evacuation.[2] The broadcast took place eight hours after the Allies had decided on the final postponement, and it is now obvious that the deciding reason was Auchinleck's view that sufficient fighter assets were not available.

The operational directive issued by the Norwegian 6th Division on May 22 resulted in a complicated and time-consuming regrouping of forces, dictated in part by logistic considerations and in part by the perceived need to give the troops a chance to rest before resuming operations. The directive, parts of which appear to have been written before the extent of the German withdrawal was known, anticipated that the Germans would be able to hold the Kuberg

Plateau against attacks from the north for a lengthy period.

The Alta Battalion's rear depot had been moved to Skoglund, about two and a half kilometers north of Bjerkvik. The farm road from Bjerkvik to Gamberg was improved to support truck traffic. Engineers had constructed a provisional bridge over the Vassdal River and supplies were moved along a track suitable for horse-drawn wagons to Fiskeløsvann, where the battalion's forward depot was located after the repositioning of forces. The battalion's own supply personnel brought the supplies from this point to the forward units.

The two battalions of the 16th Inf were supplied over two parallel routes from their rear depots at Lund and Lapphaugen. The 1/16th Inf had its depot at Lund. From there, the supplies were trucked to Bonnes and by wagons from there to the eastern end of Rauvann where a forward depot was established. A track usable for wagons led to the battalion receiving point at the western end of Rauvann. The battalion supply personnel brought the supplies to Bratbakken by horse-drawn wagons and from there to the front; they were carried by soldiers or, in some cases, by packhorses.

The 2/16th Inf was supplied from its rear depot at Lapphaugen. Wagons or sleds brought the supplies from there through Gressdal to the foot of Storebalak where a distribution point was established. From there, everything had to be carried by soldiers up the steep northern slope of Storebalak and on to the southern edge of the plateau. The terrain was too steep for packhorses. It was this supply route that Fleischer wanted changed and which must have been the primary factor for the strange rearrangement of forces that was made without consulting the battalion commander or his quartermaster.[3]

The 6th District Command had planned for some time to simplify the division's supply operations by using the main road through Gratangen to Bjerkvik. From there, it was intended to bring the supplies by sea transport to Trældal on the north side of Rombakfjord. An adequate road led from Trældal to Cirkelvann, where battalion distribution points were to be established. However, this plan was based on two assumptions that had not been realized by May 22. First, Narvik was still in German hands and this prevented all boat traffic in Rombakfjord. Second, the French had failed to secure the road from Trældal to Cirkelvann. In the end, the supply route for the two battalions of the 16th Inf remained as before but the route for the 2/16th was extended from the old distribution point at the base of Storebalak through Vassdal via Gamberg to Fiskeløsvann. This westward extension became necessary when the 2/16th was moved off the mountains.

Military operations cannot be carried out successfully unless they can be supported logistically. To that extent, logistic considerations often dictate strategy. However, this was not the case on May 22. While the old supply lines were long and cumbersome in the roadless mountain terrain, the 6th Brigade was successfully supported during its long drive to secure the high plateau and there were no apparent reasons why this could not have continued now that the weather was improving. The middle of an offensive operation was the wrong time to experiment with new supply lines, particularly those that were dependent on circumstances that were outside General Fleischer's control. The validity of Lindbäck-Larsen's claim that supply difficulties "made it impossible to bring sufficient forces to bear to pursue the enemy when he withdrew from the Kuberg Plateau" is at least questionable.[4]

It appears that Fleischer allowed logistic considerations and an overly negative assessment of the abilities of his troops to continue the offensive to dictate operations. The operational directives on May 19 and 22 left the 6th Brigade to make the main attack against Bjørnefjell, but the movement of the main supply line through Vassdal appear to have caused Fleischer to decide that the initial main effort be made against Jernvannene from the Hartvigvann area. It was decided to bring part of the 6th Brigade's troops off the mountains, leaving one battalion to hold the captured area. The rest of the brigade was withdrawn to the area southeast of Hartvigvann and readied for operations against Jernvannene.

The selection of Jernvannene as the area of main effort had unfortunate results that should have been anticipated by officers as thoroughly familiar with this area as those in the 6th Division. The watershed in this area was at flood-stage because of the thaw and all likely crossing sites were dominated by the bastion-like high ground to the south. The terrain to the east, along the Swedish border, did not present the same obstacles and the main effort was eventually shifted to that area after considerable lost time and effort.

The Norwegian troops had succeeded in driving the enemy from the high plateau and they were eager to continue taking the fight to their opponents. The Norwegians knew that the Germans had suffered considerable losses, that their own were rather low, that the Germans had practically no reserves left, that their opponents' morale must have suffered as a result of their setbacks, and that they had not had time to prepare new positions. Time was of the essence since the German flow of reinforcements into the Narvik area increased daily and General Feurstein was uncomfortably close in the south. This was the wrong time to rest the troops, redeploy them, or alter supply lines. The troops should have been encouraged to make one last super-human effort to defeat Windisch before he could organize his defense. Both the 6th Brigade Commander and his battalion commanders (Munthe-Kaas and Hunstad) disagreed with the pause in operations and the relocation of the 2nd Battalion, 16th Inf.[5] Less than three weeks later, Lieutenant Colonel Berg (later Lieutenant General) made the following statement, which Birger Godtaas includes in his book:

> I can never forgive myself for not following my first instinct to continue the advance (in May) without interruption when we first started. I believe we could have cleared the whole Rundfjell area quickly. However, the division insisted that it could be dangerous. If we met with a setback, our lines of communication were too long and difficult. I will never be convinced whether or not I made the right decision when I allowed the units to take a break.

Munthe-Kaas viewed it as a mistake to give up the high ground and recommended that his battalion be given the opportunity to rest in its positions and thereafter move eastward to join the 1/16th Inf in a decisive attack on the German positions near the Swedish border. He recommended the establishment of a forward supply point with four days of provisions and ammunition on Storeblank to support such an operation. Lieutenant Colonel Berg turned down this suggestion. It is not known if Berg discussed this with General Fleischer.

Munthe-Kaas writes that the battalions did not require more than 48-hours rest and that the units were focused eagerly on a continued and rapid advance against the Germans. If the battalion was allowed to rest in its positions, it would have been ready for continued operations on May 24. Instead, the evening of May 24 finds most of the battalion arriving at Fiskeløsvann after a stressful and dangerous march from the Kobberfjell area.

General Fleischer directed a redeployment of forces and an initial shifting of units to prepare for a resumption of the offensive. The 2/16th Inf moved laterally to the far right of the Norwegian sector while the Alta Bn moved forward to rest positions near Cirkelvann.

The 2/16th Inf began its move from the Kobberfjell area to its new assembly area at Fiskeløsvann at 2300 hours on May 23 and completed this redeployment by 2200 hours the following day. Not only is the wisdom of the move open to serious questions, but the battalion was badly split in the process. One reinforced company was left on the plateau to serve as flank security for the 1/16th Inf. The Headquarters Company moved to the south end of Hartvigvann where a depot for provisions and munitions was established. Since the battalion was now located at a lower altitude where skis were not required, these were sent to Setermoen. This action was sorely regretted when the battalion later moved into the snow-covered mountains. The 2/16th Inf was subjected to heavy German air attacks during the move.

To cover the movement of the 2/16th Inf, the 7th Brigade was ordered to send the Alta Bn forward to occupy the high ground west of Cirkelvann during the night of 22-23 May. The division directed that this battalion remain in its positions when the 6th Brigade attacked past Cirkelvann. The 2/16th Inf was ordered to advance its outpost line forward to where it made contact with the Alta Bn south of Skitdalsvann and to reconnoiter a route of advance and attack positions against Hills 456, 615, 625 and the stream junction west of Hill 529, in the area east of Øvre Jernvann. The 6th Brigade was not permitted to advance across a line between Skitdalsvann and Nedre Jernvann without orders.

The length of the new German front was approximately 21 kilometers, six kilometers shorter than it had been when they occupied the high plateau. However, some of the mountainsides of the dominant terrain on which the Germans established their new front are almost vertical, unsuitable for both offensive and defensive operations. Outside these inapproachable areas, the Germans had a front of less than 10 kilometers that they needed to occupy in strength.

The new German line was located directly south of a deep watercourse that formed a veritably impenetrable moat in front of their positions. The river between the junction of Karenelven and Holmelven varies in width from 20 feet to 150 feet and the current is rapid, particularly during the spring thaw. The Norwegians had no bridging equipment since all was lost when the Germans captured Elvegårdsmoen on April 9. A reconnaissance of possible crossing points on June 1 led the division to conclude that the river between Cirkelvann and Nedre Jernvann was so wide that it would take one full week to construct a footbridge. As Munthe-Kaas writes, this was "an unfortunate belated discovery!"

The German flanks were now more difficult to assault and roll up than they had been when they occupied the high plateau. Their right flank was anchored on the Swedish border and their left flank on Rombakfjord. The cliffs on the German left leading to Rauberget south of Lakselv are extremely steep. Dietl had little to worry about on this flank. A French attempt to advance in this area on

May 25 was repelled easily by the Germans. The French lost eight killed and seven were captured.

While the new German front presented the Norwegians with what seemed a mountain bastion, the best approach was still in the area along the Swedish border, defended by Group Schleebrügge. This group consisted of a mixture of a few mountain troops, some paratroopers who were not equipped and trained for mountain warfare, and naval units of questionable reliability. Furthermore, in the first days after the withdrawal, these units had not had a chance to prepare their defensive positions. A quick thrust at the German right flank as recommended by Munthe-Kaas on May 21 presented the best chance of success and it may well have led to the collapse of the German northern front. Instead, Fleischer chose to attack the enemy bastion from the lower terrain further west via an approach that was under easy observation by the Germans on the high ground to the south. Furthermore, the attacking forces would have to find a way to cross the raging river, without bridging equipment and in the face of German fire.

Dietl was desperately trying to win time for meaningful reinforcements to reach his forces. The Norwegians and the Allies handed it to him by suspending offensive operations in the north for over a week. The number of reinforcements reaching the Germans around Narvik in the first half of May amounted to only 133 officers and men. From May 15 to May 22, the flow increased to 239 and during the last week of May, it grew to 671. In the south, Feurstein's forces were brushing aside delaying forces and approaching Bodø.

Finally, the events that were unfolding in France and the Low Countries, should have instilled a sense of urgency in the Norwegian military leadership. It had become imperative to complete the destruction of Group Windisch before the possible transfer of Allied ground forces to the west. Dietl admitted forthrightly that he was saved from having to enter Sweden by the German attack in the west.

Fleischer could not have anticipated the frequent postponements in the operations against Narvik between May 21 and May 28. However, there was no reason to delay his operation against Bjørnefjell pending the capture of Narvik. Ziemke notes that this relative quiet on the northern front "facilitated the German withdrawal from Narvik."[6] This is an understatement. A strong attack by Norwegian and French forces on the northern front simultaneously with or leading up to the attack on Narvik was General Dietl's worst nightmare. An offensive on the northern front would have prevented the Germans from rushing all incoming reinforcements to the Narvik Peninsula to stem the French and Polish advance. The inactivity also allowed them to pull units away from the northern front for the same purpose.

By May 26 Fleischer, who was unaware of the reasons for the postponements of the attack on Narvik, directed an urgent appeal to Béthouart, pointing out that time was now working in Germany's favor. He also sent his chief of staff to Allied headquarters in Harstad in an attempt to speed up operations against Narvik.

Béthouart informed Fleischer that his intention was to attack Narvik the following night but he refused to enter into any agreements about future operations after Narvik was captured. He also told the Norwegian that the 14th Bn, CA was not capable of an offensive south of Cirkelvann. Cork and Auchinleck had briefed Béthouart earlier in the day about the evacuation decision, which limited Allied operations to the capture of Narvik.

Polish Operations on the Ankenes Peninsula

The 12th Bn CA took over on Ankenes Peninsula from the British in early May. This battalion operated initially in Håvikdal but in the period May 6-9, it occupied a number of heights overlooking Narvik harbor. Hill 295 was occupied on May 6, Hill 405 on May 8, and Hills 677, 734, and 668 on May 9. In the end, the Germans occupied only the high ground on both flanks: the hillside to the south and west of Ankenes and the area from Hill 606 to Skarvtuva.

Two Polish battalions were moved by sea from Bjerkvik to Ankenes Peninsula on May 14 to replace the South Wales Borderers, who were sent to Bodø. At about the same time, a Polish battalion from Harstad was to relieve the 12th Bn CA. The 4th Polish Bn and 2nd Half-Brigade Headquarters were brought south from Sjøvegan on May 19. This made Ankenes Peninsula a Polish area of operations except for a section of British field artillery and some antiaircraft guns.

Major General Zygmunt Bohusz-Szyszko commanded the Polish forces. He started his career in the Tsarist army and was wounded while commanding the 16th Polish Infantry Division in 1939. Lieutenant Colonel Benedykt Chlusewiez, who also started his career in the Tsarist army, commanded the 1st Half-Brigade consisting of 1st and 2nd Battalions. Lieutenant Colonel Józef Kobylecki, another Tsarist army officer, commanded the 2nd Half-Brigade, consisting of the 3rd and 4th Battalions. The troops were a mixture of escapees from Poland, Poles residing in France, and volunteers from other countries, including a detachment of veterans from the Spanish Civil War.[7]

General Bohusz-Szyszko's orders were to defend Ankenes Peninsula after relieving the British and French forces. The planned relief of the 12th Bn CA was delayed because of a strong German infantry attack on May 17 against its positions on the ridgeline overlooking Narvik harbor and Beisfjord. The Germans had two companies in this area: Co 6 in the north, holding a bridgehead around the village of Ankenes; and Co 7 in the south, holding Hills 650 (Skarvtuva), and Hill 773 (Hestefjell). The Germans attacked Hills 605 and 668. The surprise attacks almost succeeded in driving the French from the mountain ridge. The Germans reached within 100 meters of the summit of Hill 605 when the attack faltered under heavy French fire. The attack against Hill 668 was only stopped after the French committed all available resources, including a counterattack by the battalion reserve, the 12th S.E.S. The Germans lost six killed and five seriously wounded.

The South Wales Borderers were still located on Ankenes Peninsula, apparently in a defensive perimeter from somewhere southwest of Hill 405 to Haavik. The French occupied the area from Hill 405 to Hill 668. The only information about the enemy situation that the South Wales Borderers could give to Lieutenant Colonel Wladyslaw Dec, commander of the 2nd Polish Bn, was "The Germans are up there somewhere."[8]

Dec occupied a line of almost five kilometers along the ridge from Baatberget to, and including, Hill 405. The 1st Polish Bn, commanded by Major Waclaw Kobylinsky, occupied the ridgeline from Hill 677 to Hill 668. Lieutenant Colonel Chlusewiez was the overall commander of these forward forces. His reserve consisted of the 4th Polish Bn, which was moved from Sjøvegan to Tjeldebotn, west of Ballangen, on May 19. It was moved to Ankenes Peninsula in the period 22–24 May. The 3rd Polish Bn remained in the Ballangen area along with the headquarters of the 2nd Half-Brigade.

The Ankenes Peninsula became an area of bitter positional warfare until May 27. The 2nd Polish Bn tried to move its positions forward in the evening of May 17 and on May 18. With the exception of a minor forward adjustment by the left flank company, the Germans repelled these attempts at the cost to the Poles of nine killed and 15 wounded.

Bieganski writes that during this period, the Germans constantly improved their positions and their strength grew to two battalions. This is a considerable overstatement of the actual forces involved. The Germans only had one battalion of mountain troops and some naval units in the whole Narvik area.

Company 7 was reinforced by an assortment of naval personnel but its strength never exceeded that of a reinforced company. The main Polish effort after May 18 was directed against the Ankenes pocket. Company 7's thin, convex line, covering about five kilometers from Hill 650 to Hill 606 was left relatively unmolested until May 27.

Company 8 relieved Co 6 during the night of May 18-19. The company was reinforced and supplied by boats on a nightly basis in the week that followed, but all these had to be scraped together from Major Haussels' forces in Narvik, since Group Windisch was given priority in the allocation of all other forces. Parts of Major Haussels' engineer and reconnaissance platoons were brought into the pocket along with various groups of naval personnel. These reinforcements increased the strength of the defenders to between 160 and 180 men. One hundred and eighteen men from Co 2, 137th Regiment parachuted into the area near Bjørnefjell on May 25, and were sent into the Ankenes pocket by Major Haussels on May 27.

Company 8 was already engaged in heavy action on its first day at Ankenes, repelling several Polish attacks. The Germans were in an unenviable position with their backs to the sea, a numerically superior enemy on the high ground to their front, and under frequent and heavy naval gunfire from British ships in the fjord. The situation improved on May 20 when heavy German air attacks were launched against the Poles on the ridgeline. However, as soon as the planes disappeared the Poles launched another unsuccessful attack against the Ankenes pocket.

One of the greatest German fears in May was a possible Allied threat against the Bjørnefjell base area from the south. The Germans knew from prisoners that the entire Polish brigade was located on Ankenes Peninsula or in other locations on the south side of Ofotfjord. The Germans also knew that total Allied strength was approximately 20,000 and they had a hard time understanding why most of the fighting had been left to the Norwegians and French. Dietl, like Fleischer, considered Bjørnefjell the key to the survival of German forces and he and his staff had to assume that the Allies were of a like mind. A thrust from the south in combination with heavy pressure from the north and threatening gestures against Narvik could lead to a quick collapse.

The Germans knew that a road ran southeast from Elvegård, near the village of Skjomen. This road turned into a summer road when it reached the east-west valley of Norddal and continued eastward in this valley towards the Swedish border until it reached the north-south valley of Hunddal. This valley leads directly to Bjørnefjell. The route was difficult and long for troops not accustomed to mountains and snow, but even a minor threat from this direction would trouble the Germans since their reserves in this period never exceeded a company and even less than that during the last weeks of May.

The heavy Allied activities on the south side of Ofotfjord after May 10 caused the Germans to suspect that a wide envelopment could be in progress. The Luftwaffe was requested to make reconnaissance flights in this sector. Group XXI reported that there were no signs of enemy activities in the Skjomen area. Dietl was not completely convinced and he ordered a ski patrol to make a 50-kilometer deep reconnaissance to the south and southwest. Its report confirmed that there were no enemy forces in this area.

Reports from Major Haussels flowing into the headquarters of the 3rd Division towards the end of May pointed to an imminent attack directly against Narvik. These reports were based primarily on prisoner interrogations.

German Relief and Supply Operations

The situation for the German troops in Narvik was growing daily more desperate in late May. While some reinforcements were flown into the pocket and others arrived through Sweden disguised as Red Cross personnel and "specialists," they were not sufficient to replace the losses or counter the increased Norwegian and Allied buildup. Supplies were also arriving by air but most came by train from Sweden, classified as "humanitarian assistance." In the early part of the campaign, the supplies arriving through Sweden were mostly limited to rations, coal, and medical equipment. Later, they included clothing and ski equipment. The Swedes would not allow the transport of ammunition, which had to be brought in entirely by air.

With Group Windisch near collapse, Dietl needed fresh troops to shore up the front and give some of his mountain troops a chance to rest. General von Falkenhorst had only a few paratroopers at his disposal, who were sent to Narvik between May 14 and 16 On May 15, von Falkenhorst asked OKW for one parachute battalion. He argued persuasively that the valiant efforts by the troops in General Feurstein's 2nd Mountain Division would have been in vain if Narvik could not be held until they arrived. He mentioned the importance of tying down Allied forces as long as possible. His reference to the importance of holding Narvik for political and prestige reasons was no doubt intended more for Hitler than for the officers at OKW.

Falkenhorst's arguments produced results. Hitler ordered 1st Bn, 1st Para Regt made available to reinforce Narvik, the same battalion that had landed at

Fornebu near Oslo on April 9 and that subsequently participated in the operations in Holland on May 10. It was anticipated that this unit should start arriving in Narvik within a week or ten days.

In the meantime, Group XXI carried out expedited and abbreviated parachute training for some of the mountain troops. The first group, consisting of 65 men from Co 2, 137th, parachuted into the Bjørnefjell area on May 23. The Germans expected ten percent casualties in the operation, but only two soldiers sustained minor injuries. Another parachute drop was made the following day, this time involving 55 troops from Co 1, 137th. On the same day, 14 troops from Co 6, 138th arrived by seaplane. Another 54 troops from Co 1, 137th arrived by parachute on May 25, as did 44 troops from Co 2, 138th. Forty mortar and machinegun personnel arrived via Sweden on May 25.

The airborne troops began arriving on May 26 when 81 men parachuted safely into the Bjørnefjell area. Inclement weather delayed the next lift until May 28 when 46 paratroopers were dropped and one mountain howitzer with a crew of five landed by seaplane. One hundred thirty four paratroopers arrived on May 29 with the remaining 46 arriving on June 2. A further 80 "specialists" arrived from Sweden on May 31.[9] While 599 troops arrived in the Narvik area between May 23 and June 2, Dietl concluded that he needed another 1,500 to 2,000 men in order to hold out.

The resupply of weapons and ammunition was not without mishap. Seaplanes successfully flew in five antitank guns and two captured Norwegian mountain howitzers. The airdrop of 15 captured Polish antitank guns was unsuccessful. All weapons became unserviceable. About 30% of the infantry weapons (mortars, machineguns, and sub-machineguns) airdropped were damaged and unserviceable. About 20-25% of the ammunition parachuted into the Narvik pocket was damaged to the point where it was useless.

Bringing rations and ammunition to the forward troops was a major task for the Germans as it was for the Norwegians, French, and Poles. The Germans started out using two officers and 60 men for this task but this was soon increased to six officers and 460 men, including Norwegian prisoners. About 8,000 lbs of rations and 4-6,000 lbs of ammunition had to be brought forward on a daily basis.[10] Some supplies were moved by sleds but most were carried by men, at least part of the way.

The use of Norwegian prisoners in the supply effort was a serious breach of the conventions regulating the treatment of prisoners. On May 10, Hitler directed that all non-career Norwegian prisoners of war be released and allowed to proceed to their homes. This was an atypical document by the German dictator and since it is so uncharacteristic, it is worthwhile to quote its operative parts:

> … In the course of the campaign in the east German soldiers who had the misfortune to fall injured or uninjured into Polish hands were usually brutally ill-treated or massacred. By way of contrast, it must be said of the Norwegian army that not one single such incident of the debasement of warfare has occurred.[11]
>
> The Norwegian soldier spurned all the cowardly and deceitful methods common to the Poles. He fought with open visor and honorably, and he tended our prisoners and injured properly and to the best of his ability. The civilian population acted similarly. Nowhere did they join in the fighting, and they did all they could for the welfare of our casualties.
>
> I have therefore decided in appreciation for this to authorize the liberation of the Norwegian soldiers we took prisoner. Only the professional soldiers will have to remain in captivity until such time as the former Norwegian government withdraws its call to arms against Germany, or individual officers and men give their formal word not to take part under any circumstances in further hostilities against Germany.

This proclamation was a political gesture designed to win favor with the Norwegian people and to lower the fighting morale of the Norwegian troops in North Norway. Dietl was quick to point out that the release of prisoners was not possible in his active theater of operations, since those who were set free would simply rejoin their units via Sweden. However, the most serious objection to their release had to do with the loss of their use in the supply effort and he pointed out that the prisoners were far superior to the naval personnel used for that purpose because they were in better physical condition and used to the winter climate and mountainous terrain.[12] Both Group XXI and OKW were thus aware of Dietl's use of Norwegian prisoners in this manner.

After the outbreak of panic among the naval personnel on May 13, Dietl described them as "useless for combat and a danger to our troops." Group XXI had therefore arranged to bring the destroyer crews back to Germany via Sweden. Group XXI's view that the end was near for Dietl's command may have hastened these arrangements. Sweden granted permission on May 19 to evacuate these crews as "shipwrecked sailors." Dietl had now decided that these sailors, despite their shortcomings as infantry, were critical for supply duties. This was the beginning of a series of exchanges between Group XXI and the 3rd Division. In the end, it was agreed that Dietl would decide who should be evacuated and make the necessary arrangements through the naval attaché in Stockholm.

At the end of May and in early June OKW was searching frantically for ways to bring Dietl the reinforcements he needed so that he could hold out until Feurstein arrived from the south. Göring appears to have been unwilling to support the Narvik reinforcement operations. A desire not to divert resources from the western front and to conserve them for the anticipated battle for Britain may have been reasons for this reluctance. On May 16, Hitler had ordered Göring to make gliders available to bring 600 mountain troops to Narvik. After a series of procrastinations, Göring finally ordered the gliders held in Denmark on May 29. Hitler then reduced the requirement to six gliders, but the operation was never carried out.

On May 30, Hitler decided that Dietl's troops in Narvik were to be supported by all available means. This represented a change in Hitler's outlook, probably caused by the successes the Germans had achieved on the western front. Dietl was promised two parachute battalions (about 1,800 men) and another 1,000 mountain troops who were given a quick parachute course. Again, this operation was never carried out.

In the beginning of June, OKW planned a new operation, code-named *Naumburg*, to bring relief to Narvik. The plan involved landing a strong force in Lyngefjord, about 90 miles north of Narvik, at the same time as Luftwaffe paratroopers captured Bardufoss Airfield. The plan involved the transport of about 6,000 troops and a dozen tanks to Lyngefjord in the fast ocean-liners *Bremen* and *Europa*. A similar plan was discussed when reinforcements for Trondheim were considered. It died because of Admiral Raeder's opposition.

Raeder pointed out to Hitler that this operation would take too long to be of any help to Dietl and he suggested that it would be quicker and easier for the Luftwaffe to seize Bardufoss with a glider-borne force and then bring in troops by transports. Hitler decided that both operations (Lyngefjord and Bardufoss) should be carried out simultaneously. The plan envisioned that the ocean liners would proceed to *Basis Nord* near Murmansk after landing the troops.[13]

The OKW eventually agreed with Raeder's conclusion that Operation *Naumburg* would probably come too late to save the troops in Narvik. This realization led to another plan, Operation *Juno*. This plan originated with the

German Naval Staff and it was intended initially to be a diversionary operation by the fleet. The worsening situation in Narvik led the naval staff to scuttle the diversionary nature of the plan and substitute an operation that would bring direct help to Narvik.

The plan called for a naval sortie by the battleships *Scharnhorst* and *Gneisenau*, the heavy cruiser *Hipper*, and four destroyers. This fleet would undertake a surprise attack on Allied ships and bases in the Harstad area or alternatively, if reconnaissance indicated the possibility of success, an attack in Vestfjord and Ofotfjord. Hitler also wanted the coastal area between Trondheim and Bodø cleared of light Norwegian naval units that interfered with the resupply of General Feurstein's forces. The light cruiser *Nürnberg* and a number of torpedo boats were assigned this mission and dispatched to Trondheim. The German warships designated for Operation *Juno* departed Kiel on June 4. The execution of this operation is covered in the last chapter.

Allied Air Support

The Allies were slow in taking steps to provide air support for their forces in Narvik and Nordland Province and when they did, it was inadequate. This slowness is partially explained by the reliance on aircraft carriers and the relative lack of German air operations in North Norway during the first month of the campaign. The unfortunate experience in operating from frozen lakes in the southern part of the country may also have contributed to the delay in bringing in land-based aircraft.

The aircraft carrier *Furious* was present in the waters off North Norway until April 26. This carrier had no fighter aircraft aboard and this, and the difficulty in keeping aircraft serviceable, severely limited its usefulness. For most of the next two weeks, the Allies had no combat aircraft other than a squadron of seaplanes in the Narvik area. The aircraft carrier *Ark Royal* arrived off Narvik on May 6, and remained there until May 21 when the carrier *Furious* delivered a squadron of Gladiators to operate from Bardufoss. The threat to the aircraft carriers from German aircraft and submarines was a grave concern in the British Navy. While the carriers operated from well offshore in order to minimize the air threat, their aircraft and those of the Norwegians were initially able to contest German air operations, carry out attacks against shore targets, and provide limited support for ground operations.

The Allied evacuations in south and central Norway freed German air assets for use in the north. The opening of a land connection between Oslo and Trondheim allowed the Luftwaffe to base and support expanded air operations from Værnes Airfield and this soon made itself felt in the Narvik area. German close air support operations were, as already mentioned, hampered by two facts. First, the scale of Luftwaffe maps (1:1,000,000) made effective close air support practically impossible. The lack of ground-to-air communications was the second problem. While the 3rd Division received the necessary radio equipment on May 6, an air force liaison officer was not provided until May 20. His efforts increased the effectiveness of close air support operations and resulted in improved coordination and support from the air operation center in Trondheim, which directed all air operations in North Norway.

Increased German air presence in the Narvik area and the inability of the carrier aircraft to effectively contest this increased threat speeded up Allied efforts to establish shore-based air operations. The increased German air activity also began to take its toll on the British Navy. The battleship *Resolution* was withdrawn from the area after a German bomb penetrated three decks on May 18. The antiaircraft cruiser *Curlew* was lost on May 26 with many of her crew as she provided antiaircraft protection for the construction of the airfield at Skånland.

Ash writes that Admiral Cork "had been scouring the countryside for possible landing grounds since his earliest days in Norway."[14] In fact, construction of a new airfield at Skånland was started but never completed to the point where it could be used. Several fields that could be made operational with much less effort were available. There were fields at Bardufoss, Elvenes in Salangen, Banak, Bodø, and Mo but all had to be cleared of snow and improved to support fighter operations. Hundreds of civilian laborers were involved in making Bardufoss and the field at Bodø ready to receive British fighter aircraft. Within two weeks after the decision to station two squadrons of fighters at Bardufoss, a number of protective shelters for aircraft were built and snow was cleared from three 900-meter runways.

Because of the delayed decision to bring in land-based fighters, the Bardufoss Airfield was not ready to receive British fighter aircraft until May 21. The 263rd Gladiator Squadron took off from the aircraft carrier *Furious*. The weather was bad and two of the 18 aircraft crashed into a mountain on the way to Bardufoss. However, by the following day the Gladiators were established on the airfield and able to conduct air operations in the Harstad-Narvik area.

It was planned to have the 46th Hurricane Squadron operate from Skånland. This squadron took off from the aircraft carrier *Glorious* on May 26 and attempted to land at Skånland "but three out of eleven aircraft tipped on to their noses on landing as a result of the soft surface of the runway."[15] The squadron was diverted to Bardufoss from where it operated until the end of the campaign.

It was not until the middle of May that the British decided to establish an airbase at Bodø. The Norwegians provided a large labor force from the Bodø area and they had the field ready for operations on May 26. Initially, the ground proved too soft here as it did at Skånland but this was rectified when the runway was re-laid in 14 hours. Except for the three Gladiators that came down from Bardufoss, the British never used this airfield and its capture by the Germans after the British evacuated Bodø gave them an operational airfield close to Narvik.

The Norwegian air group was down to one serviceable aircraft in early May. The rest were shot down, had crashed, or were unserviceable due to lack of spare parts. The aircraft flown in from the southern part of the country performed well in support of the forward brigades but the lack of spare parts reduced their number because some aircraft had to be cannibalized to keep others flying. Some pilots without aircraft were sent to England to receive fighter aircraft training and new aircraft.

Norwegian-Allied Friction

There was growing bitterness between the Norwegians and the British as the operations in Norway progressed. Many Norwegians viewed British actions since the outbreak of war in 1939 as designed to pull their country into that conflict. The Norwegians were promised on April 9 that quick and large-scale assistance would be forthcoming. When the assistance did arrive it was inadequate in both quantity and quality. Continual promises and assurances during the operations in southern and central Norway never materialized. The displeasure over the adequacy of the assistance was closely tied to the question of strategy.

Norwegian recommendations on strategy failed to alter the British War Cabinet's preoccupation with Narvik and the iron ore. The British decision makers failed to realize that control of central Norway would lead to eventual success in North Norway, while giving up in central Norway doomed any efforts in the north. Frequent Norwegian suggestions that the Allies use forces sitting idle in the Narvik area in Nordland Province were unheeded until it was too late. They could not understand the relative inactivity of the British Navy or the Allied failure to provide adequate air resources for the forces they sent to Norway. General Ruge's comments on the air support situation in southern

Norway were shared by his fellow officers in northern Norway:

> It turned out that, as on many other subjects, the British had difficulties coping with the conditions in the country. They did not risk following our recommendations. . . . Our airmen were used to operating from frozen lakes in the winter. . . . The British pilots, not used to working under such conditions, did not venture to base their operations on such provisional arrangements and continued to search for what they called real airfields. In this way, much valuable time was lost.[16]

The British displayed an attitude of deep distrust and arrogance towards their new allies from the very beginning, often based on fallacious information. Intelligence Summary No 227 in mid-April, for example, reports that Norwegian inactivity was due to low morale, mass desertions, a country riddled with Nazi agents, and an army of disloyal elements. Reports by Auchinleck to Dill in May demonstrate disrespect for Norwegians in general and especially for their military. Reflecting on British/Norwegian relations in 1946, Ruge wrote:

> To start with, the British did not have a high opinion of Norwegian defense forces. Our apparent collapse on April 9 did not exactly improve the respect for us by a people who had not yet felt what it meant to confront the German war machine and be placed in a hopeless position by German air power. Excessive talk here at home in the days after April 9 about treason and Quisling and his followers created the impression in London that Norway was full of traitors ...[17]

It is understandable that the Norwegians were bitter towards the Allies. Norwegian operational recommendations, based on their intimate knowledge of local conditions and better intelligence on German forces, were brushed aside, often with tragic consequences. Agreed on cooperation with Allied land forces were altered without timely notification. Moulton observes that the Allies felt that the Norwegian Government and its military were unwarlike, negligent in their security, and that there was a large number of Norwegians who sympathized with the Germans.

The behavior of ill-disciplined British and French troops added to the bad atmosphere. Colonel Tue, commanding the 4th Regiment in Romsdal, reported, "Very young lads who appeared to come from the slums of London. They had taken a very close interest in the women of Romsdal, and engaged in wholesale looting of stores and houses."[18] Kersuady also attests to such behavior:

> It was hard to deny the evidence, as the Foreign Office grudgingly acknowledged shortly thereafter: 'Drunk' British troops had on one occasion quarreled and eventually fired upon some Norwegian fishermen. Again, some of the British Army officers had behaved 'with the arrogance of Prussians' and the Naval Officers were in general so cautious and suspicious that they treated every Norwegian as a Fifth Columnist and refused to believe vital information when given them. [19]

Chamberlain's speech to a very unfriendly parliamentary session on May 7 did not improve things. In trying to play down the extent of the defeat in South and Central Norway, he stated, "the German strike was made easy by treachery from inside Norway." The Norwegians felt betrayed and such statements only served to increase their bitterness.

Derry notes that the shortcomings of the Norwegian forces and their lack of morale were not helped by a lack of sympathy and continual mistrust by the British. General Moulton notes that there was enough blame to go around for both sides but claims that neither side behaved badly in southern and central Norway.

Moulton underestimates the ill feeling among Norwegians in the Narvik area. They remembered the unannounced Allied withdrawals from the southern and central parts of the country where they were kept in the dark until the last moments, resulting in large segments of their troops being placed in untenable positions and forced to surrender. This pattern continued with the withdrawals from Mosjøen and Bodø. The plan to withdraw from Bodø was kept from General Ruge despite a solemn promise to the contrary on May 16. This action, which left Roscher-Nielsen's forces isolated in Røsvik, so infuriated the Norwegian Government that the British command suspected that it might conclude peace with the Germans.

The British had the lead in the Norwegian campaign and they went to great lengths to insure that this command authority was kept intact. Auchinleck's instructions were that, in case he became ill or incapacitated, a junior British officer be temporarily promoted to lieutenant general and assume command. In the planned operation against Trondheim, again without consulting or informing the Norwegians, it was stipulated that all forces, including

Norwegians, would come under British command. Auchinleck, after taking over from Mackesy, requested authority not only to assume command of Norwegian forces but the right to regulate the non-military sector, including mass movements of civilians.

In a letter to General Dill, Auchinleck wrote, "I shall shortly have to have a wholesale clearing out of the inhabitants from the occupied areas. The place is riddled, I am convinced, with spies."[20] There is no mention of where he intended to move the civilians in this winter wilderness or how he proposed to feed and care for them after such a move. While these proposals and suggestions were never acted on, they illustrate the extent of the mistrust that existed.

There was a complete lack of systematic coordination and cooperation between the Allied military leaders in North Norway and the Norwegian authorities. The British commanders, Cork, Mackesy, and Auchinleck, never visited Ruge or Fleischer's headquarters. Fleischer had likewise not visited the Allied headquarters in Harstad until Ruge brought him along on May 16. This conference was General Fleischer's first and last direct contact with the British leadership during the campaign.

Liaison officers were exchanged but they were not provided with adequate communications and were often purposely kept in the dark about planned operations. Consequently, they had little or no influence on the planning and conduct of operations at the highest echelons. The failure to include Norwegian officers on the operations and intelligence staffs at Harstad is deplorable.

News of what had transpired in southern and central Norway made Norwegians, especially Fleischer, suspicious of Allied plans and intentions. The way the evacuations were carried out was looked upon by many as treachery, particularly since the Norwegian forces were not given an opportunity to be evacuated. The broken promises caused bitterness and dejection from cabinet level to the privates who suffered at the front.

Fleischer's suspicions were evident when Admiral Cork sent a wing commander to arrange for British use of Bardufoss Airfield for two fighter squadrons. After keeping the British waiting for twenty minutes and then listening to the request, Fleischer demanded written assurances that there would be no sudden withdrawal of aircraft and pilots. Fleischer also rejected the use of Allied troops to clear snow at Bardufoss. He no doubt thought they could be used to better purpose somewhere else. According to some, the meeting was at times heated but in the end, Fleischer agreed to British use of the airfield, arranged for a workforce to clear the field, and provided a battalion as protection. Victor MacClure writes that Fleischer's agreement was contingent on his chief-of-staff going to Harstad to present Fleischer's conditions to Admiral Cork.[21] Ash, while not mentioning any demands by Fleischer for his chief of staff to be taken to see Admiral Cork, also describes the meeting as tense and Fleischer as "completely intransigent" and says that he made it "plain that his intransigence would continue until he had evidence of some Allied will to fight."[22] Ash, who describes Fleischer as "resentful and uncooperative," notes that the general had some good reasons for his bitterness. Moulton writes that the British account is denied by Lindbäck-Larsen who termed it inaccurate and insulting.

Fleischer's distrust reached a point where he questioned the motives of Béthouart, an officer he had worked well with from the outset. In late May, Béthouart recommended that the French forces north of Rombakfjord be moved to Narvik and replaced by the Norwegian battalion that had participated in the capture of that city. Fleischer saw in this recommendation an Allied attempt to further shift the burden of fighting to the Norwegians while sparing their own forces and he refused. Béthouart's recommendation had a different motive. He had just learned about the planned evacuation and was concerned that a precipitous withdrawal of French forces from the northern front would leave the Norwegian right flank wide open.

The campaign in Norway is a textbook example of what to avoid when multi-national forces are involved in joint operations. There are numerous examples of improper behavior on both sides and it was naïve for Norwegians to expect that their own objectives should be reflected in all cases in those of a world power like Great Britain. The Allies were involved in the beginnings of a giant struggle that had worldwide implications while the Norwegian leadership was more concerned about what happened in Norway.

Relations between Ruge and Fleischer

Hovland writes that Fleischer learned about the new Norwegian administrative and military command relationships in North Norway from Ruge at their meeting with Auchinleck. It is strange that Fleischer could not tell from the meeting with Ruge on May 6, and the document issued the same day by HOK, that he was no longer commander-in-chief but would continue to direct military operations against Narvik. Fleischer's reaction to the new arrangements, as well as other episodes, suggests that he was a person who allowed his ego and pride to cloud his judgment. Fleischer's apparent unwillingness to confront people directly on critical issues may have contributed to some of the already mentioned misunderstandings that characterized the campaign. His unwillingness to deal directly with his subordinate commanders at the critical time of the invasion is a most glaring illustration. However, there are other examples such as the uncertainty about his wishes when it came to the positioning of defensive installations in Narvik before the attack, confusion about the movement of Alta Bn in the fighting at Gratangen, General Béthouart's understanding that parts of the 7th Brigade was under French command in early May, and the misunderstandings that arose between Fleischer and Getz about the destruction of lines of communications. So many examples of misunderstandings are difficult to explain except for the possibility that Fleischer may not have made himself clear.

General Fleischer wrote a protest letter addressed to the Defense Minister on May 17. The letter was a direct challenge to the competency, if not the authority, of General Ruge, Admiral Diesen, and the government. It is a damaging indictment of the government's decision, scheduled to become effective by a Royal Proclamation the following day. The appropriateness of the government taking over the civil administrative apparatus in North Norway is questioned, and Fleischer claims this would weaken the war effort. He suggests that the government's role be limited to foreign relations, the securing of resources from overseas, and dealings with those parts of the country that were already occupied.

Fleischer also challenged what he perceived as an undermining of his sole authority for conducting operations by removing the naval and air forces from his direct control. He maintained that operations in North Norway had to be viewed as a single effort and any weakening of his central authority would be damaging, both logistically and operationally. A part of his letter is worth quoting in view of his own failure for five weeks to meet with British commanders and to establish effective cooperation with them:

> Since the joint command of North Norway must rest with the Commander-in-Chief [General Fleischer], the negotiations with the Allied forces about joint operations in North Norway must absolutely remain with the Commander-in-Chief. It is difficult enough to get the Allies to conduct effective operations with Norwegian military forces. The prerequisite for any hope of obtaining such cooperation is that there is no doubt whom has operational command. Moreover, those issues that the operational commanders cannot decide or reach agreement on

must be handled on the diplomatic level between the respective governments. Any mixing of operational command and diplomatic negotiations will lead to tragedies as such mixtures always do in war. [23]

He appears to be saying that there was no good alternative to his continuing as commander-in-chief in all matters, military and civilian. He also appears to view the King, Government, and the commanders of the military services as guests in his domain who were welcomed as long as they remained inactive.

The government's decision to take over their normal civil administrative functions in the three northern provinces rather than work through the system established by Fleischer at the outset of the war was probably not the best solution and led to dissatisfaction in some quarters. Fleischer had selected Governor Hans Gabrielsen from Finnmark Province to head the civilian machinery. It may have been wise for the government to continue to use that machinery by making Gabrielsen responsible to it rather than to Fleischer.

General Ruge's earlier decision not to involve himself for the time being in the military operations in North Norway turned out to be impractical. The three northern provinces were now the only theater of operations in Norway. It was unrealistic to expect that the arrival of the government as well as the army and navy high commands would lead to harmonious relations with a commander who had little respect for some members of the government, and who disliked both General Ruge and Admiral Diesen.

The protest letter on May 17 served as a watershed in the relations between General Fleischer, the government, and especially General Ruge. While some of his objections to the reshuffling of responsibilities were valid and had merit, his uncompromising attitude led to a poisonous relationship and a failure to have some of the proposed changes accepted. His refusal to accept the new political realities and his apparent unwillingness to accept General Ruge as his superior led to a loss of influence when he tried to avoid changes that he believed would damage the war effort.

The Royal Proclamation of May 18 appointed General Ruge as Armed Forces Commander, with authority over all military branches. Diesen had passed control of naval forces to Ruge during the southern campaign. He also continued his former duties as army commander. Upon his arrival in North Norway, Ruge had two options under the regulations. First, he could continue to operate with General Fleischer as commander-in-chief within that part of the country; or second, he could take over as commander-in-chief and direct operations. It appears that his initial decision was to operate with General Fleischer as commander-in-chief. It soon proved impractical to adhere strictly to this arrangement.[24]

Hovland writes that Ruge kept Fleischer's letter from reaching the government as a part of his planned assumption of command of the campaign and that he therefore showed himself to be a man without scruples who would go to any lengths to advance his interests. He claims that the establishment of a Defense High Command was accomplished on May 18 without the government being made aware of General Fleischer's objections.

Ruge answered Fleischer's protest letter on May 23. He pointed out that in a crisis such as the country now found itself, there should not be any competence arguments or accusations, and he wanted to clarify the situation. Among other things, he pointed to the fact that North Norway had become the main theater of war. The Armed Forces High Command (FOK) was present in this part of the country and it should then automatically assume the functions that General Fleischer had taken over because of the physical and communications separation that had existed earlier with respect to the central government. The previous arrangement could no longer continue unless the FOK and the government abandoned their duties and responsibilities for defense and administration of the country.

Ruge informed Fleischer that he had not yet made the new command relationships effective because he wanted Fleischer, who had prepared the operations against Narvik, to have the honor of being in command when Narvik was recaptured. He also told Fleischer that it was his intention to give him command of the southern front (Nordland Province) as soon as the situation around Narvik was resolved or permitted such a move. In addition, he informed Fleischer that he had retained his May 17 letter since it dealt with military matters within his prerogatives and that the changes in the civil administration had been decided before he received Fleischer's letter. If Fleischer wanted to lodge a complaint with the government about Ruge or the new command relationships, such a complaint would be expedited. Fleischer requested this be done in a letter on May 24. General Fleischer's letter of May 17 was accordingly sent directly to the Minister of Defense along with all other correspondence between Ruge and Fleischer about the command relationships.

Fleischer's letter of May 24, which is missing from the archives, requested that his letter of protest be forwarded to the Defense Minister. It must have convinced Ruge that he should not wait any longer to institute the new command arrangements. He announced the reorganization in a letter to Fleischer on May

26, placing the following directly under FOK: Naval High Command, 6th Division, Norwegian Forces in Nordland Province, Sector Commanders in East and West Finnmark, and 6th District Command. Ruge noted that the District Command needed to designate and separate out a Chief of Supply and necessary service chiefs for General Fleischer. He went on to solicit Fleischer's suggestions with respect to the administrative details involving the District Command since some issues were not yet decided. He also explained why he proposed to place the Norwegian troops in Nordland directly under FOK.

> In removing Roscher Nielsen's forces from your command, it is because I believe that sooner or later it will be necessary to have a combined commander for the troops in the Salten-Bodø area. Since the Allies have the preponderance of forces there and since we are dependent on the British Navy, it should be the British commander who takes over.

Ruge's decision elicited an immediate response from General Fleischer on May 27. He accepted only that FOK should assume the commander-in-chief duties and that the Naval High Command came under FOK. The other points were unacceptable:

> … The division requests in the most urgent manner that the dissolution of the well-established command relationships not take place.
>   FOK also proposes to separate out the forces in Sør Hålogaland [Nordland Province] in order to place them under the English commander. This will place Norwegian troops in a subordinate relationship to Allied troops, which is not reciprocated by any Allied forces under a Norwegian commander in other places. It will place a stamp of inferiority on the North Norwegian units which is completely unjustified and which Norwegian commanders should be the last to facilitate …

Ruge answered in a personal letter to Fleischer where he pointed out that the latter's agreement with the main point of the proposal carried with it some inescapable conclusions:[25] "Thereby, the rest follow naturally since the various sectors and the District Command have been, and should be in the future, under the direct authority of the commander-in-chief (hereafter FOK)." Ruge agreed to allow the division's current relationship with the District Command to remain essentially unchanged to ease the transition to the new command relationship. He also agreed to leave Roscher-Nielsen and his forces in Nordland under Fleischer for the time being. He rejected Fleischer's proposal for a conference between FOK, the defense ministry, and the 6th Division, since matters concerning organization and dispositions of military forces fell within his authority and responsibility. The new command relationships were made effective in a FOK order on May 29.

Fleischer felt that Ruge handled the division's views in an unsatisfactory manner and he did not let the matter rest after the issuance of the order. In a letter as late as June 6, the 6th Division stated that, in view of developments, the FOK order of May 29 should be cancelled. For his part, Ruge wrote that this struggle over prerogatives was the only one he had experienced during the war and that it made his job more difficult than it should have been. Writing as a prisoner of war in the fall of 1940, Ruge regretted that he had not involved himself earlier and more forcefully. However, he recognized that General Fleischer probably felt he had involved himself too much into his affairs.[26]

The changed command relationships became effective so late that they had little, if any, effects on the operations. However, the continuous wrangling tells us much about the personalities involved. The spiteful atmosphere made a situation that called for the highest degree of professional behavior more difficult.

NOTES

1 Derry, *The Campaign in Norway*, p. 207 and Sandvik, *Operasjonene*, vol. 2, p. :193, n.ote 12.

2 Derry, *The Campaign in Norway*, p. 218.

3 Munthe-Kaas, *NarvikavsnittetKrigen*, p. 180.

4 Lindbäck-Larsen, *6. division*, , p. 154.

5 Sandvik, *Operasjonen*, vol. 2, p. :144 and note 50. A number of the Norwegian archives dealing with operations in the 6th Division area have disappeared. According to Colonel Tor Holm (captain and chief of staff of the 6th Brigade during the campaign), as recorded by Berg and Vollan (in *Fjellkrigen*, p.age 321), both the 6th Division and 6th Brigade archives were on hand when Major Lindbäck-Larsen began writing his book about the campaign (*6th divisjon*). Colonel Holm wrote a scathing review of Lindbäck-Larsen's book in 1947 (in the professional periodical *Hærens Offisers Forbund*, nr. 9-10, 1947). My colleague, Dr. Haga, attempted to locate a copy of the periodical. The Armed Forces Museum's Library, responsible for collecting and stocking all Norwegian Military periodicals, reported that the issue in question was missing from its archives and it had proved impossible to locate it anywhere in the Norwegian library system. It is

unfortunate and puzzling how and why the archives – apparently not destroyed at the end of hostilities – became missing and why the critique of Lindbäck-Larsen's account cannot be located.

6 Ziemke, *German Northern Theater*, p. 101.

7 Witold Bieganski, *Poles in the Battle of Narvik* (Warsaw: Interpress Publishers, 1969), p. 39.

8 Ibid, p. 60.

9 United Kingdom, Cabinet Office Historical Branch, *Notes on the Norwegian Campaign*, Appendix 1, p. 61 and Appendix 2, p. 64.

10 Ibid, Appendix 2, p. 64.

11 As quoted in Irving, *Hitler's War*, pp. 105-106.

12 *3GDKTB*, 05101200.

13 *Fuehrer Conferences 1940*, pp. 52-53

14 Ash, *Norway 1940*, p. 225.

15 Derry, 206.

16 Ruge, *Felttoget*, 72.

17 Ruge, *Krigens dagbok*, 370.

18 Lie, 189.

19 Kersuady, 169.

20 Moulton, 243.

21 Victor MacClure, *Gladiators over Norway*, 23.

22 Ash, 253 and 227.

23 As quoted in Hovland, 181.

24 As quoted in Sandvik, 2:154. Ruge wrote that, "Both the Government, Allied military commanders, and military attaches continually turned to me for decisions on matters that had to be resolved quickly and the distances were so great and communications so bad that I had to make decisions with increasing frequency without first having an opportunity to discuss them with General Fleischer. The reality that I could not avoid making decisions in the long run, forced me in the end to revise my decision not to become involved in the conduct of operations in North Norway."

25 The quotes from the exchanges between Ruge and Fleischer are from ibid, 2:157.

26 Ruge, *Felttoget*, 131-132.

16

TIME RUNS OUT

"It is, for the sake of the country, absolutely necessary
that the brigades make a renewed effort to bring
the Narvik Campaign to a conclusion."
GENERAL FLEISCHER'S MAY 30 DIRECTIVE TO HIS TROOPS.

Plans to Recapture Narvik

The recapture of Narvik and the offensive on the northern front were the two main topics dealt with at the conference between Generals Fleischer and Béthouart on May 14. The Norwegians were satisfied with the choice of the French general as the Allied ground commander in the Narvik area. They demonstrated their confidence in him by placing one infantry battalion and a motorized artillery battery under his command for the operation against Narvik. It was the first and only time during the Narvik campaign that this was done.

The 2/15th Inf and the 9th Motorized Artillery Battery moved from the Kvernmoen area to the vicinity of Skoglund, north of Bjerkvik, in the evening of May 21. The two battalions of the Foreign Legion moved off the high ground east of Herjangsfjord with the 1st Bn remaining on the east side of that fjord while the 2nd Bn moved to Øyjord. This battalion left some security detachments in the mountains as it withdrew. These detachments withdrew after the Norwegians pushed forward to the area around Cirkelvann.

The 14th Bn, CA landed at Liljedal on May 19 and moved northeast to establish a bridgehead from Hill 332 to Hergot. The 12th Bn, CA was located at Lenvik on the north side of Ofotfjord as Béthouart's reserve. The 6th Bn, CA was pulled out of the front on May 14 and moved to Gratangen to rest and recover from a very high percentage of frostbite cases. From Gratangen it moved to Sjøvegan to reorganize. The Polish troops were positioned as described in the previous chapter.

The attack on Narvik was to take place simultaneously with other attacks designed to tie down German forces in order to keep reinforcements from reaching Narvik and to cut the enemy's line of retreat. Three Polish battalions were to attack the German positions on the Ankenes Peninsula. Norwegian troops were to keep up their pressure on the northern front. The Allies also planned to make a wide envelopment from the south against Bjørnefjell, a move that Dietl anticipated.

Lieutenant Colonel Magrin-Vernerey, the commander of the 13th Demi-Brigade of the Foreign Legion commanded the Narvik landing forces. These consisted of the two battalions of Legionnaires, a Norwegian battalion (2/15th Inf), an artillery group consisting of one Norwegian and two French batteries, and two tanks.

Magrin-Vernerey's mission was to land at Ornes, establish a bridgehead as far inland as Hill 457, and seize the city of Narvik. He intended to carry out these tasks by landing 1st Bn of the Legion just east of Ornes. This battalion was to establish security towards the east by advancing along the railroad. The 2nd Bn of the Legion and 2/15th Inf were to embark at Seines and land in the same place as the 1st Bn, but the two tanks were to be landed at Taraldsvik when that place was secured. The second French battalion, with the two tanks, was to advance towards Narvik via the Framnes Peninsula. The Norwegian battalion would pass through units of the 1st Bn of the Legion and seize Taraldsvikfjell (Hill 457). The three artillery batteries would support the attack from positions at Øyjord. British warships would provide additional fire support and British aircraft were expected to keep the Luftwaffe at a distance.

There were insufficient landing craft to move the three battalions in one lift and the units were therefore divided into assault and follow-up elements. There were only three assault and two mechanized landing craft available for the operation. This limited the number of troops in each wave to 290. Some troops were transported in Norwegian fishing vessels. To insure surprise, the assault elements of the battalions were embarked at Seines, shielded from German observation by the Øyjord Peninsula. Plans were to move follow-up elements from the ferry landing at Øyjord and have them ashore about 45 minutes after the first echelon had landed.

The 1st Bn of Legionnaires was to make the initial landing with assault groups Gilbert and de Guittaut, each consisting of two rifle platoons with machineguns, in the first echelon. Group Gilbert's primary mission was to secure a small bridgehead before the arrival of the second echelon. Group de Guittaut was to seize the railroad tunnel above and to the right of the landing area. Group Bouchet, consisting of four rifle platoons, machineguns, and some regimental elements, formed second echelon. After its arrival, Group de Guittaut had orders to expand the bridgehead eastward. Later, after the Norwegian battalion had landed and moved forward past its right flank, Group de Guittaut would resume its advance towards Hill 457 (Taraldsvikfjell), the dominant terrain east of Narvik. Group Bouchet was supposed to move forward between Group Guittaut and the Norwegians. This was how the French understood the plan.

The Norwegians had a different understanding. They expected to pass through the French battalion only after that unit had seized the northern slope of Hill 457. This misunderstanding was only one of the problems facing the assault forces.

The German Defenses

The German defenders in the Narvik sector numbered about 1,100 troops but only 550 of these were mountain infantry. Major Haussels, the sector commander, faced serious problems in mounting an effective defense. He had to defend the long coastline from Straumsnes in the east, around the Framnes Peninsula, and the harbor area. Three reinforced mountain infantry companies under his command were tied down on the Ankenes Peninsula, facing the Poles. The Germans did not know where the attack would take place and had to prepare for all eventualities. This made for a thinly manned strong-point defense line and very limited reserves. Major Haussels had to assume that it would be exceedingly difficult to move his reserve or shift his forces once the attack was underway because of expected heavy naval and artillery fire.

The German right flank was held by Naval Co von Freytag, which tied into Naval Regiment Berger on its right. A naval artillery unit under Lieutenant Nöller was located in the Ornes area. Co 6, 2/139th and the battalion engineer platoon were located on the Framnes Peninsula. Company 6 had earlier occupied Ankenes village but Co 8 replaced it there on May 24. Two naval infantry companies, Co Möllmann and Co von Gaartzen, were responsible for the defense of the harbor area. A railway company of about 40 men constituted the sector reserve.

Company 7 (reinforced) held the southern front on Ankenes Peninsula while Co 8 (reinforced) held the pocket around the village of Ankenes. In addition to the approximately 900 troops mentioned by most writers, Cos 1 and 2 of the 137th Mountain Regiment were moved into the Narvik sector shortly after they parachuted into the Bjørnefjell area on May 23, 24, and 25. These reinforcements increased the strength of Major Haussels command to approximately 1,100 troops.

Company 1, with a strength of 108, was placed in reserve while Co 2, with a strength of 109, was moved across the Narvik harbor to reinforce Co 8. Haussels had ordered this move despite the reluctance expressed by General Dietl at a meeting between the two on May 27. The 3rd Division journal notes on May 28 that the movement of that company to Ankenes did not have the desired results and it could have been used to better effect as a reserve in Narvik.[1]

The battalion's heavy machinegun platoon had four guns located where they could fire on the harbor area and two at the bottom of the Fagernes Mountains from where they could support the German forces in Ankenes. There were only two 75mm mountain howitzers in the Narvik sector, located about 700 meters northeast of the railroad station. The two 105mm railway guns were not very effective since their positioning was restricted by their dependence on the rail network. There were seven 20mm and one 37mm antiaircraft guns that could be used against enemy attempts to land in the harbor as well as at Vassvik and Taraldsvik.

The Recapture of Narvik

The Germans expected an attack on Narvik at any time, but there was not much they could do about it while they did not know the exact landing sites. A German agent in Stockholm – Marina – had overheard a conversation between the Norwegian Ambassador and the embassy. Based on this conversation, she reported that coordinated attacks against Hundal from the north and across the Rombak against the railroad should be expected within the next six days.[2] This information was forwarded immediately to Major Haussels, although it turned out to be inaccurate.

The first useful information received by the Germans came around 2300 hours on May 27 when British warships entered Ofotfjord. This was the British naval fire support group consisting of the cruiser *Southampton*, the antiaircraft cruisers *Cairo* and *Coventry*, and five destroyers. Four destroyers entered Rombakfjord while the two antiaircraft cruisers and one destroyer remained in the eastern part of Ofotfjord. *Southampton*, with its 6-inch guns, remained further west in that fjord. General Béthouart was aboard *Cairo* and a flare from that ship at 2340 hours signaled the start of the attack.

The weather had been sunny and beautiful and the midnight sun provided excellent visibility at the time of the attack. A thunderous fire from the warships and artillery batteries now broke the stillness of the night. In order not to give away the intended landing sites, the fire from the warships was directed at a wide spread of targets along the whole coastline. Communications between the German units were lost within ten minutes of the start of the bombardment. The fire from the French and Norwegian batteries located at Øyjord, on the other hand, was concentrated on and around the landing area. Buchner describes the inferno:

> Without interruption, hundreds of projectiles exploded along the railway, detonated with a thunderous roar at the tunnel entrances, rained down with a shrill whine on the cliffs on Framnes, detonated between the homes in Vassvik, and broke loose large rocks that plunged down the slopes of Fagernesfjell with earth-shaking reverberations. Also over in Ankenes and Nyborg, the roar of descending fire was like the eruption of a volcano on Ankenesfjell above. In the town, in the harbor, at Fagernes, and on the coastline of Ankenes, wooden buildings burned like torches. With infernal detonations and thunder, the shells from the ships burst in stone and steel and sent a rain of thousands of iron and rock splinters in all directions … Gradually, it was possible to discern the centers of gravity of the enemy fire. It involved the outcropping of land at Ornes with its hilltops, the railroad by Tunnel 1, Hill 79 near Taraldsvik, and even Fagernes, the southern end of the harbor, and Ankenes. A thick cloud of powder smoke and dust from stone particles, continually pierced by the bright flashes of new explosions, hung over the whole coastline from Ornes to Taraldsvik.[3]

The landing craft carrying the first wave of the Foreign Legion came within sight of their target area as they rounded the Øyjord Peninsula at 2355 hours. Most of the supporting fire was now directed at the area around the landing zone. The concentrated fire hit the weakest link in the German defenses, the 50-man naval artillery unit under Lieutenant Nöller. The defenders were forced to take cover and the first wave of Legionnaires landed at Ornes around 0030 hours without meeting any resistance. Group de Guittaut crossed the 70-meter wide roof of Tunnel 1 and began the climb to the top of the 1,400-foot mountain.

Lt. Nöller was seriously wounded and his men sought refuge in Tunnel 1 where they refused demands to surrender. De Guittaut left a small force to watch the tunnel while the rest of the group continued its advance. Nöller's men capitulated later in the day after the French positioned a field gun where it could fire directly into the tunnel. Group Gilbert secured the small knoll near the railroad line by surprising its defenders (part of Nöller's force) and the French battalion commander established his CP on the northern slope of this knoll.

The landing craft had meanwhile re-crossed the fjord to pick up the second echelon of Legionnaires at Øyjord. However, German artillery fire caused a number of casualties among the French troops and necessitated shifting the embarkation to both sides of Øyjord. This delayed the flow of reinforcements for the two groups already ashore. The Norwegian battalion was not landed until 0230 hours, about one hour behind schedule. Group Bourchet, with three rifle platoons and two tanks, which were to lead the advance into Narvik, were not embarked until 0300 hours and landed in Taraldsvik at 0345.

The delay in the buildup of forces could have jeopardized the amphibious operation but the Germans were unable to take advantage of the situation. Artillery and naval gunfire kept them under cover and many sought shelter in the railroad tunnels. Furthermore, the shelling cut communications between the various units and Haussels CP near the railroad station.

The Norwegian battalion landed without losses. Three observers accompanied the battalion commander and his staff: Fleischer, his chief of staff, and his adjutant. This was a risky act on the part of Fleischer, but it undoubtedly lifted the morale of the troops in Major Hyldmo's battalion to see the general accompanying them into battle.

The Norwegians crossed the tunnel roof as had the French before them and began the climb, which was very steep for the first 1,200 feet. The area was narrow, with the drop-off into the Taraldsvik River valley on the right and a ravine on the left. The companies had to make the ascent one by one. Company 5 led the advance and it was to swing to the right after reaching the flatter terrain north of Hill 457 in order to give room for following units. Company 7, with a machinegun platoon attached, constituted the left wing of the battalion after reaching the more open terrain. The heavy weapons company (Co 8), the mortar platoon and Co 6, the battalion reserve, followed these two companies.

The Germans were still unable to communicate but Lieutenant Erich Schweiger, commander of Co 1, 137th Mountain Regiment, decided on his own initiative to counterattack. He gathered his unit from the shelter in a tunnel in the Djupvik area. Reinforced by a few engineers, some naval personnel, and a small number of mountain artillery troops, he moved to and occupied positions north of Hill 457. They soon found themselves in contact with Norwegians troops moving up the hillside.

The difference in French and Norwegian interpretations of the operational plan now led to difficulties. While the French understood the plan to be that Group de Guittaut should only advance against Hill 457 and secure the northern slope *after* the Norwegians had passed them on their right, the Norwegians understood the plan to be that they were to *pass through* the French forces after these had secured the northern slope of Taraldsvikfjell.[4] The different interpretations of the operational plan may well have been caused by language difficulties.

The Norwegians found that the French bridgehead did not extend as far forward on the hillside above the rail line as they were led to expect in the pre-operational briefings. The Norwegians encountered heavy enemy fire, first from the flank and then from the front, as they approached the area where the two companies could spread out and where they expected to pass through the French forces.

The German troops appearing in front of the Norwegians did so as one Norwegian platoon was in the process of enveloping some Germans who were giving them problems from the flank. The Norwegians were slow in firing on the troops to their front because they believed them to be part of Group de Guittaut. The Germans opened heavy fire on the Norwegians. Several soldiers were killed or wounded in the exchange and around 0400 hours, the company commander decided to reposition his troops for better cover. In doing so, there was a temporary loss of contact with the enemy.

The weather in an area at some distance from Narvik turned the situation temporarily in the Germans' favor. A heavy fog descended on Bardufoss Airfield and the Hurricanes that had provided air cover were barely able to land before the airfield was closed. The Luftwaffe appeared in the clear skies above Narvik shortly after the British aircraft were grounded.

The German bombers began an intense attack of the British warships. The ships were forced to cease their supporting fire and concentrate on avoiding the bombs that rained down from the sky. The antiaircraft cruiser *Cairo*, with Admiral Cork and General Béthouart aboard, was struck by two bombs. One landed between the smokestacks while the other hit the forward deck. The last bomb killed or wounded 30 sailors at the forward turrets. The five destroyers operating in Rombakfjord were forced to withdraw west to Ofotfjord where they could maneuver under high speed.

Cork had earlier requested that Béthouart inform him when his troops were securely ashore to allow him to minimize the number of warships in the constricted waters. Béthouart now informed Cork that he only needed the support of two destroyers and the admiral ordered most of his ships to retire at 0630 hours, leaving the antiaircraft cruiser *Coventry* and two destroyers to support the troops. Cork's desire to withdraw most of his ships is understandable, particularly in view of the loss of the cruiser *Curlew* the previous day. Béthouart moved his flag to one of the destroyers and shortly thereafter, he went ashore at his forward CP in Øyjord. The British ships avoided further losses but one Norwegian fishing vessel, loaded with ammunition, was sunk.

The German air attacks had two important results. First, the movement of the 2nd Bn of the Foreign Legion was delayed and was not completed until 1100 hours. Second, the reduction in fire support for the troops that had landed enabled the Germans to launch a counterattack against the French and Norwegians and thereby win valuable time for their comrades to begin evacuating Narvik before their route of retreat was cut.

Group de Guittart was located to the left and slightly to the rear of the Norwegians on the slopes leading to Hill 457 and the troops had become intermingled on a narrow front that prevented proper deployment. Schweiger's vigorous counterattack came as a surprise to both the French and Norwegians who had a distinct numerical superiority over the attackers.

The attack struck the weakest point in the line, the Norwegian left flank and the French right flank. Captain de Guittaut fell, along with a number of his men in the close-quarter fighting and a near panic situation developed. Some French troops began withdrawing and pulled along parts of Co 7, 2/15th Inf.

Strong leaders among the French and Norwegians prevented a debacle. Captain Hans Hanekamhaug, commander of Co 7, drew his pistol and threatened to shoot any of his troops who withdrew. The commander of the heavy weapons company grabbed an abandoned machinegun and personally operated it effectively against the advancing Germans. Major Hyldmo exhorted his troops forward by calling out that the fate of the nation was at stake. These examples of leadership in the heat of battle lifted the fighting spirit of the men and enabled them to halt the German advance. Lieutenant Schweiger was shot through the throat and killed. Most of the German officers were killed or severely wounded and this undoubtedly had a negative effect on German morale.

While the attacking Germans were able to place effective machinegun fire on the landing area, statements that the French and Norwegian troops were driven "back down the hill and on to the beaches" are not correct. However, the landing site was moved further west after Major Paris, General Béthouart's chief of staff, was killed in a landing craft.[5]

Lieutenant Schweiger's counterattack points out the value of strong reserves with aggressive leaders when defending a long line against an enemy that can strike at any point along that line. If Major Haussels had followed General Dietl's wishes and left Co 2, 137th in reserve alongside Lieutenant Schweiger's unit, it is quite possible that they could have overwhelmed the Norwegians and French and driven them back to the landing area. This might have encouraged the German naval units in the area to become more aggressive and could have spelled the end of the amphibious operation.

The situation ashore was still critical and it was worsened by friction between the French and Norwegians. Some French accounts place the blame for the setback caused by the German counterattack on the Norwegians.[6] Magrin-Vernerey complained to Fleischer that the 2/15th Inf would not advance and this placed his own troops in danger. He demanded that the general intervene to insure that his orders were followed. Fleischer wisely refused to intervene, pointing out that he had placed the battalion under French command and it was the colonel's job to lead the attack. He would not complicate the situation by intervening but agreed to have a Norwegian officer bring the colonel's orders to Major Hyldmo. He also pointed out to Margin-Vernerey that the Norwegians had again reached the plateau and were ahead of, not behind, their French allies.[7]

Major Hyldmo committed his reserve, Co 6, and a bitter close-quarter fight ensued on the edge of the plateau. The Germans were finally driven back after Norwegian forces managed to work themselves into a position on the German left flank. The last German assault was carried out by naval personnel who tried to overwhelm the Norwegians making their way towards the flat ground on the north side of Hill 457. The attack failed and it resulted in a dozen Germans killed. The Norwegian losses in the fighting for Taraldsvikfjell were relatively heavy with 18 killed, including those who died while being evacuated, and 36 wounded. Two additional soldiers were later killed and two seriously wounded in a German air attack.

Two other events contributed to the change in Allied fortunes. Lieutenant Commander S. H. Balfour, who accompanied the French as naval gunfire liaison officer, lost his signal lamps during the retreat following the German counterattack. He went back to the landing site, found a boat that brought him to the *Coventry*, where he explained the situation to Rear Admiral Vivian before heading back to the shore with new signal lamps. Vivian ordered the destroyer *Beagle* back into Rombakfjord and its 4.7-inch guns helped stabilize the situation. The second event was the departure of the German bombers because of fuel shortage, followed by the reappearance of British Hurricane fighters after the fog at Bardufoss lifted.

The 2nd Bn of the Legion was ashore by 1100 hours and started its planned advance towards the Framnes Peninsula and Narvik. The two tanks that were to lead the advance became bogged down in the soft ground near the landing site and they did not participate in the fighting. There was some sharp fighting with Co 6, 2/139th located on Framnes and with Haussels' reserve, which was now committed. This mixed group of engineers, railroad personnel, and naval infantry was unable to prevent the French from seizing Hill 79, a dominating piece of terrain southwest of Taraldsvik. The French also secured Hill 102 at the western tip of the Framnes Peninsula. Part of this success was due to a much earlier decision by Haussels to evacuate Narvik and withdraw his forces towards the village of Beisfjord.

The fighting in the mountains continued throughout the day as the Germans withdrew slowly eastward. In the process, Hill 457 was secured. Small groups of isolated Germans surrendered. It was evident to those in the mountains that the Germans were evacuating Narvik in the direction of Beisfjord. Hyldmo was ordered to move the bulk of his battalion into town, to the left of the 2nd Bn of the Legion, and to clear the city north of the railroad. Company 7, reinforced with a machinegun platoon and a section of mortars, was left to secure Taraldsvikfjell.

General Fleischer, still in the bridgehead, was concerned that French troops would enter Narvik and that there would be no Norwegian Army representation. He decided to send three officers with the French units but these halted on Hill 79 at 1200 hours. From there, the French and Norwegians had an excellent view of the city and it was obvious that the Germans had left or were in the process of leaving. The division commander returned to Bjerkvik and ordered a group of military police into Narvik.

The 2/15th Inf entered and occupied Narvik without resistance at 1830 hours, before the arrival of the military police. In a show of gallantry, the French let the Norwegians have the honor of occupying the town and Magrin-Vernerey informed the Norwegians that as long as he was in the city, "I am under your orders." The many soldiers from Narvik in the Norwegian battalion were greeted as heroes as they entered the city.

Major Haussels had a difficult time exerting operational control of his forces in and around Narvik. The naval and artillery bombardment destroyed all landline communications and he was forced to rely on runners for communicating with his units. The communications difficulties increased as units became involved in combat and small units operated independently. The failure of Lieutenant Schweiger's counterattack to drive the French and Norwegians back to the beach and the flow of fresh forces in the beachhead convinced Haussels that he could not hold Narvik. His forces were in danger of having their line of retreat cut by the Poles advancing south on the Ankenes Peninsula or the Norwegians in the mountains east of Narvik. He ordered the city evacuated at 0650 hours.

Schweiger's counterattack, while failing to achieve its primary goal, provided enough delay to enable Haussels to get most of his troops out of Narvik. The withdrawal order specified that all equipment, heavy weapons, and excess ammunition were to be destroyed and Fagernes was designated as the assembly area. Only personal and crew-served weapons along with plenty of ammunition were to be carried by the retiring troops. The Germans tried to bring along the 20mm antiaircraft guns but it proved impossible because of French fire and they were made inoperable and abandoned.

However, not all units received the withdrawal order or were in position to extricate. Two groups from Co von Gaartzen did not receive the order and went missing. Company Möllmann was later able to disengage and withdraw on its own. A heavy cloud of smoke from the many burning buildings in Narvik hung over the area and aided the disengagement and withdrawal.

The Germans occupied several delaying positions between Narvik and the village of Beisfjord. The first position was on Fagernes and occupied by a platoon from Co 6 and a machinegun section from Co 10. Their fire prevented a quick follow-up by the French along the harbor road. Company 8, at Ankenes, also provided cover for the withdrawal. The withdrawing units assembled at Fagernes, reorganized, and moved to the village of Beisfjord in trucks.

These troops occupied a security line in the Lakselv Valley behind the heavily engaged Co 7 at the southern end of the Ankenes Peninsula. Naval infantry detachment Dehnert was left at Fagernes to cover the withdrawal across Beisfjord of the rear guard on the Ankenes Peninsula. The mission of securing the road from Fagernes to the village of Beisfjord was given to parts of Co von Gaartzen, which occupied a position about three kilometers southeast of Fagernes with orders to hold until 2000 hours. A last delaying position, about 1,500 meters north of Beisfjord village, was occupied by half of Co 6 with orders to hold until the Ankenes rear guard, naval infantry detachment Dehnert, and

Co von Gaartzen withdrew through its positions. The mountain flank on the German right was covered by machineguns from Co 10.

Major Haussels' CP remained at Fagernes until after 1100 hours, by which time the rear guard from Ankenes had arrived. Parts of the two companies at Ankenes appear to have withdrawn along the south side of Beisfjord. Haussels established his new CP in the village of Beisfjord at 1200 hours.

During the afternoon, the 1st Bn of the Legion pushed east along the railroad towards Sildvik while the 2nd Bn sent a motorcycle platoon along the road to Beisfjord village where contact was made with Polish troops. Haussels had meanwhile withdrawn his troops to a line running generally from Beisfjordstøtta (Hill 1448) in the north to Durmalsfjell (Hill 844) in the east.

Narvik holds the distinction of being the first city recaptured from the Germans in World War 2. General Béthouart made the official report of this accomplishment at 2200 hours on May 28. The victory announcement transmitted to the world must have seemed ironic to the privileged few who knew about the evacuation decision taken in London and Paris four days earlier. It is difficult to establish accurate casualty figures, except for those already noted in the 2/15th Inf. Most Norwegian and Allied sources apparently base their figures on those contained in General Béthouart's official announcement on May 28 and place the French and Norwegian casualties at about 150 while they claim that 300 to 400 prisoners were taken.

Whatever the exact numbers, Churchill's statement that the operation was "effected with practically no loss" must have seemed dismissive to the French, Polish, and Norwegian troops who participated in the operation. Buchner takes exception to the number of prisoners claimed by the Allies, stating that it is much too high. His detailed account of losses in Narvik includes 41 killed, 69 wounded, and 176 missing. Since only a small number of the missing rejoined their units, and were not captured, he concludes that many of those missing were killed.

The Polish Offensive

The flare from the cruiser HMS *Cairo* at 2340 hours was also a signal for Polish General Bohusz-Szyszkos' troops to go into action on the Ankenes Peninsula. Their mission was simply to clear the Germans from this peninsula at the same time as the French and Norwegians attacked Narvik, then advance against the village of Beisfjord, and cut the German line of retreat.

While the main mission of the Polish troops was against Beisfjord, the original plan called for Polish units to make a wide encirclement through Skjomdal, Nordal, and Hundal, which would bring them into the rear of Dietl's forces at Bjørnefjell. A company from the 3rd Polish Bn made a reconnaissance in preparation for this part of the operation. The evacuation plan caused this planned envelopment to be cancelled.

There was some repositioning of the Polish forces before the attack because it became evident that the Germans had increased their forces on the peninsula. This involved the strengthening of Co 8 at Ankenes to where it numbered nearly 180 men and the movement of Co 2, 137th Mountain Inf into the pocket on May 27. The 2nd Polish Bn's mission was to eliminate the German pocket at Ankenes. The 1st Polish Bn and one company of the 4th Bn (Co 1) were given the mission of attacking Beisfjord. Company 1's task was to envelop the German positions on Hills 650 and 773 from the south at the same time as the 1st Bn attacked frontally. Parts of the 4th Bn manned positions on Hills 677 and 734 and served as a link between the 1st and 2nd Battalions. The rest of the 4th Bn was located in reserve near Klubban.

The attack against Ankenes started at midnight, when Co 3 on the 2nd Battalion's left wing attacked along the road towards Ankenes, supported by naval artillery, the British artillery battery, and two tanks. The center company in the Polish line, Co 1, began its attack towards Lyngenes and Haugen from positions southeast of Hill 295 20 minutes later. Company 2, on the battalion's right wing did not begin its attack in the direction of Nyborg until 0200 hours.

The Polish attack started out well and Co 3 reached the outskirts of Ankenes village around 0200 hours when one of the tanks hit a mine and ended up blocking the road for the second tank. At the same time, the company came under intense crossfire, suffered heavy casualties, and was forced to withdraw towards Emmenes.

Bieganski's account is somewhat different. He writes that one of the two tanks never left the assembly area because of mechanical difficulties and the other tank became entangled in a barricade on the western outskirts of Ankenes. The 2nd Bn Commander, Lieutenant Colonel Dec, who witnessed Co 3's fight through binoculars, wrote later, "I found with horror that the 3rd company was bouncing back in disarray. Some groups were moving towards Baathberget by road, others were sneaking amidst the shrubbery. Some of the men had no helmets and no arms. Others were dragging the wounded."[8]

Company 1's attack at 0020 hours drove the Germans back, but a space developed between Cos 1 and 3. Lieutenant Hermann Rieger, commanding Co

2, 137th, quickly took advantage of this opportunity. With 15 men, he launched a determined attack between the two Polish companies and captured Hill 295 at 0430 hours with his force, now down to eight men.

Lieutenant Colonel Dec personally directed the defense of this key terrain. He had no reserves and the defenders were members of the battalion staff, orderlies, telephone operators and others that he was able to scrape together. Most Poles on the hill were killed. Only the battalion commander and eight men survived. This was a serious setback for the Poles. Hill 295 was not only a dominant piece of terrain from which Lieutenant Rieger could bring flanking fire to bear on Co 1, halting its attack, but the hill was also the observation post for the Polish battalion commander, the brigade commander, and the artillery.

Company 2 on the right flank did not launch its attack until 0200 hours and it was stopped almost immediately by heavy fire from a knoll to the north of Hill 405. The company was unable to resume its advance until the commander of Co 2, 4th Bn, located on Hill 677, sent two platoons to storm the troublesome German position. Company 2 reached Nyborg around 0900 hours and found the Germans in the process of evacuating the Ankenes pocket. The boats were fired on, two overturned, and several Germans drowned.

Despite this success, the Poles were unable to capture Ankenes on May 28. The German withdrawal decision was caused as much by the success of the landings at Ornes as it was by the unrelenting Polish pressure. The French and Norwegian forces in Narvik threatened to isolate the German units opposing the Poles, much in the same way as the Polish advance threatened to isolate the German defenders in Narvik. It was important for the Germans to hold the Ankenes positions long enough to assist the withdrawal from Narvik since effective machinegun fire could be placed on anyone trying to advance along the harbor road past Fagernes. When this was accomplished, the defenders withdrew under the protection of a covering force that later escaped across the fjord in boats.

Lieutenant Rieger and his men held Hill 295 until 2000 hours when they had used up all their ammunition. They had successfully repelled three Polish attacks. Rieger and his eight soldiers managed to slip away towards Ankenes and tried to make it across the fjord but the Poles saw their boat and sank it with gunfire. Rieger was wounded and captured. Many in his company were killed, wounded, or missing.

The 1st Polish Bn also met determined resistance in its offensive near the base of the Ankenes Peninsula. The operation began around midnight, with Co

1 of that battalion attacking Hill 650 while Co 3 attacked Hill 773. Company 2 was the battalion reserve. The first attack was repelled but the German Co 7 defending this area was so exhausted after weeks of fighting that it was obvious an effective defense could not be maintained for long.

The defenses at the base of the Ankenes Peninsula assumed enormous importance in the successful extraction of Major Haussels' forces from Narvik, including the defenders in the Ankenes pocket. If the Poles could break through Co 7's positions, they could advance on and capture Beisfjord village, thereby cutting Major Haussels line of retreat. The Germans would then be caught in a trap.

Major Haussels was unable to communicate with his forces on Ankenes Peninsula as the day passed, but General Dietl was able to establish communication with Co 7 and gave orders directly to this unit since it reported that it was not only hard pressed but unable to communicate with Haussels. Dietl told the company commander to hold his positions as long as possible but to withdraw in the face of overwhelming enemy strength and establish a delaying position east of Lakselv (Salmon River).

Lieutenant Rieger's daring attack on and capture of Hill 295 now took on an importance out of all proportion to the size of his force and his actions. Like Lieutenant Schweiger's attack near Hill 457, it became another key to the successful extraction of the Germans from the Narvik area. General Bohusz-Szyszko viewed Lieutenant Rieger's attack as posing a serious threat to the facilities in his rear area and the line of communications from Håvik. He ordered the 1st Half-Brigade commander, Lieutenant Colonel Chlusewiez, to alter the attack plans and this gave the Germans the precious time they needed to make good their escape.

It is difficult to understand the Polish commander's concern. Only two platoons of his three-company reserve were already committed. The Poles should have been aware of the limited size of the German force on Hill 295 and it had a company of Polish troops on each side. He was surely aware that the French/Norwegian landings at Ornes were successful. This made the Beisfjord village the key objective in trying to trap the Germans. The Ankenes pocket had become, in the course of events, a secondary objective and the Germans on Hill 295 could easily be contained by the 2nd Bn while the full weight of the half-brigade's attack was directed against Hills 650 and 773.

Instead of doing so, the 1st Half-Brigade was directed at 0300 hours to move the reserve company located at Klubban to Emmenes. Two hours later, a string was put on Co 1 of the 1st Bn, reasoning that it might become necessary to commit it to restore the situation on the left flank of the 2nd Bn. This effectively left the 1st Bn without a reserve and slowed the tempo of its attack against the two key terrain features that constituted the doorway to Beisfjord.

General Bohusz-Szyszko also requested that General Béthouart release at least one company from his reserve, the 3rd Polish Bn, which was located in Ballangen. The request was turned down because the battalion constituted the only protection against threats from the southwest, according to Sereau. What the nature of the threat southwest was is not explained, but it was probably a concern about possible airborne landings since General Feurstein's forces in Nordland Province were far to the south and had not yet captured Bodø.

Béthouart did ask Magrin-Vernerey if he could send a company of Legionnaires to help the Poles. This elicited a rather caustic reply according to Lapie, "Do they want the 63 men guarding the luggage at Scarnes?" The state of inter-allied cooperation is further illustrated by another comment attributed by Lapie to the French colonel, "Nothing ever seems to happen in this place [Ankenes] ... And to think they want a company of mine to help those fellows! Not a single shot."[9] This was a very unfair observation. The Poles fought fiercely and bravely and took heavy losses at the same time as the French and Norwegians were fighting near Narvik.

While the Germans gained valuable time because of the Polish commander's action, the situation on Hills 650 and 773 eventually turned precarious. Although he no longer had a reserve that he controlled, Major Kobylinsky, the 1st Bn commander, continued his attack against the two hills but met heavy resistance. A German air attack between 1600 and 1700 hours made things even more difficult.

Company 1 of the 4th Polish Bn was sent on its flanking march by Lieutenant Colonel Chlusewiez as called for in the plan. This unit was able to occupy Hill 606, southeast of Hill 773, making the German positions on the two other hills untenable and this forced a general German withdrawal. They left behind one machinegun and four men on Hill 650 and these managed to hold the hill until 2100 hours, when Co 1 of the 1st Bn stormed it. Hill 773 was occupied at about the same time by Co 3. Co 1 continued its advance after securing Hill 650, occupied Beisfjord village at 0900 hours the following morning, and linked up with a motorcycle troop from the Foreign Legion.

The fighting on the Ankenes Peninsula exacted a heavy toll of both Poles and Germans. The Poles reported that they found 150 fallen Germans on the peninsula. This figure is undoubtedly too high in view of the actual numbers of Germans involved in the fighting. Bieganski reports that the German losses in the Polish sector were 190, including 60 captured. Buchner reports that Co 2/137th at Ankenes had 20 killed, five wounded, and 22 missing. No figures are given for Co 7 and Co 8 of the 139th. Polish losses are reported by Bieganski as 97 killed, 189 wounded, seven prisoners, and 21 missing.[10]

The French-Polish Drive towards Sildvik

General Dietl and his staff remained in the dark about what was happening in the Narvik area after their communication station on the Fagernes Mountain was destroyed and abandoned at 1215 hours on May 28. They knew that Lieutenant Schweiger's counterattack had failed to eliminate the beachhead, that Major Haussels had withdrawn his forces towards Beisfjord, that the three companies on the Ankenes Peninsula were under heavy pressure, and that Allied troops, supported by British warships, were pushing east along the railroad.

Dietl had to make some immediate decisions without knowing the location and status of the various units or enemy intentions. A company from the 1st Parachute Regiment, which had arrived on May 26, was sent towards Sildvik around 0400 hours and at 0700 hours, the division ordered naval infantry Regiment Berger to attack westward along the railroad with all available forces except the paratroopers.

By mid-afternoon, the division assumed that the companies on the Ankenes Peninsula were isolated and lost. Naval infantry battalion Holtorf, in positions between Fornes and the rail line needed help and a platoon of mountain infantry was dispatched to his assistance around 1400 hours. Major Haussels apparently used the prearranged code word for the abandonment of Narvik – *Berta*. The code word was intended to be used in a critical situation and called for a general withdrawal to the vicinity of Straumnes. Dietl did not think the situation that critical and he did not want the enemy to reach as far as Straumnes without serious opposition. He therefore sent out messages canceling the order for a general withdrawal.

A messenger was sent to Major Haussels around 2200 hours with orders to establish and hold a line from Lakselv to Hill 1446. General Dietl also decided to energize the leadership of the troops along the railroad by dispatching Captain Walther with a company of airborne troops from Bjørnefjell to the area around Tunnel 3 early in the morning of May 29. In addition, the parachute company in Sildvik (Co 4) was moved forward.

General Béthouart issued orders for the continuation of the offensive in the evening of May 29. The 1st Bn of the Foreign Legion and the Poles would undertake the offensive. The 1st Bn was to advance along the railroad while the 1st Polish Bn attacked across the mountains to link up with the Legionnaires in Sildvik. Thereafter, these forces were to carry out reconnaissance in force in the direction of Hundal.

The French Foreign Legion reached Tunnel 4 around midnight on May 28, but here it was stopped temporarily by units from naval infantry battalion Holtorf. However, Holtorf reported to division that he would not be able to hold unless he received reinforcements.

The situation for the Germans was still very unclear on May 29, primarily because of poor conditions for radio communications. Dietl could only communicate with Captain Walther indirectly and he had no communications with Major Haussels until mid-afternoon on May 29, when the major reported that his troops had occupied the designated positions at 0300 that morning. The lack of communications between Captain Walther and Major Haussels was even more disconcerting since there was a strong possibility that a gap had developed between the two commands that the enemy might be able to exploit. This fear was reinforced by the fact that Captain Walther, after a personal reconnaissance in the afternoon, failed to find any of Major Haussels' units in the vicinity of Hills 1448 (Beisfjordstøtta) and 970 (Resmålsaksla). Major Haussels' men had reportedly occupied these heights early that morning and it is likely, in view of subsequent events, that Walther made a map-reading mistake.

General Dietl moved additional forces into the area and adjusted his front line late in the evening of May 29. The 83 men from the 1st Bn, 1st Parachute Regiment who arrived on May 29 were rushed to the Sildvik area and the Engineer Platoon assigned to Group Windisch on the northern front was withdrawn to Bjørnefjell as a division reserve. Dietl ordered Captain Walther to pull his forces back to a point about half a kilometer west of Straumnes and to occupy Hills 1436 and 970. There appears to have been confusion at all levels. Major Haussels' forces were already on Hill 970 and Walther's troops, believing they were on Hill 1436, were actually on the western slopes of Hill 818.

There were three reasons for Dietl's redeployments. First, he wanted to make sure that Walther established contact with Haussels' forces. Second, he wanted to move the forces along the railroad out of the reach of British warships and French/Norwegian artillery batteries at Øyjord. Finally, Walther was worried about an enemy landing in his rear, and a withdrawal to the narrows at

Straumnes would alleviate this problem. The retreating Germans offered strong resistance and were able to destroy the railroad.

May 30 and 31 were days full of crises for the Germans and they did not know that the situation with respect to the French and Polish forces would stabilize at the end of that period. Captain Walther's forces along the railroad were under steady and increasing pressure from the French. The most serious situation developed in Major Haussels' area when it became apparent that the Poles were driving towards Sildvik. If they succeeded, Walther's forces would be cut off. There were no reserves available and it was estimated that the Polish drive was in battalion strength. Haussels had only weak forces in their path and the 3rd Division expected the enemy to reach Sildvik shortly.

Dietl had a telephone conversation with Group XXI in Oslo and stressed the need for immediate assistance. He then traveled to Hundal to familiarize himself with the situation at the front. At 1200 hours, he decided to send a parachute company to block the expected arrival of the Poles in the valley above Sildvik. He also ordered Walther's forces to fall back to positions at the narrow strait east of Straumnes. Naval detachment Kothe was withdrawn from Rundfjell on the northern front and moved towards Hundal while one company of mountain infantry was removed from Walther's command and transferred to Haussels to shore up his left flank at Hill 884. The division reserve, the engineer platoon, was moved to the mountains south of Sildvik. At 2245 hours it was reported that the enemy was about to break through the German positions at Straumnes Strait and the parachute company that was earlier moved to the valley above Sildvik was brought back to Sildvik in case of a breakthrough to the west.

There was still no contact between Captain Walther's left flank and Major Haussels' right flank and it was not until the evening of May 31 that it was discovered that Walther's left flank was two kilometers behind Haussels' right flank. The division ordered Walther to establish contact with Haussels' forces immediately and insure that there were no gaps between them.

The French forces reached the peninsula east of Straumnes on May 31 but did not press their attack. The Polish attack against Major Haussels' forces was hampered by heavy fog and snow. Consequently, their advance was delayed and Company 2 was not able to capture Hill 884 before May 31, at the same time as Company 3 captured Hill 970. Company 1, which was supposed to make a more or less isolated move towards Sildvik encountered unexpected resistance. After being caught in a crossfire, it withdrew to the Beisfjord village area.

The bad weather that hampered the Polish attack on May 30 and 31 also affected the Germans. The troops were beginning to show signs of exhaustion. The weather had prevented aerial resupply for three days and ammunition was running short. An attempt to airdrop ammunition in the evening of May 31 was not successful. The parachutes were improperly fastened to the loads and tore loose. Most of the mortar ammunition detonated as it hit the ground. The situation was to become worse as continued bad weather prevented air operations.

The Last Fights

The first phase of the resumed Norwegian offensive called for a move to the Nygård watershed. Alta Bn was given the mission of clearing the Germans from the north side of this watershed, capturing Hill 346 on the south side of the watershed, and thereby securing the road from Trældal to Cirkelvann, the proposed new supply line that it was hoped would be opened by a French drive from the southwest.

The Germans had positions on the north side of the watershed, on Hill 361 and between Cirkelvann and Nedre Jernvann. They were driven back across the river in a series of company-size operations by the Alta Battalion between May 24 and May 31. The 6th Division ordered the Alta Bn to seize Hill 346 by 2400 hours on May 30. The Germans had strong forces on Hill 346 and the Norwegians were unable to cross the river because there was no bridging equipment available.

Lieutenant Colonel Dahl planned to cross Jernvannene using improvised rafts made from sleeping bags stuffed with hay or straw. It was envisioned that two sleeping bags tied together would suffice to carry five soldiers with equipment. It was now light around the clock and the battalion planned a quick crossing under air cover and concealed by an artillery smoke screen. Although the battalion was suffering from scurvy, Dahl felt that it was better to attack than continue the positional warfare and relative inactivity of the past week. Safely across, the battalion planned to bypass all enemy positions and secure the highest terrain in the area. The plan was not carried out since division's operational order on June 1 directed that most of Alta Bn move east to operate in conjunction with the 6th Brigade.

New units were also arriving in the area. The 1/15th Inf assembled in Gratangen where it was reorganized since all its trains and transport were lost in the evacuation from Bodø. The battalion was eventually moved to the Lillebalak area with one company relieving part of Alta Bn and another company involved in supply operations. The reserve battalion of the 14th Inf also moved into the area from Nordland Province. This battalion, badly demoralized by its experience in that province, was given security missions in the rear, against enemy airborne operations. This mission was made more important by the frequent German parachute operations into the Bjørnefjell area.

The 6th Division's directive for the operations against Bjørnefjell was issued on May 29. The 6th Brigade was directed to advance to the border and the railroad line. It was left up to the brigade whether this was accomplished by driving the Germans southward or over the border into Sweden. The 7th Brigade's mission was to provide flank security for the 6th Brigade and serve as a link to the French forces that were expected to advance eastward at the same time. The 6th Brigade wished to locate its supply point at the east end of Hartvigvann but the division did not feel this solution was satisfactory. The decision was to establish a supply point for both brigades at the east end of Cirkelvann with the understanding that the brigades would fetch their supplies at this location. It was also decided that the 1/16th Inf, located on the far left, would continue to receive its supplies via Raudal.

The Germans held the northern front with the equivalent of three battalions. The exact composition of these battalions changed frequently as units were moved. Major Stautner's battalion held the western sector from Rombakfjord to Hill 346 with Cos 2, 3, 4, and 5. Naval infantry Co Erdmenger was located behind the left wing. Major Hagemann's battalion held the center from Hill 522 to the river junction 500 meters east of Øvre Jernvann with Cos 11, 12 (reserve), 13, 14, and 15 as well as some smaller units. Group Schlee-brügge constituted the right wing of Windisch's front from where it tied in with Hagemann's troops to the Swedish border via Hill 620. He had a mixture of units under his command, including three companies of mountain troops (Co 1, 139th, and Cos 2 and 3 of the 138th), one parachute company (Co 1, 1st Regiment), ski platoons Adler and Rohr, naval infantry company Steinecker, and naval infantry platoon Braun.[11]

The British evacuation of Bodø and the collapse of the front in Nordland Province gave new urgency to Norwegian offensive preparations. A report by Colonel Finne, the Norwegian liaison officer at Allied headquarters, also caused unease. He reported that the French plan was to capture Sildvik but not advance any further and that the Norwegians would have to take care of the rest.

On May 30, the division amended its earlier directive and ordered the operations to begin no later than 2400 hours that same day. A phrase in the amendment summed up the sense of urgency, "It is, for the sake of the country, absolutely necessary that the brigades make a renewed effort to bring the Narvik Campaign to a conclusion."[12] The 7th Brigade was asked to report immediately any French failure to participate in or support the attack.

Problems in getting the French on the north side of Rombakfjord to participate in the planned offensive continued. We have seen that Béthouart viewed the troops in the 14th Bn, CA as unfit for offensive operations and that Valentini voiced the opinion that there was no need for haste since the Germans would either surrender or intern themselves in Sweden within two weeks. Both these officers were aware of the evacuation and the prohibition against offensive operations after the capture of Narvik.

The 6th Brigade issued its attack order to the battalions on May 29 at 2130 hours. The 1/16th Inf was ordered to attack the eastern anchor of the German line at Hill 620, while the 2/16th Inf was to advance from its rest area to pre-reconnoitered attack positions and capture, as its first objectives, Hills 456 and 615. The 3rd Mountain Artillery Battalion would support the attack from positions between Kuberget and Skitdalsvann.

The 2nd Bn began its move at 0200 hours on May 30 but the terrain east of Skitdalsvann was mountainous and difficult. The battalion came under intense enemy automatic weapons fire as the units reached the high ground to the north side of the watershed near its objectives. Major Munthe-Kaas viewed the chances of success in a frontal attack as very small and made the first in a series of recommendations that the battalion move into the mountains to the east where the terrain was more favorable. The brigade turned down these suggestions and repeated attempts, frustrated by heavy enemy fire, were made to ford the river or build a footbridge. After wasting almost four days in these attempts, the brigade agreed to move the battalion into the mountains to the east at 1330 hours on June 3.

It will be recalled that the 1/16th Inf was left on the high plateau after the Germans withdrew to new defensive positions on May 22. An eastward movement, to make room for the 2/16th Inf that was getting ready to move forward from its rest area was begun on May 27. The battalion plan of attack called for Co 1 to attack Hill 620 from the east while Co 2 approached the objective from the west, with the machinegun company supporting both attacks. Company 7 was left in its positions on Hill 931 as flank security. The attack was planned for 2300 hours on May 30 but was postponed until 0600 hours on May 31 because of heavy fog.

Company 1 ended up attacking the hill from the north, not east as planned. The first attempts were unsuccessful due to German air attacks and stubborn resistance.

Company 1 reassembled on the northeast slope of the hill and the battalion altered the attack plan by directing Co 2 to attack from the east. Company 1 was to remain in its positions and support Co 2's attack with fire. Company 2 would move against the German right flank after reaching the plateau between Hills 620 and 698, and Co 1 would then attack Hill 620 on a prearranged signal. Company 2 cleared the plateau by 2300 hours on May 31 after some heavy fighting. The Norwegians were able to hold the gained terrain and Hill 620 was stormed and captured on June 1.

The Germans describe the fight for Hill 620:

From May 31 at 1300 hours, several companies advanced against Hill 620 – defended by about 90 men with one machinegun and one mortar – from the west, supported by strong supporting fire and partially in heavy fog ... In hours of bitter struggle, until late night, heavy enemy attacks, supported by six aircraft, to secure this important hill were repelled three time ... The enemy was finally able to break into and hold their positions, without securing the whole hill. In this dire situation, the last division reserve, Co 2, 138th [Lieutenant Renner)]arrived [30 men and more hand grenades and ammunition] ... After four more attacks were repelled, the hill, which had been fought over continually for 15 hours, had to be abandoned around 0800 hours [June 1].[13]

Company 2 continued its attack against Hill 698 but was stopped by heavy enemy crossfire. The battalion commander also committed Co 7 against this objective. The two companies surprised the German defenders under the cover of a heavy fog on June 2 and gained a precarious foothold on the northern part of the hill. Three Norwegians were killed and nine wounded in the attack.

Heavy fighting continued throughout the following week for Hill 698 and Border Marker 267A (Hill 623). This key objective changed hands a couple of times. Both Norwegians and Germans accused each other of violating Swedish territory. It appears that both sides were guilty. The Norwegian violation was carried out by a unit commanded by a Swedish volunteer, Lieutenant Jan Danielsen. When confronted by a Swedish officer and accused of violating the border, Danielsen is reported to have replied, "To hell with that, we have to attack the Germans wherever they are."[14] This surprise attack from the east led to the capture of this key terrain.

Lieutenant Rohr's platoon held the far right of the German line, up against the Swedish border. Rohr's report to Schleebrügge indicates that he felt that what was appropriate for one side should also be appropriate for the other:

On the 7th or 8th of June, about 40 Norwegians with at least three machineguns crossed the border into Sweden and at 0230 hours attacked our right flank on Hill 698. Our weak border security force was thrown back after two soldiers fell. Both platoons Adler and Appeln received orders to immediately retire some distance, cross the border, and attack the Norwegians from the rear.[15]

The German counterattack forced the Norwegians off the hill but eventually both sides abandoned the area around the border marker as Swedish troops appeared and hoisted the Swedish flag. In his description of the heavy fighting for Hills 620 and 698, Buchner notes that after long having neglected the deep and open German flank, the Norwegians were forced into frontal attacks against well-prepared defensive positions.

The German supply situation was becoming desperate, as was their lack of reinforcements. The bad weather during this period, with heavy fog, rain, snow, and sleet, prevented aerial resupply. Troops on both sides suffered severely and were completely exhausted. They had difficulties in moving around and fell asleep, even while under attack. While these conditions plagued both sides, Group Windisch had reached such a state of exhaustion that a total collapse was imminent.

The 3rd Division journal mentions on June 2 that there had been no resupply of ammunition for six days and that they managed only because there were no enemy attacks on the Narvik Peninsula. The journal also notes that one reason they were able to hold the front was because the Norwegians did not launch simultaneous attacks against more than one objective and this enabled the Germans to bring forward badly needed supplies to the threatened areas. It also allowed the Germans to reinforce the threatened areas in a timely manner with forces from Group Windisch's left flank and from the units facing the Poles and French.

It is ironic and tragic that the Norwegians and Allies failed to coordinate their efforts. The Norwegians remained virtually idle in the days prior to the

Narvik landings and during most of the period when the French and Poles were attacking towards Sildvik. Because of the lack of activity on the northern front, Dietl was able to commit all incoming reinforcements and some units from Group Windisch to counter the Allied drive. When the Norwegians began their offensive, the Poles and French remained inactive, and this allowed Dietl again to switch units to the threatened sector. It is very doubtful that the Germans in the Bjørnefjell area would have survived if these attacks had been coordinated in such a way as to keep maximum pressure on both fronts.

The loss of Hill 620, the threatened loss of Hill 698, and the attacks against Holmevann were direct threats against the German base at Bjørnefjell. Late on May 31, Dietl had already decided that he needed to withdraw his forces to a shorter line in order to make reserves available. On the northern front, the Germans withdrew their left flank to the western slopes of Rauberg. The front on the Narvik Peninsula was also pulled back about two kilometers. These withdrawals allowed the Germans to form a company-size reserve in each battalion.

The Norwegians were within seven kilometers of the Bjørnefjell Railroad Station and the logical next objective of the attack was Rundfjell if the German resistance on Hill 698 and north of Holmevann was overcome. With Rundfjell in Norwegian hands, the forces confronting the French and Poles would be in an untenable position and forced to withdraw. The hope was that the capture of Rundfjell would force Dietl to surrender or withdraw into Sweden.[16] The date for the final attack was set for June 8.

NOTES

1 *3GDKTB*, 05270800 and 05282300.

2 *3GDKTB*, 05241130. Marina Lie Goubonia was originally a Soviet agent in Norway who was turned into a double agent by the *Abwehr*. She apparently operated from both Sweden and Norway. Hovland writes that she came into Norway from Sweden on skis dressed as a Red Cross worker, established contacts and operated from the Bjerkvik area. As a show of appreciation for services in Narvik, the Germans allowed her to retire from her career as a spy and she settled in Spain.

3 Büchner, *Narvik*, pp. 126-127.

4 Sandvik, *Operasjone*, vol. 2, p. 207.

5 MacIntyre, *Narvik*, p. 197 and Sereau, *L'Expedition*, p. 89.

6 See, for example, Pierre Oliver Lapie, *With the Foreign Legion at Narvik* (Anthony Merryn

transl., London: J. Murray, 1941), p. 7; Marcel Jean Marie Joseph Torris, *Narvik*, (New York: Bretano, 1943), p. 222; and Jacques Mordal, *La campagne de Norvège* (Paris: Self, 1949), p. 401.

7 Lindbäck-Larsen, *6. division*, p. 138.

8 Witold Bieganski, *Poles in the Battle of Narvikk* (Warsaw: Interpress Publishers, 1969), p. 80.

9 Lapie, *Foreign Legion at Narvik*, pp. 90 and 92.

10 The figures given by Bieganski for Polish and German casualties may include the entire period from when the Poles took over from the French until the capture of Narvik.

11 Berg and Vollan, *Fjellkrigen*, p. 316 and Büchner, *Narvik*, pp. 159-163.

12 6th Division directive of May 30, 1940 as quoted in Sandvik, *Operasjone*, vol. 2, p. 265.

13 Büchner, *Narvik*, pp. 164-165.

14 Berg and Vollan, *Fjellkrigen*, p. 377.

15 Lieutenant Rohr's journal as quoted in Berg and Vollan, *Fjellkrigen*, p. 377..

16 Under German pressure, the Swedes entered into an agreement, which was actually an evacuation rather than an internment of Dietl's forces. The Germans requested the Swedish Government to provide sufficient railroad transport to move Dietl's forces to Holmesund on the Gulf of Bothnia. The Swedes agreed on the conditions that all weapons be left behind in Norway. At Holmesund, Dietl's forces were to embark on ships for transport to Germany. The Swedes held four trains in readiness near the border from the end of May until the end of the Narvik Campaign.

17

EVACUATION, ARMISTICE, AND DISASTER

"You may think we are running away from the enemy, we are not, our chummy ship has sunk, the *Glorious* is sinking, the least we can do is make a show, good luck to you all."

ANNOUNCEMENT BY LIEUTENANT COMMANDER GLASFURD TO THE CREW BEFORE TURNING HIS DESTROYER AROUND IN A DESPERATE ATTACK ON THE GERMAN BATTLESHIPS, AS RECALLED BY THE DESTROYER CREW'S LONE SURVIVOR.

Evacuation Plans

Foreign Minister Koht and Defense Minister Ljungberg were in London when the Germans attacked in the west on May 10. Lord Halifax asked to see them and they met in the afternoon of May 10. Ljungberg asked the British Foreign Secretary if the events in Holland, Belgium, and France would cause any changes in the help promised Norway in the form of troops and materiel. Halifax assured his visitors that a cabinet meeting earlier in the day had decided there would be no changes.

There is no reason to question Halifax's sincerity. In fact, two days later Churchill, who had become Prime Minister on May 10, offered Admiral Cork the 2nd French Light Division, located in Scotland. The return of this unit to France was delayed for three days pending a reply. Cork answered that, for administrative reasons, he could not receive the French troops before May 30. In a message to Cork on May 14, Churchill sounded even more positive by expressing the hope that Cork would clear out Narvik as soon as possible and thereafter work himself southward in increasing strength.[1]

Even as late as May 19, there were no hints that Churchill was thinking about a possible withdrawal. He was adamantly opposed to the Mowinkel Plan (discussed later in this chapter), which called for the neutralization of North Norway. "The main remaining value of our forces in Norway is to entice and retain largely superior German forces in that area away from the main decision.

Norway is paying a good dividend now and must be held down to the job."[2]

Churchill's tone changed the following day, May 20, after a report by the Inter-Service Planning Staff to the Chiefs of Staff. The consequences of a defeat in France and the loss or withdrawal of the British forces from that country were beginning to set in. It was emphasized that every ship, aircraft, and anti-aircraft gun was needed at home. That night, Churchill informed the new defense committee that since the Germans were now in a position of strength where they could demand troop transit through Sweden, the Allies would no longer be able to advance from Narvik to the iron ore fields and that Narvik had no significant importance as a naval base.[3] He concluded that holding Narvik drained British resources, a stark reversal of the position he had expressed the day before. However, as late as May 23, Churchill considered leaving the evacuation in a planning stage.

The situation appeared more distressing the next day as the noose around the British, Belgian, and French forces began to tighten. The Chiefs of Staff, in an appreciation of the military implications of a withdrawal from Norway, provided the necessary impetus for an evacuation order and spelled the end to any hopes the Norwegians might have had of carrying on the struggle with Allied air and logistic support. The Chiefs estimated that it would take 28 days from the time the order was given to bring the forces in Norway back to Great Britain in an operational condition. A telegram ordering the evacuation was sent to Cork that evening (May 24) and the War Cabinet approved the order on May 25, followed by the Supreme Allied War Council on May 31. While the evacuation decision proved final, there were misgivings within the War Cabinet and even Churchill toyed with the idea of leaving a garrison in Narvik.

The British also decided to proceed with the attack on Narvik. The reasons given for proceeding were to ensure that the harbor facilities were destroyed and to cover the evacuation, which are difficult to square with the actual situation. In anticipation of losing the city, the Germans had carried out a thorough and systematic destruction of the harbor facilities, starting on April 22. The German troops were in no position to interfere seriously with an Allied evacuation. In fact, it is arguable that it would have been simpler to evacuate from the positions occupied by the Allies prior to Narvik's capture than it was after they had advanced into the interior. However, operations in the final days of May and early June diverted German attention away from any thoughts that the Allies were about to depart. They were completely unaware of the evacuation since they considered that the Norwegians and Allies were in ideal positions to undertake a final push that they felt incapable of containing.

The real reasons for capturing Narvik before the evacuation were probably due to pride and prestige or, as argued by General Béthouart in retrospect, because a victory was needed for Allied morale. In the process, several hundred Allied and Norwegian soldiers and sailors gave their lives without any major benefits. The delay, although impossible to foresee by the planners and decision-makers, meant that it took place at the same time as the German fleet made a sortie that brought a calamity to the British Navy.

The British government had instructed Cork and Auchinleck to keep the evacuation a close secret, with knowledge limited to senior British and French officers. The need for secrecy is understandable. Allied mistrust of Norwegians continued and any leakage of information would jeopardize the evacuation.

The Allied commanders had a distasteful task. Not only were they required to abandon a campaign when final victory was within reach, but they were required to keep that knowledge from the Norwegians and they no doubt felt that they were again abandoning their comrades on the field of battle. General Béthouart said as much, "I am operating with Norwegian troops whom for reasons of national honor, I will not abandon in difficulties on the battlefield."[4] Auchinleck's feelings are summed up in a hand-written letter he sent to General Dill on May 30, one day after Churchill decided that the Norwegians still could not be told about the evacuation. "The worst of it all is the need for lying to all and sundry in order to preserve secrecy. The situation vis-à-vis the Norwegians is particularly difficult and one feels a most despicable creature in pretending that we are going on fighting, when we are going to quit at once."[5]

The Norwegians reacted very angrily to the British evacuation of Bodø, leading the British to believe that they were discussing an armistice with the Germans. While there was no serious consideration on the part of the Norwegians to negotiate with the Germans, the meeting between Ambassador Dormer and the Norwegians on May 30 was very heated. Mr. Hambro told Dormer that Norwegians could no longer trust the British and he complained about the apparent lack of cooperation between the British Navy and the British Army. This elicited a sharp reply from Dormer that Hambro was in no position to pass judgment on such matters, and cooperation was in fact excellent. Hambro replied that if this was true, the situation was even worse than he had thought.

In view of these strong statements about the Bodø evacuation, the Allies could not be sure what the reaction would be to far worse news. The carefully worked out deception plan for the evacuation was as much directed at misleading the Norwegians as it was to conceal the operation from the Germans. There were those in Allied headquarters who felt that telling the Norwegians was tantamount to informing the Germans. The movement order, codenamed *Alphabet*, had an appendix, which informed people privy to the evacuation how to answer questions from individuals who were not in on the evacuation plans. There were three main points: 1) The capture of Narvik allowed forces to be redeployed to better advantage for future operations; 2) A planned move of the Allied base of operations from Harstad to Tromsø to minimize German air threats; and 3) The need to prepared to move forces to the Finnmark Province in case of German or Soviet threats in that area.

Despite concerns by Cork and Auchinleck about worsened relations with the Norwegian as result of not telling them about the impending evacuation, Churchill decided on May 29 that there should still be a few days delay in informing the Norwegians. To soften the blow of the eventual disclosure of the evacuation to the Norwegians, he told Admiral Cork to offer them "the alternatives of evacuation or being left in positions capable of further defence."[6]

By the end of the month, it became obvious that the Norwegians had to be informed since it would be next to impossible to disengage French and Polish forces without their knowledge and acquiescence. It was also impossible to conceal all evacuation operations since some of the supplies and heavy equipment were shipped out before the end of May.

Admiral Cork sent a message to London on May 31, stressing the necessity to inform the Norwegians about the evacuation and received the necessary authority to do so that same day.

It fell to Ambassador Dormer to fly to Tromsø to carry out this distasteful task. Dormer gave the bad news to the Norwegians on June 1. Auchinleck's biographer writes, " ... when the truth was told them, the Norwegians reacted with generosity and courage. It is arguable that, even at some risk of security, it would have been wiser, as well as more friendly, to have taken them into confidence earlier." Admiral Cork wrote that the Norwegians "... after a very natural display of great disappointment continued to co-operate loyally to the end, although they might, with some justification, have decided to lay down their arms at once and so gravely prejudice our withdrawal."[7]

The Mowinkel Plan
The message to Admiral Cork from the Foreign Office on May 31 also gave the green light for the Norwegians to explore the so-called Mowinkel Plan. This plan

had surfaced earlier but rejected by both the British and Norwegians. The plan originated with the Swedes and it was designed to keep the war in Scandinavia from dragging out with the distinct possibility that Sweden might become involved. At the same time, the plan also protected Swedish commercial interests. It called for the neutralization of North Norway, with both the Germans and Allies withdrawing. Swedish troops would occupy Narvik and the Norwegian King and Government would continue to function in the pacified area. If the belligerents accepted the plan, it would reduce the chance of Sweden becoming involved in a protracted conflict and would protect their export of iron ore to both sides. According to Sandvik, the first approach to the Germans came in early May in conversations that a private Swede Dahlerus had with Göring.

Dahlerus reported his conversations with Göring to the former Norwegian Prime Minister, Lars Mowinkel. Nothing developed until a conversation between Mowinkel and the Swedish Foreign Minister, Christian Günther, on May 13, followed by a visit by the Permanent Undersecretary of the Norwegian Foreign Office to the Swedish Foreign Office on May 14. Günther assured the Norwegians that it was not a question of peace negotiations but hinted at the possibility of a demarcation line in North Norway. He stressed that the suggestion had to come from the Norwegians, with British agreement. Sweden would then present the proposal to Germany. Günther stated that the Germans might be more likely to look favorably on the plan if it called for the Swedish occupation of Narvik.

The reactions by Norwegian officials were mixed. Some were opposed to Swedish military occupation while others opposed the whole scheme. The Norwegian Ambassador in Stockholm had asked the Norwegian Ambassador to Great Britain, Colban, for his opinion and Hambro discussed the plan with the British Ambassador in Stockholm in the evening of May 14. The Norwegian Government also discussed the plan, but in the end, the idea was rejected.

There were two reasons for this rejection. First, the Norwegians did not want to take any action that could be interpreted as disloyalty to their brothers-in-arms. Second, they viewed a demarcation line as a risky proposition, since the forces at their disposal after an Allied withdrawal would be unable to cope with a German breach of the agreement. The British reaction was also negative. While the British Foreign Office expressed interest in the idea, others felt that the operations in North Norway could be brought to a successful conclusion and suspected that the plan had originated in Berlin.

Churchill was adamant in his opposition to the Mowinkel Plan on May 19 but had changed his opinion by the end of the month. In the May 31 message to Cork, it was clear that the Mowinkel Plan had full British backing. The message pointed out that the time for negotiations was short, and that the Germans would be sure to reject the plan if they had any inclination that an evacuation was contemplated.

The Norwegian Government decided to make the attempt. Foreign Minister Koht flew to Luleå on June 3 and met with his Swedish counterpart. Koth, who had delivered the rejection of the plan a week before, told Günther why his government had changed its position. A proposed agreement was drafted by Koth and approved by Günther. The Swedes were asked to position troops on both sides of the demarcation line as well as in Narvik. Günther stated that he would submit the proposed agreement to his government and hoped to have it on its way to Berlin that evening.

Koth ran into a hornets' nest when he returned to Tromsø and informed the government of his actions. Most were upset that Koth had found it necessary to tell his Swedish counterpart about the evacuation. Everyone believed that the negotiations would fail and many concluded that this was the best outcome. A formal Norwegian investigation after the war found that Koht acted correctly when he gave his counterpart in Sweden the true reasons for the changed Norwegian position on the Mowinkel Plan.

In their discussion about Koht's revelation to the Swedes, Berg and Vollan refer to a note made in Lieutenant Rohr's journal on June 3 about a rumor, brought from the division by a parachute lieutenant. The rumor was a demand by General Dietl that his troops hold out for at least five more days. All were waiting in anticipation for this 'Miracle of Narvik.' Berg and Vollan suggest that this indicated that Dietl knew about the evacuation.

This is not so. First, Dietl was completely unaware of the evacuation and did not believe it even when it was discovered that French and Polish troops had abandoned their positions east of Narvik. Second, Koht met with Günther on June 3 and the proposal was not presented in Berlin until June 4. The rumor referred to in Rohr's journal probably had a basis in the anticipated arrival of the 1,800 paratroopers and 1,000 mountain troops Hitler had ordered be parachuted into the Narvik area.

The Swedes did not tell the Germans about the evacuation. It was not in their interest to do so since the acceptance of the plan would be of considerable advantage to Sweden. The German successes on the western front and in

Norway since the idea first surfaced made the Swedish proposal, presented in Berlin on June 4, of little interest and the Swedes received no immediate answer. The German Foreign Ministry believed correctly that the reason for the current interest in such a plan was connected to an impending Allied withdrawal. The OKW did not draw the same conclusion because it was inconceivable to them that the Allies would abandon the venture now that it was so close to a complete success. OKW therefore continued to finalize the plans for Operation *Naumburg*, to be executed during the last week of June.[8]

Norwegian Government Opts for Exile

On June 1, the Norwegian Government faced decisions of enormous consequence for the future of Norway. There were three choices: 1) Stay in the country and continue to resist; 2) Stay in the country and seek an immediate armistice or peace with the Germans; or 3) Go into exile and continue the war.

Ruge, when he received the news of the evacuation from the British liaison officer, was eager to have the evacuation delayed long enough to permit the final attack on the Germans. He maintained that Dietl could be brought to terms within a few days if all the Allied troops were used in the attack. The Norwegian troops could only carry on the war alone if Dietl was first driven across the Swedish border or surrendered. Even under these circumstances, the Norwegians would need Allied air support and supplies.

Cork and Auchinleck responded to Ruge on June 3. They pointed out that all arrangements for the evacuation were made and that a postponement was out of the question. They also stated that the Norwegians should not count on air support or supplies after the Allied withdrawal in view of the situation in France.[9] Generals Ruge and Fleischer were summoned to a meeting with the king and government in Tromsø on June 3. In Ruge's view, the war should be continued unless there was no hope of further Allied support. In that case, the king and government should go into exile. The two generals found that the government had already made decisions in line with Ruge's thinking. Ruge recommended in the strongest terms that the attack against Bjørnefjell be allowed to continue.

There was also a discussion about what forces should be brought to England and it was decided to take all capable naval vessels, aircraft, and volunteers. Crown Prince Olav suggested that he remain in the country and try to do what he could for the people and the nation, but his proposal was rejected by the government.

There was also the question of who should be the commander of the Norwegian forces overseas. The government wanted Ruge to fill this position but he was opposed. He pointed out that he had already been required—in South Norway—to leave his defeated troops. He would not do so again. He recommended that Fleischer accompany the government into exile. The government was not convinced and voted unanimously on June 4 to ask him to assume command of Norwegian troops outside Norway. Ruge considered the government action an order but still voiced his disagreement. Everyone appears to have viewed the matter as settled, but at the last moment it was changed.

The Norwegian General Staff intervened and implored Ruge to remain behind since they believed that to do otherwise in this crisis would have a severe negative effect on the morale of the army and the people. Ruge told his officers that he had debated the issue as far as possible with the government but that he had no problems with others trying to bring the government to a different decision. A delegation met with the President of the Parliament and various members of the government and the result was that the cabinet decided on June 7 to transfer all authority in North Norway to General Ruge when the government departed. The same decision ordered General Fleischer to accompany the government to England.

Hovland's biography of Fleischer is very critical of the decision to leave Ruge behind to handle the demobilization and surrender in North Norway. He claims that Ruge wished to remain at home in Norway and that he used his influence with politicians to achieve this goal and that it would have been logical for Ruge to accompany the government while leaving the affairs in North Norway in Fleischer's hands. Hovland asserts that Ruge's campaign to be allowed to remain in Norway focused on weakening the government's faith in Fleischer.

It is difficult to find a personal benefit for Ruge in remaining behind and spending five years in German prisoner of war camps. There is no evidence that he tried to use this fact to his advantage after the war. It is true that some members of the government had less faith in Fleischer's than in Ruge's abilities to handle the political–military situation in North Norway after the departure of the government. This lack of faith may have more to do with a protest letter from Fleischer to the government about their decision to leave the country than it had with any attempt by Ruge to discredit his fellow officer.

When Fleischer returned to his headquarters in Soløy after meeting with the government on June 3, he discussed the situation with his chief of staff. A letter to the government was prepared for the general's signature. Lindbäck-Larsen does not state in his report or book who wrote the letter. Hovland writes that Lindbäck-Larsen "returned to Fleischer in the afternoon of June 4 and stated that he found it unacceptable to surrender the whole country to German troops after the division had covered the withdrawal of the Allies unless all other possibilities had been tried."[10] Hovland writes that Lindbäck-Larsen thereupon presented Fleischer with a draft document. The document stated that since the government had decided that it would not continue the war in Norway, it should enter into negotiations with the Germans for an armistice and peace. If the enemy refused, the Norwegian Army should cross the border to Sweden and Finland and be interned. The letter warned the government not to leave the country and implored the king to remain to insure that peace was concluded.

It is, as noted by Hovland, a strange document that far exceeds the authority and prerogatives of a division commander. It challenged a political decision already taken and called for a separate peace with Germany. Hovland maintains that the document only makes sense by understanding the desperate situation in which Fleischer and Lindbäck-Larsen found themselves and that it should be regarded as an attempt to secure peace and maintain a reasonable degree of independence in part of the country. This would have been a settlement along the line of that reached by the Soviet Union and Finland. However, if this was their thinking, they failed to recognize the fundamental political-military differences between the situation in Finland and that in Norway.

Fleischer and his chief of staff flew to Tromsø on June 5 to brief the government on the military situation and to present the document that represented their view to the ministers of foreign affairs and defense. According to Fleischer, the document was not looked upon favorably and according to Lindbäck-Larsen, it was withdrawn. Fleischer writes that he asked the foreign minister not to forward it to the king or other members of the government. In answer to a question from the Investigative Commission in 1945, Koht did not remember Fleischer withdrawing the document. However, he noted that Fleischer, in their conversation on the way to England, gave every indication that he supported the decision by the government and royal family to leave the country.[11]

While the document did not receive serious consideration, it was obviously not withdrawn as claimed by Lindbäck-Larsen and Fleischer. It was reported to the prime minister and discussed by the government in a conference on June 6. Lie writes that, "After the prime minister had read the letter, we agreed that the general's thinking was a little unclear" and "the Government decided to stand by its earlier views about departing Norway if it could not be avoided, in order to organize and carry on the war outside the country's borders."[12] This document was not forgotten and, according to Hovland, had later repercussions for General Fleischer.

In what appears to be an astonishing attempt to revise history, General Hovland shifts the blame for the letter to General Ruge. He writes, "In retrospect, the letter appears to mirror Ruge's ideas and it is not improbable that Lindbäck-Larsen was influenced by the General Staff."[13] This damaging accusation is not documented and a review of Ruge's writings, memoranda, or statements reveals nothing to support Hovland's contention. On the contrary, Ruge had argued consistently since he assumed command of the army that the country should carry out active resistance against the Germans and he supported the government's decision to depart the country in order to carry on this resistance.

Hovland is right in criticizing Ruge for not providing Fleischer with a staff as he left the country. Fleischer left without his own staff or members of the Norwegian General Staff. These remained in Norway. While Fleischer overcame this difficulty as competent officers flocked to Great Britain, the assistance of experienced officers from the general staff would certainly have eased the task of setting up a new headquarters in a foreign country and organizing and training military formations for future operations.

Evacuation

Admiral Cork and General Auchinleck were preoccupied with planning and executing the evacuation, especially after the recapture of Narvik. In order to give the Norwegian Government time to negotiate the Mowinkel Plan, Ambassador Dormer asked Cork to postpone the evacuation by one or two days. As a result, the first evacuation was scheduled for the night between June 3 and 4.

It was not an easy task to evacuate about 25,000 troops from various points in the Narvik/Harstad area, including disengaging those at the front without giving the enemy or the Norwegians any suspicions about what was transpiring. The bad weather that kept supplies and reinforcements from reaching General Dietl at the end of May and beginning of June also curtailed German air operations, shielded evacuation activities, and kept German bombers away when they could have caused serious damage to the operation.

The evacuated men and equipment were divided into a series of convoys and the first of these, carrying supplies and some French guns and tanks, left before the end of May. Cork had the cruisers *Southampton*, *Vindictive*, and *Devonshire*, the antiaircraft cruiser *Coventry*, 10 destroyers, one escort, and 13 armed trawlers at his disposal to cover the evacuation. He asked Admiral Forbes on May 31 to place naval escorts at his disposal for the convoys that were to carry the troops to Great Britain. Forbes ordered the aircraft carriers *Ark Royal* and *Glorious* to North Norway and they were offshore on June 2. Their mission was first and foremost to cover the evacuation with their fighter aircraft. Recovering the land-based aircraft operating from Bardufoss Airfield was a secondary mission.

Fifteen large troop transports were sent to evacuate the troops, but only 13 were used. To avoid air attacks, these transports rendezvoused 180 miles offshore and approached the coast in groups of two. The troops were ferried to the transports by destroyers and Norwegian fishing vessels. After taking aboard the troops, the transports proceeded back to the rendezvous point. During the nights of June 4-6, 14,700 troops were moved to six transports. These six fast ships made up the first convoy, assembled at the designated rendezvous point, and started out for Great Britain in the evening of June 7 escorted only by the old cruiser *Vindictive*.

The seven transports of the second troop convoy took aboard 9,800 troops during the nights of June 7 and 8. The convoy departed its rendezvous in the morning of June 9, escorted by the cruisers *Southampton*, *Coventry*, and five destroyers. Cork, Auchinleck, and Béthouart were aboard the *Southampton*. The aircraft carrier *Ark Royal* escorted by three destroyers attached herself to this convoy.

Eight transports were dispatched to Harstad to bring away equipment. This convoy, which sailed in the evening of June 7, was called the "slow" convoy and was protected by the destroyer *Arrow*, the sloop *Stork*, and ten armed trawlers. Another equipment and supply convoy consisting of three transports, one tanker, and a number of Norwegian merchantmen departed Tromsø. Its escorts were the destroyer *Campbell* and three armed trawlers. Vice-Admiral J. Cunningham in the cruiser *Devonshire* accompanied the convoy initially but they apparently parted company after reaching the open sea.

The naval protection provided for the convoys was woefully inadequate. Except for the ships coming from Tromsø accompanied by the cruiser *Devonshire* and one destroyer, the supply and equipment convoys had only armed trawler protection until destroyers that were involved in other duties could join them. The first troop convoy, carrying nearly 15,000 troops, had no escort initially except the aged and partially disarmed *Vindictive* because all destroyers were used to transport troops from embarkation points to the transports. The second troop convoy, carrying about 10,000 troops, had better protection although still inadequate in case of a German surface attack.

There were several reasons for the inadequate naval protection. First, the British were lulled into a false feeling of security since their numerous convoys between Great Britain and Norway had sailed unmolested for two months. Second, the British naval planners did not believe the German Navy was capable of or willing to make a determined sortie into northern waters, much in the same manner as they had miscalculated on this issue earlier in the year. Much of the convoy routes were outside the range of air protection but except for notifying the commander of Coastal Command in the strictest secrecy that an evacuation was underway, even long-range Sunderland aircraft were not employed to reconnoiter the routes. Finally, Allied naval resources were stretched thin. The events on the western front naturally caused the British to concentrate their ships against a cross-Channel invasion and few resources were diverted from this task. However, there were major units of the Home Fleet in Scapa Flow or in the waters between the Faeroes and Iceland.

The Norwegian Government held its last meeting on Norwegian soil in the afternoon of June 7. The king, crown prince, members of the government, the diplomatic corps, including Ambassador Dormer, boarded the cruiser *Devonshire* a few hours later.

All serviceable Norwegian naval vessels, aircraft with adequate range, and merchant ships were ordered to Great Britain. The remaining flyable aircraft were ordered into internment in Finland. The 1,500-ton *Fridtjof Nansen* carried the Norwegian Foreign Minister, Admiral Diesen, General Fleischer, and their families. The ship left Norway in the afternoon of June 8 and arrived in the Faeroe Islands in the morning of June 13 without any mishaps.

Most small warships reached their destination, but not all and not without difficulties. The patrol vessel *Nordkapp* and the armed trawler *Kvitøy* became involved in a gun duel with the British ships *Raven* and *Northern Gem*. Two hits were registered on *Raven* before the British ceased fire and headed out to sea.[14] There was no serious damage or loss of life on either side. *Kvitøy* was damaged in an air attack and forced to return to Norway where it was captured.

The armed trawler *Svalbard II* started its journey, but on June 11 its crew found numerous bodies floating in the ocean. Around noon, it encountered a raft with five men aboard in very poor condition. Steen reports that there were originally 32 men on the raft but 27 had been thrown overboard as they died.

The captain of the trawler decided to bring the wounded British seamen back to Norway for medical assistance. One died before they reached shore but the other four were hospitalized. *Svalbard II* was captured by the Germans.

Submarine *B3* and the armed trawler *Honningsvåg* departed together in the morning of June 8. There was a battery explosion aboard the submarine after the two ships had reached a position about 100 miles from shore. They returned to Norway to see if the damage could be repaired. When this proved impractical, the submarine was scuttled in deep waters and *Honningsvåg* departed for a second time and joined one of the British convoys.

The five Norwegian merchant ships, *Nova*, *Hestmannen*, *Prins Olav*, *Finnmarken*, and *Ariadne*, which tried to link up with the British convoy were not as lucky. *Finnmarken* was forced to return to Norway by German aircraft. *Prins Olav* and *Ariadne* were attacked by six to eight German aircraft late in the evening of June 9. *Ariadne* was hit by several bombs and set on fire from stem to stern. Nine crewmembers were killed and others were wounded. The crew managed to lower lifeboats and those who jumped overboard were rescued, including Captain Askim, commander of the coastal defense ship *Norge*. Forty-five were saved.

Prins Olav tried to avoid the bombs by evasive maneuvers but one exploded so close that the engine stopped and it was not possible to get it restarted. The order to abandon ship was given but the Germans continued to attack as the personnel were entering the lifeboats. A bomb hit the ship after the crew had left and the explosion tore it apart. One crewmember was killed and three wounded. Thirty-six were saved.

Prins Olav managed to send a radio S.O.S. but the operator was not able to report the position before the antenna was destroyed. However, Admiral Cunningham knew that Norwegian merchant ships were trying to join his convoy and assumed correctly that the call for help came from one of those. The British convoy was also attacked by German aircraft but fire from the escorts kept the attackers at a distance. Cunningham sent the destroyer *Arrow* towards where he assumed the Norwegian ships were located. *Arrow* found the 81 survivors and brought them aboard before rejoining the convoy. *Nova* and *Hestmannen* joined the convoy on June 11.

Armistice and Demobilization

The planned final Norwegian attack never took place. The troops were not told about the evacuation even after Fleischer learned what was about to happen. His chief of staff wanted to inform the brigade commanders immediately but Fleischer stated this would be a breach of the word of honor to the British. While the 6th Division staff was preparing demobilization orders, the brigades at the front were still fighting without knowing what was happening.

While there were clear signs of an imminent German collapse, such as contact by the Swedes to make arrangements for an orderly internment of the German troops and the exhausted condition of prisoners, it also became obvious that the Allies were up to something. Their preparations for evacuation did not pass as unnoticed as they may have believed. Many Norwegians had concluded that the Allies might withdraw but they did not think that such a withdrawal would take place before the German forces east of Narvik were destroyed.

Rather than holding back offensive operations after learning about the Allied withdrawal, Ruge and Fleischer increased their efforts to complete the destruction of Dietl's forces as quickly as possible. Their reasoning was that the Allies would be more amenable to leave air and naval support in place after such a victory and that with such support, the Norwegian forces would be able to block General Feurstein's advance.

After returning from Tromsø on June 5, Fleischer ordered the 6th Brigade to attack immediately, that same night, if possible. Fleischer, knowing that the French were withdrawing, agreed to assume responsibility for the whole area north of Rombakfjord and he moved the 1/15th Inf from Narvik into positions vacated by the French.

General Fleischer was called to Tromsø early on June 7. Shortly after arriving in Tromsø, he telephoned his chief of staff and told him he would not be returning, that the chief of staff should sign all future orders, and that the troops should eventually be told that it was not his wish to leave the division.

The division staff completed the demobilization orders and the brigade commanders were ordered to report to the division headquarters at 2000 hours on June 7. This order was later cancelled, but the 6th Brigade commander, Lieutenant Colonel Berg, was already underway. He was finally briefed on the situation and it was left up to him to decide if he wished to use the last 24 hours to continue the attack. He was told that there would be no air support. The 6th Brigade notified the battalions the next morning (June 8) at 0545 hours that the planned attack was not to be carried out and that preparations should be made to move units and trains to the rear.

Lindbäck-Larsen met Ruge at 1430 hours on June 8. He was informed that the king, government, and Fleischer had left the country and that the campaign was to be concluded. Ruge was briefed on and accepted the demobilization order prepared by the division. The subordinate commanders within the division were then briefed by Lindbäck-Larsen.

The order to execute the demobilization plan was received by the division at 2300 hours on June 8. The units were ordered to leave small security detachments in the forward positions while the rest moved to the rear and were demobilized, or transported to their home district to be demobilized. The operation was carried out in good order and the Germans did not interfere. However, the troops were in a state of shock and disbelief. Birger Gotaas, the press officer with the Norwegian General Staff, asked Lieutenant Colonel Berg how the troops reacted to the news of a cease-fire, Berg answered:

> It was the saddest moment in my life, to see the boys as they headed home. They looked at me with questioning eyes. They did not understand what was happening. They had fought and advanced inch by inch and week after week. They knew as well as I that within a few days, at most, the whole Rundfjell and Bjørnefjell areas would be cleared of Germans. They would have no recourse except to surrender or be interned in Sweden. And then, the boys were ordered back! I will never forget the depressed looks directed at me as they marched past.[15]

At 2200 hours on June 8, General Ruge notified General von Falkenhorst that he was ready to initiate negotiations for a cease-fire. In a telegram received by Ruge at 1500 hours on June 9, von Falkenhorst responded that all hostilities had to cease by 1600 hours that day. Negotiators with full authority were to be sent to General Dietl and to the German commander in Trondheim. Ruge answered that the deadline demanded by von Falkenhorst could not be met and that he had ordered his units to cease operations at 2400 hours. This was accepted by the Germans.

Two lieutenant colonels, with full powers to enter into agreements, were sent to the two headquarters designated by General von Falkenhorst. Lieutenant Colonel Harald Wrede Holm was sent to General Dietl's headquarters while Lieutenant Colonel Roscher-Nielsen was sent to Trondheim. The representatives had written authorizations from General Ruge as well as verbal instructions. General Hovland has directed sharp criticism against Ruge and the agreement he entered into with the Germans. He writes:

As became known later, Ruge immediately initiated negotiations about capitulation. He was not satisfied with a cease-fire agreement for North Norway, but allowed himself to be led into comprehensive capitulation negotiations with General Falkenhorst's staff that resulted in the Declaration of Capitulation of June 10, 1940, which fails to mention that the war should continue, led from overseas, and could therefore rightly be interpreted as a total Norwegian capitulation.[16]

This is a serious charge that is not supported by statements, documents, and reports. It would certainly be strange for the German military to agree to and sign a document that recognized and acknowledged continued Norwegian resistance from overseas and one should therefore not be surprised that this subject is not mentioned. Ruge was empowered by the government to make all arrangements dealing with the German assumption of authority in North Norway. Both representatives initiated their contact by stating that the king, government, navy, and air force had left the country and that Norway, as a state, continued now and in the future to be at war with Germany. In this regard, it may be of interest to quote from Roscher-Nielsen's description of events when he reported to the German headquarters in Trondheim: [17]: "The negotiations began with Colonel Buschenhagen [von Falkenhorst's chief of staff] asking what kind of negotiating authority I had, whether I came to negotiate a peace or a cease-fire. I answered that I was exclusively authorized to negotiate a cease-fire for the 6th Division in North Norway, which for various reasons no longer could continue the fight."

Buschenhagen then asked Roscher-Nielsen if he was empowered to act on behalf of the Norwegian Navy and Air Force to which the Norwegian answered that he did not have such powers. As to the location of the navy and air force, Roscher-Nielsen answered that he did not know but believed they were outside the country. Roscher-Nielsen's report continues:

"Good," said v. B. "It was really what we had expected and based on that assumption we have prepared a draft for an agreement to a cease-fire, which we will now go through. However, I wish to point out to you in advance that you will have full opportunity to present your objections about the various points and your objections will be carefully weighted and, if possible, accepted."

The OKW situation report from June 10 confirms Roscher-Nielsen's account, "... the negotiator emphasizes strongly that despite the end of fighting in Norway, the war continues. It is stressed that the Norwegian naval and air forces have left Norway with the Allies."[18] Furthermore, the nine-paragraph document signed by Roscher-Nielsen starts with the following statement of purpose, which clearly limits its scope: "In view of the Norwegian 6th Divisions courageous conduct, it is accorded the honorable conditions set forth below in laying down its weapons."[19] The other paragraphs in the document deal with the release of prisoners, weapons, ammunition, equipment, fuel, vehicles, airfields, and the disposition of Norwegian forces along the Soviet border. These forces were permitted to continue their functions under the authority of the provincial governor until German forces could take over those functions. Non-career officers, NCOs, and troops were allowed to proceed to their homes. Career officers and soldiers could chose between giving their word of honor not to participate in hostilities against Germany or its allies in the current war or entering an honorable prisoner-of-war status. Officers were permitted to retain their personal weapons.

General Ruge became a prisoner of war, but he was treated with courtesy and generosity by Dietl, and no efforts were made to interfere with the Norwegian demobilization. Dietl visited Ruge's headquarters on June 12 and Ruge made a reciprocal visit to Dietl's headquarters the following day. Walter Hubatsch takes note of what General Ruge said in his proclamation to the Norwegian people on June 9. The statement "But the war continues on other fronts – Norwegians are participating in that war ..." towards the end of the proclamation are hardly words describing a "total Norwegian capitulation."[20]

Operation *Juno*

The evacuation from Norway was not completed without serious losses. The Germans, without any knowledge about the Allied evacuation, had launched a naval operation in northern waters. In mid-May, OKW held a bleak view of the situation in Narvik. It appeared that Dietl would not be able to hold out much longer, that the weather in the Narvik area was too unpredictable for effective reinforcements by air, and that General Feurstein's troops would not reach Narvik in time to save the 3rd Mountain Division. It was decided to employ German naval forces against the Allied bases and ships in the Harstad-Narvik area in order to reduce the pressure on Dietl's forces. The mission was expanded on May 16 to include protection of sea supply routes for General Feurstein's troops. The operation was given the codename *Juno*.

Admiral Saalwächter issued the directive for the operation to Admiral Wilhelm Marschall, the Commander-in-Chief of the fleet, on May 29. The main objective was to enter Andfjord and Vågsfjord to destroy enemy warships, transports, and base facilities. If the fleet commander found a penetration of Ofotfjord to Narvik possible, that would become the main mission. The protection of the sea routes for supplies to the 2nd Mountain Division was a secondary objective. The forces placed at Admiral Marschall's disposal included the battleships *Gneisenau* (his flagship) and *Scharnhorst*, the heavy cruiser *Admiral Hipper*, and the destroyers *Karl Galster, Hans Lody, Erich Steinbrinck*, and *Hermann Schoemann*.

The German fleet departed Kiel at 0800 hours on June 4 and proceeded northward through Storebelt. It had a rotating escort of He-115s and 111s for portions of the voyage and aggressive air reconnaissance was carried out from bases in Norway. The fleet passed the latitude of Bergen during the night of June 6 and reached a position at the latitude of Harstad, 200 nautical miles southeast of Jan Mayen in the morning of June 7.

Marschall was informed by Group Command West that an analysis of British radio traffic indicated that the British were unaware of the presence of the German fleet. Group Command West kept Marschall informed about the location and movement of British surface units. A report in the evening on June 6 informed Marschall that the battleship *Valiant*, the aircraft carriers *Glorious* and *Ark Royal*, the cruisers *Devonshire, Southampton, Vindictive, Coventry* and about 15 destroyers were in North Norway. A message the following morning reported seven ships about 360 nautical miles northwest of Trondheim on a southwesterly course. These were the ships of the first convoy, carrying about 15,000 Allied troops. Marschall was about 110 nautical miles north of the reported sighting when he received the message. These fast liners were already out of reach of the German fleet. Marschall may have assumed that they were empty ships returning to England and the report did not cause him to change his plan to attack the Harstad area.

Heavy units of the Home Fleet were engaged in a chase after two mysterious warships reported by a British armed merchant ship. These mysterious naval vessels were 200 nautical miles northeast of the Faeroe Islands with a course towards the Faeroe-Iceland gap. Admiral Forbes, fearing a German breakout into the Atlantic, sent a strong naval force consisting of the battle cruisers *Renown* and *Repulse*, the cruisers *Newcastle* and *Sussex*, and five destroyers to chase this sighting. This left the battleships *Rodney* and *Valiant* at Scapa Flow. *Valiant* was sent to meet the first troop convoy, escort it around the Faeroe Islands, and repeat the operation for the second troop convoy two days later.

Marschall assembled his ship captains aboard his flagship in the evening of June 7 to discuss the attack on Harstad, which he intended to carry out during the night of June 8-9. While this conference was taking place, Marschall received a radio report from Group Command West (2155 hours) which read:

> Air reconnaissance reports one cruiser, two destroyers, and two large transports at 1325 at the northern entrance to Andfjord on a westerly course at moderate speed, and two destroyers at 1345, 25 nautical miles from Andenes on a northerly course. Two aircraft carriers and two destroyers were dead in the water at 1400 about 45 nautical miles north of Andenes.[21]

This intelligence was several hours old when received, but it caused Marschall to revise his estimate of the situation. He became convinced that the numerous reports of British ship movements on different courses away from the Norwegian coast indicated that a major movement of warships and transports were underway and that the most important targets would not be found in the fjords around Harstad. An entry in his war journal reads, "It strikes me that that the noteworthy westerly movement [of British ships], may indicate a British evacuation of Norway, and that the convoys on a westerly course present valuable targets."[22]

Marschall decided to operate against the British ships that had been sighted and to await further intelligence before moving against Harstad. He informed Saalwächter of his decision at 0400 hours on June 8. Saalwächter disagreed with Marschall's decision and sent a message stating that the main mission remained as before, the destruction of enemy naval forces in the Harstad-Narvik area. There appears to have been some differences between Saalwächter and the German Naval Staff on this issue, resulting in a compromise which permitted the *Hipper* and the destroyers to search for the merchant convoy.

The Germans encountered the British tanker *Oil Pioneer* and its escort, the armed trawler *Juniper* at 0600 hours on June 8. *Hipper* sank the trawler with gunfire and 29 survivors were taken aboard the German ships. The Germans removed the crew from *Oil Pioneer* and sent the ship to the bottom with torpedoes. The two British ships were unable to send out messages warning other ships.

Aircraft were launched by *Hipper* and *Scharnhorst* to look for the convoy. This led to the sighting of the passenger vessel *Orama* and the hospital ship *Atlantis*. The liner *Orama* was one of the troop transports not used in the evacuation. It was short of fuel and water and she was sent on her way along with the hospital ship without an escort. *Hipper* sank the 20,000-ton *Orama*, carrying 100 German prisoners, and successfully jammed her last radio message. Two hundred seventy-five survivors were taken aboard the cruiser and two destroyers. In accordance with the rules of war, the Germans did not attack *Atlantis*, carrying over 600 wounded, and in accordance with the same rules, *Atlantis* did not report the presence of the German ships until she made a visual signal to the battleship *Valiant* about 24 hours later.

Hipper's reconnaissance aircraft also reported seeing an enemy cruiser and a merchant ship to the south and the two German battleships and the destroyers searched unsuccessfully for these ships while *Hipper* took care of *Orama*. The reported sighting must have been a mistake since there was no British cruiser near that location. It is possible that the aircraft had spotted the *Devonshire* but if this is the case it was serious mistake in position and direction since that cruiser was located to the northwest of the German fleet.

Soon after this encounter, Marschall sent *Hipper* and the destroyers to Trondheim to refuel and to participate in that part of his mission that called for securing the sea route along the coast of Nordland Province. He discontinued his search for additional British transports and headed north with the two battleships, intending to operate between Harstad and Tromsø. He was particularly interested in the two aircraft carriers, which had been reported repeatedly.

Several groups of British ships were meanwhile well within range of the German battleships. Two divisions of the slow convoy were approaching from the northeast. The second troop convoy, carrying about 10,000 troops and escorted by the cruisers *Southampton* and *Coventry*, the aircraft carrier *Ark Royal*, and five destroyers, was also approaching from the northeast. This convoy was heavily outgunned by the two German battleships. The cruiser *Devonshire*, carrying the Norwegian royal family, Government, and Allied diplomats and their families (400 passengers), was located only 80 nautical miles northwest of the German battleships. Then there was the aircraft carrier *Glorious* with its two destroyers, *Acasta* and *Ardent*, about 100 nautical miles behind *Devonshire*.

The land-based British fighter aircraft had maintained their patrols over the evacuation area until the very last moments around midnight on June 7. The original plan was to destroy the aircraft but it was decided to try to land them on the aircraft carriers despite expert opinions that the flight decks were too short for Hurricanes. *Ark Royal* had a slightly longer flight deck, but since the aircraft could not be brought under deck because their wings could not be folded, it was decided that they should land on *Glorious*. The ten Gladiators and eight Hurricanes landed successfully on this aircraft carrier in the early hours of June 8. The landings on an aircraft carrier by pilots who had never before done so and in aircraft not intended for carrier operations was a courageous accomplishment. However, problems for air operations were thereby created. The Gladiators and Hurricanes, whose wings could not be folded, made for a disorderly storage situation.

Glorious and her escorts were thus about 100 nautical miles behind *Devonshire* when one of the worst calamities in British naval history began to unfold. The catastrophe could have been far worse if the Germans had their reconnaissance aircraft aloft since they would undoubtedly have discovered both the *Devonshire* and the second troop convoy.

At 1645 hours on June 8, the lookout on *Scharnhorst* sighted smoke off the starboard bow. The Germans immediately altered course and headed towards the sighting. As they approached they recognized the silhouette of an aircraft carrier. *Glorious*, recognizing the danger, turned away and tried to escape from her pursuers. Admiral Marschall continued on a course that would bring his battleships to the windward of the carrier, forcing that ship to turn towards the Germans if she attempted to turn into the wind to launch her aircraft.

Gneisenau opened fire with her secondary armament against the escorting destroyers at 1728 hours and *Scharnhorst* opened fire on the carrier with her 11-inch guns four minutes later, at a range of 25,000 meters. *Gneisenau* opened fire on the *Glorious* with her main armaments at 1746 hours. This distance far exceeded the range of the 4.7-inch guns on the aircraft carrier. The radio operators on *Glorious* tried to report the presence of the Germans but the Germans believed that they had succeeded in jamming the transmission. The British version is that the initial report was interrupted when a salvo from *Scharnhorst* struck the bridge. No signals were received from the two destroyers, which is strange. The *Devonshire* received a garbled and incomplete message with the words "2 PB" (2 Pocket Battleships). Its authenticity was suspect and Cunningham decided not to break radio silence and possibly give away his position because of the important passengers the cruiser was carrying.

Scharnhorst found the range with her third salvo and a projectile penetrated and exploded in the forward hanger among the Hurricanes that were stored there. The spreading fire made it impossible to get any of the Swordfish aircraft aloft. About 1800 hours, an 11-inch shell hit the carrier's bridge, killing the captain and destroying the steering controls. The two destroyer escorts laid a smoke screen that successfully concealed the carrier, now on a southeasterly course, for about 20 minutes.

The destroyer *Ardent* turned back through the smoke and launched her torpedoes at *Gneisenau*. The German battleship avoided the torpedoes by evasive maneuvers that bought the carrier a few more minutes of survival but both German ships opened fire at the British destroyer with their secondary armaments. The devastating German fire tore the British destroyer apart and caused her to capsize and sink within four minutes.

Glorious now emerged into view from behind the smoke and both German battleships opened fire on her with their main armaments. An 11-inch shell struck the aft part of the carrier and this sealed her fate. At 1820 hours, the order to abandon ship was given and the Germans ceased firing at the sinking ship at 1843 hours as the carrier was showing a 40-degree list. It sank at 1908 hours.

With *Ardent* sunk and *Glorious* sinking, no one would have faulted Lieutenant Commander C. E. Glasfurd, the captain of *Acasta*, if he had tried to disengage and save his destroyer. For a while, it appeared to the crew that he had chosen this course. Leading Seaman C. Carter, the only survivor from *Acasta* tells the story:

> On board our ship, what a deathly calm, hardly a word spoken, the ship was now steaming full speed away from the enemy. Then came a host of orders, prepare all smoke floats, hose-pipes connected up, various other jobs were prepared. We were still steaming away from the enemy, and making smoke, and all our smoke floats had been set going. The Captain, then had this message passed to all positions: "You may think we are running away from the enemy, we are not, our chummy ship has sunk, the *Glorious* is sinking, the least we can do is make a show, good luck to you all."[23]

After that message to his crew, Lieutenant Commander Glasfurd made a 180-degree turn into his own smoke. As the destroyer exited the smoke, it made a starboard turn and fired its port torpedoes against *Scharnhorst* at a distance of 14,000 meters. Despite evasive action, one torpedo hit the battleship on the starboard side near the aft turret at 1840 hours as she was coming back to her original course, killing two officers and 46 men. The explosion put the aft turret out of commission and caused flooding that forced the shutdown of the amidships and starboard main engines. This reduced the battleship's maximum speed to 20 knots. *Acasta* reentered the smoke screen without receiving fire but as she emerged from the smoke for another torpedo attack, the Germans were ready. The *Gneisenau*, which had tried to keep the enemy in sight, sent a rain of projectiles from her secondary armament at a range of 10,000 meters against the destroyer, registering a number of hits. One hit in the aft of the ship caused a violent explosion. *Acasta*, making only five knots and partially shielded in the smoke, kept firing her guns at the adversary and scored a hit near Turret C on the *Scharnhorst* without causing any severe damage. *Gneisenau* turned away at 1916 hours to look after *Scharnhorst*, leaving *Acasta* motionless with fires covering two-thirds of the ship. *Acasta* sank shortly thereafter. Leading Seaman Carter continues his story:

> I will always remember the Surgeon Lieutenant [Lieutenant H. J. Stammers], his first ship, his first action. Before I jumped over the side, I saw him still attending to the wounded, a hopeless task, and when I was in the water I saw the Captain leaning over the bridge, take a cigarette from a case and light it. We shouted to him to come on our raft, he waved "Good-bye and good luck" – the end of a gallant man.

The German reports are full of praise for the gallant and skillful actions of the two British destroyers. The two German battleships had fired a total of 387 11-inch and 1,448 6-inch shells against the British. This was a lot of munitions but represented only 20% of what they had available and there was therefore plenty left to continue the operation.

Instead, Marschall decided to break off the operation and escort the damaged *Scharnhorst* to Trondheim. Based on the information at hand, his decision is understandable. However, the wisdom of his earlier decision to send *Hipper* and the four destroyers to Trondheim to refuel in preparation for a secondary mission is questionable. If he had not done so, he could have sent the damaged *Scharnhorst* back to Trondheim with a destroyer escort and continued the operation with the *Gneisenau* and the heavy cruiser. There is a high probability that these ships would have encountered the second troop convoy steaming unknowingly towards the scene of the disaster. However, this is only apparent in retrospect.

Hindsight is not needed to see the grievous mistakes made by the British Admiralty and Forbes. While the British were preoccupied with events in France and the threat of a cross-Channel invasion, this does not explain why the heavy units of the Royal Navy were kept at anchor in Scapa Flow or in the waters north of Scotland. The Home Fleet was not responsible for either the operations in the Channel or off Norway but, as pointed out by Moulton, the "cover for both was surely its prime responsibility." Admiral Forbes had the battle cruisers *Repulse* and *Renown*, the battleships *Rodney* and *Valiant*, and several cruisers and destroyers at his disposal. Part of this powerful force was sent north to reinforce the Northern Patrol and to investigate reports of a German landing in Iceland.

It appears that the battleship *Valiant* and four destroyers were sent out to meet the first troop convoy more as an afterthought. When *Valiant* learned from the hospital ship *Atlantis* on June 9 that two German battleships were in the waters off Norway, she headed for the second convoy at full speed. *Valiant* also notified Forbes who finally left with the *Rodney, Renown,* and six destroyers. He also ordered the *Repulse,* two cruisers, and three destroyers, still near Iceland, to join him.

In the official British history, Derry concludes that Operation *Juno* "achieved by luck a considerable success for which it was not designed." This may be technically true but it is also misleading. The British were the ones who were lucky. Had it not been for the gallant self-sacrifice of the two destroyers and Glasfurd's lucky torpedo, Marschall would have continued his operation and probably located and destroyed the *Devonshire* as well as the second convoy. The sinking of *Devonshire* would have had far-reaching political repercussions and would have been a severe blow to Britain's naval reputation. The loss of this ship, a second carrier, and the second convoy with approximately 20,000 troops, passengers, and crewmembers would truly have been calamitous.

The Admiralty and Forbes made the dangerous error of assuming that the lack of evidence for actual or intended German naval operations off Norway meant that they did not intend or were incapable of such operations. As in the case of the invasion in April, they based their decisions on what they viewed as the most likely German course of action rather than on German capabilities and the most dangerous course of action.

Captain MacIntyre may be correct in his conclusion that divided authority on the British side contributed to the disaster. Churchill's appointment of Admiral Cork, much senior to Admiral Forbes, to command an area within the Home Fleet's region of responsibility was bound to create confusion and misjudgments but it is also a damaging conclusion about the professionalism at the highest levels of the Royal Navy at this stage of the war. Marschall was recalled for his perceived errors during Operation *Juno*. No action was taken against commanders of the Home Fleet.

The loss of one of the four carriers available was severe for the British Navy. Few survivors were rescued. The Norwegian ship *Borgund* rescued 38 men from *Glorious* and the lone survivor from *Acasta* on June 11 and brought them to the Faeroe Islands. Two were also rescued by a German seaplane. In all, 1,515 lost their lives. All aircraft and pilots from Norway that could have been used in the looming Battle of Britain were lost.

Admiral Marschall took the *Gneisenau*, *Hipper*, and four destroyers back to sea on June 10 to continue the operation against the convoys. The sortie did not lead to any contacts and was cancelled by Naval Group West when it concluded that the Allied evacuation was completed and there was therefore nothing of importance to be accomplished in the north. Marschall brought his ships to Trondheim in the morning of June 11. On that day, 12 aircraft from Bomber Command carried out an unsuccessful attack against the German ships. Early on 13 June, 15 Skuas from *Ark Royal* attacked the German ships in their anchorage in Trondheim. One 500-lb bomb struck *Scharnhorst* but rolled overboard without detonating. Eight British aircraft were downed by antiaircraft fire and fighters.

Admiral Lütjens took *Gneisenau* and *Hipper* back to sea on June 20. He headed for the Iceland-Faeroe Island gap in an attempt to divert British attention from *Scharnhorst's* return to Germany. *Gneisenau* was hit by a torpedo from the British submarine *Clyde* shortly before midnight on June 20 while 40 nautical miles off the Norwegian coast. The torpedo tore a large hole through both sides of the forward portion of the battleship. No armaments were affected and there were no casualties. However, the sortie was aborted and the ships returned to Trondheim to make emergency repairs.

It was decided that the battleship needed to return to Germany in order to make more extensive repairs. A fleet consisting of *Gneisenau*, *Hipper*, the light cruiser *Nürnberg*, and the destroyers *Galster*, *Ihn*, *Lody*, and *Jacobi* left

Trondheim on July 25. Five torpedo boats were later added as escorts. The torpedo boat *Luchs* happened to be in the track of a torpedo fired at *Gneisenau* by a British submarine. The torpedo boat sank after a violent explosion. The German ships arrived in Kiel in the morning of July 28. Operation *Juno* was concluded after eight weeks.

NOTES

1 Sandvik, *Operasjone*, vol. 2, p. 201.

2 As quoted in Derry, *The Norway Campaign*, p. 174.

3 Halvdan Koht, pp. 138-139. It is worth noting the very accurate impression Foreign Minister Koht arrived at as a result of his visit to Paris and London. "This idea about the Swedish iron ore had become so deeply imbedded among the English and French that it appeared they believed that this was the factor which would decide the whole war. In addition, I have no doubt that it was this idea that made Narvik such a main element in Allied war plans. Otherwise, Narvik had little strategic value. When I returned to Norway, it was expected that it was only a matter of days before the Germans in Narvik had to give up and my belief that the Allies then planned to enter Sweden and occupy the iron ore district grew in strength."

4 Sereau, *L'Expedition*, p. 84.

5 As quoted in Connell, *Auchinleck*, pp. 139-141.

6 Moulton, *Study of Warfare*, p. 248.

7 Connell, *Auchinleck*, pp. 145-146.

8 Hubatsch, 253 and Ziemke, *The German Northern Theater*, p. 103.

9 Steen, *Norges Sjøkrig 1940-1945*, vol. 4, p. 272.

10 Hovland, *Fleischer*, p. 220.

11 The report in a private archive of an interview with Koht on June 26, 1947 is cited by Hovland, *Fleischer*, p. 223.

12 Lie, *Norge i Krig*, pp. 233-234.

13 Hovland, *Fleischer*, p. 221.

14 Steen, *Norges Sjøkrig 1940-1945*, vol. 4, p. 282. This accidental engagement is described differently by Captain MacIntyre (pp. 205-206): "Sir Geoffrey Congreve's irregular command, the self-styled H.M.S. *Raven*, was given the task of destroying the oil tanks at Solfolla, north of Bodo. Having duly set them ablaze, she encountered an enemy corvette considerably more heavily armed than herself, but boldly went after it in company with a trawler. A strange game of hide-and-seek followed amongst the narrow channels between the islands; but unable to come to grips with the faster enemy vessel, his solitary long range gun, an Army Bofors, having only time-fused self-destroying ammunition, Congreve was forced to abandon the pursuit and continue his interrupted journey to Scapa Flow."

15 Birger Godtaas, *Fra 9. april til 7. juni. Episoder og opplevelser fra krigen i Norge* (Oslo: J. Dybwad, 1945), p.235, as quoted in Berg and Vollan, *Fjellkrigen*, p. 418.

16 Hovland, *Fleischer*, p. 236.

17 Reports by Lieutenant Colonels Holm and Roscher-Nielsen as quoted in Sandvik, *Operasjone*, vol. 2, p. 310.

18 Hubatsch, Annex A, Die Lageberichte des Wehrmachtführungsstabes über die Besetzung von Dänemark u. Norwegen 7. April – 14. Juni 1940, p. 373.

19 As quoted in Munthe-Kaas, *Krigen*, p. 213.

20 Hubatsch, p. 256 and Ruge, *Felttoget*, p.195.

21 As quoted in Steen, *Norges Sjøkrig 1940-1945*, vol. 4, p. 269.

22 As quoted in loc cit.

23 Churchill, *The Gathering Storm*, p. 655.

EPILOGUE

"It was a marvel—I really do not know how—I survived and maintained my position in public esteem while all the blame was thrown on poor Mr. Chamberlain."

CHURCHILL'S REFLECTION ON THE NORWEGIAN CAMPAIGN IN HIS DRAFT OF *THE GATHERING STORM,* AS QUOTED BY DAVID REYNOLDS.

The Human and Material Costs of the Campaign

In comparison to other theaters of operations in World War II, the losses in lives in Norway were small. However, when viewed against the number of combatants involved (about 100,000 German, 55,000 Norwegians, and 38,000 Allied), the number of casualties in the 62-day campaign came to over six percent. Even today, some of the statistics covering losses vary and are misleading, particularly as they apply to specific actions. Ash's statement that "German Army casualties were a good third higher than the casualties of the Norwegians and all the Allied units put together," even when losses at sea are discounted, is not supported by figures released by the various participants. Norwegian and Allied casualties on land were about 25% higher than those of the Germans.

One example of these discrepancies is the two-day engagement between British and German troops at Kvam, in which 54 British soldiers fell and are buried at the Kvam Cemetery. Norwegian and British eye witness accounts, which prevailed in the postwar period, told about a large number of German killed and that their bodies were cremated on large wooden funeral pyres. Kersaudy, writing in 1989, claims that there were over 50 Germans killed at Kvam.

Official German sources give different statistics for this action that are confirmed by records of the Norwegian War Cemetery Service. The Germans claimed that they lost ten killed in the Kvam engagement and Norwegian cemetery records show that 13 Germans were buried in Kvam, three of those apparently killed in nearby areas. Furthermore, it was not customary for the Germans to cremate their fallen, at least not at this stage of the war.

Another problem that should be kept in mind when looking at the casualty figures is the very low number of wounded in relation to the number killed. Historically the ratio of wounded to killed in land combat is greater than 3:1. This ratio has increased over the years as means of evacuation and field medical services have improved. Nevertheless, Norwegian statistics show a ratio of less than 1:1. Similarly, the ratio resulting from German figures for land combat losses, gives us a ratio of killed to wounded of roughly 1:1.2. It is possible that the Germans and Norwegians used a more restrictive classification for those that they listed as wounded. For example, they may not have counted as wounded troops that were able to return to duty during the campaign. The terrain and climatic conditions under which the fighting took place contribute to this low ratio. Evacuation of wounded in a timely manner was difficult. Most British, French, and Polish sources do not break down the figures into killed, wounded, or missing and their losses at sea are not included. By using the figures that are available, it appears that there were about 12,000 military casualties in the 62-day campaign. Probably about 70% of these were killed.

The official German figure for losses in the Norwegian campaign is 5,296 killed, wounded, and missing. Hubatsch and Moulton give a figure of 5,660 but this includes the small number that died in the invasion of Denmark. German records break the 5,296 figure into 1,317 killed, 1,604 wounded and 2,375 lost at sea. This last number includes over 1,000 who were killed when *Blücher* was sunk in the Dröbak Strait.

On the Allied side, British casualties are listed as 1,869 killed, wounded, and missing while those of the French and Poles are given as 533. These do not include losses at sea where at least 2,500 perished.

Norwegian losses have not been established with complete accuracy, even today. Most sources list about 860 killed. Lindbäck-Larsen places the number of killed and wounded at about 1,700, not including the approximately 400 civilians who died during the campaign.

The loss of military equipment was most serious for the Allies. Most losses occurred in the five evacuations that they undertook from Åndalsnes, Namsos, Mosjøen, Bodø, and Narvik. The Germans ended up with a net gain in this area, due primarily to the sudden capture of Norwegian depots and the surrender of Norwegian Army units.

The naval losses in the campaign were significant. The German Navy was prepared for the loss of more than half its fleet. That expectation was largely realized. Among the larger units of the German Navy, both battleships were damaged. Of the three heavy cruisers involved in the operation, one was sunk, one badly damaged, and the third sustained moderate damage but it returned to service during the campaign. Two of the four light cruisers were sunk and one was damaged. Ten destroyers, six submarines, two large torpedo boats, and 15 lighter units were also lost. Six destroyers sustained various degrees of damage, as did many lighter units. Churchill stresses the importance of these losses:

> On the other hand, at the end of June, 1940, a momentous date, the effective German Fleet consisted of no more than one eight-inch cruiser, two light cruisers, and four destroyers. Although many of their damaged ships, like ours, could be repaired, the German Navy was no factor in the supreme issue of the invasion of Britain.[1]

Churchill overstates the case. It is debatable whether the German Navy as it existed before the invasion of Norway could have seriously interfered with the Dunkirk evacuation or tempted the Germans to undertake an invasion of Great Britain in 1940 unless they also achieved air superiority. There is no doubt, however, that the German naval losses gave the British considerable comfort during a period of continuous bad news.

The Norwegians effectively lost their whole navy. Two destroyers made their way to Great Britain from western Norway. A number of smaller ships escaped to England from both western and northern Norway. However, for the most part, the naval units were sunk, scuttled, or captured. Within a relatively short period, the Germans put about 50 captured vessels into service. With the exception of a minelayer and two destroyers, these were small or obsolete units.

The Allies also sustained heavy, but not crippling, naval losses. The most serious was the aircraft carrier *Glorious*. In addition, the British lost two cruisers, seven destroyers, one sloop, four submarines, and a number of armed trawlers. The French and Poles each lost one destroyer and one submarine. The British also had six cruisers, eight destroyers, and two sloops disabled but repairable.

Aircraft losses in the Norwegian Campaign were relatively light and had minor effects on the future conduct of the war. Statistics given for aircraft losses vary significantly. Kersaudy writes that the Luftwaffe lost 240 planes, including 80 transports. These are essentially the same numbers used by Derry. Ziemke puts German air losses at 127 combat aircraft and this is ten more than given by Hubatsch. Levsen, quoting official German sources, place the total number of German aircraft lost at 90.

Except for some aircraft flown to England or interned in Finland, the Norwegians lost all their aircraft. British air losses are placed at 112. These losses had little effect on future operations, because the Gladiators were too slow and cumbersome to have made a difference in the Battle of Britain.

The losses in transports and other merchant ships were significant, especially for the Germans. They lost 21 transports with a tonnage of 111,700, or about ten percent of available shipping. Levsen writes that the Allies lost over 70 transports. This number, if correct, must include Norwegian ships.

Von Falkenhorst assessed the losses in the Norwegian Campaign as surprisingly light, justified, and acceptable. He writes that much greater losses were expected, particularly because of British and French naval superiority. It must be remembered that he wrote the assessment against the background of the horrible losses sustained during the remainder of World War II.

Achievement of Objectives

The Germans achieved most of their objectives in what must be viewed as a stunning military success in the face of overwhelming odds. The source of iron ore was secured and the navy was able to remove some of the limitations imposed on it by geography. The occupation of Norway not only complicated British blockade measures but also cracked open the door to the Atlantic for possible interference with the British supplies coming from overseas. The air threat to the Baltic by a British presence in Norway was avoided, as was the possibility of Sweden falling into the Allied orbit.

If the diplomatic effort had been as thoroughly prepared as the military, the German success could have been even more spectacular and the campaign might have been avoided. The fault must be placed at Hitler's feet. Ribbentrop and his Foreign Office were kept in the dark about the plans for Scandinavia for security reasons.

By April 10, it was obvious that the Norwegians would resist and that a solution along the lines achieved in Denmark could only be achieved by modifications in the original ultimatum. Colonel Eriksen's action had saved the government from capture and the Germans knew that the Norwegians were mobilizing. The German demands were not modified and Hitler's action in allowing Quisling to form a government in Oslo only served to increase Norwegian defiance. Finally, German attempts to capture or kill the Norwegian Government by Captain Spiller's raid and the bombing of Elverum, removed all possibilities of coming to an understanding.

French objectives, primarily to avoid or reduce the threat to their homeland by opening a new theater of war, were not achieved. The protracted war in Scandinavia and the consequent drain on German resources did not materialize. In divisional strength, only about five percent of the German Army was employed in Norway when Hitler attacked in the west. The conquest of Denmark was so quick that the combat forces employed there were available for use in the west by May.

British desires to get the Germans involved in an operation in Scandinavia were achieved but the quick victories that had been envisioned were unrealized. The German source of iron ore from Sweden was in fact secured. Sweden came under the sway of Berlin and the supply route through the Baltic was safer than before the operation.

Churchill did get Germany to react to earlier violations of Norwegian neutrality and the possibility that the Allies intended to establish themselves in Norway. However, rather than a reaction to the Allied mining, it was a full-fledged preemptive invasion that had been in planning for three months. The hope that quick victories could be achieved by enticing the Germans into an area where they would confront enormous British naval superiority was not realized. While the German Navy sustained heavy losses, the hoped for easy victories turned into a humiliating defeat.

For Norway, its policy of neutrality backed by inadequate military resources brought disaster to the country and increased suffering to its people during a five-year occupation. It is doubtful if Hitler would have undertaken the invasion if Norway had possessed a military establishment on the scale and quality, which wiser political and military leaders had provided for in World War I.

Some Reasons for German Military Success

When looking at the reason for Norwegian/Allied failure, it is most convenient to break the analysis into two periods. The first period covers the time leading up to and including the landings. The second period covers subsequent operations. Much of the German success in the initial part of the operation was due to luck and the Norwegian and Allied failure to act in a rational manner.

There can be no doubt that the German invasion would have met with disaster if Norway and the Allies had responded appropriately to the many warnings they received in the week or two leading up to April 9. A full or partial mobilization between April 5 and April 9 would have changed the events on April 9, as well as the conduct of subsequent operations. Even more limited defensive measures, such as laying minefields, full manning of coastal fortresses, and adequate infantry protection for airfields, would have made the task of the invading forces more difficult. Such measures may have prevented the quick capture of mobilization centers and depots as well as the German success in capturing the airfields at Fornebu and Sola.

The Allies and Norwegians placed too much faith in the Royal Navy and consequently underestimated German capabilities and the potential threat to the western and northern portions of Norway. The pre-conceived notion that Germany could not undertake operations in these areas led to a rejection of some of the more explicit warnings.

The British Navy could have done much more to hinder the German invasion. The obsession of its leaders with a possible German breakout into the Atlantic caused them to overlook possibilities even more damaging to their own interests by failing to search for German naval units in areas where they could be expected to be found in an invasion scenario.

Admiral Forbes' delay in sailing from Scapa Flow to a central location in the North Sea after the sighting on April 7, allowed the main German fleet to pass the latitude where it could be intercepted. The concern with a breakout continued even after the composition of the various German flotillas indicated that they were not structured for high sea operations.

The Admiralty insistence on overwhelming superiority also worked in the Germans' favor. *R4* was abandoned at the very moment when the situation for which it was held in readiness arose. If the panic-like debarkation of the troops for *R4* had not taken place, these could have been committed much earlier and with all their equipment intact. This damaging decision, taken solely by the navy, caused a chaotic equipment and supply situation for the forces when they were eventually deployed.

The Admiralty's interference in operational matters on four different occasions in the critical 24-hour invasion period resulted in an amazing series of miscalculations and missed opportunities. First, the cruiser screen on the Norwegian coast south of Bergen was removed only hours before they would have encountered Task Force 3. Then the attack on Bergen was cancelled at a time when the Luftwaffe threat was still a minor factor. The withdrawal of the naval units in the Vestfjord approach to Narvik and Admiral Whitworth's subsequent withdrawal from the area left the gate to Narvik unguarded. Finally, Warburton-Lee's destroyer flotilla was dispatched to Narvik under unfavorable conditions. These actions had a great effect on subsequent operations.

The paralyzed behavior of the Norwegian Government in the immediate aftermath of the German landings, the irrational mobilization decision, and premature withdrawals in the region around Oslo facilitated the efforts by the Germans to secure their beachheads. Likewise, the failure of the Allies to settle quickly on an appropriate strategy and the hurried dispatch of disorganized and ill-equipped forces without clear missions created delays and uncertainties.

Without Admiralty interference and Whitworth's withdrawal, Narvik might have remained in Norwegian hands and the divisive debate over strategy – Narvik versus Trondheim – would not have taken place. In the debate over strategy, Churchill's insistenced on the importance of Narvik led to an unfortunate compromise that split the Allied effort, with the best troops employed in Narvik. This compromise apparently ignored the fact that Trondheim was the key objective. Capturing and holding central Norway would have made the German position in Narvik untenable. The recapture of Narvik at the expense of giving up the Trondheim area had little effect on the eventual outcome of the campaign.

The invasion of Norway was history's first three-dimensional military campaign and it illustrated the dangers of not using the three elements in harmony. The Luftwaffe has been identified by most writers as a factor of decisive importance. Derry and Roskill emphasise its undermining of sea power and conclude that the period of fleet operations without air cover was over. Moulton and Liddell-Hart view British failure to understand the concept of three-dimensional warfare as a root cause for the defeat. It was not only the physical damage inflicted by the Luftwaffe but the psychological effects of its domination of the skies over the battlefield and the rear areas that had to be taken into account. In his after-action report on operations in Norway, General Auchinleck writes, "that to commit troops to a campaign in which they cannot be provided with adequate air support is to court disaster."[2]

The British air force was never much interested in the Norwegian operations. It was responsible for the defense of Great Britain and the forces in France and saw the operations in Norway as an unwelcome distraction. This is at least a partial explanation for the failure to provide adequate air units to support operations in Norway. The fleet air arm proved incapable in countering the German air threat. This was partially due to the type of aircraft employed but also because the carriers stayed so far offshore that they could not effectively support the troops fighting in the valleys of eastern Norway or north of Trondheim.

The movement of troops, equipment, and supplies into Norway by air was history's largest airlift operation up to that time. The Norwegians and the Allies also underestimated the German capability to move reinforcements and supplies by air to isolated beachheads. This was an important factor in saving General Dietl's forces at Narvik and supplying General Feurstein's drive through Nordland Province. The air-bridge established to Oslo and from Oslo to Trondheim allowed for a rapid build-up of forces in both areas.

Operations in Norway gave the Allies their first taste of the German doctrine of close air support for ground operations. Norwegian and British forces were unable to counter the devastating effectiveness of coordinated German ground and air operations. In this respect, the operation in Norway was a curtain raiser for what was soon to follow on the western front.

The Allies also failed to provide their troops with adequate artillery and anti-tank weapons, leaving their troops helpless against German employment of only a few light tank units in eastern Norway.

The British command structure was not geared for quick decision-making. The time-consuming coordination between the British cabinet and its subsidiary committees was nothing short of disastrous when trying to cope with the tempo of German operations. Most issues requiring quick decisions were debated and studied in a leisurely manner more appropriate for a peacetime environment. Studies and recommendations were thrown back and forth between committees until it was too late. The events leading to the cancellation of *Hammer* is a typical example. The only member in the War Cabinet with any experience in military matters was Churchill, and it is not an overstatement to say that his experience and views were primarily focused on naval matters.

The Norwegian campaign revealed the glaring inadequacies in inter-allied cooperation and coordination. Mistrust, suspicions, and too much emphasis on national versus coalition objectives infected the decision-making apparatus. The cavalier and insensitive manner in which the British treated their brothers-in-arms, particularly the Norwegians, had a deleterious effect on the campaign.

One aspect of the campaign in Norway that is often neglected is the effect of differences in operational philosophies. These differences, and their effects, are illustrated repeatedly in this book. German officers and NCOs were taught to expect the unexpected on the battlefield and were instructed to deviate from plans in order to achieve their goals. Higher German commanders intervened in operations of subordinate units to a far lesser extent than the Allied commanders, who tended to be schooled in a much more centralized operational philosophy. The Germans expected quick decisions and equally quick execution, a cornerstone in the German military doctrine. The speed at which operations at all levels were executed resulted in keeping an opponent, operating under more centralized and methodical guidelines, off balance. There is a long-standing principle that one of the most lucrative objectives for a military commander is the mind of the enemy commander. The Germans achieved this objective by confusing, demoralizing, and paralyzing the enemy through unrelenting pressure.

The operations in eastern Norway, in Trøndelag, and in Nordland Province are full of examples of how well the differences in the two doctrines worked to Germany's advantage.

In their after-action and lessons learned reports, the Germans show a relatively high regard for the operations of smaller Norwegian units, particularly in defensive operations. Special mention is given to ski units and to the marksmanship abilities of the average Norwegian soldier. However, they held a rather low opinion of how larger units functioned. The Norwegian lack of large-scale maneuvers and exercises in the 1930s was telling, and their rather rigid operational philosophy translated into weakness on the battlefield.

The Germans viewed the British units as having low morale, poor self-reliance, and lacking fighting qualities and spirit. This is an interesting observation in view of General Auchinleck's confidential report on June 19, 1940. An abridged version of this report was published in 1947 but two paragraphs were suppressed:

> The comparison between the efficiency of the French contingent and that of British troops operating under similar conditions has driven this lesson home to all in this theatre, though this was not altogether a matter of equipment.
>
> By comparison with the French, or the Germans, either for that matter, our men for the most part seemed distressingly young, not so much in years as in self-reliance and manliness generally. They give an impression of being callow and undeveloped, which is not reassuring for the future, unless our methods of man-mastership and training for war can be made more realistic and less effeminate.[3]

As later years in the war would demonstrate, a great deal had to do with poor training and inadequate equipment.

The Long Term Effects

There is no doubt that the occupation of Norway was a constant drain on German resources. At times, nearly a half million men from the armed forces were tied up in Norway. Nevertheless, it is highly unlikely that the resources tied up in Norway could have had any major influence on the events in other theaters of war.

Hitler, like Churchill, had what can be characterized as an unhealthy preoccupation with Scandinavia, particularly Norway. Hitler was extremely proud of having pulled off the "sauciest" military operation of the war, against virtually all military principles except surprise and against the almost unanimous views of the renowned German General Staff. He undoubtedly viewed Norway as a trophy attesting to his military genius and wanted to protect that trophy at nearly any cost. He continued to maintain, "Norway is the zone of destiny in this war" and demanded unconditional obedience to all edicts pertaining to its defense.[5] Concern about Norway after the British/Norwegian commando raid on Vågsø in December 1941 was the reason for ordering the battleships *Scharnhorst, Gneisenau,* and the heavy cruiser *Prinz Eugen* to make the famous Channel dash in February 1942 and for subsequently stationing most of the German fleet in Norway.

Was this expenditure of resources warranted by the advantages obtained? Let us first look at what is considered a primary motive for Hitler's move against Norway, iron ore. While the harbor facilities in Narvik were so damaged that the first shipments of iron ore from that port could not tale place for over seven months, the Germans shipped over 600,000 tons through Narvik in 1941. This amounted to no more than 25% of what had flowed through that port in 1939 but by 1943, it was back up to 1.8 million tons. Shipments from Swedish ports more than compensated for the reduced volume going through Narvik. While the successful German offensive in the west secured a 14 million ton annual supply of iron ore from the French and Luxembourg mines, Hubatsch claims that the flow of Swedish ore made the great battles of 1942-44 possible for the Germans.

While the German Navy obtained bases for a wider starting line against the British, the problem was that the naval losses sustained in the invasion and the cancellation of most of the building program in the famous *Z plan*, made obtaining these bases rather meaningless. Furthermore, the German Navy acquired excellent harbors on the Atlantic after the fall of France but this could also not have been anticipated. The advantages secured by a less restricted access to the Atlantic were countered by the British occupation of Iceland in May 1940. Aircraft operating from Iceland and the Faeroe Islands were able to patrol the gateways to the Atlantic, including the strait between Iceland and Greenland. While the movement of the heavy units of the German fleet to the fjords of northern Norway in 1942 presented a potent threat against the Murmansk convoys, the concentration of most of the German fleet in Norwegian waters was welcomed by the Royal Navy.

German occupation of Norway complicated British blockade measures. They were also forced to prepare to defend against air and naval threats from the Scandinavian Peninsula. However, these threats were more than offset by the resources Germany needed to employ to defend against the reverse threat of Allied raids and possible invasion.

Nevertheless, all of this fails to address adequately the question of advantages versus disadvantages. We have to place ourselves in the position of the German planners and ask what the situation would have been for the Germans if the Allies had seized strategic points in Norway. This would have allowed them to exert pressure on Sweden and Finland and eliminate Swedish export of iron ore to Germany. Allied air power would be more effective in the Baltic and over German ports on the southern shores of that sea. An Allied presence in Norway would probably have kept Finland from joining Germany in its attack on the Soviet Union and Stalin would not have had to worry about an Arctic front or a threat to his supply line from the United States. While the wisdom of the German preoccupation with Norway was an advantage or an unnecessary drain on its resources is debatable, Hitler was not paranoid when he concluded that an Allied occupation of Norway would be of decisive importance for the outcome of the war.

Those in Germany who secretly hoped for a failure in Norway that would weaken Hitler's hold on power were silenced. In fact, the stunning success strengthened Hitler's popularity. His military advisers became increasingly reluctant to argue against his plans. To some, he took on the qualities of a genius. The incidents of Hitler losing his nerve when confronting the possibility of failure were forgotten in the elation of success and they did not resurface as serious issues until the military reverses in the east and in North Africa. Hitler's international standing was also elevated by the series of military successes from Poland, to Norway, to the Low Countries and France. This was offset by the hardening of public opinion against Germany in neutral countries, particularly in the United States.

The initial effect on the British was negative. Their inability to confront the Germans successfully in Norway reduced their standing as a military power and this was reinforced by the calamity in France. In a strange twist of history, Churchill, who was largely responsible for some of the most serious mistakes in Norway not only survived politically but also became Prime Minister. His eloquence and determination became factors of immense importance as he became the personification of Allied determination to prevail. Churchill himself was surprised by his political survival. In the initial draft about these events he wrote, "it was a marvel – I really do not know how – I survived and maintained my position in public esteem while all the blame was thrown on poor Mr. Chamberlain."[6]

The British put their lessons from Norway to good use but there remained resistance to the recognition of the problems and the necessary corrective actions. Although Churchill had toyed with the idea of restructuring the cumbersome command structure earlier, the fiasco in Norway gave impetus to the effort. The reorganization did away with some of the maze of committees involved in planning and decision-making. A Ministry of Defense was created and a system of theater commanders was established. These reorganizations eliminated some of the most serious command structure problems that had plagued the operations in Norway.

The operational lessons were also taken to heart. British troops were not again sent into battle in the sad state that they were in Norway. There was increased emphasis on training. The problem of close air support for ground troops was addressed and it became an increasingly important factor in future operations. The British were impressed by the innovative German use of airborne and air assault forces to seize airfields and this gave an impetus to the development of similar capabilities.

While the lessons from the Norwegian campaign led to important improvements in the planning and conduct of combined operations, their importance should not be overstated. As Kersaudy points out, some of the mistakes were repeated at Dakar, Crete, and Dieppe and it was only through the resistance of military advisers, that Churchill was kept from carrying out major landings in Norway later in the war.

Improved inter-allied cooperation and coordination was forced on the British more by the developing situation than by lessons learned from Norway. As the war became worldwide, the British sometimes found themselves in the unaccustomed situation of being a junior member of a coalition of great powers.

This uncomfortable position required a revision of some traditional thinking and the establishment of new command structures. The eventual success of the more compromising approach was due in large measure to the leadership of Churchill and Roosevelt. They recognized that coalition warfare requires compromises and accepted the necessity that coalition goals take precedence over more parochial ones.

The Allies obtained the willing service of the 4.8 million ton Norwegian merchant fleet. The service and sacrifice of this fleet was a vital factor in the survival of Britain, particularly in the critical period 1940-1942.

The German invasion had a profound effect on Norwegian policies over the next two generations. There was no return to the policy of neutrality. Norway embraced collective security and became a charter member of the North Atlantic Treaty Organization. While Norway has elected not to become a member of the European Union, there remains strong support for the traditional security system that came into being after the war.

NOTES

1 Churchill, *The Gathering Storm*, p. 657.

2 PRO, *WO* 106/1882 45965 – "Extract from report on Operations in Northern Norway from 13 May to 8 June 1940 by Lt Gen CJE Auchinleck."

3 PRO, *WO* 106/1882 45965 and Connell, *Auchinleck*, p. 149. Churchill was unhappy with Auchinleck's performance as illustrated by a notation quoted in Adams, *The Doomed Expedition*, p. 281: "I hope before any fresh appointments is given to General Auchinleck, the whole story of the slack and feeble manner in which the operations at Narvik were conducted, and the failure to make an earlier assault on Narvik town, will be considered …" The general's frank critique of the operations probably did not improve his standings in certain circles in London.

5 Joseph H. Devins Jr., *The Vaagso Raid* , (Philadelphia: Chilton Book Company, 1968), p. 202.

6 As quoted in David Reynolds, *In Command of History* (New York: Random House, 2005), p. 125.

MAPS

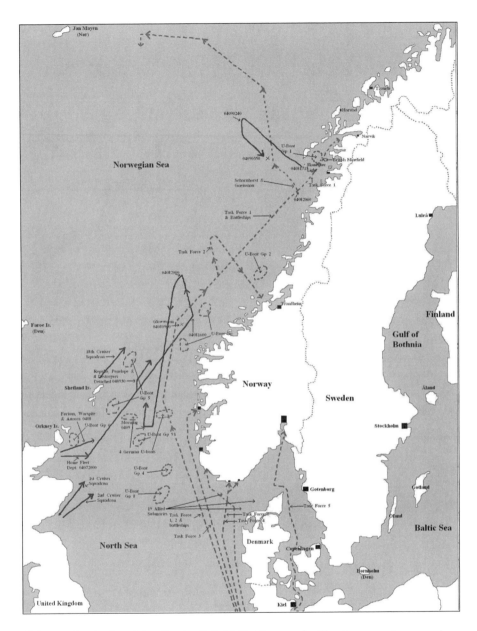

Ships passing in the night. On April 8, 1940, German flotillas, in a surprise operation, were able to slip through the teeth of British naval superiority to begin the invasion of Norway.

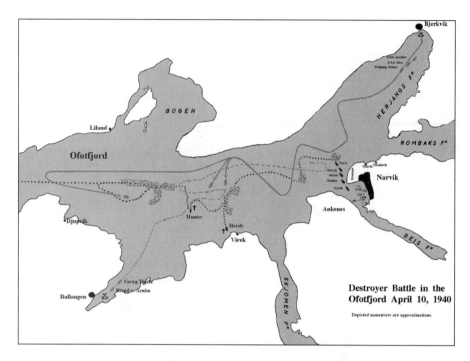

Above: British warships attacking the Germans on the approaches to Narvik. Below: The Battle of Bjørnefjell on April 16 saw German troops surprising and defeating a larger Norwegian force, thus securing the all-important railway line to Sweden.

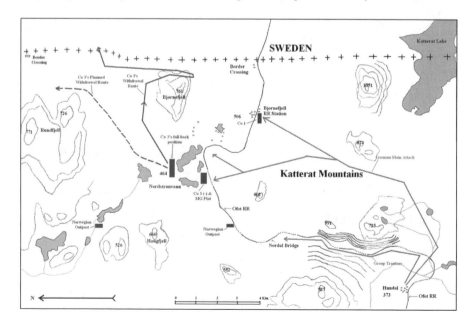

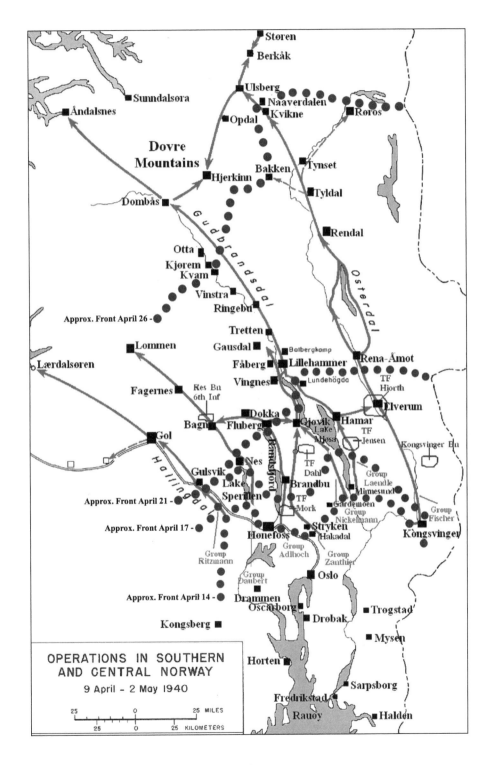

Støren
Berkåk
Ulsberg
Naaverdalen
Kvikne
Røros
Opdal
Sunndalsøra
Åndalsnes
Dovre
Mountains
Hjerkinn
Bakken
Tynset
Tyldal
Dombås
Rendal
Gudbrandsdal
Osterdal
Otta
Kjørem
Kvam
Vinstra
Ringebu
Approx. Front April 26 -
Tretten
Gausdal
Balbergkamp
Lommen
Fåberg
Lillehammer
Rena-Åmot
Lærdalsøren
Vingnes
Lundehögda
TF
Hjorth
Fagernes
Res Bn
6th Inf
Dokka
Gjøvik
Hamar
Elverum
Bagn
Fluberg
Lake
Mjøsa
TF
Jensen
Kongsvinger Bn
Gol
Nes
Randsfjord
TF
Dahl
Group
Laendle
Mimesund
Gulsvik
Lake
Sperillen
Brandbu
Group
Nickelmann
Group
Fischer
Hallingdal
TF
Mork
Gardemoen
Approx. Front April 21 -
Approx. Front April 17 -
Stryken
Hakadal
Kongsvinger
Hønefoss
Group
Adlhoch
Group
Zanthier
Group
Ritzmann
Oslo
Group
Daubert
Approx. Front April 14 -
Drammen
Oscarsborg
Drøbak
Trøgstad
Kongsberg
Mysen
Horten
Sarpsborg
Fredrikstad
Halden
Rauøy

OPERATIONS IN SOUTHERN
AND CENTRAL NORWAY
9 April – 2 May 1940

25   0   25 MILES

25   0   25 KILOMETERS

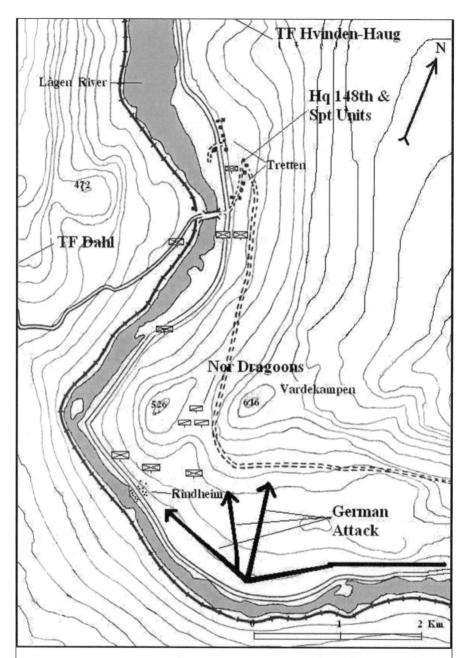

The Battle of Tretten, in which the Germans defeated a combined British-Norwegian force, and the British 148th Brigade all but ceased to exist.

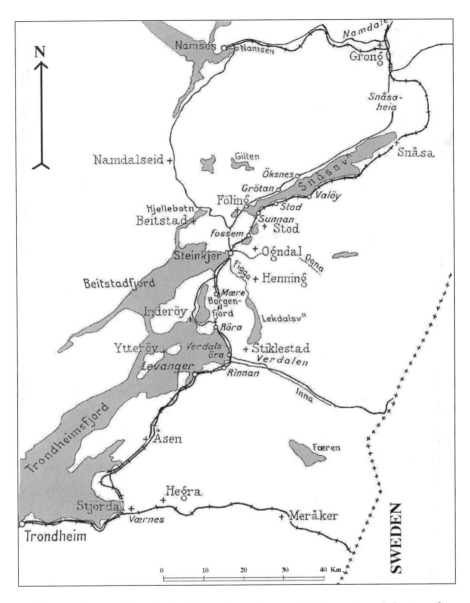

The area between Trondheim, Norway's ancient capital (bottom), and the city of Namsos (top).

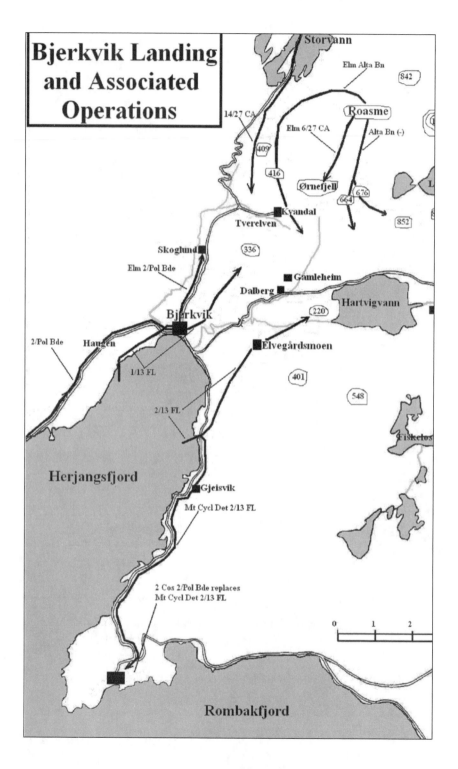

Bjerkvik Landing and Associated Operations

Storvann

Elm Alta Bn

842

14/27 CA

Roasme

Elm 6/27 CA

Alta Bn (-)

409

416

Ørnefjell

676

664

Kvandal

852

Tverelven

Skoglund

336

Elm 2/Pol Bde

Gamleheim

Dalberg

Hartvigvann

Bjerkvik

220

2/Pol Bde   Haugen

Elvegårdsmoen

1/13 FL

401

548

2/13 FL

Herjangsfjord

Fiskelos

Gjeisvik

Mt Cycl Det 2/13 FL

2 Cos 2/Pol Bde replaces
Mt Cycl Det 2/13 FL

0   1   2

Rombakfjord

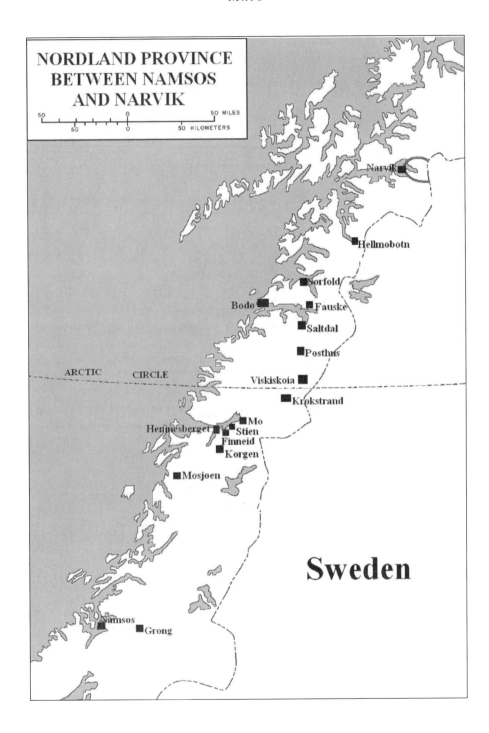

NORDLAND PROVINCE
BETWEEN NAMSOS
AND NARVIK

50 MILES

50 KILOMETERS

Narvik

Hellmobotn

Sorfold

Bodo · Fauske

Saltdal

Posthus

ARCTIC CIRCLE

Viskiskoia

Krokstrand

Mo
Stien
Hennesberget Finneid
Korgen

Mosjoen

Sweden

Namsos Grong

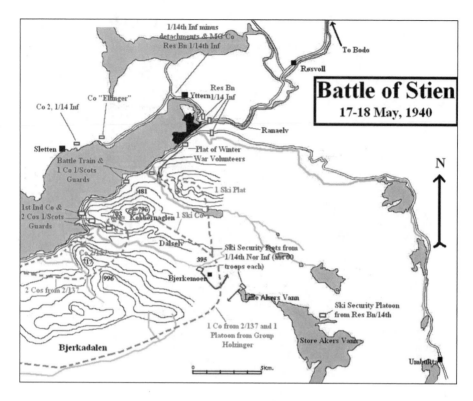

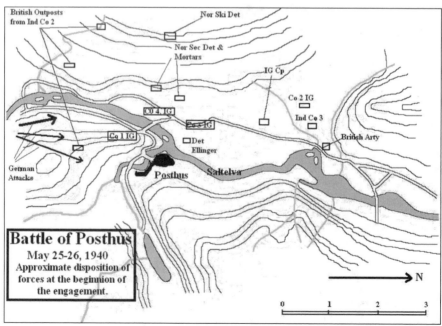

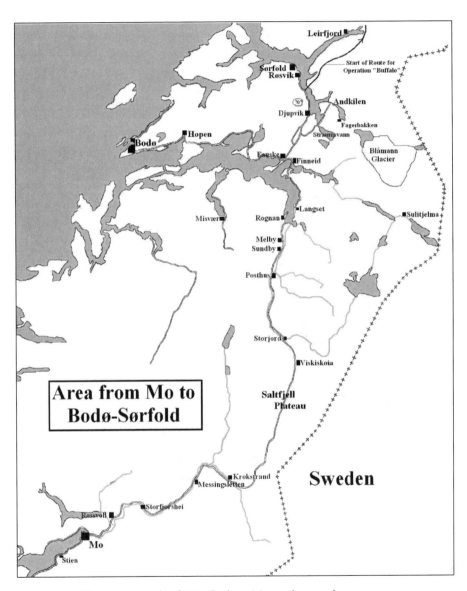

The region south of Narvik along Norway's central west coast.

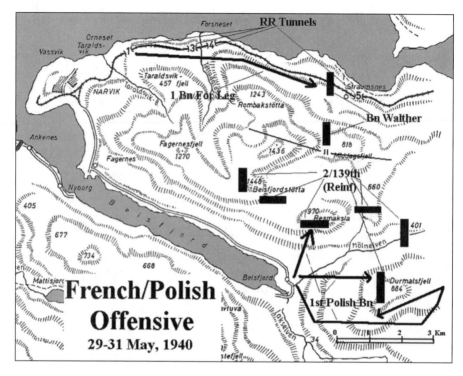

French/Polish Offensive 29-31 May, 1940

The Allies repeatedly attempted to break the German grip on Narvik until events in France forced efforts to cease.

Norwegian forces persisted in attacking after the Allied evacuation had begun, but finally capitulated to the Germans on June 10, 1940.

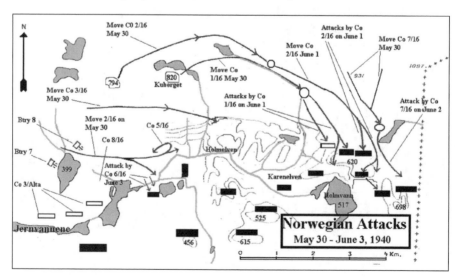

Norwegian Attacks May 30 - June 3, 1940

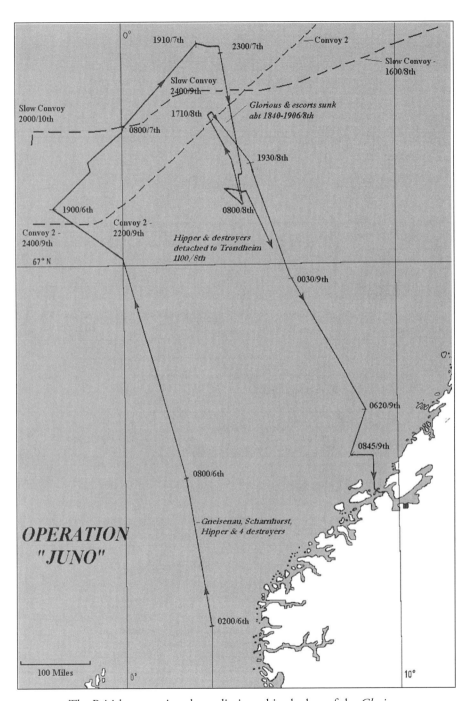

The British evacuation that culminated in the loss of the *Glorious*.

COMMAND STRUCTURES

Allied Command Structure in Norway

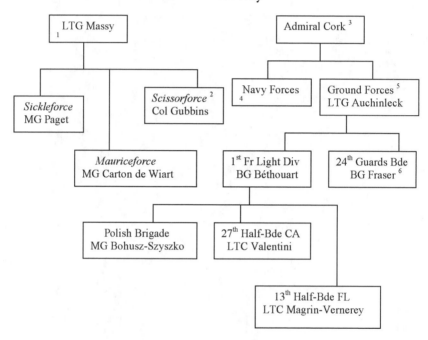

1 General Massy never left London but operated from the War Office. British commanders in Central Norway did not command naval or air forces associated with their operations. Those forces took their orders from their respective service.

2 *Scissorforce* and Colonel Gubbins remained under General Massy's command until May 7 when the command was transferred to General Auchinleck.

3 Initially, Admiral Cork commanded only the naval forces and reported to the Admiralty. Major General Mackesy, replaced by Lieutenant General Auchinleck on May 16, reported to General Ironside. Admiral Cork assumed command of both sea and land forces on April 20.

4 All naval forces operating within 100 nautical miles of Harstad.

5 Lieutenant General Auchinleck assumed command from Major General Mackesy on May 16.

6 Brigadier Fraser commanded the 24th Guards until he was evacuated to England at which time Gubbins, promoted to brevet Brigadier General, assumed command of that unit as well as the Independent Companies.

German Command Structure for Operations in Norway

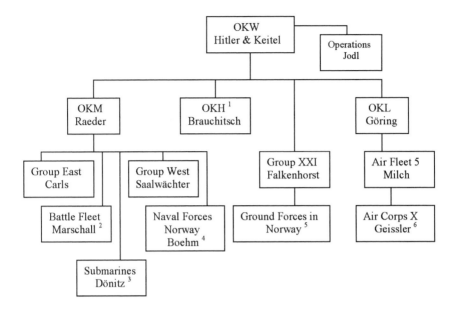

1 *Weserübung Süd*, under General Kaupisch, was subordinate to von Falkenhorst until April 12 when it was placed under OKH.

2 The Battle Fleet operated under the orders of Group West in the North Sea but directly under OKM for operations in the Atlantic.

3 The submarine command was subordinate to OKM but parts were under the operational control of the Fleet Commander during fleet operations.

4 Boehm was subordinate to von Falkenhorst within Norway but he was subordinate to OKM for naval operations.

5 General Dietl (3rd Mountain Division) operated directly under OKW in the period April 18 to May 5.

6 General von Falkenhorst did not command the air forces in Norway. General Milch's 5th Air Fleet absorbed Air Corps X as well as the territorial air commands within Norway. Geissler was not subordinate to Falkenhorst. Theoretically, all requests had to go through the chain of command but after the establishment of regional air commands, many requests were handled laterally between army and air force commands.

Norwegian Command Structure [1]

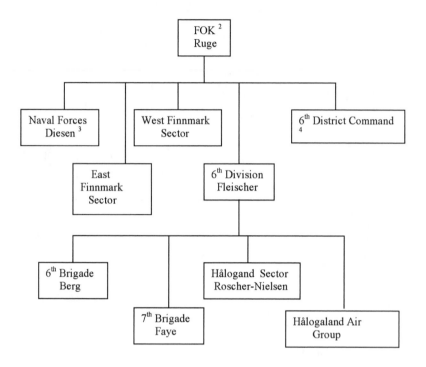

1 This is the command structure in North Norway that became effective after the reorganization in late May. Before hostilities, the army and navy commanders (General Laake and Admiral Diesen) reported directly to the Ministry of Defense and General Fleischer, like the other division commanders, reported to the army commander. After hostilities commenced, Fleischer became commander-in-chief in North Norway and reported directly to the Ministry of Defense.

2 While commander-in-chief of the armed forces, General Ruge continued to also occupy the position as commander of the army. The two headquarters operated as one.

3 Admiral Diesen had placed himself and his forces under General Ruge's command during the campaign in Central Norway. The May reorganization made this arrangement official.

4 As a result of the reorganization, 6th District Command became the army's support organization, responsible for supporting all army organizations. It was directed to separate out a staff, which would concentrate its efforts on supporting General Fleischer's forces.

Operational Code names

Alphabet	Allied evacuation of Narvik in May/June 1940.
Avonmouth	Planned Allied expedition to Narvik and the Swedish iron ore districts.
Biene	German operation to clear out Norwegian naval units along the Nordland coast and open a coastal supply route for General Feurstein's forces..
Büffel	German relief operation through the mountains between Bodø and Narvik.
Catherine	Plan for British fleet in the Baltic to sever German's supply of Swedish iron ore.
Juno	German naval operation against shipping off North Norway.
Hammer	Planned Allied attack on Trondheim.
Maurice	Allied operation against Trondheim from Namsos. Force involved was called *Mauriceforce*.
Naumburg	German plan to land forces in West Finnmark and Bardufoss for relief to Narvik.
Plymouth	Allied plan for operations against the Germans in southern Sweden.

R4	Allied plan to occupy Narvik, Trondheim, Bergen, and Stavanger in conjunction with Operation *Wilfred* when German intention to land in Norway was evident.
Royal Marine	Allied plan to drop mines in the Rhine River and its channels simultaneous with Operation *Wilfred*.
Rupert	Allied operations to recapture Narvik. Units involved were labeled Rupertforce.
Scissorforce	British Independent Companies operating in Nordland Province.
Sickle	Operation against Trondheim from Åndalsnes. Force was labeled *Sickleforce*.
Stratford	Allied plan in February 1940 to occupy Trondheim, Bergen, and Stavanger
Weserübung	German operations against Denmark and Norway. *Weserübung Sud* = Denmark and *Weserübung Nord* = Norway.
Wildente	German amphibious and air assault operation against Hemnesberget.
Wilfred	Allied mining operations in Norwegian territorial waters.

BIBLIOGRAPHY

The Norwegian language contains three letters – æ, ø, and å – that appear at the end of its alphabet. To avoid confusion, they are given here in the English language alphabetical order.

*Adams, Jack. *The Doomed Expedition. The Norwegian Campaign of 1940*. London: Leo Cooper, 1989.

Aftenposten. June 6, 1945 and June 14, 2005.

*Ash, Bernard. *Norway 1940*. London: Cassell, 1964.

Askim, Per. *Rapport fra sjefen for Norge og Ofotavdelingen til Kommanderende Admiral av 20 april 1940*. Six page typed manuscript.

*Assmann, Kurt. *The German Campaign in Norway*. Admiralty: Naval Staff, 1948.

Baudouin, Paul. *Neuf mois au gouvernement*. Paris: Table Ronde, 1948.

Berg, Johan Helge and Olav Vollan. *Fjellkrigen 1940. Lapphaugen – Bjørnefjell*. Trondheim: Wennbergs Trykkeri A.S., 1999.

Berg, Johan Helge and Olav Vollan. *I Trønderbataljonens fotspor – 50 år etter*. Trondheim: Wennbergs trykkeri, 1990.

*Béthouart, Marie Émile. *Rapport*. Eleven page typed manuscript in Norwegian with a penned date of August 8, 1944.

*Béthouart, Marie Émile. *Cinq années d'espérance. Mémoires de guerre, 1939-1945*. Paris: Plon, 1968.

*Bieganski, Witold. *Poles in the Battle of Narvik*. Warsaw: Interpress Publishers, 1969.

Bjørnsen, Bjørn. *Det utrolige døgnet*. Oslo: Gyldendal, 1978.

*Bjørnsen, Bjørn. *Narvik 1940*. Oslo: Gyldendal Norsk Forlag, 1980.

Böttger, Gerd. *Narvik im Bild*. Oldenburg: Gerhard Stalling Verlag, 1941.

*Breckan, Hans. *Tapte skanser. IR 14 i april, mai, juni 1940*. Brønnøysund: Eget forlag, 1986.

*Büchner, Alex. *Kampf im Gebirge*. München-Lochhausen: Schild-Verlag, 1957.

*Büchner, Alex. *Narvik. Kämpfe der Gruppe Dietl im Frühjahr 1940*.

Nechargemünd - Heidelberg: Scharnhorst Buchkameradschaft GmbH, 1958.

Buckley, Christopher. *Norway. The Commandos. Dieppe.* London: HMSO, 1951.

Butler, James Ramsay Montagu. *Grand Strategy.* London: HMSO, 1956–1976. 6 volumes.

Busch, Fritz Otto. *Die Deutsche Kriegsmarine im Kamp. Schiffe und Taten.* Berlin: Vier Tannen Verlag, 1943.

Busch, Fritz Otto. *Die Kriegsmarine in der Aktion Dänemark-Norwegen.* Berlin-Grunewald: Franz Schneider Verlag, 1940.

Busch, Fritz Otto. *Narvik. Vom Heldekampfe deutscher Zerstörer.* Verlag C. Bertelsmann Gutersloh, 1940.

*Christensen, Chr. *De som heiste flagget.* J. W. Cappelens Forlag, 1986.

*Churchill, Winston S. *The Gathering Storm.* Boston: Houghton Mifflin Company, 1948.

Ciano, Galeazzo. *Ciano's Diplomatic Papers.* London: Malcolm Muggeridge, 1948.

*Clarke, Dudley. *Seven Assignments.* London: Jonathan Cape, 1948.

*Connell, John. *Auchinleck.* London: Cassell, 1959.

Cosgrave, Patrick. *Churchill at War, Alone 1939–1940.* London: 1974. Volume I.

Dagbladet. January 14, 1939. Give article title and author.

*Dahl, Arne Dagfin. *Med Alta bataljon mot tyskerne.* Oslo: H. Aschehoug & Co., 1945.

Dahl, Greta. *Fem tunge år. En husmors dagbok fra krigstidens Narvik.* Skien: Grøndahl & Søn Forlag A.s

Dahl, Hans Fredrik, Guri Hjeltnes Nökleby; Nils Johan Ringdal, and Øystein Sørensen (eds.). *Norsk Krigsleksikon 1940-1945.* Oslo: J. W. Capelen Forlag A/S, 1995.

Den Krigshistoriske Avdeling. *Krigen i Norge 1940. Operasjonene i Rogaland og Haugesund – Indre Hardangeravsnittet.* Haugesund: Skoglands Boktrykeri A.s., 1952.

*Derry, T. K. *The Campaign in Norway.* London: HMSO, 1952.

Deutsch, Harold C. *Hitler and his Generals. The Hidden Crisis, January-June 1938.* Minneapolis: The University of Minnesota Press, 1974.

*Deutsch, Harold C. *The Conspiracy against Hitler in the Twilight War.* Minneapolis: The University of Minnesota Press, 1968.

*Devins, Joseph H. Jr. *The Vaagso Raid.* Philadelphia: Chilton Book Company, 1968.

*Dickens, Peter. *Narvik: Battles in the Fjords.* Annapolis: Naval Institute Press, 1974.

*Dietl, Gerda-Louise and Kurt Hermann. *General Dietl.* Münich, 1951.

Dildy, Douglas C. *Denmark and Norway 1940: Hitler's Boldest Operation.* Botley: Osprey Publishing, 2007.

Eade, Charles (Compiler). *The War Speeches of the Rt Hon Winston S. Churchill.* Volume 1 of 3 volumes. Boston: Houghton Mifflin Company, 1953.

*Ellinger, Tage. *Den Forunderlige Krig.* Oslo: Gyldendal Norsk Forlag, 1960.

Erskine, David. *The Scots Guards 1919-1945.* London: William Clowes and Sons, Limited, 1956.

*von Falkenhorst, Nikolaus. *Bericht und Vernehmung des Generalobersten von Falkenhorst.*

Faye, W. *Krigen i Norge 1940. Operasjonene i Østfold.* Oslo: Forsvarets Krigshistoriske Avdeling, 1963.

*Fergusson, Bernard. *The Watery Maze.* London: Collins, 1961.

*Feurstein, Valentin. *Irrwege der Pflicht, 1938-1945.* Munich, Verlag Welsermühl, 1963.

Fitzgerald, Desmond J. L. *History of the Irish Guards in the Second World War.* Aldershot: Gale & Polden Ltd, 1952.

*Fleischer, Carl Gustav. *Efterlatte papirer.* Tønsberg: Tønsbergs aktietrykkeris forlag i kommisjon hos T. Landberg, 1947.

Fuller, J. F. C. *A Military History of the Western World.* Minerva Press, 1956. Three volumes.

*Fure, Odd-Bjørn. *Norsk utenrikspolitiske historie.* Volume 3, *Mellomkrigstid 1920–1940.* Oslo: 1996.

*Gamelin, Maurice Gustave. *Servir.* Paris: Plon, 1946-47. Three volumes.

*Gemzell, Carl-Axel. *Raeder, Hitler und Skandinavien. Der Kamp für einen maritimen Operationsplan.* Lund: C.W.K. Gleerup, 1965.

*Gemzell, Carl-Axel. *Organization, Conflict, and Innovation. A Study of German Naval Strategic Planning 1888-1940.* Lund: Esselte Studium, 1973.

Der Sieg im Norden. Berlin: Volk und Reich Verlag, 1941.

Fuehrer Conferences On Matters Dealing With the German Navy 1939. Translated and printed by the Office of Naval Intelligence, Navy Department, Washington, D.C., 1947.

Fuehrer Conferences On Matters Dealing With the German Navy 1940. Translated and printed by the Office of Naval Intelligence, Navy Department, Washington, D.C., 1947.

Fuehrer Directives and Other Top-level Directives of the German Armed Forces 1939–1942.

Kampf um Norwegen. Berichte und Bilder zum Kriege gegen England. Berlin: Oberkommando der Wehrmacht. Zeitgeschichte-Verlag Wilhelm Andermann, 1940.

Kriegstagebuch der Seekriegsleitung 1939-1945. Herfrod: E. S. Mittler & Sohn, 1988.

Germany – War Diaries.

Gruppe XXI Kriegstagebuch.

Halder Diary.

Jodl Diary.

Kriegstagebuch der Seekriegsleitung.

3. Gebirgsdivision Kriegstagesbuch.

*Getz, Ole Berg. *Fra krigen i Nord-Trøndelag 1940.* Oslo: Aschehoug & Co., 1940.

Goerlitz, Walter. *History of the German General Staff 1657–1945.* New York: Praeger, 1957.

Gotaas, Birger. *Fra 9. april til 7. juni. Episoder og opplevelser fra krigen i Norge.* Oslo: J. Dybwad, 1945.

Graf, Georg Engelbret. *Unser Kampf in Norwegen.* München: F. Bruckmann Verlag, 1940.

Hambro, Carl Joachim. *I saw it happen in Norway.* New York: D. Appleton-Century Co., 1940.

Hankey, Maurice Pascal Alers. *Politics, Trials, and Errors.* Chicago: H. Regnery, 1950.

*Hansen, Kenneth P. "Raeder versus Wegener: Conflict in German Naval Strategy." *Naval War College Review*, September 22, 2005.

*Harvey, Maurice. *Scandinavian Misadventure.* Tumbridge Wells: Spellmount Limited, 1990.

von Hase, Georg. *Die Kriegsmarine erobert Norwegens Fjorde.* Leipzig: Hase & Koehler Verlag, 1940.

Hauge, Andreas. *Kampene i Norge.* Krigshistorisk Forlag, 1995.

Herzberg, Niels. *Krigen i Norge 1940. Operasjonene på Ringerike og Hadeland.* Oslo: Forsvarets Krigshistoriske Avdeling, 1960.

*Hewins, Ralph. *Quisling. Prophet without Honour.* New York: The John Day Company, 1966.

Heye, August Wilhelm. *Z13 Von Kiel bis Narvik.* Berlin: Mittler & Sohn, 1941.

*Hobson, Rolf and Tom Kristiansen. *Norsk Forsvarshitorie. Bind 3 1905–1940. Total krig, nøytralitet og politisk splittelse.* Bergen: Eide Forlag, 2001.

Hoffmann, Heinrich. *Für Hitler bis Narvik.* München: H. Hoffmann, 1941.

*Hovland, Torkel. *General Carl Gustaf Fleischer. Storhet og fall.* Oslo: Forum-Aschehoug, 2000, third edition.

*Hubatsch, Walter. *Die deutsche Besetzung von Danemark und Norwegen 1940.* Gottingen: Wissenschaftlicher Verlag, 1952.

Hubatsch, Walter. *Weserübung. Die deutsche Besetzung von Dänemark und Norwegen 1940.* Gottingen: Musterschmidt-Verlag, 1960.

*International Military Tribunal. *Trial of the Major War Criminals before the International Military Tribunal, 14 November 1945 – 1 October 1946.* Nuremberg: 1947-49.

*Irving, David. *Hitler's War.* New York: The Viking Press, 1977.

*Ismay, Lord. *The Memoirs of Lord Ismay.* London: Heinemann, 1950.

Jacobsen, Hans Adolf (ed.). *Kriegstagebuch des Oberkommandos der Wehrmacht (Wehrmachtführungsstab) 1940–1945.* Frankfurt am Main: Bernard and Graefe: 1961–1965.

Jensen, Jørgen. *Krigen på Hedemark.* Oslo: Tanum, 1947.

Journal of the Royal United Service Institution, December 1970.

*Kennedy, Sir John. *The Business of War: The War Narrative of Sir John Kennedy.* Edited by Bernard Fergusson. London: Hutchinson, 1957.

*Kersaudy, François. *Norway 1940.* New York: St. Martin's Press, 1987.

*Koht, Halvdan. *Frå skanse til skanse. Minne frå krigsmånadane i Noreg 1940.* Oslo: Tiden norsk forlag, 1947.

Koht, Halvdan. *Norway. Neutral and Invaded.* New York: Macmillan, 1941.

Kräutler, M. and K. Springenschmidt. *Es war ein Edelweiss. Schicksal und Weg der zweiten Gebirgsdivision.* Leopold Stocker, Graz, 1962.

*Ladislas, Fargo. *The Game of the Foxes.* New York: D. McKay Co., 1971.

*Lapie, Pierre Oliver. *With the Foreign Legion at Narvik.* London: J. Murray, 1941. Translated by Anthony Merryn.

Levsen, Dirk. *Krieg im Norden. Die Kämpfe in Norwegen im Frühjahr 1940.* Hamburg: E. S. Mittler & Sohn, 2000.

Liddell-Hart, Basil H. *History of the Second World War.* New York: G. P. Putnam's Sons, 1971.

Lie, Trygve. *Leve eller dø. Norge i krig.* Oslo: Tiden norsk forlag, 1955.

*Lindbäck-Larsen, Odd. *6. division.* Oslo: Gyldendal, 1946.

*Lindbäck-Larsen, Odd. *Krigen i Norge 1940.* Oslo: Forsvarets Krigshistoriske Avdeling, 1965.

*Lindbäck-Larsen, Odd. *Rapport om 6. Divisjonskommandos virksomhet under nøytralitetvakten 1939–40 og felttoget 1940.*

Lindemann, Timothy F. *Weserübung Nord: Germany's Invasion of Norway, 1940.* A joint operations case study (AU/ACSC/0146A/97-03) at the Air Command and Staff College, March 1997.

London Gazette, Supplement, 10 July 1947.

*Loock, Hans-Dietrich. *Quisling, Rosenberg und Terboven. Zur Vorgeschichte und Geschichte der nationalsozialistischen Revolution in Norwegen.* Stuttgart: Deutsche Verlags-Anstalt, 1970.

Lossberg, Bernhard von. *Im Wehrmachtführungsstab. Bericht eines Generalstabsoffiziers.* Hamburg: H. H. Nölke, 1949.

Lucas, James. *Alpine Elite. German Mountain Troops of World War II.* New York: Jane's Publishing Incorporated, 1980.

*MacIntyre, Donald. *Narvik.* London: Evans Brothers Limited, 1959.

*Macleod, Roderick and Denis Kelly (eds.). *Time Unguarded. The Ironside Diaries 1937–1940.* New York: David McKay Company, Inc., 1963.

MacClure, Victor. *Gladiators over Norway.* London: W. H. Allen & Co., 1942.

Mann, Chris and Christer Jorgensen. *Hitler's Arctic War: The German Campaigns in Norway-Finland, and the USSR, 1940–1945.* Hersham: Ian Allan Publishing, 2002.

Mannerheim, Marshal Carl von. *The Memoirs of Marshal Mannerheim.* Translated by Count Eric Lewenhaupt. New York: E. P. Dutton & Company, Inc., 1954.

Manvell, Roger and Heinrich Fraenkel. *The Canaris Conspiracy. The Secret Resistance to Hitler in the German Army.* New York: Pinnacle Books, 1972.

Maund, Loben Edward Harold. *Assault from the Sea.* London: Methuen, 1949.

Medlicott, William Norton. *The Economic Blockade.* London: HMSO, 1952–1959.

*Mordal, Jacques. *La campagne de Norvège.* Paris: Self, 1949.

*Moulton, J. L. *A Study of Warfare in Three Dimensions. The Norwegian Campaign of 1940.* Athens, Ohio: The Ohio University Press, 1967.

*Munthe-Kaas, Otto H. *Krigen i Narviksavsnittet 1940.* Oslo: Gyldendal Norsk Forlag, 1968.

Munthe-Kaas, Otto H. *The Campaign in Northern Norway. An Account of the Norwegian 6th Division's Advance Against the Germans in the Narvik Area April 9th–June 9th, 1940.* Washington, D.C.: The Royal Norwegian Information Service, 1944.

Norwegian News Company. Hans Olav and Tor Gjesdal editors. *Norway.* Brooklyn: Arnesen Press, Inc. 1941.

Nygaardsvold, Johan. *Norge i krig: 9. april-7. juni 1940.* Oslo: Tiden norsk forlag, 1982.

Osen, Marcus Einarson. *Sjøslaget i Ofotfjorden 9.-10. og 13. april 1940.* Hundevåg: Norsk Tidsskrift for Sjøvensn, 2003.

*Østbye, Gudbrand. *Krigen i Norge 1940. Operasjonene på Vestsiden av Mjøsa–Follebu-Gausdal.* Oslo: Forsvarets Krigshistoriske Avdeling, 1960.

*Ottmer, Hans-Martin. *Weserübung. Der deutsche Angriff auf Dänemark und Norwegen im April 1940.* Oldenburg: Militärgeschichtliches Forschungsamt, 1994.

Petersen, Ib Damegaard. "Aksen OKW-OKM." *Historisk Tidsskrift.* Copenhagen: 1966.

*Petrow, Richard. *The Bitter Years. The Invasion and Occupation of Denmark and Norway April 1940–May 1945.* New York: William Morrow and Company, Inc., 1974.

Polish Ministry of Information. *Polish Troops in Norway. A Photographic Record of the Campaign at Narvik.* London: M. I. Kolin Ltd, 1943.

Pruszyânski, Kaawery. *Droga wiodla przez Narvik.* London: M. I. Kolin Ltd., 1941.

Puttkamer, Karl Jesko von. *Die unheimliche See.* Vienna: Verlag Karl Kuhne, 1952.

Quarrie, Bruce. *German Mountain Troops.* Tucson: AZTEX Corporation, 1980.

Raeder, Eric. *My Life.* Henry W. Drexel, transl. Annapolis: United States Naval Institute, 1960.

"Rapport fra sjefen for Norge og Ofotavdelingen til Kommandrende Admiral av 20 April 1940."

Reynaud, Paul. *La France a suave l'Europe.* Paris: Flammarion, 1957.

*Reynolds, David. *In Command of History.* New York: Random House, 2005.

Roskill, Stepehn Wentworth. *The War at Sea 1939–1945.* London: HMSO, 1954.

*Ruef, Karl. *Odyssee einer Gebirgsdivision. Die 3. Geb. Div. im Einsatz.* Stuttgart: Leopold Stocker Verlag, 1976.

*Ruge, Otto. *Felttoget: General Otto Ruges erindringer fra kampene april-juni 1940.* Edited by Olav Riste. Oslo: Aschenhoug, 1989.

Ruge, Otto. *Krigens Dagbok. Annen verdenskrig i tekst og billeder.* Oslo: Halvorsen & Larsen, 1946.

*Salewski, Michael. *Die deutsche Seekriegsleitung 1935–1945*. Volume I: 1935–
1941. Frankfurt am Main: Bernard & Graefe Verlag für Wehrwesen,
1970.

*Sandvik, Trygve. *Operasjonene til lands i Nord-Norge 1940*. 2 volumes. Oslo:
Forsvarets Krigshistoriske Avdeling, 1965.

*Seraphim, Hans-Guenther. *Das politische Tagebuch Alfred Rosenbergs aus den
Jahren 1934/35 und 1939/40*. Göttingen: Musterschmidt-Verlag, 1956.

*Sereau, Raymond. *L'Expedition de Norvège 1940*. Baden-Baden: Regie
Autonome des Publications Officielles, 1949.

Shirer, William L. *The Rise and Fall of the Third Reich*. New York: Simon and
Schuster, 1960.

*Steen, E. A. *Norges Sjøkrig 1940-1945*. 1. *Sjøforsvarets nøytralitetsvern 1939-
1940. Tysklands og Vestmaktenes planer og forbe-redelser for en Norgesaksjon.*
Oslo: Den Krigshistoriske Avdeling, Forsvarstaben. Gyldendal Norsk
Forlag, 1954–1958.

*Steen, E. A. *Norges Sjøkrig 1940–1945*. 2. *Det tyske angrepet i Oslofjorden og
på Norges sørkyst*. Oslo: Den Krigshistoriske Avdeling, Forsvarstaben.
Gyldendal Norsk Forlag, 1954–1958.

Steen, E. A. *Norges Sjøkrig 1940-1945*. 3. *Sjøforsvar-ets kamper og virke på
Vestlandet og i Trøndelag i 1940*. Oslo: Den Krigshistoriske Avdeling,
Forsvarstaben. Gyldendal Norsk Forlag, 1954–1958.

*Steen E. A. *Norges Sjøkrig 1940-1945*. 4. *Sjøforsvar-ets kamper og virke i Nord-
Norge i 1940*. Oslo: Den Krigshistoriske Avdeling, Forsvarstaben.
Gyldendal Norsk Forlag, 1954–1958.

Strabolgi, Lord Joseph Montagua Kenworthy. *Narvik and After. A Study of the
Scandinavian Campaign*. London: Gainsborough Press, St. Albans by
Fisher, Knight & Co., Ltd, 1940.

*Sundell, Olof. *9. april*. Stockholm: Sohlmans, 1949.

*Tamelander, Michael and Niklas Zetterling. *Niende april. Nazi-Tysklands
invasjon av Norge*. Oslo: Spartacus, 2001.

Taylor, Telford. *The March of Conquest. The German Victories in Western
Europe, 1940*. New York: Simon and Schuster, 1958.

Tessin, G. *Verbände und Truppen der deutschen Wehrmacht und Waffen-SS*.
Frankfurt-am-Main: Mittler and Sohn, 1966.

Torris, Marcel Jean Marie Joseph. *Narvik*. New York: Bretano, 1943.

Unger, Hellmuth. *Die Männer von Narvik*. Oldenburg i. O./Berlin: Gerhard
Stalling Verlagsbuchhandlung, 1941.

United Kingdom. *Parliamentary Debates, House of Commons*. Volumes 359–60.

United Kingdom. *Notes on the Norwegian Campaign*. London: Historical Branch, Cabinet Office, 1951.

United States, Office of United States Chief of Counsel for Prosecution of Axis Crimes. *Nazi Conspiracy and Aggression*. Washington, D.C.: Government Printing Office, 1946–1948. 8 vols and 2 supplemental vols.

United States. *German Mountain Troops*. Washington, D.C.: War Department, Military Intelligence Department. Special Series 28, December 1944.

Waage, Johan. *The Narvik Campaign. An Eye-Witness Account*. Translated from the Norwegian by Ewan Butler. London: George G. Harrap & Co. LTD, 1964.

Warlimont, Walter. *Inside Hitler's Headquarters 1939–45*. Translated from the German by R. H. Barry. Novato: Presidio Press, 1962.

Wegener, Wolfgang. *Die Seestrategie des Weltkriges*. Berlin: E. S. Mittler & Sohn, 1929.

Wheeler-Bennett, John W. *The Nemesis of Power: The German Army in Politics 1918–1945*. New York: St. Martin's Press, Inc., 1954.

*Woodward, Llewellyn. *British Foreign Policy in the Second World War*. London: HMSO, 1970.

Ydstebø, Palle. *Geostrategi, trusselvurdering og operativ planlegging. Forsvaret av Nord-Norge 1880–1920*. Tromsø. University of Tromsø, 2000.

*Ziemke, Earl F. *The German Northern Theater of Operations 1940–1945*. Washington, D.C.: Department of Army Pamphlet 20–271, 1959.

*Zbyszewski, Karol. *The fight for Narvik: Impressions of the Polish Campaign in Norway*. London: L. Drummond, 1941.

Zeska, Theodor von. *Der Kampf gegen die Westmächte im ersten Vierteljahr 1940 und die Eroberung Norwegen*. Berlin: E.S. Mittler & Sohn, 1941.

Zoepffel, Kurt. "Mit Kreuzer 'Blucher' nach Norden" in George von Hase, *Die Kriegsmarine erobert Norwegens Fjorde*. Leipzig: v. Hase & Koehler Verlag, 1940.

INDEX